# Advertising Works 21

Proving the payback on marketing investment

Case studies from the IPA Effectiveness Awards 2012

Open to all agencies, media owners and clients worldwide

**Edited and introduced by**
**Marie Oldham**
Convenor of Judges

First published 2013 by Warc
85 Newman Street, London W1T 3EX
Telephone: 0207 467 8100
Fax: 0207 467 8101
Email: enquiries@warc.com
www.warc.com



A CIP catalogue record for this book is available from the British Library

ISBN: 978-1-84116-226-3

Typeset by HWA Text and Data Management, London
Printed and bound in Great Britain by The MPG Books Group

# Contents

# Foreword

**Lindsey Clay**
Managing Director, Thinkbox

The most successful businesses advertise. They know that advertising is an investment in market share and growth. So it is essential that there is a body of hard evidence to prove the value of this investment.

That is why Thinkbox has sponsored the IPA Effectiveness Awards for eight consecutive years – since we were set up, in fact. They are the pre-eminent advertising awards because they celebrate what advertising actually does: changes behaviour, builds the strongest businesses and, ultimately, expands the economy.

So you couldn't invent an award scheme that has more in common with what Thinkbox is committed to: helping businesses get the most out of advertising.

Obviously Thinkbox is focused on the effectiveness of TV advertising in all its many forms – broadcast, on-demand, interactive, mobile – and it is gratifying that so many of this year's IPA Effectiveness Award winners once again have TV at the heart of their campaigns (33 of the 35 winners, in fact).

And once again our thanks go to those clients and agencies that didn't stop at creating an effective campaign, but tested it and measured it and submitted it for the scrutiny of the Awards judges. Their efforts to demonstrate how advertising has worked for them benefit everyone.

The communication landscape is ever more complex. Options and opinions abound but these Awards stand out as a testament to the simple fact that, however complex it might be, advertising remains the cornerstone of so much success and growth.

So, congratulations to all the award winners, with Effectiveness Agency of the Year winner Abbott Mead Vickers BBDO and Grand Prix winner John Lewis – with Adam & Eve and Manning Gottlieb OMD – leading from the front. The winners' creativity, innovation and dedication to proving the worth of advertising deserve all the acclaim we can give them.

# Sponsors

The success of the 2012 IPA Effectiveness Awards is in no small part down to its sponsors, and the IPA would like to thank the companies listed here for their continuing support. We are particularly grateful to Thinkbox, its overall sponsor, for their commitment to sponsor this competition.

IN ASSOCIATION WITH

campaign

# Acknowledgements

Many people worked hard to make the Awards a success, especially the following: Richard Exon, ex Chairman of the IPA Value of Advertising Group (recently renamed Value of Creativity Group), Marie Oldham, Convenor of Judges, and Lorna Hawtin, Deputy Convenor of Judges.

At the IPA, the core team were: Bryony Clare, Bethany Hamlin, Danielle Davies, Tessa Gooding and Kathryn Patten.

We also owe a debt of gratitude to:

## The IPA Awards Board

| | |
|---|---|
| IPA Chairman of VCG, Karen Buchanan | Publicis |
| 1988/90 Convenor of Judges, Paul Feldwick | Consultant |
| 1992/94 Convenor of Judges, Chris Baker | Consultant |
| 1996 Convenor of Judges, Gary Duckworth | Consultant |
| 1998 Convenor of Judges, Nick Kendall | BBH |
| 2000 Convenor of Judges, Tim Broadbent | Ogilvy & Mather Beijing |
| 2002 Convenor of Judges, Marco Rimini | Mindshare |
| 2004 Convenor of Judges, Alison Hoad | RKCR/Y&R |
| 2005 Convenor of Judges, Les Binet | Adam & Eve/DDB |
| 2006 Convenor of Judges, Laurence Green | 101 |
| 2007 Convenor of Judges, Richard Storey | M&C Saatchi |
| 2008 Convenor of Judges, Neil Dawson | HMDG |
| 2009 Convenor of Judges, Andy Nairn | Dare |
| 2010 Convenor of Judges, David Golding | Adam & Eve/DDB |
| 2011 Convenor of Judges, Charlie Snow | DLKW Lowe |
| 2012 Convenor of Judges, Marie Oldham | MPG Media Contacts |
| 2014 Convenor of Judges, Lorna Hawtin | TBWA\Manchester |
| IPA Director General, Paul Bainsfair | |
| IPA Director of Communications, Tessa Gooding | |
| IPA Events & Awards Senior Manager, Kathryn Patten | |
| 1982/80 Convenor of Judges, Simon Broadbent *(d)* | |
| 1986/84 Convenor of Judges, Charles Channon *(d)* | |

## The IPA Value of Creativity Group

| | |
|---|---|
| Karen Buchanan (Chairman) | Publicis |
| Bridget Angear | AMV BBDO |
| Les Binet | Adam & Eve/DDB |
| Lucas Brown | Total Media |
| James Devon | MBA |
| Ken Dixon | Newhaven |
| Simeon Duckworth | Mindshare |
| Rachel Hatton | Ogilvy |
| Lorna Hawtin | TBWA\Manchester |
| Gavin Hilton | RAPP |
| Nick Kendall | BBH |
| Sophie Maunder-Allan | VCCP |
| Richard Morris | Vizeum UK |
| Andy Nairn | Dare |
| Marie Oldham | MPG Media Contacts |

# The Judges

**Marie Oldham**
*Convenor of Judges*
Chief Strategy Officer
MPG Media Contacts

**Lorna Hawtin**
*Deputy Convenor of Judges*
Disruption Director
TBWA\Manchester

## STAGE 1: INDUSTRY SPECIALISTS

**Janey Bullivant**
Founding Partner,
The Effectiveness Partnership

**Peter Dann**
Director,
The Nursery Research and Planning

**Phil Danter**
Consultant

**Liz Donaldson**
Founder,
Liz Donaldson Associates

**Roger Gane**
Research Consultant

**Eric Edge**
Head of Marketing Communications,
EMEA, Facebook

**James Hayr**
Head of Specialist Sales,
Microsoft Advertising UK

**Melanie Howard**
Co-Founder and Chair,
Future Foundation

**Jennifer Laing**
Non Executive Director,
InterContinental Hotels Group

**Carole Lee**
Managing Director,
London Brand Innovations

**Noelle McElhatton**
Editor,
Marketing

**Neil Mortensen**
Research and Planning Director,
Thinkbox

**Emma Newman**
Marketing Director,
Clear Channel UK

**Rufus Olins**
Chief Executive,
Newsworks

**Lizzie Palmer**
Owner, On Your Feet and Professional
Training & Coaching

**Mark Rapley**
Founder,
The Garden Recruitment

**Linda Smith**
Executive Chair,
RAB

**Nick Southgate**
Behavioural Economics Consultant

**Thomas Twigg**
Communications Manager,
Velti

## STAGE 2: CLIENT JURY

**Lord Hollick**
former CEO United News and Media,
former Non Executive Director of Diageo
Chairman of Judges

**Jo Blundell**
Marketing Director UK,
Burger King

**Carolyn Bradley**
Group Brand Director,
Tesco

**David George**
Marketing Director,
Mercedes-Benz

**Will Harris**
Chief Marketing Officer,
Belvedere Vodka, LVMH Group

**Catherine Kehoe**
Brands and Marketing Director,
Lloyds Banking Group

**Mary McGovern**
Media Country Manager and
Associate Director,
P&G

**Andy McQueen**
Divisional Director of Customer Strategy
& Marketing,
Nationwide Building Society

**Sheila Mitchell**
Marketing Director,
Department of Health

# Introduction

**By Marie Oldham**
Chief Strategic Officer, MPG Media Contacts
Convenor of Judges 2012

The IPA Effectiveness Awards is a little like the Olympics of communications effectiveness. Following years of hard work, sheer effort, commitment, and striving for excellence, the best of the best came to London in 2012 to see who would make it into the medals table. The aspiration of all entrants is to reach gold, but to get any medal at all requires robust evidence that competitors have leveraged genuine insight to create big ideas; have created communications that can engage consumers on many levels; and have contributed to the success of client organisations. This year we saw papers entered from Brazil, China, France, Germany, Hong Kong, India, Norway, Shanghai, Singapore, Spain, UK and the US. The bar is set high and winners have to reach beyond everyday good work to demonstrate leadership, new learnings or innovative use of emerging communications channels. Beyond this, papers must seek to pull together a body of evidence which can persuade the judges, beyond reasonable doubt, that powerful communications can be proven to drive positive return on marketing investment and can contribute to the bottom line of client organisations.

Just as the Olympics is not like any other sporting event, judging the IPA Effectiveness Awards is not like judging any other awards on the planet. It is more akin to doing an MBA in the power of creative thinking to deliver effective business results. All 30 judges involved agree that, whilst it is hard work, involves early mornings, late nights and commitment beyond the call of duty, it is worth it to be able to peep under the bonnet of some of the greatest brand stewardship in the UK and beyond.

The IPA Effectiveness Awards were set up to demonstrate that advertising was not an isolated, unaccountable, sub-set of marketing but could in fact prove how insight, rigorous planning and smart media thinking can pay back to the bottom line. Thirty-two years later we can claim to have met that objective; the 2012 shortlisted papers alone have a combined marketing spend of over £1.7bn and proven incremental profit of £6.8bn. But, the world has moved on, audience interaction with brands has become more complex, our thinking often needs to span paid, owned and earned communications channels, and measurement can encompass monitoring internet chatter, last click analysis and a working knowledge of behavioural economics. However, at the same time as we develop our understanding of campaign effectiveness on a micro level, we must not lose sight of the fact that agencies add most value when they are capable of delivering big creative ideas that inspire bravery, can shape and lead organisations, and that money invested in those ideas can be proven to pay back both on an individual channel level and a holistic basis.

With 32 years under our belt we are also in a position to look back at the world's most effective campaigns as a way of understanding long-term vs. short-term effects. The work done by Peter Field and Les Binet in 2012 is a must read for anyone involved in genuine brand stewardship (all of us?). Topline findings are outlined in Chapter 6 and the study underpins previous analysis of the Gunn Report with both approaches aiming to allocate a quantitative value of the power of creativity in achieving more effective ROI levels. Their finding that award winning creativity can enhance effectiveness to the power of ten is all the evidence we need to justify the value IPA agencies bring to client organisations.

At our best, agencies and clients work together to turn logic into magic, to create a culture of bravery underpinned by measurement and deliver creative solutions to commercial problems. Entries from brands such as Boots, Dove, McDonald's, Snickers, The Metropolitan Police, The National Lottery, Virgin Atlantic, Walkers, Cadbury and Waitrose, amongst others, demonstrate innovative thinking (see Metropolitan Police on knife crime) as well as clarity of understanding of the real business issues facing modern brands (try LV=). Within this year's entries I also think we are finally seeing work that can provide guidance for all of us on how emerging technologies from customer loyalty cards to social networks can act not only as marketing tools but also measurement tools to understand the effect of communications (read Boots and John Lewis).

Each Awards has its own particular 'flavour' and this year is no different. The judges felt that the pick of the crop showed genuine understanding of the post-credit crunch world and particularly leveraged the deeper consumer needstates and values driving brand choice in a recessionary market. Consumers have moved beyond the world of bling; and brands that leverage the power of family, that offer meaningfulness across a number of dimensions and provide multi-platform access to consumers were all rewarded for meeting consumer needs. In particular, those who managed to engage entire organisations behind a big brand idea (e.g. John Lewis, Snickers, Shangri-La Hotels, and British Gas) saw the added benefits of providing a unifying thought for staff, consumers and other key stakeholders.

All is not rosy in our world however; we still have a long way to go in measuring emerging channels and we need to look beyond econometrics in our measurement tool kit. Again and again the judges wondered why so few have moved beyond 'Likes' as a measurement of social success. Very few papers used the wealth of knowledge that can be gained from analysing social sentiment, from visualising the digital footprint of an idea as it goes truly viral or harnessing the power of digital media in making TV more engaging and, ultimately, effective. Wieden+Kennedy's Martin Weigel (Chapter 3) has some strong opinions on our failure to move away from traditional models when we have the opportunity to define a more insightful and directional language for future communications models. One paper that didn't quite make the shortlist but did take a brave approach to understanding new communications models was LateRooms and it is worthy of tracking down on the database for that reason alone.

That said, reading the IPA Effectiveness Awards papers will help you do your job better, so watch the brilliant brand films on www.ipaeffectivenessawards.co.uk, or log onto the Databank via EASE (www.ipa.co.uk/ease) and get yourself in training for your entry into the effectiveness Olympics of the future.

SECTION 1

# New learning

**Chapter 1**

# Tapping into the nation's dreams

## The power of emotion in driving effectiveness

**By Marie Oldham**
Chief Strategy Officer, MPG Media Contacts
Convenor of Judges 2012

### The decline of the stiff upper lip

Chris Hoy does it, Andy Murray did it and even the Queen did it in 2012: Great Britain is busy reconnecting with our emotions and shedding a tear in public is no longer seen as weak or embarrassing. The post credit crunch world has seen the re-emergence of family values, a focus on supporting local business and creating support networks to inform everything from our parenting styles, where we go on holiday or where to get the best value car insurance. 'Reality TV' has moved on from Big Brother and we now want to see personal histories unfold on *Who Do You Think You Are?*, we are inspired by Mo Farah's story and John Bishop's tears as he cycled for Sports Relief gaining an audience of 6 million and 391,000 Facebook likes. Who could have predicted that the nation would respond to the tragic death of Claire Squires during the London Marathon by actively visiting a stranger's fundraising page; over 64,000 people collectively donating £1m plus. Like it or loathe it, Facebook and Twitter offer us an outlet for emotional outpouring, whether it is to comment on a human tragedy, shame a banker into resigning or salute a hero. Anyone who witnessed the singing volunteers at the Olympics, or the sweeping brush-toting residents of London who cleaned up after the 2011 riots can see that Great Britain is no longer the home of the stiff upper lip. Equally, we are starting to realise that the spend, spend, spend years of the 80s and 90s may have clouded our view of what's really important and that wanting your children to succeed in life is a deeper human motivation than wanting to have the most expensive car in your street.

## Getting beneath the skin of consumers

Successful communications campaigns often tap into the zeitgeist to reflect the emerging trends and feelings of the moment, positioning brands as relevant and 'for people like me'. However, I would argue that genuinely transformative big ideas tap into something much deeper. Agencies and clients who understand that human beings are driven by powerful needstates such as Belonging, Conviviality, Security, Recognition and Vitality can gain deeper insight from which to build ownable territories. These are some of the needstates that shape our aspirations and behaviours around family, our need to belong to communities, our need to feel accomplished and our need to feel secure in our lives.

For example, the closely connected needstates of Power, Vitality and Recognition explain why men throughout history have volunteered to go to war, needed to sail the seven seas in search of adventure and to climb treacherous mountains. The same needstates today are satisfied through adventurous gap year travels, running marathons or even the desire to parade every moment of your exciting life on Facebook and amass hundreds of friends who reinforce your personal Vitality by 'liking' your every comment. In order to gain rich insight into the purchase decisions made by parents you need to understand how creating a home is not about furniture but is about creating a safe haven from the nasty world for your children, how a barbecue with friends makes us feel valued, accepted, connected and how using fabric softener is an act of love.

The strongest entrants into this year's IPA Effectiveness Awards immediately demonstrated to the judges that they not only understood what makes human beings tick but also that times have changed, and for many audiences the recession has offered a much needed chance to reassess the lifestyle choices we are making and a chance to return to what is important in life.

## Making the nation cry, talk, and buy

John Lewis certainly delved deep into our emotional lives and the world beyond price to remind people of the role of their brand at life-defining moments and of the emotion imbued in many purchases we make. The campaign succeeded not through the power of advertising weight (it was outspent by many competing brands) but through the power of emotion. In addition to personal yet universal storylines, longer time-lengths and anthemic music were used to draw consumers into each film and engage them in a rich experience. In return, viewers were inspired to talk about the campaign at home, with friends face-to-face and online, to share the films widely and to let the staff know what they felt when they went to store. British Gas more overtly taps into the belief that we strive to create a world of warmth and safety and that trust is a defining KPI even for brands that deliver services and utilities. In a world of negative press, energy price rises, category confusion and increased competition, the unifying idea and the conversion of rational product message into emotional consumer benefit is starting to win through for the former monolith.

The Nikon paper is also worth a read as an example of human understanding completely changing the direction of a brand. The 'I AM' insight offers the brand a strong platform from which to tap into the increasing image culture emerging on our phones, laptops and tablets, a great example of technology facilitating our deep seated human need to define our lives by creating and capturing happy memories in forms that we can share in our virtual world as well as display in our physical world. Interestingly, different needstates come to the fore as we move through life; and The Art Fund paper highlights this with a brand that for too long depended on Accomplishment and Philanthropy needstates amongst older life stages as the core of its revenue base, but needed to get to grips with the social needs of younger consumers in order to win new members.

The IPA Effectiveness Awards are not the only place where this shift in consumer values is being understood and leveraged. We have all seen how Proctor & Gamble are making the seismic shift to recognise 'Mums' and the powerful role they often have as family 'glue'. Mums whose aspirations and desires are delivered into our lives daily as home-cooked food, healthy lunchboxes, soft towels, shampoo that won't hurt your eyes and hundreds of miles spent driving kids to swimming, hockey and horse riding – not to get the kids off their hands, but to give them the best chance in life. Proctor's positioning as the champion of Team GB's 'Nearest & dearest' was inspired; the 'Thank you mum' platform obviously has legs both globally and beyond the Olympics so you can look forward to seeing more of it in the future.

The need to tap into consumer needstates on a more meaningful level is also outlined in research carried out by Mumsnet for the 'venus2mars' event in 2011. Mumsnet asked women which ads connected with them and why. Campaigns such as Aldi, John Lewis (old couple), Dove and VW's Darth Vader got positive mentions because of their authenticity, understanding of the human condition and a sense that these situations could happen to 'real people'. Equally, some campaigns were slated for having no warmth or humanity. Campaigns that involve a group of women sitting around a kitchen table discussing what products they use for 'tummy troubles' were widely derided. Though sheer weight of ratings make these ads remembered, it is not likely that they achieve cut-through on a more meaningful level or build any long-term value.

## Insight-rich campaigns drive effectiveness in both the long and short term

It is not rocket science to say that the power of emotion shone through in many of this year's successful entries. However, the latest datamine analysis into long- and short-term effects of advertising provides four very robust findings:

1. emotional advertising has much broader effects than rational approaches – it tends to move *all* the dials;
2. emotional effects last much longer than rational effects;

3. this means that emotional effects build up over years in a way that rational effects do not;
4. these longer and broader effects of emotion mean that the ultimate paybacks from emotion are much higher.

However, what I believe we really learnt is that emotional responses which are deeply rooted in human values are the critical factor. Our world has changed significantly in the last five years; older consumers are getting back to the values they believe in, and modern families are creating homes and lifestyles that are not about bling and designer labels but are about shared experiences, being connected to the world and brands that offer value beyond just price. We also mustn't forget that the children and teenagers of today are growing up in this new world, and the brands they respect (Moshi Monsters, Nike, CBBC, Apple) offer multi-dimensional access, rich experiences and strong brand values. Whenever you set out to communicate in this new world, be sure you know what makes your audience tick on a human level.

# Comment

## Looking for the golden insight nuggets

**By Melanie Howard**
Co-Founder and Chair, Future Foundation

Genuine, fresh insights lie at the heart of good advertising. Understanding the motivations and needs of consumers remains critical to the creation of effective communications – a fact borne out by most of the winners in this year's crop of entries. This is particularly true of the big emotional, TV-led campaigns that play to the enduring dreams of the individuals, families and communities that make up the rich tapestry of modern society such as John Lewis and British Gas. Here, as Marie Oldham describes above, the insights are often about providing a new twist on something familiar, revealing the deep archetypes and desires that continue to shape our world in the face of the deluge of digital communications and flexible social structures.

However, my strong impression from all the entries taken together is that insight is failing to play as significant and pivotal a role as it should in inspiring, innovative and exciting new ideas and work. There seem to be two reasons for this: first, in the way papers are written, there is generally not enough emphasis on explaining either the insight itself and how it was derived. Nor, is there sufficient explanation of how the insight was really used to make a difference. Clearly the Nikon paper does do this, but in many it seems that insight has become another box to be ticked rather than the well-spring of greater understanding of the nature of an emerging strand of consumer behaviour or the discovery of something quite new.

All too often there were tantalising glimpses of a process that promised to be ground-breaking, but not enough detail provided to explain how new research methods were used and combined with other sources of knowledge to transpose the underlying proposition into new territory. One entry mentioned brain science and semiotics in passing but it would certainly be of great benefit to future entries if more time was given to unpicking how new insights were arrived at and used – not the whole process in detail, but articulating the components that gave rise to the 'aha' moment as many of Future Foundation's clients like to describe them. Shangri-La Hotels' decision to engage staff in the development of their campaign was a good example that made a real difference.

Second, and clearly connected, it seems that the role of insight in many agencies is in danger of becoming secondary and mechanistic rather than primary and transformative. The IPA's main business theme this year is innovation, and it is notable that innovation in the sources and uses of insight are remarkably thin on the ground amongst the majority of entries. This is particularly true in the area of digital communications and social media. With a few notable exceptions, IBM being the most outstanding, the way in which newer channels have been used appears to be a nod to the reality of digital interpenetration across consumers' lives these days, rather than as a significant route to effective behaviour change.

We see that TV remains the most commonly used medium across the entries received, followed by press advertising. Nothing wrong with that, but given the stunning growth in expenditure on digital media in recent years, it is disappointing that digital hasn't been deployed with greater verve in many instances. Thus the lack of new inspiration may well be working to reinforce established campaign models – big TV to generate big emotional responses with other media playing a subservient role. Most often the cases demonstrate how social media can help spread a stunning TV creative execution rather than seriously engage customers – such as with the Walkers example. The most pressing challenge must surely be to find ways of unlocking the real creative potential to generate strong emotions and powerful connections in the new spaces created by digital media.

The largest areas of new expenditure for brands nowadays are in the expanding domains of 'earned' or 'owned' media – both of which remain tantalisingly unmeasured and, by the evidence of the entries, largely unexploited. The Art Fund provides a great example of where a small organisation partnered with *The Guardian* to create a jointly branded proposition that generated impressive results. But with PR agencies rapidly encroaching on the more diffuse digital territory and social media spaces, it will be important for advertising agencies to forge and proclaim proven techniques here too. Search too was lamentably underrepresented in my view. So often the life blood of smaller brands on the internet, it was only used in 13 entries, despite being shown to have great effect such as in the paper for Which?.

Many of the Future Foundation's clients are talking about their insight teams becoming the 'think tank within', responsible for generating and communicating new ideas about customers that are changing their businesses at every level. Are agencies falling behind in this area where they used to lead? The planning revolution of the 1980s, which was predicated on using consumer research to improve advertising resonance and thus effectiveness, was a trailblazer and put agencies at the forefront of thinking about the real role of brands in customers' lives. For decades agencies were seen as guardians of NPD as a result by many clients. No longer – I would suggest that a reappraisal of the nature and role that insight plays in each and every campaign and how it can inspire genuinely innovative work in the use and integration of new digital channels in order to achieve a powerful emotional connection with the consumer is essential to driving the development of new models that go beyond the tried and tested. Innovation should be the order of the day in every part of the industry if it is to prove its continuing value to clients in the future. There are some great cases this year, but from the insight perspective definitely not enough to reassure me that insight is working its transformative magic throughout.

## Chapter 2

# The employee works

## From audience and message to brand medium, mentor and maker

**By Lorna Hawtin**
Disruption Director, TBWA\Manchester
Deputy Convenor of Judges

To remain remarkable in today's fast-paced business environment, companies need employees who embody this level of engagement and motivation. Which employer wouldn't want a workforce which is driven and passionate about their organisation's success and who is empowered by the brand and its purpose to know how they can personally contribute?

Brand marketers should be wary of treating their internal stakeholders as a secondary audience, merely informed about a new campaign in the final weeks before it launches. After all, a willing engaged employee has been shown to contribute directly to the bottom line of a business.[1] Equally, a disengaged employee can be a drain on both energy and productivity. The shocking reality is that, according to a Gallup poll, 71% of UK employees remain unengaged or even worse are actively disengaged. So in a period of unprecedented change, could employee engagement be a catalyst for resurgence that brand marketers have been overlooking?

### Employee as audience

In the past, employee responses to a campaign were largely an addendum to the 'main' results section rather than being a core objective. There are signs in this year's papers that employees are becoming a far more central and varied consideration. Cases such as John Lewis, British Gas, Snickers and Shangri-La Hotels made particular reference to the role and importance of employee engagement in both the development *and* execution of their campaigns.

Of course employees have always been susceptible to the external behaviours of the brand, and will always look for purpose and leadership in the communications they see pushing out into the world. After all, everything that exists between the brand and the customer is media and the same, of course, is true of the employee. Indeed, the British Gas paper this year continues to reiterate the value of communications as an internal engagement tool.

*It makes you feel really good about working for British Gas, really proud, especially when you get the chance to be in the ads. It makes us want to really look after customers as best we can.*

But this dimension was not simply included as an incremental effect in the case; it is clear that the campaign was founded in this objective, created to help unify the divisions of the organisation as well as reach out to customers. In tough times, employee-specific objectives can only become more important.

In the case of Shangri-La, the *first* manifestation of the idea was employee-facing: a manifesto in the form of a pocket book which was distributed to all employees along with internal advertising, training programmes and experiential launch events representing a significant proportion of the overall budget.

Similarly, John Lewis talked about the importance of making the staff feel part of the campaign and also demonstrated how employees felt personally proud and excited when they saw the campaign on air. This is obviously key for John Lewis as they are a 'Partnership' and staff are encouraged to take personal responsibility for delivering a quality service and customer satisfaction. There is a huge pride in working for John Lewis among staff; they therefore needed to feel huge pride in the campaign as a reflection of themselves.

## Beyond employees as message

Aside from the employee as an audience, we're also familiar with the starring role played by employees in advertising campaigns over the years. Now we're seeing the extent of this relationship deepening as employees become far more than simply a creative vehicle or 'reason' to believe in advertising.

Again, the Shangri-La story shows how they put their people at the heart of the whole strategy, not just creative execution; and by doing so created immense and lasting ownership of the brand idea and not just the communications idea.

*Shangri-La's version of outstanding customer service is based on employees' personal values: respect, humility, courtesy, helpfulness and sincerity.*

Staff training and engagement in the campaign received significant investment and the belief was that staff at their best led to happier customers and return visits. This signalled inwardly the belief and respect that they had for their people, whilst setting an ideal towards which employees could continue to aspire.

*The campaign objectives were to motivate employees in the Shangri-La way while also stimulating more stays. Establishing a service ideal in the public domain inspired employees to live up to a higher standard. It brought out the best in them: their inherent kindness and desire to treat guests well.*

Indeed, this type of case may be paving the way for a much more integrated and holistic approach to the role and importance of employee stakeholders in both campaign development and implementation. Productivity in one way or another is no longer the end of the story; they are not just audience or the brand message these days, we are seeing them as brand media, brand mentors and brand makers too.

## Employee as brand mentor and content maker

If at all, employees have historically been included in the creative development process as casual mentors. Just consider for a moment the eponymous 'tea lady test'. Their contribution has largely been sporadic and rather secondary, more a case of lip service than true collaboration. Perhaps with co-creation systems and cultures facilitating a wave of collaborations across the brand–consumer divide, we can start to realise the potential of employees too as more influential mentors in the development of branded content.

Furthermore, we could envision employees as curators and co-creators of the brand experience both in literal delivery of the promise, but also in their ability to shape, develop and personally contribute to brand behaviour ideas in a broader sense. So how would we allow them to *add value* to the idea we're propelling into culture as a means to foster a deeper sense of ownership?

After all, the ability to attract and retain talent remains central; and with employees increasingly looking beyond compensation to non-monetary factors such as advancement, recognition, pride and corporate social responsibility, the opportunity to shape the future direction of a business and claim a real stake in the process can only help to strengthen the employee–employer connection.[2]

## Employees as brand medium

This is key, because now more than ever, employees are able to multiply a brand's presence and message across a much larger network than ever before. Employees are the new influencers. Indeed, Tesco recently identified that their workforce has the potential to connect them to over two-thirds of the UK population. This kind of reach and personal influence should place employees ever more central in the communications planning process.

Part of the story of future campaign development must be the way in which we equip the workforce to carry the brand experience and message outwards. What knowledge, what incentive, what level of ownership, and what ideas can we equip employees with to help them seed the intent of the brand to the public at large?

Essentially, where do marketing campaigns start and where does service delivery stop these days?

Take as examples *Twelpforce* (a collective force of Best Buy technology pros offering tech advice in Tweet form), or amongst this year's papers, the John Lewis case. There, the retailer's employees were rewarded and engaged by a bonus which was linked to campaign-linked growth. This goes beyond the ephemeral brand campaign and employee relationship, to contribute to the business model itself. It seems we can stretch further than simple advocacy strategies, weaving them into our brand behaviour plans so that they can become a fundamental and cherished contributor in themselves.

## Making it happen more often

It remains the norm in many companies for the curation of a brand's behaviour to be divided internally across functions and geographies. Frequently HR, internal communications, customer and consumer marketing teams each pursue what remain in many cases rather disassociated agendas. How do we bring together teams with often separate agency relationships, contrasting notions regarding strategy and execution and even disparate geographies?

Indeed, is it even possible to create a planning, process and budgeting culture that not only enables global marketing teams to be cooperative, but draws in human resources and internal communications teams to work seamlessly with external marketing? To do so, agencies may need to broaden their relationships horizontally, reaching out to *all* those in the client business who have a responsibility to deliver and build a brand's relationships. The benefits can be valuable for all parties.

In the Snickers example, the core 'Stop being a diva' idea was developed in the US and was later informally adopted across markets fostering a significant increase in global marketing alignment. In addition to discussing the success of the advertising, the paper shares how it could not have succeeded without bringing the internal stakeholders on the journey. The idea would have remained a localised phenomenon if it had not harnessed the will of the employees and freed up organisational resources to help a great idea take hold.

Thinking more outwardly, if we are to connect these central co-ordinating teams more effectively with the peripheral curators of the brand, be they consumers or employees, we need to be willing to relinquish some control. We must recognise that the relationship between brand and audiences which has latterly been shaped by the marketing team, their agency partners and even consumers is now ready to be shaped and delivered by empowered and equipped employees too. Ultimately, employees may become the channel through which consumers increasingly receive branded content in the future, and it is our duty to ensure that employees are as connected to the external message and internal purpose of the brand as indeed we are.

Agencies will still therefore remain essential facilitators by creating a shared agenda, an inspirational sense of purpose, a common way of behaving and a benchmark that can become the catalyst for collaboration. Ultimately however, we must strive for a 'one brand' view. Searching for those magnetic creative properties which have the potential to entrance and engage all of a brand's audiences, and by doing so challenge the increasingly out-dated delineation between internal and external brand strategy once and for all.

## Notes

1 Towers Perrin has found that companies with engaged employees boosted operating income by 19% compared with companies with the lowest percentage of engaged employees, which saw operating income fall 33%. Watson Wyatt further found that companies with highly engaged employees experienced 26% higher employee productivity, lower turnover risk, greater ability to attract top talent, and 13% higher total returns to shareholders over the last five years. Additionally, highly engaged employees are twice as likely to be top performers – and miss 20% fewer days off work. They also exceed expectations in performance reviews and are more supportive of organisational change initiatives. A study by Towers Perrin similarly linked employee engagement to a 6% higher net-profit margin, and Aon Hewitt tied high levels of engagement (65% or greater) to outperforming the total stock market index and posting total shareholder returns 22% higher than average in 2010.

2 Constellation Research have found that engaged workers – those who participated in a forum, helped out a colleague in a chat, or provided feedback on an enterprise initiative – are 37% more likely to stay with their employers.

# Comment

**By Jo Blundell**
Marketing Director UK, Burger King

At Burger King, it may only take four people to sign off an idea but it takes 47 signatures at local, EMEA and global level to get that creative on to TV or into restaurant, and most importantly 25,000 internal stakeholders across the business – from crew to franchise operators – to believe in the brand, own the idea and make the message a reality that is grounded in truth.

In an age of heightened scrutiny and transparency with even greater channels for our guests to give feedback and comment on their experience, the onus is on marketing to ensure that every stakeholder, every function, every point of contact with the guest lives up to the promise: the story needs to add up. Any chink in the chain of evidence will be found and commented on.

Across the industry, every piece of communication is not only asked to prove its commercial worth but also to demonstrate a perceived and real value to all internal and external stakeholders as well as to the consumer.

So we talk of 'alignment' but this all too often is synonymous with compromise.

The fact that the winning papers have elegantly proven that the communications as an isolated factor met the commercial imperatives is a given. What marks them out from the rest is that they found a way of using 'buy in' to resonate internally and externally. And in these papers, we find the inspiration to strive for the highest common denominator and redefine 'alignment'.

Mars provides hope for any agency that sees the words 'global campaign' and groans. By finding a human truth, the team created a campaign vehicle that transcends borders and delivers global brand synergy. However, it also recognised the downfall of a 'one size fits all' approach to the execution and a lack of local ownership, especially against a backdrop of commercially and creatively successful country-led films, by allowing local culture to add additional emotional connection.

And then to the hotly debated British Gas and John Lewis papers: the discussion for the Grand Prix winner's position was fiercely focused on the scale of the task – the need to reflect back the personal responsibility for delivering the customer promise encouraged in 'partners' who are financially wedded to the success of the communications versus the need to unpick a disenfranchised set of businesses into one seamless service, turning a faceless commodity into a brand that warms the heart of the home. Both required the organisation to live up to the promise. Both achieved it.

But they also pay testament to the fact that great advertising delivers great results and also remind us that 'media changes. The rules of great creative do not' (@leeclowsbeard).

So I salute the marketers and the agencies celebrated in this book. They can rightfully take pride in the positive spirit they no doubt engendered within their organisations and the undeniable results delivered. For they have provided the evidence points for Mark Twain's observation that 'fiction is obliged to stick to the possibilities. Truth isn't'.

## Chapter 3

# TV and digital

## Are we there yet? Or do we even have a map?

**By Phil Danter**
Consultant

Despite many judges' hope that this would finally be the year of digital effectiveness becoming predominant, TV still dominated this year's entries, in many instances as a solus or near-solus medium. Great examples of campaigns which relied almost exclusively on TV include Gü, which used all its emotive power to portray the brand's 'innocent pleasure', and Snickers, which created a classic fame-driving idea ('You're not you when you're hungry') which was adapted brilliantly across markets.

Campaigns like these re-assured many judges who felt it was great to see that the growth in new channels does not equal the death of TV. We all know that TV viewing is growing; 40% of Twitter content during peak time each evening is about TV content, and chatting about content on Facebook whilst viewing only serves to enhance the viewing experience.

What was really interesting was to see the clear emergence of smart brands using distinct models of how TV and digital media can work together to achieve transformational campaigns and results. From this year's shortlist, what emerges are four models for combining TV with digital (by which we mean social platforms, websites, search and blogs facilitating dialogue and participation) – no doubt more will emerge as we all start to understand how these key media best combine to deliver effective ROMI.

### 1. 'Top-down' model

The first is a 'top-down' model whereby TV is used as the primary launch platform for the campaign message with digital media providing a 'social extension' of this theme. This is a model favoured by the John Lewis Partnership, whose entries for John Lewis and Waitrose both used TV to establish their campaign themes and then extended these themes on social platforms with dedicated content. Waitrose's 'School of magic' Christmas theme launched with 90" TV ads, but also gained 1.5 million views of related in-depth video on YouTube and a 'hub' of dedicated Facebook content. Crucially this all drove shopper volumes in a market dominated by 'value' messages.

## 2. 'Bottom-up' model

The second model is the polar opposite: a 'bottom-up' approach where significant levels of social/online activity is generated (usually with direct consumer participation/co-creation), which is then selectively 're-broadcast' via TV to a wider audience. Yorkshire Tea's campaign idea resounded in the relationship it had developed with its community of Facebook friends living as expats. They would alert Yorkshire Tea about their various 'tea crises' as a consequence of living abroad, and this became an experiential campaign whereby a Yorkshire Tea-branded van ('Little Urn') drove across the United States, rescuing UK expats from bad tea. Customers helped design the route and seven long-form films of the road trip were placed on a dedicated 'BrewTube' channel. TV was then used to broadcast the trip and specifically the consumer involvement/interaction – a classic bottom-up approach. Crucially, this helped them move from the number three tea brand to number two.

The highly successful anti-smoking campaign from Singapore used a similar bottom-up model, creating a real social 'movement' to salute quitters which tied in with government cessation programmes. The campaign then used TV to get the wider public to support quitters and create a national consciousness for the programme.

## 3. 'Prequel/teaser' model

The third model uses digital channels as a 'prequel' to TV launches, seeding often longer-form video to establish some buzz around campaigns before they launch more 'traditionally'. This is a new spin on the very well established 'teaser' model, but differs to 'bottom-up' as it doesn't involve online consumers directly in content development. Examples from this year's shortlist include Magnum Gold?!, whose creative idea of a 'heist movie' meant that a 2'30" trailer was a perfect digital 'prequel' for the TV campaign, gaining 1.9 million views. Similarly, VO5 Extreme Style created an unbranded teaser film for social platforms and their own website to hype their TV launch.

## 4. 'Recruitment' model

The fourth model sees TV take on a very specific role in relation to digital, which is to recruit viewers to online/social programmes and activities, thereby maximizing the levels of participation. Walkers' 'Do us a flavour' campaign is a classic example of this model, inviting consumers to suggest new flavours of crisps, the top six then being manufactured and participants voting on an eventual winner. Whilst this campaign involved various stages of flavour suggestions and voting, TV was clearly crucial to prompting mass engagement, helping to achieve 1.2 million flavour entries, 1.1 million votes and 4.3 million site views.

These four models of TV/digital integration naturally overlap, and many of this year's entries combined more than one – for example, Magnum Gold?! not only used digital channels for their prequel, but also used a top-down approach by taking the TV 'movie trailer' theme as the basis for a 'create your own blockbuster/movie poster' online competition, which generated 387,000 video entries. Similarly, VO5 (who also used the prequel model) also used the top-down model, extending the TV campaign online with a 'mockumentary' of the ad's production, out-takes and a number of styling 'how to' videos. Likewise, Walkers have experimented with all four models since they started integrated TV and digital/social activity in 2008.

However, what struck me most as I waded through 35 papers, is that few authors were clear and overt about their TV & digital strategy; both were often positioned as media decisions rather than core communications platforms which were planned in order to shape how the message was received and engaged with. No one has yet taken a stance as to which of these models might be most effective, in particular from the point of view of how to optimize the balance of investment/presence between TV and digital channels. As none of this year's entries were able to clearly separate the effects of different media (an issue which still makes econometricians lose sleep at night), we do not yet seem to have the tools to engage in the debate that will shape communications significantly in the next five to ten years.

For example, with the bottom-up model, it is logical to assume that TV copy created from existing social programmes would be highly meaningful to consumers and thus highly effective, given it is born from genuine consumer engagement (rather than the old model of creative teams imagining what might be motivating to them). However, what no one knows is whether this theoretically more engaging form of creative work *is* more effective, and thus how much *less investment* it might need compared to a more traditional top-down TV ad. Until we are able to answer these sorts of questions, clients may be rightly sceptical about the extent to which agencies know how best to balance TV/digital investment.

Given the most recent developments in TV, with Sky looking to beta-test single-household targeted TV spots next year, one way to initially judge these four models is on the basis of which might be more effective in the context of household-specific TV targeting, which will fast become a reality.

In a hyper-segmented world, the top-down model looks least likely to survive, as it runs contrary to the opportunity for multiple executions for increasingly discreet segments – tempting though it might be for some creative agencies to try and rack up production budgets by suggesting the need for multiple top-down TV executions.

The bottom-up model naturally works much better in a hyper-segmented future, as the significant amounts of content and data generated by 'grassroots' social programmes would enable agencies to produce multiple TV executions at relatively low cost. This approach would also use data analysis to understand how best to distribute multiple TV executions across hyper-segmented households.

The last two models of TV/digital integration (the 'prequel/teaser' and 'recruitment' model) would both be able to exploit the testing potential of single-household-targeted TV. Indeed, 'seeding' TV copy 'online' would no longer be necessary when TV can be targeted by household, as this would facilitate seeding on any scale via TV itself before a wider roll-out. Similarly, multiple incentives/calls to action for recruitment to social programmes could be tested in selected households before being scaled up.

The future will see the line between TV and digital as we define it today become increasingly blurred and even non-existent. You can also be sure it will be consumers who lead this, as they integrate their TV and digital platforms without thinking, using YouView, Smart TVs or dual screening. This will mean chapters like this will be utterly meaningless and agencies who are still debating how to integrate TV and digital operations will be fast running out of clients.

# Comment

## TV and digital: the real opportunity

**By Martin Weigel**
Head of Planning, Wieden+Kennedy Amsterdam

While the 'traditional' and the 'digital' have, at least in some quarters, regarded each other with suspicion (and occasionally outright hostility), in this latest collection of effectiveness stories, we're seeing smart agencies and clients harnessing what happens when TV and digital come together. Crucially, for demonstrable commercial gain.

John Lewis, for example, led its unlocking of the nation's tear ducts with TV. What might have been deemed a good ol' fashioned campaign (and there's nothing wrong with that) was deliberately orchestrated with an eye on social channels, with the advertising running in highly social programmes, i.e. those that generated a high amount of Twitter conversation.

In contrast, Walkers led its bid to get us to eat more crisps at lunchtime with live events designed to produce news content and conversation. Judicious use of TV both fuelled the intrigue around these stories and joined the dots, revealing the story behind the news reports.

Examples such as these rightly encourage us to explore the whole spectrum and variety of TV/digital combinations (and this has been done brilliantly by Phil elsewhere in this chapter). I would argue that they should also encourage us to be much more imaginative and specific in defining the role of different campaign elements in shaping people's attitudes and behaviours.

Rather than thinking of TV as being the primary vehicle that we 'blow out' in secondary channels, we might think about TV:

- as *signposting*... directing people to other destinations and interactions;
- as *ignition*... for a longer experience or programme;
- as *fuel*... intensifying interest in content experienced elsewhere;
- as *explainer*... elaborating the purpose or motivations behind other interactions.

And we can get more specific about the contribution and role of digital:

- as *propagating*... giving people things to *share*;
- as *involving*... giving people things to *do*;
- as *informing*... giving people resources that answer *questions*;

- as *amplifying*... giving people things to further *explore*;
- as *fulfilling*... turning interest into *purchase*.

The IPA's own Databank has already demonstrated that campaigns utilizing both online and TV achieved a 10% increase in effectiveness. This feels like progress. Though as the ancient Sufi wisdom advises, 'You think that because you understand "one" you understand "two" because one and one make two. But you must also understand "two".'

So perhaps it is time to erase the increasingly unhelpful distinction between 'TV' and 'digital' and focus on what really travels across platforms, channels and touchpoints: ideas.

These winners remind us that while they by no means have the monopoly on the outcome, digital interactions can help make our ideas properly *three-dimensional* ideas. That is, they can extend the physical and mental real estate an idea occupies in people's lives; they can extend the life of that idea across time, as well as the depth it has (see Figure 1).

Figure 1: The 3D idea

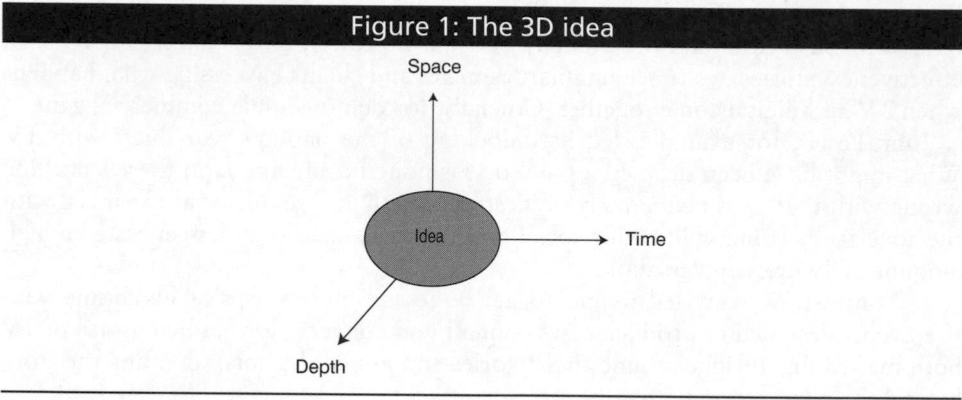


And perhaps that's the question we should be asking not of channels and touchpoints, but of our *ideas*. In other words what – in the light of the business challenge and audience – can we do to give our ideas more relevant time, more space and more depth?

## Chapter 4

# From clicks to yardsticks

## How digital media can help measure creative effectiveness

**By Simeon Duckworth**
Global Head of Analytics, Mindshare

Many of the latest digital media measurement techniques were on show in this year's IPA Awards entries. But there are some tricks that are still being missed. Digital measurement is no longer about post-campaign justification, but increasingly about understanding human behaviour in an adaptive environment.

### Digital media: new methods for understanding decision-making

We know from countless studies that digital media has a significant impact on brand metrics and sales, particularly in combination with other media. But the great thing about digital media is that, largely because it is interactive, it offers new and insightful ways to understand consumer reaction and response that go beyond traditional research.

*Interaction and engagement*

There is a huge amount of data available to understand how people seek and engage with advertising online. The Met case study, for example, shows how Facebook was used to target and engage 13–17-year-olds in dialogue about a complex issue, Joint Enterprise. Communication engagement was six times the average, with 60% of hosted videos watched in full. Importantly, we know that engagement is not only informative as a metric, but it can also help improve brand and message impact.[1]

### *Reaction, message take-out and issue insight*

Our actions, views and intentions are increasingly sedimented in digital data. Search terms, Twitter, Facebook posts, blogs and product reviews all have the potential to uncover the ways we are reacting to communications. So, for instance, share of search or natural search position are indicators of salience; positive and negative sentiment can be tracked and overlaid with communication weight; likes and re-tweets can be forms of endorsement and recommendation. A good example from this year's entries is the Singapore anti-smoking campaign, which used sentiment analysis to show how online conversation became more disposed to quitting.

### *Simpler experiments to measure brand impact*

The ability to conduct almost gold-standard control testing is an important way to measure brand affinity or sales impact and sets digital apart from other media.[2] The Met case study shows how by following up with people who liked the communication on Facebook, they were able to keep the debate going. With some careful design, this could have been extended to testing how kids exposed to the communication thought differently from a control group.

The John Lewis case study effectively illustrates many of these measures and techniques:

- How search (vs. competition) can be used to show relative popularity of the ad.
- How YouTube views and Facebook Likes (vs. competition) show relative reach and enjoyment.
- How YouTube drop-out rates through the duration of the ad measure engagement (it would have been interesting to see how this compared to the Neuroscience measures).
- How Twitter sentiment analysis can measure positive and negative sentiment (although not benchmarked).
- How Twitter can be used to select TV programme environments that are 'social' (although the rationale for why this is important is not clearly explained).

## Isolating influence

Digital media might be the most measurable media, but it is also the easiest to misinterpret. While its interactivity – constantly asking people to make decisions and choices – creates many very useful metrics, it is also, sadly, the very reason that can make it difficult to understand what influences these decisions. Unpicking cause and effect in digital media is riddled with nuance.

*Benchmarks and targets*

The most common mistake in digital measurement is to simply quote the number of fans, views, clicks or impressions. Size always needs a comparison, if not always a yardstick. So, the expected number of fans will depend systematically on the category, the strength and size of the brand, the country, the target audience and so on. Traditional research has known this for years and has developed sophisticated ways of creating norms taking into account factors such as brand size. Digital benchmarks need to do the same.

*Selection bias*

We are quite used to the idea that the online or Twitter population is different from the general population (but that it can still be very informative). We also know that Facebook fans are likely to be drawn from the most loyal consumers, so the value of a fan (three times the average consumer or whatever) tells you very little about the value of creating new fans. However, the deeper problem is that behaviour online and exposure to marketing is commonly driven by intent – the more I want to buy a product the more likely I am to see related media about it. If I intend to buy a Canon camera from Amazon, I am more likely to use Canon-related search words, to see Canon display ads (particularly with re-targeting) and even to be a fan on the Canon Facebook page. But none of this has influenced my decision to buy. Sadly, this 'selection bias' matters a lot. In a recent thorough study, it was found that naïve measurement can be biased to the tune of 1000%.[3] Great care needs to be taken when looking at simple correlations between offline and online metrics. Best practice should include test and control measures wherever possible, even with econometric models.

*Homophily*

As social media has grown, we have become more interested in how ideas propagate, through peer-to-peer networks and/or through mass media. The temptation is to see viral communication everywhere. Clusters of similar people tend to congregate together and may look like they are influencing each other, but are in fact responding to the same external stimulus – seeing a 'Quit smoking' ad on TV, for example. This is known as a 'homophily' – or more simply the idea that 'birds of feather flock together'. In some academic studies, over half of what looks like a cascade is actually 'homophily'.[4] The implication is that TV and other mass media may be more important than at first sight.[5] For example, this may not mean that the overall effectiveness of the Singapore anti-smoking campaign is different, but that the role of creating a movement is less important.

## Three tips to improve digital measurement

*1. Start early, plan evaluation, and implement test and control experiments*

Digital campaign measurement and evaluation is going on all the time, but it is often geared to short-term optimisation rather than measuring the wider impact of a creative idea. Account planners and media planners, who are often the stewards of IPA papers, should not only include digital measures within the existing evaluation plan, but importantly consider any test and control experiments. This requires quite a bit of forethought and pre-planning in comparison to the evaluation of more traditional media and metrics. Not everything can be tested. But, for example, regional tests of Google or Facebook activity could be included within econometric models or re-contact studies to measure brand metrics.

### *2. It's about more than clicks. Use online to evaluate brand behaviour and message take out*

Only one in six people have ever clicked on an ad, so it is perhaps no surprise that there is no correlation between clicks and brand impact. A good way of measuring brand impact is through re-contact studies – and it is a shame that none of the studies in this year's awards used this approach. It would have been interesting, in particular for the Met and Singapore anti-smoking campaigns, to have seen differences in attitudes between engaged and control groups.

### *3. Think about novel ways to connect online data sources*

Increasingly there is the option to use online panels to connect digital data and behavioural response in a single source. For example, Facebook and Google have connected loyalty card data with cookies to isolate the sales impact of their ad formats through controlled tests. Typically, IPA papers are looking at effectiveness more broadly than the role of individual channels, but the opportunity of using single source data (e.g. Kantar's Compete panel) in combination with econometric modelling and controlled testing offers powerful potential for understanding the chain of influence (including the role of targeting). For example, in the John Lewis case study, it would be valuable to know from the econometric model the extent to which online exposure drove sales online vs. offline.

## Future development

It seems likely that we are only really starting to realise the potential of digital measurement to uncover new insight. Over the coming years, IPA papers are likely to address:

- the importance of engagement to drive sales;
- how channels and owned assets interact to drive sales;
- the value (or not) of targeting;
- new ways to quantify online conversation with text analytics.

As with offline media before it, the IPA has the opportunity to guide digital measurement through its formative years and help shape standards for the future.

## Notes

1 Microsoft Advertising (2010) Dwell on branding.
2 Controlled tests are the cornerstone of isolating the impact of digital channels on brand (e.g. Millward Brown's Dynamic Logic) and on sales (e.g. Facebook's joint research with DataLogix).
3 Farahat, A. & Bailey, M. (2012) How effective is targeted advertising. WWW 2012, 16–20 April, Lyon, France.
4 Aral, S. & Walker, D. (2011) Identifying social influence in networks using randomized experiments. IEEE Intelligent Systems.
5 Watts, D. (2007) Viral marketing for the real world. *Harvard Business Review*.

# Comment

## The future is just beginning

**By Nick Southgate**
Behavioural Economics Consultant

The IPA Awards exist to prove advertising is effective. However, one of the real joys of reading papers is the ingenuity used in proving that effectiveness.

As the Awards enter their fourth decade one might imagine there are simply fewer ingenious ways left to be discovered, but also hope that the challenges of digital advertising might spur people on.

The bulk of shortlisted papers build on what has gone before. Large campaigns backed by plentiful data produce well-argued and incontrovertibly proven papers often backed by econometric models. The excellence is in the solidity not the invention.

There are also papers shortlisted that show real ingenuity in using limited data with persuasive intelligence. Both of Tim Broadbent's papers, the first for Shangri-La Hotels and the second for an anti-smoking campaign in Singapore, use well-selected and convincing benchmarks for limited data to make what is available work harder.

IBM provide a fascinating story about the appearance of the Watson super-computer on the quiz show *Jeopardy!*. The paper's central challenge is to connect content placed in a mass-market consumer channel with the nitty-gritty of B2B sales conversion. We will surely see more papers grapple with such extended chains of causation in the future.

But does the shortlist show breakthrough leaps in measurement and argument? I think not.

However, the long list most surely does.

I want to draw attention to two of these near misses. They point the way to a brave, exciting and innovative future. They were held back by a lack of data or gaps in the argument. However, those gaps were created by the leaps they tried to make. That ambition is celebrated here.

The Late Rooms paper argued for their client's success by comparing not campaigns, but overall business models. This is brilliant. For digital businesses the investment in digital presence cannot be regarded as optional for their business. It *is* their business. Imagine agencies helping clients build advertising into their business models and proving this model more effective because of advertising. That's a powerful shift in our offering to the client community and a proof of our worth as a creative business.

Similarly, the TV Licensing entry subtly combined issues of compliance, social acceptance and business processes for collection and enforcement with more traditional concerns of impact and effectiveness to produce an intriguing demonstration of how multiple agencies can collaborate with a client to change results by changing the way business is done.

These attempts at new models moved towards what might be called 'Return on idea' rather than return on investment. Agencies are at their best when ideas as well as financial investment drive a client's business. We have shown to clients what it costs them to cut investment in media and advertising. We need to show what it costs them to stop investing in ideas in business as well. To measure that would put the industry on a new footing. In this year's entries many steps were taken towards that future.

Chapter 5

# Econometrics

## An able servant but never the master

**By Louise Cook**
Consultant, Holmes & Cook

Writing this chapter has been both a vivid trip down memory lane and a realisation as to how far the industry has advanced in using econometrics to evaluate communications over the last 30 years. This is not just in terms of the quantity of econometrics being undertaken but also the quality and variety of what is being produced. In 2012, half of all the IPA papers submitted included modelling, and not only for UK brands but also for Latin American, Chinese and Indian ones. This is the highest ever proportion of papers to include econometrics, underlining its increasing importance as a means of demonstrating effectiveness and allocating media funds.

It seemed that fewer models were constructed specifically for the Awards than has previously been the case. Most were existing tools used for media or brand planning. Many papers incorporated multiple models either of different sales channels, products or SKUs. At the extreme, the Boots case was based on over 40 models, one for every key sales category. And although much of the modelling relied on well tried and tested approaches, some papers, like McDonald's, did use leading-edge techniques.

In a fast-moving industry there will always be aspects of our modelling we should review and things we could improve, but we should take a moment to celebrate the significant advancements we have made and to remember the pioneers, especially perhaps Dr Simon Broadbent, who was so very involved with these Awards for many years and whose legacy is the concept of adstock used in almost all the models submitted.

The first paper to include econometrics as we would recognise it today was Dulux Natural Whites in 1984. By contemporary standards the model was very simple. In the 1980s, sales data was at best monthly, often bi-monthly, limiting the factors you could sensibly include. But the context was also less complicated – TV plus supporting press or outdoor to extend reach. No ambient, no experiential, no social. No integration to try and unpick.

In the 80s and early 90s, much of the modelling in IPA papers was FMCG or financial. It was 1996 before modelling appeared in telecoms and retail papers; 1998 for cars; 2000 for dot.com; 2004 for transport; 2006 for the public sector. Almost all these categories were represented in 2012, along with pay TV, lottery and charity. All present their own challenges with respect to theory, available data and difficulty of task.

As the use of econometrics in IPA papers grew over the years, it became clear that not all models were equal, nor was the way they were explained within the context of wider results. Some papers included modelling which was far from robust and detracted from other evidence, causing significant issues for judging and even heated debate!

As early as 1988, in *Advertising Works 5* Paul Feldwick wrote:

> *This year's entry was also characterised by numerous examples of the use and abuse of econometric modelling. At its worst, this manifested itself as an apparent belief that to mention the existence of a model was sufficient evidence to justify any conclusion, without necessarily giving any further details. (In at least one case it was not only impossible to see how the model had been done, but even unclear as to what the dependent variable was.)*

One of the difficulties with econometrics is that it is so hard for non-technicians to judge whether it is sound. Any academic paper including econometrics would be expected to demonstrate the validity of the models used via a range of statistical tests checked by reviewers. Although the IPA judging panel has included econometric technical judges since 1998, prior to 2012 only a minority of IPA papers adhered to anything like academic standards of reporting, making it tricky even for them to confirm suspected flaws.

This year the technical judging system was changed. A guideline specification for an econometric technical appendix was circulated to all entrants, and it was asked that wherever a model was quoted it be accompanied by the appropriate technical detail. There were then three judges (experienced econometricians) whose sole task was to evaluate the econometrics, both on the basis of what was reported in these appendices and on how the results were incorporated in the paper itself. This enabled the main judging panel to focus on all other aspects of a submission and avoid the distraction and dissent that questionable models create. Having three econometricians also meant that where there truly was dissent, there wouldn't be a hung jury.

The industry judges have said how much easier this made the short-listing process. More importantly it has coincided with a major step-change in the quality of econometric submissions, even when compared with 2010. Being an econometrician, I should be wary of claiming causality – we may of course as an industry have been quietly pulling our collective socks up anyway. But one of the things that has been notable and must be welcomed is that, where we would generally have appendices only from certain suppliers, most have complied this year and some to a very high standard. Transparency can only benefit us all. Many clients are still extremely wary of what they view as a 'black box'. If we publicly demonstrate that our work is beyond reproach, blind faith could be exchanged for a trust which is well-placed.

A personal issue with much current modelling is its almost single-minded focus on ROI, and in some papers this is practically its only use. Strictly speaking, econometrics is a tool to test our theories as to how particular factors or particular types of communication affect sales. It should thus be able to help unravel some of the 'how' communication works, not just the 'how much'.

To be fair there are some good examples of this amongst 2012 entries, where modelling of intermediate KPIs, like key equity measures, aids both understanding and argument. For Aviva we see individual campaigns for motor and life policies feeding into Aviva's masterbrand equity. McDonald's use modelling to establish the role that re-building trust played in driving sales metrics.

In our current multi-dimensional media world, no one research technique has all the answers, making our biggest challenge to pull together their findings to provide genuine insight. Econometrics is a very powerful technique and capable of breaking new ground, but its dependence on theory means that it is often in conjunction with other research that it is most likely to do this.

So, econometrics adds maximum value to a paper where it is interwoven with other research, where approaches corroborate one another or provide a logical chain of evidence as to how an effect came about. In many instances though, planners appear not to fully understand the results they have and so do not fully utilise them. This is most obvious in the section discounting non-communication factors. Action: econometrician to check what has been written and to advise.

My first involvement with the Awards was in 1988 and I can honestly say that since then they have been pivotal in working out how to stretch what econometrics can do and how to combine its results with other research. Because our world is moving so fast and because theory as to the nature of the response doesn't always exist, we often find ourselves developing it as part of the evaluation. Being set a challenge is therefore an important way of providing a development framework.

The introduction of the Longer and Broader category in 1990 was the first time I had thought to do something now so obvious – use data other than time-series to corroborate results. Here it was to show that PG Tips and Tetley tea were indistinguishable in blind taste tests, therefore the observed response differences (PG's lower price elasticity and more muted response to Private Label growth) weren't product related, but had to be the result of stronger brand equity and thus PG's long-running TV campaign.

In 2004 the gauntlet was thrown down to evaluate integrated campaigns. The IPA mandate was to show effects by medium, but we realised quickly that there simply wasn't enough granularity in our data to separate most media from the dominant sound of TV across 20 different creative executions. Here the task was thus very much to determine via other research and benchmarks what the econometric results actually meant and what they said about integration. This truly involved a 360°

inspection of all research results and much discussion to establish how they fitted together and what they implied.

The next challenge will be to nail social media and word of mouth. How do these impact sales theoretically? Does the data support those theories? Can we reconcile the output of different methodologies? What contribution can econometrics make to this whole process? Should we be more widely applying some of the modelling techniques developed in recent years such as panel approaches or else combining econometric results with those of techniques like agent-based modelling?

Fascinating times ahead!

# Comment

**By Richard Bateson**
Commercial Director, Camelot Global

For many marketing-focused organisations, econometrics can be both a godsend and an albatross, and I fear this issue may be replicated in IPA Effectiveness Awards papers. In many ways a good econometric model can be the holy grail, separating out the key influences on sales shifts and allowing you to evaluate the ROMI of factors as diverse as TV advertising, promotions, the weather, the economy and competitor communications – who wouldn't want one? Another dimension of econometrics I find particularly powerful is the ability to look across a diverse brand portfolio and understand the interdependencies of each of your products, halo effects and even potential cannibalisation. Many marketers I have worked with have found modeling to be hugely informative as a marketing tool, both as a measurement tool in understanding the effectiveness of past activity, but also as a planning tool for future activity. Within the National Lottery, econometrics is particularly important as we need to be answerable to our players and all our stakeholders as to where we invest our budgets and how much we return to National Lottery Good Causes for every marketing pound spent. It cannot answer all questions, but does provide one strong tool within our measurement suite.

And therein lies the rub – I believe that econometrics is only one tool and should not be treated as gospel or looked at in isolation. When looking at the effect of past activity, results should align with your gut instinct, you should be able to see the same indicators in your other tracking tools, and even qualitative consumer research should back up your findings. My main concern with econometrics is the danger of thinking 'if it says it in the model it must be true' – models are only as good as the data put into them, the skills of the analyst and the other information available in order to look at the outputs holistically. Lots of murky factors can be hiding in the base figure and, perhaps more importantly, ground-breaking new activity which is driving a valuable ROMI into the business can be lost because it is not robust enough to be picked up in a model which learns from the past and from deviation.

My second concern is therefore that dependency on models which tell us what worked in the past can make us risk averse in the future. Few clients would take a leap into social if all eyes are on the econometrics model, the Orange association with cinema probably doesn't stack up in the world of econometrics, and no-one would ever develop 90 second films. Marketing still needs bravery alongside the science bit. So my words of advice to any potential author of an IPA Awards entry in the future are: use your econometric findings wisely; do not let jargon dominate; do not fall into the trap of thinking it is the only proof you need; explore all avenues to make your case stack up; don't use econometrics as your end goal – use it to say 'the model suggests this is what is happening, do we have more evidence to support that?'.

## Chapter 6

# Creativity and effectiveness

## Never lose sight of the power of the idea

**By Bridget Angear**
Joint Chief Strategic Officer, Abbott Mead Vickers BBDO

For the purposes of this chapter, I've defined creativity as the use of the imagination to produce original ideas, and effectiveness as the ability to prove that these ideas have had a demonstrable effect.

In some ways I think it's a bit odd that as an industry we still feel the need to prove that there is a link. I think most of us who work in this crazy, chaotic, frustrating and wonderful business take it for granted that creative communications work better than uncreative ones. Why else would we toil long into the night in the quest for an original idea? I wanted to work in advertising because of what Nick Kamen did for Levis 501 back in 1984. This was an ad that got everyone of my generation talking about it. I wanted to be part of an industry that could, overnight, change people's perceptions of a brand. At the time I was just reacting to it emotionally. I didn't know that 'fame', which is what it created for Levis, has proven to be the real key to business success.

So, here's the thing. Perhaps because creativity is such a subjective thing, we have been reluctant to put an objective number on just how effective it is. The IPA Awards pride themselves on being 'objective' by disentangling creativity from the measurement of effectiveness. And of course it is probably necessary to approach judging this way in order to focus on absolute proof and genuine business results. However, can we go on deluding ourselves that creativity is not intrinsically linked to effectiveness?

There are two seminal studies that tackle this issue. And they both conclude that creative campaigns are more than ten times more effective than others.

The first of these is a paper entitled 'Advertising's greatest hits: profitability and brand value' by Karl Weaver and Paul Dyson which concludes that after market size, creative execution is the second most important factor in determining advertising profitability.[1] They calculated a profit multiplier of ten.

The second study, 'The link between creativity and effectiveness', published in 2011, fused together the Gunn Report database of creatively-awarded campaigns with the IPA Effectiveness database and concluded that creatively-awarded campaigns are more efficient than non-awarded ones in terms of the level of market share growth they drive.[2]

These studies give us a chance not merely to assert that creativity works, but to demonstrate just how well it works. I believe it is clients in particular who we need to share these findings with. We need to reinforce to the client world the value of working with creative agencies who aspire to achieve the best results for all clients, who understand the value to business of powerful ideas and who invest in talented individuals and the right resource to deliver this.

Understanding the impact of creative thinking on effectiveness can help clients bear with the frustrations, time delays and extra expense almost always incurred in the quest for originality. I don't know if it is apocryphal but the story is told that the Guinness surfers ad was so late and so over budget that the question was asked 'do we really need the horses?'. Thankfully, the client remained committed, but perhaps having numbers like the ones above might have helped sooth the furrowed brows of both senior agency and client personnel?

So, we can prove just how well creativity works. We also know a lot about how it works that is worthy of sharing more with our clients.

For example, the paper 'The dangers of common sense marketing' by Les Binet concludes,[3]

> *Evidence from the IPA databank suggests that there are some fundamental flaws in assumptions that most marketing people work by…as an industry we are too easily seduced by clever theories and not interested enough in testing them… all pre-testing systems are based on some model of how advertising works. If that model is wrong, then pre-testing will give misleading results.*

His analysis of IPA cases found that those which used pre-testing data reported much smaller business effects than those that didn't. Could data such as this provide the start point for a conversation with clients and research agencies about the need to develop new frameworks and approaches to testing creativity? This seems so much more productive than railing against those which we know don't.

The IPA has commissioned many seminal studies on behalf of its member agencies, including some of those cited above. Many have used the databank of 32 years of IPA Effectiveness Awards entries for the analysis. That databank now has over 1,000 cases – what a treasure house of learning these are. Brands from BMW to Barnado's, from Drug Awareness to Dulux, from M&S to Milkmen have won the Grand Prix – in the words of Donald Gunn 'the crème de la crème of effectiveness'.

The latest analysis, carried out by Peter Field and Les Binet, looks at long-term campaigns vs. short to understand the difference in effect and ROMI.[4] There is significant evidence of the wider effects of long-term campaigns. However, in terms of creativity and effect, the team found that, across all time periods, campaigns which are highly awarded for their creativity are ten times more efficient than others. They have broader business effects, bigger effect on market share and are particularly good at reducing price sensitivity. Original thinking has the power to create 'fame', and fame magnifies effectiveness and efficiency.

The IPA has always been an extraordinary content creator and going forward it will find new ways to extract learning from the databank of case studies. But it seems fitting for the digital age that the IPA also becomes a content distributor and finds new ways to share its learnings with key audiences (especially clients), not only through a diverse mix of channels but also more often. There's a chapter in *Switch* by Chip and Dan Heath where they suggest that the way to motivate people to change is to concentrate on 'bright spots' – things that have worked really well – and then to be forensic in your analysis of why and how they worked in order that others can replicate them.[5]

Greatness does not come easy. Behind every outstanding creative idea that has made it into the world is an outstanding client. A client who has committed to it when others doubted, and backed it all the way even though the road to getting there will have been anything but smooth. We need to celebrate these clients, help others learn from them and hear their stories of what it is like from their side. What they've learnt about how to get the best from their agencies and create the right conditions for creativity to flourish. To understand their motivations, fears, hopes and aspirations. Because they are the ones that make everything we do possible.

And a few final questions I have been pondering:

- How could we make it the norm for everyone working in this industry to have the maximum possible exposure to all the best thinking that is on offer?
- How could we build the right habits from the start?
- Should we insist on client and agency people being trained together more often?
- Should everyone have to read the very best IPA cases every year as part of their CPD?
- Should everyone have to have read a collection of the very best theses our industry has produced?

Because it is my belief that, although we work in a business driven by creativity, analysis and measurement need to be given an equal voice if we are to continue to serve clients and ourselves well.

## Notes

1 Source: D2D Limited 2006.
2 The link between creativity and effectiveness. New findings from the Gunn Report and the IPA Database in association with Thinkbox.
3 Binet, L. (2009) The dangers of common sense marketing. *Market Leader*, Quarter 3, June.
4 Field, P. & Binet, L. (2013) Advertising Effectiveness: the long & the short of it.
5 Heath, C. & Heath, D. (2011) *Switch: How to Change Things When Change is Hard*. London: Random House Business Books.

SECTION 2

# Prize winners

# SPECIAL PRIZES

**GRAND PRIX**
John Lewis

**BEST CHANNEL PLANNING**
Digital UK

**BEST INTERNATIONAL**
Snickers

**BEST DEMONSTRATION OF CONSUMER PARTICIPATION**
Metropolitan Police Service

**BEST USE OF INSIGHT**
Cadbury Dairy Milk

**THE CHANNON PRIZE FOR BEST NEW LEARNING**
Metropolitan Police Service

**THE BROADBENT PRIZE FOR BEST DEDICATION TO EFFECTIVENESS**
Waitrose

**EFFECTIVENESS COMPANY OF THE YEAR**
Abbott Mead Vickers BBDO

# GRAND PRIX

**Adam & Eve and Manning Gottlieb OMD for John Lewis (pp. 53–92)**

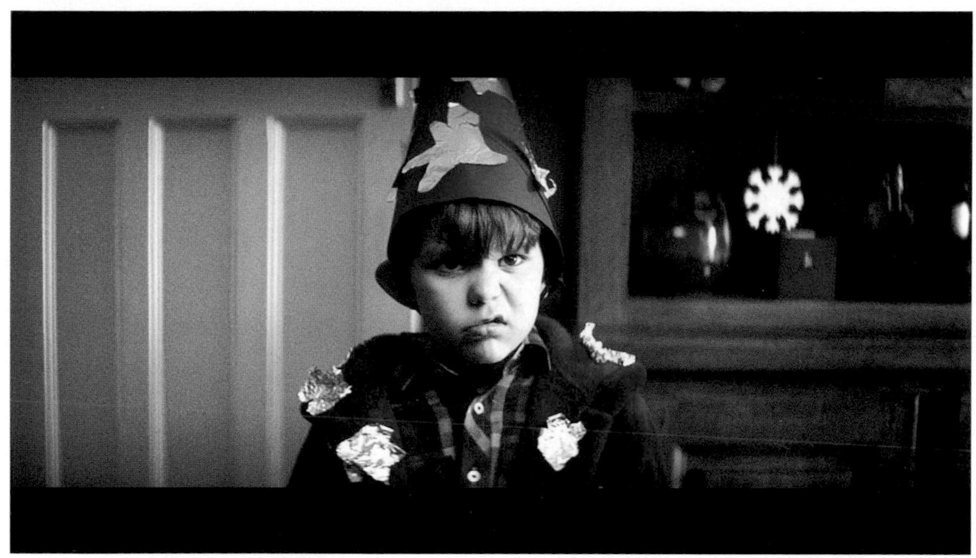

# GOLD AWARDS

**McCann Manchester for Aldi (pp. 93–118)**

**CHI & Partners for British Gas (pp. 119–144)**

**Ogilvy & Mather India for Cadbury Dairy Milk (pp. 145–164)**

**Leo Burnett for Department for Transport (pp. 165–195)**

**DLKW Lowe, Digital UK, MediaCom and Switchover Help Scheme for Digital UK (pp. 197–233)**

**Ogilvy & Mather Shanghai for Dove (pp. 235–255)**

**Ogilvy & Mather Singapore for Health Promotion Board Singapore (pp. 257–276)**

# SILVER AWARDS

**101 for Art Fund (pp. 447–460)**

**RKCR/Y&R for Danone Activia (pp. 461–491)**

**Ogilvy & Mather New York for IBM (pp. 493–511)**

**Lowe and Partners and Lola Madrid for Magnum Gold?! (pp. 513–538)**

**Jung von Matt AG for Nikon (pp. 539–559)**

**Lew'Lara\TBWA for Nissan (pp. 561–583)**

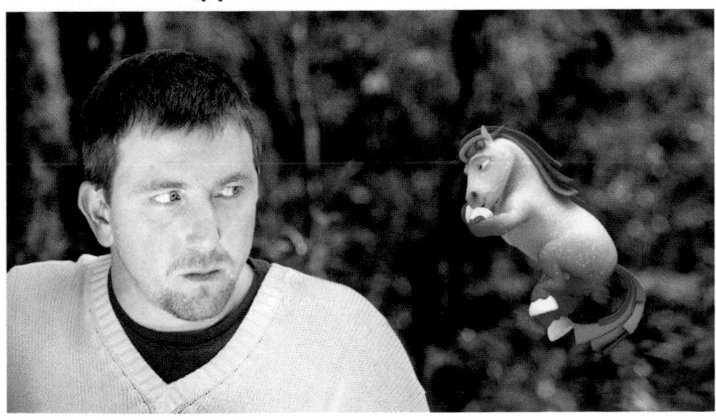

**MPG Media Contacts for The National Lottery (pp. 585–605)**

**Euro RSCG London for VO5 Extreme Style (pp. 607–630)**

**Bartle Bogle Hegarty for Waitrose (pp. 631–654)**

**Beattie McGuinness Bungay for Yorkshire Tea (pp. 655–679)**

SECTION 3

# Gold winners

## Chapter 7

# John Lewis

## Making the nation cry ... and buy

**By David Golding, Adam & Eve;**
**Helen Weavers, Real World Planning and**
**Paul Knight, Manning Gottlieb OMD**
Contributing authors: Sam Veitch and Lesley Turnbull, BrandScience
Credited companies: Creative Agency: Adam & Eve; Media Agency: Manning Gottlieb OMD; Production Company: Blink Productions; Research Agency: Neuro-Insight; Research Agency: Millward Brown; Client: John Lewis

**Editor's summary**

In mid-2009 John Lewis was struggling in a very challenging financial climate. Recent advertising investment had been ineffective and a new approach was required. A bold decision to use highly emotional advertising, particularly on TV, generated a huge amount of interest in the brand which resulted in more visitors, coming more frequently who spent more money. The campaign generated £1,074m of incremental sales and £261m of incremental profit in just over two years. Thousands of Partners also benefited as the profitability of John Lewis communications enhanced the annual bonus that they share.

Both judging panels wondered if we too were being taken for an emotional roller coaster journey with this paper. Who could not love the epic, heart tugging films that link John Lewis to the important things in life such as family and friends? Were we just being swept along by the feel-good factor or did this campaign genuinely deliver? Following rigorous debate and thorough challenging of all claims we agreed that, yes, this is quality. This is the work we all aspire to do in order to change both perceptions and behaviours around brands and to strengthen our clients' business now and for the future.

## Introduction

Few people would dispute that in 2012 John Lewis is one of the most talked about and admired advertisers in the UK. But it's easy to forget how recently that wasn't the case and how rapid the turnaround in the brand's communications effectiveness has been. This paper tells the story of how a bold decision to use highly emotional advertising, in a very challenging economic climate, has delivered a highly impressive £1,074m of incremental sales and £261m of incremental profit since Christmas 2009.

Not only has the John Lewis business benefited greatly but so have all the Partners, who share an annual bonus based on profits. This paper proves how emotional advertising has directly enriched the lives of thousands of people, and brought a tear to the eye of millions.

## About John Lewis

The first store bearing the John Lewis name opened in 1864, but the brand as we know it today was born in 1929 when John Spedan Lewis inherited the business on his father's death. John Spedan was a visionary thinker who believed that commercial success would result from putting the happiness of workers at the heart of everything the company did. He created a Partnership structure in which every permanent employee is an owner of the business.

While the idea at the heart of John Lewis was radical, in other respects John Lewis has been a very conservative organisation. It wasn't until 2005 that all stores were open seven days a week.[1] It wasn't until 2007 that all but two of the stores took full John Lewis branding.[2] There are still only 36 stores, compared with almost 350 for M&S[3] and more than 150 for Debenhams. And, unusually for a retailer, the company has been very reluctant to spend significant amounts of money on marketing and advertising. John Lewis is an inherently modest organisation. Between 1997 and 2006 it spent an average of £5.7m per year on advertising, compared to £26.4m for M&S and £12.9m for Debenhams.[4]

## Setting the scene

Our story covers the period from early 2009 to the end of 2011. Throughout this period life has been very difficult on the UK high street. The financial downturn has driven consumer confidence to record lows (Figure 1) and the housing market has collapsed (Figure 2), particularly impacting on retailers with reliance on home-related categories.

As a result, retail sales growth has been very muted or non-existent through this period (Figure 3) and numerous retailers have been forced to announce closure or administration (Table 1).

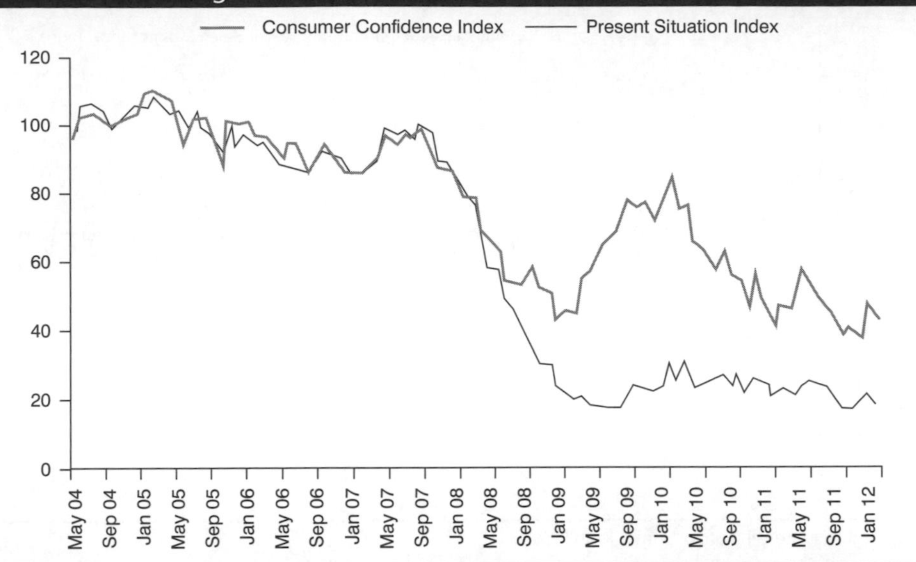


Source: Nationwide, in partnership with TNS

## Figure 2: Mortgage approvals and average house prices

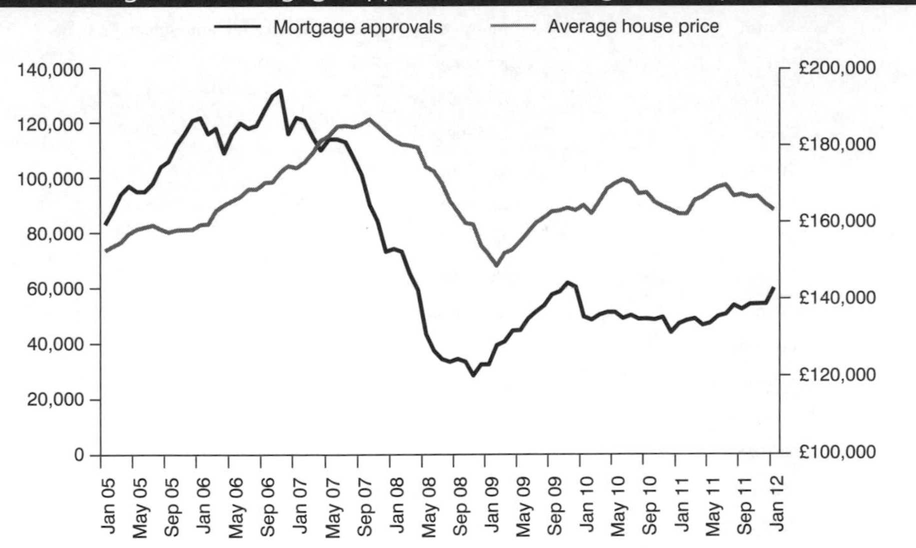


Source: Bank of England, Nationwide

## Figure 3: Sales growth (like-for-like) amongst UK non-food retailers

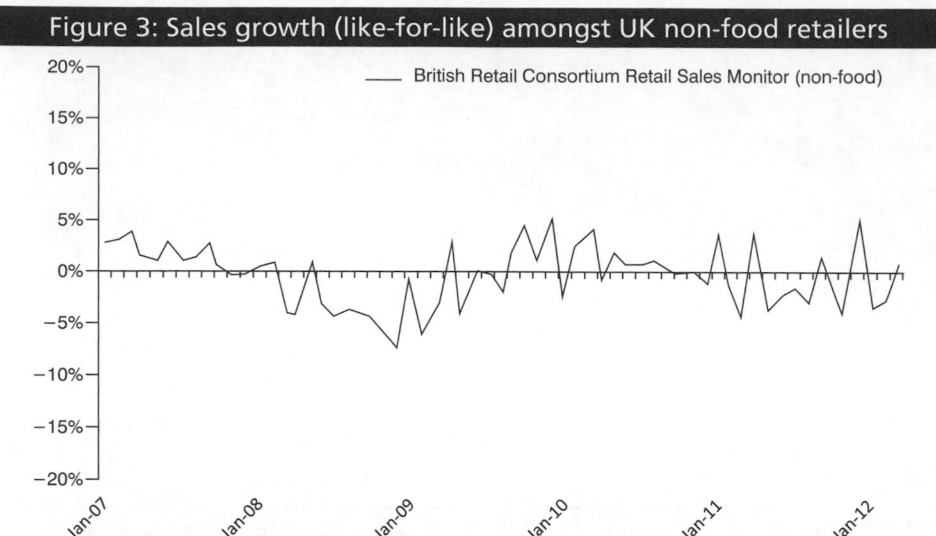


Source: British Retail Consortium;[6] John Lewis

## Table 1: UK retailers in John Lewis categories announcing closure/administration

| Brand | Month that closure/administration announced |
|---|---|
| MFI | Nov 2008 |
| Woolworths | Dec 2008 |
| Zavvi | Dec 2008 |
| The Pier | Dec 2008 |
| Land of Leather | Jan 2009 |
| Allied Carpets | Jul 2009 |
| Borders | Nov 2009 |
| Adams | Dec 2009 |
| Confetti | Aug 2010 |
| Suits You | Oct 2010 |
| Focus DIY | May 2011 |
| Habitat | Jun 2011 |
| Jane Norman | Jun 2011 |
| TJ Hughes | Jun 2011 |
| Lombok | Aug 2011 |
| Best Buy | Nov 2011 |
| Barratts | Dec 2011 |
| La Senza | Jan 2012 |
| Peacocks | Jan 2012 |
| Fenn Wright Manson | Mar 2012 |
| Game | Mar 2012 |

Source: Press coverage

## John Lewis in 2009: a retailer suffering more than most

After years of solid growth, John Lewis was under intense pressure. Gross sales were -0.1% and like-for-like sales -3.4% for the financial year ending Jan 2009. Operating profit had dropped by 26% and the annual Partner bonus was the lowest for five years (Figure 4).

**Figure 4: Media coverage of John Lewis financial results 2009**

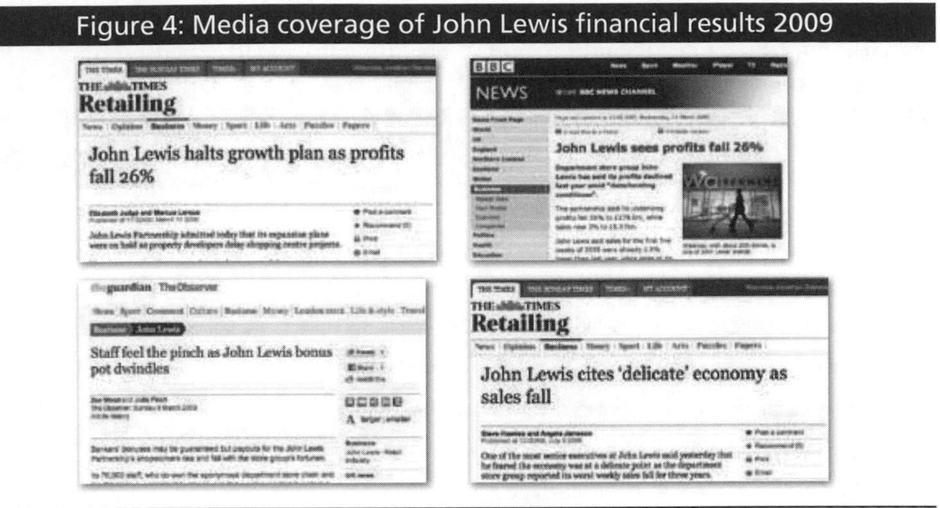

THE TIMES
Retailing
John Lewis halts growth plan as profits fall 26%

BBC NEWS
John Lewis sees profits fall 26%

the guardian The Observer
Staff feel the pinch as John Lewis bonus pot dwindles

THE TIMES
Retailing
John Lewis cites 'delicate' economy as sales fall

For all but two of the previous 18 months, like-for-like sales had been negative and often more so than the British Retail Consortium's average (Figure 5). John Lewis wasn't just suffering in line with the rest of the market, it was suffering more.

**Figure 5: Sales growth (like-for-like) amongst UK non-food retailers vs. John Lewis prior to mid-2009**

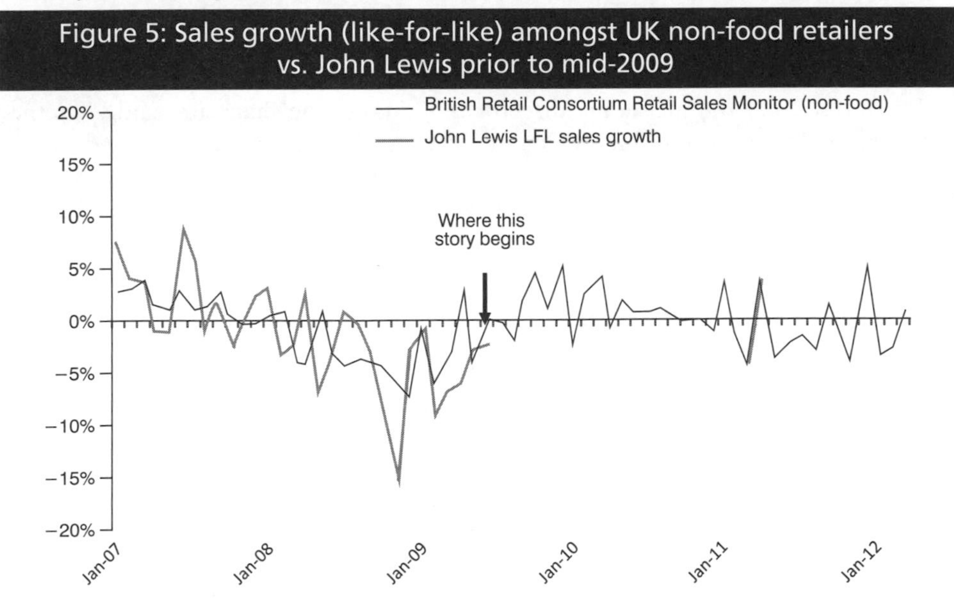


Source: British Retail Consortium; John Lewis

As Andy Street, the Managing Director (and Partner since 1985), said at the time: 'Last year was probably the most tricky in my time at the Partnership ... The year ahead is going to be equally difficult, if not harder.'[7]

While John Lewis had been making steady progress to make its business more competitive and appealing (stores had been refurbished, the website was receiving investment), the brand overall remained a bit of a sleeping giant: it kept a low profile and was respected rather than loved. It was considered more for functional items than for emotional ones (Figures 6 and 7). For some it seemed expensive and out-of-synch with the times.

**Figure 6: Qualitative research summary of the strategic challenge for John Lewis**

**Reaffirming the strategy**

- Drive 'blinkered' shoppers' consideration of John Lewis for desirable as well as functional items
- Their current barriers are:

  These shoppers are 'stuck' in their functional approach to the store – only visiting certain departments

  But they also perceive John Lewis as quite old-fashioned

  They therefore don't think it will have truly contemporary lifestyle items

  Nor is it an image they want to associate with when it comes to these more desirable items

Source: The Nursery qualitative research, Jan 2005

The marketing team was convinced that communications could play a significant role in re-energising the brand and business. However, they faced an internal challenge: John Lewis had recently significantly increased its investment in advertising ... but to little apparent positive effect.[8]

The various campaigns in TV and print across 2007 and 2008 had been product-focused and lacking in consistency. They had struggled to cut through, were poorly branded and had failed to impress Partners. Their average Awareness Index was 2.[9]

In March 2009 the marketing director left. Marketing magazine said 'Whether Inglis [Craig Inglis, head of brand communications] has inherited a poisoned chalice is open to debate. He certainly faces a considerable challenge, given that weekly sales at the upmarket department store have been sliding since the beginning of the year.'[10]

## The communications solution

A new communications approach was required. The team felt that the emphasis needed to be far more emotional, to make existing customers more conscious of what makes John Lewis special. John Lewis serves people at some of the most emotional times in their lives (moving into or refurbishing a home, getting married, having babies, preparing for Christmas) yet the brand had never brought to life the emotional role it plays.

Analysis of previous IPA effectiveness cases had demonstrated the power of emotional strategies to drive significant business effects,[11] and learnings from neuroscience were demonstrating that the most effective role for communication is

## Figure 7: Analysis of drivers of 'bonding' (a measure of loyalty)

Loyalty to department stores in general is driven most strongly by emotional affinity and perceived popularity, with rational affinity in third place and perceived price in fourth place.

| | | Importance ranking 2008 |
|---|---|---|
| Recommend to friends; Want to be seen using; Appeal to you more; Have a higher opinion of; Meets your needs; Trust more than others | Emotional affinity | =1 |
| Most popular; Unaided awareness | Popularity | =1 |
| Better customer service; Have a wider range of products; Sell better quality products; Make shopping easier | Rational affinity | 3 |
| Charge more acceptable prices than other stores | Price | 4 |
| Growing more popular; Setting trends | Leadership | 5 |
| Offer something different | Difference | 6 |

John Lewis does much better than expected (given the size of the brand and relative to its competitive set) in the area of rational affinity but no better than expected on emotional dimensions and significantly worse than expected on perceived popularity and value.

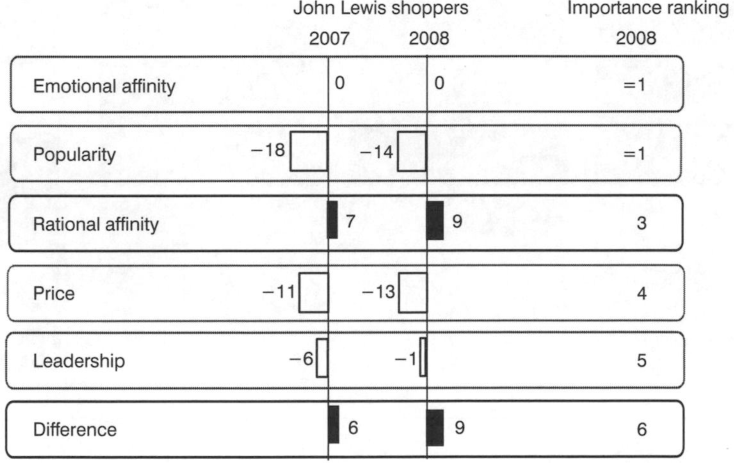


Source: BrandZ/Millward Brown 2008, base department store/John Lewis last 12 month shoppers at bonding level

to plant positive emotional memories in people's minds, so the time felt right to try a more emotional approach.

The primary objective was to encourage existing shoppers to visit a little more and spend a little more. On a secondary level it was hoped that communications could get those who hadn't shopped at John Lewis recently to see the brand in a fresh light and decide to visit again or for the first time.

There have been two main strands of communications (both led by TV advertising), plus a continuation of support (mostly in press) for topics like Clearance[12] and fashion.

### *1. Christmas*

Christmas 2009 became the first test of this new strategy. Christmas is hugely important to John Lewis sales so the stakes were high.[13]

At Christmas most retailers showcase gifts and emphasise how easy and fun they will make Christmas shopping. Celebrities, sparkle and over-excitement are involved. However, John Lewis chose to position itself as the home of thoughtful gifting, celebrating those who put more care into what they choose and how they present it.

The Christmas 2009 commercial 'Remember the feeling' (Figure 8) showed children unwrapping adult gifts with undisguised delight. It used a well-known moving track re-recorded by a contemporary artist, a model which all subsequent commercials followed (Table 2).

**Figure 8: 'Remember the feeling' TV ad and other Christmas 2009 communications**

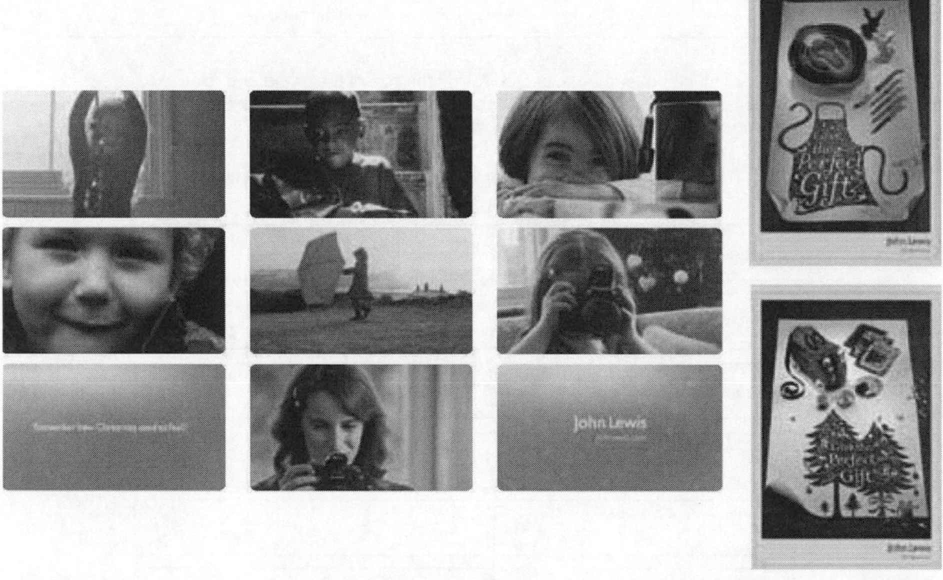


**Table 2: Music tracks used in the TV ads**

| Track | Original artist | Artist |
|---|---|---|
| 'Sweet child o' mine' | Guns N' Roses | Taken by Trees |
| 'Always a woman' | Billy Joel | Fyfe Dangerfield |
| 'Your song' | Elton John | Ellie Goulding |
| 'Please please please' | The Smiths | Slow Moving Millie |

In Christmas 2010 the campaign was spearheaded by the TV ad 'For those who care' (Figure 9a) and for Christmas 2011 'The long wait' was created (Figure 9b).

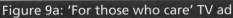

Figure 9a: 'For those who care' TV ad

Figure 9b: 'The long wait' TV ad and other Christmas 2011 communications

*2. 'Never knowingly undersold'*

John Lewis's commitment to 'Never knowingly undersold' was introduced by John Spedan Lewis in 1925.[14] He intended it not just as a price promise but as a total trading philosophy, meaning not only that if a customer can find the same product cheaper elsewhere, John Lewis will refund the difference, but also that all products will be the best quality for the price and expert advice will add additional value. However, 'Never knowingly undersold' had been allowed to become rather recessive and purely price-focused in meaning (Figure 10).

Figure 10: 'Never knowingly undersold' communication pre 2010

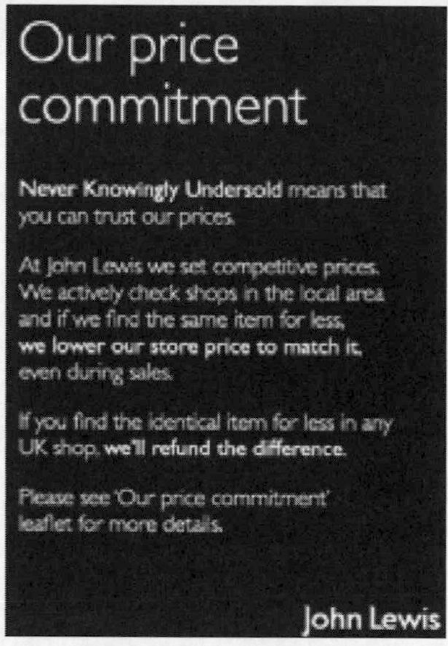


As the recession continued it was felt that the time was right to return to the broader meaning of 'Never knowingly undersold' and put it back at the heart of the brand. A new mark (Figure 11) was introduced on all products and touchpoints, and there was a desire for communications to highlight the refreshed philosophy. But how to do that within an emotional approach?

Figure 11: New 'Never knowingly undersold' communication from 2010

**Never Knowingly Undersold**
**on quality | on price | on service**

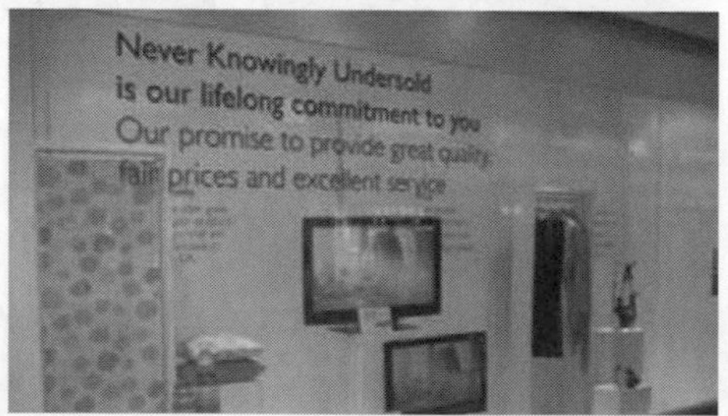

The resulting commercial 'Always a woman' (Figure 12) was an emotional demonstration of John Lewis's constancy through the key moments of a customer's life, implying that in a world that now felt very changeable, John Lewis remains a beacon of stability, offering permanent and multi-dimensional good value.

Figure 12: 'Always a woman' TV ad, May 2010

In Autumn 2011, John Lewis decided to again support the 'Never knowingly undersold' promise but this time focusing on one of its three key 'directorates': Electrical & Home Technology. The price-matching commitment had been recently extended to the John Lewis website and to matching competitors' online prices, which made John Lewis more competitive. However, John Lewis wasn't always seen as somewhere to go for the latest technology products and desirable brands.

The commercial 'Through the ages' (Figure 13) cleverly continued the 'passage of time' idea but using the insight that people enjoy reminiscing about entertainment products that have played a big role in their lives over the years.

## The media approach

John Lewis's media approach has worked hard to optimise the emotional strategy and ensure an integrated approach. The two main channels have been TV and press (Table 3).

### *1. TV*

TV is central due to its unparalleled ability to engage large audiences emotionally. Time lengths have been long (at least 60" for the lead version of each commercial) and airtime bursts brief, making the ratio of production cost to media spend high.

**Figure 13: 'Through the ages' TV ad and other electricals communications, September 2011**

However, at John Lewis, communications are seen as a customer touchpoint just like a new product line or store opening, so they must reflect the brand's quality standards.

TV buying has ensured that the ads are experienced within emotional programming (e.g. X Factor/Britain's Got Talent, dramas, soaps) and that as many people as possible see the ad for the first time within a short period (since this is when word-of-mouth and sharing are most likely).

While the typical John Lewis customer was not an early adopter of social media, it became clear in 2009 that people were talking about the advertising on Facebook

## Table 3: Media plan

| | 2009 | | 2010 | | | | | | | | | | | | 2011 | | | | | | | | | | | |
|---|---|---|---|---|---|---|---|---|---|---|---|---|---|---|---|---|---|---|---|---|---|---|---|---|---|---|
| | Nov | Dec | Jan | Feb | Mar | Apr | May | Jun | Jul | Aug | Sep | Oct | Nov | Dec | Jan | Feb | Mar | Apr | May | Jun | Jul | Aug | Sep | Oct | Nov | Dec |
| TV | 'Remember the feeling' | | | | | 'Always a woman' | | | | | | | 'For those who care' | | | | | 'Always a woman' re-run | | | | | 'Through the ages' | | 'The long wait' | |
| Cinema | | | | | | | | | | | | | | | | | | | | | | | | | | |
| Press | | | | | | | | | | | | | | | | | | | | | | | | | | |
| Outdoor | | | | | | | | | | | | | | | | | | | | | | | | | | |
| Online display | | | | | | | | | | | | | | | | | | | | | | | | | | |

and Twitter. Since Christmas 2010, the TV ads have launched on the brand's Facebook page the day before they first air on TV. By Christmas 2011, TV buying was prioritising the programmes seen to be highly 'sociable' (provoke a much higher number of Tweets within 24 hours than you'd expect from their coverage levels – Figure 14).

### *2. Print (press/outdoor)*

Print channels are important to add more rational messaging about products, prices, stores and Clearance periods to the emotional story told on TV. However, even here a more emotional approach has been developed using richer colours, stylish photography and more emotive copy (Figure 15).

## Figure 14: Analysis of 'sociability' of TV programmes

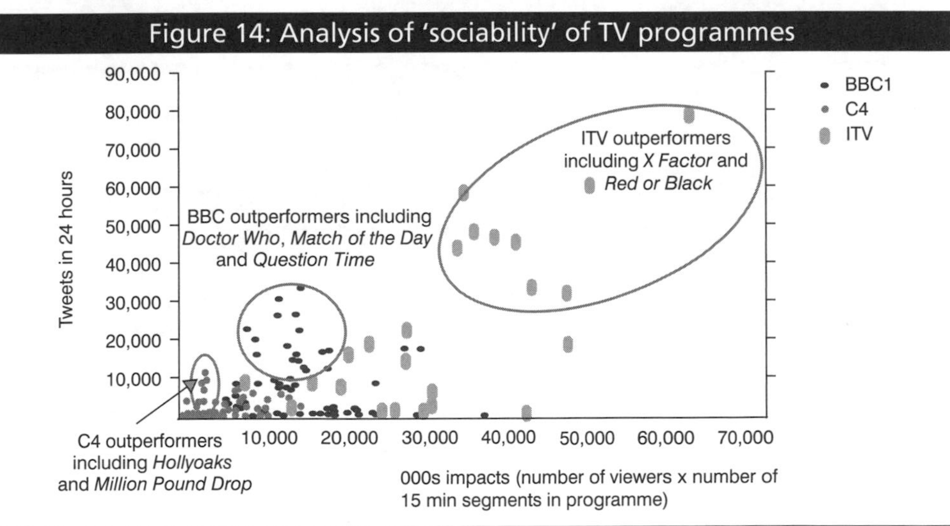


Source: Data Science. The horizontal axis takes account of how long a programme is, since this affects how likely it is to generate Tweets

Figure 15: Examples of more emotional print communications

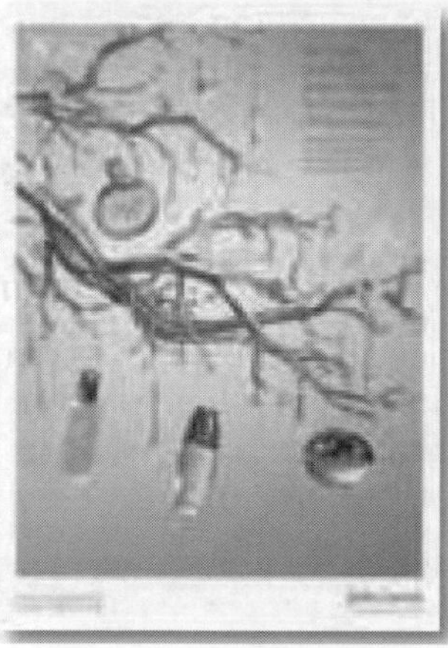

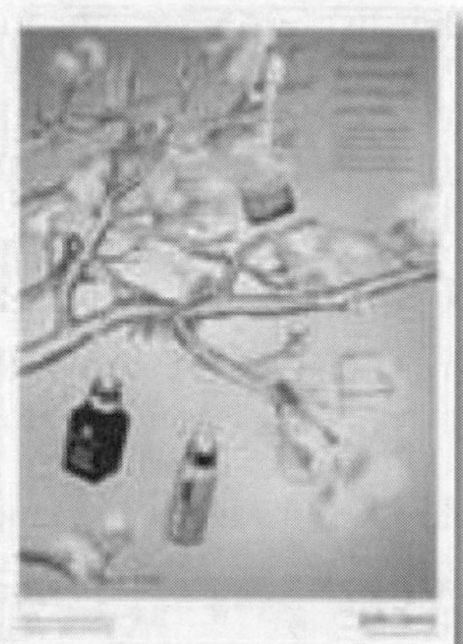

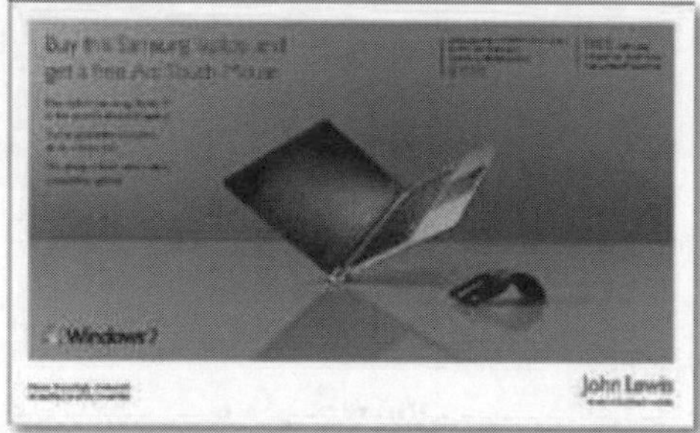

A consistent look and feel has created a strong tonal 'handwriting' for the brand across all product categories and types of message. This improves branding and communications efficiency, contributing to media spends remaining far lower than those of key competitors (Table 4). M&S's annual TV spend is greater than John Lewis's entire annual advertising spend.[15]

**Table 4: John Lewis above-the-line spend and share of voice**

| | 2009 | 2010 | 2011 |
|---|---|---|---|
| ATL spend | £15.2m | £21.3m | £26.3m |
| ATL share of voice | 7.5% | 7.9% | 9.4% |
| TV spend | £2.3m | £8.9m | £10.0m |
| TV share of voice | 2.6% | 6.5% | 6.6% |

Source: Nielsen AdDynamix

## The results

The John Lewis campaign has become one of the most popular and successful marketing stories of recent years. We will review the impact of the communications in a number of ways.

1. The communications were noticed and enjoyed.
2. The communications were sought out, talked about and shared by consumers.
3. The communications were talked about by the media and entered popular culture.
4. Brand perceptions improved.
5. Penetration, frequency and average spend increased.
6. The business grew and outperformed the competition.
7. The communications directly contributed to significant sales and profit uplifts.
8. The communications had other indirect business effects.
9. The communications made Partners very happy.

### *1. The communications were noticed and enjoyed*

Tracking shows that existing customers, our primary audience, have noticed the advertising to an extent previously unseen (Figure 16) and have really enjoyed it, with the music contributing strongly to appeal (Figure 17).

Figure 16: Total brand communication awareness and TV ad awareness

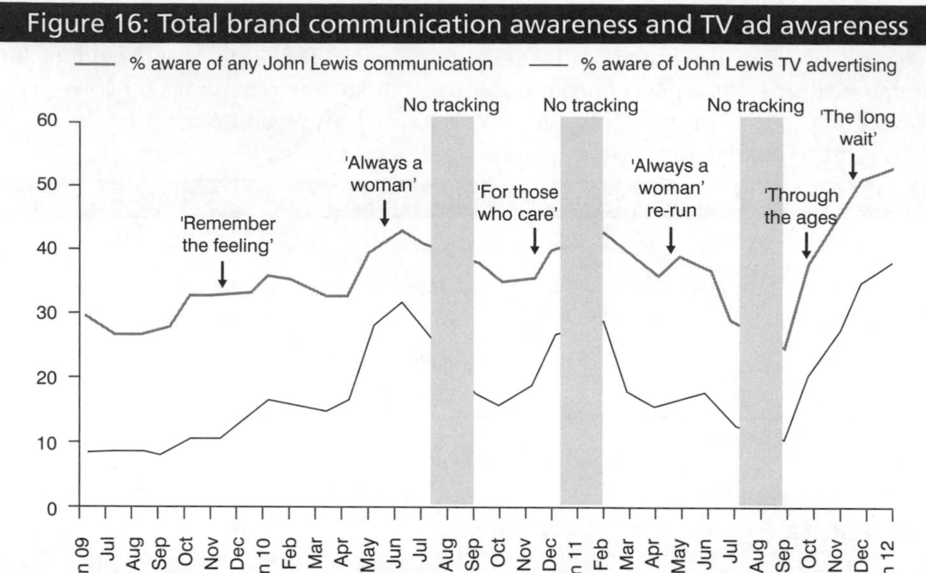


Source: Millward Brown tracking amongst John Lewis shoppers[16] in catchment areas (rolling 8 week data). Gaps represent breaks in fieldwork

Figure 17: Advertising enjoyment and music enjoyment

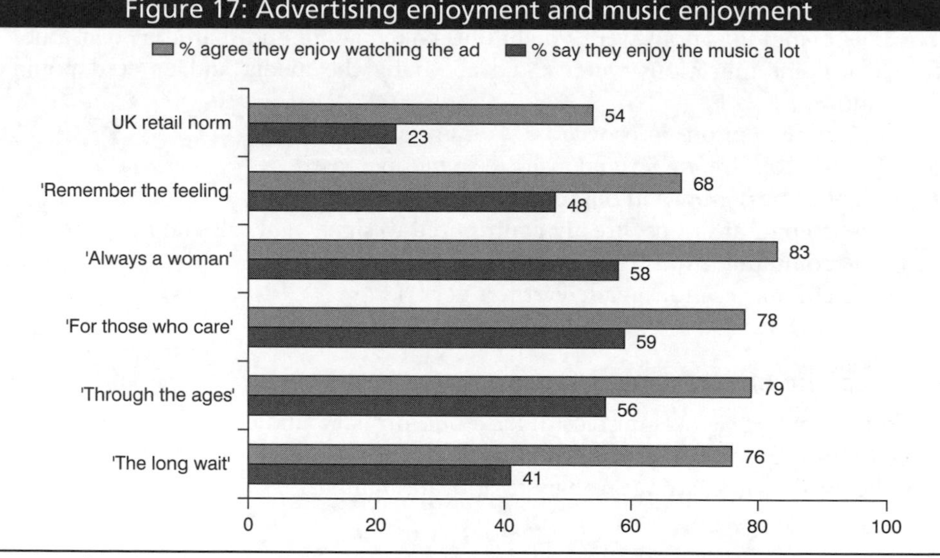


Source: Millward Brown tracking amongst John Lewis shoppers in catchment areas

As intended, the ads triggered positive emotions amongst customers (Figure 18).

We also have evidence that memorability and emotional engagement extend beyond John Lewis customers to a wider audience. In *Campaign* magazine's 'Punter Appeal' research, 'The long wait' achieved the highest rating to date for a private sector ad (Table 5); and in a *Daily Mirror* poll (Figure 19) the John Lewis Christmas 2011 ad was strongly preferred.

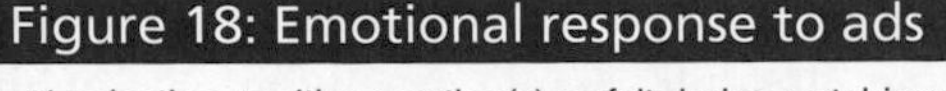

## Figure 18: Emotional response to ads

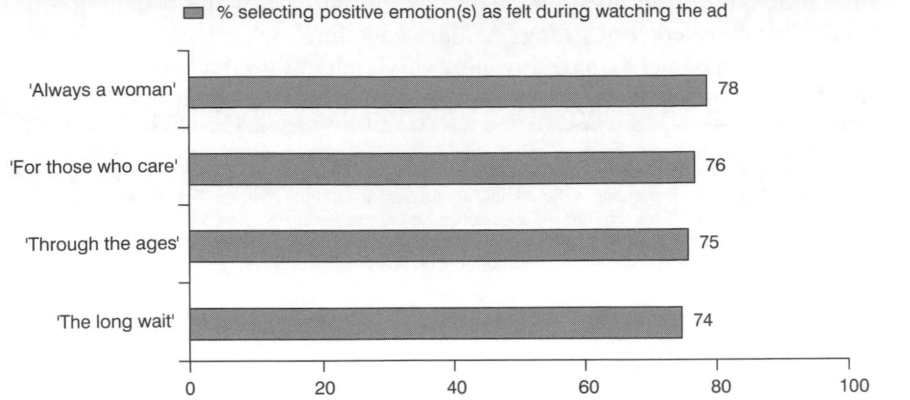


Source: Millward Brown tracking amongst John Lewis shoppers in catchment areas. These questions weren't asked for Christmas 2009 and there isn't a norm

## Table 5: 'Punter Appeal' scores [17]

| | Consumer rating |
|---|---|
| John Lewis 'The long wait' | 6.49 |
| Met Police 'Choose a different ending' | 6.45 |
| T Mobile 'Royal wedding' | 6.37 |
| Cadbury's Dairy Milk 'Clothes dance' | 6.33 |
| M&S 'Everybody dance' | 6.30 |
| Virgin Atlantic 'Love at first sight' | 6.29 |
| Barclaycard 'Rollercoaster' | 6.24 |

Source: Campaign magazine

## Figure 19: *Daily Mirror* poll

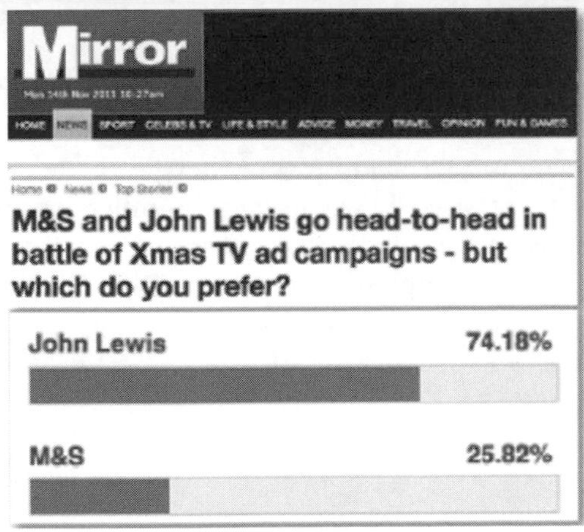

Mirror

HOME NEWS SPORT CELEBS & TV LIFE & STYLE ADVICE MONEY TRAVEL OPINION FUN & GAMES

**M&S and John Lewis go head-to-head in battle of Xmas TV ad campaigns - but which do you prefer?**

John Lewis 74.18%

M&S 25.82%

Source: *Daily Mirror* website

A more sophisticated piece of evidence is from a neuroscience study (Figure 20). The brain activity of an all-adult sample was monitored while watching 'Always a woman'. This revealed very strong 'memory encoding', which correlates highly with subsequent purchase behaviour, driven by very high emotional engagement.

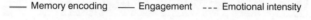

**Figure 20: Neuroscience tracking of 'Always a woman'**

A form of brain-imaging technology called steady-state topography records electrical signals at the scalp in order to build a second-by-second picture of activity in the brain. 114 adults 18–64 were shown TV ads within a TV programme, without knowing the purpose of the research. For 'Always a woman' there are peaks of left-brain response at or above typical maximum levels throughout the narrative, indicating very strong memory encoding, including at the moment of branding. Engagement and emotional intensity are both very high throughout, indicating a strong sense of personal relevance.

— Memory encoding — Engagement --- Emotional intensity

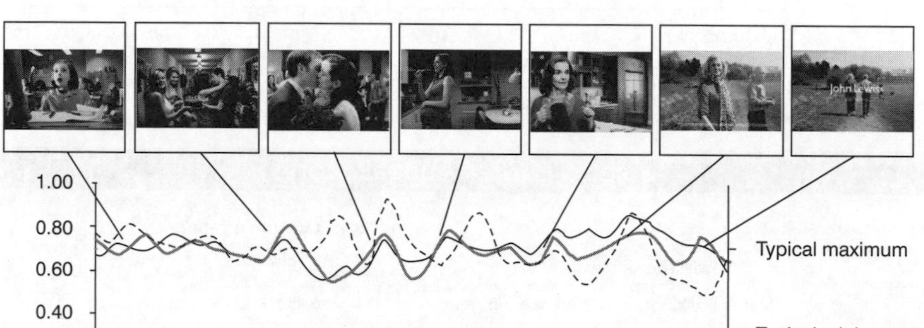


Source: Neuro-Insight

### *2. The communications were sought out, talked about and shared by consumers*

Not only were the communications noticed and enjoyed at the time of viewing but people talked about them, looked for them online and shared them, thus greatly amplifying the effect of the bought media and implying an active engagement that is more likely to lead to behavioural change than merely passive consumption of paid-for airtime.

First, the evidence for our primary target audience of existing customers: tracking shows that they were unusually likely to say they've talked about the advertising (Figure 21), they contacted John Lewis in large numbers to praise the advertising (Figure 22) and many following John Lewis on Facebook commented, shared the ads and even formed groups to champion them (Figure 23).

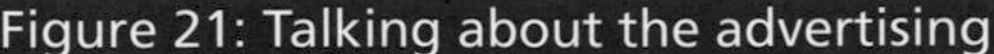

## Figure 21: Talking about the advertising

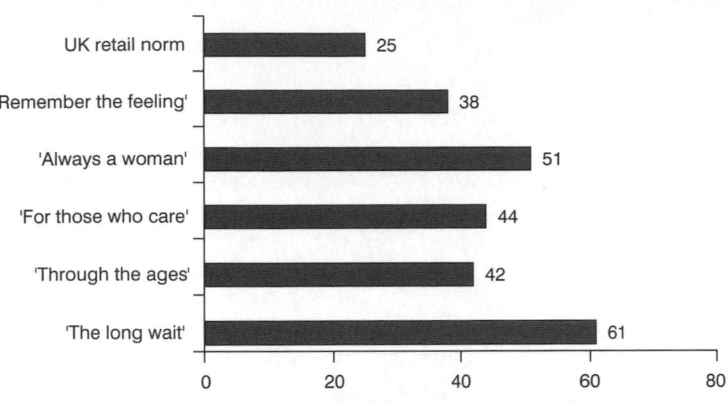


Source: Millward Brown tracking amongst John Lewis shoppers in catchment areas

## Figure 22: Examples of direct feedback from customers

'I just wanted to say thank you for the wonderful tv advert. 10 out of 10! The best thing on tv at the moment. Something very touching about it! Well done indeed – and congratulations on a fabulous store in Liverpool.'

'Apologies if this is not the correct email address, but I just wanted to say 'Thank You' for producing such a beautiful, life affirming advert. It's very moving and speaks volumes about your company and its proposition.'

'I have just watched your TV advert on Channel 4 tonight, absolutely brilliant. It said everything why my partner Ann and I love about your stores, food and service.'

'Dear Sirs, I thought that I should write to you to tell you how wonderful I feel your current advertisement on the television is. I am a rather elderly gentleman, who has recently lost his wife after 54 years of very happy marriage.
I must admit I found the way this advertisement was made was very very moving, and although I admit that I am still easily moved to tears this is so well done. By the way, I shop, eat, and park at your wonderful store in Norwich, my first stop when in town.'

Source: John Lewis

There is also a wealth of evidence of active engagement by a broader audience beyond just existing customers. Searches for 'john lewis ad' or similar vastly exceeded searches for 'm&s ad' or similar, or 'comparethemarket ad' or similar during this period (Figure 24).

Figure 23: Facebook response to Christmas 2011 ad

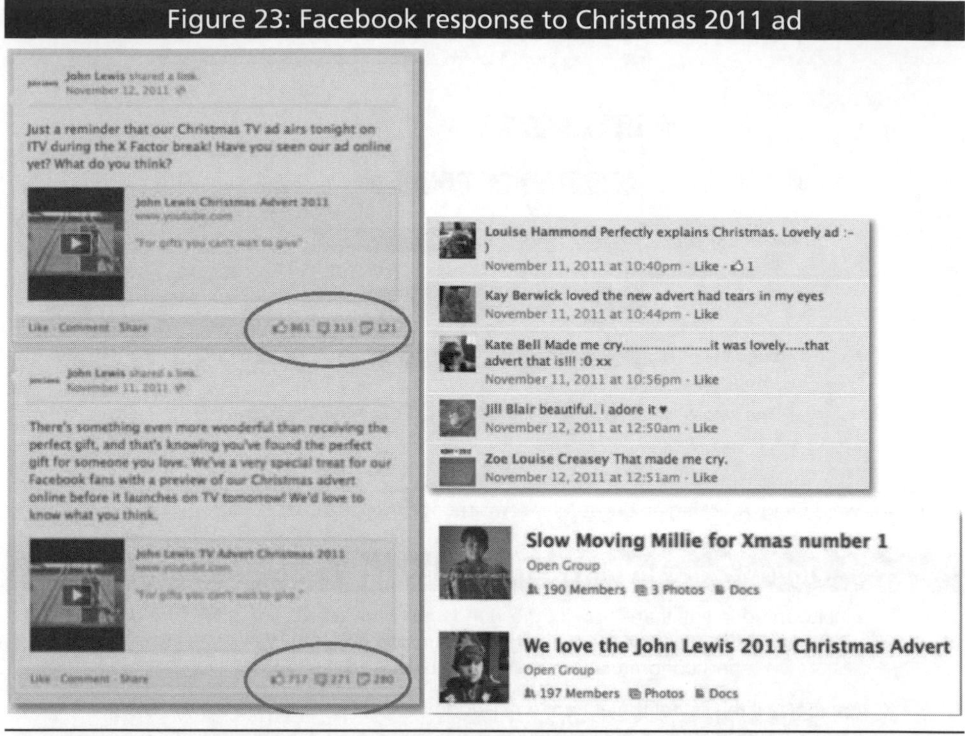


Figure 24: Consumer searches for advertising

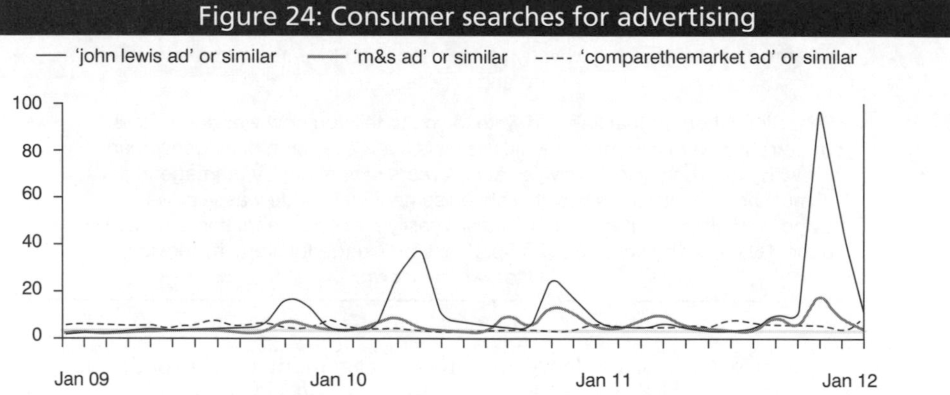


Source: Google Insights for Search.[18] The numbers on the vertical axis don't represent absolute search volume numbers but relative ones: the data is normalised and presented on a scale from 0 to 100; each point on the graph is divided by the highest point or 100.

Huge numbers of people have viewed the John Lewis TV ads on YouTube (Table 6), with many spoof versions created and shared too.

People continue to come back to the ads months after they have aired, debating which is the best and asking about the tracks. Many of the comments mention the ads making viewers cry (Figure 25).

## Table 6: YouTube viewing of ads

| | YouTube views | YouTube likes | YouTube dislikes | YouTube comments |
|---|---|---|---|---|
| John Lewis ads: | | | | |
| 'Remember the feeling' | 338,319 | 457 | 19 | 263 |
| 'Always a woman' | 806,718 | 1,875 | 40 | 764 |
| 'For those who care' | 858,930 | 1,796 | 244 | 1,517 |
| 'Through the ages' | 353,410 | 388 | 87 | 309 |
| 'The long wait' | 4,167,209 | 18,933 | 939 | 6,518 |
| | | | | |
| M&S Christmas 2009 ad | 174,823 | 191 | 11 | 352 |
| M&S Christmas 2010 ad | 170,446 | 221 | 27 | 215 |
| M&S Christmas 2011 ad | 410,062 | 818 | 420 | 1,130 |
| | | | | |
| Comparethemarket meerkat launch ad 2009 | 552,142 | 632 | 46 | 602 |

Source: YouTube, 2 April 2012. Several versions of these ads exist on YouTube: views for all non-spoof versions have been combined

## Figure 25: Example YouTube comments

*'Remember the feeling'*

I cant believe a 1min bit of film can get me all worked up:) The first time an advert has brought me to tears...
Beautfly shot and very astute with a purposeful message.
tomboz777

I'm 16 and miss that childhood excitment that this advert captures perfectly.
Disft 47

*'Always a woman'*

thumbe up if you cried at the end :'(
ohhbrackett10 10

We had an assembly on this today. The teacher said it makes him cry.. :)
Simowl

*'For those who care'*

john lewis have the BEST christmas adverts. :-)
FabBluewho

Is it bad that I welled up a wee bit? :)
tangerinesonrisa

Such a good advert. Almost makes me cry whch is unusual for an advert. It's so beautiful and festive. Roll on Christmas 2011.
robynrobyn94

I wish all ads were as good as this one.
mareinx 87

*'Through the ages'*

love these sort of adverts. I was only born in 95 but seeing all those different periods in time made me feel as old as my grandparents lol. I love pretty much every scene and song in this ad. Only John Lewis. :)
kingofkeyboards

I normally hate adverts but this played on the telly yesterday morning during the Rugby and really captured us! I love it. Maybe it replays some of our youth or something - the tapes, the Ska music, the Sixth Form common Room, the Sony Walkman .......... it's great!
simmyechoes

I can't get enough of this commercial...I love it!!! The Smiths, Sade, "1982"...my coming of age years....makes me so nostalgic!!! Thanks for posting :))
cleanheart13

*'The long wait'*

There's just something in my eye.
And in my other eye.
And in my heart.
13mungoman13

One of the best adverts all of 2011
Medrum101 2

That was so adorable. So adorable.
sparklingselly

ammmmm its so cute
misspotatoheads

Makes me cry every time i watch this:')
ZoeChisholm

Source: YouTube

The John Lewis ads are particularly likely to be watched to completion on YouTube (Figure 26), whereas the dropout rate for many ads is high.

**Figure 26: YouTube viewer retention throughout John Lewis ads, relative to films of a similar length**

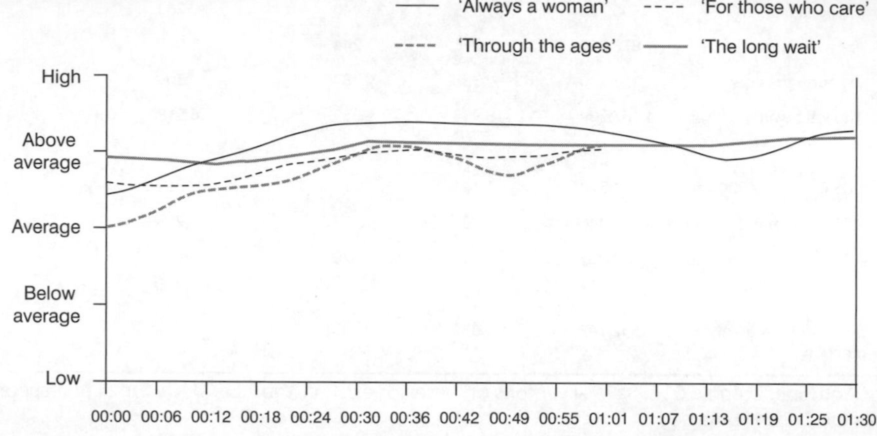


Source: YouTube

Such was the Twitter interest in 'The long wait' that it trended – globally – within six hours of it being launched online, even before it had been on TV (Figure 27). This is a phenomenal achievement given John Lewis is a UK-only chain of 36 stores and it was Armistice Day. On the day the ad launched on TV, Twitter mentions of John Lewis were up more than 1,500% (Figure 28). Even celebrities expressed their enthusiasm to their followers (Figure 29).

**Figure 27: Twitter worldwide trending topics on the day 'The long wait' launched on Facebook**

| Trending Now |
|---|
| **#lestweforget** |
| **#armisticeday** |
| **#LadiesWeWantAnswers** |
| **Today is 11/11/11** |
| **John Lewis Christmas** |
| **WW1** |
| **Mike Tindall** |

Source: Twitter, 11 November 2011

## Figure 28: Tweets mentioning John Lewis pre and post 'The long wait' launch

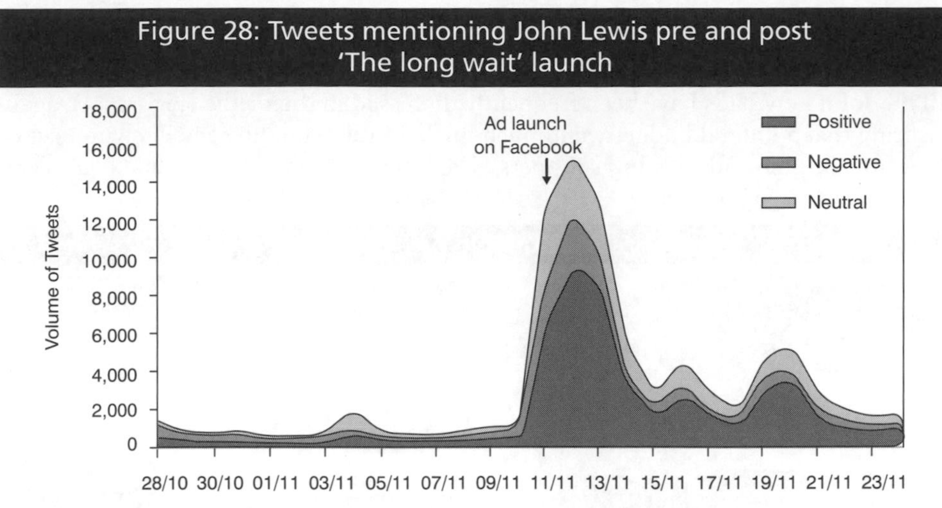


Source: Analysis by Precise (media monitoring company) of Twitter 'storms' in 2011

## Figure 29: Celebrity Tweets about 'The long wait'

Source: Twitter

It is unlikely that these extremely high levels of online engagement could be achieved if only existing customers were involved. Indeed some of the comments bear that out (Figure 30).

## Figure 30: Examples of comments from non-customers

'That has got to be the best TV advert i have ever seen! I don't think i have ever shopped at John Lewis, but I'll have to from now on!'

im going to start shopping at john lewis...
Manategers

Source: Email to John Lewis; Facebook

### *3. The communications were talked about by the media and entered popular culture*

All the John Lewis ads have been frequently discussed in the media (Figure 31), again ensuring that a limited budget went much further and extending the likely impact of the campaign beyond existing shoppers. The estimated 'advertising value equivalent' of all the coverage is £4.2m.[19]

Figure 31: Example press coverage

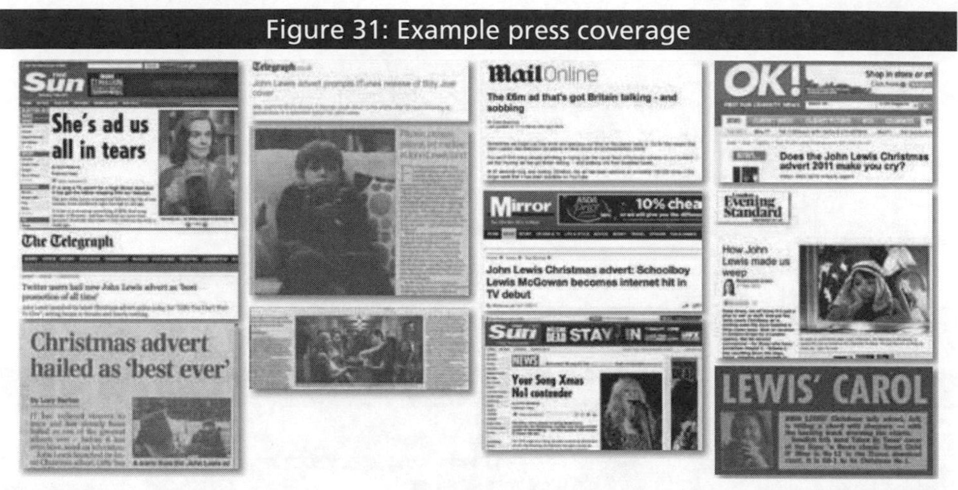


'The long wait' was spoofed by Channel 4 to promote Gordon Ramsay's Christmas show and by Sky to promote Soccer AM (Figure 32), and became inspiration for cartoonists (Figure 33).

Figure 32: Soccer AM spoof of 'The long wait'

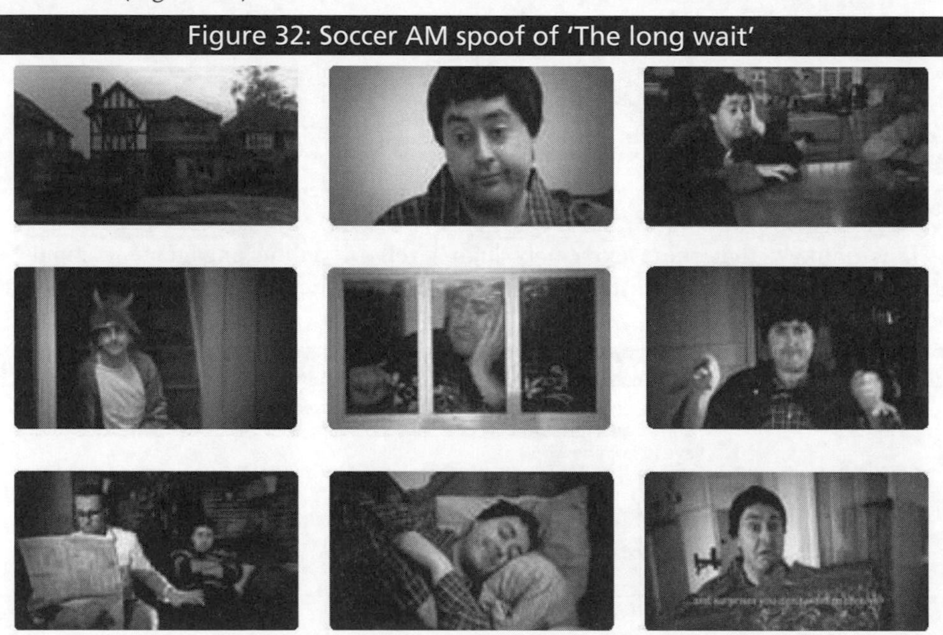

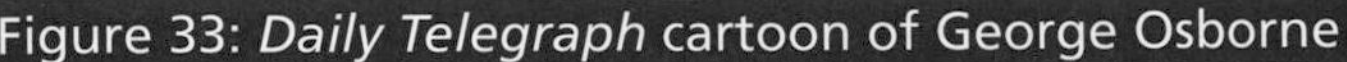

Figure 33: *Daily Telegraph* cartoon of George Osborne

'Always a woman' was the subject of 'Thought for the Day' on BBC Radio 4's *Today* programme,[20] and an exam topic for AS Media Studies. 'The long wait' became an official subject for church sermons and school assemblies: over 7,000 schools (teaching over a million pupils) downloaded an assembly guide devoted to the ad (Figure 34).[21]

Figure 34: Assembly guide involving 'The long wait'

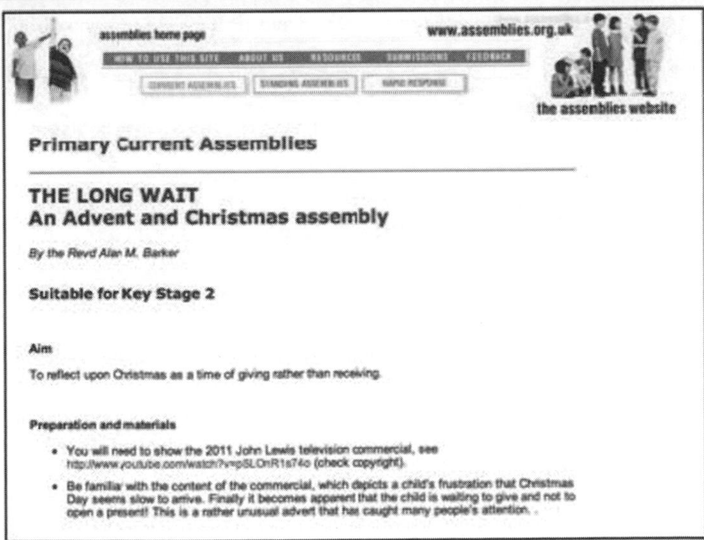

assemblies home page

www.assemblies.org.uk

HOW TO USE THIS SITE | ABOUT US | RESOURCES | SUBMISSIONS | FEEDBACK

CURRENT ASSEMBLIES | STANDING ASSEMBLIES | RAPID RESPONSE

the assemblies website

**Primary Current Assemblies**

**THE LONG WAIT**
**An Advent and Christmas assembly**

*By the Revd Alan M. Barker*

**Suitable for Key Stage 2**

**Aim**

To reflect upon Christmas as a time of giving rather than receiving.

**Preparation and materials**

- You will need to show the 2011 John Lewis television commercial, see http://www.youtube.com/watch?v=pSLOnR1s74o (check copyright).
- Be familiar with the content of the commercial, which depicts a child's frustration that Christmas Day seems slow to arrive. Finally it becomes apparent that the child is waiting to give and not to open a present! This is a rather unusual advert that has caught many people's attention.

Source: assemblies.org.uk

The music has been an important part of the advertising's entry into popular culture. The tracks have charted after the ads launched and featured heavily in radio airplay (Table 7). Ellie Goulding's *Your Song* was even chosen as the first dance at the wedding of the Duke and Duchess of Cambridge.

Table 7: Popularity of music tracks from the ads

| Track | Artist | UK single sales | UK radio plays |
|---|---|---|---|
| 'Sweet child o' mine' | Taken by Trees | 46,000 | No data available |
| 'Always a woman' | Fyfe Dangerfield | 216,957 | 66,314 |
| 'Your song' | Ellie Goulding | 694,537 | 51,075 |
| 'Please please please' | Slow Moving Millie | 78,964 | 5,836 |
| Total | | 1,036,458 | 123,225 |

Source: Record companies. 'Sweet child o' mine' single sales for month 1 only

To our knowledge no-one has quantified the business benefit of advertising tracks achieving radio exposure, so we have attempted to do so (Figure 35) and suggest an 'advertising value equivalent' of about £14.6m. Given the TV media spend was only £17.7m, this free coverage almost doubles the investment and demonstrates for the first time the considerable value of advertising using music that gets radio airplay.

Figure 35: Estimate of the value of the music from the John Lewis advertising receiving radio airplay

The tracks will have been played on both national and local stations, both BBC and commercial, and we have no information about dayparts so can only approximately estimate the likely coverage achieved by the tracks.

Taking Heart London as an average station that played the tracks:

One airplay of a track would achieve about 132 impacts (coverage of 132k adults) so 123,225 airplays would achieve 16.3 million impacts.

A national average Cost Per Thousand for a 30" radio ad is about £1.50, so the CPT for three mins (the length of a track) would be £9.00.

Therefore the advertising equivalent cost of the radio airplay is about £146.4m (16.3 million impacts × £9.00).

Making a conservative assumption that John Lewis is thought about perhaps 10% of the time the tracks are played, we get a value of about £14.6m for the radio airplay.

Source: Manning Gottlieb OMD with guidance from the RAB

In November 2011, John Lewis released a charity album of the tracks from the ads (Figure 36).[22] 17,349 copies have so far been sold.[23]

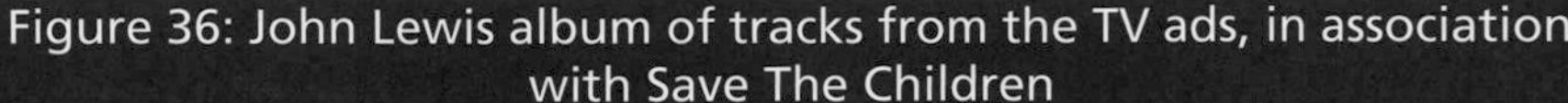
Figure 36: John Lewis album of tracks from the TV ads, in association with Save The Children

### *4. Brand perceptions improved*

The key question here is: do customers now find John Lewis more emotionally relevant? Unfortunately we don't have a direct post-advertising equivalent of Figure 7 but we do have tracking evidence for some of the emotional affinity measures mentioned (Figure 37). Trust and perceived modernity have improved markedly over the period of the campaign (with more rational measures such as 'better quality' and 'better service' also increasing).

Figure 37: Agreement with brand image statements

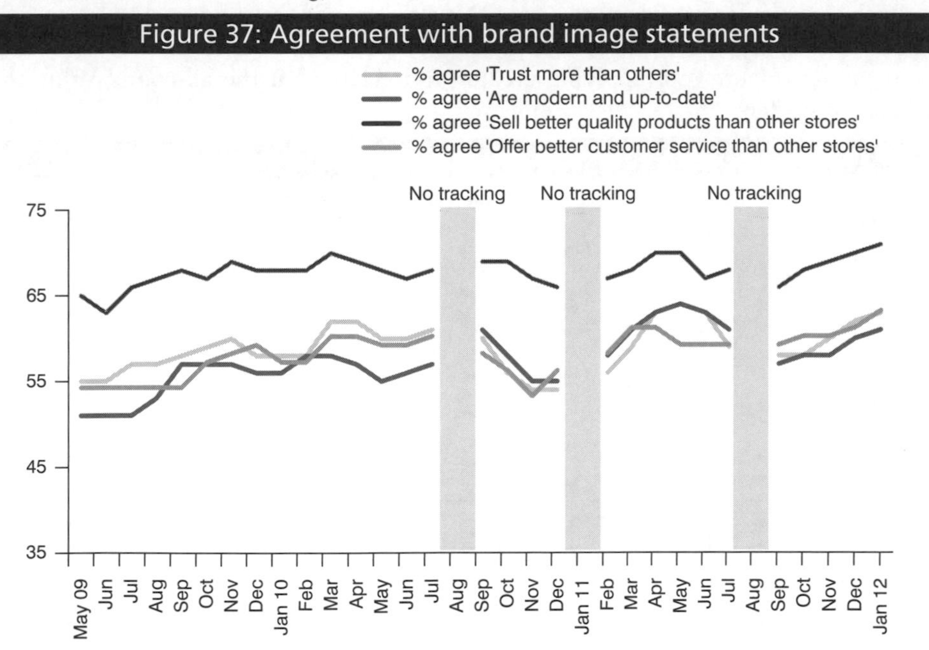


Source: Millward Brown tracking amongst John Lewis shoppers in catchment areas (rolling 12 week data). Gaps represent breaks in fieldwork

Customers are prepared to directly attribute the advertising with making the brand more appealing and making them feel good about shopping at John Lewis (Figure 38).

Figure 38: Brand 'feel good' generated by the advertising

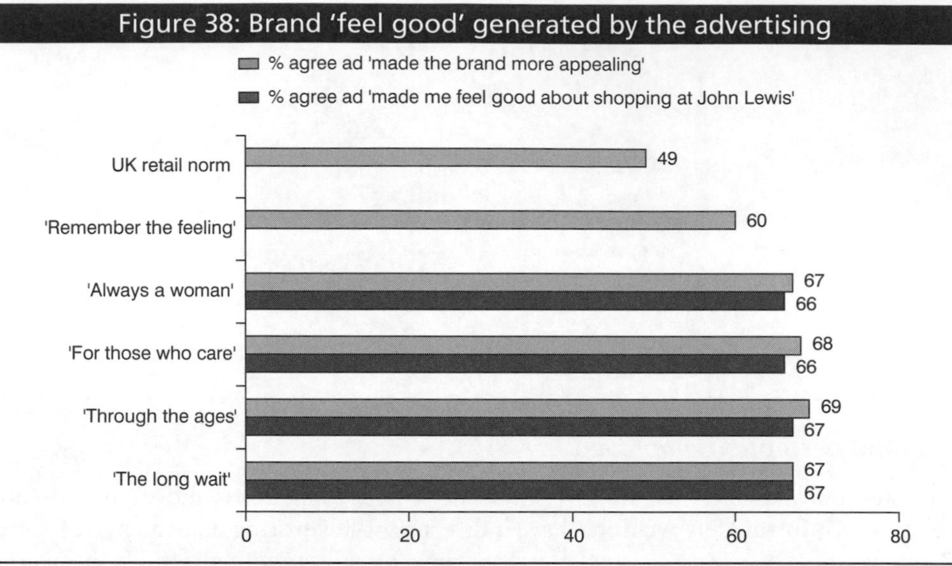


Source: Millward Brown tracking amongst John Lewis shoppers in catchment areas.
The 'feel good' question wasn't asked for Christmas 2009 and there isn't a retail norm

With particular respect to the 'Never knowingly undersold' strand of communications, awareness of the promise has grown every time these ads have been on air (Figure 39), implying greater appreciation of the all-round value that John Lewis offers.

Figure 39: Percentage aware of 'Never knowingly undersold'

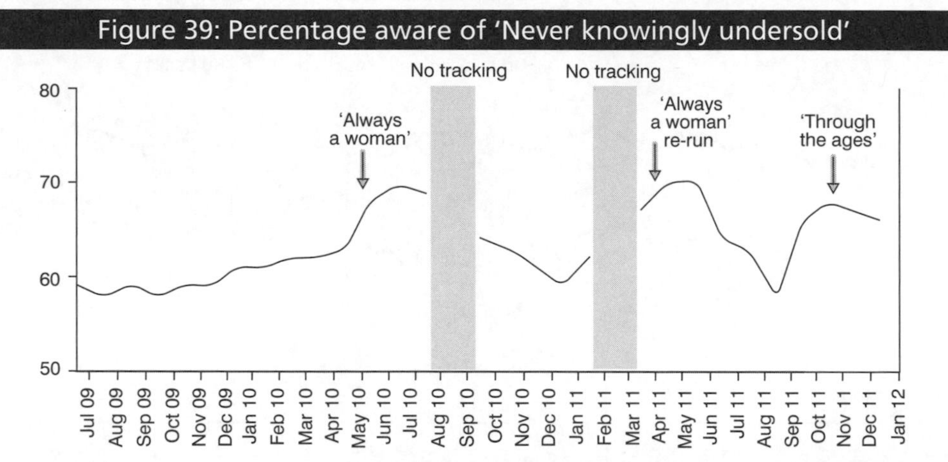


Source: Millward Brown tracking amongst John Lewis shoppers in catchment areas (3 month rolling data)

## *5. Penetration, frequency and average spend increased*

We have seen that perceptions of John Lewis have changed during the campaign period, but has behaviour?

Our primary objective of getting existing shoppers to visit more and spend more has indeed been achieved (Table 8). While increases of 3% may seem small, combined they mean that average annual spend has grown by 6% (Figure 40), and for a retailer of John Lewis's scale, that has a massive impact.

**Table 8: Average number of visits per year and average spend per visit (indexed on 2009)**

| | 2009 | 2010 | 2011 |
|---|---|---|---|
| Average number of visits per year | 100 | 101 | 103 |
| Average spend per visit | 100 | 102 | 103 |

Source: John Lewis analysis of payment card data (not possible prior to 2009 because EPOS system not in place)

**Figure 40: Average annual spend per John Lewis customer**

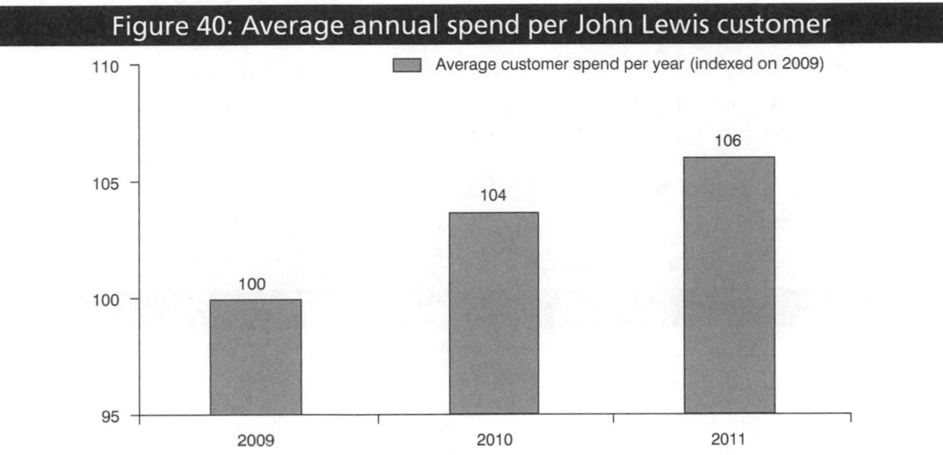


Source: John Lewis analysis of payment card data (not possible prior to 2009 because EPOS system not in place)

Furthermore, our secondary objective of increasing penetration has also been achieved (Figure 41). The ability of the advertising to actively engage a broad audience (apparent in the earlier social media evidence) has resulted in John Lewis acquiring 10% more customers. This makes the frequency/spend growth more significant, since you would expect marked increases in penetration to result in lower frequency and spend, since the customer base contains more new and occasional shoppers. The implication is that existing customers increased their visiting frequency and spend per visit by significantly more than the 3% overall figures.

## Figure 41: Number of John Lewis customers

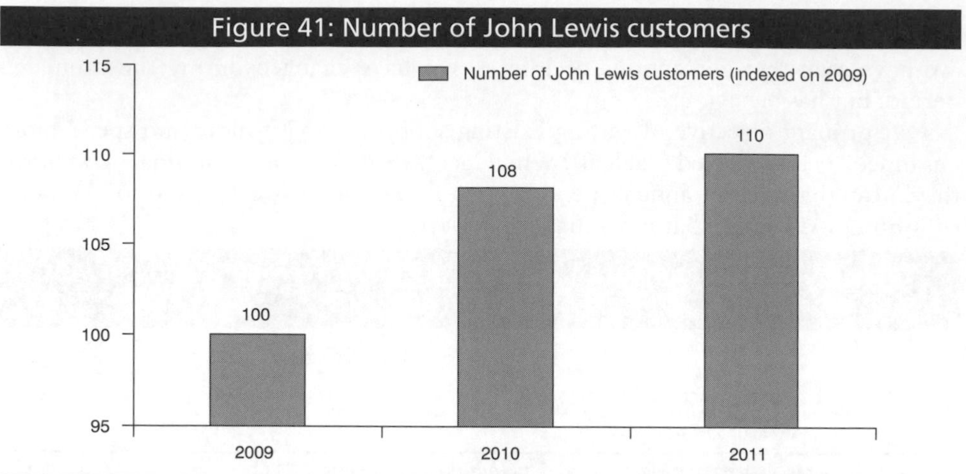


Source: John Lewis analysis of payment card data (not possible prior to 2009 because EPOS system not in place)

Some penetration growth will be due to new stores opening, but the new stores were mostly the smaller John Lewis At Home format and in existing catchment areas. We demonstrate later via modelling the limited impact that new stores have had on sales growth, distinct from the effect of communications.

### *6. The business grew and outperformed the competition*

Following a difficult 2008 where sales declined slightly, John Lewis returned to growth from 2009 onwards (Figure 42).

## Figure 42: John Lewis gross sales

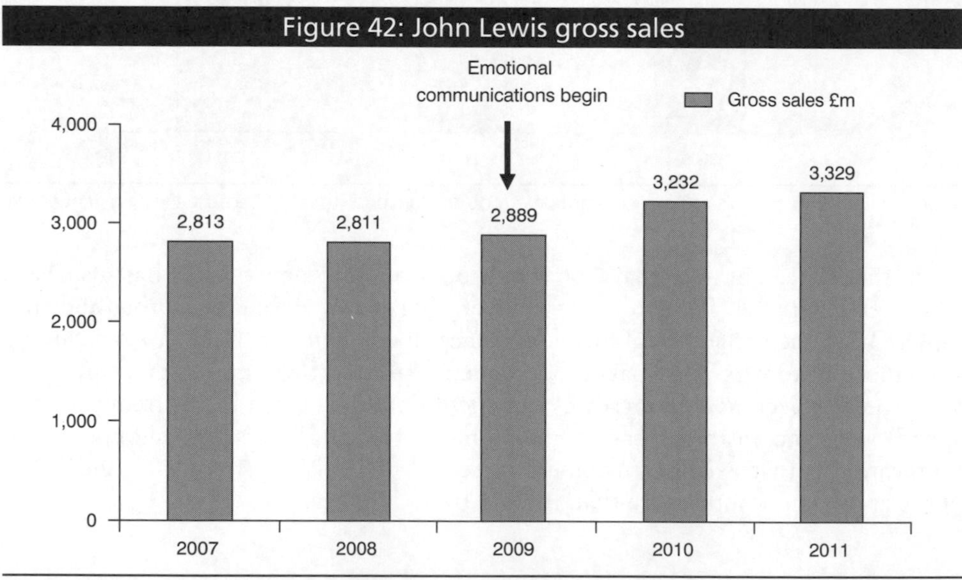


Source: John Lewis financial reports (John Lewis financial years run Feb to Jan but have been taken as equivalent to the relevant calendar year)

Like-for-like sales growth has become positive again (Figure 43), although 2011 was a particularly challenging year for John Lewis in line with the rest of the high street.

Figure 43: John Lewis like-for-like sales growth

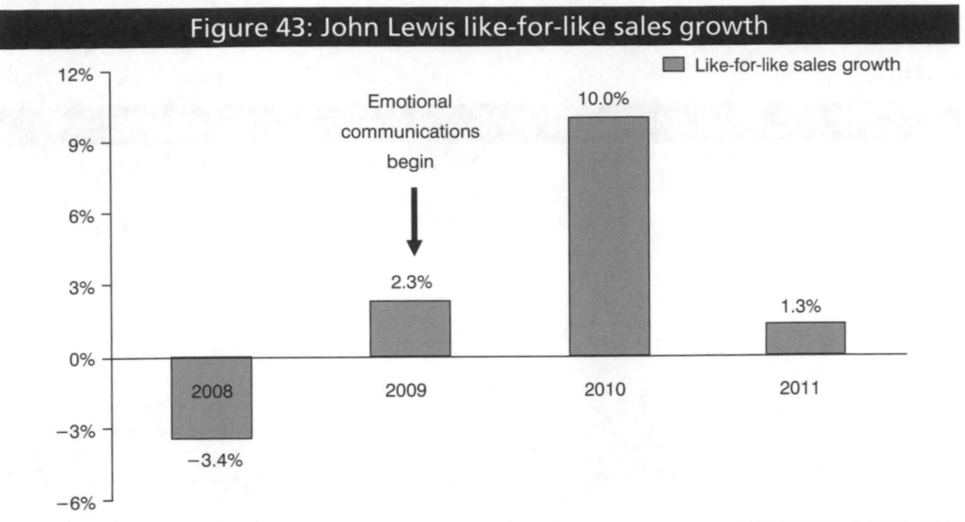


Source: John Lewis financial reports (John Lewis financial years run Feb to Jan but have been taken as equivalent to the relevant calendar year)

Focusing on the pre-Christmas periods so crucial to retailers, John Lewis's December sales have been particularly impressive since the new advertising began, outperforming most of the rest of the high street (Figure 44) and setting new internal records every year.

Figure 44: Christmas period like-for-like sales growth

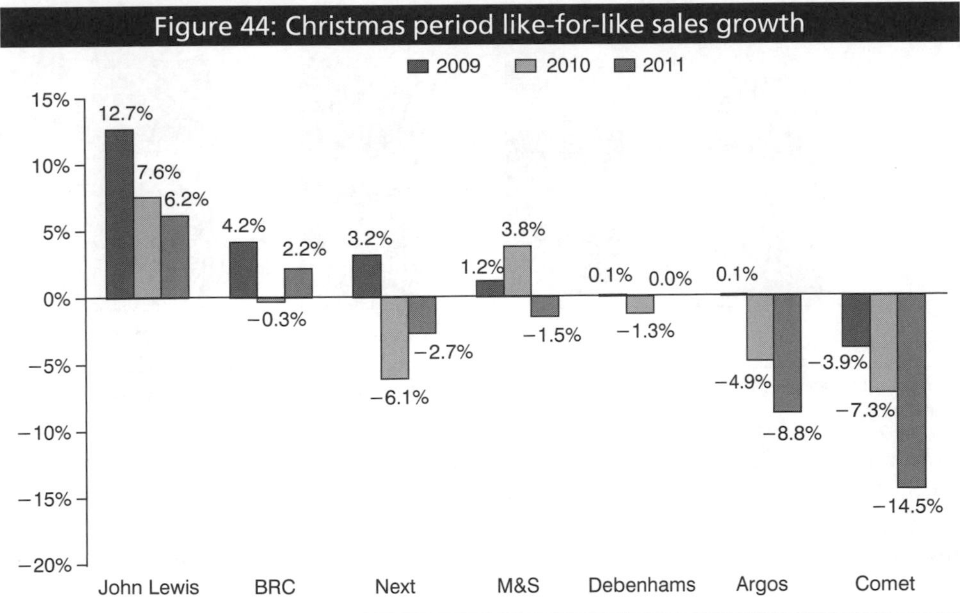


Source: Published financial information;[24] BRC: British Retail Consortium Retail Index (non-food)

As Neil Saunders of retail consultancy Conlumino said: 'I think relative to the rest of the high street they've been doing very well. They've gained market share ... Their performance has been robust compared to others.'[25] Market share growth is indeed evident, both at overall department store level (Figure 45) and for the two of the three directorates for which we have market share information (Figure 46).[26]

**Figure 45: John Lewis share of department store sales**

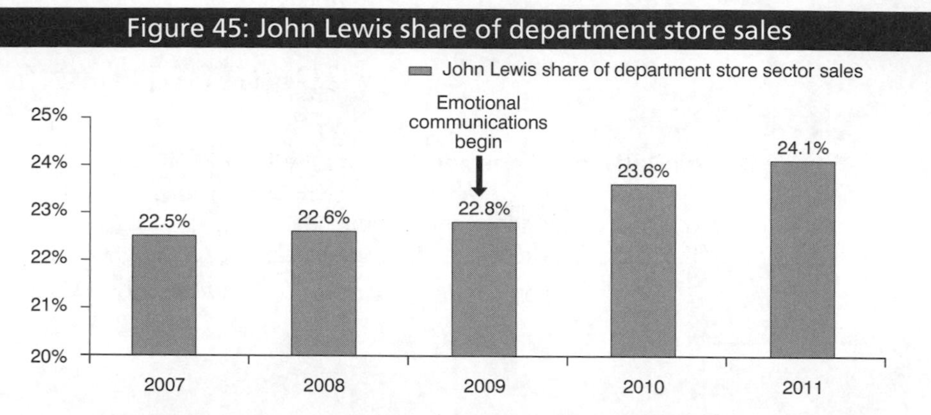


Source: John Lewis gross sales (including VAT) versus Mintel's department store sector sales (including VAT) in 'Department Store Retailing', Mar 2012

**Figure 46: John Lewis share of Home and Electricals categories**

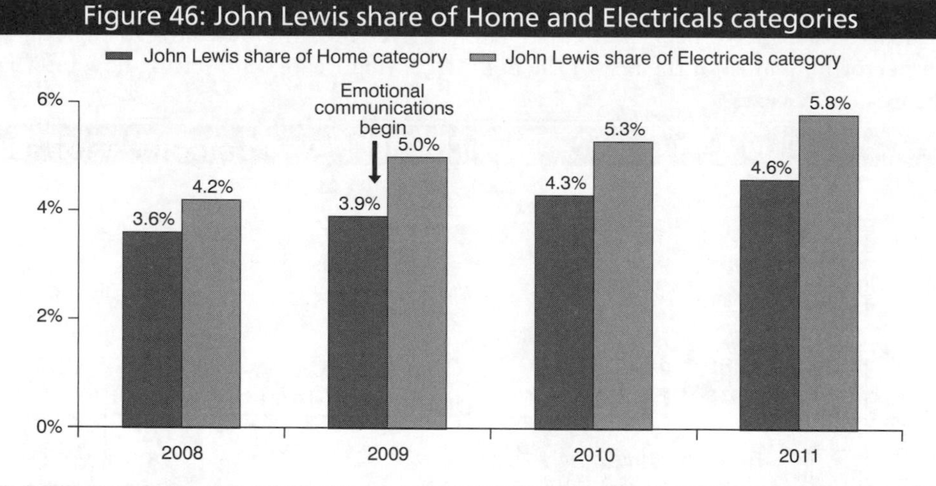


Source: John Lewis estimates using Verdict reports for Homewares, Furniture & Floorcoverings and DIY & Gardening; GfK

In terms of sales growth versus the high street, during this period John Lewis has outperformed the British Retail Consortium average for every month except one (Figure 47). As Howard Archer of the economic forecasting organisation IHS Global Insight said: 'John Lewis has been seen as a bellwether for the state of consumer spending, but it has been very much an outperformer in recent years'.[27]

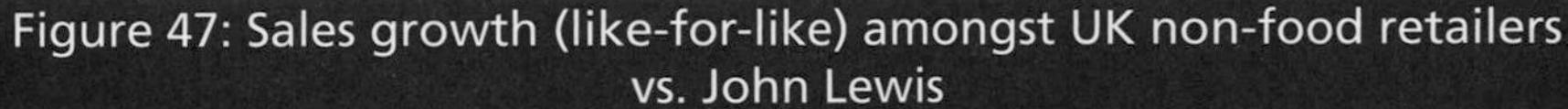

Figure 47: Sales growth (like-for-like) amongst UK non-food retailers vs. John Lewis

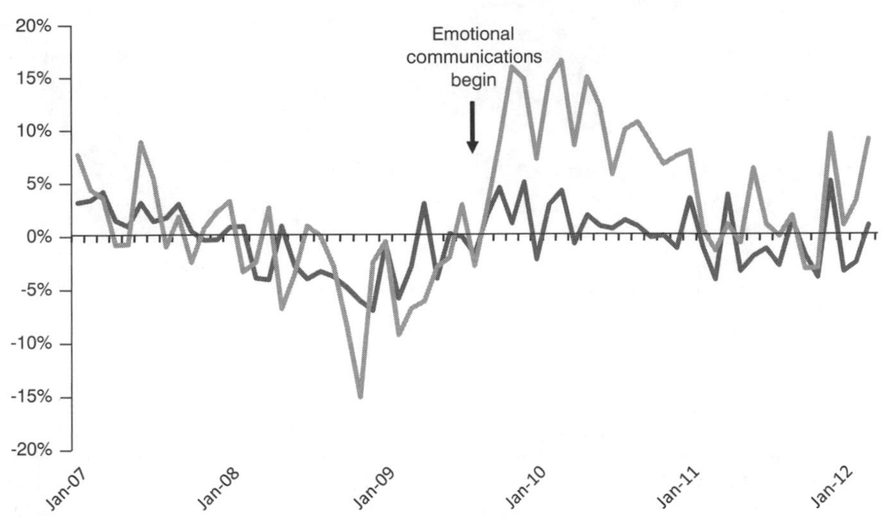


Source: British Retail Consortium; John Lewis

### *7. The communications directly contributed to significant sales and profit uplifts*

It's clear that John Lewis's business did very well during this period, but the critical question is: to what extent are communications driving this, versus other factors?

The sales of any large multi-channel retailer are affected by numerous variables, and John Lewis uses sophisticated econometric modelling to isolate the contributions of different factors. The model distinguishes between factors which drive variation in base sales and in incremental sales. The effects of the number of stores, the weather, consumer confidence and growth in internet shopping are all observed at the level of base sales (Figure 48).

Of the factors which drive incremental sales, above-the-line activity is the single biggest component, accounting for £1,074m (14% of total sales) from Nov 2009 to Jan 2012 (Figure 49).

Online activity such as search marketing and emails have a significant impact, with changes to the store experience, promotional activity such as the Clearance sales periods and below-the-line activity playing smaller parts.

## Figure 48: Model decomposition of the key drivers of base sales only (in-store and online)

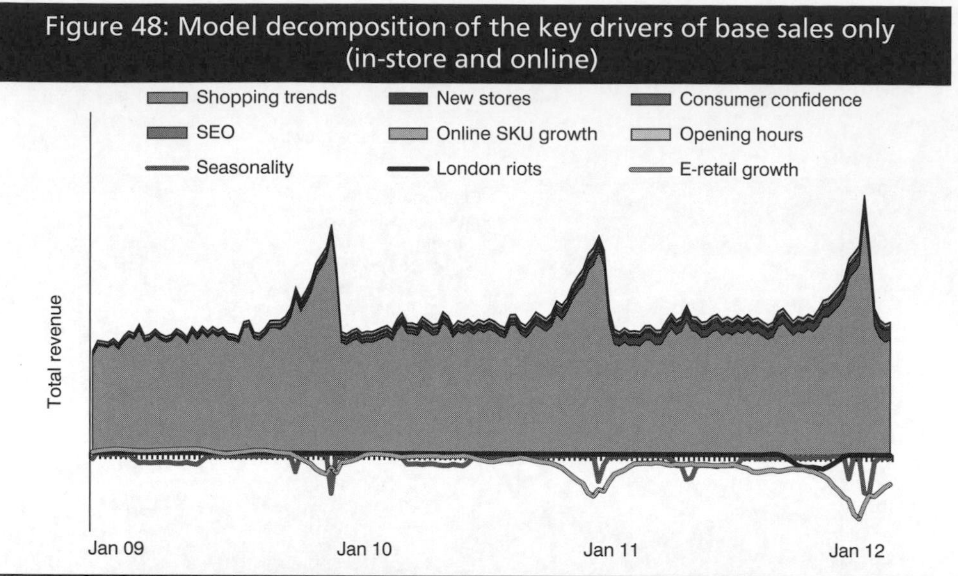


Source: Econometric modelling by BrandScience. The numbers have been removed from the y axis for confidentiality reasons. E-retail growth = IMRG Capgemini e-Retail Sales Index which tracks the overall growth in online retail, which exerts a negative effect on total John Lewis sales (while exerting a positive one on John Lewis online sales). Seasonality = Bank Holidays, weather effects, etc. SEO = search engine optimization. Online SKU growth = the growth in the number of lines stocked by johnlewis.com

## Figure 49: Model decomposition of the key drivers of incremental sales (in-store and online)

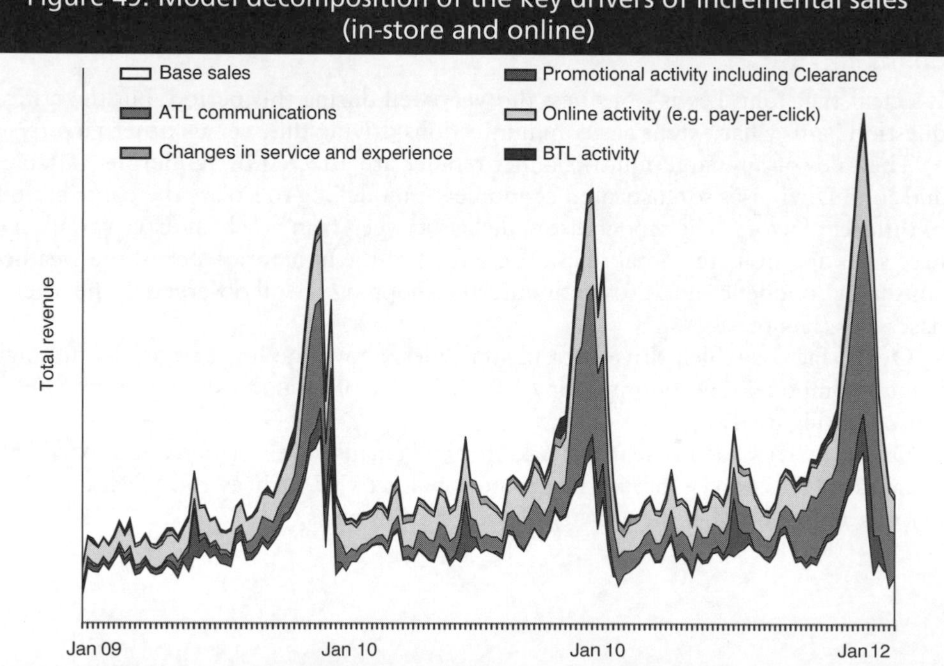


Source: Econometric modelling by BrandScience. The numbers have been removed from the y axis for confidentiality reasons. Online activity = pay-per-click search, price comparison, other affiliates and emails. BTL activity = direct mail, inserts, etc.

The incremental revenue generated by communications translates into impressive incremental profit, since (as is typical) the brand's marketing contribution margin is far higher than its net profit margin (which includes fixed costs). In a little over two years John Lewis communications have delivered £261m incremental profit, meaning that for every £1 spent £5.02 is returned to the business (Table 9).

**Table 9: Contribution of above-the-line communications to incremental sales, 2009 to 2011**

| ATL communications (TV, press, outdoor, radio, cinema, online display) | Nov–Dec 2009 TV only | Feb 2010–Jan 2011 | Feb 2011–Jan 2012 | Total |
|---|---|---|---|---|
| Spend (media, production, fees) | £3.2m | £19.0m | £29.7m | £51.9m |
| Total incremental revenue (including VAT) | £71.6m | £363.3m | £584.3m | £1019.2m |
| Total incremental revenue (excluding VAT) | £59.7m | £302.7m | £487.0m | £849.4m |
| Net profit ([incremental revenue excluding VAT x marketing contribution margin] – spend) | £13.7m | £97.5m | £149.8m | £261.0m |
| Profit ROI (Net profit/spend) | £4.24 | £5.13 | £5.04 | £5.02 |
| ROMI (% return on marketing investment) | 424 | 513 | 504 | 502 |

Source: Econometric modelling by BrandScience.[28] For Nov 2009 to Jan 2010 only the TV advertising is included here (print is excluded), which is why the total incremental revenue figure of £1,019m is lower than the figure of £1,074m quoted earlier

The Christmas TV ads have been particularly hardworking, with the latest two delivering extremely high profit ROIs of over £9 (Table 10).

**Table 10: Contribution of TV ads to incremental sales, 2009 to 2011**

| TV advertising | 'Remember the feeling' | 'Always a woman' (2010 & 2011 bursts combined) | 'For those who care' | 'Through the ages' | 'The long wait' | Total |
|---|---|---|---|---|---|---|
| Spend (media, production, fees) | £5.7m | £6.9m | £4.4m | £5.7m | £4.7m | £27.4m |
| Total incremental revenue (including VAT) | £71.6m | £76.9m | £146.6m | £66.1m | £148.7m | £509.9m |
| Total incremental revenue (excluding VAT) | £61.0m | £65.1m | £124.8m | £55.1m | £124.0m | £430.0m |
| Net profit ([Incremental revenue excluding VAT x marketing contribution margin] – spend) | £13.7m | £19.0m | £45.3m | £13.5m | £43.1m | £134.6m |
| Profit ROI (Net profit/spend) | £4.24 | £2.75 | £10.20 | £2.39 | £9.14 | £4.91 |
| ROMI (% return on marketing investment) | 424 | 275 | 1020 | 239 | 914 | 491 |

Source: Econometric modelling by BrandScience

To provide some context, in the IPA dataMINE analysis of effectiveness case studies, only 8% of those correctly disclosing payback achieved ROMIs of 800% or above.[29] Given the dataMINE work has demonstrated the higher effectiveness of emotional involvement campaigns, we wanted to compare our results with that more demanding competitive set. Peter Field has provided us with previously unpublished data regarding ROMI levels for emotional campaigns (Table 11). Against this tougher benchmark our Christmas TV advertising still ranks amongst the top 6% of cases.

**Table 11: Incidence of reported levels of ROMI (profit ROI)**

| ROMI range | All cases (39) | Emotional cases (18) | |
|---|---|---|---|
| <=50 | 26% | 11% | |
| 50–100 | 8% | 17% | |
| 100–200 | 23% | 28% | |
| 200–400 | 21% | 6% | |
| 400–600 | 10% | 28% | ← John Lewis communications overall |
| 600–800 | 5% | 6% | |
| >=800 | 8% | 6% | ← John Lewis Christmas TV ads 2010 & 2011 |

Source: Marketing in the Era of Accountability, Les Binet and Peter Field, 2007; Peter Field[30]

All the figures described above refer only to short-term sales impact. The TV advertising is very memorable with notably long adstocks (carryover rates) (Table 12), meaning that there will be a significant longer-term effect, as in years to come memories of the advertising will continue to trigger brand consideration, and changed shopping habits will continue to provide incremental sales. A commonly cited study[31] suggests a multiple of 2.5 be applied to short-term sales effects to estimate the longer-term impact. Given our total short-term sales contribution of £1,074m, the longer-term effect might be as much as £2,685m.

**Table 12: Adstocks (advertising carryover rates)[32]**

| | Adstock for in-store sales | Adstock for online sales |
|---|---|---|
| 'Remember the feeling' | 50% | 50% |
| 'Always a woman' | 90% | 90% |
| 'For those who care' | 65% | 65% |
| 'Through the ages' | 90% | 90% |
| 'The long wait' | 85% | 75% |

Source: Econometric modelling by BrandScience

## *8. The communications had other indirect business effects*

Beyond the direct contribution of communications to sales and profit, we can identify some additional profitable business developments, believed internally to result partly from the effect of communications on a broader audience beyond customers.

Since the advertising began, John Lewis's desirability to supplier brands (especially premium ones) has increased dramatically (Table 13). Brands that were previously reluctant to be stocked in John Lewis have sought to be distributed there and allocation of stock and exclusives has improved. These developments greatly increase John Lewis's competitiveness and are extremely valuable. They are largely due to the hard work of Partners and improvements to store environments, but the business believes the advertising has contributed to driving faster reappraisal by these premium brands.

**Table 13: Premium brands that have become available at John Lewis since 2009**

| | Electrical & Home technology | Fashion | Beauty |
|---|---|---|---|
| **New brands stocked** | Loewe (returned after 5 year absence)<br>Bang & Olufsen (JL are only chain stockist)<br>Monster Beats<br>Bowers & Wilkins<br>Manfrotto<br>Smythson accessories | Ralph Lauren<br>Hugo Boss<br>Whistles<br>Tom Ford<br>Prada<br>Valentino<br>Thomas Pink<br>Ghost<br>Temperley<br>Day Birger et Mikkelsen<br>Hoss Intropia<br>Links | Hugo Boss<br>Prada<br>Aveda<br>Jo Malone<br>Burberry Body<br>Nars<br>Bare Minerals<br>Kiehls |

Source: John Lewis

Tangible evidence of suppliers' increased commitment to John Lewis is their greater preparedness to contribute to funding the advertising. Supplier funding has more than doubled since 2009 (representing an increase of almost £10m) (Table 14). The modelling does *not* take into account supplier funding – i.e. the cost to John Lewis of the advertising is actually lower than stated, so communications are even more profitable.

**Table 14: Growth in supplier funding since 2009**

| | Supplier funding of advertising (indexed on 2009–2010 figure) |
|---|---|
| 2009–2010 | 100 |
| 2010–2011 | 117 |
| 2011–2012 | 175 |
| 2012–2013 (estimated) | 217 |

Source: John Lewis

### *9. The communications made Partners very happy*

The Partnership's overall stated purpose is 'the happiness of all its members, through their worthwhile and satisfying employment in a successful business.[33] This adds a unique perspective to John Lewis's definition of marketing effectiveness: in contrast to most businesses whose main ambition is to pass on more profit to a small group of often corporate shareholders, John Lewis truly desires to make its Partners happy.

Communications have contributed to the fulfilment of this objective, not only by giving Partners advertising that they have enjoyed and felt proud of (Figure 50), but also by increasing the size of the annual bonuses they have been given.

**Figure 50: Partner feedback about the advertising**

'Sir: I sat transfixed to the screen on Friday (23 April) at 7.45pm to what I can only describe as a very beautiful and touching advert. I think it has to be one of the best I have ever seen. The music was perfect, the way the story of a customer's life was shown with our products in her home updating was very clever. All in all it left me with a tear in my eye and a lump in my throat. Very well done!'
Yours, etc IMPRESSED PARTNER

'Firstly who do I congratulate on the most intriguing advertisement campaign recently aired on Television from John Lewis. I absolutely loved it, I understood immediately how the girl/woman interacted with the brand, I even recognised some merchandise from our shop floor myself.'

'Gorgeous, sentimental, spell-binding and perfectly sums up a brand we have every reason to be proud of. Absolutely love it.'

'I would firstly like to congratulate you on a truly fantastic and moving Christmas advert. The first time I saw it, I cried!'

'We have been watching the new advert in the Partners entrance – its lovely. You have nearly every woman in Wycombe in tears. I think we all started recognising our own daughters and then flipped to seeing ourselves in the advert. Brilliant!'

'Just shown it, great reaction tears and applause and huge thumbs up.'

Source: Letters to John Lewis Gazette, emails to marketing department

John Lewis is the UK's largest employee co-operative. The directness and scale with which employees share in the business's success is perhaps unique. Every March the board decides on a percentage of pay to be given as a bonus to all permanent employees regardless of position or salary, depending on the profitability of the Partnership overall. For the three financial years that this activity straddles, both John Lewis and Waitrose have gone from strength to strength, so bonuses have been generous at 15%, 18% and 14% of annual salary (equivalent to seven to ten weeks' pay – an unprecedented level of generosity in retail) (Figure 51). £511m has been given away over the three years to an annual average of 75,300 Partners, so the average payout over the period was £6,786.

Due to a need to keep bonus calculation methodology confidential we cannot publish the direct contribution John Lewis communications made to Partner bonuses. However, we have already demonstrated the considerable impact John Lewis communications have made to the success of the business during this period, contributing over £1bn or 14% of total John Lewis sales and a substantial proportion of Partnership profit, and hence making a major contribution to the bonus pool shared by every Partner.

It is very unusual to be able to make a link between marketing effectiveness and employee happiness, but it is a fact of immense pride to all concerned that we can, and we would hope to the founder of John Lewis himself.

Figure 51: Partners celebrate the bonus announcement, March 2011

## Summary

This paper tells the story of how, in a little over two years, John Lewis communications have propelled the brand into the nation's hearts, achieved a return on investment of over 500% and made every Partner better off.

We have also offered some new perspectives on communications evaluation, with an estimate of the business benefit of music tracks from advertising being played on the radio, an illustration of the new insights that neuroscience tracking can provide, and previously unpublished ROMI data for emotional campaigns.

## Notes

1 Traditionally John Lewis was closed on both Sundays and Mondays.
2 Many stores retained their original department store names (e.g. Robert Sayle in Cambridge) until very recently. Peter Jones in London and Knight & Lee in Southsea still retain their original names.
3 There are almost 350 M&S stores that aren't food-only (there are over 700 stores in total). Source: Mintel 'Department Store Retailing', March 2012.
4 Source: Nielsen Media Research.
5 The Consumer Confidence Index is an average of 1,000 adults' appraisal of current economic conditions, expectations regarding economic conditions six months hence, appraisal of current employment conditions, expectations regarding employment conditions six months hence and expectations regarding their total family income six months hence. The Present Situation Index is an average of respondents' appraisal of current economic conditions and current employment conditions.
6 The British Retail Consortium-KPMG Retail Sales Monitor is an accurate monthly measure of retail sales performance that acts as both a benchmark for participating retailers and as a key economic indicator. It measures changes in the actual value of retail sales based on figures supplied by about 70 participating companies.
7 Source: *Daily Telegraph*, 11 March 2009.
8 Advertising spend had totalled £48.7m during 2007 and 2008. Source: Nielsen Media Research.
9 Source: Millward Brown.
10 Source: *Marketing* magazine, 27 May 2009.

11 Source: Binet, L. & Field, P. (2007) *Marketing in the Era of Accountability*. Henley-on-Thames: Warc.
12 John Lewis has two annual sales periods called Clearance.
13 The four weeks leading up to Christmas typically deliver about 20% of John Lewis's annual sales and about 40% of annual profit. Source: John Lewis.
14 Prior to taking over John Lewis in 1929, John Spedan was the Managing Director of Peter Jones and instigated the 'Never knowingly undersold' policy there.
15 Source: Nielsen AdDynamix.
16 John Lewis's tracking has always focused on existing shoppers, 18+ ABC1C2.
17 2,000 members of the public are asked to rate TV ads from a particular agency. The average rating is a combination of how impressed people are with the ad, how much the spot makes them like the brand and how likely they are to share it with others.
18 Search terms used: John Lewis: john lewis ad + john lewis advert + john lewis christmas ad + john lewis christmas advert
M&S: m&s ad + m&s advert + m&s christmas ad + m&s christmas advert + marks & spencer ad + marks & spencer advert + marks & spencer christmas ad + marks & spencer christmas advert
Comparethemarket: comparethemarket ad + comparethemarket advert + compare the market ad + compare the market advert + meerkat ad + meerkat advert.
19 Source: John Lewis PR department.
20 Canon Lucy Winkett of St Paul's Cathedral, 29 April 2010.
21 Source: assemblies.org.uk.
22 £2 from the sale of each album goes to Save The Children.
23 Source: John Lewis.
24 Weeks included in Christmas trading updates: John Lewis 5, BRC 5, Next 21, M&S 13, Debenhams 19, Argos 18, Comet 11. M&S figure is for general merchandise only (food excluded).
25 Source: *The Guardian*, 2 March 2012.
26 John Lewis's share in Fashion is very small and robust share information for this category is hard to come by.
27 *Evening Standard*, 13 April 2011.
28 Net profit is calculated using incremental revenue excluding VAT because the marginal contribution figures John Lewis use relate to VAT-exclusive revenues. Separate marketing contribution margins for store sales and online sales have been used.
29 Source: Binet, L. & Field, P. (2007) *Marketing in the Era of Accountability*. Henley-on-Thames: Warc.
30 A caveat here is that ROMI figures are heavily affected by the innate profitability of the sector and of the company.
31 Source: Broadbent, T. (2011) 'How advertising pays back'. *Admap* 422, November. Used in this way in the Hovis and Essential Waitrose papers of 2010, amongst others.
32 An adstock of 85% means that 85% of the ad's effect carries over to the following week, then 85% of that effect to the next week, and so on. Christmas ads usually have shorter adstocks because their subject matter is time-limited.
33 Source: John Lewis Partnership Constitution.

## Chapter 8

# Aldi

## The 'Like brands' campaign

**By Ian Lloyd Jones and Sibel Akel Saoulli, McCann Manchester**
Credited companies: Creative Agency: McCann Manchester; Media Agency: Universal McCann; Consulting Firm: The Effectiveness Partnership; Econometric modelling agency: Ohal; Client: Aldi Stores Ltd

### Editor's summary

Recession had not helped Aldi sales. Consumers were returning to brands they trusted which Aldi did not sell. The objective was to get back into double figure growth. This paper explains how Aldi applied a martial arts technique – harnessing and redirecting an oncoming force to its marketing communications. The 'Like brands' campaign was unusual in a number of respects. It targeted Aldi's least loyal customers and positively endorsed brands that Aldi did not sell, which grew market share by 43% and delivered a ROMI of 14.5:1.

The judges really liked the way this paper encapsulated the challenger brand mentality. By focusing their energy on a simple idea and challenging the 'branded' competition head on, the Aldi team delivered a campaign that is brilliant in its simplicity. Classic techniques (e.g. blind taste tests, price comparisons) are leveraged to good effect and delivered with a twist of inspiration. A brave idea.

This paper tells the story of how an unusual creative communications strategy helped transform Aldi from retail underdog to fastest growing supermarket chain in the UK, along the way creating the UK's favourite TV ad of 2011.[1]

Martial arts such as Judo and Ju-jitsu are well known for using an opponent's force against them, borrowing and redirecting their power so that even a stronger attacker can be disarmed. Aldi faced much larger opponents in the Big 4 supermarkets – Tesco, Asda, Sainsbury's and Morrisons – and it was beginning to lose the tussle. Appropriate, then, to see if martial arts thinking could help gain the upper hand in marketing communications against competitors with much greater resources.

The 'Like brands' campaign was introduced in February 2011, and propelled Aldi's market share growth from a virtual standstill to +43% up on the previous year.[2]

This paper will show how the 'Like brands' campaign delivered the biggest sales growth in Aldi's history, by increasing shopper basket size and frequency of shopper visits.

It will also demonstrate how the whole strategy was fuelled by a deep dive into the hearts and minds of consumers, producing insights which led to the conclusion that the best prospects for growth lay in an unlikely place – Aldi's most disloyal customers.

## Category context

Aldi held an average market value share of just 2.4% in 2010, making it a relatively small player in the UK supermarket sector. [3] It had to compete for every pound of consumer grocery spending with the Big 4 who together accounted for three quarters of all grocery sales (Figure 1).[4]

Figure 1: Aldi market share vs. the Big 4 supermarkets

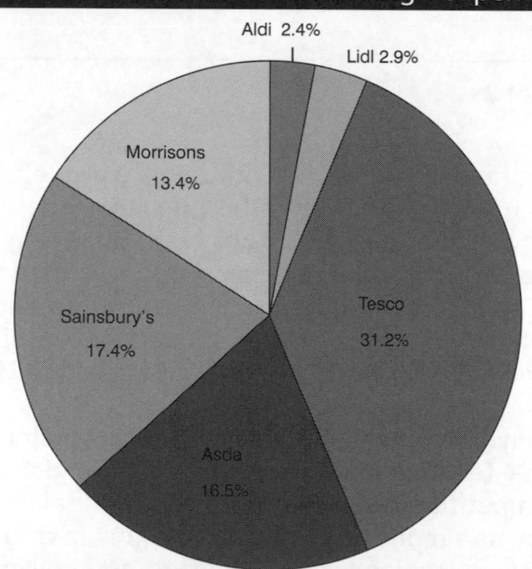


Source: Nielsen Homescan total FMCG (excluding Non Food); 52 week ending 24 December 2010

As the planning cycle commenced in September 2010, the picture was rather bleak. The economic downturn had not benefited Aldi. Its growth rate had been dropping and whilst some corrective actions had been taken, growth remained at a worryingly low level (Figure 2).

**Figure 2: Aldi's declining value share growth**

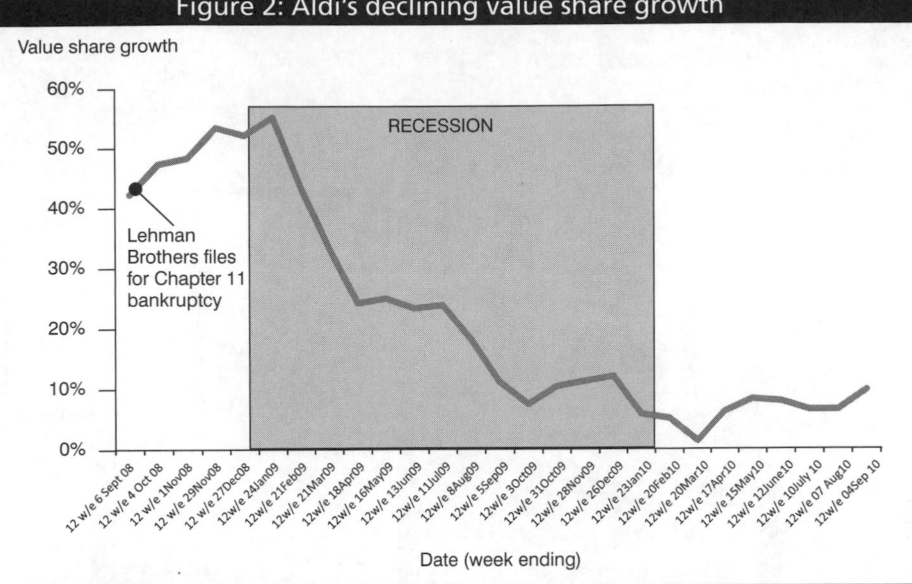


Source: Nielsen Homescan total FMCG (excluding Non Food); 12 week ending 6 September 2008–4 September 2010

To the casual observer this weak performance may seem surprising. Surely in recession people make sacrifices and traditional discounters like Aldi do well? If only it were that simple. Recession had made consumers more risk averse. It had fundamentally impacted consumer confidence[5] and led to them seeking tried and tested brands rather than experimenting with new ones.

To make things worse, the value for money mantle was being claimed by other supermarkets, and they all enjoyed more heritage and consumer trust than Aldi. The major supermarkets were all dropping prices and upping promotional spends (Figure 3).

In a direct attack on Aldi, Tesco launched a major campaign claiming to be 'Britain's Biggest Discounter'. As part of this initiative it introduced a huge range of new products with names and identities similar to those found in Aldi. In-store these were supported with shelf edge strips showing that their prices matched those of Aldi. The intended message was clear: Tesco shoppers did not need to go to Aldi as Tesco matched their offer.

Figure 3: Supermarkets' focus on value for money messages

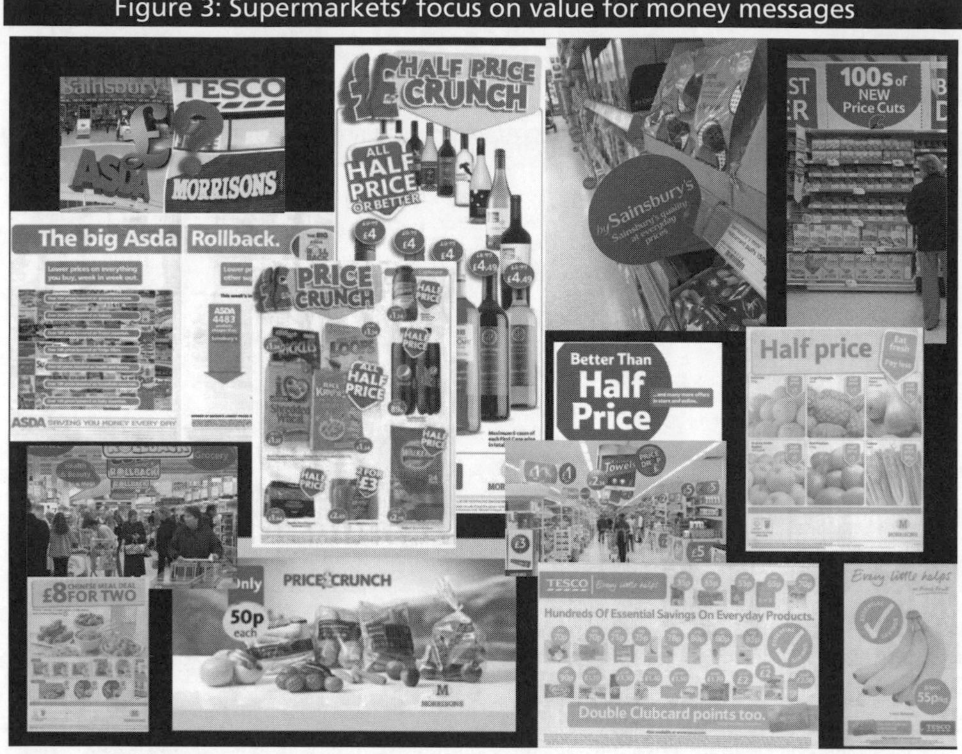


Source: Adynamix

## A word on the Aldi business model

Aldi does not operate the same way as other supermarkets. First, as supermarkets go, the stores are relatively small. Constructed around four or five main aisles, all the stores follow the same simple format. Little money is wasted on displays and signage. Aldi stocks about 1,200 product lines; larger supermarkets frequently offer more than 25,000. Most notably, Aldi doesn't list famous brands, preferring to create and sell its own product range at lower prices. In short, Aldi delivers a very different shopping experience from the one British shoppers are used to (Figure 4).

During the recession, these fundamental differences in the way Aldi conducts business had become a bigger barrier. It was proving difficult to persuade shoppers to adopt the different approach that Aldi offered. To make things worse, the recession had made consumers more sensitive about being seen shopping at Aldi. Many shoppers thought shopping at Aldi was a sign of financial desperation and shopping there seemed to add to their feelings of financial hardship (Figure 5).

## Figure 4: Aldi brands vs. famous and Own Label brands

## Figure 5: Negative perceptions of Aldi

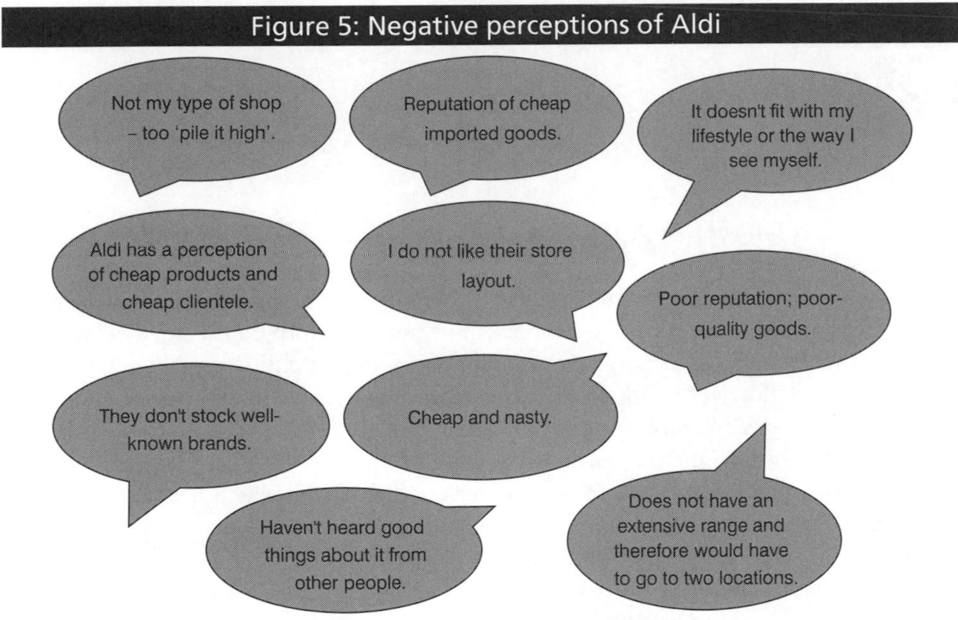


Source: Harris Interactive, Aldi Brand and Market Assessment, 2010

## Gathering consumer insights

Aldi management were determined that performance should be improved. We knew that fresh consumer insight – really understanding what was affecting consumers' shopping behaviours – was the key to unlocking the growth opportunity.

We turned to research to inspire our strategic thinking and designed a deep dive into the hearts and minds of grocery shoppers. Using a mix of qualitative and quantitative research techniques,[6] we uncovered three main insights:

### *1. The majority of Aldi shoppers are highly disloyal*

To get the most out of the Nielsen Homescan data we went beyond standard reports and commissioned a special analysis of shopping patterns. We knew that Aldi was a 'top-up' rather than a 'main shop' for most people but, even so, the results astonished us:

- Over 80% of Aldi shoppers displayed an extremely low loyalty level. Their average visit frequency was just six times across a full year and on average they were giving Aldi just 2% of their grocery spending.[7]
- Around a third of households shopped at Aldi in a full year but Aldi was a 'sometimes' shop for almost all of these (73%).[8]

These findings were a total eye-opener. For many, Aldi clearly was a shop they felt they could take or leave. The predominant pattern was to use Aldi only occasionally and for only a few basic items. A quantification of the business opportunity amongst high, medium and low loyal Aldi customers was undertaken and this showed clearly that the low loyals offered the greatest scope for increasing sales.

### *2. Brands are synonymous with quality*

Focus groups were conducted amongst Aldi shoppers[9] and confirmed what we already suspected people believed:

> *'I can't do a full shop at Aldi because they don't sell the brands I need.'*[10]

The surprise was the degree to which this was stopping people from diverting more of their expenditure to Aldi. Consumers, it seemed, simply could not live without the big name brands, and many claimed that partners and children were more brand conscious than they were and would reject Aldi products as being inferior. The least loyal Aldi shoppers appeared most emotionally attached to big name brands.

Further digging led us to a core insight (Figure 6).

Aldi's price positioning was clearly understood, but this was not converting into an image of true value for money because Aldi brands' quality credentials were in question. Cheap prices at Aldi were not simply the same as cheap prices at any of the Big 4. The Aldi brand did not carry the weight of assurance that more established supermarkets like Tesco or Sainsbury's enjoyed.

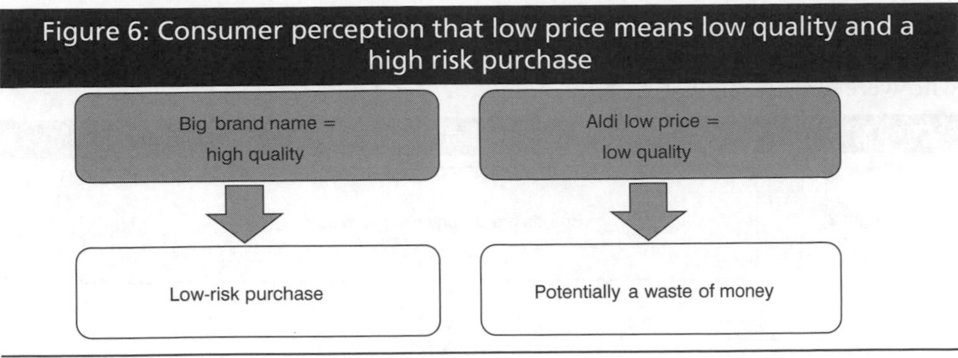

Figure 6: Consumer perception that low price means low quality and a high risk purchase

*3. Lack of emotional connection*

The final insight was that consumers were emotionally distant from the brand.

Conventional supermarkets offered a much wider range of services – butchery counters, fishmongers, in-store bakeries, cafés, toilets, petrol, reward schemes, home delivery and so on – which the Aldi business model did not permit. These add-ons made larger shops feel more welcoming.

Aldi would need to create empathy in other ways – in ways that would give Aldi an authentic voice and make it a strong brand on a par with the Big 4.

## Campaign strategy

Armed with these insights, the next step was to develop a campaign strategy. For each of the three insights we came up with a strategic response and in this way established a three-pillar communications strategy (Figures 7–9).

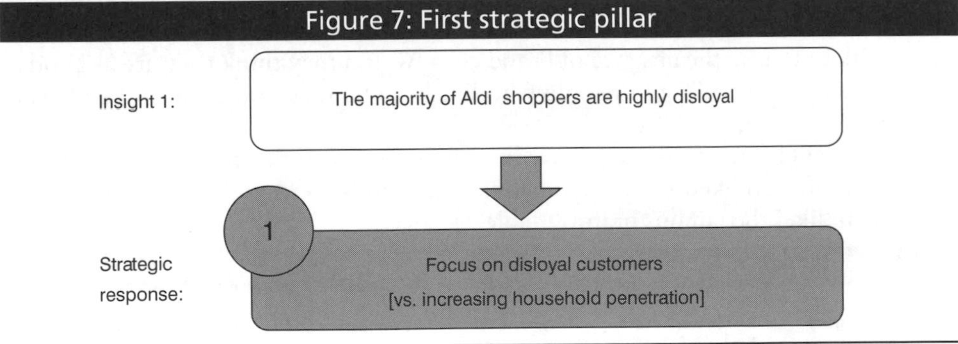

Figure 7: First strategic pillar

Given Aldi's tiny market share, the most obvious strategy would have been to chase new customers. However, our deep dive had revealed that there was an easier target to go for: the vast number of disloyal customers who only occasionally shopped at Aldi. These disloyal customers made up 80% of Aldi's existing customer base, yet spent around £20bn per year in other supermarkets, and primarily in the Big 4. Diverting a fraction of this to Aldi would deliver much higher growth rates.

We judged that instead of acquiring brand new customers, the 2011 campaign should instead spend its money more wisely and persuade these disloyal shoppers, who were already familiar with the brand, to spend more at Aldi.

Figure 8: Second strategic pillar

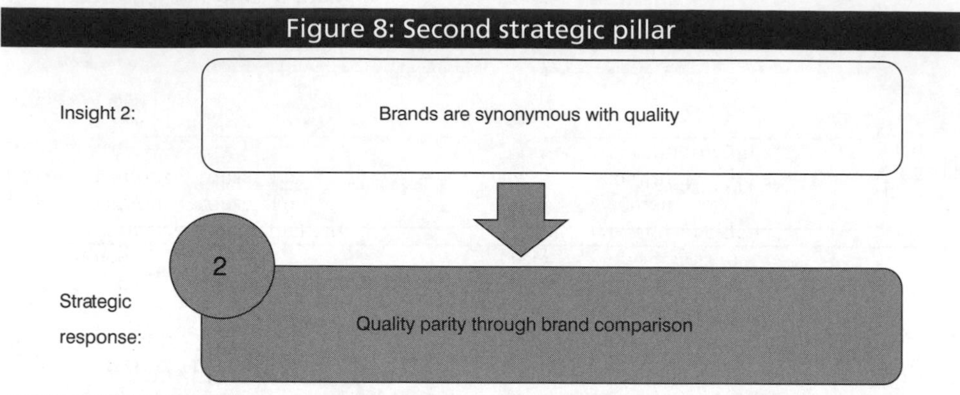
Insight 2:
Brands are synonymous with quality
2
Strategic response:
Quality parity through brand comparison

We had been hearing repeatedly on our journey:

*Low prices = Low quality -> Potential waste of money -> Little willingness to shop at Aldi*

Consumers were craving the power of big name brands – Heinz, PG Tips, Fairy Liquid, etc. These brands stood for quality and were the missing link for Aldi.

The killer question was, how could we convince our disloyal customers that Aldi brands were of similar quality despite their significantly lower prices and unknown names?

To help us come up with a solution, we decided to run blind taste tests among a cross section of shoppers. Our objective was to figure out what people really thought of the Aldi brands in the absence of brand cues. Would they think they are as good as their famous cousins? Would people who liked the famous brands also like the Aldi versions?

To our delight, the tests confirmed that the majority of the people who liked the famous brand also liked the Aldi version. Aldi brands were not inferior; they were very much 'like' the famous brands (Table 1).

Table 1: Aldi blind taste test results for key product categories

| Category | Benchmark famous brand | Total sample | Like famous brand | Also like Aldi brand |
|---|---|---|---|---|
| Tea | PG Tips | 167 | 80% | 78% |
| Beans | Heinz Baked Beans | 206 | 81% | 79% |
| Fish fingers | Birds Eye | 200 | 90% | 91% |

Source: Parklane Research, Aldi Hall Tests, quantitative research, 2011

The solution was starting to take shape in our minds: we had to simply tell the untold truth about Aldi's products – that people liked them just as much as the more expensive brand names.

Figure 9: Third strategic pillar

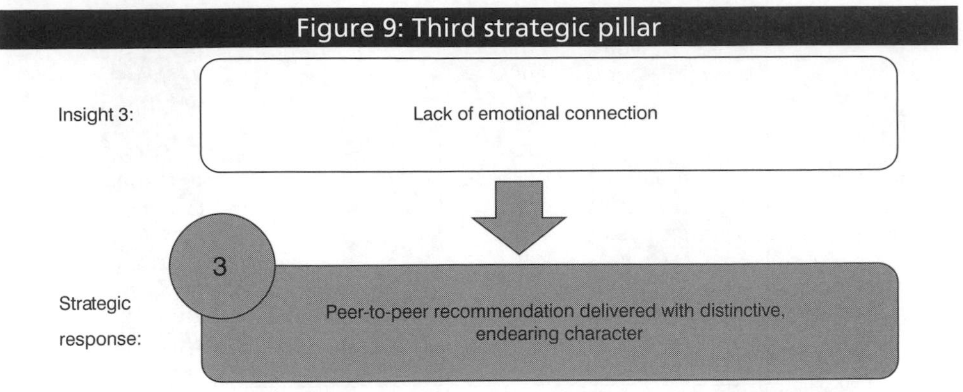


Whilst we could not change the Aldi business model to overcome the lack of goods and services, we could develop a powerful creative idea, personality and style that would challenge consumers' perceptions of Aldi and reach beyond Aldi's small share of voice.

We had frequently witnessed in focus groups that respondents would swap stories about their favourite Aldi products,[11] and leave saying 'Well, I'm going to try that now after hearing what you've said.'

It was confirming an age-old consumer truth: people trust people, ordinary people, people like themselves. For our campaign to succeed, we had to find a way to unlock the power of peer-to-peer recommendation.

## Setting objectives

We had a clear goal: to improve Aldi's overall sales revenue growth rate. To do that we had to deliver in three areas:

### *1. Business objectives*

Sales were forecast to end 2010 at £1.8bn. A target was set to hit £2bn in 2011 – a growth rate back into double figures at 11%, generating an additional £200m of turnover (Figure 10).

Achieving this would increase market share from a forecast 2.4% for 2010 to 2.65% for 2011 as measured by Nielsen.

Figure 10: Aldi target for 2011 value sales

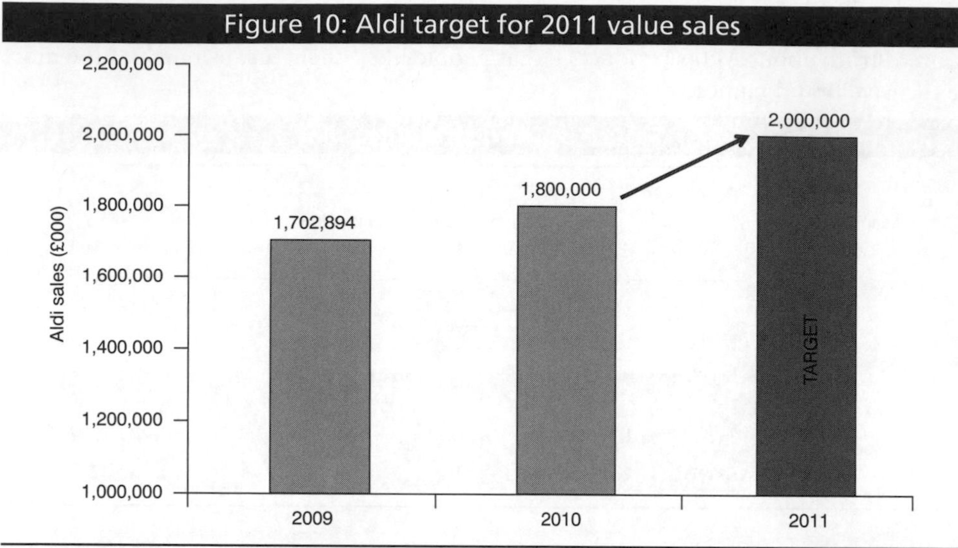


Source: Aldi sales data

### *2. Marketing objectives*

- Increase basket size
  To increase average annual household spend on groceries from £166 to £176. This meant roughly one extra item in the trolley for every customer per visit (at roughly six visits per year).
- Increase frequency
  To increase the proportion of shoppers using Aldi as their 'most often top-up shop' from 13% to 15%.

### *3. Communications objectives*

If we wanted our most disloyal customers to shop at Aldi more frequently and for a bigger proportion of their grocery shop, we had to shift Aldi's negative perceptions.

To achieve this we needed to develop creative communications that resonated strongly and effectively, making the relatively small budget (in comparison to the Big 4) work the hardest it possibly could.

## Developing the 'Like brands' creative strategy

The brief to the creative team was:

*Motivate disloyal Aldi consumers to buy more at Aldi by making them see that Aldi brands are on par with the famous brands and by reassuring them through peer-to-peer recommendations.*

To make the leap from logic to magic, the team looked into what has always been at the heart of Aldi's ethos: simplicity.

Wouldn't it be great if the advertising tuned into that ethos and delivered its message in the simplest way possible? Such a campaign would be authentically 'on brand', would deliver its key message without distraction, and would feel honest and straightforward.

A decision was taken to feature real people so as to be more emotionally appealing. The goal was to make ads that did not look like ads. Initially at least they would need to feel more like home videos, casually shot by 'normal' people who like famous brands as well as the cheaper Aldi versions. The characters were selected to represent the families and friends of our *disloyal* audience, so we cast everyone from kids to grannies. None were professional actors.

Humour was at the heart of each ad. This disarming but quintessentially British humour based on everyday observations lent a high degree of charm to each ad. The aim was to create warmth and affection for Aldi, and hence help close the emotional gap (Figure 11).

Figure 11: The journey from consumer insights to creative idea

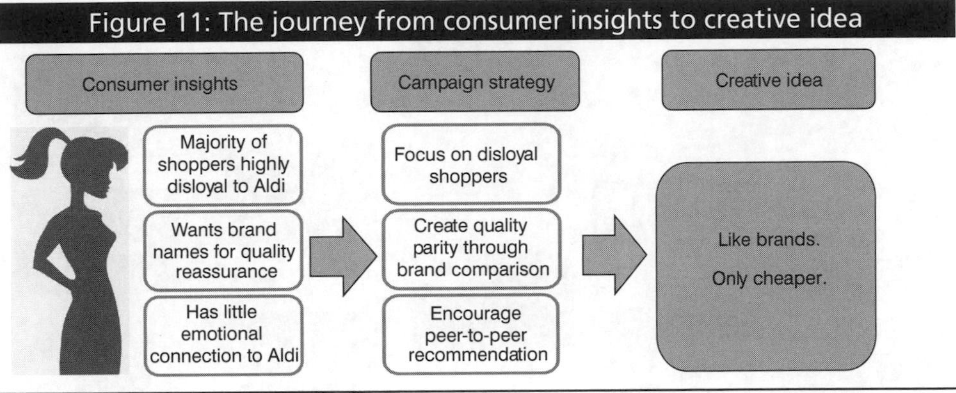


Perhaps the most crucial leap creatively was the decision to feature big brands within the advertising. The 'martial arts' approach was born. Competitors' great advantage was that consumers trusted the brands they sold; Aldi would leverage that strength against them.

Each 20-second TV ad focused on a single staple product category. It showed one iconic brand as the benchmark for quality side by side with the corresponding Aldi brand. This was probably the first time ever that an advertiser had endorsed a competitor brand that it did NOT sell. Each ad ended with the tagline *'Like Brands. Only Cheaper'*, which summed up beautifully what Aldi was about (Figures 12 and 13).

None of the ads were set in store, thus assuming a degree of familiarity which disloyal Aldi customers would already have. Our aim was not to educate new users, but to give our existing users permission to buy more at Aldi – and more often.

Figure 12: Aldi baked beans and tea ads

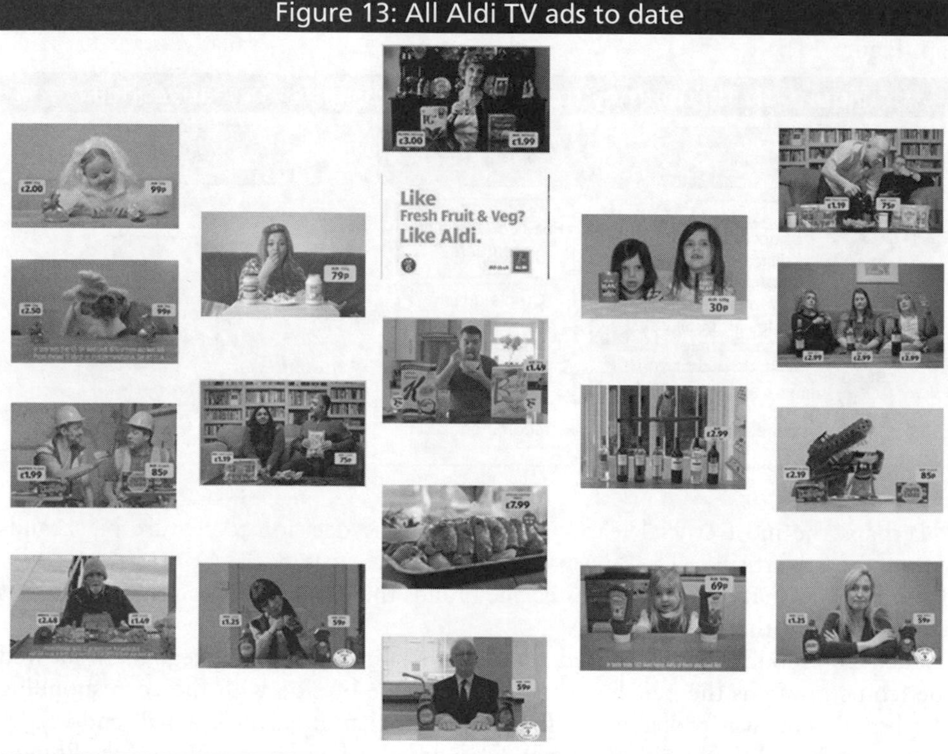


Figure 13: All Aldi TV ads to date

## Media strategy

To ignite growth for Aldi, we knew we had to be on TV. This was the medium that would deliver rapid cut-through and maximum engagement. However, Aldi did not have the same budgets as the Big 4; we had to be clever about our flighting and the choice of programming.

The first challenge was how to create visibility against the Big 4's 'always on' scheduling. Instead of conventional four-weekly 'bursts', we decided to go for short two-week 'mini bursts'. The key to our strategy was to create as many conversation opportunities as possible with our target audience during these mini bursts. Thus we decided to go for programming that was not only hugely popular with Aldi's disloyal customers – mainly made up of housewives with kids – but also fitted with the cheeky and everyday tone of the ads (Table 2).

**Table 2: Aldi choice of programming**

| **ITV1** | **Channel 5** | **Satellite channels** |
|---|---|---|
| • Emmerdale | • Neighbours | Sky1 |
| • Coronation Street | • Big Brother | • An Idiot Abroad |
| • I'm A Celebrity Get Me Out Of Here | • Home and Away | • Glee |
| | • CSI/NCIS | • House |
| • This Morning | • The Mentalist | Living |
| • Loose Women | | • Criminal Minds |
| • X Factor | | • America's Next Top Model |
| • Britain's Got Talent | | • Katie |
| • Take Me Out | | ITV2 |
| • Downton Abbey | | • Celebrity Juice |
| • Britain's Best Dish | | • The Only Way Is Essex |
| • Dancing On Ice | | E4 |
| | | • Big Bang Theory |
| | | • Desperate Housewives |
| | | • Made In Chelsea |

In addition to the TV ads, the campaign also extended dialogue with its customers through social media and a Facebook page (Figure 14).

**Figure 14: Aldi Facebook page**

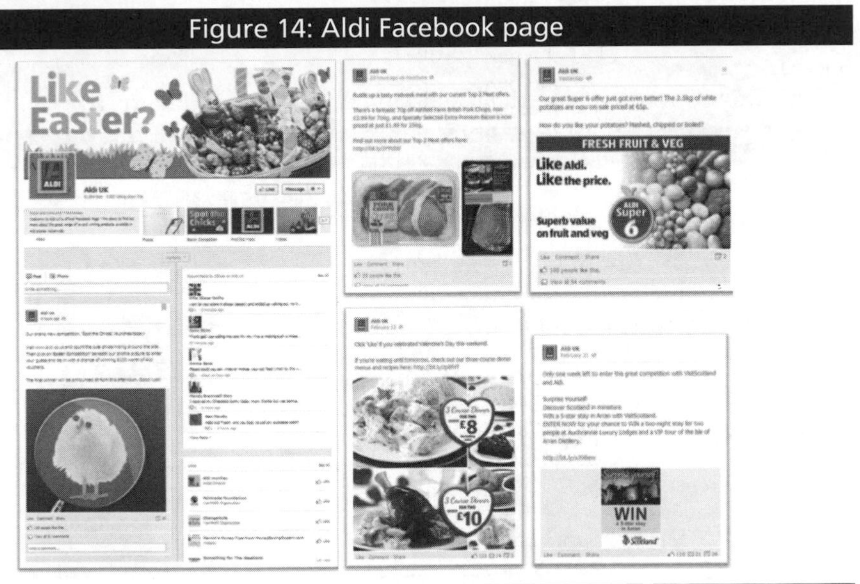


Source: Aldi Facebook page

Finally, we also introduced print and in-store poster executions within the 'Like brands' theme to extend reach and to drill down deeper to the product level (Figure 15).

Figure 15: Some examples of 'Like brands' print and poster executions

## Results against business objectives

The business objectives were clear. Aldi was seeking 11% growth in value sales year on year.

This was not only achieved but substantially exceeded (Figure 16).

Figure 16: Aldi annual value sales growth vs. objectives

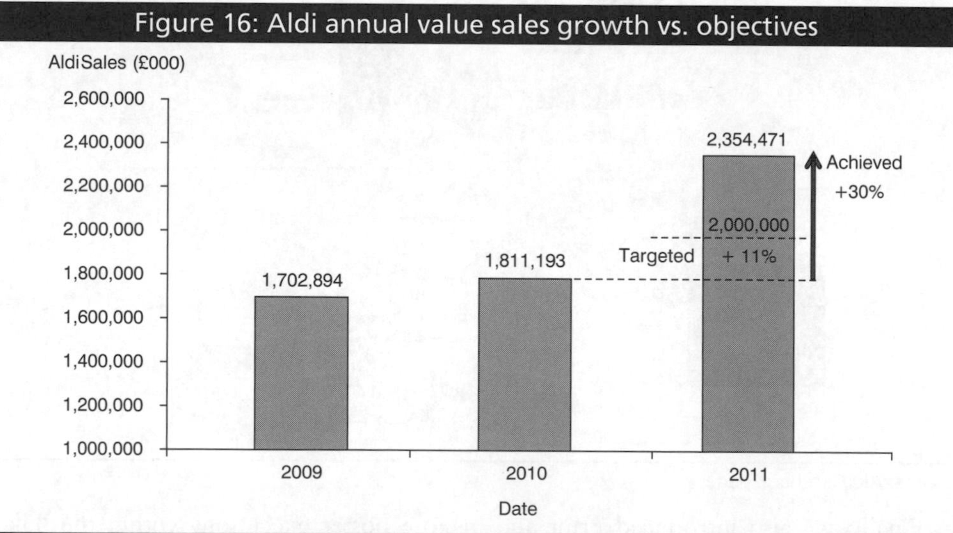


Source: Aldi sales data

The campaign also delivered above target value market share growth: from 2.4% to 3% (vs. the targeted 2.65%). This meant +25% growth vs. the previous year (Figure 17).[12]

Figure 17: Aldi annual value market share growth vs. objectives

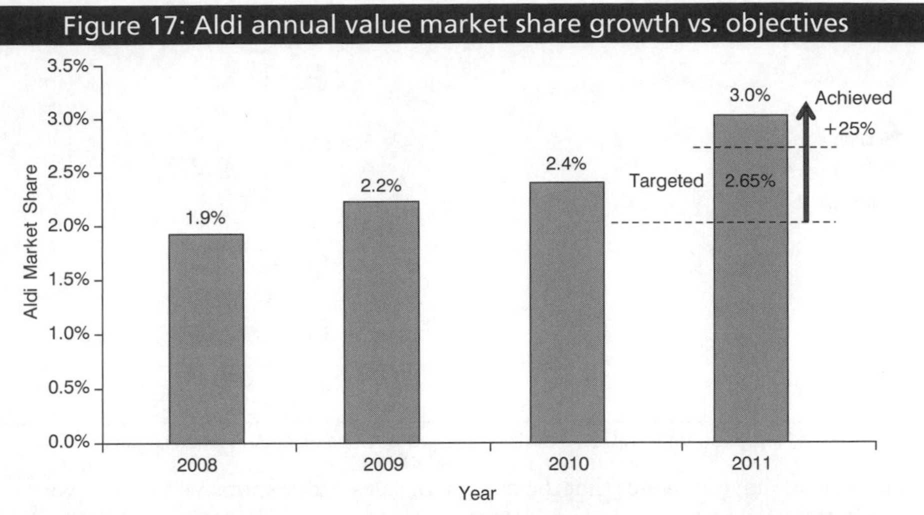


Source: Nielsen Homescan total FMCG (excluding Non Food); 52 week ending 25 December 2011

The four-weekly figures show the sustained performance of the campaign delivering up to 3.5% value market share (Figure 18).

Figure 18: Aldi value market share growth 2011 vs. 2010

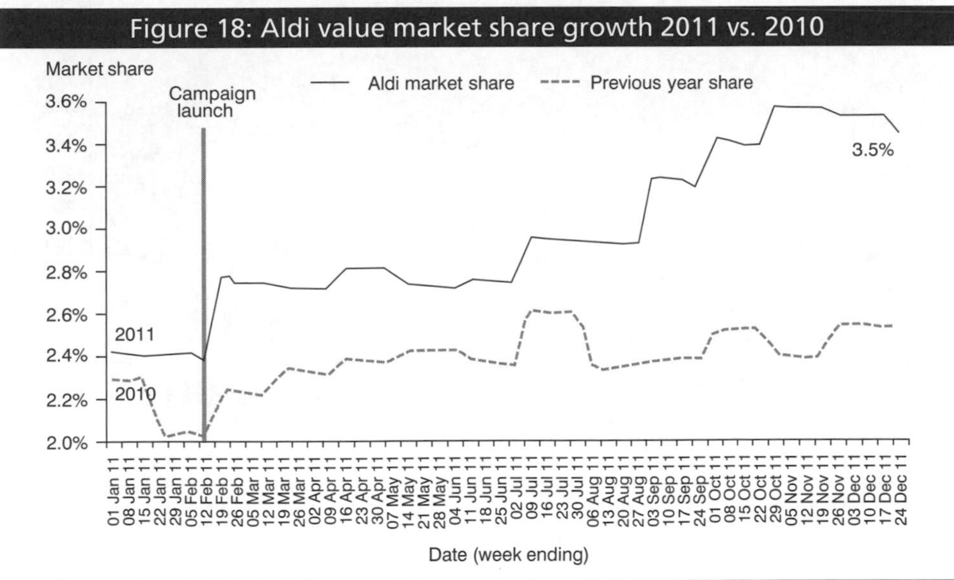


Source: Nielsen Homescan total FMCG (excluding Non Food); four-weekly data to 24 December 2011

Figures for the last quarter of the year show the campaign to still be gathering momentum with Aldi outperforming all other supermarkets (Figure 19).

Figure 19: Aldi value share growth vs. competitors

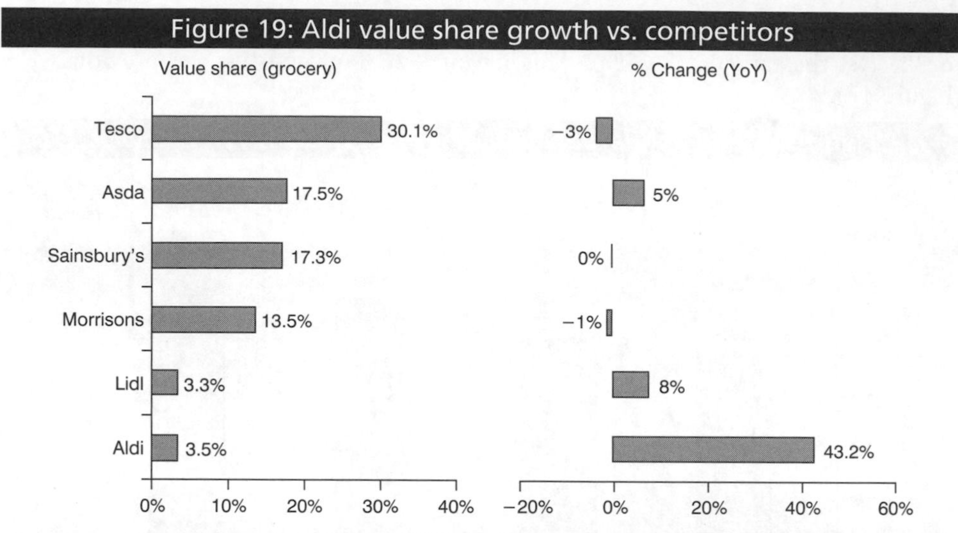


Source: Nielsen Homescan total FMCG (excluding Non Food); 12 week ending 24 December 2011

Further, we have evidence that the pattern of sales was responsive to the advertising (Figure 20), also explained in more detail in the econometrics section.

Figure 20: Aldi value market share vs. campaign TVRs

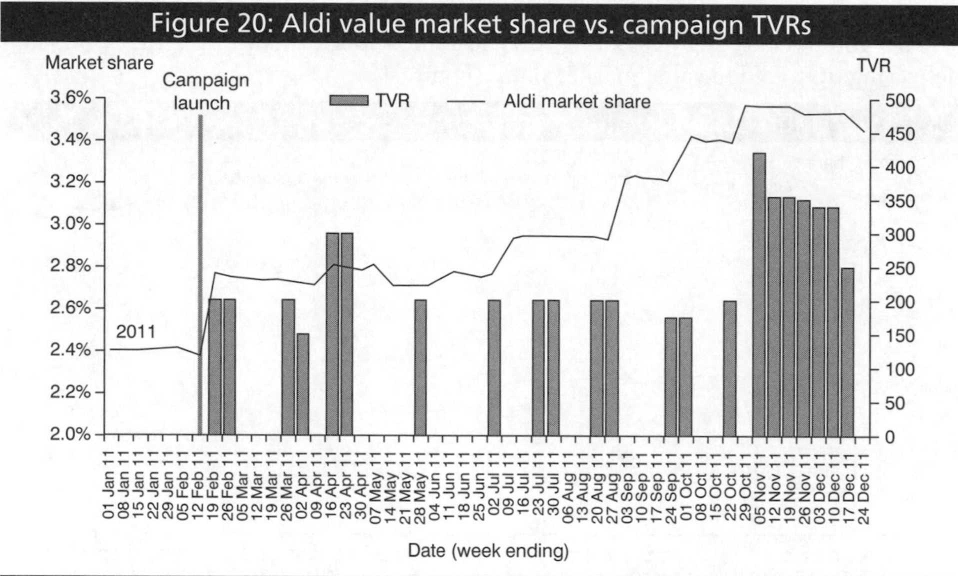


Source: Nielsen Homescan total FMCG (excluding Non Food); four-weekly data to 24 December 2011

## Results against marketing objectives

Finally, the campaign achieved above-target annual household spend growth and 'most often top-up shop' scores, showing that the campaign worked as intended on the disloyal customers (Table 3).

**Table 3a: Aldi annual household spend growth**

| | Full year 2010 | Target full year 2011 | Achieved full year 2011 | Year-on-year change |
|---|---|---|---|---|
| Average annual spend per household | £166 | £176 | £212 | 28% |

Source: Nielsen Homescan total FMCG (excluding Non Food); 52 week ending 24 December 2011

**Table 3b: Use of Aldi as the 'most often top-up shop'**

| | Oct 2010 | Target Oct 2011 | Achieved Oct 2011 | Change |
|---|---|---|---|---|
| Most often top-up shop | 13% | 15% | 18% | 38% |

Source: Harris Interactive Aldi Brand and Market Assessment, 2011

## Results against communications objectives

In the rest of the paper, we shall demonstrate that the 'Like brands' campaign was instrumental in creating Aldi's exceptional performance. Specifically, we will address the following:

1. Show that the advertising worked exactly as intended.
2. Show that no other factors could wholly explain Aldi's success during the campaign period.
3. Use econometric modelling to precisely identify and quantify the contribution of advertising to Aldi's sales over this period.

### *1. Advertising worked as intended*

'Like brands' TV ads generated a level of enthusiasm and, dare we say, 'love' among our target audience not common in the world of advertising and marketing these days. This was a priceless catalyst in shifting negative perceptions of Aldi (Figure 21).

The campaign was also praised for its positive framing of 'cheap'.

> *So in short, bravo Aldi. It's a fun campaign that nicely fits your brand values. It pushes 'cheap' in a positive way that makes it seem like the sensible choice rather than cutting back. I like it.*
>
> *Marketing Week*, 'I like the Aldi Christmas Adverts', December 2011

Aldi's own tracking study also confirmed the positive impact on Aldi's brand metrics, from overall brand perception to key image attributes such as quality and savings (Figure 22).

## Figure 21: Public's comments on the campaign

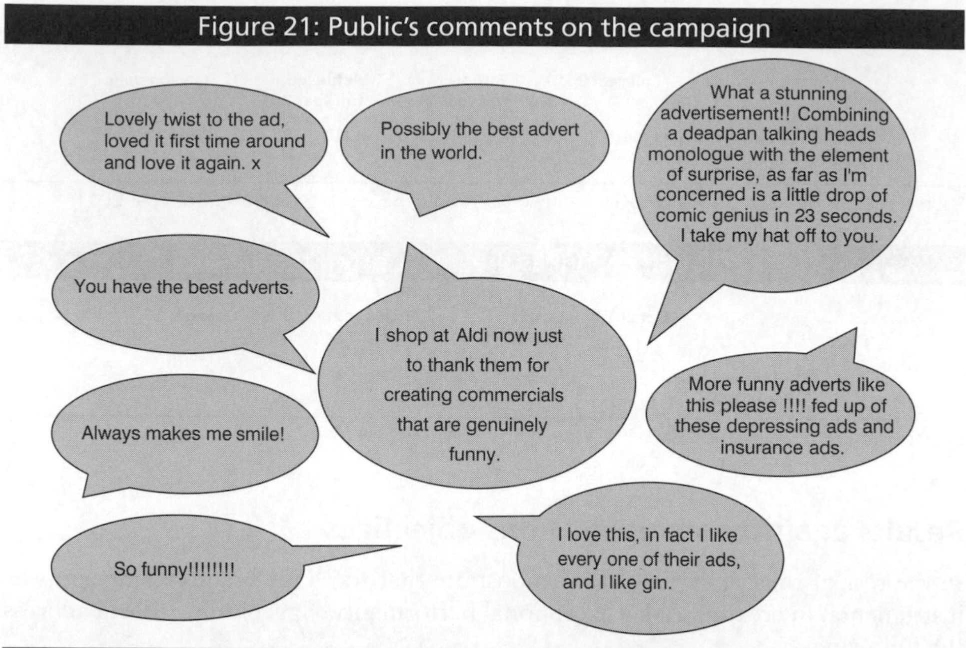


Source: Facebook/YouTube

## Figure 22: Tracking study results, changing perceptions of Aldi

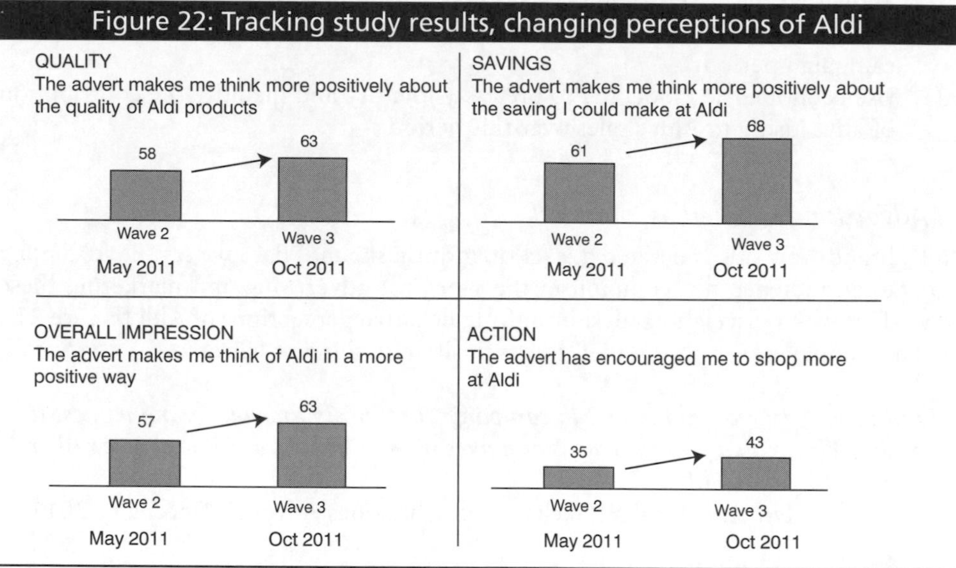


Source: Harris Interactive Aldi Brand and Market Assessment, 2011

Finally, all of the above also helped Aldi become one of the stars in UK customer satisfaction league tables, elevating it to the same level as Waitrose at 12th place:[13]

*Aldi has become one of the UK Customer Satisfaction Index stars over the last year. The public's perception of a good value, high quality product and excellent complaint handling set it apart from many of its competitors.*

The Institute of Customer Satisfaction, 'How Aldi's service shines in difficult economic times', July 2011

## *2. No other factors could wholly explain Aldi's success*

### a) Recession

Recession couldn't have been the main driver as Aldi's sales actually decreased during that period (Figure 23).

**Figure 23: Aldi's declining value share growth**

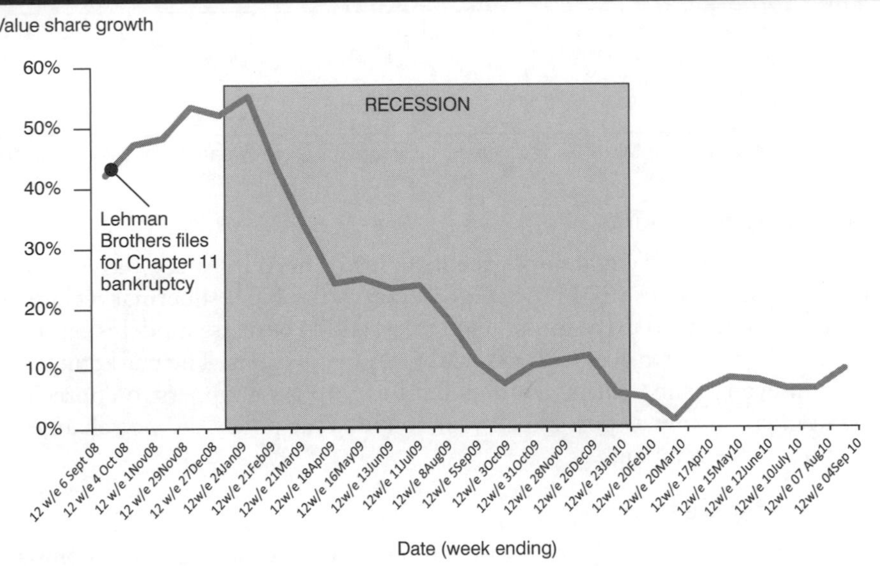


Source: Nielsen Homescan total FMCG (excluding Non Food); 12 week ending 6 September 2008–4 September 2010

### b) Discount sector growth

Although both Aldi and Lidl – the two main players in the UK's discounter sector – have increased their market share in 2011, Aldi's sales increased at a much higher rate than Lidl (Figure 24). Thus, Aldi's success can't be attributed to discounter category effect.

Figure 24: Aldi vs. Lidl value market share growth

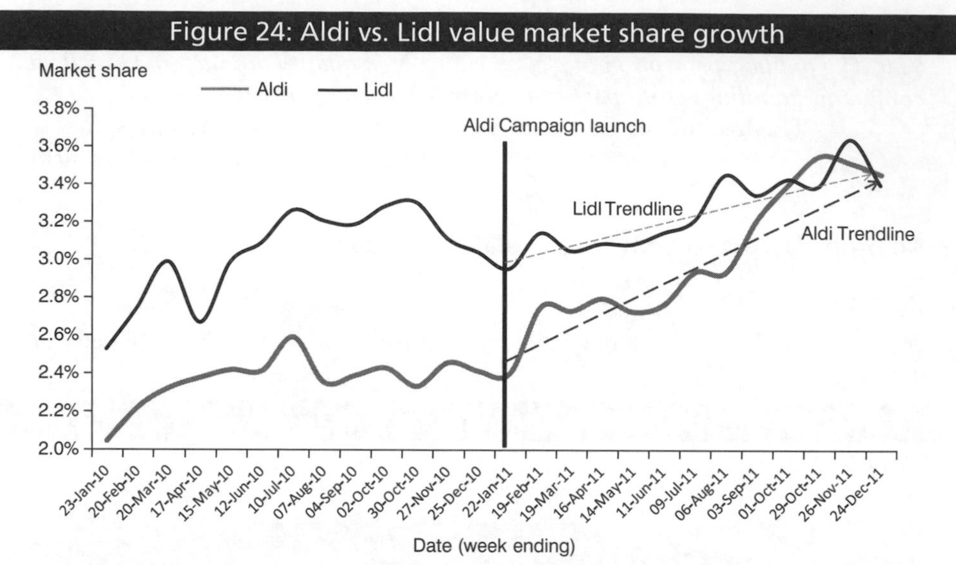


Source: Nielsen Homescan total FMCG (excluding Non Food); four-weekly data to 24 December 2011

## c) Radical price discounts

Radical price discounts could not be the main factor in Aldi's success as Aldi operates an Everyday Low Prices (EDLP) strategy. Whereas the Big 4 supermarkets use waves of price promotions to drive footfall and sales, Aldi's business model is built around offering everyday low prices with minimal price fluctuations. The marketing policy is not to run eye-catching cut-price offers but to try to get shoppers to appreciate that prices are kept as low as possible all year round. This policy did not change during the period of the campaign.

## d) Increased share of voice

Although Aldi's media budget increased 2009–2011, its share of voice compared to the Big 4 supermarkets and other grocers stayed relatively stable (Figure 25).

Figure 25: Aldi share of voice vs. competitors

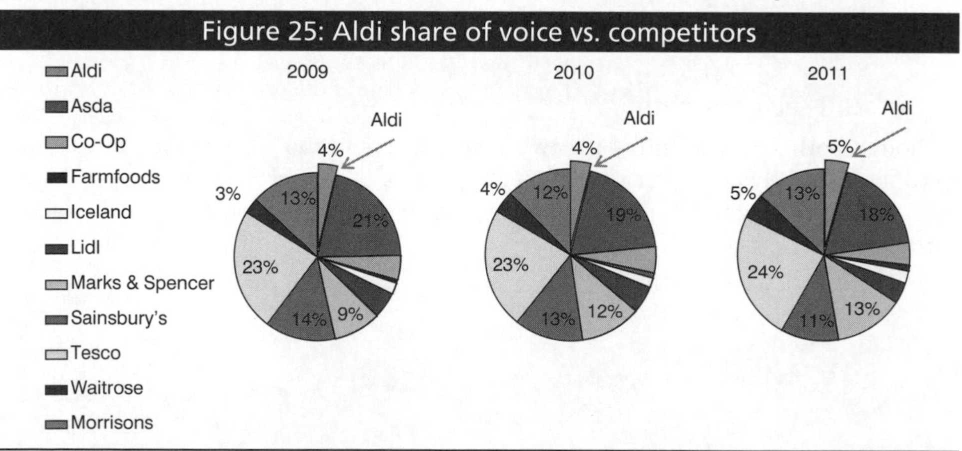


Source: Nielsen addynamix

## e) Increased distribution

Increased distribution cannot be the reason behind Aldi's success, as Aldi's store count remained stable 2009–2011 (Figure 26).

Figure 26: Aldi vs. competitors store count

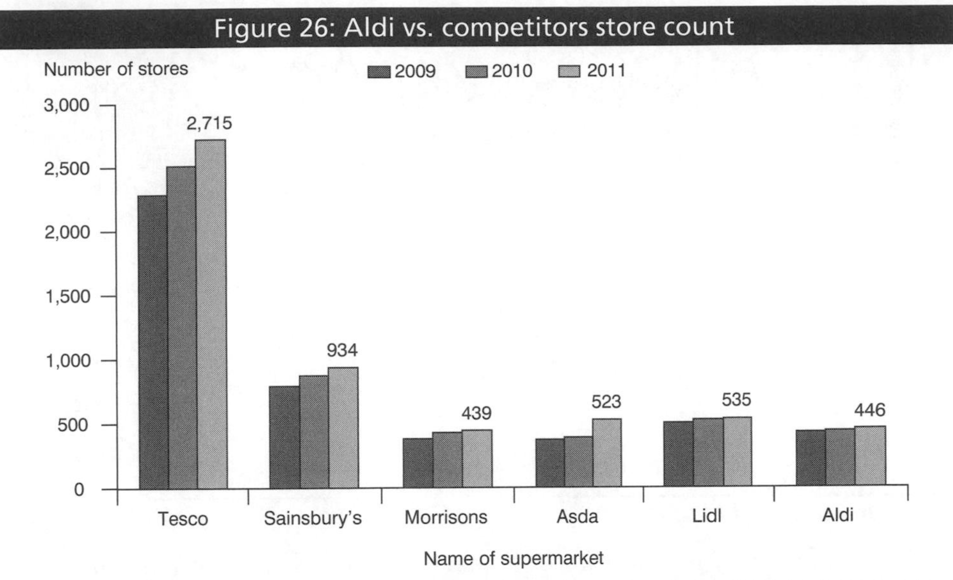


Source: Mintel

### *3. Econometric modelling to precisely identify and quantify the contribution of advertising*

Ohal has constructed a robust econometric model using historic data from 2008 and also including the first five months of the campaign from February to June 2011. As the campaign has been continuing uninterrupted for 14 months since its launch in February, the below results only reflect a fraction of the campaign's contribution to the total sales.

Based on the econometric model of the first five campaign months, the total contribution from the Aldi campaign was just over 15% of total sales. This equates to total incremental revenue from the Aldi campaign of £118m, with a revenue ROMI of 8.97:1 and a profit ROMI of 2.24:1 based on the industry average of 25% profit margin.[14]

Yet, as the campaign was heavily skewed towards TV, it would make sense to take the TV contribution as the main ROMI figure. The Aldi TV campaign has been estimated to have generated almost 9% of total Aldi sales, equating to an incremental revenue of £72m, giving a revenue ROMI of 14.52:1 and a profit ROMI of 3.63:1 based on the industry average of 25% profit margin.

Figure 27 is the actual versus fitted sales chart from the Ohal model. The model accounted for 97% of sales with a standard error of 6.1%.

**Figure 27: Aldi actual vs. fitted value sales**

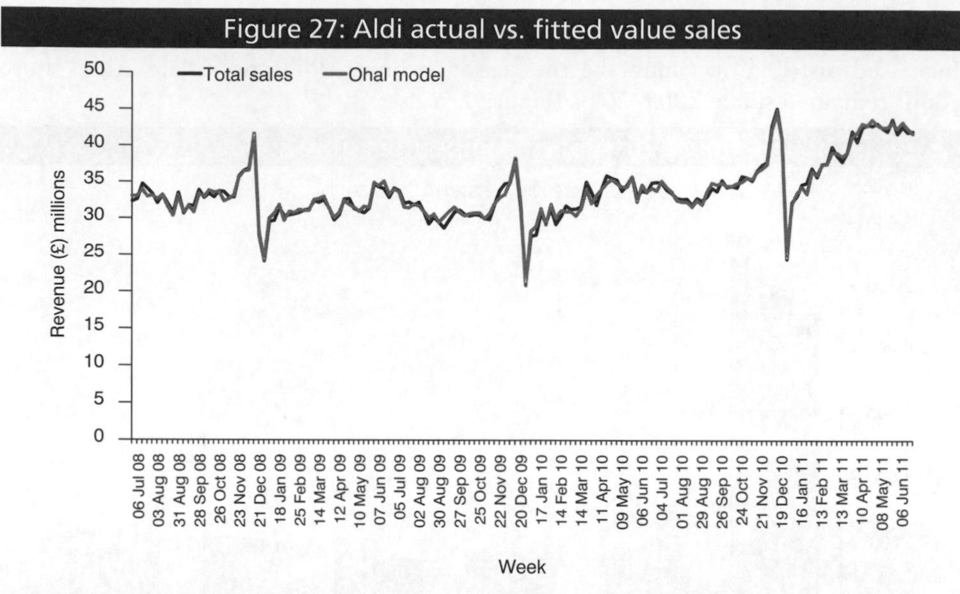


Source: Ohal 2012

Figure 28 is the 'with and without communications' chart, showing what would have happened if the campaign had not run.

**Figure 28: Aldi sales with and without communications**

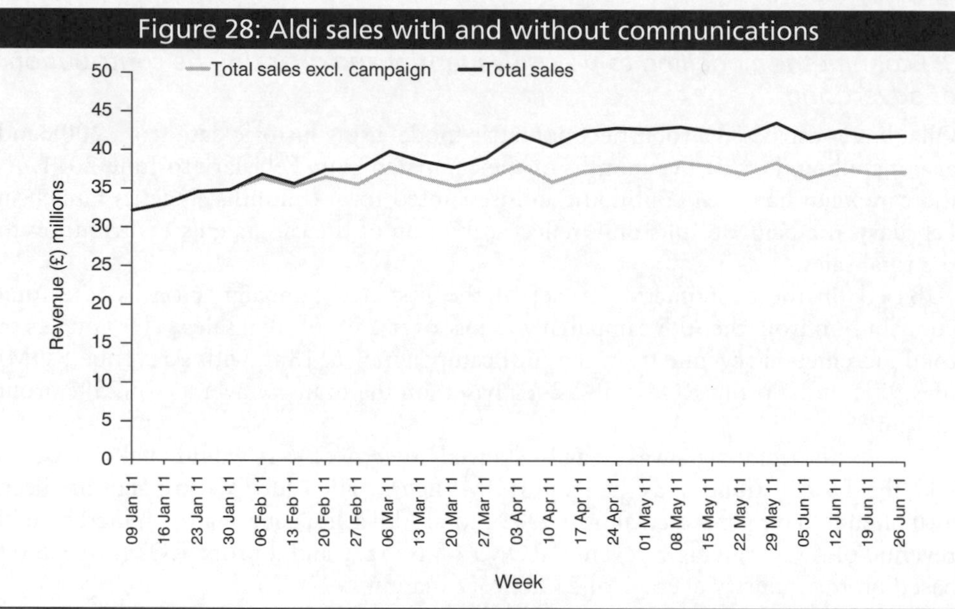


Source: Ohal 2012

Through the Ohal Ad Model for TV, a long-term effect from the campaign has been measured. Over 50% of the TV impact measured has been found to occur post-campaign (Figure 29).

Figure 29: Aldi TV campaign long-term effect

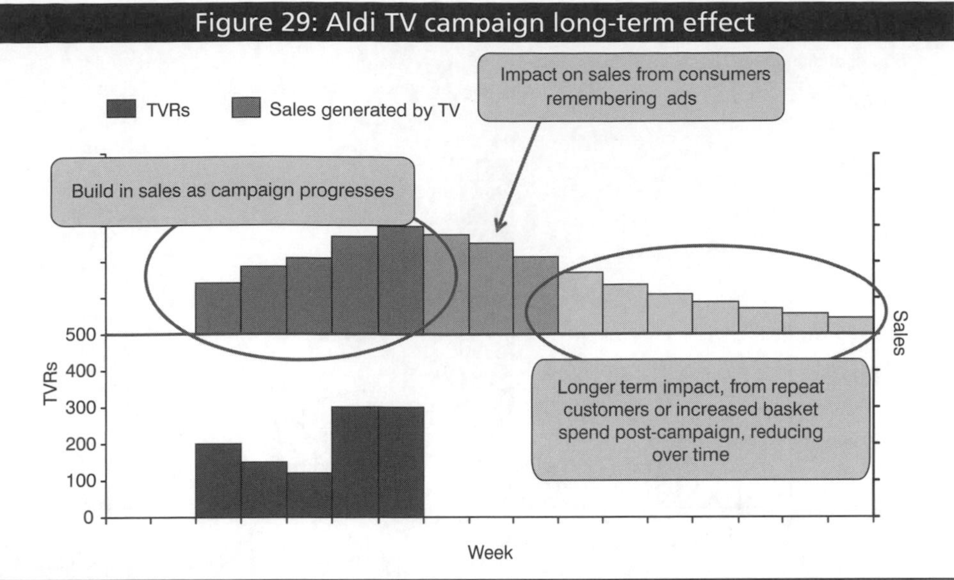


Source: Ohal 2012

A long-term effect was also measured through press activity; over 35% of the press impact measured has been found to occur post-campaign (Figure 30).

Figure 30: Aldi print campaign long-term effect

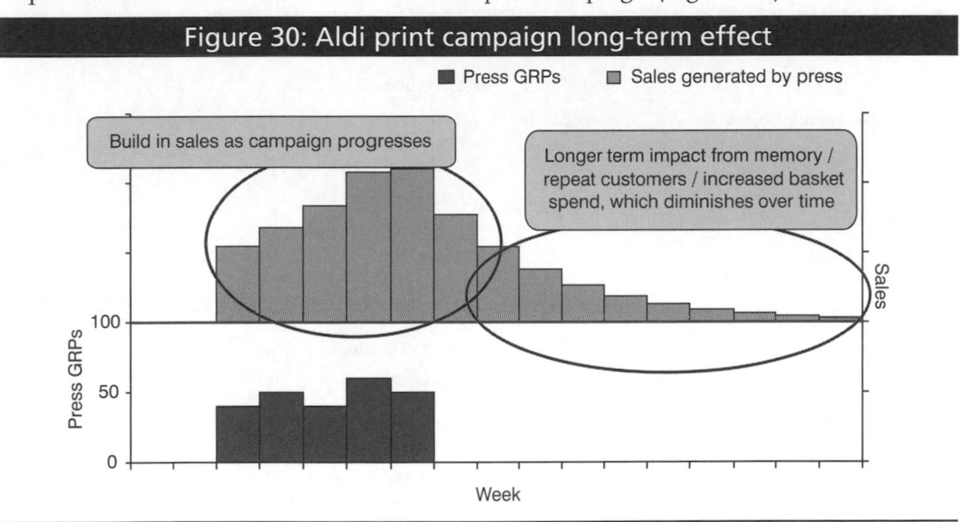


Source: Ohal 2012

## Additional evidence showing 'Like brands' worked as intended

The campaign experienced considerable social media buzz, with the 'Tea' ad having been watched by over half a million people online (Figure 31).

Aldi's Facebook page also proved to be very popular with over 68,000 'likes' to date.[15]

## Figure 31: Aldi's most popular ads on YouTube & Twitter

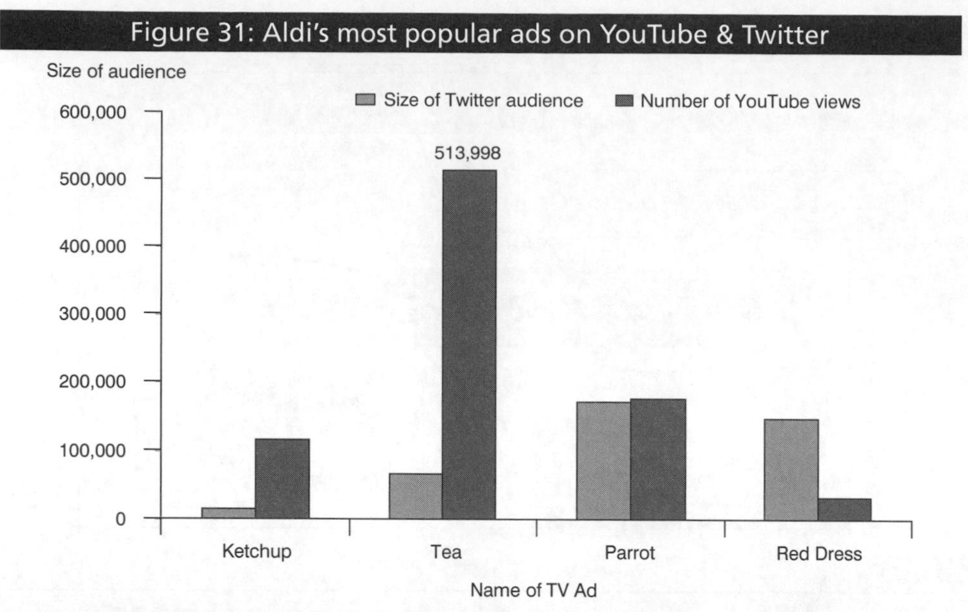


Source: Twitter and YouTube

The campaign has also been awarded by various industry bodies (Table 4).

## Table 4: Aldi industry awards to date

| Award | Date | Description |
|---|---|---|
| Campaign Big Awards | Oct 2011 | Aldi 'Like brands' campaign took the top prize in the Household, Grocery & Soft Drinks category for Best TV campaign of the year |
| The Grocer Marketing, Advertising and PR awards 2011 | Nov 2011 | TV & cinema campaign of the year |
| Utalk Marketing.Com – People's Choice | July 2011 | Aldi Tea TV ad |
| Epica | Jan 2012 | Gold – Film – Retail services for Like brands campaign |
| British Arrows | Nov 2011 | Best new Director for Aldi Tea ad |
| Nielsen | Dec 2011 | The most liked TV ad of 2011: Gin-loving pensioner TVC |
| ITV ad of the year | Dec 2011 | 4th place |
| Creative Circle | Mar 2012 | 'Like brands' campaign won the gold award for the Best campaign of 2011, as well as winning two silvers for Best commercial under 30 seconds and Best direction |
| British Arrows | Mar 2012 | Gold Arrows: Best UK TV series, Best 20-second commercial in non-alcoholic beverages category |

## Learnings and conclusion

At the heart of all martial arts lies the philosophy of 'making the weak equal to the strong'.

Aldi has been a relatively weak player in the UK supermarkets league compared to the Big 4 'muscle' supermarkets. Like in the film *Karate Kid*, by learning how to use its own powers Aldi has managed to turn its weakness into strength.

'Like brands' has shown how a combination of thorough understanding of consumer decision making, unconventional creative thinking, and a pinch of irreverence can work wonders.

This campaign marks a breakthrough in Aldi's history in the UK. It has given the brand a degree of self-confidence that is becoming more apparent as the campaign evolves. Fourteen months since its launch and over 20 TV executions later, 'Like brands' continues to gather momentum and flex creatively into new territories.

Aldi has stood its ground against stronger opponents, increasing its value share by a whopping +43%.

As for the wider marketing community, this case study should give all 'underdog' brands across all categories hope that it is possible to be small and mighty.

> *The results of our 'Like brands' campaign speak for themselves. It has been a remarkable year for Aldi with the business going from strength to strength. The contribution of the McCann team and the exceptionally strong and highly effective advertising campaign cannot be underestimated.*
>
> Tony Baines, Aldi Managing Director, Buying

## Notes

1 Nielsen (2011) The 2011 most-liked ads of the year in the UK, December (Table 5).

**Table 5: The 2011 most-liked ads of the year in the UK**

| Rank | Brand | Ad caption | Likeability Index |
|---|---|---|---|
| 1 | Aldi Supermarket | I buy this tea for my husband | 205 |
| 2 | CompareTheMarket | Sarah Roberts – Congrats from village of Meerkovo | 195 |
| 3 | Volkswagen Passat | Little Boy dressed as Darth Vader | 189 |
| 4 | John Lewis | For gifts you can't wait to give | 179 |
| 5 | Walkers Crisps | 4 comedians, 4 new flavours | 174 |
| 6 | Foster's Beer | Warren from Halifax – Girlfriend's new haircut | 168 |
| 7 | Skittles Candy | Everything Tim touches turns to Skittles | 168 |
| 8 | Boots Pharmacies | Here come the girls – Christmas Mission Impossible | 163 |
| 9 | Dreamies Cat Treats | Cat bursts through wall | 163 |
| 10 | PG Tips | Put the kettle on | 163 |

Source: Nielsen (2011)

2 Nielsen Homescan (2011) Total FMCG (excluding Non Food), 12 week ending 24 December 2011.
3 Nielsen Homescan (2010) Total FMCG (excluding Non Food), 52 week ending 24 December 2011.
4 Ibid.
5 Gfk NOP (2010) Consumer Confidence Barometer, December.
6 Qualitative and quantitative sources used: Nielsen Homescan Data (a comprehensive source of supermarket shopping data based on 14,500 homes), the Aldi brand tracker (a national survey, undertaken by Harris Interactive, tracking key brand measures), shopper focus groups by Blue Banana, TGI (consumer measures based on a sample of c. 25,000). Alongside these, we studied every available report and article on supermarket shopping to ensure we could locate our thinking in the real world.
7 Nielsen Homescan Special Analysis (2010) 52 week ending 25 December 2010.
8 Harris Interactive (2010) Aldi Brand and Market Assessment, October.
9 Blue Banana (2010) Aldi Pulse Research and Insight Programme, November.
10 Ibid.
11 Ibid.
12 N.B. Share growth lower than sales value growth due to growth in total market value.
13 Institute of Customer Service (2012) Customer Satisfaction: Sector League Table, February.
14 Ohal modelling takes account of media costs, plus any variable costs within the Aldi business when estimating profit ROMIs.
15 Number of Fans as of 14 April 2012.

## Chapter 9

# British Gas

## Taking British Gas back to the future

**By Neil Goodlad and Chrissy Jamieson, CHI & Partners**
Contributing authors: Karl Weaver, David Hartley and David Bassett, Data2Decisions
Credited companies: Creative Agency: CHI & Partners; Digital Agency: Outside Line; Direct Marketing Agency: Ogilvy One; PR Agency: Blue Rubicon; Media Agency: Carat; Client: British Gas

**Editor's summary**

Following privatisation, British Gas was declared Britain's most popular brand. Twenty years later it was just another energy company, losing 40,000 accounts every month. This is the story of how a communications idea drew on a once-great brand's past and future, to give it purpose and pride, and most importantly, return it to growth. The idea was 'Looking after your world', an animated multi-platform campaign rendering consumers' homes on individual planets, displaying the new ways British Gas could look after Britain's homes. It generated £82.7m profit from £45.5m investment, giving a profit payback of £1.82 for every marketing £1 invested. It also galvanised necessary organisational change, leaving the business ready to face the future with confidence.

Given the wide-ranging changes within the organisation that took place alongside much of this campaign, judges debated hotly whether all of the ROMI could be explained by paid-for communications activity. However, no one will deny that the task was enormous. To rebuild the brand, to take it beyond slugging it out in the gutter with its competitors and to drive genuine reappraisal beyond price, demonstrates the corporate buy in and commitment to this idea. By taking a leadership stance and demonstrating its understanding of the role British Gas plays in the lives of its customers, by focusing unequivocally on its existing customers, British Gas has regained its leadership status and its mojo.

## Summary

Following privatisation, British Gas was pronounced Britain's most popular brand. Twenty years later it was just another energy company, losing 40,000 accounts every month. This is the story of how a communications idea drew on a once-great brand's past and future, to give it purpose and pride, and most importantly, return it to growth. The idea was 'Looking after your world', and its impact was profound: £82.7m profit from £45.5m investment, giving a profit ROMI of £1.82 for every marketing £ invested. More than this, it galvanised necessary organisational change – leaving the business ready to face the future with confidence.

## The background: how British Gas lost its way

### *1986: Brand of Britain*

Think back to 1986. *Back to the Future* was the biggest movie in Britain, *Don't Leave Me This Way* the biggest single. *Only Fools and Horses* was our favourite TV show. And the 'Brand of Britain'? That honour went to British Gas.[1] Following a highly successful privatisation,[2] British Gas was surrounded by optimism, officially a national treasure.

> *We chose British Gas as our 'Golden brand' of 1986 because of its iconic advertising and the goodwill consumers felt towards the brand at the time – a brand in its hey-day and a worthy recipient of our award which was voted for by our members.*
>
> Gemma Greaves, Marketing Director, The Marketing Society

For the next 12 years, British Gas continued to enjoy a comfortable monopoly over Britain's gas supply.

### *1998: Brand under siege*

In 1998 all that changed. Deregulation of the UK's energy market saw new European competitors, hungry to grow and spurred by the regulator OFGEM, trigger a relentless price war. Their biggest target? The UK's largest energy provider, of course. Challenged so explicitly, British Gas felt obliged to respond in kind and a seemingly inevitable 'race to the bottom' began (Figure 1).

**Figure 1: A communications price war**

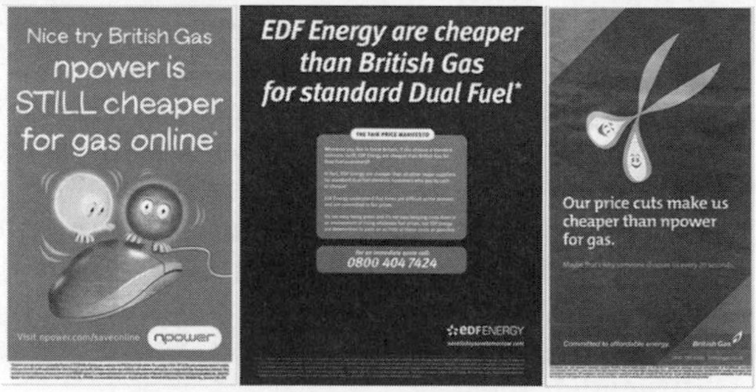

Source: British Gas

The market was flooded with hundreds of new tariffs. OFGEM and the emerging comparison websites urged 'switching'. And as long as the market was presented solely through the prism of price, British Gas had a major problem. It couldn't always compete on these terms. How things would shake out for these new competitors was unclear, but for an ex-monopoly, the only way was down.

### *2008: Brand in free-fall*

As wholesale prices increased over the course of the Noughties, the picture for British Gas continued to darken. 2008 brought the worst recession for decades, and consumer apathy turned to anger at rising energy costs. The media made British Gas its whipping boy – shorthand for 'profiteering' energy companies (Figure 2).

**Figure 2: As prices rose, British Gas took the brunt of negative press**

Source: Various newspaper cuttings

It didn't help itself either. The business had actually made significant strides post-deregulation. Not only supplying electricity as well as gas, but also expanding its 'home services' beyond boiler maintenance and into plumbing, electrics and appliance care. There were aspirations too for 'new energy': sustainable solutions like solar installation and smart meters.

Yet these business divisions were just that: divisions. Operating in silos, pulling in different directions, the company was unfocused and fragmented. At war with the competition *and* itself.

> *At that time, there was very little synergy between the Energy and the Home Services side of the business, despite there being significant customer overlap.*
>
> Chris Jansen, Managing Director Services & Commercial, British Gas

Communication reflected the disharmony (Figure 3). The energy business favoured 'flame' characters. Home services insisted on real engineers.

**Figure 3: Poorly integrated communication reflected the internal disharmony**

Source: British Gas

The various visual identities of contrasting campaigns contributed to the sense of a brand without unifying direction or purpose. The result was communication drifting off the consumer radar (Figure 4).

**Figure 4: Communications were failing to cut through across the market**

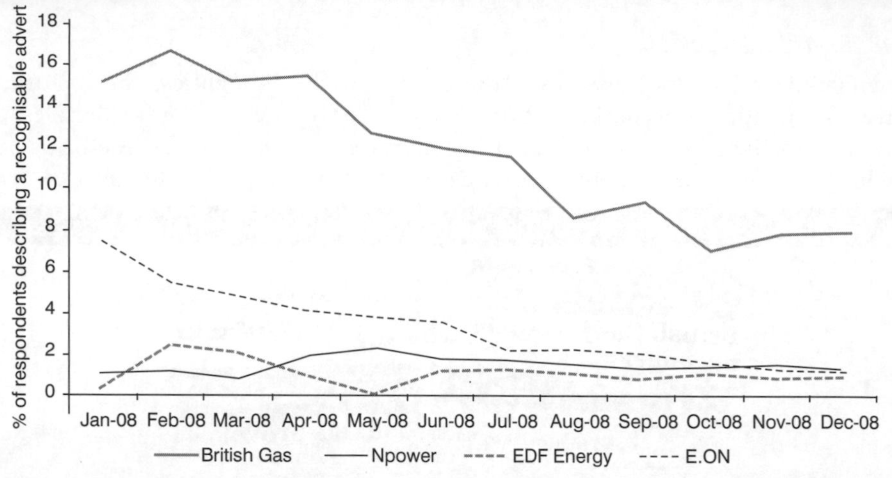


Source: TNS. Base: total sample. Typical sample size is 600

Little wonder the commercial reality was so stark. British Gas was losing 40,000 customer accounts[3] every month (Figure 5).[4] Pre-occupied by the competition and internal rivalries, and out-of-touch with customers, people were deciding British Gas was no longer for them.

**Figure 5: British Gas continued to lose accounts**

Total Energy Accounts (m)
19.0
18.5
18.0
17.5
17.0
16.5
16.0
15.5
15.0
2003 2004 2005 2006 2007 2008

Source: Centrica Annual Reports

Continued decline seemed inevitable. At the current rate of losses, the business would lose top spot within a decade (Figure 6).

Figure 6: British Gas was losing share

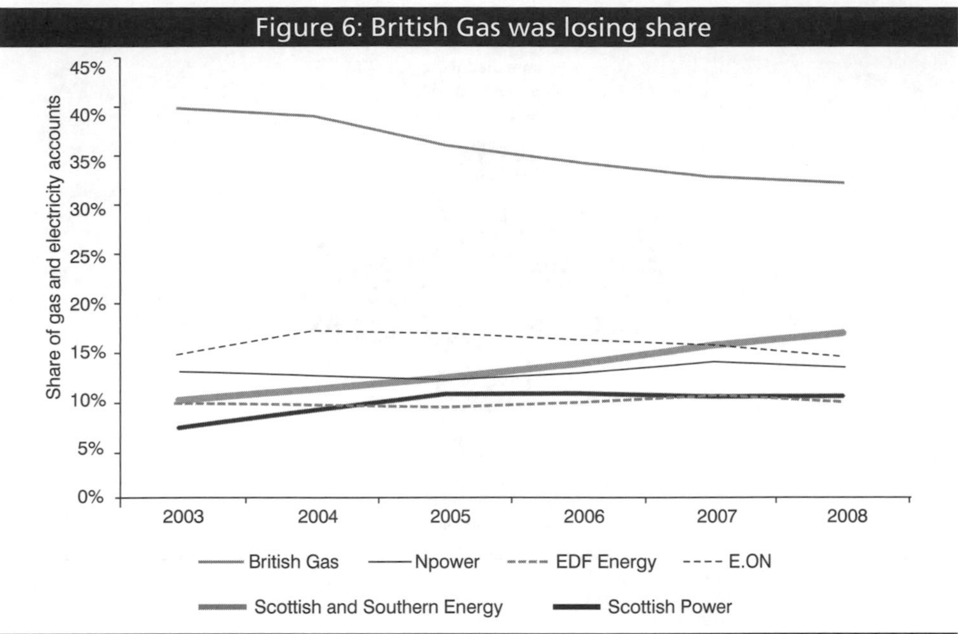


Source: Datamonitor, Cornwall

## The challenge: getting back to great

2008 had to be a line in the sand. The new Managing Director, Phil Bentley, took urgent action to turn the business round. He outlined a two-year vision to '*Get back to great*' and set a hugely ambitious target: *put the business back into growth in two years.*

This wasn't about acquisition: British Gas attracted 2.2 million new accounts in 2008, 4% of the market. The problem lay in the 2.6 million that were leaving to other suppliers. Reduce the churn to a more sustainable level and growth was a possibility.

For his part, Bentley committed to creating 'One British Gas', where all aspects of the business would come together as a single team: energy, services, business and new energy. Collectively they needed to end the business's unhealthy introspection and focus their attention on those who mattered most – customers.

CHI, British Gas' communications agency, had a vital role to play in understanding the contemporary customer. Their response was to find an idea big enough to be the catalyst for 'great': galvanising internally, convincing externally, true today and inspiring tomorrow (Figure 7).

Figure 7: The challenge

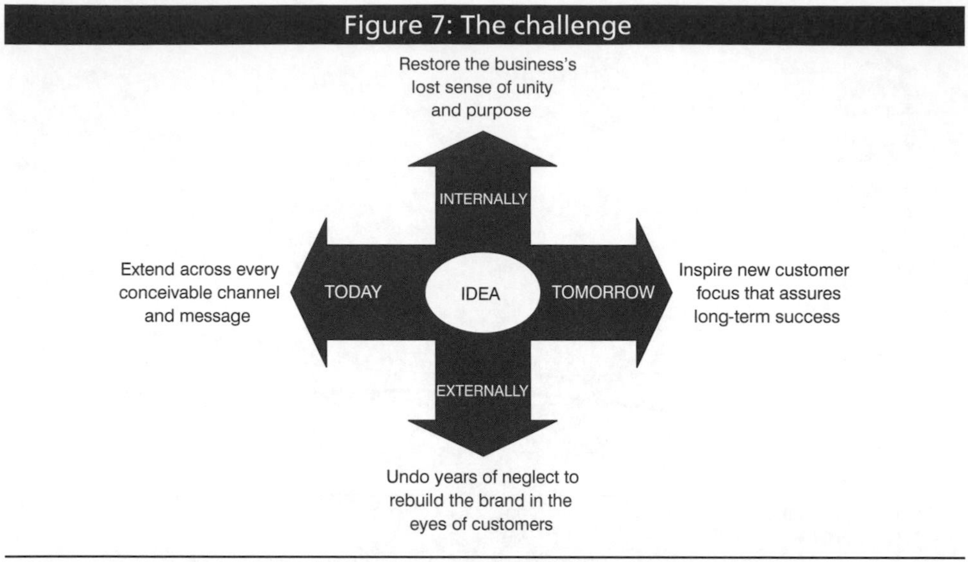


## The communications model

Beyond this broader challenge, CHI designed a communications model that would deliver greater customer commitment. Tasks and metrics were identified that would provide a roadmap to success. Crucially, we knew communications had to differentiate British Gas in an increasingly commoditised sector. Communications would need to command attention more consistently, broaden people's perception of the brand and restore their affinity with it (Figure 8).

Figure 8: The communications model

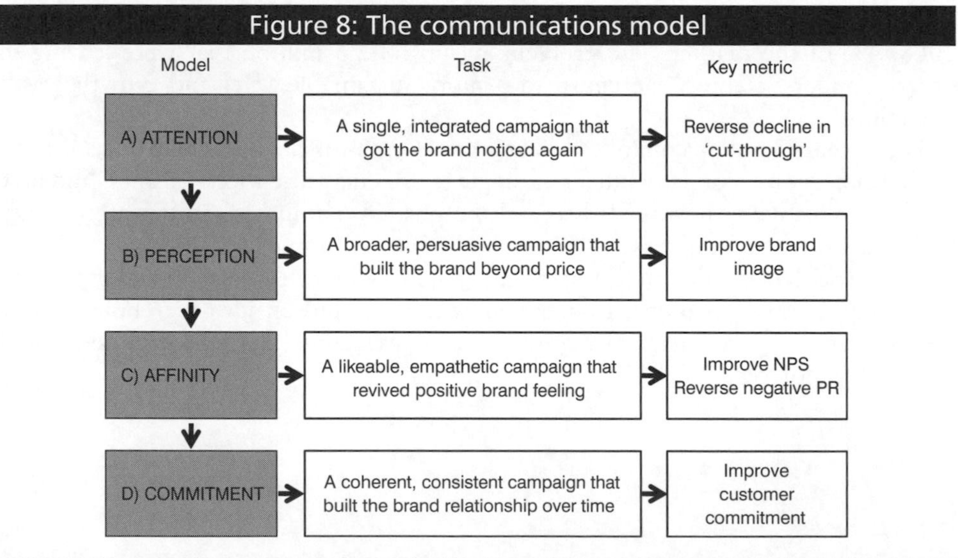

## The idea: Looking after your world

CHI recognised that the key to the idea would be a compelling definition of the contemporary role British Gas could play in its customers' lives. It commissioned research to explore this single question:

*What is the role that 'One British Gas' could play in the life of today's customer?*

The research found people surprised by the breadth of what British Gas could do for them and their homes. The dominant price conversation had obscured the fact that British Gas was now, more than any of its rivals, more than just an energy company. This shone a harsh light on the existing communications thought, 'Your energy experts', which described too narrow a role to do justice to the brand and its ambitions. Moreover, some questioned if British Gas did in fact have more expertise than any other energy company.[5]

'Energy experts' also lacked warmth. These were uncertain times. And people's homes are emotive things. Yet this thought felt cold, even arrogant, lacking the care and reassurance respondents were looking for, especially where their homes were concerned.

The research also led to a second, deeper conclusion. People's homes are so emotive because their homes are their worlds. Where they eat, sleep, laugh, cry, live. And in recession, they're where they 'hunker down' until the worst is over.

> *Home is very important. It is where people escape from the real world and retreat to their own world to feel safe, secure, and comfy. Their home is their castle.*
>
> British Gas Customer, CML Creative Development Research, 2008

They're a retreat, and not every person – or brand – is welcome over the threshold. Yet, crucially, British Gas was still one of them. In spite of everything that had happened over the last 20 years, it still had the credibility to care. People had grown up with its familiar logo, ubiquitous vans and friendly engineers. It didn't just pump gas through pipes, it kept many of Britain's homes going. Yet its warmth had been frozen out by the aggressive cold-calling feeding frenzy the energy market had become.

CHI saw the opportunity to go 'back to the future'. To revive goodwill towards the brand, but reframe it in the context of the new ways in which British Gas could look after Britain's homes:

*Your home is your world. Count on British Gas to look after it.*

Here was the insightful, emotive definition of British Gas's role that was needed. 84% of consumers said they related to it.[6] Competitors didn't have the legacy or range of services to emulate it. Abbreviated to 'Looking after your world', it became the basis of the communications idea.

## The campaign: Planet Home

The idea found an involving creative expression in 'Planet Home'. The thought was simple: if people's homes really are their worlds, why not show them as such?

Customers' homes were rendered quirkily, on their own individual planets. These planets hung in an engaging space-scape, populated by helpful engineers flying dynamic space-vans (Figures 9–11). Not only did this allow any proposition to become a warm, witty and insightful story of British Gas looking after customers' worlds, it had the potential to become the brand's universe and deliver distinctiveness and branding.

Figure 9: TV stills

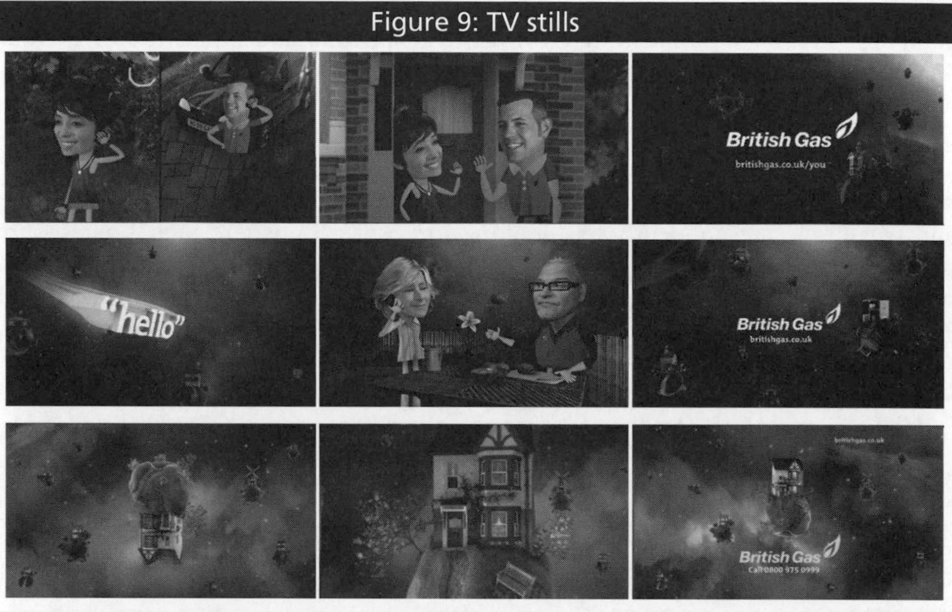


Figure 10: Print

Figure 11: Direct mail

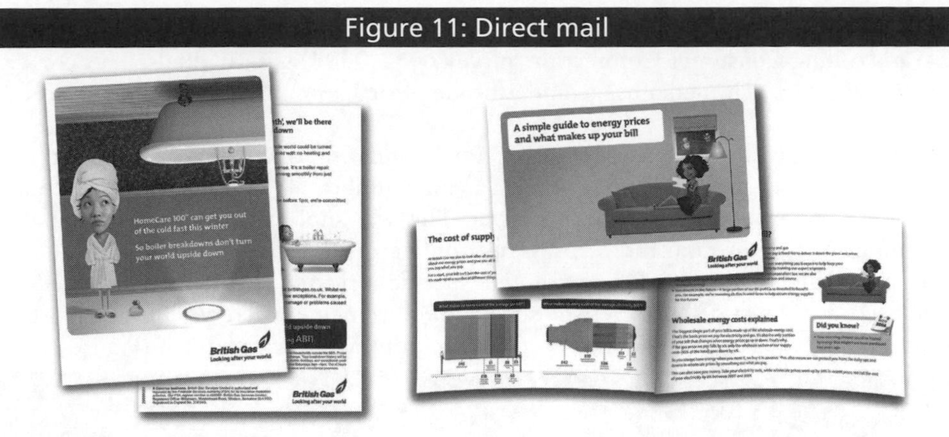


The idea and campaign had the potential to deliver in every way it had been challenged to (Figure 12).

Figure 12: A campaign with potential

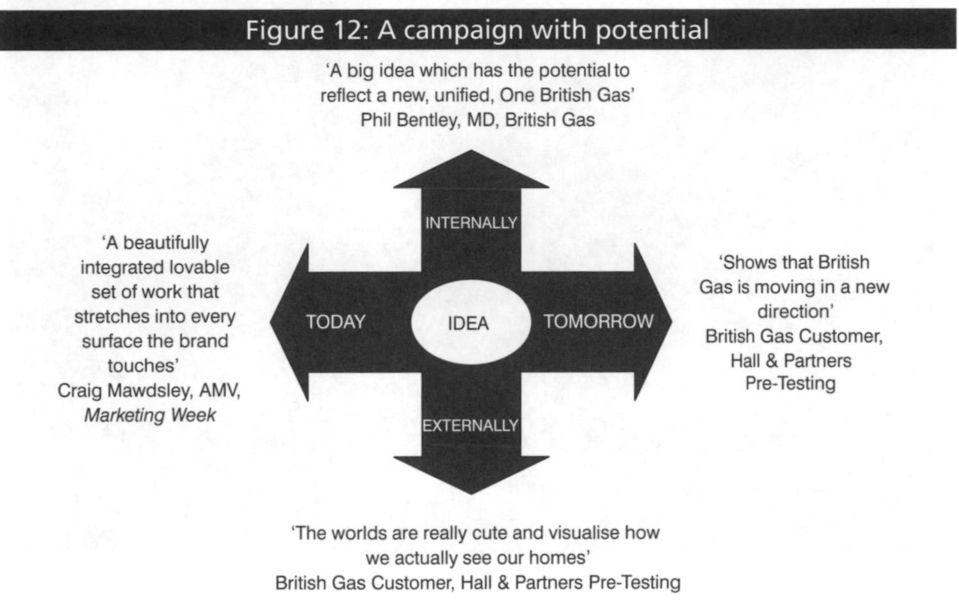

'A big idea which has the potential to reflect a new, unified, One British Gas'
Phil Bentley, MD, British Gas
INTERNALLY
TODAY
IDEA
TOMORROW
EXTERNALLY
'A beautifully integrated lovable set of work that stretches into every surface the brand touches'
Craig Mawdsley, AMV, *Marketing Week*
'Shows that British Gas is moving in a new direction'
British Gas Customer, Hall & Partners Pre-Testing
'The worlds are really cute and visualise how we actually see our homes'
British Gas Customer, Hall & Partners Pre-Testing


## The media approach

The campaign had to be established as quickly and as powerfully as possible amongst a broad audience. British Gas needed to engage customers from 20 to 80 years old, from all walks of life. However, various propositions within 'Looking after your world' would have differing relevance amongst customer segments. So both broadcast coverage and more selective placements were needed to reflect these differences.

To best achieve this, a new British Gas customer segmentation was fused with Carat's rolling Consumer Connection Survey of 11,000 UK individuals. This created a single view of rich media usage and attitude information combined with customer behaviour.

From launch in early March 2009, rapid and broad coverage was built and sustained through multiple bursts of TV: a medium unbeatable for building the affinity the new campaign was designed to deliver. This was supported by more segmented communications through radio, press and online display, allowing for more depth and personal communications with the specific priority segments. Out-of-home was used more tactically to deliver specific requirements, such as Opinion Former engagement, via a unique Westminster tube station takeover at launch (Figure 13).

Figure 13: Planet Home takeover of Westminster tube to engage Opinion Formers

## The results

### *The desired impact on retention*

Returning to growth was never going to be easy for a once-nationalised monopoly. Everybody over the age of 30 had been a British Gas customer, but many had left dissatisfied, so it would be hard to win them back. With British Gas's remaining market share still large, new customers would, by definition, be hard to find. Yet with the Planet Home campaign, growth was achieved.

In the first two years from launch, churn fell from a frightening 2.6 million customer accounts per year, down to a much more sustainable 1.8 million (Figure 14).

Figure 14: Energy account losses fell dramatically

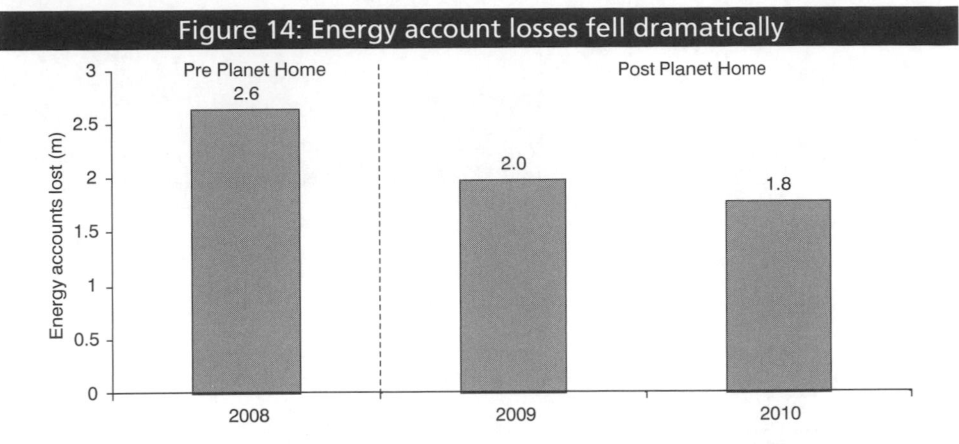


Source: British Gas

Crucially, this decline meant British Gas was now acquiring new customer accounts faster than it was losing them (Figure 15).

Figure 15: British Gas began acquiring more energy accounts than it was losing

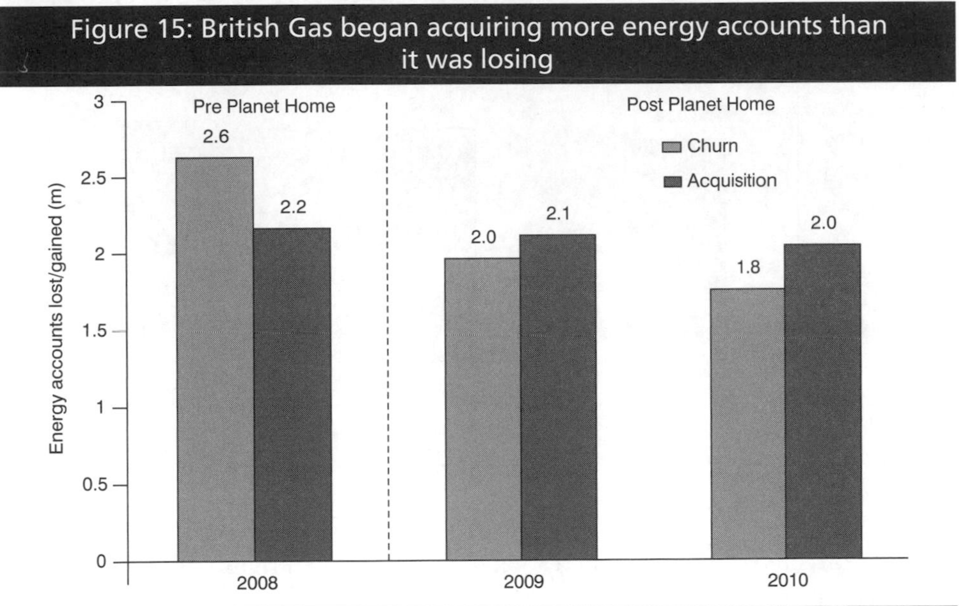


Source: British Gas

As a result, British Gas entered its first period of energy account growth since privatisation (Figure 16).

Figure 16: Planet Home reversed the decline in energy accounts

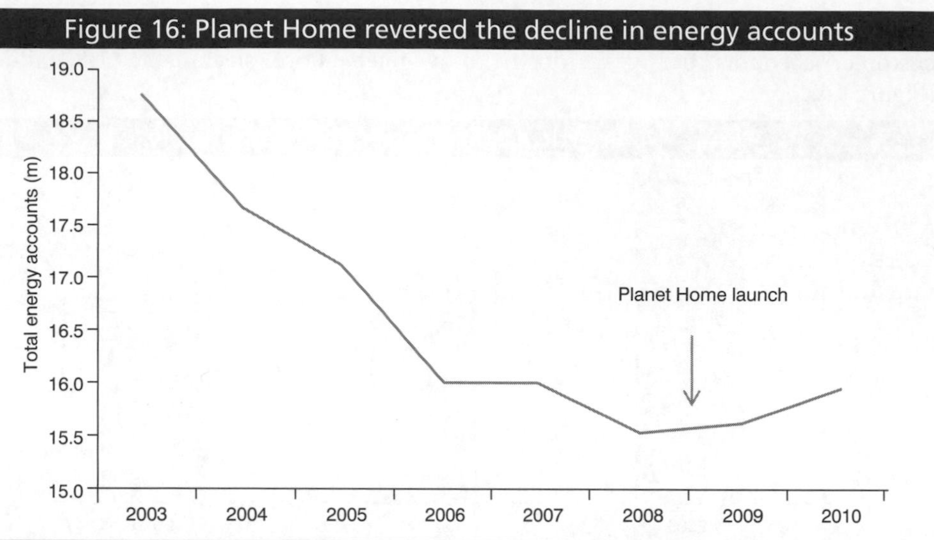


Source: Centrica Annual Reports

The home services side of the business also experienced customer account growth (Figure 17).

Figure 17: Home services account growth

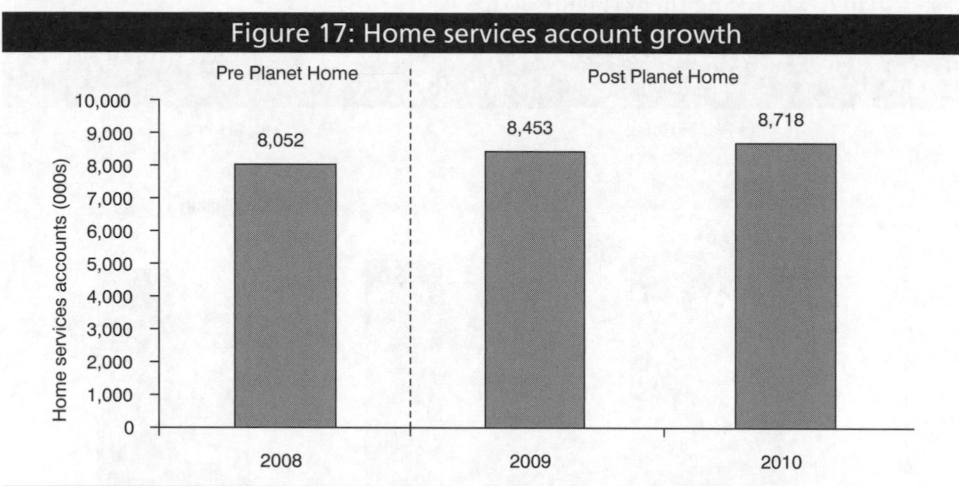


Source: British Gas

The commercial transformation is clear. The following sections will demonstrate that Planet Home was pivotal in creating this remarkable turnaround:

- Hard and soft measures show that the campaign worked as intended at each stage of the communications model outlined above.
- The 'above and beyond' objectives for the campaign were met.
- All other factors that influence British Gas are examined and shown not to be responsible.

- Controlled regional tests of advertising weight prove how up-weighted regions performed better.
- Econometric analysis isolates and quantifies the overall commercial impact.

### *1) The campaign worked as intended*

Improvements across all KPIs show how each task in the communications model was achieved, leading to more committed customers, and ultimately, the reduction in churn (Figure 18).

Figure 18: The campaign delivered against our key intermediate metrics

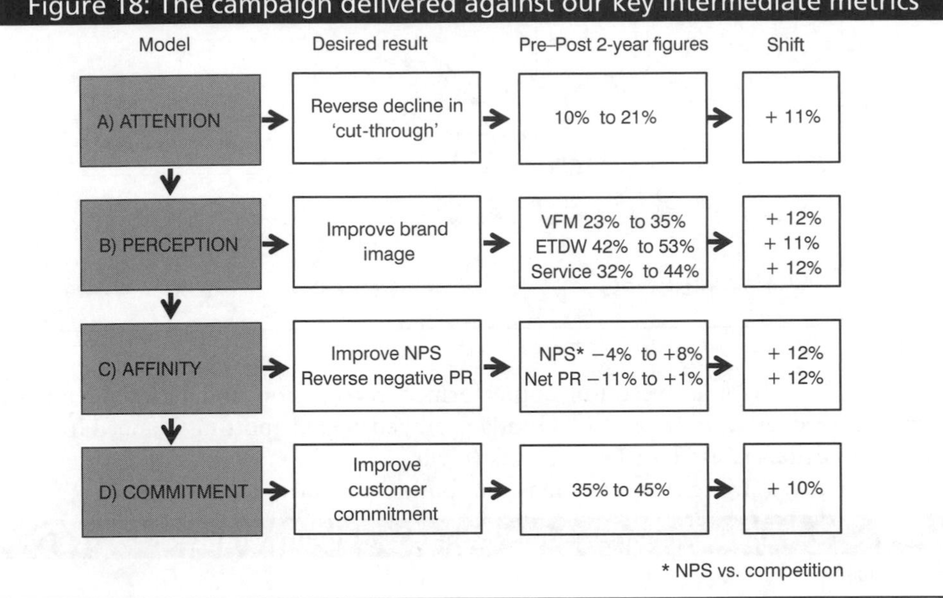


### a) Attention: A single, integrated campaign that got the brand noticed again

As previously illustrated (Figure 4), communications from British Gas and competitors had failed to stand out, perhaps unsurprisingly, given the relatively low interest in the category in general and the creative inconsistency of British Gas in particular. Consumers just didn't notice anyone's advertising, despite significant spend (energy total TV spend alone was £28.8m in 2008).[7]

Planet Home reversed this trend for British Gas, whilst competitors continued to struggle. Part of this can be accounted for by an increased share of voice (SOV) on TV, up 36%,[8] but the improvement in TV cut-through was three times greater, at 109% (Figure 19).[9]

Figure 19: Planet Home stood out from the competition

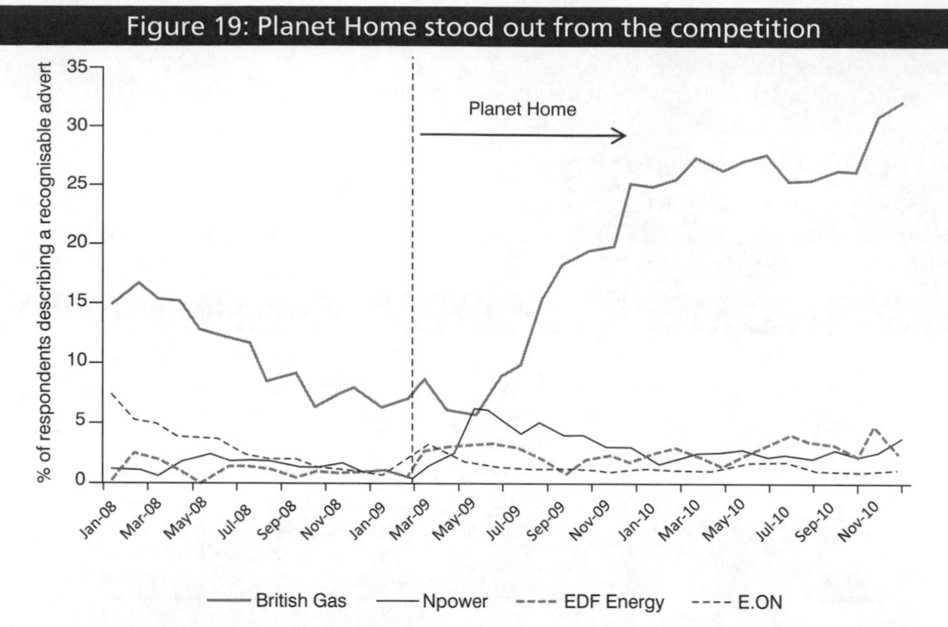


Source: TNS. Base: total sample. Typical sample size is 600

Every Planet Home execution outperformed recognition and branding norms. Campaign recognition across the TV ads averaged 66%,[10] putting Planet Home in the top quartile against TNS benchmarks (Figure 20).

Branding was strong from the outset but built over time.

Figure 20: Planet Home ads are excellently branded

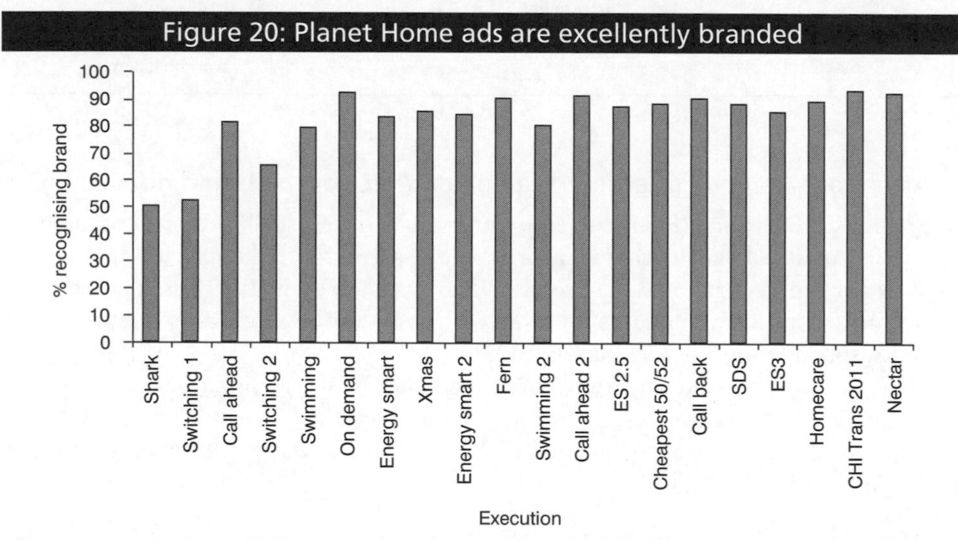


Source: TNS. Base: total sample. Typical sample size is 600

This impressive performance had been anticipated in qualitative and quantitative pre-testing:

> *You've achieved an Awareness Index of 9. This compares to an average of 6 across all UK ads, and an average of 4–5 for low interest (non-FMCG) categories and services.*
>
> Millward Brown Research, 2009

> *This is appealing advertising with the potential to punch through and catch the attention, differentiate British Gas and be remembered.*
>
> Grant Litchfield, Founder, CML Research, Creative Development, 2008

The result was work that continually outperformed every benchmark:

> *These are impressive results, beating all our norms on brand salience, involvement and persuasion.*
>
> Helen Law, Director, Hall & Partners, Pre-Testing, 2008

### b) Perception: A broader, persuasive campaign that built the brand beyond price

The campaign was not only well recognised, but its key message was convincing for consumers. People believed British Gas was the energy company that could be most relied upon to look after their home (Figure 21).

**Figure 21: British Gas staked out a distinctive identity: 'Count on us to look after your home'**

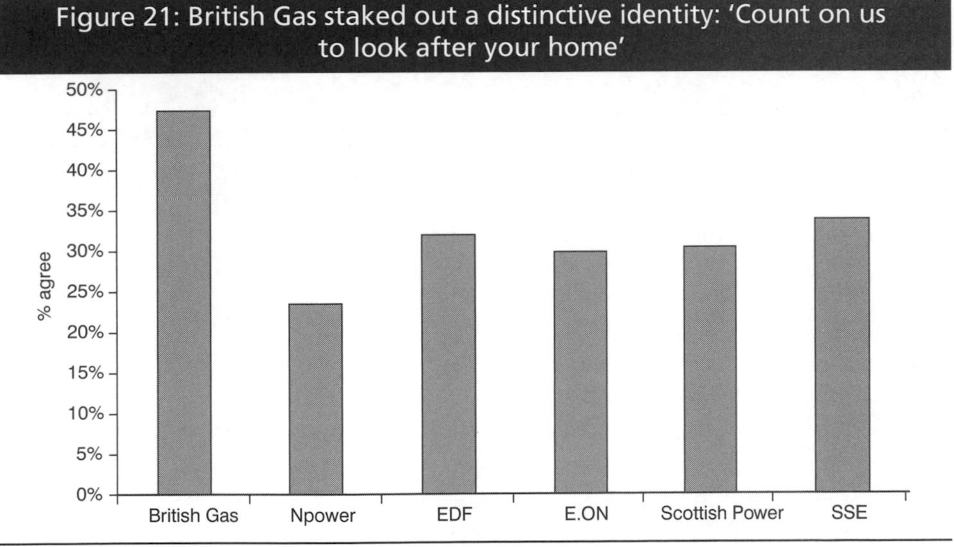


Source: TNS. Q: Here is a series of statements and we'd like you to tell me for which of the companies below each statement applies. You can mention as many or as few as you like... Which of these companies do you associate with...? Response was added in Nov 2009. Figures shown are average Nov 2009 to Dec 2010. Base: Aware of. Average base sizes per period: BG n=c220, npower n=c95, EDF n=c100, E.ON n=c130, Scottish Power n=c85, SSE n=c100

Part of the challenge had been to create a campaign flexible enough to deliver a broad variety of messages. Over the two years from launch these included Call Back,[11] Call Ahead[12] and EnergySmart.[13] Again, tracking measures showed these messages 'landing', with perceptions of British Gas out-performing rivals in key areas (Figure 22).

Figure 22: Attitudes to British Gas improved across several dimensions

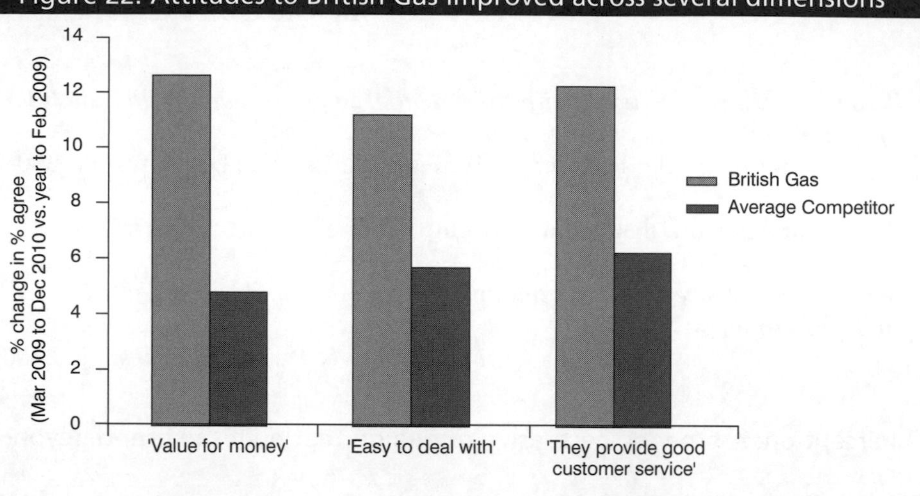


Source: TNS. Q: Here is a series of statements and we'd like you to tell me for which of the companies below each statement applies. You can mention as many or as few as you like... Which of these companies do you associate with…? Base: Aware of. Average base sizes per period: BG n=c220, npower n=c95, EDF n=c100, E.ON n=c130, Scottish Power n=c85, SSE n=c100

### c) Affinity: A likeable, empathetic campaign that revived positive brand feeling

Beyond these more rational attributes, the campaign needed to revive positive sentiment towards the brand. It helped that consumers liked the campaign:

> *These are happy adverts that make you smile.*
>
> British Gas Customer, Hall & Partners, Pre-Testing, 2008

> *It's lovely, the little individual worlds, quirky people and there's always something funny within the story.*
>
> British Gas Customer, Litchfield Research, Campaign Development, 2009

This translated to affection. British Gas assessed its status as a 'national treasure' by a broad measure of how people rated it as a large company and saw a statistically significant shift here that none of its peers emulated (Figure 23).

Figure 23: British Gas was becoming a national treasure again

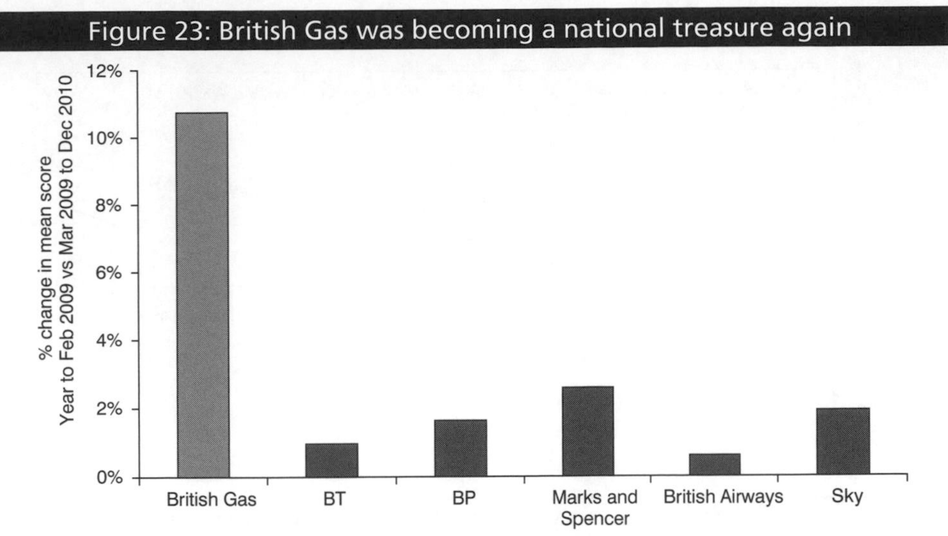


Source: TNS. Q: Taking into account everything that you look for in a large company, how would you rate each of these companies? (Where 10 is perfect in every way and 1 is terrible)

Consumers' willingness to recommend British Gas improved markedly, reflected in a dramatic improvement to its net promoter score (NPS), widely recognised as a key indicator of brand health (Figure 24).

Figure 24: Consumers' affinity with British Gas improved

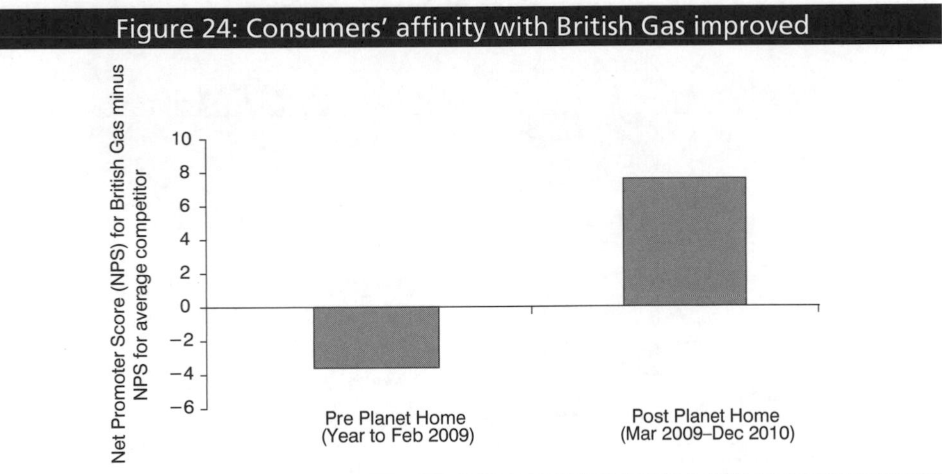


Source: TNS. Q. On a scale of 0 to 10 with 0 being definitely not recommend and 10 being definitely recommend, how likely is it you would recommend…? Base: total sample excluding 'don't know'. Average monthly sample sizes: All British Gas 182, Competitor average 164

This strengthening of customer affinity helped make the brand more resilient in the prevailing tough market conditions. The price rises still generated a fair degree of negative PR, but now these negative stories were more quickly forgotten by consumers, rather than a lingering problem that damaged the brand (Figure 25).

Figure 25: The brand became more resilient to negative PR

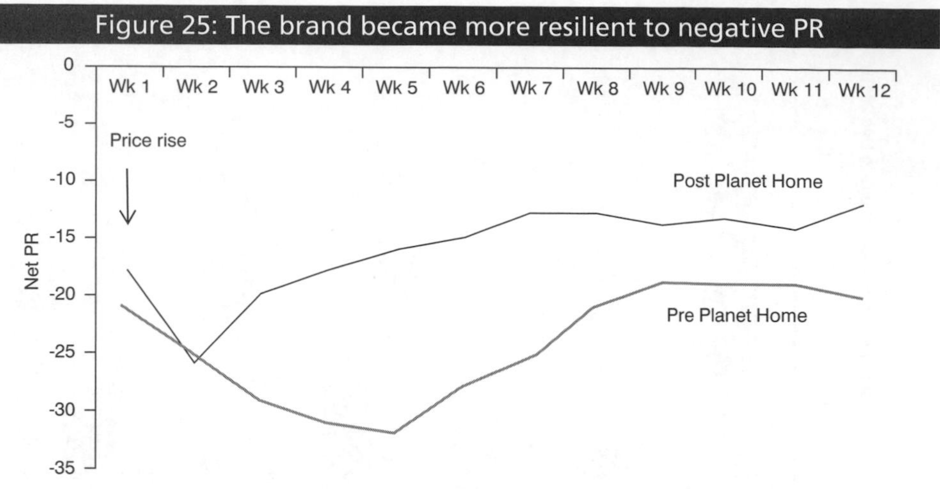


Source: TNS. Q: Thinking now about the news [on TV, newspapers, magazines, radio, online, etc.] and also what you might have heard through your family, friends and associates, which companies that supply gas, electricity and other services to the home can you think of, that you have heard favourable/unfavourable or positive/negative information for recently? Net PR is % positive respondents minus % negative respondents. Base: total sample. Sample size = c. 600 per week

In fact, consumers' perceptions of PR tipped from being highly negative, to slightly positive (Figure 26).

Figure 26: PR perceptions changed from negative to positive

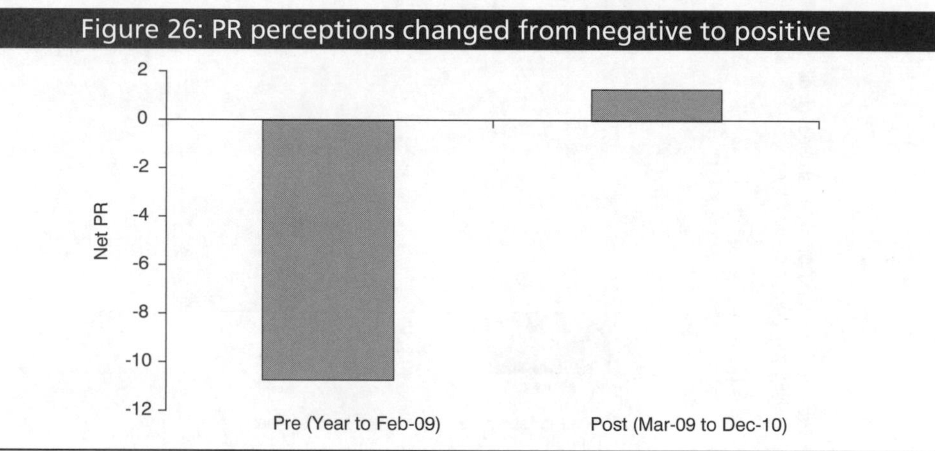


Source: TNS. Q: Thinking now about the news [on TV, newspapers, magazines, radio, online, etc.] and also what you might have heard through your family, friends and associates, which companies that supply gas, electricity and other services to the home can you think of, that you have heard favourable/unfavourable or positive/negative information for recently? Net PR is % positive respondents minus % negative respondents. Base: total sample. Sample size = c. 600 per week

### d) Commitment: A coherent, consistent campaign that built the brand relationship over time

In combination, more noticeable communications building deeper emotional ties and stronger rational associations led to a more committed customer base (Figure 27).

Figure 27: Customers became more committed

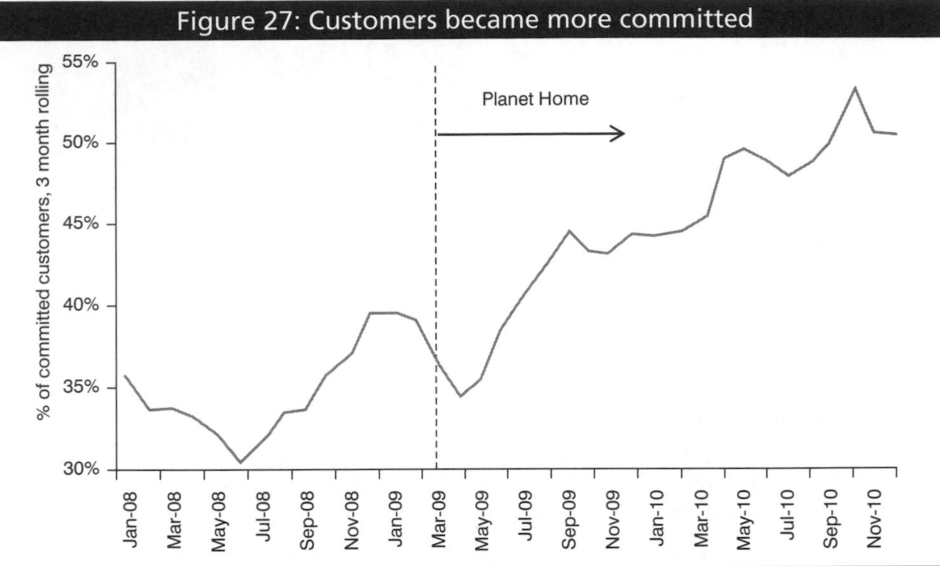


Source: TNS. Base: British Gas customers. Sample size c. 300 per month

### *2) Additional benefits*

Phil Bentley's vision to harmonise the business into 'One British Gas' laid down further internal objectives for the campaign that were also met. The campaign was as well received internally as it was by consumers. Employees really got behind the core 'Looking after your world' idea and embraced it.

> *It makes you feel really good about working for British Gas, really proud, especially when you get the chance to be in the ads. It makes us want to really look after customers as best we can.*
>
> Rami Ryatt, Technical Engineer, British Gas

Whereas earlier campaigns had contributed to a divided business, the core idea behind Planet Home brought the divisions together.

> *Presenting a united front to our customers via a cohesive idea and campaign helped further unite us internally.*
>
> Chris Jansen, Managing Director Services & Commercial, British Gas

Though a direct link cannot be drawn, the period of the campaign coincided with a sharp increase in staff satisfaction (Figure 28).

Figure 28: Staff satisfaction improved

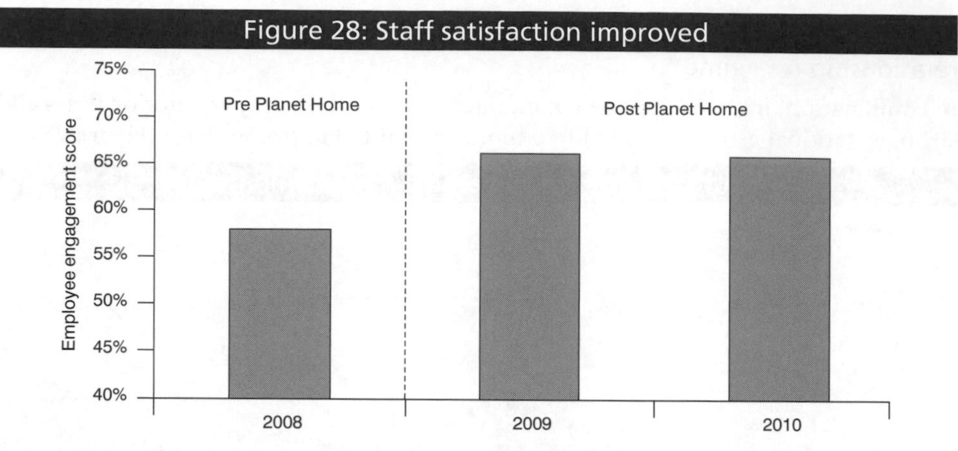


Source: British Gas. Employee engagement is an average of multiple measures covering working life at British Gas

### *3) Eliminating the impact of other factors*

These results show a dramatic turnaround in British Gas's fortunes. But was the Planet Home campaign responsible for this success? A number of other factors are in play over the period, but mostly these are stable and cannot account for such impressive results. British Gas also has a suite of econometric models to evaluate the impact of marketing (maintained with assistance from Data2Decisions), and these can further help to isolate the impact of these other factors. The payback calculations are based upon these models, demonstrated shortly, but first each of these factors is given due consideration.

*Market size:* The number of households in the UK has grown slightly over the period and with it the number of energy accounts available across the market. However, this does not account for the growth seen, as market share has increased too (Figure 29).

*Weather:* The weather impacts revenue per customer; in general the colder it is, the more energy used. However it only has a small effect on customer accounts, which has been accounted for in the econometric models.

*Product:* The basic energy supply offer remained the same, insofar as energy is a commodity. British Gas had entered the electricity market back in 1997, and market share quickly rose to 23%. It peaked in 2003 however and had been in decline with the rest of the business until Planet Home.

Another important change within the market place was the shift towards energy companies providing 'dual fuel' contracts of both gas and electricity, but these are offered by all competitors and so provide no competitive edge to explain the reversal.

*Higher media spend:* Though there is some increase in spend, SOV is relatively stable over the period in question. SOV was at 48% in the two years prior to Planet Home and 50% for the two years since the campaign launched.[14] This modest increase is taken account of in the econometric model. Executions from the Planet Home campaign have higher ROI than earlier activity.

Figure 29: Market share grew

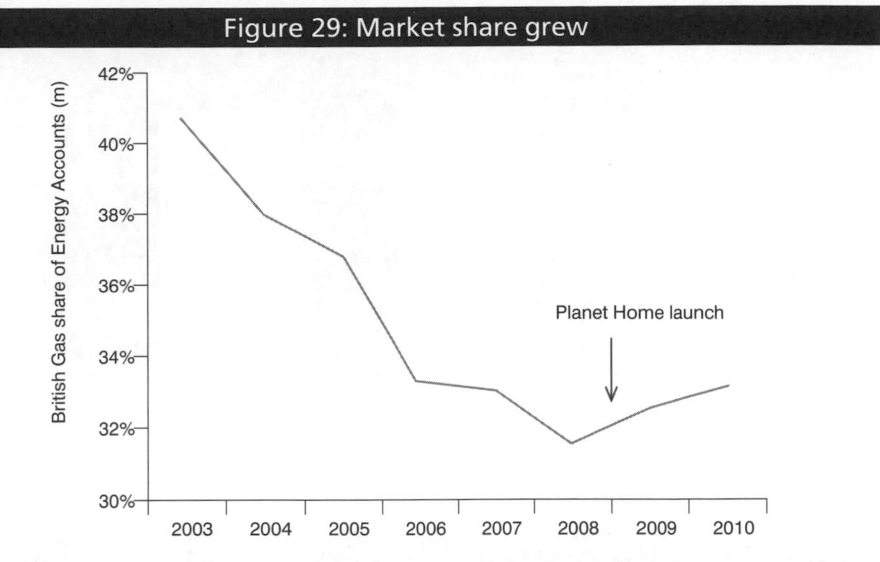


Source: Centrica Annual Reports

*Direct Marketing:* British Gas also invests considerably in 'below-the-line' communications. This activity cannot account for the turnaround in fortunes, however: investment levels have remained broadly stable, as have the response rates from this activity. Moreover, very little of this investment is directed towards customer retention, which is where the improvements have been made (Figure 30).

*Changes to competitive landscape:* The market landscape has not changed significantly over the last ten years, with the 'big 6' suppliers accounting for 99% of the energy market over this period.[15]

*Distribution:* The only major change to sales channels used by British Gas over the period in question was a *reduction* in the number of field sales agents over the period (field sales agent numbers dropped from 1,075 full-time equivalent agents in January 2008 to 424 by the end of Q1 2011).[16] In terms of market dynamics, increased internet penetration and the growth in usage of price comparison sites over the period in question only intensified the drive towards increased switching.[17]

*Price:* Consumer prices are primarily determined by energy prices on the wholesale markets and so all providers tend to change their prices around a similar time. In general, the providers' prices are fairly consistent with one another, with some differences arising thanks to the timing of futures buying in the wholesale markets. Recently there has only been a minimal difference between British Gas's price and the average price across the rest of the market (Figure 31).

Figure 30: Direct Marketing spend remained constant

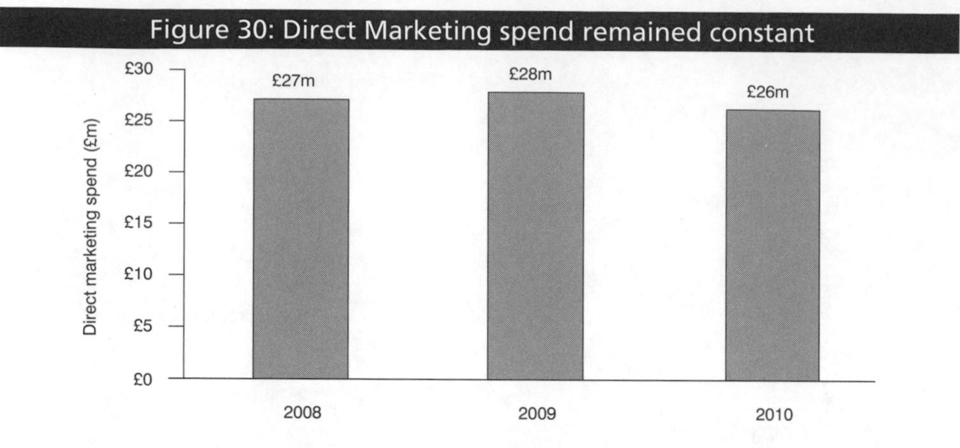


Source: Nielsen

Figure 31: Prices have typically been close to competitors

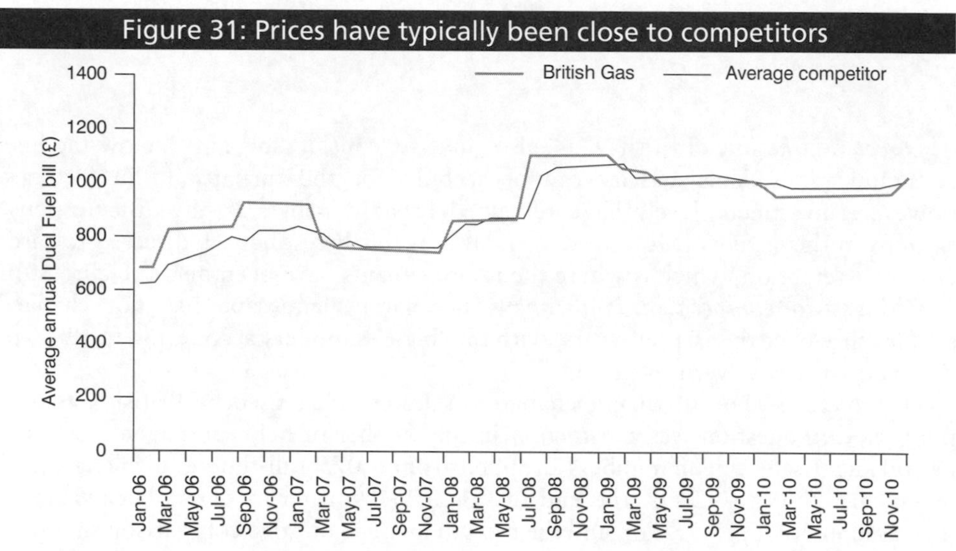


Source: British Gas

Although recently British Gas's pricing has been broadly in line with its competitors, it has a legacy of being expensive. Many consumers still consider British Gas to be less competitively priced than the newer market entrants (Figure 32).

Figure 32: British Gas is thought to be less competitively priced

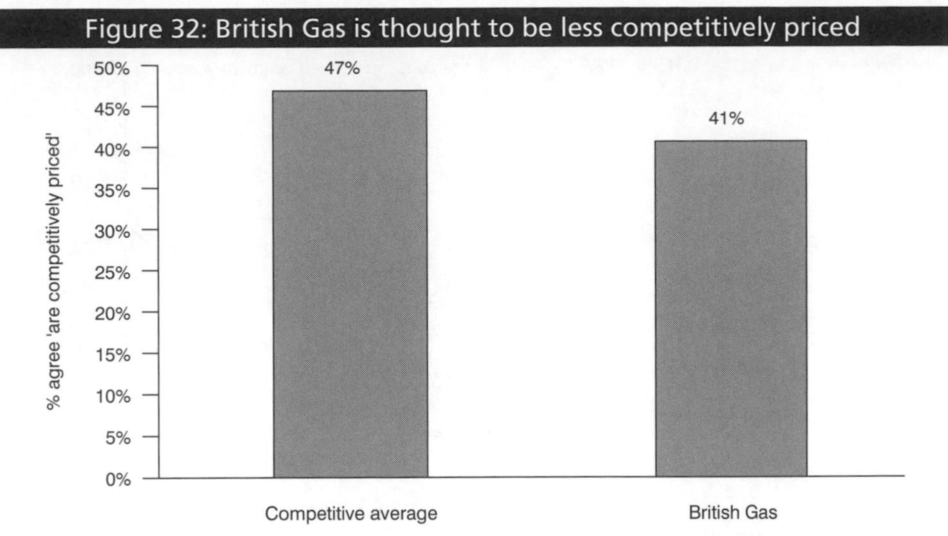


Source: TNS. Base: Energy customers for each brand. Sample size c. 220 per month

Other complications arise because of newer 'dual fuel' tariffs, where consumers receive good rates for getting both their gas and electricity from a single provider, and 'websaver' tariffs, which lock in competitive rates over a longer time period to add security in a time of rising prices. Neither of these innovations is unique to British Gas, however, and regardless, Figure 32 includes their effects in a single measure of the average annual dual fuel bill.

The modest variation in relative price shown in Figure 32 has influenced British Gas's fortunes over the campaign period.[18] These effects are not sufficient to account for the remarkable turnaround, however.

### *4) Regions with more exposure to the campaign performed better*

Part of the transition to greater customer focus involved greater scrutiny of marketing investment. The econometric models built were part of this effort, but in addition, British Gas employed Ebiquity to conduct regional tests of their communications by business division. Figure 33 is an example of their analysis of a TV execution, showing how those regions that received more weight performed better.

There is also variation in the weight of advertising that different regions received over a longer time frame, showing the impact of the campaign as a whole. Churn fell more in those regions that received greater weight (Figure 34).

Figure 33: Up-weighted test regions show clear sales uplifts

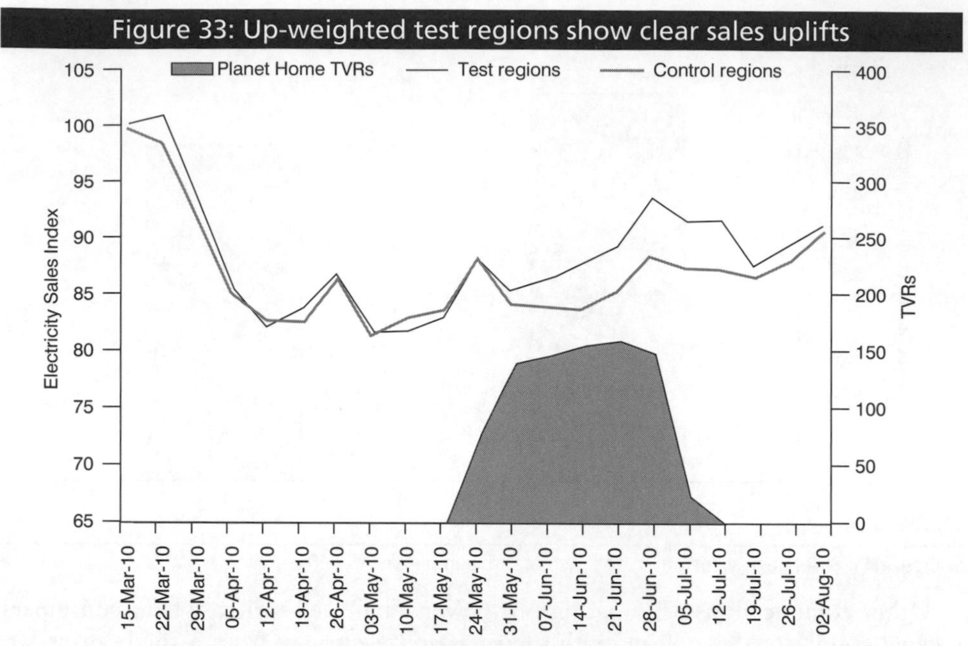


Source: Ebiquity. Sales indices are 3-month rolling sales in test/control groups, indexed to 15 March 2010

Figure 34: Up-weighted regions had bigger reductions in churn

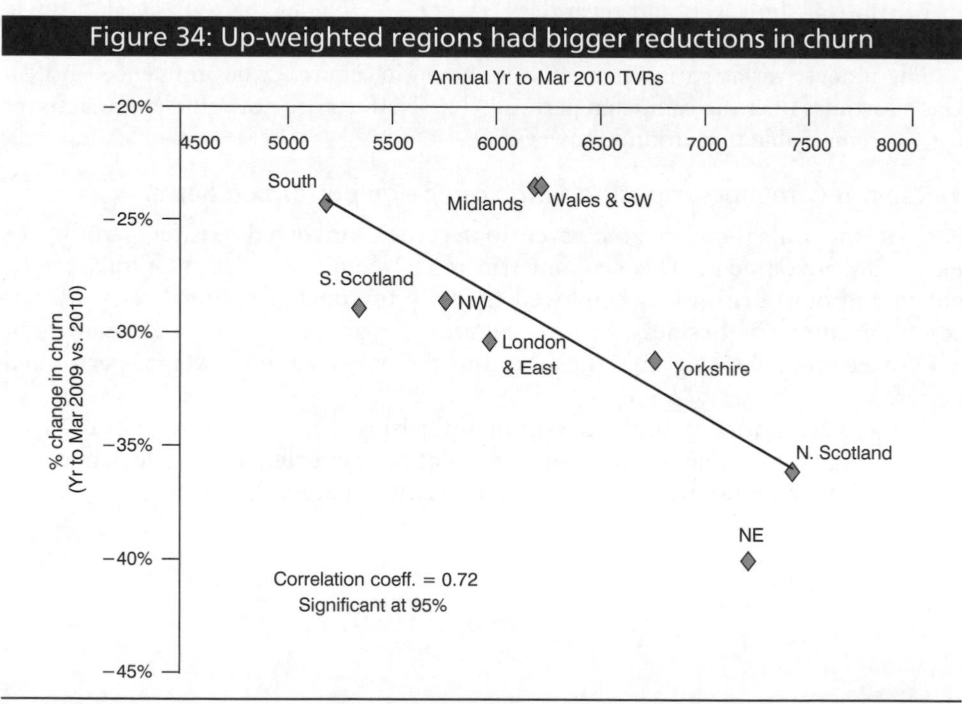


Source: British Gas

*5) Econometric payback*

Econometric modelling shows that in the two years post-launch, the Planet Home campaign drove an additional 103,000 new gas customer accounts and 168,000 new electricity customer accounts. Gas customer churn was reduced by 108,000 accounts and electricity churn reduced by 102,000 accounts as a direct result of the Planet Home campaign.

Clearly, each of these customers has an indeterminate lifetime value to the business. British Gas calculates existing customer profitability across a range of different timeframes. We are using a five-year timeframe in these figures but it is worth noting the lifetime value of these customers will be substantially more. Whilst we cannot disclose specific customer profitability due to client confidentiality, the overall profit contribution for these energy accounts on a five-year basis is £82.7m. It is worth noting that British Gas energy customers also hold other insurance-based services products (central heating care, etc.) and so retaining energy customers will inevitably lead to increased retention for services, although this is excluded from our ROI calculations.

The overall investment from this period (media, production and agency fees) was £45.5m. This implies a £1.82 profit return for every pound spent.

## New learning

The lessons of this paper are two-fold. First, a salutary reminder that even a modernising business, eyes firmly focused on the future, can draw inspiration and equity from its past. 'Looking after your world' was a role British Gas could perform better now than ever before, but it had a historical resonance too, and it was that legacy which encouraged customers to believe and embrace it.

Second, it demonstrates the power of a big idea, founded on a potent insight, to unite and motivate an organisation. To reverse its spiralling fortunes, British Gas had to become a genuinely joined-up home energy and services provider; 'Looking after your world' captured this mission in a way the whole business could sign up to and proved an important cohering force as it shed old rivalries and practices.

## Conclusion

This paper has demonstrated how a communication idea, 'Looking after your world', brought British Gas back into people's lives and the business back into growth.

It showed that by 2008, British Gas looked less and less relevant to its customers. The problem was compounded by the fragmented way in which British Gas operated and communicated, and the net result was 40,000 customers leaving every month.

As the business set a two-year timeframe to get its house in order, a communications idea was sought that would help to heal internal divisions, work flexibly across the business's multiple communication requirements, and ultimately rebuild the relationship with customers, securing their commitment and reducing churn sufficiently to put the business back into growth.

For the answer, the agency went back to the future; by defining the brand's role as 'Looking after your world', it tapped into the warm welcome customers had once given the brand, while inviting them to see it now as a broader service provider, not just an energy supplier.

The effect of the resulting 'Planet Home' campaign was striking: communication got noticed, affinity grew, perceptions improved, commitment rose. Internally, everyone liked and aligned behind the campaign and staff satisfaction grew. Most importantly, churn dropped dramatically and the decline in customer accounts was reversed. The business had momentum again.

The paper has examined and eliminated other variables that might have accounted for this turnaround and used econometric modelling to isolate and value the contribution of the campaign at £1.82 profit for every £1 spent.

Finally, this is a true campaign, in that its usefulness has extended well beyond the initial timeframe. The idea has proved itself broad and resilient – most recently extended to the business-to-business audience. Communication ideas on this scale don't come along very often, but when they do their impact is profound.

## Notes

1 Marketing Society, 1986.
2 The privatisation raised £9bn, which was the highest equity offer in British history.
3 The KPI shown throughout this paper is of total energy accounts (the sum of gas and electricity accounts). Dual fuel customers are counted as having both gas and electricity accounts, as is consistent with British Gas and the industry's usual reporting methods.
4 This is a net figure. 220,000 accounts were leaving each month with 180,000 accounts joining.
5 The Nursery, Brand Key Research, November 2008.
6 Hall & Partners Pre Testing, 2008. Base: 350 British Gas customers.
7 Source: Nielsen Addynamix.
8 Source: Nielsen Addynamix. Based on: Jan 2008–Feb 2009 vs. Mar 2009–Mar 2011.
9 Source: TNS. Based on: Jan 2008–Feb 2009 vs. Mar 2009–Mar 2011.
10 Source: TNS.
11 Call Back was a service whereby customers wouldn't have to wait on the phone when they called the call centres if the wait was more than 60 seconds. They could request to get called back by British Gas.
12 Call Ahead was a service promise that meant engineers would call to let customers know they were on their way so they didn't have to wait in.
13 EnergySmart was a new online service customers could sign up to in order to monitor their energy usage over time and submit meter reads to receive accurate billing.
14 Source: Nielsen.
15 Source: Mintel.
16 Source: Centrica.
17 UK total population Internet penetration grew from 59.8% in 2005 to 82.5% in 2010 (Source: Nielsen/ITU).
18 Econometric models account for these effects in our ROI calculation.

## Chapter 10

# Cadbury Dairy Milk

## A meetha journey

**By Ganapathy Balagopalan and Nirav Parekh, Ogilvy & Mather India**
Contributing authors: Kawal Shoor and Madhukar Sabnavis, Ogilvy & Mather India
Credited companies: Creative Agency: Ogilvy & Mather India; Media Agency: Madison Media; Research Agency: The Third Eye; Brand and advertising tracking: TNS India; Client: Cadbury India

**Editor's summary**

This paper demonstrates how an exceptional piece of insight can redefine a brand and open it to new audiences and markets. Despite a strong sweet (meetha) market in India, chocolate was seen as a foreign treat that lacked the same popularity. Research revealed that while meetha were enjoyed as part of collective celebrations, such as at festivals and parties, chocolate was seen as a pleasure that was generally enjoyed alone. The solution was to therefore repurpose Cadbury Dairy Milk as meetha, and to communicate this message via television, radio, outdoor, digital and point of sale advertising. The campaign resulted in an increase in revenue and profits, and grew the business from 3% to 23% in seven years. To achieve such growth from a hugely bold strategy change in a relatively short space of time thoroughly excited the judges.

## Summary

This case shows how advertising reinvented the very essence of the product, so it became something different, and by doing so, unlocked brand growth for Cadbury Dairy Milk.

It did this *by transposing culture codes* that got a new target audience to view a familiar brand in a new light; it became a new product, generating a desire for purchase.

The scale of the success is remarkable. After falling 78% in value, we will show how the campaign grew the business from 3% to 23% within seven years of the campaign launch.[1]

The case shows how this growth led to a huge increase in revenue and profits, and was made possible by the advertising.

## Background

### *Origins in India*

Cadbury Dairy Milk (CDM) came to India in 1948, a year after the independent country's birth and the English had left Indian shores. This English icon has over the years grown into one of the most loved and recognised brands in India. CDM is a part of sweet childhood memories, for millions of Indians.

### *Circa 2004*

Cadbury was the biggest player in the chocolate market in India with nearly 65% share of the category and CDM its flagship brand with 31%.[2]

CDM accounted for over half of Cadbury India's chocolate revenue in 2004, and this obviously meant Cadbury India's fortunes (read profitability) were tied to CDM's fortunes (compared to Nestlé Munch its nearest competitor, which was less than 10% of Nestlé India in 2004,[3] in spite of being more widely available than CDM).[4]

CDM was obviously Cadbury India's bread and butter brand and to most Indians:

Chocolate = Cadbury = Cadbury Dairy Milk.

## Market situation

While the 1990s were kind to Cadbury, by the early 2000s growth began to dry up (Figure 1).

The flattening of sales is obvious – between 2000 and 2004, CDM growth rate dropped by 78% over the previous four-year period from 1996 to 2000 (Figure 2).[5]

CDM growth was running out of fuel. We had to find new triggers to fuel growth. However, given CDM's criticality to the Cadbury bottom line, we had to manage growth without compromising profits.

## Business objective

Grow CDM top line (sales value) without compromising profitability.

Figure 1: Indexed sales volume of CDM and chocolate category

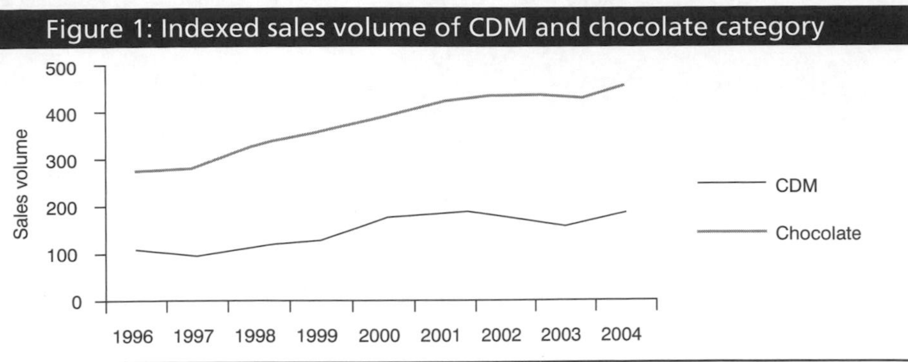


Source: AC Nielsen sales data. Sales volumes indexed at 100 for CDM 1996 figures

Figure 2: Compounded Annual Growth Rate for CDM

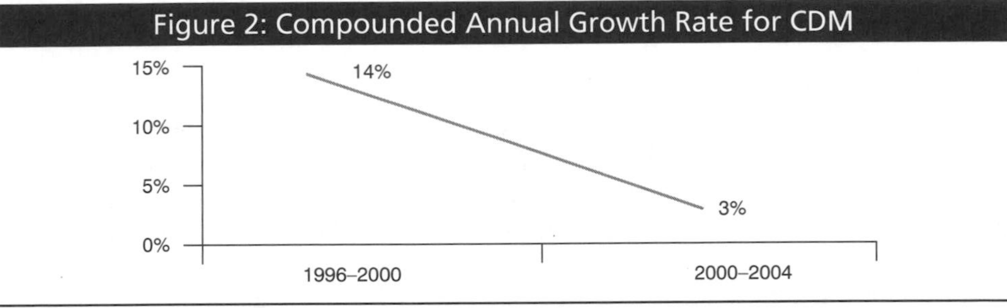


Source: AC Nielsen sales data

## Choosing the growth driver

a. Market share of all Cadbury brands put together was already 65%.[6] Playing a share game would inevitably entail cannibalising own brands.

b. CDM's competition came primarily from VFM offerings[7] (chocolate-coated wafer biscuits had lower chocolate content or, worse, used chocolate substitute; and this meant these brands offer more for less – discernibly bigger bars than CDM for the same price). Clashing with them for share was bound to be unprofitable.

c. Rising trend of commodity prices (cocoa) would only add to the pressure on sales volumes, testing the brands price elasticity. While prices fluctuated, they had nearly doubled over four years from 2000 to 2004 (Figure 3).

d. Possibility of share gain through promotions was bound to be expensive and unlikely to sustain long-term growth. Moreover, the inevitable competition response, compounded by price pressures discussed in point c) above, would further erode profitability.

All these factors appeared to suggest growing market share may not be the most profitable growth avenue for CDM.

Figure 3: Cocoa prices from 2000 to 2004

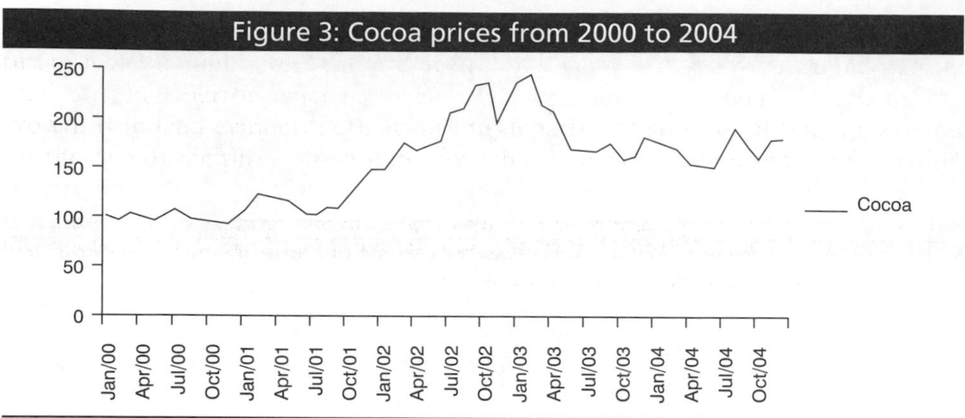


Source: World Bank statistics. Cocoa prices indexed at 100 for January 2000 figures

## The way to growth

Cadbury had started out by selling to kids, as it was felt it is easier to develop a new taste with kids than with tradition-bound adults; but the approach created an unexpected roadblock for further growth. It had become an occasional foreign treat 'for kids'. As people grew up, they grew out of chocolate instead of growing up with it.

Consumption among teens and adults was very low (Table 1).

Table 1: Chocolate penetration and frequency of consumption

| **Chocolate penetration Metros + Mini-metros** | **1995** | **2002** |
|---|---|---|
| SEC A, B, C | | |
| Kids | 80% | 85% |
| Teens | 73% | 72% |
| Adults | 48% | 59% |
| All | 69% | 71% |
| **Frequency of consumption Metros + Mini-metros** | **1995** | **2002** |
| SEC A, B, C | | |
| Kids | – | 8.0 |
| Teens | – | 6.1 |
| Adults | – | 4.9 |
| All | – | 6.4 |

Source: Cadbury Data – Listing studies, 1995, 2002. Frequency of consumption measured yearly

## Marketing objective

Increase CDM penetration among teens and adults.

## Communication challenge

Indians had made the English language, tea and, of course, cricket their own, but strangely an innocuous sweet treat, chocolate, had got the cold shoulder from the average, tradition-bound, Indian adult.

It's not as though they lacked a sweet tooth.

The size of the traditional *meetha* (sweets) market was more than 19 times that of chocolate; valued at approximately US$4.2bn, while chocolate was merely about US$215m (Figure 4).[8]

Figure 4: Market size estimates 2004 – US$m

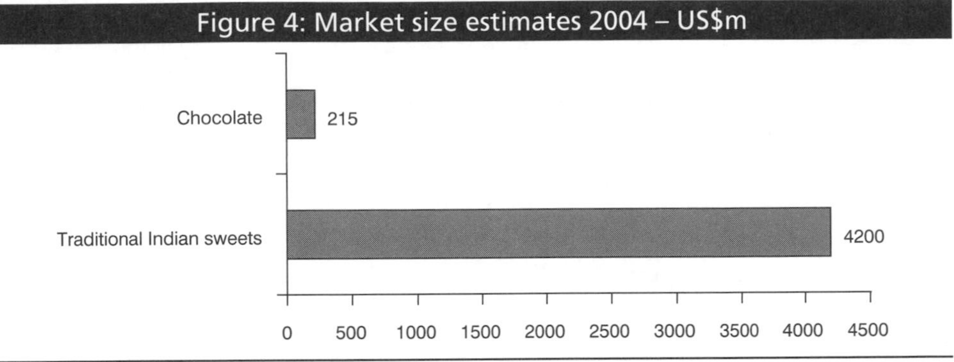


Source: Cadbury estimates, 2004

The magnitude of the opportunity was matched by the magnitude of the challenge.

A culturally antagonistic product, chocolate was a foreign sweet-treat trying to change sweet-eating habits of a country with a vast indigenous sweet tradition of its own that was several centuries old.

Chocolate had not found its barrier-breaker.

## Strategy

Our growth strategy was simple. Grow chocolate consumption by making it part of Indian *meetha* consumption behaviour.

To do this, we attempted to understand why we were not considered in traditional '*meetha*' eating occasions, by mounting an ethnographic research of sweet consumption behaviour. This exploration led us to a defining strategic discovery.

The difference in cultures and cultural perspectives of happiness between the East and the West was the crucial link to understanding differences in sweet consumption behaviour and their implications for communication.

The West has a strong belief in independence and autonomy of the self (individualism). The self is believed to be the centre of thought, action and motivation; and happiness is to be found in personal striving and fulfilment of desires. Chocolate was mostly a private craving, a means for self pleasure. A lot of chocolate advertising, e.g. Cadbury Gorilla, Dove/Galaxy campaigns, reflect this individualistic cultural perspective of happiness.

In sharp contrast, happiness in India is 'collective'. In East-Asian cultures, the self-in-relationship-with-others (collectivism) is the locus of thought, action and motivation. Consequently, happiness tends to be defined in terms of interpersonal connectedness and realisation of social harmony.

This connects strongly to sweet consumption behaviour/occasions in India. Most happy occasions tend to be collective and are ritually accompanied by *meetha* consumption. Festivals, celebrations, and traditions and cultural markers of anticipated happiness (child birth, success in exams, starting a new business, etc.) are never in short supply!

One could argue that it is not as if people in the West did not celebrate such happy occasions together, but surely there is no ritual mandating sweet consumption. Only in India does sweet perform the role of a happiness ritual.

In sum:

- Chocolate = self indulgence
- *meetha* = shared happiness ritual

In hindsight, we realised that as a consequence of its Western heritage, much of CDM's communication in India before 2004 reflected these Western, individualistic happiness codes and was, hence, not considered on *meetha* consumption occasions.

This understanding of how '*meetha*' was different from 'chocolate' was the heart of our new strategy.

We decided to repurpose chocolate (CDM) as *meetha* in order to get a share of *meetha* occasions.

### *Creative solution*

Associate CDM with Indian sweet consumption occasions so that it gets consumed on *meetha* occasions.

How did we do this?

If we had to make CDM synonymous with *meetha*, we needed the word *meetha* to become synonymous with the brand.

Traditionally, people sweeten other people's mouths when something good happens to them or when they want to wish others happiness. Festivities/celebrations are its natural outcome. This practice is popularly captured by the Indian/Hindi phrase *Muh meetha karna*.

We made this more actionable by reinventing it. CDM advertising signed off with an invitation: *Kuch Meetha Ho Jaaye!* – A call to have something sweet.

### Turning the Kuch Meetha Ho Jaaye idea into advertising

Over the years, our executions have spanned all traditional *meetha* occasions: celebrations, ShubhAarambh (new beginnings of all kinds – journeys, new jobs, new purchases, starting a job, forming new relationships – all typically Indian collective sweet consumption occasions).

The *meetha* consumption ritual is an inevitable part of these occasions.

### CDM tone of voice

- *meetha* NOT Chocolate.
- **Collective** NOT Individual.

- **Relevance** (Occasion) NOT just a feeling.
- **Indian/Hindi** NOT English.

## Media logic

Given that we were targeting the masses, it was important to reach a very wide audience. TV proved to be the most efficient medium for this. For all the campaigns, TV was the lead medium of advertising, with 80–90% of investments put into TV (Table 2).

**Table 2: Comparison across media – efficiency and reach**

| Media | TV | Print | Radio | Internet |
|---|---|---|---|---|
| Efficiency of media (with TV efficiency indexed at 1) | 1 | -4.1 | -8.0 | -4.4 |
| Reach of each medium | 93% | 64% | 26% | 30% |

Source: TAM data

The rest of investments were spread across radio, outdoor, digital and POS, with the objective of maximising impact and driving engagement with the consumers.

The communications history since 2005 is illustrated in Figure 5 and Table 3.

**Figure 5: CDM communications history 2005–2011**

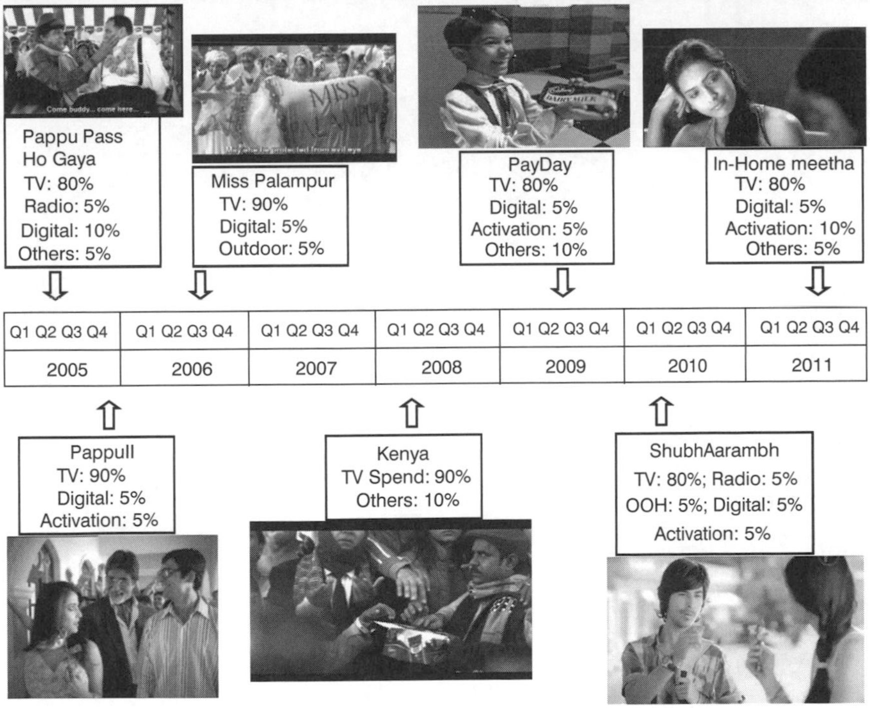

Pappu Pass Ho Gaya
TV: 80%
Radio: 5%
Digital: 10%
Others: 5%

Miss Palampur
TV: 90%
Digital: 5%
Outdoor: 5%

PayDay
TV: 80%
Digital: 5%
Activation: 5%
Others: 10%

In-Home meetha
TV: 80%
Digital: 5%
Activation: 10%
Others: 5%

| Q1 Q2 Q3 Q4 | Q1 Q2 Q3 Q4 | Q1 Q2 Q3 Q4 | Q1 Q2 Q3 Q4 | Q1 Q2 Q3 Q4 | Q1 Q2 Q3 Q4 | Q1 Q2 Q3 Q4 |
|---|---|---|---|---|---|---|
| 2005 | 2006 | 2007 | 2008 | 2009 | 2010 | 2011 |

PappuII
TV: 90%
Digital: 5%
Activation: 5%

Kenya
TV Spend: 90%
Others: 10%

ShubhAarambh
TV: 80%; Radio: 5%
OOH: 5%; Digital: 5%
Activation: 5%

Source: CDM

**Table 3: CDM campaigns and messages 2005–2011**

| Year | Campaign | Message |
|---|---|---|
| 2005 | Pappu Pass Ho Gaya – I | Celebrate happy moments with meetha (CDM) |
| 2005 | Pappu Pass Ho Gaya – II | |
| 2006 | Miss Palampur | |
| 2007 | Out of Body | |
| 2008 | Kenya | |
| 2009 | PayDay | |
| 2010 | ShubhAarambh | Eat meetha (CDM) as a good-luck ritual, before starting something new |
| 2011 | In-home meetha | Eat meetha (CDM) as dessert after meals |

Source: CDM

Consistency of the 'KMHJ' proposition over the last seven years has helped CDM become *meetha* (Figure 6).

**Figure 6: How the campaigns worked**

The campaigns became famous, and were much enjoyed

Campaign popularity led to brand becoming popular as *meetha*

Leading to more people eating CDM

CMD growth zoomed

Sales growths led to profits

Source: CDM

## Results

What happened:

### *1. Business objective*

Grow CDM top line (sales value) without compromising profitability.

CDM growth zoomed (Figure 7).[9]

Moreover, despite being the biggest brand in the category (and therefore having a larger base compared to others), CDM managed to grow faster than every competitor brand (Figure 8).[10]

Sales grew (Figure 9).

Figure 7: Sales volume growth

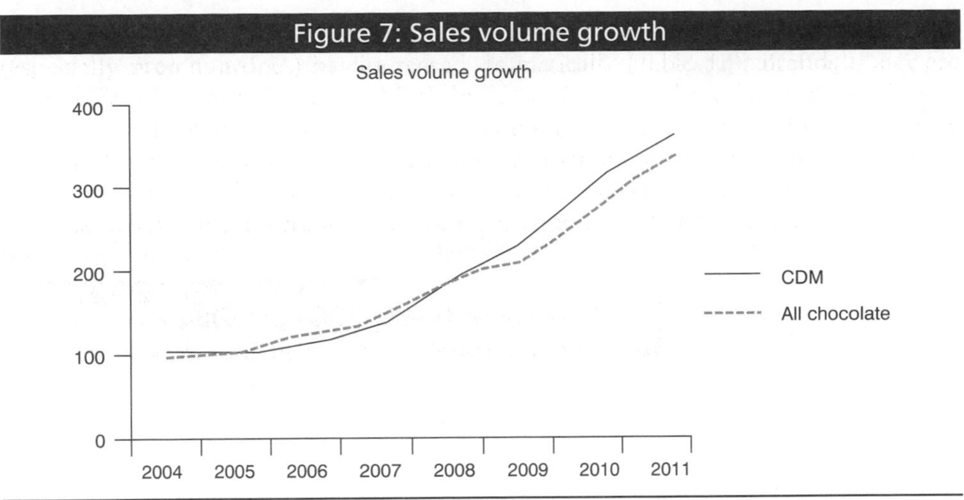


Source: Figures indexed at 100 for 2004 sales volume figures respectively

Figure 8: CDM and competition CAGR, 2004–2011

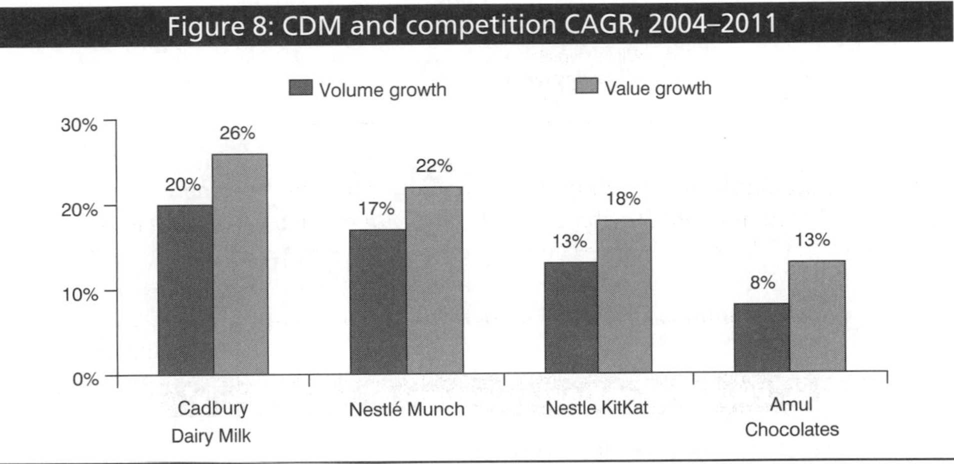


Source: AC Nielsen sales data

Figure 9: CDM Sales volume – CAGR

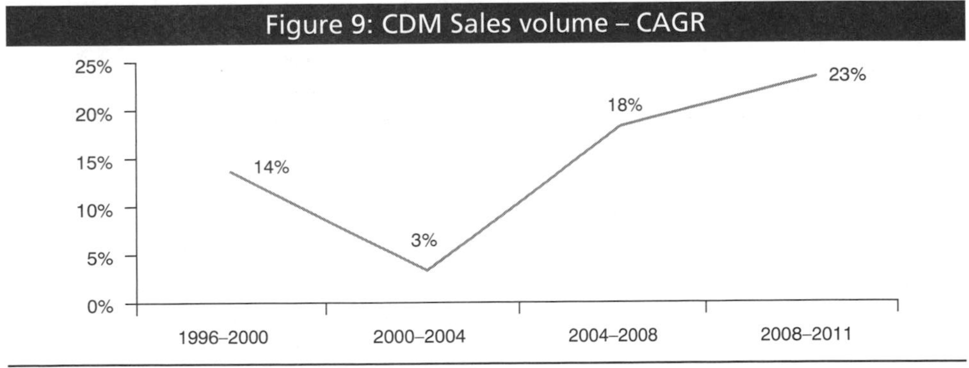


Source: AC Nielsen sales data

Clearly, the shift in strategy and the *Kuch Meetha Ho Jaaye* campaign not only reversed the flattening growth rate, but also super-charged CDM growth.

### *2. Marketing objective*

Increase CDM penetration among teens and adults.

Leading to more people eating chocolate/CDM (Figure 10).

**Figure 10: Media coverage on chocolate replacing traditional sweets**

Afternoon
DESPATCH & COURIER

NEWS FLASH | N IPL FIFTH EDITION | APPLE CEO TIM COOK GET

HOME | CITY NEWS | SPORTS | BUSINESS | EDITORIAL | TECHNO STUFF

Special Section | Quick Links >> | TOWN & ABOUT | FILM REVIEW

Home > City news > Chocolates now replacing mithais

**Chocolates now replacing mithais**

Monday, October 24, 2011
By Gayatri Sahasrabuddhe & Priyal Dave

The festive season of Diwali is essentially a time when your dining table, and probably every other table, is loaded with boxes of traditional sweets ranging from kaju katlis, barfi to kalakand. Lately, the trend of chocolates replacing these sugary delicacies has been catching up.

newKerala.com
NEWS • INFORMATION • ENTERTAINMENT

**Chocolates replacing Mithai, in demand for festivities**

Mumbai, Oct 24 : This Diwali chocolates would be replacing the traditional mithai box and in a year or two there will be a Chocolate boom in the metropolis

OUTLOOK india.com

So far the Euromonitor repot on India's expanding chocolate market, which predicted a 22 per cent increase in the market size in 2010, has been bang on with more Indians turning to gifting chocolate during the festive season

THE TIMES OF INDIA

The Gifts

TNN Aug 23, 2010, 09.55pm IST

It is no longer the same old 'laddoo' and 'gulabjamun' galore festival as the chocolate and dry fruit packs are scoring over 'desi mithai' (sweetmeat) this Rakshabandhan. Chocolates are clearly the toast of the moment.

THE TIMES OF INDIA

Chocolate, cookies score over mithai, dryfruit

Aparna Ramalingam & Nidhi Mukundan, TNN Oct 15, 2009, 06.01am IST

Source: Websites of respective publications

As targeted, the shift in strategy did show results. It got noticed and reported by newspapers too, that chocolate was being considered on occasions when traditional *meetha* were the original choice.

The impact showed up in our tracking studies too. By 2011, penetration of chocolate was over 90% for both teen and adult segments. As we will see later, CDM was the biggest brand capitalising this explosive growth in the chocolate category (Table 4).

**Table 4: Chocolate penetration**

| **Chocolate penetration Metros + Mini-metros** | **1995** | **2002** | **2011** |
|---|---|---|---|
| SEC A, B, C | | | |
| Kids | 80% | 85% | 99% |
| Teens | 73% | 72% | 96% |
| Adults | 48% | 59% | 92% |
| All | 69% | 71% | 93% |

Source: Listing Studies – 1995, 2002, 2011

Why it happened:

### *3. Communications objective*

#### Campaigns became famous and much enjoyed.

CDM campaigns enjoyed the highest recalls across all brands advertised during the seven-year period (Figure 11).

Figure 11: Branded recall of campaigns: 2005–2011

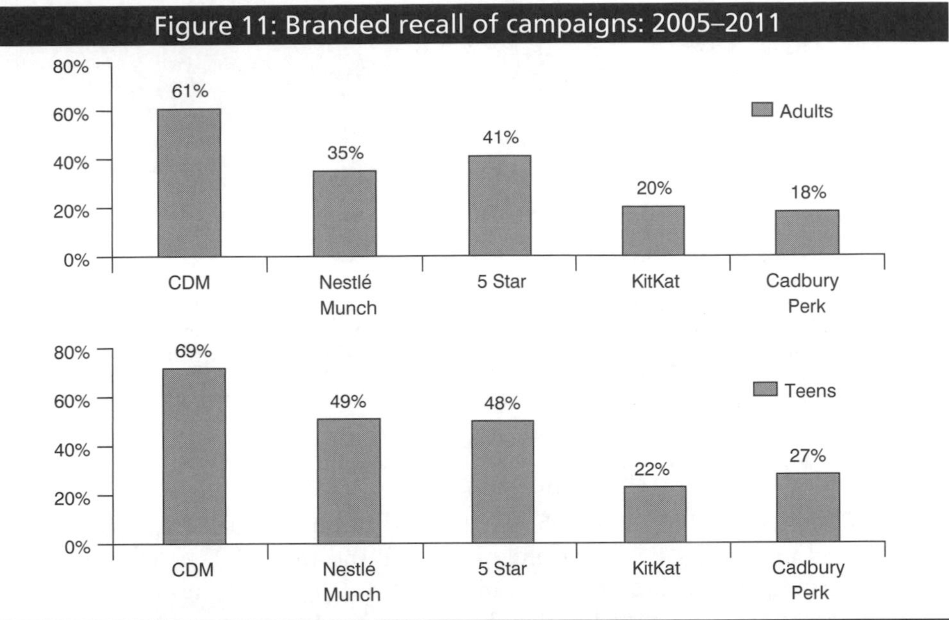


Source: TNS Brand tracking studies, 2005–2011

'Cadbury's buzz definitely emanates from its advertising', reads 'India's Buzziest Brands' list compiled by afaqs.com, India's largest website on advertising and media industry. Cadbury has consistently been in the top 20 brands from 2006 to 2012, and it has climbed up the ranks over the years.[11]

The 2012 report said: 'In a list dominated by digital and mobile brands, Cadbury was the only FMCG brand in the top ten of the 7th edition of the list.' (Figure 12).

Figure 12: Rankings of 'India's Buzziest Brands' 2012

7TH EDITION OF INDIA'S BUZZIEST BRANDS

**THE HONOURS BOARD**

| RANK 2012 | RANK 2011 | BRAND | CATEGORY | RELATIVE SCORE |
|---|---|---|---|---|
| 1 ▲ | 9 | Airtel | Telco | 100.0 |
| 2 ▼ | 1 | Facebook | Online | 90.2 |
| 3 ★ | - | Flipkart | Online | 83.4 |
| 4 ★ | - | Hero | Auto | 64.7 |
| 5 ▲ | 18 | Samsung | Electronics | 52.0 |
| 6 ▲ | 7 | Google | Online | 51.7 |
| 7 ★ | - | Snapdeal | Online | 45.4 |
| 8 ■ | 8 | Cadbury | FMCG | 41.0 |
| 9 ▲ | 23 | Iphone | Handset | 36.9 |
| 10 ▲ | 14 | Twitter | Online | 36.4 |

Source: www.afaqs.com

Rediff.com, India's leading news and entertainment portal listed CDM's 'ShubhAarambh' campaign as one of the most viewed ads of 2010 (Figure 13).[12]

Figure 13: 'Most viewed advertisements of 2010' on Rediff.com

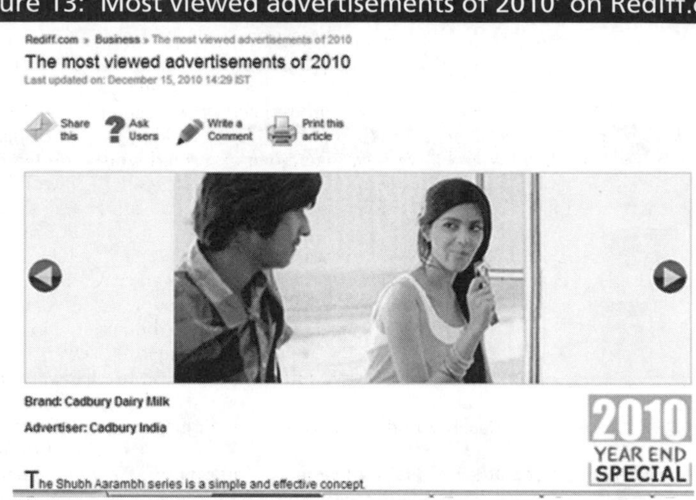


Source: Rediff.com

## People chose to see and share the campaign

On YouTube, CDM's ShubhAarambh (2010) and In-Home (2011) campaigns have been viewed more than 1 and 1.2 million times respectively.[13] This led to Cadbury India's YouTube channel becoming the third most watched YouTube channel in India in 2011.[14] Madison data estimates that 2.2 million YouTube views translate to a free PR valuation of about INR 1 crore (about US$ 200,000) – equivalent to what many brands spend on their Internet campaigns in India in a year.

On Facebook too, CDM is more popular than its competitors. While Nestlé Munch does not have a presence on Facebook, Nestlé KitKat has fewer likes and fewer people talking about it, compared to CDM (Figure 14).

Figure 14: Likes of Facebook pages and number of people talking about...

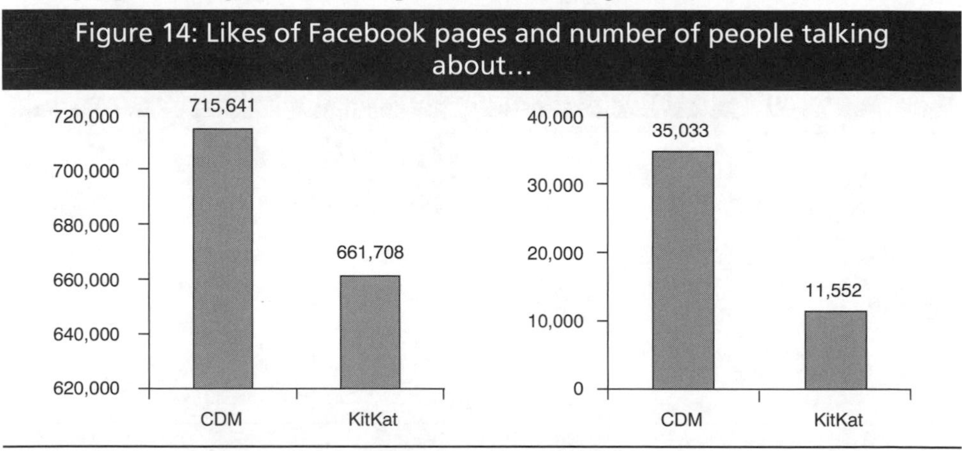


Source: Official Facebook pages for 'Cadbury Dairy Milk India' and 'Break Banta Hai' (KitKat)

User comments on YouTube and Facebook depict how engaging and loved the ads were:

- Awesome ads from cadbury....good ads love to see it again and again Yeay.!! This ad is back on tv. !! <3 <3
- After a long time, I have seen a nice TVC. Today I asked my wife and she was surprised when I told her, would you give me a bite of chocolate? Ha hahaha.
- No matter how many times I watch this...I can't get enough of this ad. It's short, sweet and it expresses the same emotions in 40 secs that a movie takes about 3 hours to say.
- Real moment is when I share my preserved Dairy Milk with my family... n smiles on everyone's face makes me feel like heaven...
- Today is a '*Kuch Meetha Ho Jaaye*' moment 4 me... Coz finally my exams got over...

### *Campaign popularity led to brand becoming popular as meetha*

#### Cultural popularity

The signoff line '*Kuch Meetha Ho Jaaye*' got used by many newspapers and websites as headlines for articles on sweets, sugar, chocolate, etc. (Figure 15). Not just that, a 2005 Bollywood movie, on people drifting apart in their relationships and coming back together, used the line as its title.

**Figure 15: Media adapting CDM's line for news articles**

Source: Websites/editions of respective publications

Even the lines used in the sub-campaigns got mashed up and used in newspaper headlines. In fact, a tabloid adopted the line 'Pappu Pass Ho Gaya' (our 2005 campaign) for advertising itself!

Moreover, the line from our 2009 'PayDay' campaign – *Khush Hai Zamana Aaj Pehli Tarikh Hai* (Everyone's happy because today's PayDay) – was used by the Minister of Finance in his Budget speech. He said: *Khush Hai Zamana Aaj Budget Ki Tarikh Hai* (Everyone's happy because today's Budget Day).

His pro-middle class budget led to a newspaper headline quipping 'PayDay for Bharat' the next day.

Impact was seen at a personal level too. The strong 'celebrations' connect with CDM led to trends like using the packaging of CDM as a wedding invitation card.

### Impact seen in brand track results

1. The campaign *created a new need-state hitherto unheard of* – the need to celebrate happy moments (Table 5).[15] Data on this need-state is not available post 2007. This is because from 2007 onwards, tracking shifted from happy moment as a need-state, to specific occasions on which CDM was preferred.

**Table 5: Preference for chocolate for various need-states**

| Need-states | Total | |
|---|---|---|
| | **2004** | **2007** |
| Hunger | 6% | 15% |
| Mental lift | 14% | 14% |
| Celebrate a happy moment | 0% | 14% |
| Craving | 6% | 10% |
| Energy | 1% | 2% |

'Celebrate a happy moment' emerged as a significant need-state over the four years from 2004 to 2007.

Source: TNS Brand Tracking Studies, 2004–2007

2. From 2004 to 2007, preference for CDM across all TGs saw a big increase across celebratory occasions; an average of 34% in large towns, and even higher at 40% in small towns (Figure 16).[16]
3. In 2010, the 'ShubhAarambh' campaign tapped into a cultural habit of eating something sweet as a good-luck ritual before starting something new, and asked consumers to replace *meetha* with chocolate on those occasions. In less than a year's time, this attitudinal change received high acceptability among teens, and moderate acceptability among adults (Figure 17).

Further, among those who said they would have chocolate before starting something new, 86% of teens and 79% of adults said they would consume CDM.[17]

Evidently, our advertising again created a new occasion for consuming chocolate (and CDM): 'before starting something new'.

Figure 16: Preference for CDM in large towns and small towns

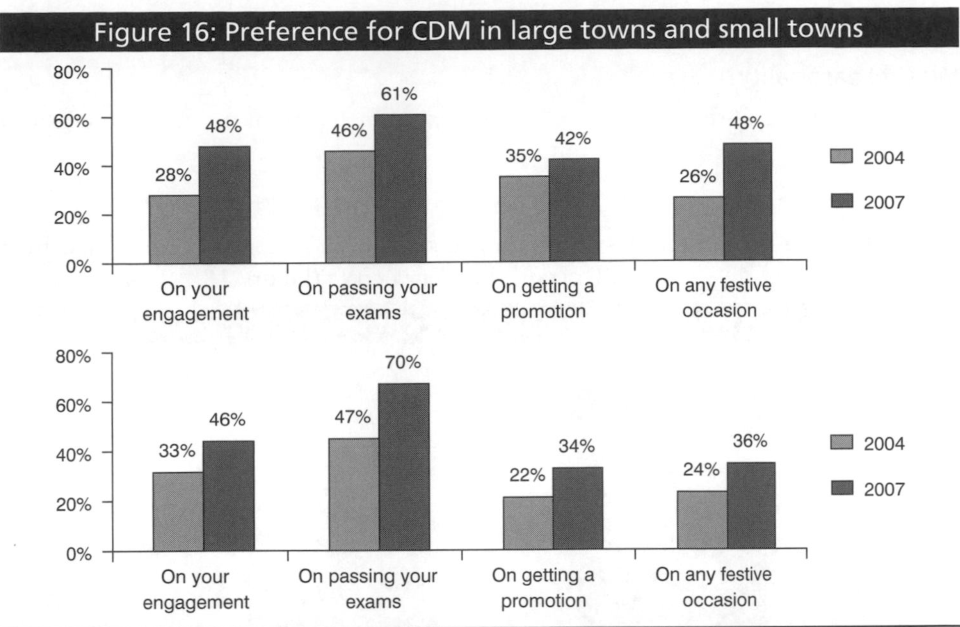


Source: TNS Brand Tracking Studies, 2004–2007

Figure 17: What would you prefer to eat, before starting something new?

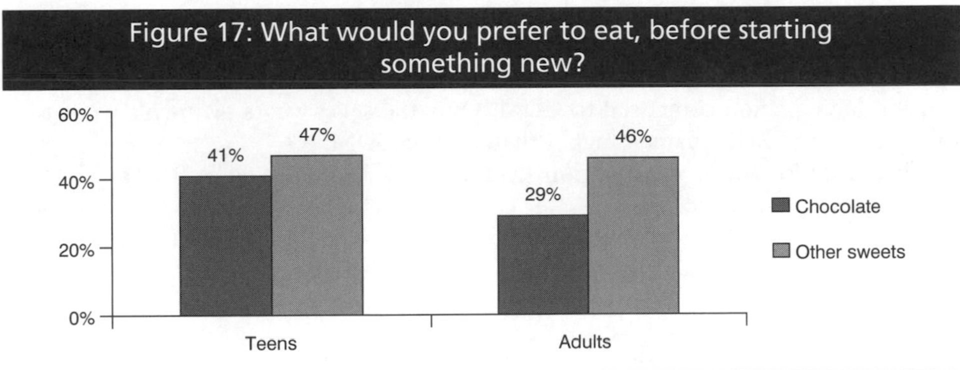


Source: TNS Brand Tracking Study 2010

## Appreciation from industry

Accolades haven't stopped since the *meetha* campaign began in 2004. A special mention in the context of this case is what Mr K.V. Sridhar, the National Creative Director of Leo Burnett, said after the 2010 'ShubhAarambh' campaign:

> *Cadbury has shown the path for others to follow and create a meaningful difference in the lives of people. So, let us not tell ourselves that we're 'just' in the business of making ads but rather in the business of transforming human behaviour.*[18]

### *4. Proving advertising grew sales and not other factors*

#### Was it seasonality?

No. Given the long-term nature and consistent annual rate of growth, the effect of seasonality is obviously not relevant.

#### Was the growth because of better price-value equation for CDM?

No. Volume growth came despite grammage reduction. This was compelled by a global increase in raw material (cocoa, sugar, etc.) costs (Figure 18).

Figure 18: Weight (grams) for pack with selling price of Rs. 5

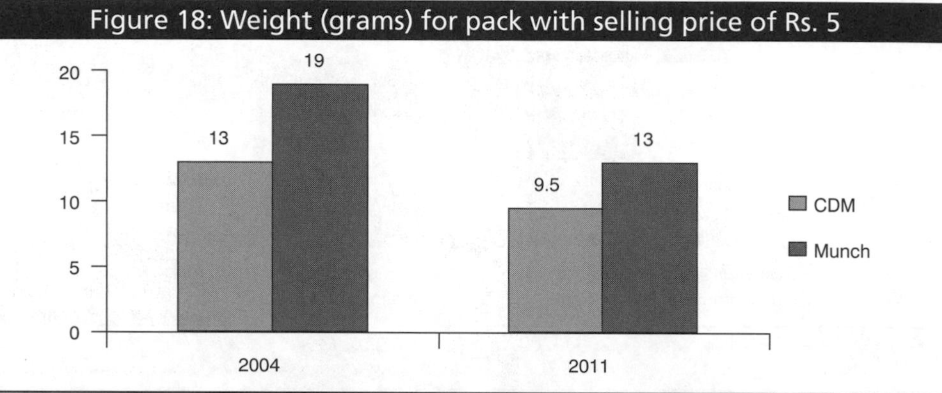


Source: AC Nielsen sales data

Not just that, CDM's key competitor, Nestlé Munch, consistently offered a better price–value equation compared to CDM. Over the seven years, Munch's weight for the same-price SKU remained higher than that of CDM.[19]

This is important as competition (Munch) was less affected by the commodity price increase, due to it being a wafer coated in chocolate (requiring less chocolate and, moreover, it made use of cocoa-butter substitute, a cheaper input material).

This indicates that *advertising helped make the brand price-inelastic,* and helped the brand to command a relative price premium.

#### Was it because of promotional activities?

No. Given price pressures, promotions were few and far between.

#### So, was it distribution?

Distribution has, indeed, increased over the seven-year period, but one could argue about the extent of causality between distribution and sales. While it could have led to growth in penetration, it would have limited the impact, if any, on growth in the frequency of CDM consumption.

As data in Table 6 shows, frequency of CDM consumption grew by more than 3.5 times from 2002 to 2011. To this extent, impact of distribution is definitely not the driving factor in CDM's growth.

Additionally, the growth in Per Dealer Off-take[20] shows that the growth in CDM sales was not achieved purely by adding new outlets. The fact that this growth was much higher than that of Nestlé Munch further proves this point (Figure 19).

Table 6: Frequency of consumption

| Frequency of consumption Metros + Mini-metros | 1995 | 2002 | 2011 |
|---|---|---|---|
| SEC A, B, C | | | |
| Kids | – | 8.0 | 30.2 |
| Teens | – | 6.1 | 25.4 |
| Adults | – | 4.9 | 20.0 |
| All | – | 6.4 | 23.8 |

Source: Cadbury Listing Studies – 1995, 2002, 2011

Figure 19: Per Dealer Output (INR): CDM vs. Nestlé Munch

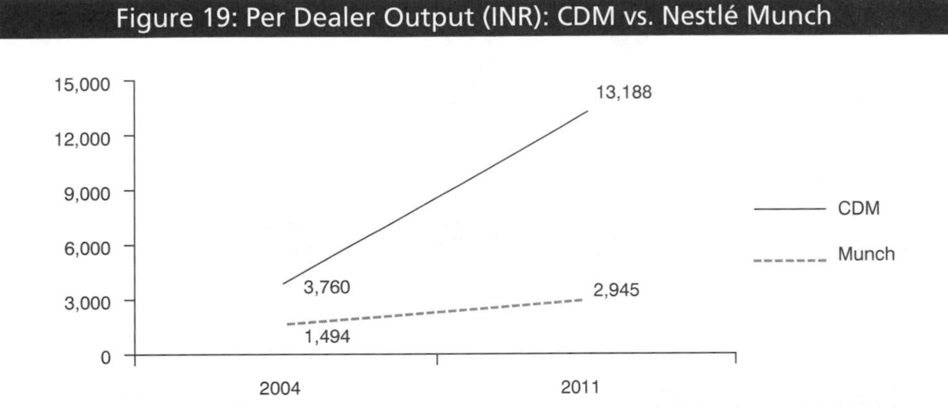


Source: AC Nielsen sales data

Moreover, if distribution was the key sales driver, Munch should lead over CDM in sales; since throughout the seven years, Munch was more widely available than CDM (Figure 20).

Figure 20: Numeric distribution: CDM vs. Nestlé Munch

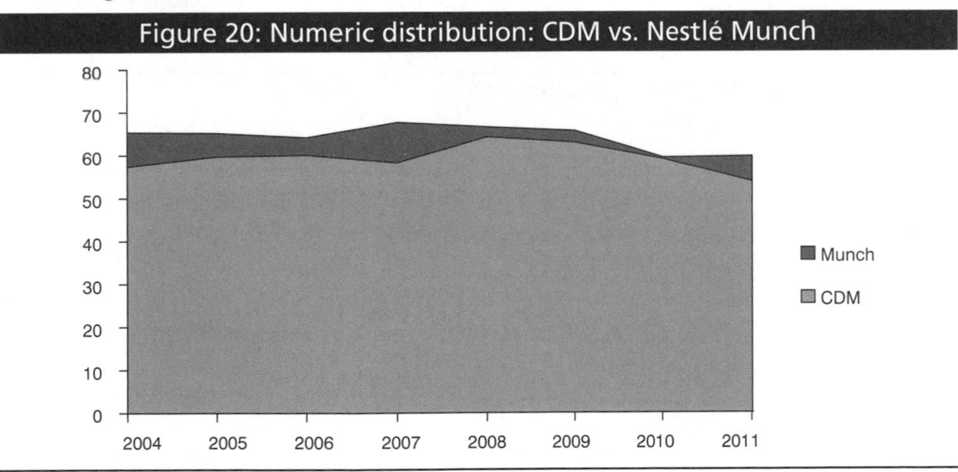


Source: AC Nielsen sales data

Although Munch has the value advantage, and is more widely distributed, CDM outperforms Munch on both absolute sales and rate of growth, as shown earlier.

### Is it that CDM's growth, then, was because of product?

No. The product taste has stayed unchanged for over a decade! And no new SKUs have been launched since 1998.[21]

### Was it packaging then?

No. CDM underwent just one marginal packaging change (to accommodate global brand guidelines; and the change was not advertised). Clearly, given the long-term nature of the results, packaging change impact cannot be the growth engine.

### Was it because of lower competition in the chocolate category?

No. The period 2005–2011 saw the launch of 25 new chocolate brands, and the launches were supported by TV advertising too.[22]

### Was it high SOVs then?

No. An analysis of sales and GRP inputs for the campaigns, using econometric modelling, shows that the effectiveness of our media inputs improved over the years (Figure 21).

Figure 21: Effectiveness across campaigns

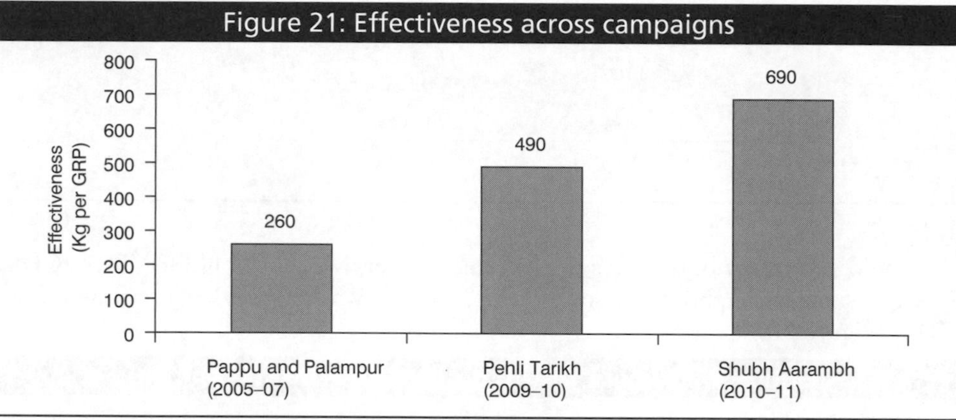


Source: Cadbury's estimates based on its econometrics analysis

### Was it macro-economic variables then, like growth in indulgent behaviour?

No. In fact, these years saw an increase in incidences of diabetes and other lifestyle diseases in India.[23] Further, there was no reduction in advertising related to healthy eating and sugar-free products (Figure 22).

In addition to these points, the high correlation between CDM sales and GRPs (0.933) goes on to show the extent of the contribution that advertising has made to sales growth (Figure 23).

All this leads us to conclude that CDM's advertising is the key driver for its superior growth.

That advertising contributed significantly to sales growth and ROI is further validated using econometric modelling.

Figure 22: Health category GRPs

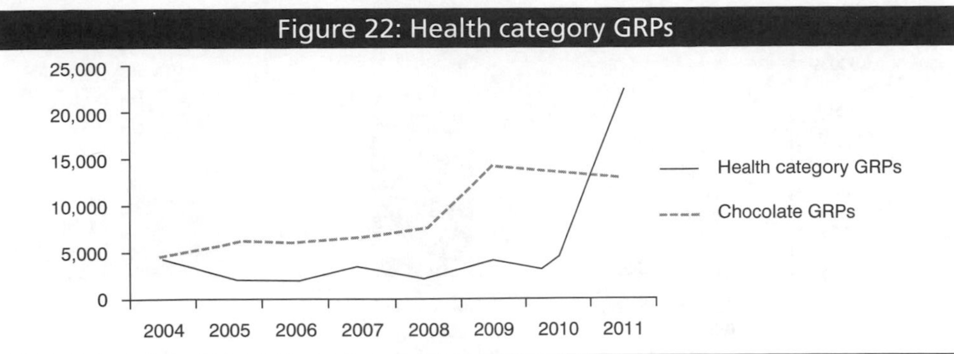


Source: TAM Media data. Products considered for health category: artificial sweeteners, sugar-free beverages and pro-biotic drinks

Figure 23: CDM sales and GRPs

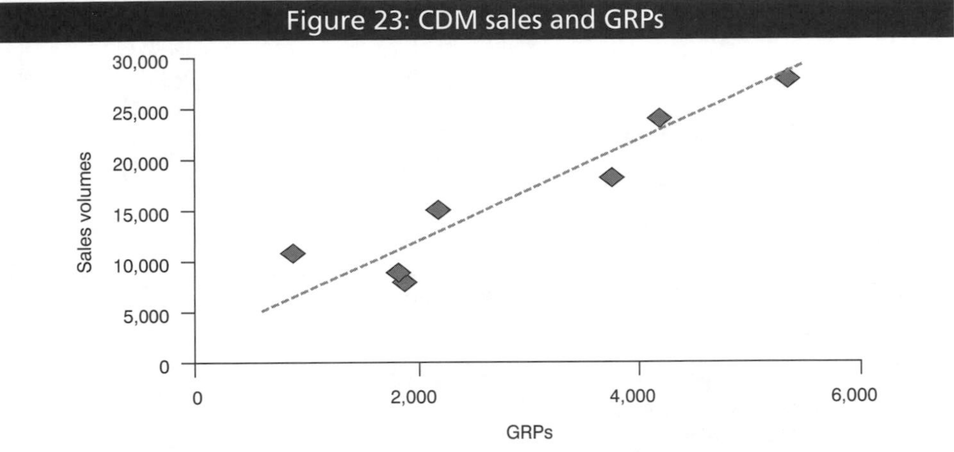


Source: AC Nielsen and TAM media data

### *5. Payback and ROMI*

Cadbury India is a private company and, as a company policy, does not share financial data. So the exact contribution of advertising must remain confidential. Hence, they have been presented only as estimates.

We already know that over the campaign period of 2005 to 2011, brand revenues have grown by 26% Compounded Annual Growth Rate (CAGR). Additionally, brand profits grew at an impressive 28% CAGR.[24]

The econometric model further asserts that both revenue and profit ROI for individual campaigns have consistently grown over the years (Figures 24 and 25).

Figure 24: Revenue ROI by campaign

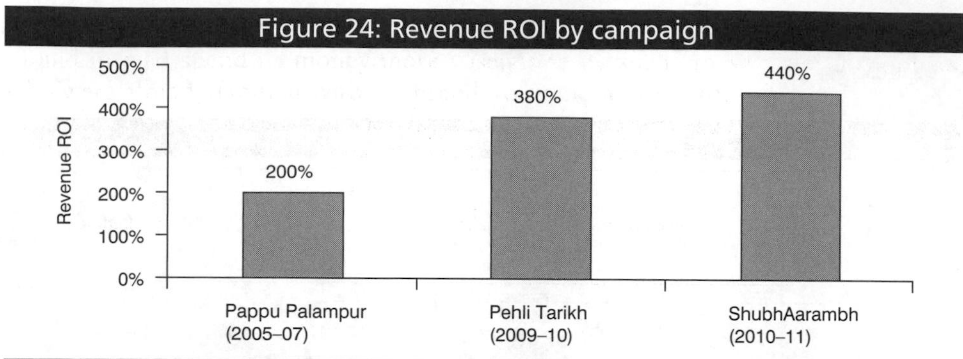


Source: Cadbury's estimates based on its econometrics analysis

Figure 25: Profit ROI by campaign

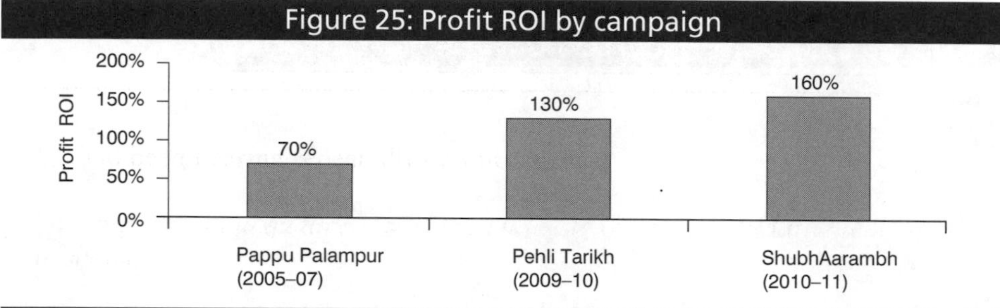


Source: Cadbury's estimates based on its econometrics analysis

## Notes

1 Source: AC Nielsen sales data.
2 Source: AC Nielsen sales data.
3 Source: Nestlé India reports (Nestlé India is a public limited company).
4 Source: AC Nielsen sales data.
5 Source: AC Nielsen sales data.
6 Source: AC Nielsen sales data.
7 VFM offerings: Nestlé Munch, Nestlé KitKat (along with Cadbury Perk) accounted for 30% of the chocolate category. These were all chocolate-coated wafer biscuits.
8 Source: Cadbury estimates, 2004.
9 Source: AC Nielsen sales data.
10 Source: AC Nielsen sales data.
11 Source: www.afaqs.com – articles on its annual list of 'India's Buzziest Brands'.
12 Source: Rediff.com. Online at: http://www.rediff.com/business/slide-show/slide-show-1-the-most-viewed-advertisements-of-2010/20101215.htm
13 Source: Statistics for video links on www.youtube.com, available on the page itself.
14 Source: Channel statistics for Cadbury India's channel 'CadburyTVCs'.
15 Source: TNS Brand Tracking studies 2004–2007.
16 Source: TNS Brand Tracking studies 2004–2007.
17 Source: TNS Tracking Study, 2010.
18 Source: http://www.business-standard.com/india/news/transforming-human-behaviour/414063/
19 Source: AC Nielsen sales audit data.
20 Per Dealer Off-take (PDO) is an AC Nielsen measure. PDO = average sales of the brand from across the number of dealers that stock the brand.
21 Source: Cadbury India data.
22 Source: TAM Media data.
23 Source: WHO health statistics for India.
24 Source: Cadbury's estimates based on its econometrics analysis.

GOLD AWARD

Chapter 11

# Department for Transport

## How 30 years of drink drive communications saved almost 2,000 lives

**By Josh Bullmore and Steve Watkins, Leo Burnett**
Credited companies: Creative Agency: Leo Burnett; Econometric modelling agency: Holmes and Cook; Client: Department for Transport

**Editor's summary**

This paper reveals how communications changed drink driving behaviour over the course of 30 years from 1979 to 2009 by tackling drink driving attitudes, acceptability, denial and decisions. This relentless pursuit of potential drink drivers saved almost 2,000 lives, prevented over 10,000 serious injuries, and created a value to society of £3bn. For the second, third and fourth periods of the campaign, every £1 spent on communications saved society £154, £12 and £38 respectively.

This paper is a seminal tribute to changing models of communications over three decades and the ability of a genuinely big brand idea to flex and evolve as its market environment changes and as consumer opinion is buffeted by market forces, peer behaviour and media comment.

## Summary

This is the story of how communications changed drink driving behaviour over the course of 30 years from 1979 to 2009.

Four successive periods of communication tackled drink driving attitudes, acceptability, denial and decisions.

This relentless pursuit of potential drink drivers saved almost 2,000 lives and prevented over 10,000 serious injuries.

The value of this to society is £3bn. We estimate that for periods two, three and four of the campaign, every £1 spent on communications saved society £154, £12 and £38 respectively.

The campaign offers powerful learning for all who seek to change behaviour over the long term.

## Introduction

In 1979, 28 people were killed or seriously injured (KSI) on our roads every day in drink driving accidents. By 2009 this had fallen to just four a day.

We intend to demonstrate the role of communications in this decline.

This is a challenging task. We must show what *hasn't* happened. The people who *didn't* drink then drive. The people who *didn't* die or become injured as a result. And do so across 30 years in which boom, bust, legislation, traffic volumes, safer vehicles and an array of road safety initiatives have all had an effect on levels of drink driving.

However, we can, and will, demonstrate the lives saved and injuries prevented using a model that delicately teases out the effect of communications.

We'll also show *how* communications have achieved these effects. Social science[1] has identified three key factors in changing drink drive behaviour that communications can influence:

1. Attitudes – particularly one's understanding of the risks of drink driving.
2. Norms – one's perceptions of what others think of drink driving.
3. Drink driver image – how one's image of drink drivers compares with self image.

Reviewing communications strategy across the 30 years against these factors reveals four distinct periods of communication (Table 1) which we will explore in turn.

**Table 1: Four distinct periods of communication**

| Period | 1 | 2 | 3 | 4 |
|---|---|---|---|---|
| Years | 1979–1987 | 1987–1992 | 1992–2002 | 2002–2009 |
| Behaviour change focus | Attitudes | Norms and drink driver perceptions | Norms and attitudes | Attitudes |
| Communications strategy | Heightening the perception of risk | Creating social unacceptability | Confronting drivers in denial | Pinpointing the moment of decision |

## Chapter 1: 1979 to 1987 – Heightening the perception of risk

**Table 2: Period 1: 1979–1987**

| Period | 1 | 2 | 3 | 4 |
|---|---|---|---|---|
| Years | 1979–1987 | | | |
| Behaviour change focus | Attitudes | | | |
| Communications strategy | Heightening the perception of risk | | | |

Drink and driving have combined to devastating effect since motor vehicles first appeared on the road in 1897.[2] The government tightened drink drive legislation in 1932, and by the 1960s had conclusively demonstrated the effects of alcohol on driving,[3] paving the way for landmark legislation in 1967.[4] Supported by a one-off communications campaign, this initially reduced the proportion of accidents involving alcohol, but this rose throughout the 70s until the government turned to communications to help reduce an unacceptable level of casualties.[5]

1979 is the first year for which accurate records of drink drive attitudes, behaviour and KSIs are available. In that year alone nearly 10,000 KSIs were caused by drink driving.

Young male drivers in particular were over-represented in these statistics and to understand what was driving their behaviour we look at the factors from the behaviour change model.

*Attitudes:* Young male drivers had little sense of the risks of drink driving:

- They typically estimated the legal limit to be two pints, but believed they could drink three pints without affecting their driving.[6]
- They felt there was little danger of being stopped by the police and facing legal consequences. Over half believed that it was just bad luck if you were caught.[7]

*Norms:* The levels of drink driving surrounding these young men were hardly conducive to positive behaviour. Over half of all male drivers and nearly two thirds of young male drivers were drink driving on a weekly basis.[8]

*Drink driver image:* Given these levels of drink driving, young men's images of drink drivers were based on friends and family and likely to be aspirational. This was reinforced by popular culture. Prime-time television showed drinking every six minutes, but rarely showed negative consequences.[9]

### *The solution*

The combined Department for Transport (DfT) and agency team began by tackling young men's attitudes towards drink driving.[10]

Their strategy was to offset the *rewards* of drinking pleasure with a heightened sense of the *risks* of drink driving. Advertising would surround them with a range of messages that left no room for doubt about the risks that drink drivers posed to themselves and to others.

Communications throughout the period focused on two areas (Figure 1).

1. *The effects of drinking*: Educating drivers on the effect of even small amounts of alcohol on their driving performance and the terrible effect on others of their actions.
2. *The chances of detection*: Highlighting that if they did drink and drive then they risked being caught, and showing the legal consequences they could face.

The advertising was targeted at young men, but intended to be overheard by all drivers. The media strategy surrounded them with multiple executions across television, cinema, radio, print and poster advertising. Activity initially focused on the peak season for drink driving – Christmas – and later ran during the summer, when warmer weather leads to a second peak. This bi-annual approach became the model for most subsequent activity.

### *The results: how heightening risk worked*

This section will demonstrate that in this period:

- communications helped change attitudes towards drink driving;
- communications reduced drink drive behaviour;
- drink drive road casualties fell.

Figure 1: Advertising 1979 to 1987: heightened drivers' perceptions of risks

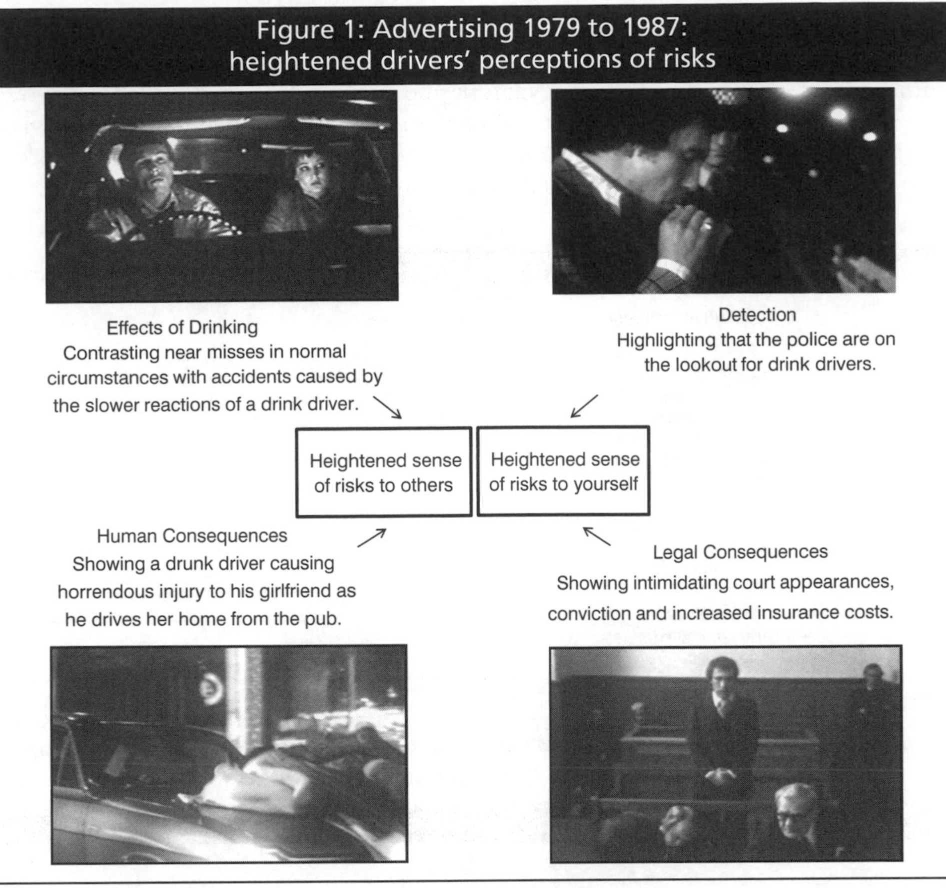

Effects of Drinking
Contrasting near misses in normal circumstances with accidents caused by the slower reactions of a drink driver.
Detection
Highlighting that the police are on the lookout for drink drivers.
Heightened sense of risks to others
Heightened sense of risks to yourself
Human Consequences
Showing a drunk driver causing horrendous injury to his girlfriend as he drives her home from the pub.
Legal Consequences
Showing intimidating court appearances, conviction and increased insurance costs.


Source: agencies Wasey Campbell-Eswald, Lowe and Davidson Pearce

In Chapter 5, we look holistically across all periods to demonstrate the casualties prevented by communications, the associated savings to society and the return on marketing investment.

## Communications helped change attitudes towards drink driving in Period 1

Attitudes targeted by communications saw substantial changes. The period saw decreases in attitudes related to both the effects of drinking and detection (Figure 2).

The period also saw a reduction in young male drivers' perceptions of their own personal limits,[11] and of the legal limits (Figure 3).

Figure 2: Changes in drink drive attitudes: Period 1 young male drivers

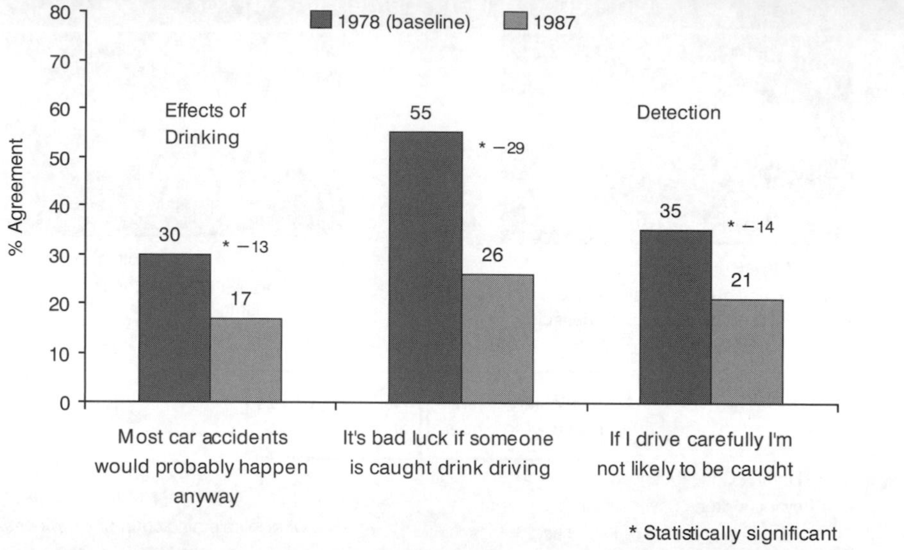

1978 (baseline)
1987
% Agreement
Effects of Drinking
Detection
30
17
* −13
55
26
* −29
35
21
* −14
Most car accidents would probably happen anyway
It's bad luck if someone is caught drink driving
If I drive carefully I'm not likely to be caught
* Statistically significant

Source: DfT Tracking Research International

Figure 3: Young male drivers changes in Period 1: Changes in perceived alcohol driving limits

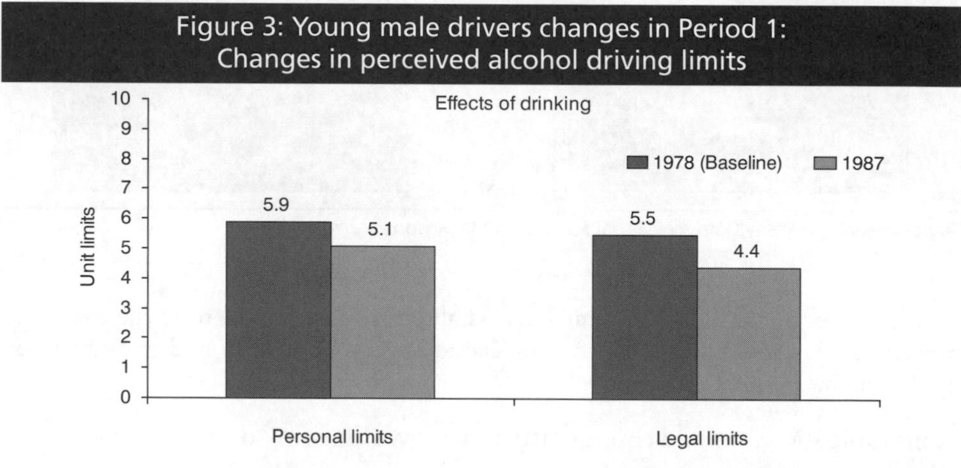

Effects of drinking
1978 (Baseline)
1987
Unit limits
5.9
5.1
5.5
4.4
Personal limits
Legal limits

Source: DfT Tracking Research International

### Communications reduced reported drink drive behaviour in Period 1

First we look at how behaviour changed across the whole period. DfT research offers an accurate picture of drink drive behaviour changes via reported behaviour.[12]

The percentage of male drivers who drove after any drinking fell from 51% to 37%, and fell from 60% to 44% amongst young male drivers (Figure 4).

Figure 4: Reported behaviour – proportion of audiences drinking and driving, Period 1

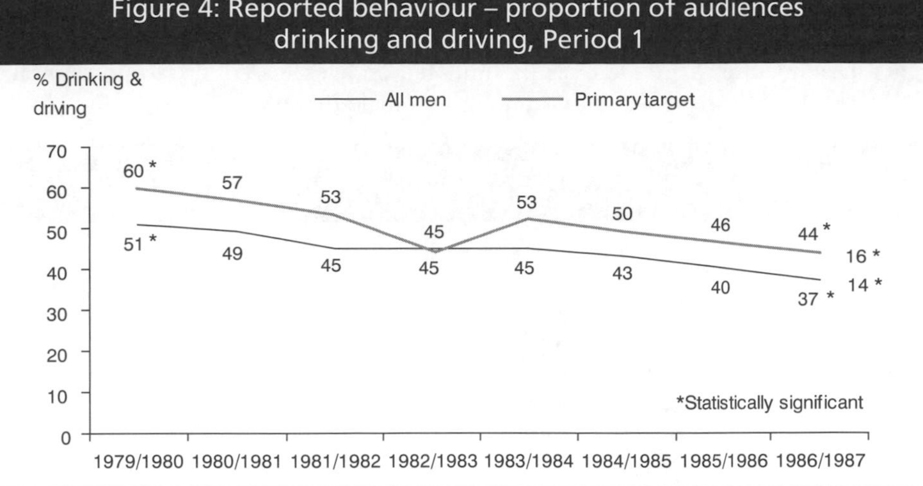


Source: DfT Tracking R.I.

The percentage of male drivers who drove after drinking six or more units (around three pints of beer) fell from 21% to 12%, and fell from 15% to 6% amongst young men (Figure 5).

Figure 5: Reported behaviour – proportion of audiences drinking and driving (6+ units), Period 1

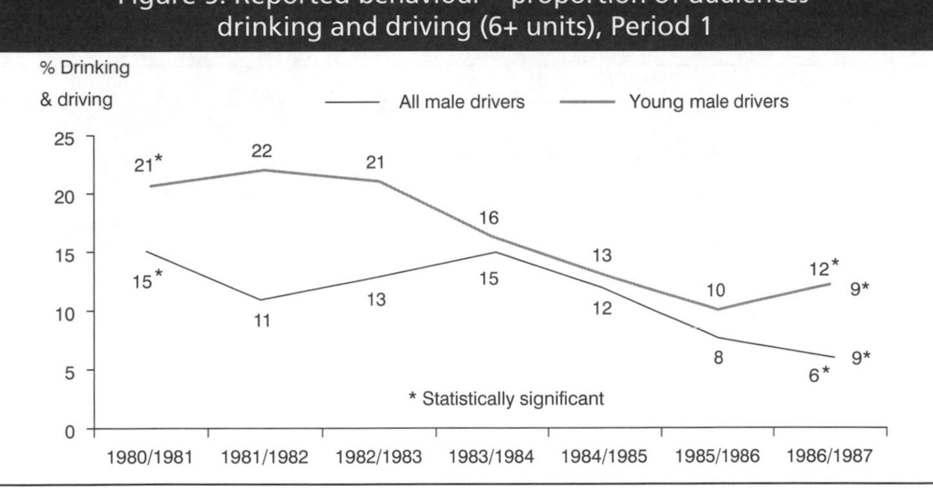


Source: DfT Tracking Research International

### *Communications impact on reported behaviour in Period 1*

To see the direct effect of communications on reported behaviour we look at the average change between behaviour measures taken immediately pre and post individual activity bursts (Figure 6):

- Driving after any drinking fell on average 7% pre to post amongst young male drivers and 3% amongst all male drivers.
- Driving after drinking over six units fell on average 4% pre to post amongst young male drivers and 2% amongst all male drivers.

**Figure 6: Campaign average pre versus post, proportion of drinking and driving, Period 1**

% Drinking & driving

| | Campaign mean pre | Campaign mean post | Change |
|---|---|---|---|
| Young males | 49 | 42 | *-7 |
| Men | 45 | 42 | *-3 |
| Young males 6+ unit | 16 | 12 | *-4 |
| Men 6+ unit | 11 | 9 | *-2 |

*Statistically significant

Source: DfT Tracking Research International

## Drink drive road casualties fell in Period 1

Drink drive KSIs fell by a quarter from 9,940 in 1979 to 7,430 in 1986 (Figure 7).

**Figure 7: Number of drink drive-related KSIs per year**

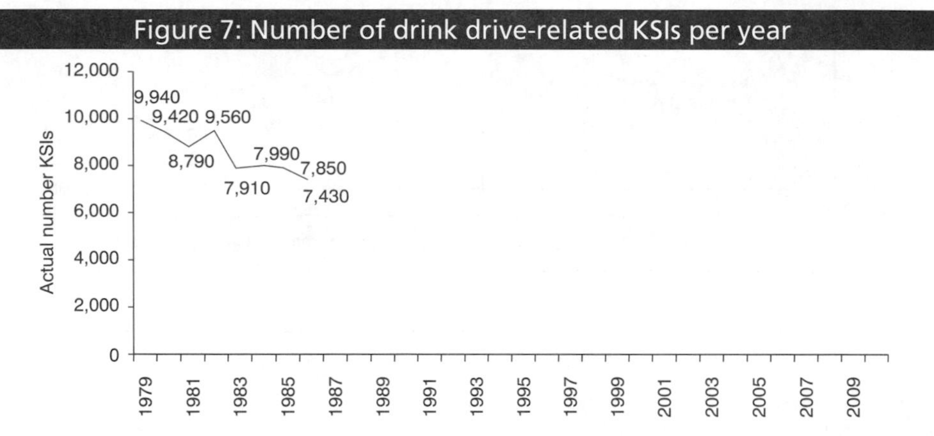


Source: Department for Transport

## Chapter 2: 1987 to 1992 – Creating social unacceptability

**Table 3: Period 2: 1987–1992**

| **Period** | **1** | **2** | **3** | **4** |
|---|---|---|---|---|
| Years | 1979–1987 | 1987–1992 | | |
| Behaviour change focus | Attitudes | Norms and drink driver perceptions | | |
| Communications strategy | Heightening the perception of risk | Creating social unacceptability | | |

Referring back to the behaviour change model, we can take stock of the situation in 1987:

*Attitudes:* had improved dramatically across the preceding period. However, drink driving casualties remained unacceptably high.

*Norms:* The team became concerned by the continued social acceptability of drink driving. Perceived levels of peer pressure had not fallen in line with other measures in previous years (Figure 8).

**Figure 8: Perception of social pressure to drink drive: 'it's difficult to avoid some drinking and driving if having any social life'**

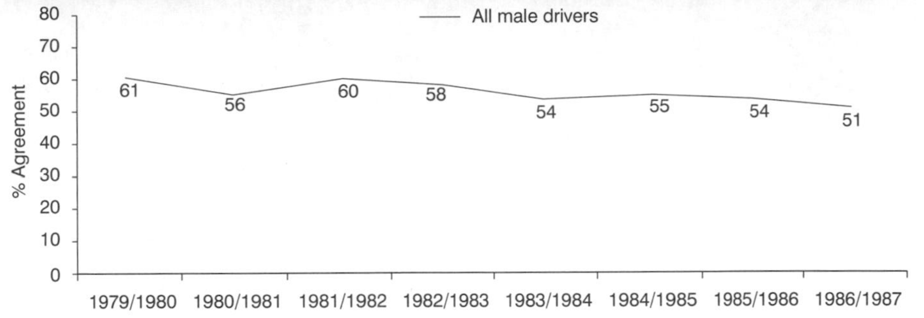


Source: DfT Tracking Research International

The team saw an opportunity. They believed that if young men felt that their friends, family and community shunned those that drank and drove, they would think twice before getting behind the wheel after a few pints.

They set out to create a sea-change in the social acceptability of drink driving. The Transport Minister at the time described this as 'changing the water in which the fish swim'.

This represented a fundamental change in strategy. Rather than targeting young men directly, communications would be aimed at society as a whole. Rather than encompassing a breadth of messages, communications would be resolutely single-minded. Rather than focusing on *attitudes,* they would change *norms* and make drink driving socially unacceptable.

The brief was to create nothing less than disgust at those who drank then drove.

The creative approach was to show the heart-rending emotional responses of people involved in drink drive tragedies: such as school-children reacting to the death of a class-mate, or a fireman to a crash scene involving a mother and baby (Figure 9).

Television and radio advertising told these emotive stories across both the Christmas and summer seasons.

**Figure 9: Advertising 1987 to 1992: creating disgust at those who drank then drove**

The Children's Story
School-children's heart-breaking reaction to the death of a class mate.

Mourning Family
A narrator tells the story of how a young man lost his life, whilst we see images of his family coping with the loss.

The Fireman's Story
A fireman breaks down after seeing a crash scene involving a mother and baby.

Rehabilitation
A man struggles to learn how to walk again after a drink drive accident.

Wheelchair
A young man recounts the accident that caused his paralysis.

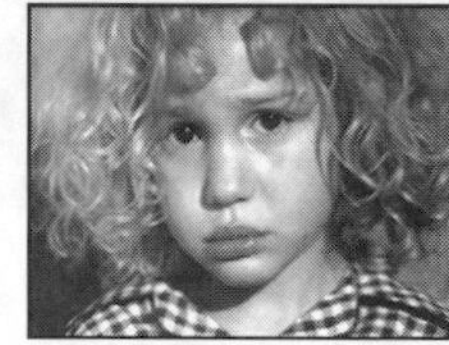

Kathy
A young girl cries whilst we overhear her mother berating her father for killing a little boy.

### *The results: how making drink driving socially unacceptable worked*

In this period communications:

- reduced the social acceptability of drink driving;
- reduced drink driving behaviour;
- reduced drink drive casualties.

### Communications reduced the social acceptability of drink driving in Period 2

Across this period, communications helped drive substantial falls in the level of perceived peer pressure (Figure 10).

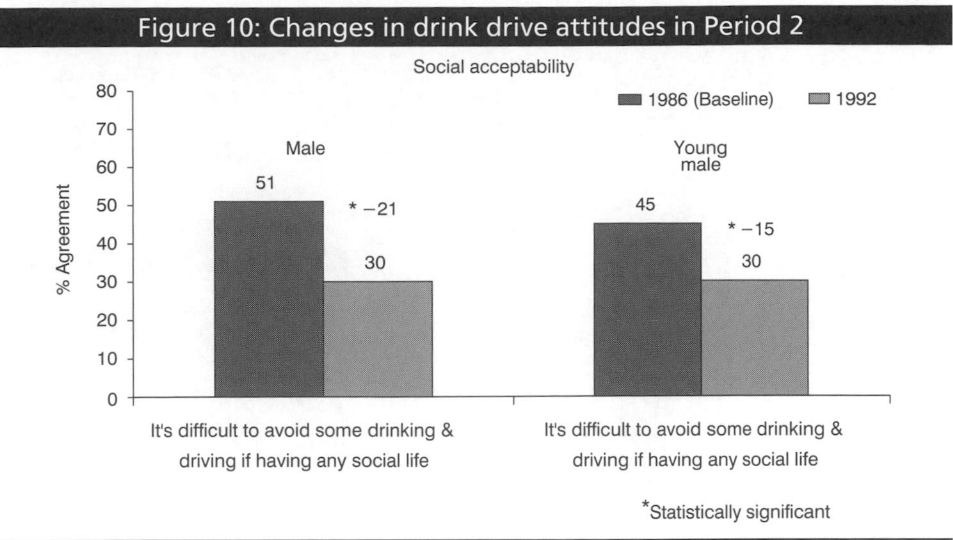


Figure 10: Changes in drink drive attitudes in Period 2

Source: DfT Tracking Research International

What's more, we see a communications effect in decreased levels of perceived peer pressure between tracking immediately pre and post activity (Figure 11).[13]

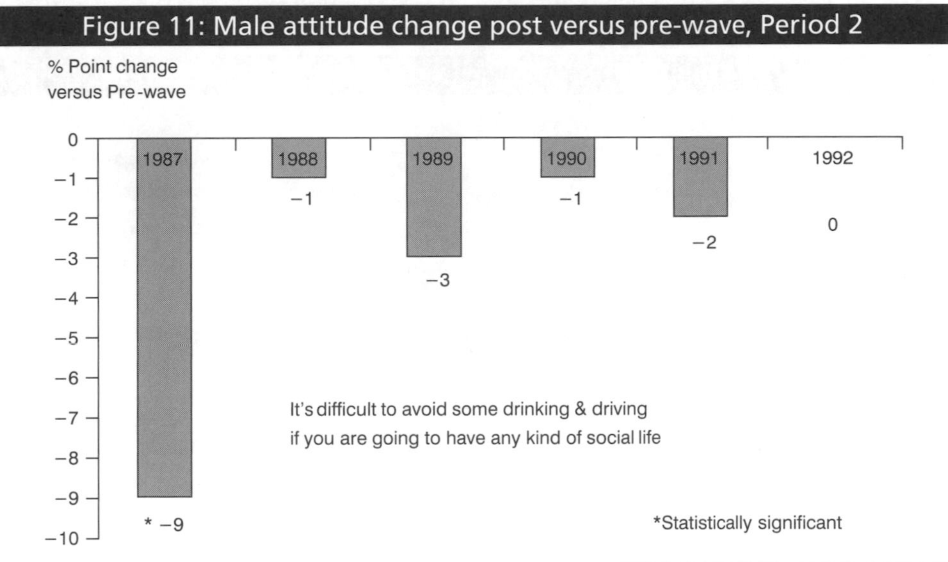


Figure 11: Male attitude change post versus pre-wave, Period 2

Source: DfT Tracking Research International

We also see corresponding increases across the entire period in perceptions that 'people I know criticise drink driving more often' (Figure 12).

Figure 12: Changes in drink drive attitudes, Period 2

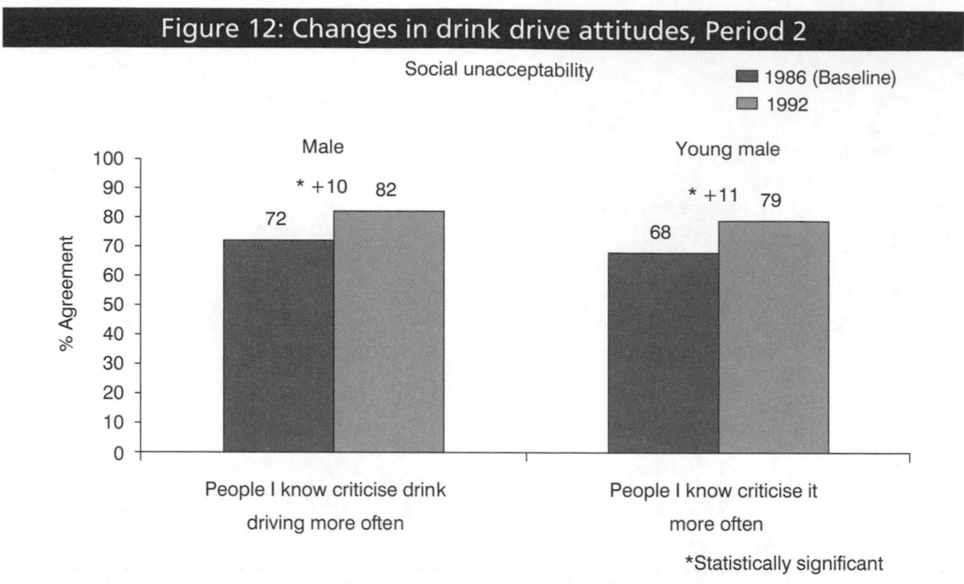


Source: DfT Tracking Research International

Again, we see a communications effect in increased perceived levels of criticism immediately pre and post activity (Figure 13).[14]

Figure 13: Male attitude change post versus pre-wave, Period 2

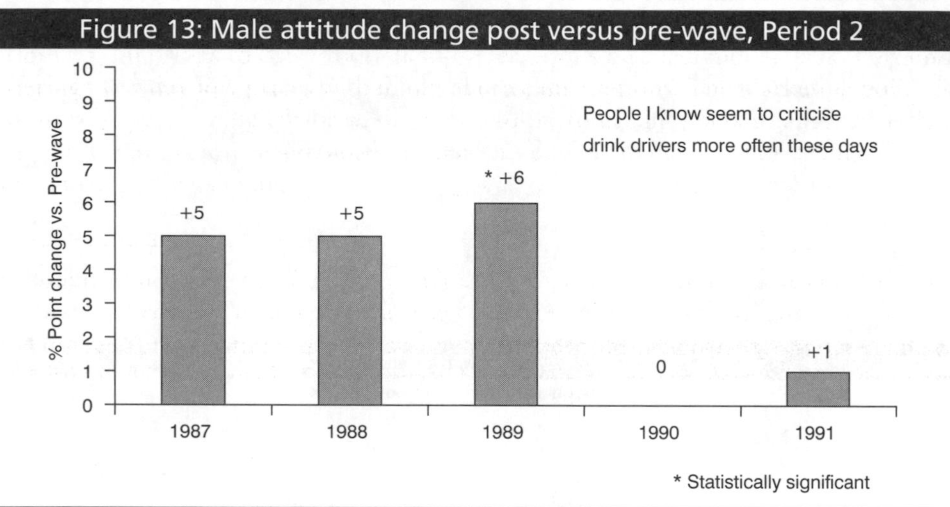


Source: DfT Tracking Research International

## Communications reduced drink driving behaviour in Period 2

The percentage of young male drivers driving after six or more units (around three pints and above) more than halved in this period (Figure 14). These are similar declines to Period 1 despite the fact that in Period 2 they started from a lower base,[15] indicating an acceleration in behaviour change in Period 2. We also see a 13% drop in young male drivers driving after any drinking (Figure 15).

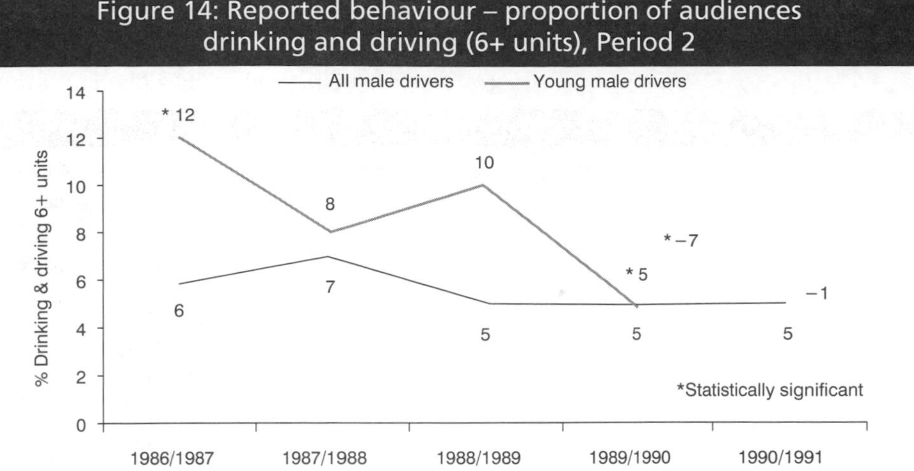


Figure 14: Reported behaviour – proportion of audiences drinking and driving (6+ units), Period 2

Source: DfT Tracking Research International

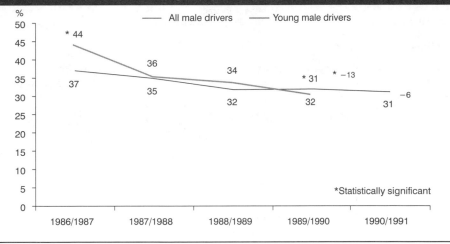

Figure 15: Reported behaviour – proportion of audiences drinking and driving, Period 2



Source: DfT Tracking

### *Communications impact on reported behaviour in Period 2*

We see a communications effect in the average change between behaviour measures taken immediately pre and post individual activity bursts (Figure 16). The decreases here show the effect of communications on behaviour:

- Driving after any drinking fell on average 2% pre to post activity amongst young male drivers and 4% amongst all male drivers.

**Figure 16: Campaign average pre versus post proportion of drinking and driving, Period 2**

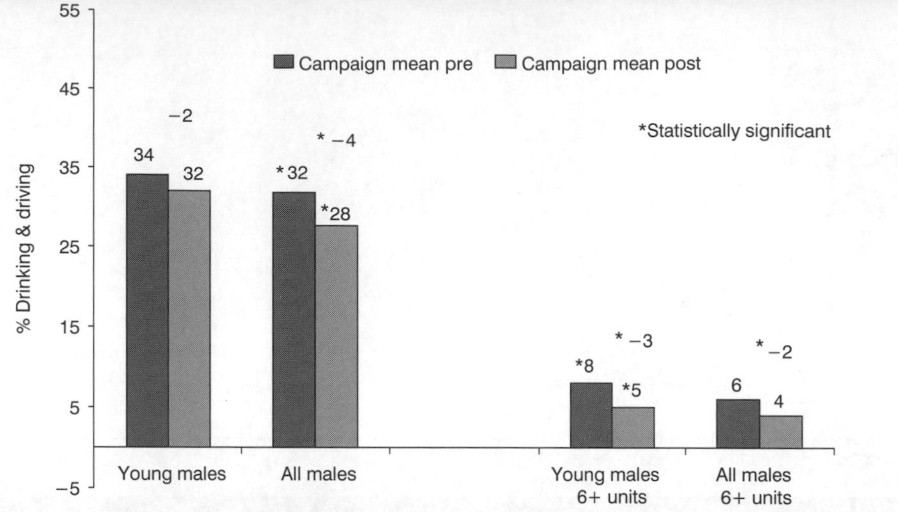

% Drinking & driving
55
45
35
25
15
5
−5
Campaign mean pre
Campaign mean post
*Statistically significant
Young males: 34, 32 (−2)
All males: *32, *28 (* −4)
Young males 6+ units: *8, *5 (* −3)
All males 6+ units: 6, 4 (* −2)

Source: DfT Tracking Research International

## Communications reduced drink drive casualties in Period 2

*Helping deliver substantial reduction in KSIs*

KSIs dropped from 6,820 in 1986 to 4,270 in 1992. A decrease of 37%. As we will see in Chapter 5, communications accounted for a substantial proportion of the casualties prevented in Period 2 (Figure 17).

**Figure 17: Number of drink drive-related KSI's per year**

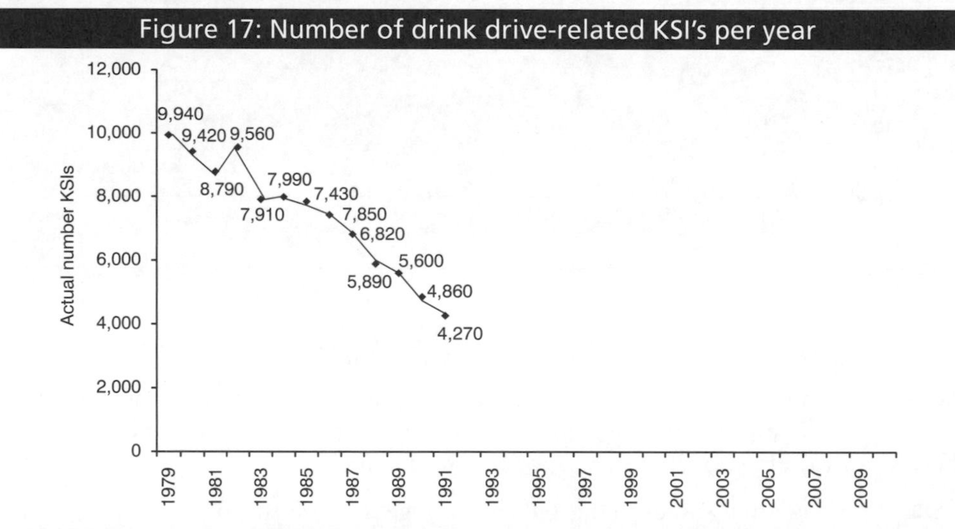


Source: Department for Transport

## Chapter 3: 1992 to 2002 – Confronting drivers in denial

**Table 4: Period 3: 1992–2002**

| **Period** | **1** | **2** | **3** | **4** |
|---|---|---|---|---|
| Years | 1979–1987 | 1987–1992 | 1992–2002 | |
| Behaviour change focus | Attitudes | Norms and drink driver perceptions | Norms and attitudes | |
| Communications strategy | Heightening the perception of risk | Creating social unacceptability | Confronting drivers in denial | |

The first decade of concerted drink drive communications had proved a success. Major inroads had been created by heightening an awareness of the risks and then building on this to create social unacceptability. The next decade was to prove tougher by comparison.

The social context was becoming ever more conducive to drink driving.

### *A new culture of intoxication*

*Norms:* A 'culture of intoxication'[16] was dramatically changing norms around broader drinking behaviours amongst young people:

- Alcohol consumption doubled across the 90s,[17] after relative stability in the 70s and 80s.[18]
- Higher sessional consumption was fuelled by stronger drinks (alcopops, stronger lagers and so on), targeted aspirational advertising and redesigned pubs and bars.[19]
- Norms that had previously constrained drunkenness, such as social condemnation of visible loss of self-control, were disappearing.[20, 21]

*Drink driver image:* The consumption of alcohol and its consequences were increasingly disconnected in popular culture. Drinking featured every four minutes on prime time television, with few depictions of negative outcomes. An explosion of 'lads' media[22] offered equally unbalanced portrayals of drinking.[23]

*Attitudes:* Qualitative research[24] revealed that young men now had a strong sense that drink driving was socially unacceptable. However, they were failing to apply this powerful moral condemnation to their own behaviour. Why? Because they defined a *drink* driver as someone who was clearly *drunk*. They admitted to driving after a 'quick drink' but joined in society's disdain for those who drove after a 'skinful' without seeing any contradiction.

### *1992–1998: Targeting attitudes to low level drinking*

The next six years focused on changing how young male drivers thought about driving after a 'quick drink'. They also aimed to create clearly negative images of drink drivers and reinforce drink driving norms to counteract wider drinking permissiveness.

These 'quick drink' campaigns became increasingly hard-hitting as research revealed ways to increase their impact (Figure 18).

- 1992: a 'quick drink' can cause a horrendous accident
  Starting to dial up the consequences of low level drinking.
- 1993–1994: building greater seasonal relevance
  Tailoring campaigns by showing festive and summer occasions shattered by the effects of a quick drink.
- 1994–1995: tragic consequences for even the nicest people
  Showing an otherwise responsible man who kills the parents of two children at Christmas.
- 1995–1997: the guilt of harming a loved one
  Graphically portraying the guilt-inducing consequences caused by a quick pint.
- 1997–1998: the scale of harm for which young drink drivers are responsible
  Emphasising that careless irresponsibility harmed thousands.

**Figure 18: Advertising 1992 to 1998: targeting low level drinking**

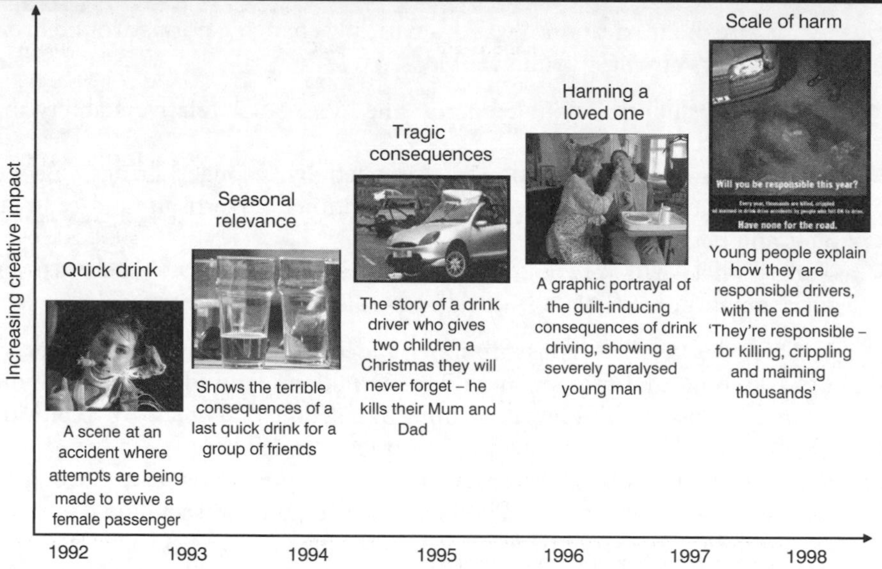

Increasing creative impact

Quick drink
A scene at an accident where attempts are being made to revive a female passenger

Seasonal relevance
Shows the terrible consequences of a last quick drink for a group of friends

Tragic consequences
The story of a drink driver who gives two children a Christmas they will never forget – he kills their Mum and Dad

Harming a loved one
A graphic portrayal of the guilt-inducing consequences of drink driving, showing a severely paralysed young man

Scale of harm
Young people explain how they are responsible drivers, with the end line 'They're responsible – for killing, crippling and maiming thousands'

1992 1993 1994 1995 1996 1997 1998

Source: agencies D'Arcy Masius Brenton Bowles and Abbott Mead Vickers

### *1998–2002: Confronting young men with reality*

Towards the end of the 90s, qualitative research revealed an issue with this escalating creative arms race. Young men 'knew the people in ads were just actors and actresses playing a role'. They were not real, so people post rationalised that the seriousness of the message was 'not real' either.[25]

The team responded by confronting young male drink drivers with the stark reality of what faced them that night if they chose to drink and drive (Figure 19):

- 1998–2000: 'someone will die tonight, don't let it be you
  A series of real road accidents were graphically reconstructed to show that this was what was happening right now on the roads.
- 2000–2002: 'one tradition we could do without'
  Familiar Christmas songs were juxtaposed with horrific accident scenes taken from real police footage.

**Figure 19: Advertising 1998 to 2002: confronting young drivers with reality**

1998–2000
Someone will die tonight, don't let it be you

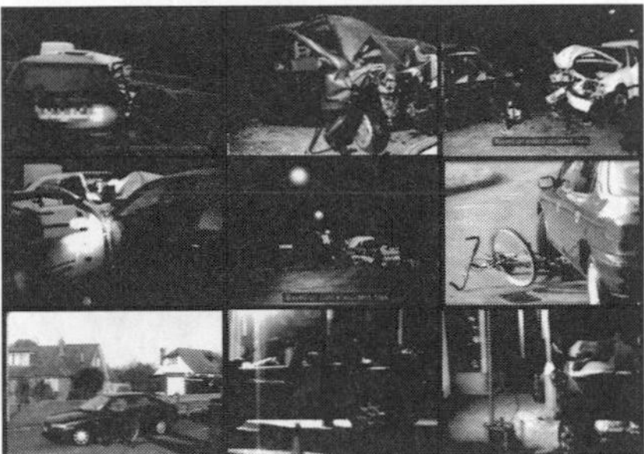

Reconstructing a series of real road accidents in graphic detail. Viewers were confronted with 15 different ads to convey the sense that this was what was happening right now on the roads.

2000–2002
One tradition we could do without

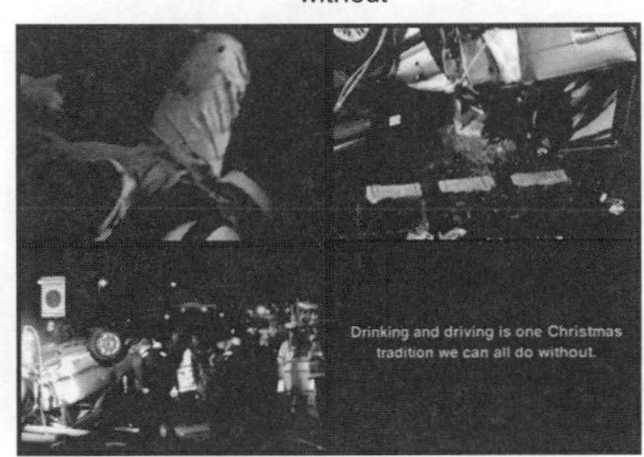


Juxtaposing familiar Christmas songs with horrific accident scenes taken from real police footage, bringing to life the stark reality of the consequences of drink driving.

Source: agency Abbott Mead Vickers

### *The results: how tackling young male drivers' denial worked*

In Period 3, communications drove further improvements to drink drive attitudes and behaviour, in turn helping reduce drink drive casualties. These gains were slim. However, in the context of the wider drinking context, holding onto previous gains and making slight improvements in key areas represented a real achievement.

#### Drink drive communications changed attitudes to driving after a quick drink

We see gains on a range of measures related to the 'quick drink' messaging in communications.[26] Amongst all male drivers and young male drivers, agreement that

'Even one drink makes me a worse driver' and 'It's wrong to drive even after a couple of drinks' increased significantly (Figure 20).

Figure 20: Changes in drink drive attitudes in Period 3

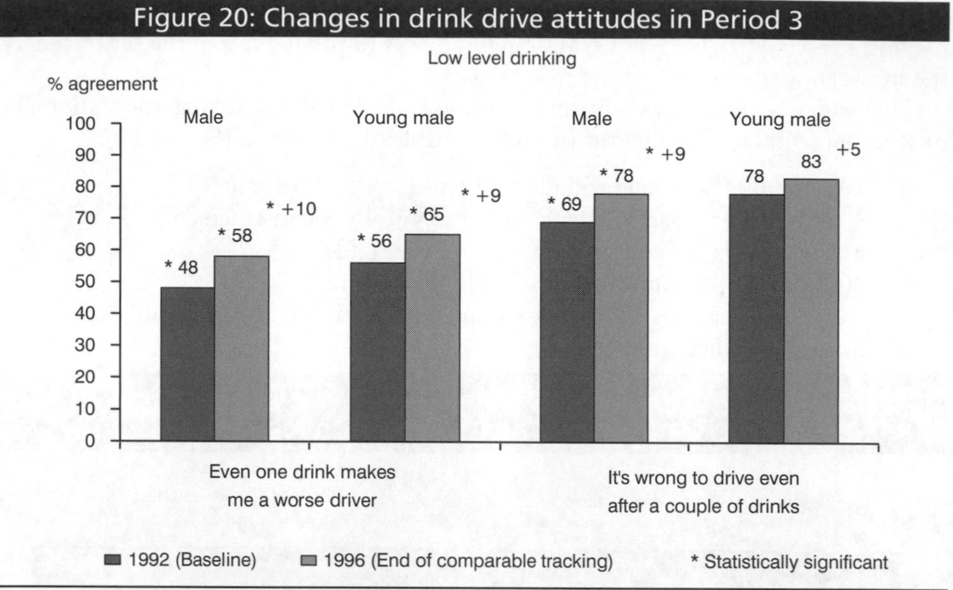


Source: DfT Tracking Research International

As in previous periods we see a comms effect in the change in these attitudes immediately pre and post activity (Figure 21), and tracking showed similar pre to post increases for 'It's wrong to drink even after a couple of pints'.

Figure 21: Young male drivers attitude change post versus pre-wave, Period 3

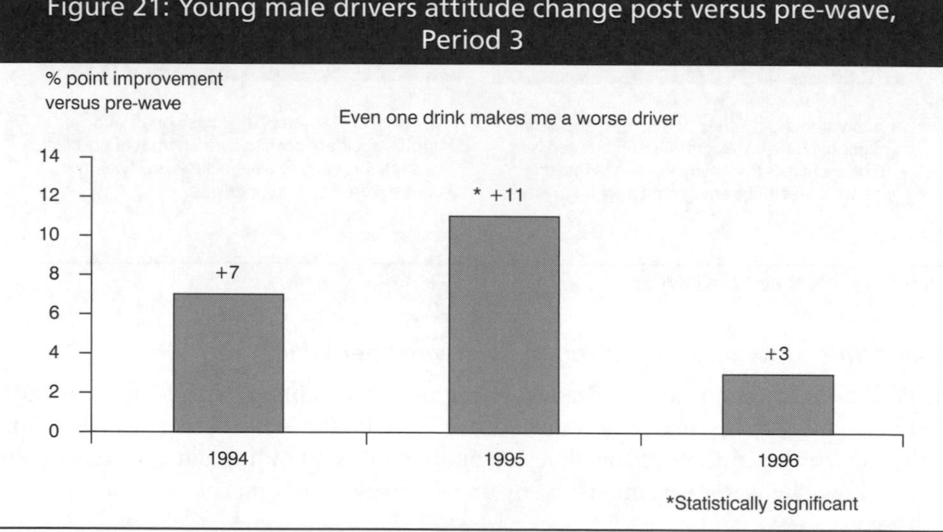


Source: DfT Tracking Research International

Between 1997 and 2002 we see a continuing trend in agreement with the dangers of drink driving, albeit at a slower pace (Figure 22).

Figure 22: Changes in drink drive attitudes, Period 3

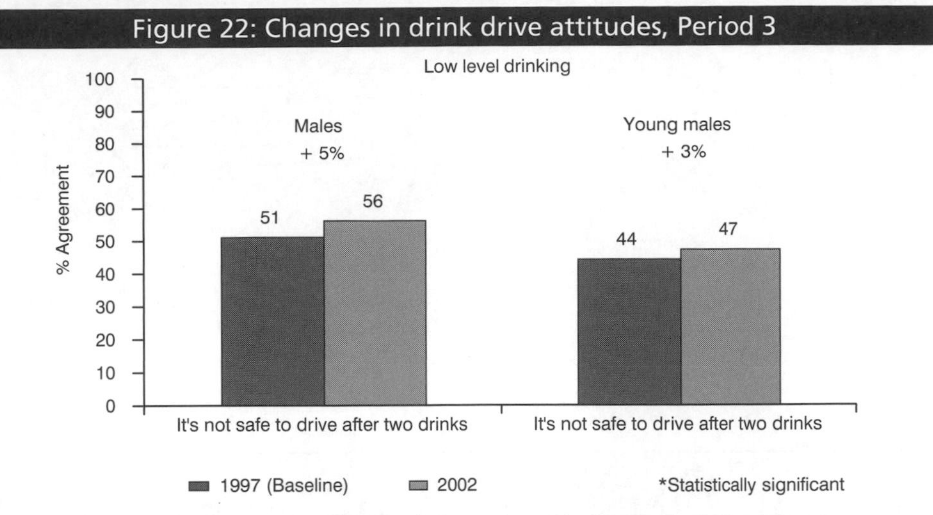


Source: DfT Tracking TNS

We see a communications effect in the average decrease between pre and post campaign measures from 1997 to 1999 (Figure 23).

Figure 23: Males average pre versus post attitude change in Period 3

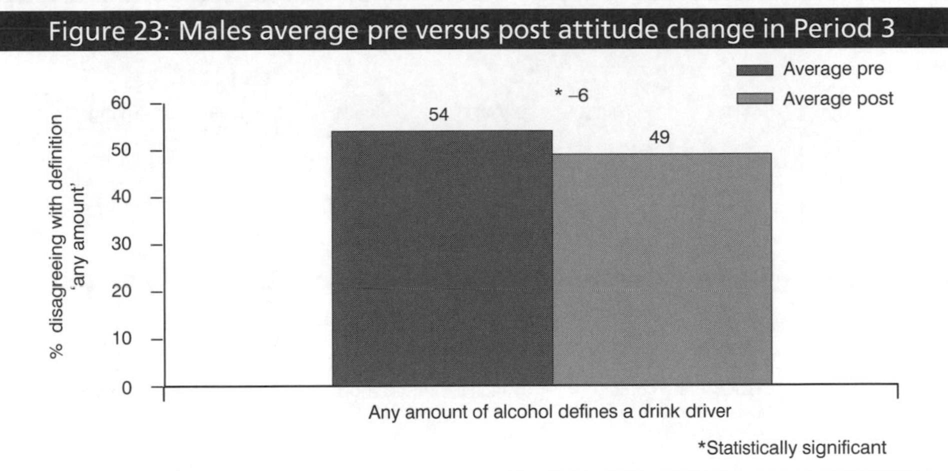


Source: DfT Tracking TNS

## Communications helped reduce drink drive behaviour in Period 3

The focus of communications was reducing the 'quick drink' and we see a corresponding decline in 'any' (i.e. low level) drinking (Figure 24).

Figure 24: Reported behaviour – proportion of audiences drinking and driving, Period 3

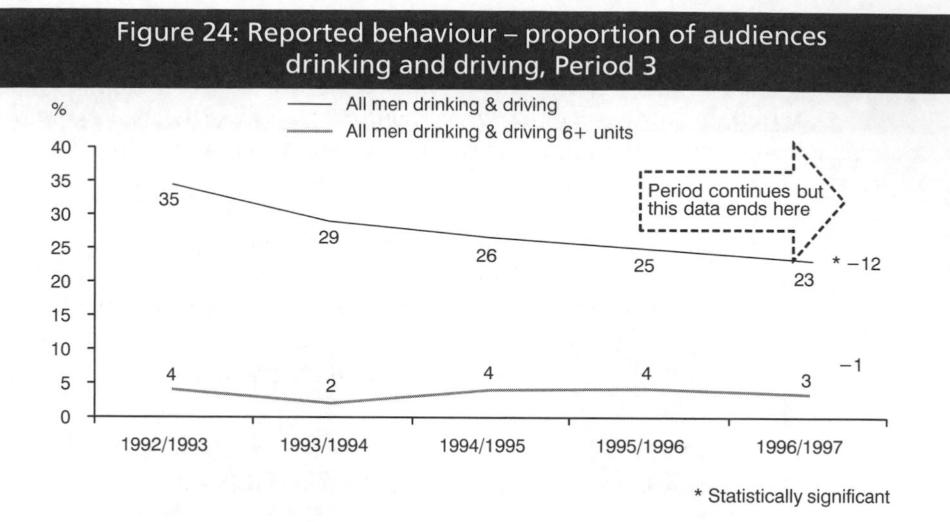


Source: DfT Tracking Research International

Further indication of changing behaviours amongst all male drivers and young male drivers is shown by the increased levels at which they claimed to adopt strategies to avoid drink driving (Figure 25).

Figure 25: Males changes in drink drive attitudes, Period 3

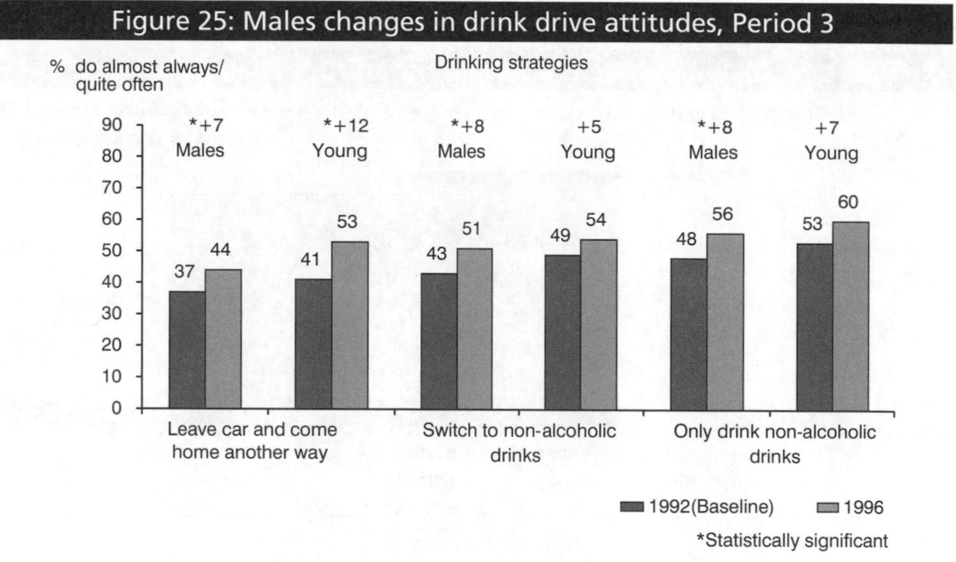


Source: DfT Tracking Research International

## Communications helped reduce drink drive casualties in Period 3

KSIs dropped from 3,380 in 1992 to 3,230 in 1986 (Figure 26). This is a smaller decrease than previous periods, but one that was achieved despite the substantial increase in wider anti-social alcohol-related behaviour. In Chapter 5 we will demonstrate the level of casualties that would have occurred in Period 3 in the absence of communications.

Figure 26: Number of drink drive related KSI's per annum (killed and seriously injured)

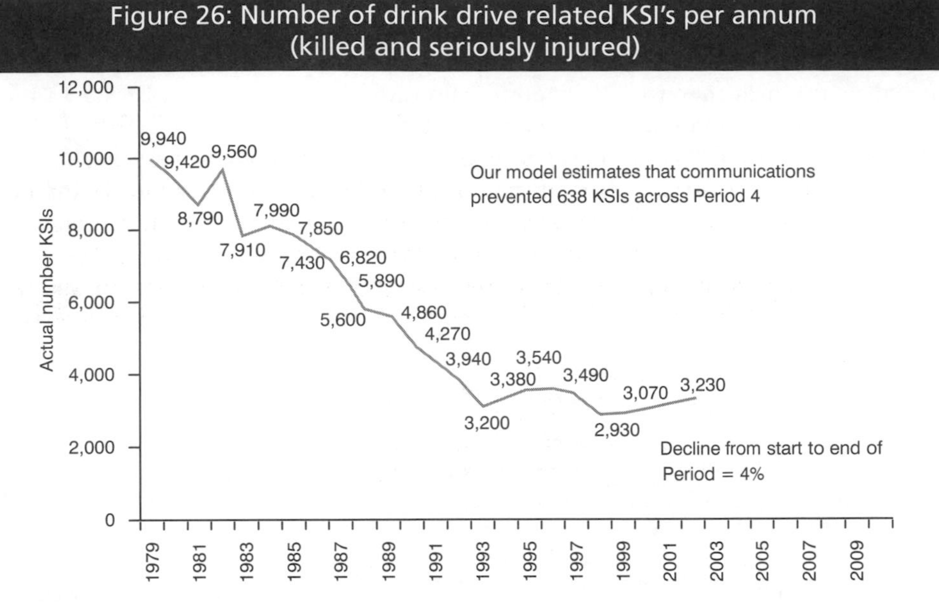


Source: DfT Tracking Research International

## Chapter 4: 2002–2010: Pinpointing the moment of decision

Table 5: Period 4: 2002–2010

| **Period** | **1** | **2** | **3** | **4** |
|---|---|---|---|---|
| Years | 1979–1987 | 1987–1992 | 1992–2002 | 2002–2009 |
| Behaviour change focus | Attitudes | Norms and drink driver perceptions | Norms and attitudes | Attitudes |
| Communications strategy | Heightening the perception of risk | Creating social unacceptability | Confronting drivers in denial | Pinpointing the moment of decision |

*Norms and driver images*: The storm of changed drinking norms and images described in the previous chapter continued to rage throughout the noughties.[27] The Government, however, was determined to turn the tide.

*Attitudes*: Young men felt that the legal alcohol limit was there specifically to give them permission to drink a certain amount and then drive. The problem was that they were unsure what this limit was. In the absence of any definitive information[28] they all created a personal rule of thumb where roughly one pint was seen to be safe, but three pints put them into risky territory.[29]

The team now identified the critical point as the decision to drink that second pint, where they weighed up the potential consequences of their behaviour. This was the stage at which they were not too impaired to control themselves, when a one-pint-after-another domino effect could still be short-circuited and where they could be realistically prevented from becoming dangerous drink drivers.

The challenge was to change attitudes in a way that would resonate in the heat of the moment. The team set out to seed doubt in the minds of the potential drink driver at the very moment in which they decide to have a second pint.

Three successive campaigns found increasingly compelling ways to contrast consumption with its consequences and pinpoint the moment of second pint decision through both creative and media (Figure 27).

- 2002–2003: tackling the excuses behind the decision
  Tackled universal excuses used to justify the decision to have that extra pint.
- 2004–2006: juxtaposing decision with consequences to *others*
  Showing a pub table at which young men are just about to have a second pint crash into a passing girl.
- 2006–present: juxtaposing decision with consequences to *you*
  As a young man orders another drink a barman acts out the legal and personal consequences – being processed, prosecuted, losing your license, job and the respect of others.

### *The results: how tackling drivers' denial worked*

In this period communications successfully got inside the heads of young male drivers, ensuring that changed attitudes and an understanding of the consequences of drink driving resonated at the moment of second pint decision, helping reduce drink drive casualties.

#### Drink drive communications got inside young male drivers' heads in Period 4

Campaigns in this period delivered higher awareness and cut-through than had previously been achieved, particularly so amongst the young male driver target audience. In addition, half of young male drivers felt that the moment of decision message 'really stuck in their minds' (Figure 28).[30]

#### Drink drive communications helped change attitudes towards the 'second pint'

We see gains on the key measure related to the second pint decision. These are slight as we might expect given the difficulty of incremental attitude change with entrenched audiences (Figure 29).

## Figure 27: Advertising 2002 to present: the decisive moment

| 2002–2003<br>Excuses | 2004–2006<br>Crash | 2006–Present<br>Moment of doubt |
|---|---|---|
|  |  |  |
| Challenging the universal excuses men use to justify their decision to drink drive, this time resulting in hitting a young girl on a bike. | Juxtaposing the decision to have another pint with the consequences to others. A pub table hits a passing woman, like a car on the road. | Showing the legal and personal consequences of drink driving, focusing advertising and media on the specific moment when the second pint decision is made. |

Source: agencies Abbott Mead Vickers and Leo Burnett

## Figure 28: Campaign salience – spontaneous awareness of drink drive publicity and TV campaign recognition, Period 4

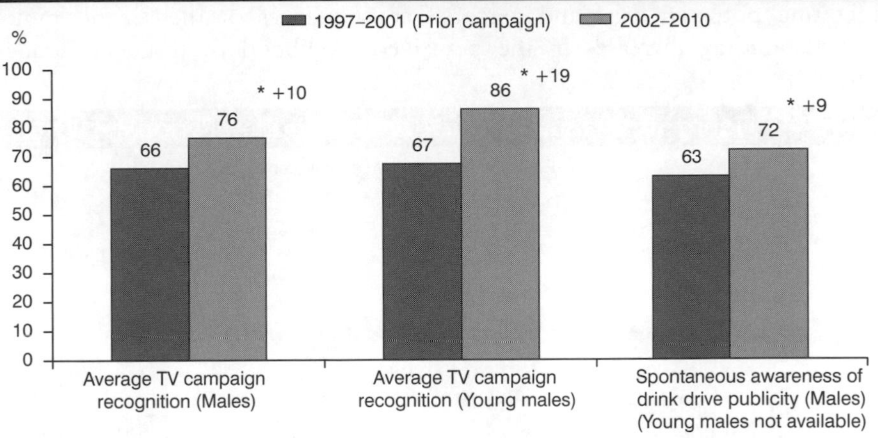


Source: DfT Tracking TNS/BMRB

Figure 29: Changes in drink drive attitudes, Period 4

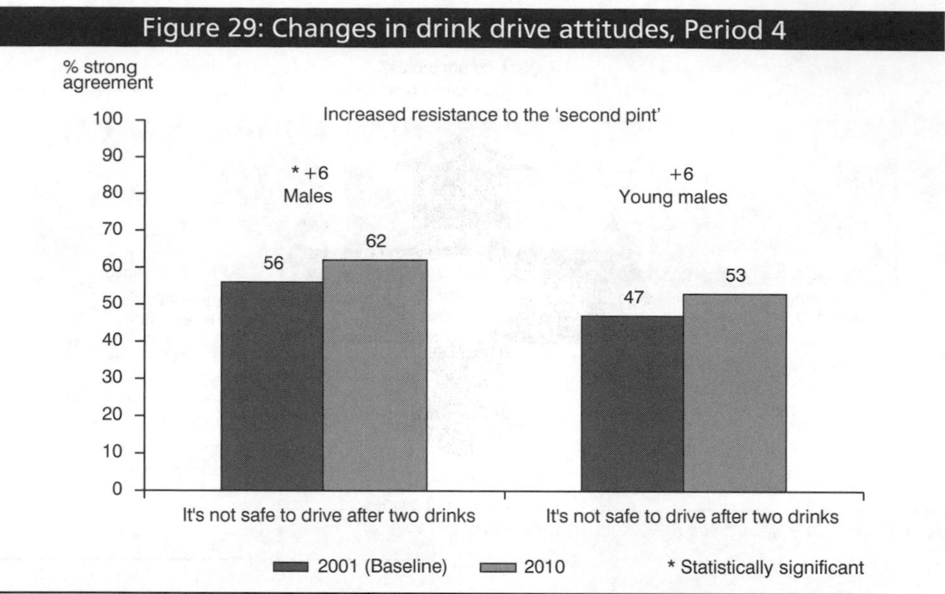


Source: DfT Tracking TNS

The last campaign found a compelling way to tackle the decision moment – highlighting potential legal and personal consequences of the second pint. We see corresponding increases in the perceived likelihood of those consequences (Figure 30).

Figure 30: Changes in drink drive attitudes, Period 4

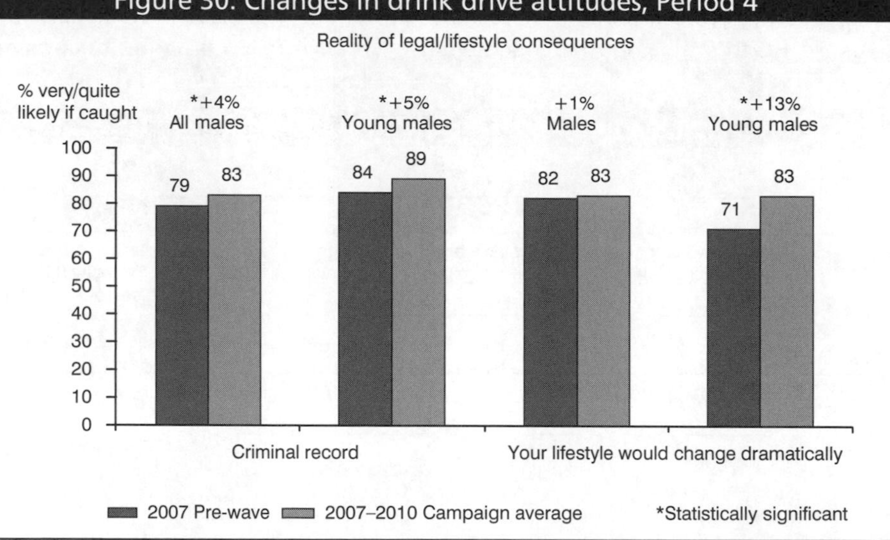


Source: DfT Tracking

In addition, we see a campaign effect in the increased perceived likelihood of those consequences amongst campaign recognisers (Figure 31).[31]

Figure 31: Male ad recognisers vs. non-recognisers (campaign aggregate)

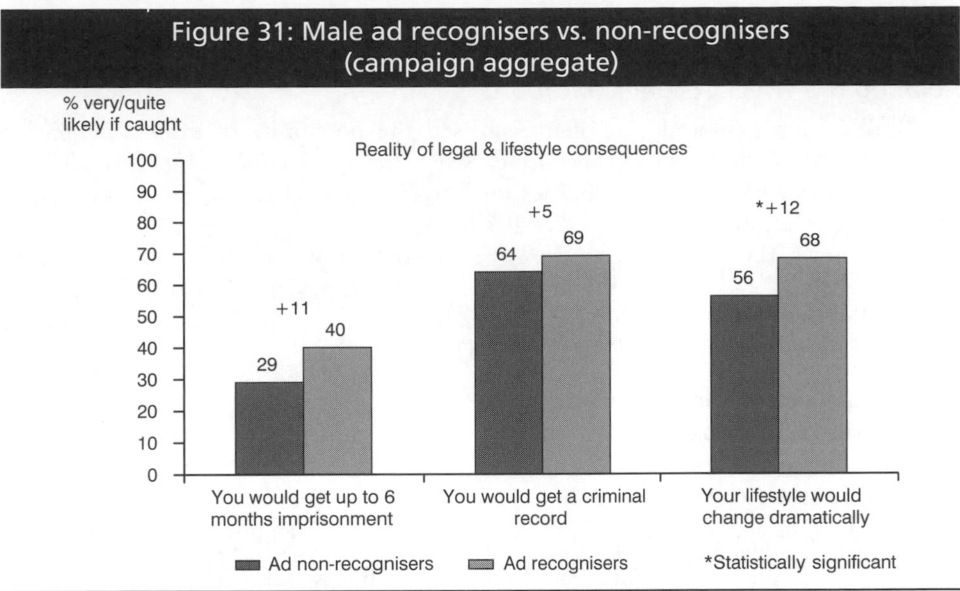


Source: DfT Tracking

## Drink drive communications helped reduce drink drive casualties

*Helping deliver substantial reduction in KSIs*

Annual KSIs more than halved, dropping from 3,340 in 2002 to 1,480 in 2010. Communications were responsible for a substantial proportion of casualties prevented (Figure 32).

Figure 32: Number of drink drive related KSIs per annum

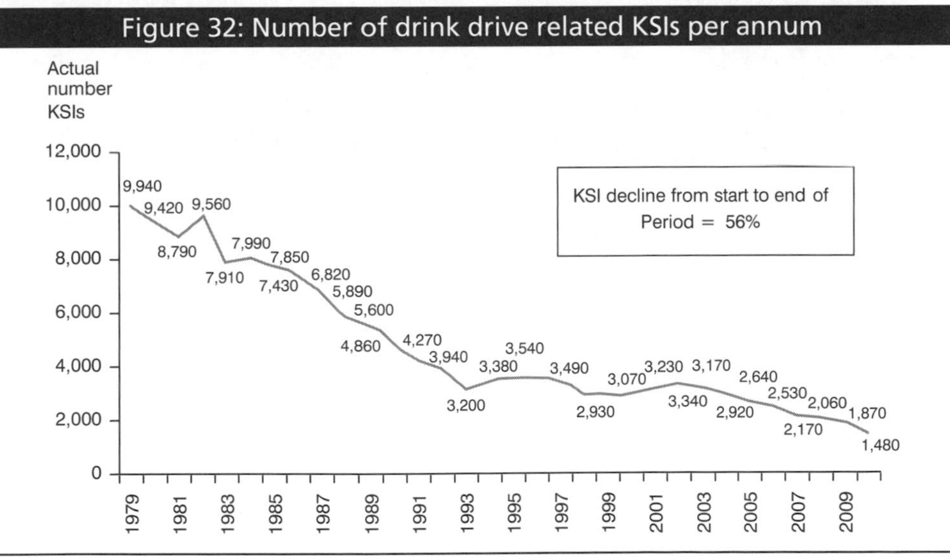


Source: Department for Transport

## Chapter 5: Calculating the savings to society

### *Isolating the effect of communications*

In 2010 a team explored and then dismissed the possibility of evaluating recent communication effects on drink drive KSIs through econometric modelling.[32] However, in reviewing the possibilities for longer term evaluation, Holmes & Cook identified a solution which was elegantly simple.

Significantly, this model is based on the *proportion* of total KSIs represented by drink drive KSIs, rather than the absolute *level* of drink drive KSIs. As such, some potentially powerful factors that can reasonably be deemed to equally affect KSIs of all types can be excluded from the model. These include:

- improvements in vehicle safety;
- road engineering;
- traffic volumes;
- wider road safety legislation.

Holmes & Cook investigated the effect on drink drive KSIs of a range of factors known or hypothesised to influence drink driving behaviour.[33] The key factors are accounted for in the model:

- drink drive enforcement – represented by volumes of breath tests, the police's key enforcement measure;
- drink drive legislation – represented by 1991 legislation[34] and, implicitly, by 1983 legislation introducing evidential breath testing that is reflected in breath test volumes;
- economic factors – represented by unemployment rates;[35]
- weather conditions;[36]
- drink drive communications – represented by media spend across the four periods.[37]

A number of other factors were explored but discounted as either having no effect on drink drive KSIs or being influenced by factors already included:

- petrol prices;
- number of pubs;
- the smoking ban.

### *Quantifying the effects of communication on drink drive KSIs*

The impact of communication on drink drive KSIs can be derived directly from the model (Figure 33). From 1988 onwards we see an increased proportion of KSIs that would have been represented by drink drive KSIs in the absence of communications.

Figure 33: Drink drive KSIs as a proportion of all KSIs – actual vs. without communication

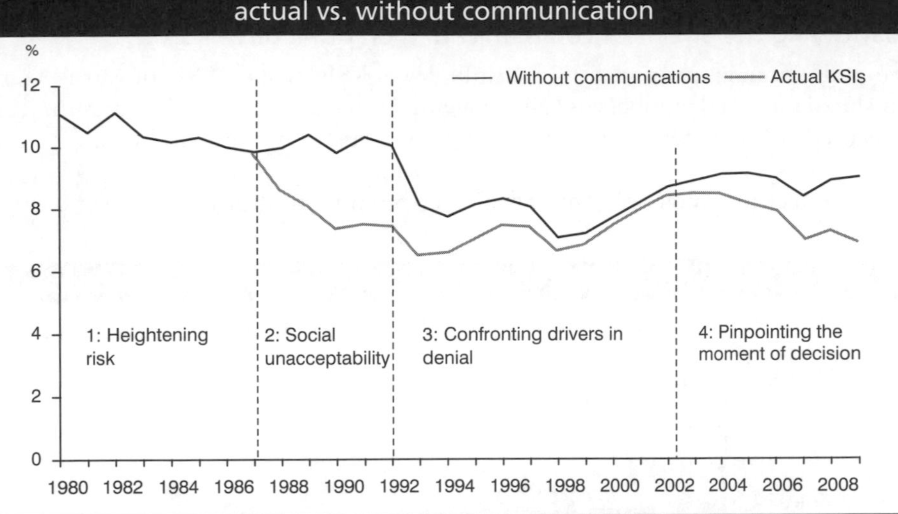


Source: Holmes & Cook

### *Assessing the effect of each period of communication*

The marked attitudinal changes seen in Period 1 (1979–1987) are not reflected in a reduction in the proportion of drink drive KSIs within the same period. However, they appear to have laid the groundwork for substantial KSI prevention in Period 2 (1987–1992).

The model shows that, without communication in Period 2, the drink drive proportion of KSIs would have remained around 10% throughout the late 80s until recession in the early 90s, driven by a buoyant economy and relatively low levels of breath testing.

Instead, communications that made drink driving socially unacceptable delivered major immediate reductions in KSIs. These reductions persisted, building with campaign weight over a number of years.

In Period 3 (1992–2002), in the face of a wider culture of intoxication, we see that communications focusing on the 'quick drink' held drink drive KSIs to lower levels than would otherwise have been seen.

The change of strategy in Period 4 to focus on the second pint moment proved decisive, with another more persistent reduction between 2003 and 2009.

Interestingly, in Periods 2 and 4 the model reveals a hitherto undetected longevity of effect for drink drive communications. Thirty per cent of their total effect came in year one with three-quarters by year four. This offers significant learnings for the planning of future activity.

*Return on investment*

## Quantifying the effects of communication on drink drive KSIs

The reduction in proportion of drink drive KSIs from 1988 onwards can be translated into total numbers of KSIs prevented (Figure 34). In total, communications prevented 12,305 people being killed or seriously injured as a result of drink driving.

This effect is comparable with road safety communications effects demonstrated previously.[38]

Figure 34: Drink drive KSIs prevented as a result of communications

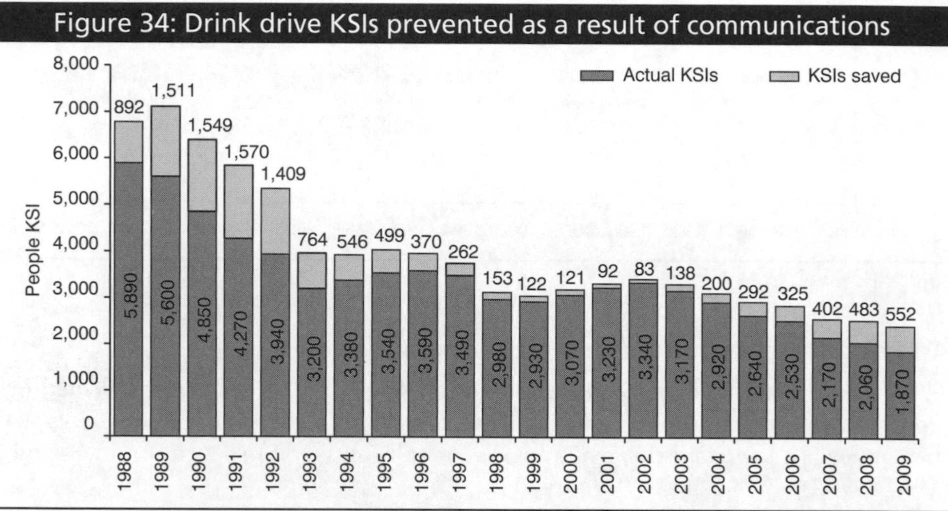


Source: Holmes & Cook

## Calculating the value of drink drive KSI reductions to society

The DfT calculates the cost of casualties to society based on a willingness to pay (WTP) approach encompassing human costs (e.g. pain, grief and suffering), direct economic costs (e.g. lost output) and medical costs.

These costs are high and so any reduction delivers huge savings (Table 6).

Table 6: Cost to society per casualty

| Casualty type | Cost per casualty (£) |
|---|---|
| Fatal | 1,585,510 |
| Serious | 178,160 |

Source: Reported Road Casualties in Great Britain, 2010 Annual Report

### *Calculating ROI*

Calculating a single ROI figure for a period of 30 years becomes unworkable, as media costs have varied so greatly in that time. Instead we show the ROI for each period (Table 7).

**Table 7: ROI breakdown**

| Period | Strategy | Media spend £m (current prices) | Lives saved | Serious injuries prevented | Value of lives and injuries saved £m[39] | Ratio of value to media spend |
|---|---|---|---|---|---|---|
| 1979–1986 | Heightening the sense of risk | 5,234 | | | | |
| 1987–1991 | Creating social unacceptability | 7,810 | 1,512 | 7,937 | 2,006 | 154 |
| 1994–2001 | Tackling drivers in denial | 15,444 | 102 | 536 | 183 | 11.8 |
| 2002–2009 | Targeting the moment of decision | 20,440 | 355 | 1,863 | 786 | 38.4 |
| | **Totals** | | **1,969** | **10,336** | **2,975** | |

Given the role of Period 1 in laying the groundwork for Period 2, the ROI for these periods is combined showing a ROI of £154 for every £1 spent. In the tough cultural conditions of Period 3 this fell to a return of 11.8 to 1, before rising to 38.4 to 1 in Period 4.

These represent significant savings to society, and compare well to a wide range of ROI on Government campaigns. The TDA Teacher Recruitment campaign demonstrated an ROI of 101:1.[40] Recent crime prevention papers have shown payback between 14:1[41] and 28:1.[42]

Against any of these high standards, this activity has been very successful.

### *Behaviour change learnings*

This review reveals a powerful approach for reducing negative behaviour:

1. change attitudes;
2. create powerful new norms around desired behaviour;
3. force those in denial to apply these norms to their own behaviour;
4. make their new understanding resonate at the moment of decision.

*This paper clearly demonstrates that communications can effect significant behavioural change and sustain that change. Through impactful, insight-led creative approaches advertising has successfully tackled even the more entrenched drink drivers.*

Emma Stranack, Deputy Director, External Communications, Department for Transport

## Notes

1 Andrew Darnton's 'Overview of behaviour change models and their uses' for Government Social Research (2008) identifies Gibbons and Gerrard's Prototype/Willingness Model (2003) as the best model for predicting and influencing drink driving behaviour. These three factors are taken from that model.
2 That very year, one George Smith was the first person to be charged with drink driving when he crashed his taxi into the front of 165 New Bond Street.
3 Drew, G.C. (1959) *Effect of Small Doses of Alcohol on a Skill Resembling Driving*. London: Medical Research Council.
4 The Road Safety Act of 1967 introduced a blood alcohol limit and a new drink driving criminal offence.
5 The proportion of crashes where alcohol was a factor had fallen from 25% to 15% from 1967 to 1968; however, from 1968 to 1975 this rose steadily to exceed 35% (DfT statistics).
6 BMRB Tracking for DfT, 1979.
7 Ibid.
8 Ibid.
9 Breed, W. & De Foe, J.R. (1950–1982) Drinking and smoking on television. *Journal of Public Health Policy*, 5, 2 (June 1984). Over the next 30 years alcohol portrayal in the media would become ever more pervasive without becoming any more representative of the dangers. Source: Coyne, S.M. & Ahmed, T. (2009) Fancy a pint? Alcohol use and smoking in soap operas. *Addiction Research & Theory*, 17, 4, pp. 345–359.
10 At least nine creative agencies have worked with DfT on this campaign. For simplicity, we refer to them collectively as 'the team' throughout: 1979–1982: Wasey Campbell Ewald; 1983: Lowe; 1984–1986: Davidson Pearce; 1987–1989: Waldron Allen Henry; 1990: Miller and Leaves, W/K&R; 1991–1997: D'Arcy Masius Benton & Bowles; 1998–2004: Abbott Mead and Vickers; 2004–present: Leo Burnett.
11 The amount they felt they could safely drink without it affecting their driving.
12 The DfT tracking methodology from 1979 to 1997 used a diary approach to get an accurate picture of drink drive behaviour. It disguised interest in drinking and driving by looking separately at drinking occasions and how the respondent left the venue. The recorded levels proved consistent with behaviour from other sources and therefore, although provided by respondents, they offer a more reliable indicator than more standard 'claimed behaviour' approaches in this field.
13 Small sample sizes preclude comparison with young male drivers on this measure.
14 Small sample sizes preclude comparison with young male drivers on this measure.
15 Young male drivers drinking 6+ units fell 9% from 21% to 12% over the six years from 1979 to 1986 compared with a drop of 7% in just five years in Period 2, and this was coming from a lower (i.e. more difficult) baseline.
16 Measham, F. & Brain, K. (2005) Binge drinking, British alcohol policy and the new culture of intoxication. *Crime, Media, Culture: an International Journal*, 1, 3.
17 Measham, F. (2002) 'Binge drinking': the meanings, motivations and management of contemporary alcohol consumption. Unpublished conference paper, American Society of Criminology Annual Meeting, Nashville, USA.
18 Duffy (1991), May (1992) referenced in Aldridge, J., Measham, F. & Williams, L. (2011) *Illegal Leisure Revisited: Changing Patterns of Alcohol and Drug Use in Adolescents and Young Adults*. New York: Routledge.
19 Brain, K. & Parker, H. (1997) *Drinking with Design: Alcopops, Designer Drinks and Youth Culture*. London: The Portman Group.
20 Brain, K. (2000) Youth Alcohol and the Emergence of the Post-Modern Alcohol Order. Occasional Paper No.1, London Institute of Alcohol Studies.
21 Measham, F. & Brain, K. (2005) Binge drinking, British alcohol policy and the new culture of intoxication. *Crime, Media, Culture: an International Journal*, 1, 3.
22 The circulation of the top four young men's magazines more than doubled from 1995 to 2002. Source: ABC.
23 *Loaded*'s launch issue in 1994 proudly proclaimed '*Loaded* is...drinking, eating, playing and living. *Loaded* is the man who believes he can do ANYTHING.' James Brown, Editor. *Loaded Magazine*, 1, May. IPC Publishing.
24 Annie Wicks, APG Creative Planning Awards, 1995.
25 Tara Macleod, APG Creative Planning Awards, 1997.
26 Due to a questionnaire change in 1996 we are unable to compare attitudes at the start and end of the Period, but we can look separately at 1992 to 1996 and then 1997 to 2002.

27 Measham, F. (2006) The new policy mix: alcohol, harm minimisation, and determined drunkenness in contemporary society. *International Journal of Drug Policy,* 17, pp. 258–268.
28 The amount of alcohol an individual would need to drink to be considered drink driving varies depending on weight, gender, age, what they've eaten, metabolism and so on.
29 Davies McKerr qualitative research for DfT throughout Period 4.
30 TNS Tracking for DfT throughout Period 4.
31 Recogniser–non-recogniser data is unavailable for young male drivers as too few did not recognise the communication to create a sufficient sample size.
32 From DfT, Leo Burnett and Holmes & Cook.
33 This is a widely researched area, with many sources to draw on.
34 The Road Traffic Act of 1991 introduced a new offence of 'Causing death by driving while under the influence of alcohol or drugs' which carried a compulsory prison sentence of up to five years. Media spend and any effects of it in the two years following the introduction of the act are inseparable from the legislative effect and so have not been included in the ROI calculations shown later.
35 Employment rates produced better statistical and forecasting properties than variables such as GDP and alcohol affordability.
36 Good summer weather, which affects road usage and drinking behaviour.
37 Wider road safety communications did not show an effect on the proportion of drink drive KSIs.
38 The 2010 THINK! IPA paper demonstrated that up to 6,594 KSIs were prevented by THINK! activity between 2000 and 2008. The drink drive model estimates that, over this period, drink drive communications accounted for 2,258 of these, or just over a third. Drink drive communications represented 55% of total road safety media spend in that period, so might be expected to represent a significant proportion of the KSIs prevented. Docherty, N., Harris, R., Hodge, W. & Dorsett, J. (2010) THINK! 2000–2008: how one word helped save a thousand lives. Institute of Practitioners in Advertising: Silver, IPA Effectiveness Awards 2010.
39 Calculated by taking the total KSIs prevented in that period, dividing between Killed and Seriously Injured in line with overall ratio and multiplying by appropriate value from WTP valuation for the period.
40 Boyd, D., Vass, A., Smith, A. & Caig, J. (2010) TDA teacher recruitment best in class: how influencing behaviour with a new media strategy helped nudge teacher recruitment to record levels. Institute of Practitioners in Advertising: Gold, IPA Effectiveness Awards 2010.
41 Huntley, A., Roberts, E. & Sawers, S. (2008) Home Office – cutting the cost of crime. Institute of Practitioners in Advertising: Gold, IPA Effectiveness Awards 2008.
42 Cook, L. & James, E. (2006) The Home Office: crime doesn't pay – but advertising to stop it does: how communications empowered the nation to protect themselves from vehicle crime. Institute of Practitioners in Advertising: Gold, IPA Effectiveness Awards 2006.

## Chapter 12

# Digital UK

## Leaving no-one behind

**By Beth Thoren, DIGITAL UK; Rachell Fox, SWITCHOVER HELP SCHEME; Chris Baker, DLKW Lowe; Emma Reeve and Anthony Morrison, MediaCom; Carola Breuning, DIGITAL UK**

Contributing authors: Sophie Reeve, DIGITAL UK; Jon Wilson, MediaCom; Richard Warren and Zoe Verrion, DLKW Lowe

Credited companies: Creative Agency: DLKW Lowe; Direct Marketing Agency: Elvis; Media Agency: MediaCom; JointEntrant: DIGITAL UK; JointEntrant: MediaCom; Client: DIGITAL UK

### Editor's summary

The scale and complexity of digital switchover presented a huge implementation challenge. The fear of blank screens, which could cause the programme to be derailed, was very real. The UK had to be 100% ready, but success depended on providing information, help and reassurance to the last 10% of analogue viewers who were often fearful of change. Working together, Digital UK and the BBC Switchover Help Scheme overcame that challenge by focusing on those people most marketers leave behind: older, disabled and minority audiences. The end result, beyond the large net benefits realised, was to transform a potentially negative situation into a quiet success story. It is estimated the campaign returned a minimum payback of £4.70 for every £1 spent. Given the Herculean challenge Digital UK faced in communicating the digital switchover to the population, this campaign represents an extraordinary marketing achievement. The judges also felt the paper was a brilliant example of meticulous channel planning.

*Analogue switchoff is vastly more complex, with more potential for chaos and consumer revolt than any other civilian project in our history, including North Sea gas conversion and decimalisation.*

David Elstein, then CEO of Channel 5 – Commons Select Committee, 2005

As we near successful completion of digital switchover, it's hard to remember just how challenging the task looked when announced in 2005.

Strong concerns were voiced at the Select Committee,[1] many centred on the risk that the old and vulnerable would lose their TV lifeline. Media coverage was predictably negative, with nervousness in the highest places, right down to concerns about the negative effect of a problematic Granada switchover in late 2009 on the General Election result (Figure 1).

Figure 1: A sample of media coverage

Despite its benefits, switchover presented a huge implementation challenge, with little precedent in the scale and complexity of delivery involved.[2]

Blank screens on switchover days could have led to the project being aborted, or delayed, costing the government between £250m and £300m a year in lost revenue from spectrum sales (as well as political embarrassment).[3]

'Leaving no one behind' was central to our remit from government. So while most marketers naturally focus on the easiest-to-convert target consumers, our critical success factor was the complete opposite – ensuring 100% of UK households were ready, which depended heavily on converting the last 10% of analogue viewers, often highly resistant to or fearful of change.

This paper focuses on regions completed by the end of 2011[4] and the essential roles played by communications – via both Digital UK and related Switchover Help Scheme campaigns – to deliver digital switchover:

- *Effectively* – hitting targets set with the government to achieve switchover with minimum consumer or media backlash.

- *Cost-efficiently* – savings versus initial budgets via continuous improvement, and versus alternative courses of action and external benchmarks.
- *Protecting the vulnerable* – leaving no-one behind and making the experience as stress-free as possible.

## Digital switchover – background

### *The public context*

Following the announcement of digital switchover, Digital UK (DUK) was set up at the request of government to manage the process. At this point (April 2005) one third of households (nearly 9 million homes) – and over half of over-75s – were analogue-only, watching just channels 1 to 5. A quarter of the UK could not get digital TV through an aerial (Freeview) because the power of the digital signal had to be kept down so as not to interfere with analogue TV.

Digital penetration was increasing, but in 2004 DTI/Generics[5] forecast that (without switchover) digital take-up would plateau at 70% to 80%, and the remaining 5 million to 8 million homes would never adopt digital TV. They also noted a lack of public enthusiasm for switchover:

> *Switchover is an unpopular policy that people see as coercive.... After being informed of the practicalities and implications of switchover, 38% of respondents agreed with switchover and 50% disagreed.*
>
> DTI/Generics Report 2004

Most people were affected, many needing to pay a significant amount for something they didn't necessarily want (OFCOM estimated households would pay over £100 on average). In Autumn 2005, the DUK/OFCOM tracker survey showed that more than a third of the UK thought that switchover was 'unfair or unjust' (Figure 2).

**Figure 2: Which of these statements best describes what you think about switchover?**

| | |
|---|---|
| Unfair | 36% |
| Have to get on with it | 41% |
| Benefits for me or UK | 19% |

Source: DUK/BMRB, November 2005

### *The remit from government*

DUK's objectives were set by government:

- ensure universal access to digital versions of public service channels via an aerial (i.e. Freeview);
- ensure the interests of older people and other vulnerable groups are protected;
- clear 14 frequency channels for reuse, releasing this 'spectrum' for sale.

We had to bring people with us, making switchover as stress-free as possible, and also be commercially impartial. Funding for the communications campaign was via a ring-fenced portion of the BBC licence fee – with any underspend returned to government.[6]

Digital UK worked in close partnership with the BBC's Switchover Help Scheme. Above-the-line communications for both DUK and Help Scheme elements were delivered initially by AMV BBDO, then DLKW Lowe since 2010, and MediaCom.

### *The Switchover Help Scheme*

This government designed scheme provided everything people aged 75 or over or eligible disabled needed to switch one TV to digital – information, equipment, installation, retuning and aftercare. It offered a range of choices – with a standard option costing £40, free if on income-related benefits (Figure 3). 7.15 million households were eligible.

**Figure 3: A Switchover Help Scheme press ad**

Don't lose your TV channels.
If you're 75 and over or eligible disabled you can get help switching to digital TV.
The switch to digital TV is coming, so you need to get ready. The Switchover Help Scheme has helped hundreds of thousands of people switch to digital and can provide everything you need to keep watching your TV.
• Easy-to-use equipment
• An approved installer to supply and install the equipment for you
• A 12 month aftercare service including a free helpline
This service is available for just £40 all-inclusive or is free if you're eligible and on certain income-related benefits.
Everyone who is entitled to help will receive an information pack from the Help Scheme.
But if you'd like to apply now, call us free on 0800 40 85 900
BBC The Switchover Help Scheme is run by the BBC

*Operational challenges*

The switchover timetable was operationally driven, rolling out regionally across 60 transmitter areas, with different switchover dates, footprints and local media availability (Figure 4).

Figure 4: Switchover roll-out

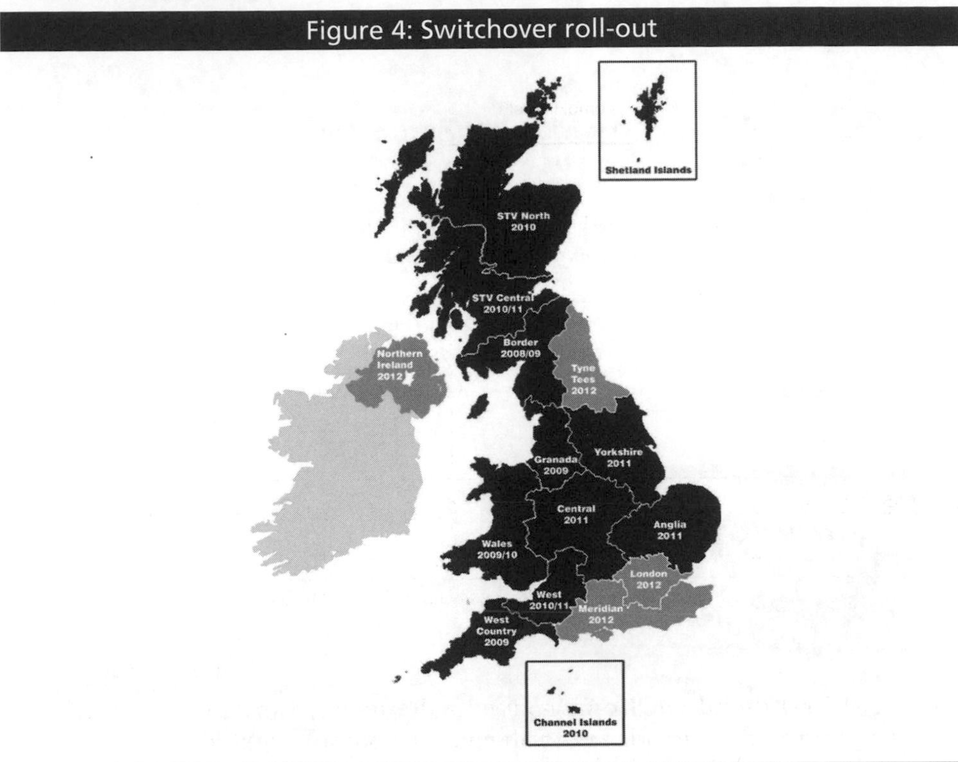


When communications started in 2006 it was estimated that:

- 79% of households were affected – needing to upgrade to digital and/or retune their Freeview equipment at switchover.
- 10% of households also needed rooftop aerials upgrading.
- 14% needed to replace an internal set top aerial; video recorders were also affected.
- Only the 21% who were entirely satellite or cable were unaffected.

The task was complicated further by:

- Millions with Freeview assuming they were unaffected.
- A vast amount of information to deliver, some affecting only small numbers of people in targeted locations (e.g. aerial issues, redundant equipment).
- DUK's need to be impartial meant we had to present *all* digital options.
- Overlapping transmitter areas (houses on the same street could switch at different times!), meaning communications had to be tightly targeted and caveated (Figure 5).

## Figure 5: Examples of complex consumer messaging requirements

**IMPORTANT:** Don't lose your channels. Prepare for the digital switchover on 29 February* 2012

If you have:

**Freeview, BT Vision, or Top Up TV**
Re-tune on 29 February and 14 March to avoid losing channels.

**Sky TV, Freesat from Sky, freesat or Virgin Media**
If you have one of these services on **all** your TVs, you won't need to do anything.

**Analogue TV (i.e. five channels or fewer)**
Convert your TV to digital or you will lose your channels.

**WARNING:**
**Freeview* viewers will lose TV channels at switchover**

Two Stages: 7 September
21 September

To get your channels back, re-tune your digital TV or box on or after 7 September and again on or after 21 September.

Switchover dates vary depending on where you live. To check your dates, enter your postcode at **digitaluk.co.uk** or call **08456 50 50 50.**

How to re-tune using your TV remote

Make sure your Freeview TV or box is on and in digital mode. Press 'menu' on your remote control.

Select the 'set up' or 'installation' option. If you see picture icons, select the tool box, satellite dish or spanner. If you are prompted for a code, try 0000 or 1234.

Select the **full re-tune** option. This is sometimes called 'first time installation', 'factory reset', 'default settings' or 'shipping conditions'. Do not select 'channel update' or 'add channels'. Press 'OK' if your equipment asks if you want to delete all your channels. Don't worry, this is normal.

Channels will automatically be installed. This may take a few minutes and your equipment may shut down and restart.

These instructions are a guide only. Product specific instructions can be found at **digitaluk.co.uk/retuning.**

**For more information on re-tuning call 08456 50 50 50** **get set for digital**

**Your Help Scheme options summary**

**Each of these options is explained in more detail on the following pages.**

| | Options | Equipment, delivery and installation cost |
|---|---|---|
| Freeview | 1. Standard option - Freeview digital box | £40 |
| freesat | 2. freesat digital box and satellite dish | £60 |
| Freeview | 3. Freeview HD digital box | £158 |
| | Freeview+ digital TV recorder | £202 |
| | Smart Talk Freeview digital box | £119 |
| freesat | 4. freesat HD digital box | £111 |
| | freesat+ HD digital TV recorder | £249 |

There are no subscriptions with any of these options.

*Consumer challenges*

These technical issues meant that the population was highly segmented in terms of what they had to do and the specific information they needed, as well as their capability/propensity to engage and respond to switchover communications.

Figure 6 shows the change in digital penetration from the start of DUK communications to the beginning of 2011. While digital penetration had increased, 71% still had to do something in upcoming 2011 and 2012 areas.

While the Freeview retune task mushroomed, analogue main set households declined to 9% and remain at circa 10% in areas not switched yet.

Figure 6: Digital status 2006–2011

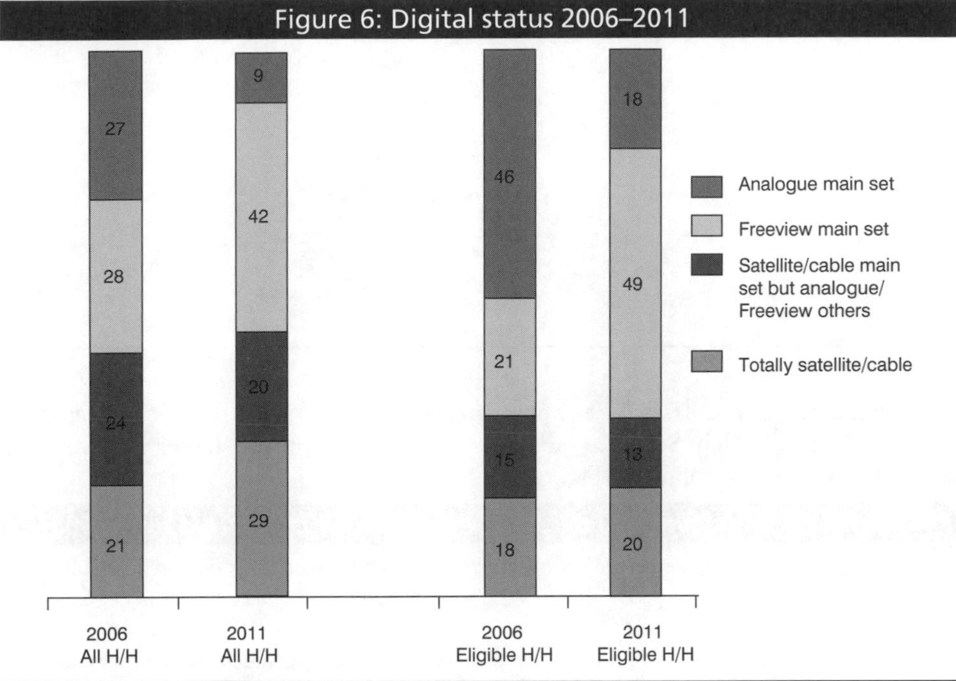


Source: All households – 26 million. Help Scheme eligible households – 7.15 million.

2006 data April/June, total UK (start of national DUK comms); 2011 based on Jan–March, only areas still to complete switchover

Those within the last 10% presented a real challenge. Indeed, seven years after the announcement of switchover, and with hundreds of millions[7] spent by Sky, Virgin, BT and Freeview selling digital TV to UK households, we are still facing circa 10% analogue-only households in the final 2012 switchover areas (as well as big secondary set tasks).

Though diverse, the 'last 10%' tend to be resistant to change, fearful of technology, often C2DE women 55+ living alone. (Half of this group was eligible for the Help Scheme, half was not.)

Some – with information, reassurance and support from family or friends – could cope themselves. Our challenge was to address those who 'don't do technology', or would otherwise struggle for different reasons (chaotic lives, dementia, learning difficulties, isolation) (Figure 7).

Figure 7: Understanding the last 10%

Understanding the last 10% was a major focus for the extensive research undertaken by the Help Scheme and DUK,[8] and became a prime factor in brand and communications development (Figure 8).

Figure 8: Research with vulnerable people (The Futures Company 2008)

'I just don't want the change… we just want to be left to get on with our old age.'
'2012 – I might not be here then!'
75+, Cardiff

'The thought of all things going like this sort of actually terrifies me. I mean I have never used, ever used a DVD player. I never used a video recorder, never got into the hang of using them.'
Professional carer, Birmingham

'If you're talking to people who have only got 5 channels you're going to bamboozle them if you start saying 200 channels you know people are going to get absolutely… confused… scared to death.'
Mental health, Birmingham

'They're getting a government licence to take advantage of vulnerable people.'
Informal carer, Glasgow

We carried out extensive qualitative research with carers and charities, as well as group and depth interviews with a huge range of eligible people: those aged 75 or over, and those with disabilities including those who were blind or partially sighted, or had mental health problems, learning disabilities and physical disabilities. While all are likely to resist or have difficulties switching to digital presented challenges, the most at risk was a highly socially isolated group comprising circa 1% of all households, neither likely to engage with conventional campaigns themselves nor having a strong support network (Figure 9).

**Figure 9: Consumer letter**

**"I need a TV because my family have died and I have no other support. "**

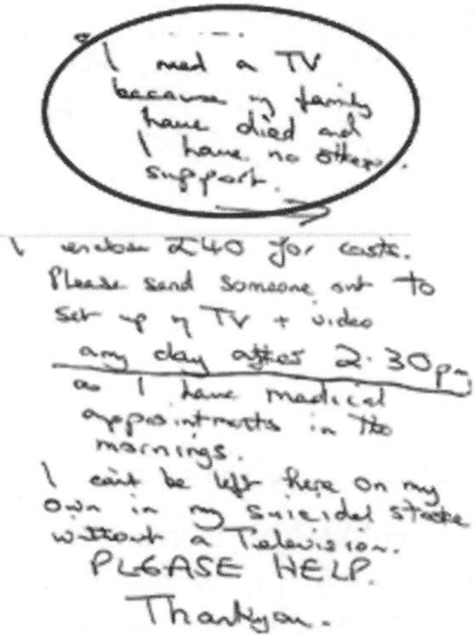

I need a TV because my family have died and I have no other support.

I enclose £40 for costs.
Please send someone out to set up my TV + video any day after 2.30pm as I have medical appointments in the mornings.
I can't be left here on my own in my suicidal state without a Television.
PLEASE HELP.
Thankyou.

*In summary – a very challenging task*

See Figure 10.

**Figure 10: Switchover: a challenging task**

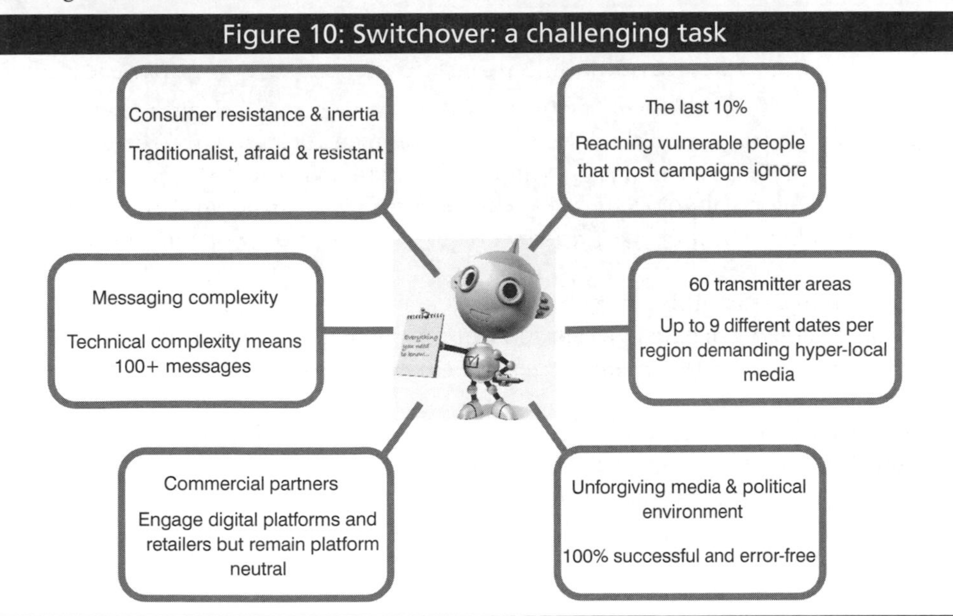
Consumer resistance & inertia
Traditionalist, afraid & resistant
The last 10%
Reaching vulnerable people that most campaigns ignore
Messaging complexity
Technical complexity means 100+ messages
60 transmitter areas
Up to 9 different dates per region demanding hyper-local media
Commercial partners
Engage digital platforms and retailers but remain platform neutral
Unforgiving media & political environment
100% successful and error-free

## What we learned and what we did

### *Research and learning*

Throughout the process we have maximised opportunities to learn and refine during regional roll-out. In addition to extensive qualitative research, a monthly face-to-face tracker monitored key awareness and switchover status metrics. This ran in every sub-region during switchover, amongst both people eligible for the Help Scheme and the broader audience. Awareness tracking informed media planning, ensuring that targets were consistently met without unnecessary spend.

This, and learnings from other IPA Award-winning campaigns such as London Congestion Charging and Stroke Awareness, produced a number of key insights that drove the development and evolution of communications and their effectiveness.

### *Brand development and creative evolution*

#### Learning: Attempts to 'sell' the benefits of a mandatory change are seen as disingenuous.

They are also counterproductive, as the key barrier for many remaining analogue viewers is discomfort with technology and change. People want clarity on what they have to do, and help doing it.

The fundamental need to provide help and reassurance guided our brand values and permeated everything we did – identity, iconography, call centre and web support and on-the-ground help (Figure 11).

Creatively, we needed to develop a vehicle that could visualise 'help', which we did with 'DigitAl', the friendly robot.

Figure 11: Brand values

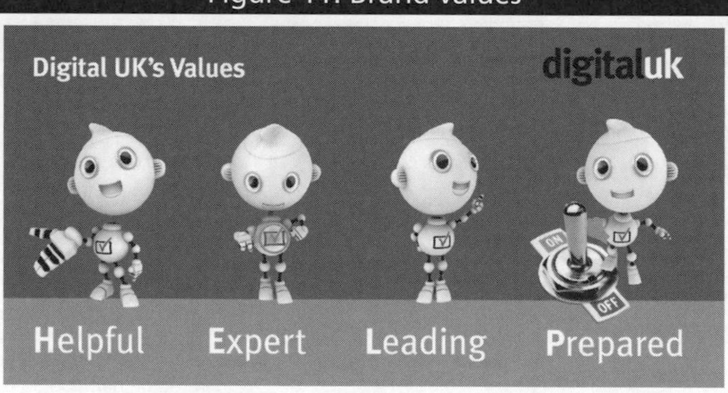


We created an 'open source' set of brand assets with the 'get set for digital' logo that partners such as retailers, manufacturers and local government could use, creating a groundswell of support (Figure 12).

We developed a partner brand for the Help Scheme, also using DigitAl but a different colour scheme and imagery explicitly reflecting older and disabled people (as they are rarely targeted by advertisers and easily assume advertising is not for them) (Figure 13).

Figure 12: Examples of third party asset use

We put great emphasis on making technical messages accessible to a multitude of audiences. Our 20-page leaflet, despite necessarily containing over a hundred different messages, was considered 'easy-to-understand' by 94% of consumers.

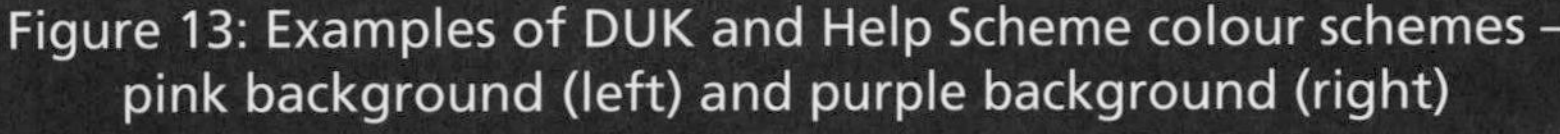
Figure 13: Examples of DUK and Help Scheme colour schemes – pink background (left) and purple background (right)

Working with expert organisations such as RNIB, Mencap and the COI we produced multiple formats including large print, audio, BSL storybook and Braille. We similarly tailored communications to minority ethnic audiences (using 10 to 50 languages depending on the area), using ethnic media channels and relevant imagery (Figure 14).

Figure 14: Minority ethnic communications

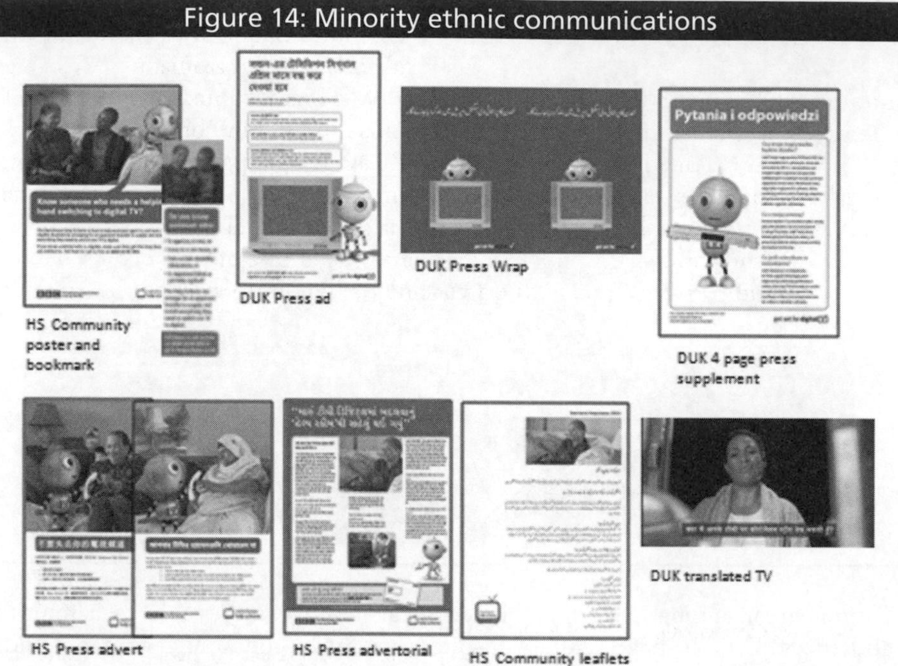


### Learning: Don't cloud the message with entertainment or humour – use a 'say it and see it' approach where messaging is supported by imagery.

Across the board, but particularly in communicating to older audiences, clarity is key. We found that older audiences do not decode advertising in the same way that younger audiences do. They tend to see 'entertaining' ads as just that – entertainment. Message take-out is low.

Charm and engagement was important, but should not obscure the message. We applied the 'say it and show it' approach from DLKWLowes' Stroke Awareness campaign to develop more impactful ads that made it easier to consistently hit our targets (Figure 15).

### Learning: Use messaging that directly targets friends and neighbours – most won't help unless prompted.

People immediately disconnect if they think an ad is not relevant to them – so do not engage enough to think about who else they know who might be affected. So we created a suite of communications explicitly targeting family, carers and other community-minded people (Figure 16).

## Figure 15: Help Scheme TV ad

Music throughout (Everybody's Talking). Open on Digit Al walking down a street carrying a bag. It is full of letters.

**VO: Are you 75 and over?**

**VO: Or eligible disabled?**

We see Digit Al handing the letters to Asian pensioners getting off a bus.

**VO: If so you will receive a letter from the Help Scheme.**

We see Digit Al give a letter to a Down's syndrome affected man.

**VO: About the help you can get to switch one TV to digital.**

Cut to Digit Al walking past a Help Scheme van parked in a drive. We see a uniformed installer helping connect a digital box for an old lady.

**VO: For £40, they can arrange for an approved installer to supply and install everything you need. For some eligible people, it's free.**

**VO: Call free on 0800 40 85 900**

## Figure 16: Help Scheme targeted press ads

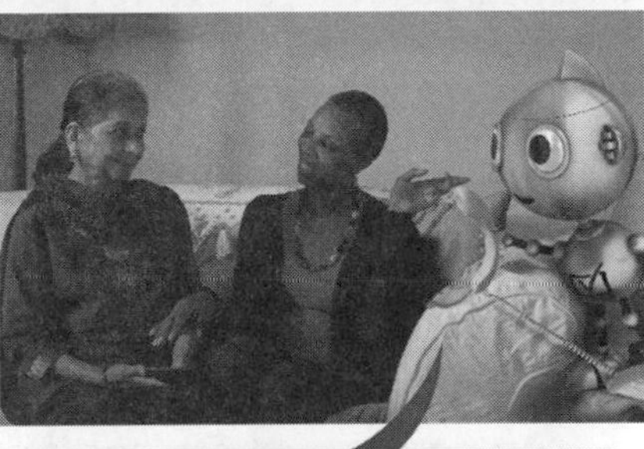

## *Messaging and phasing*

### Learning: Giving early warning lessens resistance to change – but few act until the end

We knew from research that people wanted a three-year warning. The launch with national advertising in May 2006 helped put switchover on the nation's radar early – and also energised the retail trade and digital platforms to stimulate equipment supply and promotion.

From 2008, as rolling regional switchover began, all investment shifted to local campaigns focused on the six months preceding each area's switchover – 84% of the £40m media spend[9] to date has been regional (rising to over 90% by completion later this year).

### Learning: Unsettle. Lead with harder messaging, follow with reassurance

We initially underestimated the degree to which people who were already digital would ignore our messaging because they believed they were already ready. As a result we built a phase into our communications called 'unsettle', using hard-hitting messages of blank screens aimed particularly at Freeview viewers.

The campaign evolved into three phases:

- 'Launch' phase at six months – as an early warning for remaining analogue homes.
- 'Unsettle' phase at three months – to engage existing digital viewers.
- 'Action' phase at one month – to convert final homes and get Freeview viewers to retune.

Time and again research showed people wanted hard-hitting messages, followed by support (Figure 17–20).

**Figure 17: DUK TV ad**

Music (Everybody's talking). Open on Digit Al with a TV in the background. On the TV are the Freeview, BT Vision and Top Up TV logos.
**VO: If you use any of these digital TV services...**

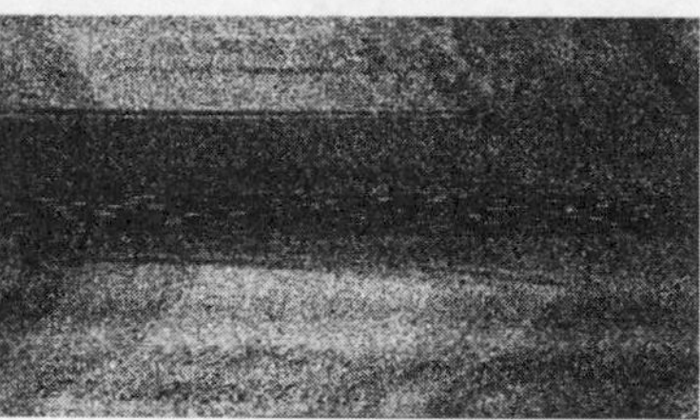

At this point the whole picture goes to 'snow' (i.e. no picture) and the music comes to an abrupt stop.
**VO: ...you'll start to lose TV channels at switchover**

Cut back to Digit Al in front of a TV. He's holding the remote for the TV.
**VO: To get them back just re-tune using your remote.**

## Figure 18a: Lose channels TV ad

Music throughout (Everybody's Talking)

Through the window of a house we can see a lady watching TV.

Suddenly the picture disappears and is replaced by static snow.

We see Digit Al open the front door in his house. It's the lady neighbour, with a coat over her shoulders. She asks him: **My telly's not working. Can I watch Corrie on yours Al?** Al politely nods and lets his neighbour in.

We next see various houses in the neighbourhood as the flicker from their TVs goes off too.

**VO: The old analogue signal is being switched off for good. If your TV isn't ready by 3rd August you'll start to lose your channels.**

We see Al's front room is filled with all the neighbours crowded round his TV.

3 August

08456 50 50 50

get set for digital

**VO: Call if you're unsure what to do.**

## Figure 18b: Options TV ad

Music throughout (Everybody's Talking)

Digit Al and his driver are continuing their journey around the country in their famous pink van informing and helping people with the digital switchover.

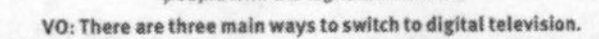

**VO: There are three main ways to switch to digital television.**

**VO: Convert your existing TV yourself with a digital set-top box or recorder.**

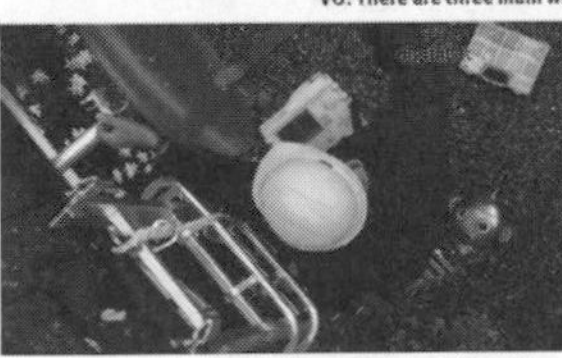

**VO: Get a service like satellite, cable or broadband TV installed for you.**

**VO: Or you can get a new TV with digital built-in.**

08456 50 50 50

**VO: For friendly impartial advice on the options available where you live, call Digital UK on 08456 50 50 50**

## Figure 19: Press ads

# Important announcement affecting your TV services.

**If you have Freeview**
If you watch TV using Freeview, BT Vision or Top Up TV, you will lose channels at digital switchover. To get them back you will need to re-tune every digital TV, box or recorder in your home.

**If you have satellite or cable**
If you have satellite or cable on ALL your TVs you won't need to do anything.

**Analogue TV (i.e. five channels or fewer)**
Your TV will lose its channels at switchover. You can convert your existing set using a digital box or recorder, install a satellite or cable TV service or get a new TV with digital built in.

The digital TV switchover comes to this area in **August**, so make sure you're ready. For more information go to **digitaluk.co.uk** or call **08456 50 50 50**

get set for **digital**

# Dear reader,

There are now just a few weeks to go before most homes in West and South Yorkshire start their switch to digital TV on **7 September**.

For anyone who has Freeview services* or an old analogue TV there are two important stages to remember:

**7 September – Switchover stage one:**
The switchover begins. Analogue BBC Two will be switched off permanently and the higher powered BBC digital services will launch. All Freeview TVs and boxes will need to be re-tuned on or after this date.

**21 September – Switchover stage two:**
The remaining analogue channels will be switched off and the rest of the digital services launched. All Freeview TVs and boxes will need to be re-tuned again.

Your switchover dates depend on where you live. To check your dates, enter your postcode at digitaluk.co.uk/postcodechecker or call 08456 50 50 50. Switchover makes Freeview available to virtually every home, including those that can't currently receive it, as it allows the digital signal to be strengthened and transmitted for the first time from the local relay transmitters.

Most homes will be able to receive more than 40 channels and some will receive around 15. It will also provide additional services such as audio description for viewers with disabilities. Homes who have satellite or cable on all their TV sets will not need to do anything.

**If you have questions go to digitaluk.co.uk or call 08456 50 50 50.**

Thank you,

**John Askew**
**Regional Manager, Yorkshire**
**Digital UK**

**Call 08456 50 50 50**
**or visit digitaluk.co.uk**

get set for **digital**

# Having trouble with your Freeview TV channels?

It may be due to the digital TV switchover happening in your area.

**Lost some of your channels?**
First, make sure you have correctly re-tuned. Choose 'first time installation' or 'factory reset' to remove all the old channels and load the new ones (just selecting 'add channels' won't work).

**Channels still missing?**
If you've done that and are still missing channels, you may need to do a 'manual re-tune.'

**Got the wrong regional channels after re-tuning?**
Your preferred services are probably a bit further down the list of channels. You can add the channels to your 'favourites' list if your equipment has one.

**Don't have a favourites option?**
You will need to do a 'manual re-tune.' This will enable you to put your channels where you want them on the channel list.

For more information or help go to **digitaluk.co.uk/retuning** or call **08456 50 50 50**

get set for **digital**

# On 7 September your TV channels will start to disappear.

If you have Freeview, BT Vision or Top Up TV your channels will disappear at switchover and you will need to re-tune on or after 7 September to get them back.

If you haven't converted your TV to digital yet, you will need to do this in time for switchover.

Switchover dates vary depending on where you live. To check your dates, enter your postcode at **digitaluk.co.uk** or call **08456 50 50 50**.

get set for **digital**

DON'T FORGET

Re-tune if you lose channels between August and September.

digitaluk.co.uk

get set for **digital**

Satellite and cable TV sets will not be affected

Figure 20: Help Scheme Options guide

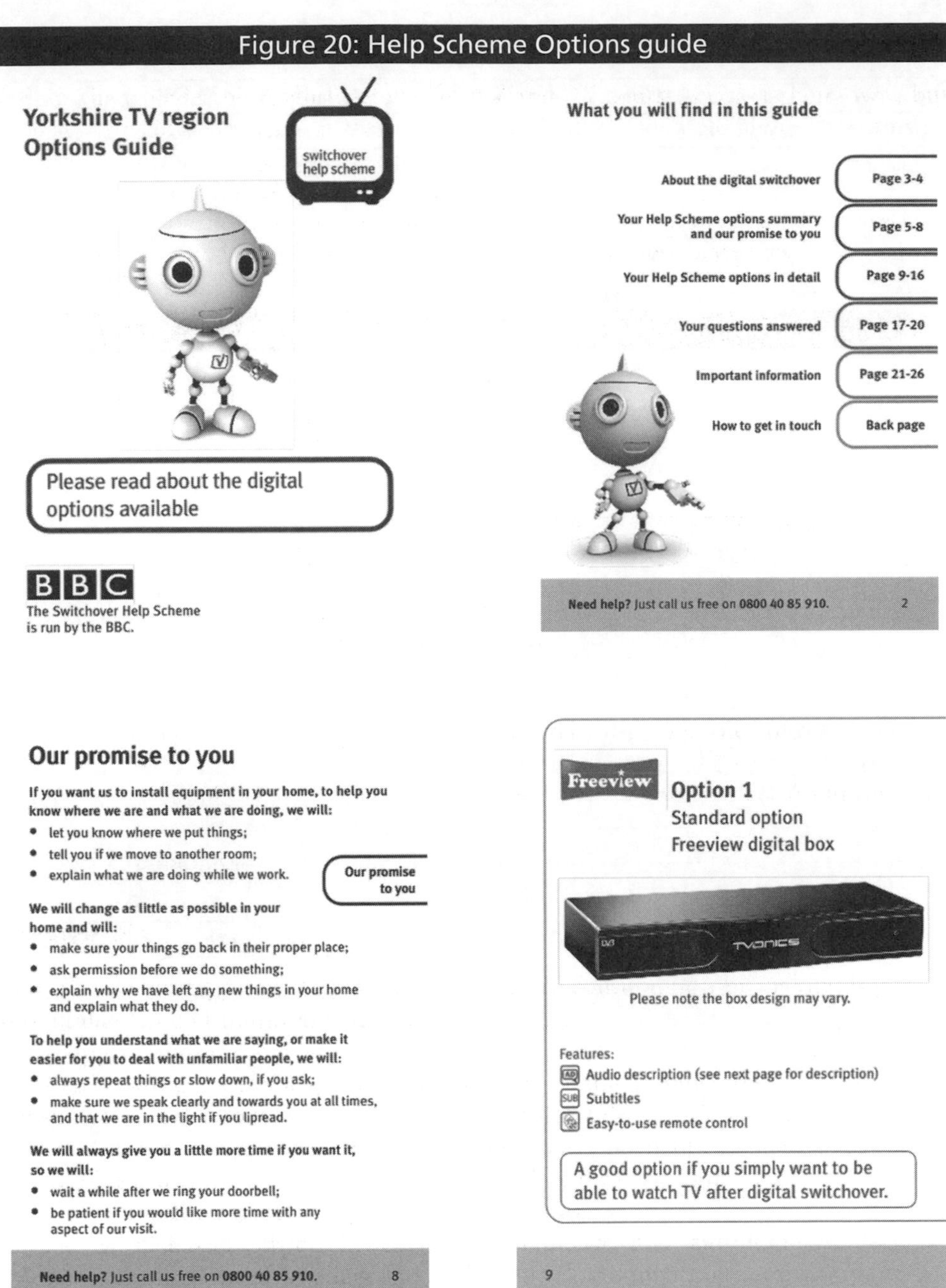


Table 1 shows a typical media laydown, based on Yorkshire, followed by more examples of the creative. NB: DUK awareness and Help Scheme communications were planned as a single campaign, with a spend split of 72%/28%.

## Table 1: Typical media plan

| January | February | March | April | May | June | July | August |
|---|---|---|---|---|---|---|---|
| **–7 month** | **–6 months** | **–5 months** | **–4 months** | **–3 months** | **–2 months** | **–1 month** | **0 months** |
| Launch/Prepare | | | | Unsettle | | Action | |
| Lose channels with date | No new TV | Options | | Look for the leaflet | | Lose channels | Having problems |
| (TV) | (TV) | (TV) | | (TV) | | (TV) | (Press and radio) |
| | Recorders | | | All TV sets, Recorders | All TV sets | Retuning | Retuning, overlaps |
| | (Radio) | | (Radio promo) | (Press and radio) | (TV) | (TV, radio, MHEGs, press, outdoor) | (TV, press and outdoor) |
| | Date | | Date | | | | |
| | (Press) | | (TV) | (TV and lamp posts) | (TV, lamp posts, press, radio) | (Press and lamp posts) | |
| | Flats DM | | | 3 mo leaflet | | | |
| | | | | | | | |
| **We can help** | | | | | | | |
| (TV) | (TV, press, radio, bus headliners) | (TV, press) | (TV, advertorial) | (TV) | (TV, community media) | (Community media) | |
| | Look for mailing | | | | | | Are you struggling? |
| | (TV) | | | | | | (Press) |
| | | | Good neighbours | Friends & Family | Good neighbours | | |
| | | | (TV) | (Press) | (TV, radio) | (Radio) | |
| | | | | Aftercare | | | |
| | | | | (TV) | | | |
| | We can help | | | 2nd sets | | Urgency | |
| | (Wave 1 mailing & care homes mailing) | | | (Wave 2 mailing) | | (Wave 3 mailing) | |

**Phase 1- Launch/prepare**
*Objectives*
DUK - Focus on analogue
- Explain what will happen at switchover and what to do
- Address misconceptions e.g. no new TV, recorders
- Raise awareness of date

*Help Scheme*
- Raise awareness amongst eligible people
- Drive to the letter

**Phase 2- Unsettle**
*Objectives*
DUK - Shift focus to all adults
- Drive to the leaflet
- Unsettle Freeview users with relevant messaging - every set, recorders
- Keep date awareness high

*Help Scheme*
- Raise awareness amongst eligible people
- Activate friends and family, and good neighbours to make eligible people aware of the Help Scheme
- Educate around aftercare offering

**Phase 3- Action**
*Objectives*
DUK - Focus on all adults
- Final reminder for those who need to invest in equipment
- Remind Freeview viewers to re-tune
- Keep date awareness high
- Provide helpline details

*Help Scheme*
- Raise awareness amongst eligible people
- Remind 'Good neighbours' to pass the message on
- Provide helpline details

The technicalities of switchover mean a lot *has* to be communicated. At launch, political sensitivities pushed us to put many messages above the line so people couldn't miss them. Over time, research enabled us to prioritise messaging and use media to maximum effect, relying on our 20-page leaflet to carry the detail (Figure 21).

Figure 21: The DUK leaflet

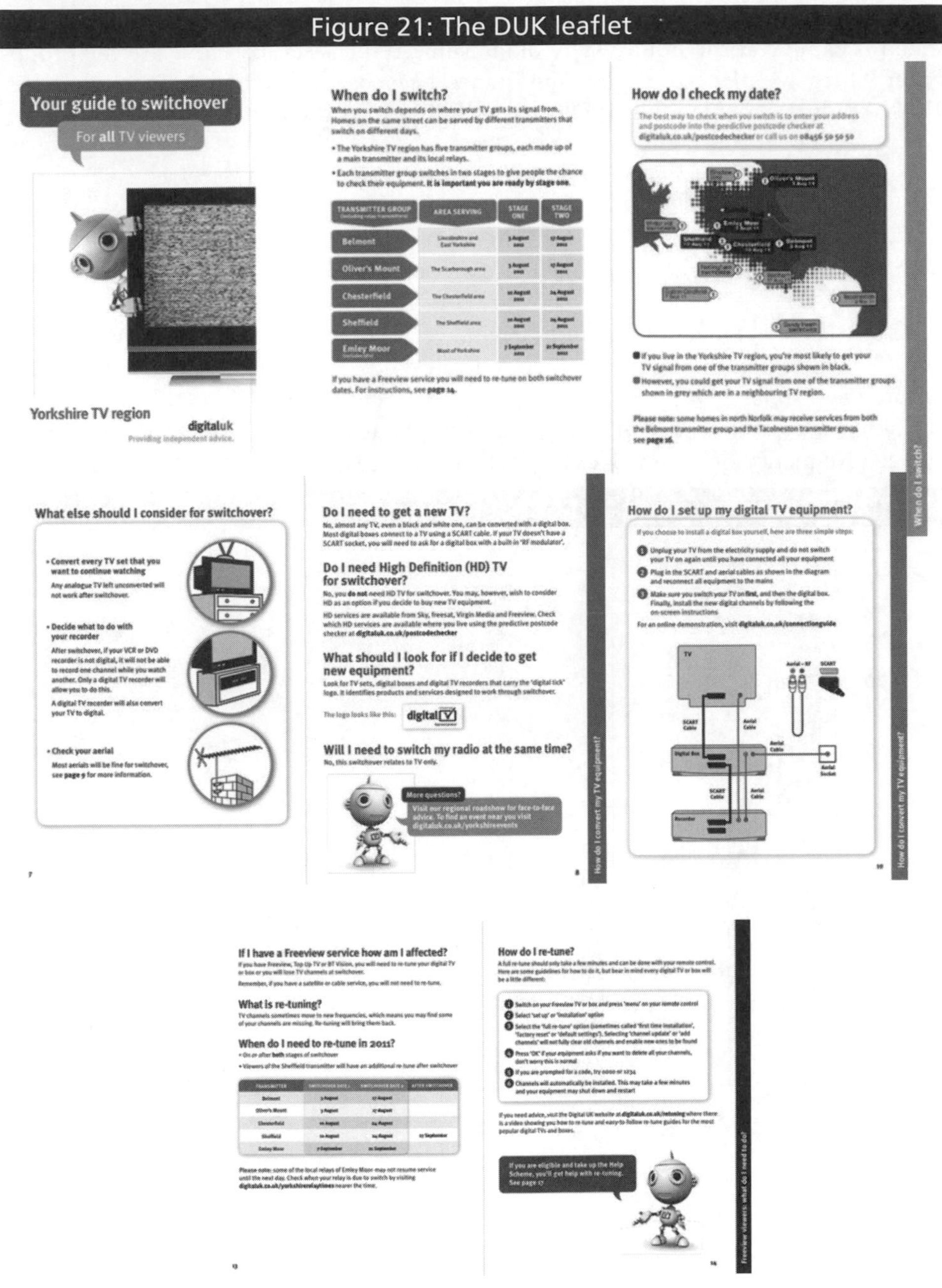

### *Media approach*

'Effectiveness' is often confused with 'Efficiency' and maximisation of Return on Marketing Investment, rather than maximisation of the *overall effect*.[10]

Our approach was the opposite to most brands in the commercial world, where often hard-to-reach audiences are disregarded as too complex or costly to reach, and spend is capped at the point where diminishing returns set in. These are the groups upon which we place the most importance because of our imperatives to deliver 100% readiness (demanding 100% reach) and protect the most vulnerable.

*Excellence = effectiveness + efficiency + protecting the vulnerable*

Constant monitoring of how tracking metrics grew as switchover progressed in each region gave insights that enabled us to maximise cost efficiencies within the media mix.

As switchover rolled out region-by-region, a truly local approach was used to 'hot-house' each region, maximise impact and relevance, and utilise varied touchpoints to catch *everyone.*

Taking a typical area (Yorkshire), the campaign achieved 100% reach with an average frequency of 23 (media plus DM) (Figure 22).

Figure 22: Spend and GRP split by media (all areas to date)

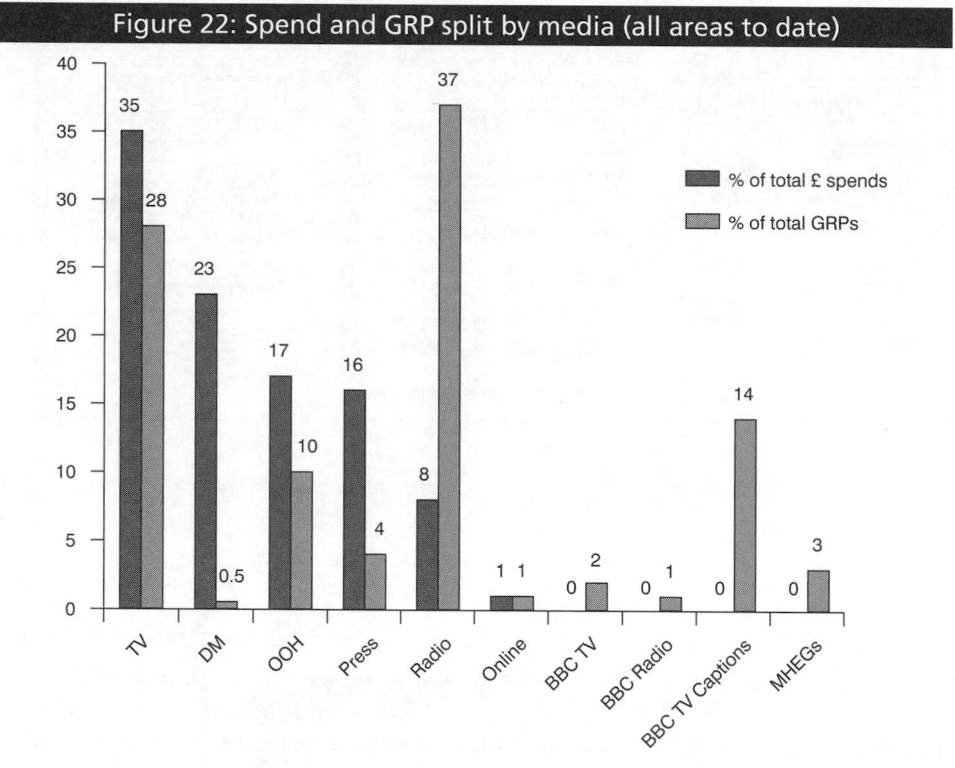

### Learning: It's counter-intuitive that a sub-regional programme would be cost-effective, but it was

By moving area-to-area, we delivered efficiencies via:

- increased relevance when messages are about people's local area;
- the multiplier effect of seeing messages in many places in a short period of time;
- on-the-ground teams and assets that can be transferred area-to-area;
- learnings that improve effectiveness as we go.

Continuous media effectiveness monitoring led more investment into TV and on-screen captions, and away from online and standard radio commercials (promotions being more effective) (Figure 23).

**Figure 23: Locally relevant messaging**

Please make sure you have a digital TV or digital set top box by **4 November**, or you will start losing TV channels. Questions? Call **digitaluk** on **08456 50 50 50**.

On screen captions

Your guide to switchover
For all TV viewers
Yorkshire TV region
digitaluk


Regional leaflet

ATM machines

Outdoor posters

Lamp posts

Ticket gateways

Micro-region TV

## Learning: Traditional media routes on their own will not meet a goal of leaving no-one behind

Research highlighted the need to go beyond traditional media to reach some of the most vulnerable and isolated people in the UK. So we also used media and PR at a more granular, community level:

- library bookmarks;
- post office and Healthcare Network TV;
- pharmacy bags;
- leaflets mailed to libraries;
- leaflets distributed to Meals-on-wheels and Dial-a-ride;
- PR complemented above-the-line messages with a 100-day countdown to each switchover, and a 'Helping Hand' campaign targeting local communities and 'human interest' case histories for local publications;
- roadshows visited key towns in each area.

To help support the most isolated people we trained up individuals and 'trusted voices' in their communities. Our community outreach pack, with DVDs and promotional materials, went to charities and parish councils, with recipients encouraged to disseminate information at community events and home visits. We even developed a schools pack for Key Stage II students.

In a ground-breaking initiative we formed a new charity consortium comprising Age UK, CSV and Foundations to identify, train and provide grants to local charities, who in turn facilitated switchover education meetings and community outreach.[11] By working with them via their established channels, we reached far into communities to provide help and advice through connections people trusted (Figure 24).

### *Location-specific targeting and project management*

In addition to reaching the vulnerable, we faced challenges of different transmitter areas (each switching on different dates) not matching the footprint of the media available. We had to create the same level of awareness and engagement in the Outer Hebrides as in Central Manchester, which demanded finding and using hyper-local media including newspaper supplements, lamp-posts, ATMs and TV captions (on-screen messaging).

The scale of the delivery challenge was unique:

- multiple messages x multiple media channels;
- hyper-local targeting to deliver the correct date in the correct location;
- managing multiple areas at a time.

Error-free delivery demanded exceptional project management across all aspects of the programme.

## Figure 24: Community media and outreach

Post office and GP surgery screens

Leaflets in post offices, libraries and CABs

Pharmacy bags

Library bookmarks

School pack

Community posters

Beer mats

### *What we did – in summary*

We took a very complicated technical subject and developed a campaign that motivated 20 million households to act. These households included the most vulnerable in society. We achieved this through a clear effective campaign, continuous improvement and error-free project management.

## 3. What we have achieved – evaluation

ROI calculations are essentially binary in this case – switchover either 'worked', running smoothly on time, or it didn't. Our communications weren't the only factor,[12] but seven years after the announcement of switchover, circa 10% still had not switched in upcoming areas (as well as the big Freeview retune task we faced).

Without communications and the related Switchover Help Scheme we would not have addressed the last 10% and achieved 100% readiness in advance of switchover – avoiding problems or delays that could have caused the programme to be derailed. In this sense, the whole net benefit of switchover could be attributed to the effectiveness of the communications campaign.

But while the effectiveness case might be straightforward, could switchover have been delivered at a lower cost?

So our case for excellence goes beyond effectiveness to demonstrate cost efficiency, as well as excellence in engaging vulnerable audiences.

### *Digital switchover will deliver benefits well in excess of costs*

The government's cost benefit analysis in February 2005 established a *net* benefit of circa £1.7bn for digital switchover – but a decrease in that benefit of £250m to £300m for every year of delay in completion beyond 2012. This took account of all costs, including those to consumers and the communications campaign.[13]

These are conservative estimates in two respects. Benefits did not reflect the full value of sale of frequencies released to mobile networks as this was uncertain at the time – the auction for this, shortly to commence, is predicted to realise billions. Additionally, as we shall see, overall Digital UK and Help Scheme costs are projected to come in substantially below the original budgets set.

### *Effectiveness = 100% readiness at switchover (not afterwards!)*

With switchover completed in 66% of the country, our tracking survey shows a steady transition to 100% readiness in advance of switchover in every one of the 20 regions/sub-regions switched to date (i.e. by end 2011) – including successfully converting 'the last 10%' (Figure 25).[14]

Importantly, 100% readiness has been achieved smoothly by bringing consumers with us, without undue stress for the great majority:

- Tracking shows, by switchover day, 93% of all households (all areas to date) are comfortable with the process (very happy/ok/not bothered by it).
- Complaints to Digital UK about any aspect of switchover have been minimal, 0.001% of households switched to date (= 1 in 100,000) (see Table 2).
- 9 out of 10 press stories (during regional roll-out) have been positive or neutral.

Inevitably, for a very small minority, there was a degree of angst which the Help Scheme and Digital Outreach worked hard to address. As a result, switchover has run smoothly with no 'outrages', either technical or public. With no cancellation or delay, the above net benefits have been fully realised.

Figure 25: Main set readiness by area

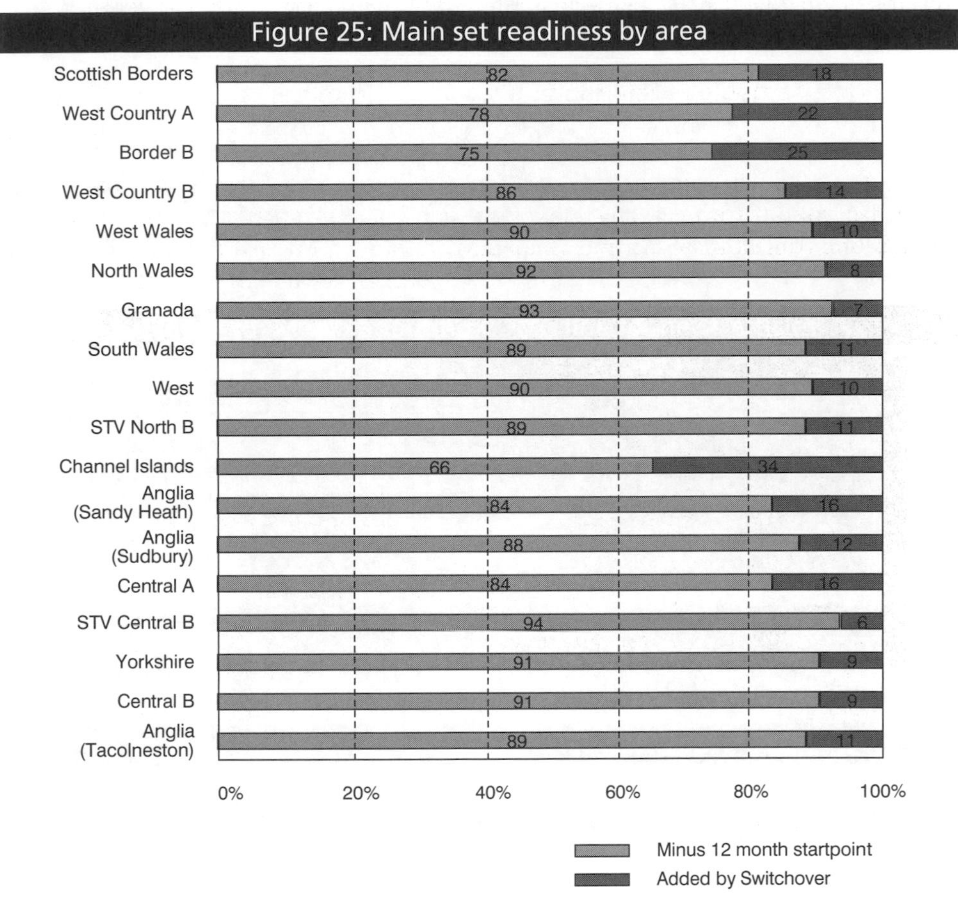


Source: Ipsos Tracking survey. Startpoint data is the lowest % main set readiness measured in the 6–12 months before switchover date

**Table 2: Complaints tracking: Digital UK complaints by letter, email and phone**

| | 2011 | | 2010 | | 2009 | | 2008 | |
|---|---|---|---|---|---|---|---|---|
| Region | Number of letters, emails and calls | Complaints as % of households | Number of letters, emails and calls | Complaints as % of households | Number of letters and emails | Complaints as % of households | Number of letters and emails | Complaints as % of households |
| Border | 4 | 0.0012% | 14 | 0.004% | 8 | 0.002% | 2 | 0.001% |
| West Country | 4 | 0.0005% | 21 | 0.003% | 25 | 0.003% | 1 | 0.000% |
| Granada | 5 | 0.0002% | 24 | 0.001% | 43 | 0.001% | 1 | 0.000% |
| Wales | 12 | 0.0009% | 41 | 0.003% | 9 | 0.001% | - | 0.000% |
| West | 11 | 0.0008% | 41 | 0.004% | 5 | 0.000% | - | 0.000% |
| STV North | 3 | 0.0005% | 31 | 0.005% | 1 | 0.000% | - | 0.000% |
| STV Central | 54 | 0.0029% | 12 | 0.001% | 1 | 0.000% | - | 0.000% |
| Channel Islands | 1 | 0.0059% | 2 | 0.004% | - | 0.000% | - | 0.000% |
| Central | 139 | 0.0037% | 63 | 0.002% | 14 | 0.000% | - | 0.000% |
| Anglia | 90 | 0.0044% | 15 | 0.001% | 3 | 0.000% | - | 0.000% |
| Yorkshire | 78 | 0.0027% | 35 | 0.001% | 1 | 0.000% | - | 0.000% |
| Meridian | 44 | 0.0015% | 22 | 0.001% | 39 | 0.002% | 1 | 0.000% |
| London | 36 | 0.0007% | 6 | 0.000% | 3 | 0.000% | - | 0.000% |
| Tyne Tees | 2 | 0.0001% | 3 | 0.000% | - | 0.000% | 1 | 0.000% |
| N Ireland | 3 | 0.0004% | 1 | 0.000% | - | 0.000% | - | 0.000% |
| **UK total** | **486** | **0.002%** | **331** | **0.001%** | **152** | **0.001%** | **6** | **0.000%** |

### *Communications demonstrably linked with hitting targets*

In consultation with government, we set awareness targets to be met in every switchover area (Table 3).

**Table 3: Awareness metrics and targets**

| | **Switchover awareness** | **Date understanding** | **Understand of need to retune** | **Main set readiness** | **Help Scheme awareness** | |
|---|---|---|---|---|---|---|
| | All adults | All adults | Analogue/ DTT adults | Homes | All adults 35+ | Eligible adults |
| **Target** | 100% | 75% | 70% | 100% | 75% | 70% |

Targets for each of these metrics were met in all 20 areas switched to date – from a total of 117 individual measures, targets have been met (within statistical error margin) for 95%, and missed only narrowly in the other 5% (Table 4).

**Table 4: Performance vs. targets summary**

| | Measure: | Switchover awareness | Date Understanding | Understand need to re-tune | Main set readiness | Help Scheme awareness | |
|---|---|---|---|---|---|---|---|
| | **Base:** | **All adults** | **All adults** | **Analogue/ DTT adults** | **Homes** | **All adults 35+** | **Eligible adults** |
| | **Targets:** | **100%** | **75%** | **70%** | **100%** | **70%** | **70%** |
| Switched | Scottish Borders | | | n/a | | | |
| | West Country A | | | | | | |
| | Border B | | -1 wk 70% | | | | |
| | West Country B | | | | | | |
| | West Wales | | | | | | |
| | North Wales | | | | | | |
| | Granada | | | | | | |
| | South Wales (Wenvoe) | | | | | | |
| | West | | -1 wk 69% | | | | |
| | STV North A | | | | | | |
| | STV North B | | | | | | |
| | STV Central A (Torosay) | | | | | *No Help Scheme boost* | |
| | Channel Islands | | | | | | |
| | Central A | | | | | | |
| | STV Central B | | | | | | |
| | Yorkshire | | | | | | |
| | Central B | | -1 wk 66% | | | | |
| | Anglia (Sandy Heath) | | | | | | |
| | Anglia (Sudbury) | | | | | | |
| | Anglia (Tacolneston) | | | | | | -1 wk 64% |

| Key | |
|---|---|
| Actual above target | |
| Actual within statistical error margins of target | |
| Actual outside statistical error margin of target | |

Meeting these targets has not become significantly easier over the roll-out period. Figure 26 is based just on households in areas yet to switch over at a given time, and shows that since 2009 we have still faced a hard core of circa 10% analogue main set homes in each upcoming area. At the same time, the number of Freeview retuners has increased greatly.

Figure 26: Main set ownership

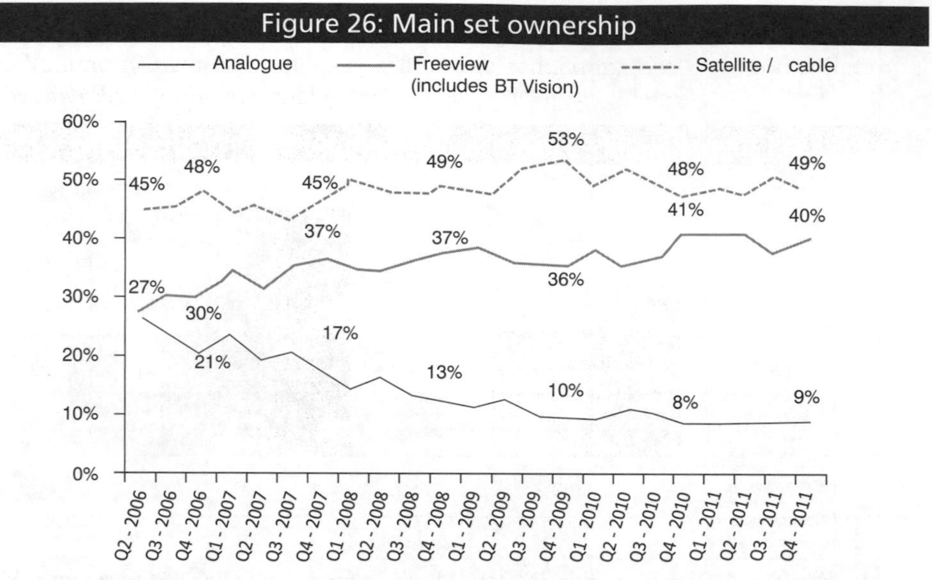


The pivotal role communications played in meeting these targets is clear from the consistent correlation between campaign phasing and increases across awareness metrics. Figures 27–30 are based on the first transmitter area in each region using the 6-month contact strategy.

Figure 27: Average date (month) awareness by month

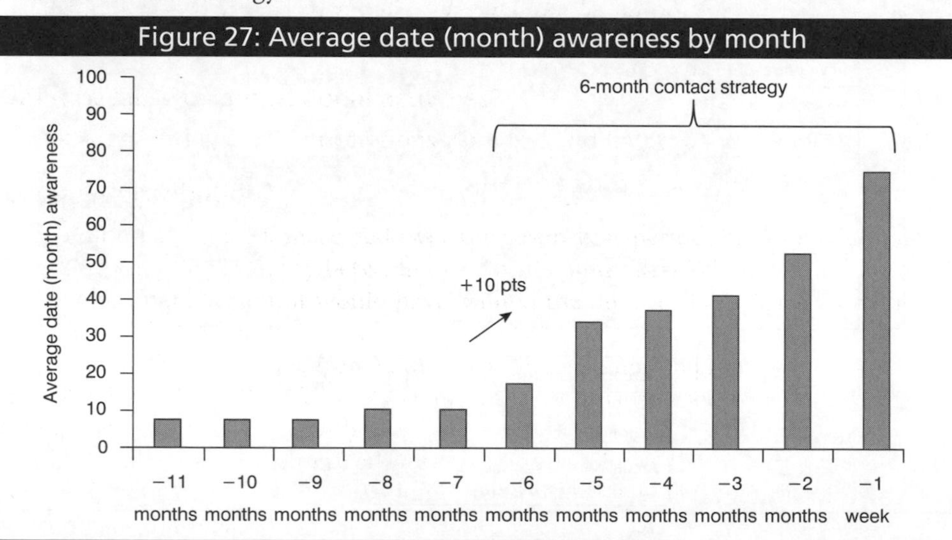

## Figure 28: Average re-tune awareness by month

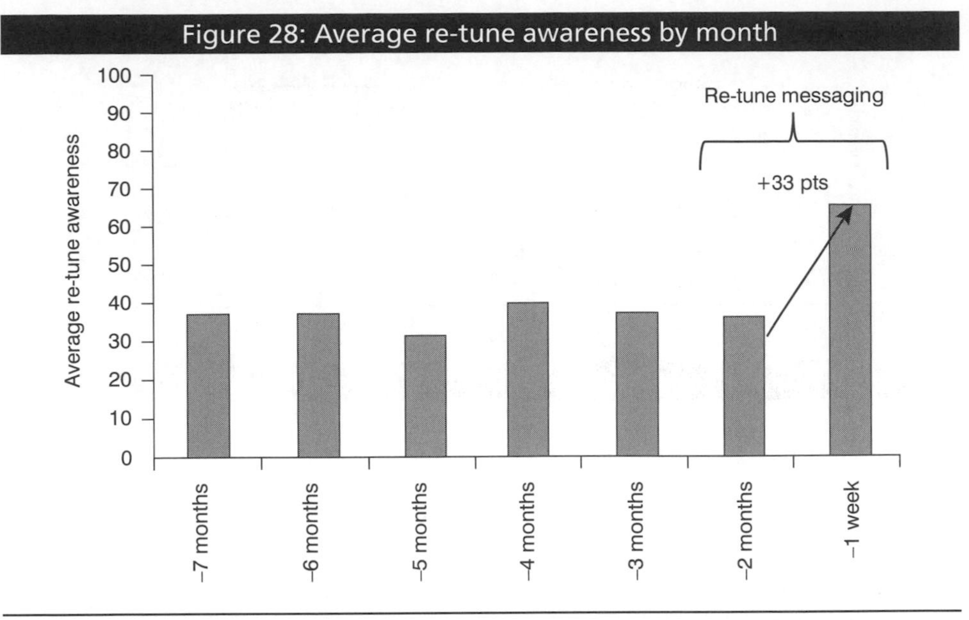


## Figure 29: Average Help Scheme awareness for all adults

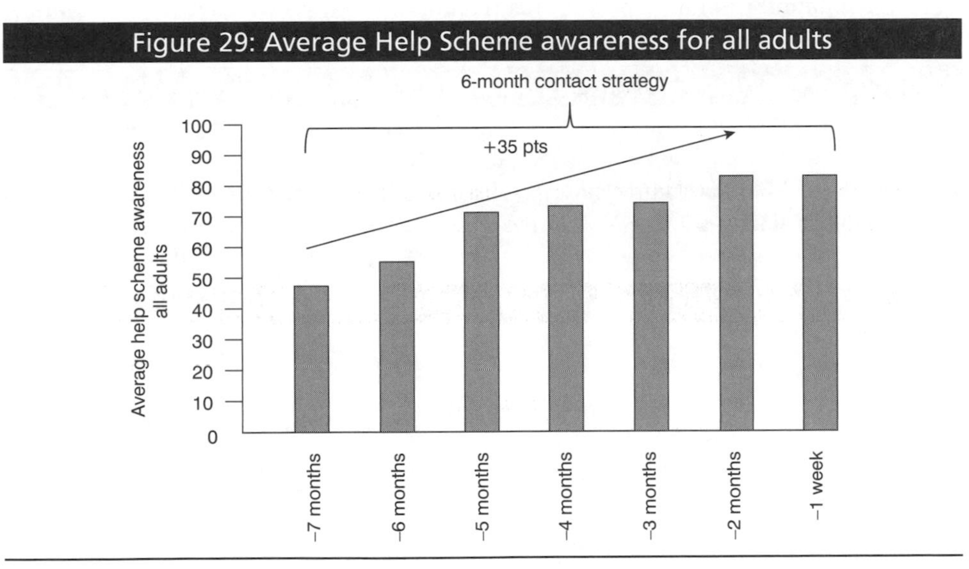

Figure 30: Average Help Scheme awareness for all eligible

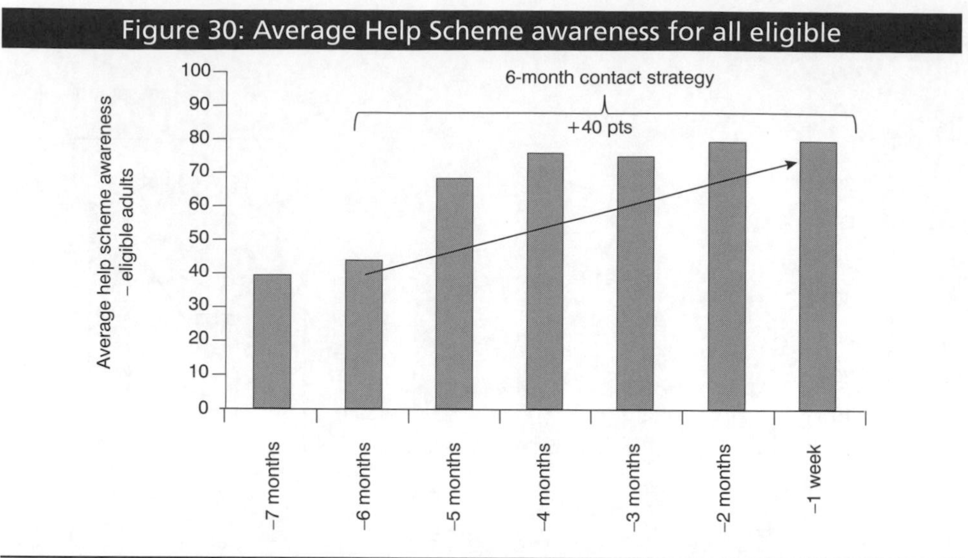


We show Yorkshire to provide a more granular example of how awareness moved against communication in a specific area (Figures 31–34) (as we have seen in Table 4, awareness metrics were met across all switchover regions to date).

Figure 31: Date (month) awareness in Yorkshire

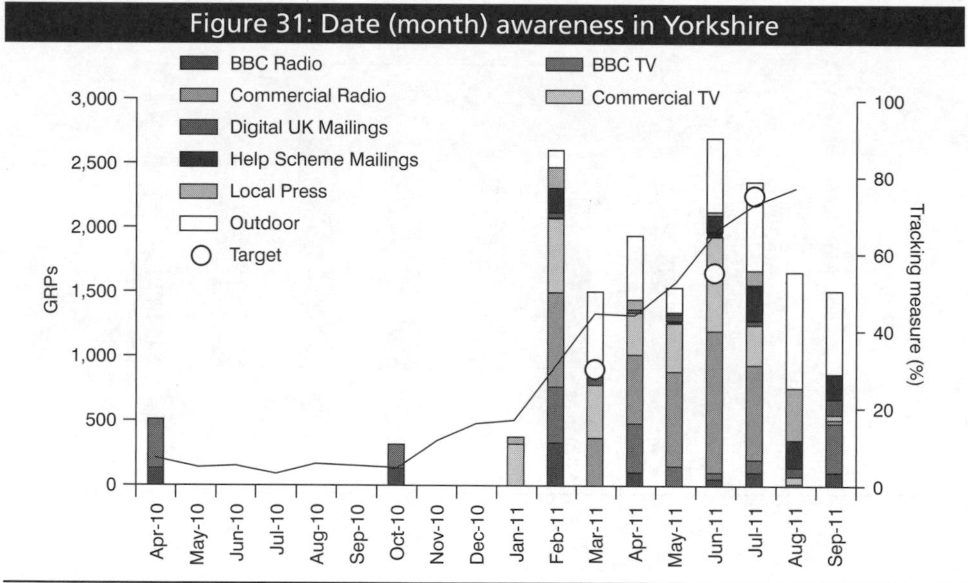

## Figure 32: Re-tune awareness in Yorkshire

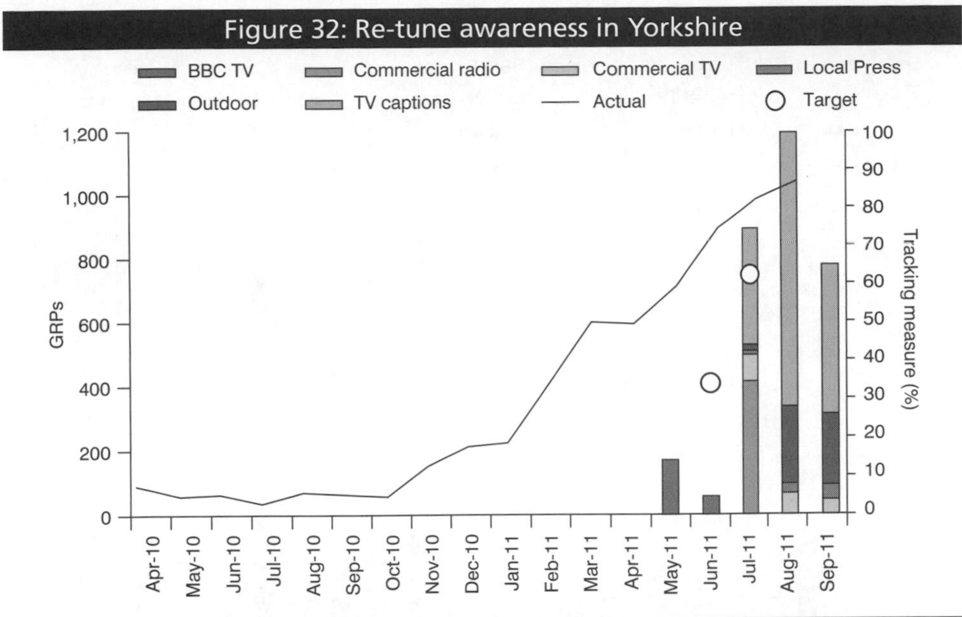


Source: MediaCom Tracking data analysis

## Figure 33: Help Scheme awareness for all adults in Yorkshire

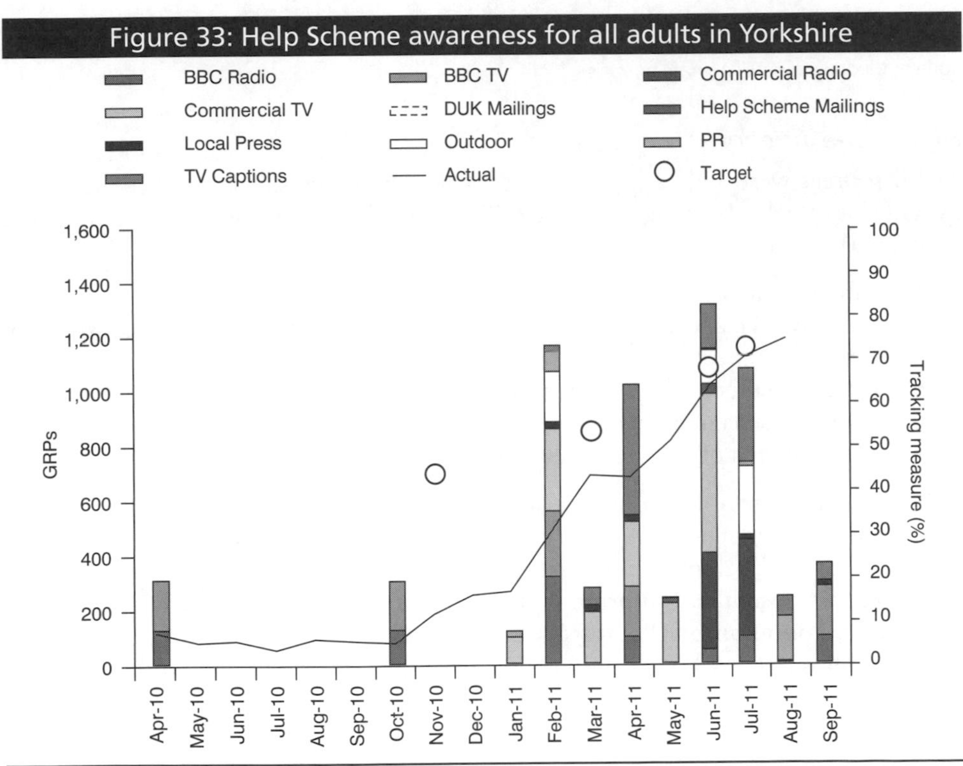


Source: MediaCom Tracking data analysis

Figure 34: Help Scheme awareness for all eligible in Yorkshire

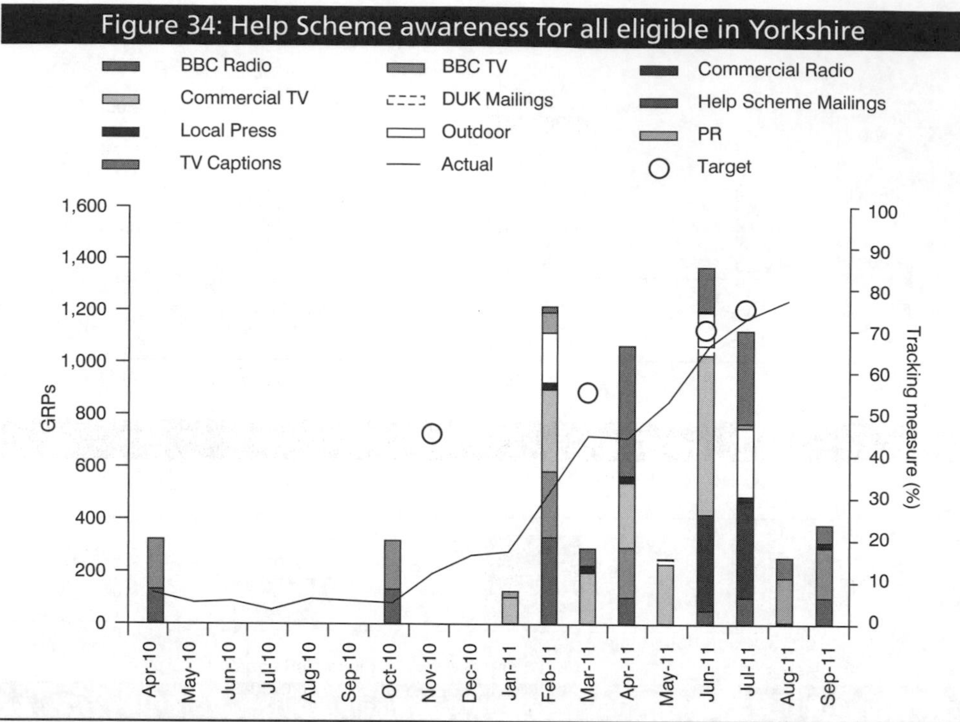


Source: MediaCom Tracking data analysis

### *High cost-efficiency*

The first areas were high risk – we had to make absolutely sure it worked – but also provided a valuable learning experience. This helped fuel our relentless focus on cost saving and continuous improvement on all fronts:

- independent benchmarking covering circa 80% of total expenditure, including audits of all media by Billets/Ebiquity (where we were shown to be consistently better than the market);
- sharp procurement via tightening scope of work;
- improvements in copy and media efficiency;
- simplification of messages (few 'pieces', reduced production costs).

Specifically from a media (and related creative) point of view, targets have been met while reducing spend.

Each area is different – not least media availability, cost and the fit of media versus each transmitter footprint – but there is a very clear downward trend in media cost. For instance, KPI targets were met and switchover successfully delivered for a third less cost per household in Yorkshire (2011) than adjacent Granada (2009) (Figure 35).

Figure 35: Media cost per household (DUK and Help Scheme combined)

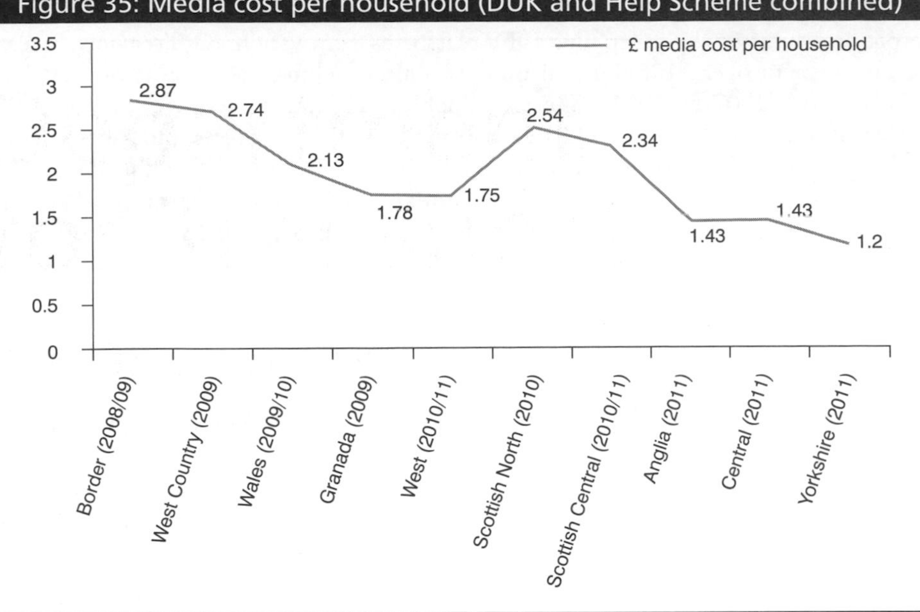


The bottom line is that we are projecting major savings versus the original budgets agreed with government:[15]

- In 2007, Digital UK was allocated a budget of £201m – we will complete the programme with a saving of more than 30% on this.[16] The savings from Advertising, Direct and Production will also be more than 30%.
- Total Help Scheme spend is projected to be circa 50% below budget[17] (although the majority of this budget, and so savings, relates to the delivery of the subsidised assistance package rather than the associated marketing).[18]
- An overall saving of circa £360m (unused allocation from the Licence Fee settlement) will be rebated to government.

### *Could we have done this differently for less?*

### What if we left the market to itself, i.e. no analogue switch off?

The 2004 DTI/Generics report forecast that without switchover, 20% of households would stay analogue – a quarter of households could not receive digital via an aerial unless analogue was switched off, plus there was high resistance amongst many to paying for multi-channel via satellite or cable. Hardly any of the benefits (which greatly exceed costs) in the DTI/DCMS cost benefit analysis could have been realised without analogue switch-off.

### What if we delegated switchover to the digital platform providers?

Before and during switchover, digital TV platforms (Sky, Virgin, BT, Freeview, Freesat, etc.) have spent over £100m a year on media alone selling the benefits of digital TV (£711m from 2007 to 2011). This is valuable – indeed we work closely with the platforms – but understandably they are in competition and promoting switching to their particular platform. Most of their sign-ups are churners from other digital platforms and, as we have seen, they have made little impact on the residual 10% of remaining analogue homes (often confused and turned-off by their competing offers).

### What if we did nothing, just pulled the plug?

Around 10% of households could have ended up with blank screens on switchover, and there would have been a great deal of confusion and lost channels in Freeview homes. This was socially and politically untenable – the programme would not have survived the first area due to public uproar (as well as a vast loss of advertising revenue for commercial broadcasters). Benefits of up to £300m would be lost for each year of delay, as well as additional operational costs of restaging.

### What if we did less, e.g. as in some other countries?

Digital switchovers are happening elsewhere, though they started *after* we commenced so could only provide limited learning. The complex nature of the UK broadcasting landscape means that there are no close 'role models'. Technical factors meant we had to switch across multiple regions in multiple years, while many countries could switch in one go. Transition has been successfully undertaken in Sweden and Germany with relatively limited communications – but with cable TV services dominant and few analogue homes, switchover was a much simpler exercise than in the UK.

In the US and Spain a lack of communication has caused major problems. The US switch was actually delayed because of people and retailers not understanding, and thus misusing the voucher system put in place to help the more disadvantaged. We did what we needed to reach the awareness targets set (carefully monitored to do just enough, nothing more) – if we'd missed these targets, similar problems may have occurred, and the scheme's benefits not been realised.

### What if we gave everybody who needed one a Freeview box?

This was in fact scoped out (including aerial upgrades where necessary) in 2005 with the cost estimated at £1,055m – many times more than the communications costs (and there would still have been the need for an enhanced Help Scheme for the vulnerable).

### What if we visited and 'switched' all vulnerable households?

We would necessarily have used similar eligibility criteria to those of the Help Scheme. But as we have seen, only circa 50% of the remaining analogue households were in fact eligible for help. The others would have been left with no information or phone advice to tell them what to do or provide reassurance (resulting in a lot of blank screens).

Secondly, many eligible do not in practice want help – preferring to sort things out using their own resources and/or support networks, supported by information and advice and the choice of help if needed (i.e. offered, but not imposed).

Thirdly, 'enforced' universal provision is enormously wasteful. Based on Help Scheme experience, installation (plus equipment and necessary follow-ups) would cost £200 per visit. Even discounting the circa 15% of eligible people already fully satellite/cable, this would have cost circa £1.2bn (7.15 million homes x 85% x £200) versus circa £300m for the current scheme (circa 20% take-up).

### *Protecting the vulnerable*

The consistent achievement of 100% readiness means that nobody has been left with a blank screen. We have seen that this was achieved without undue stress (90+% comfort with the process), very low levels of complaints and little negative press during the switchover process itself.

This was in part due to the successful communication and delivery of the Help Scheme – to date 20% of eligible households have taken up the Help Scheme's service, with satisfaction scores very high (95% recommendation). But this was also due to the information, reassurance and support from DUK for those not eligible for the Help Scheme.

Potentially vulnerable people have been helped and feel positive about it – not least those who, with information and support, feel good about mastering the change themselves, and helping others do so too (Figure 36).

**Figure 36: Quotes from and about people with difficulties we have helped**

'Staff were happy to see that one of their visitors from yesterday had returned with a huge smile on her face. When she (first came in) she was very agitated and nervous about switchover and doubted that she would be able to retune her digi box. However after staff at the Advice Point spent some time talking her through the re-tuning process, she went home and managed to re-tune first time! She then went to two of her elderly neighbours' homes to show them how to re-tune, and when she bumped into one of her friends in the street later that day, was able to talk her through the re-tuning process too! The lady was so pleased that she had managed to re-tune, and that she had been able to help her friends, that she went back to the Advice Point to say a big thank you to the staff that had helped her'

'An elderly gentleman came into the AP (Advice Point) and was given retune advice. He called back the following day (the AP was in the WVRS café and he went in there each day anyway) to say he was struggling. One of the home visit trained WVRS volunteers popped round to the gentleman's home and helped him retune – he was very grateful'

'My mum had the switchover ... and Vista (for registered blind) gave her a leaflet telling her about a help scheme ... so she had help and they came and sorted her out. It was brilliant'

'I rang this helpline when my mum's channels all disappeared and they explained what to do and they all came back straight away'

'I have a mate of mine who was at school with me – he has learning difficulties, so I was able to help him set it up. I helped three people in all'

'I'm no longer frightened by computers or frightened by trying different things, it might take me a while to get things back to the way it should be if I press the wrong button on the remote, but I don't think I've damaged anything other than my pride.'

*In summary*

*Switching to digital TV is the biggest project in UK broadcasting history and has been a real success. The project is on-time and has run brilliantly smoothly. Switching to digital TV provides people with more channels while freeing up valuable spectrum.*

Ed Vaizey, Communications Minister

*... who knows, all the dire predictions made to the Select Committee might suddenly come true. But I would say that so far, it's gone pretty well and for those who did fear that this could turn into an electoral or technological disaster I would pay tribute to Digital UK – I think they have done a great job and the fact that my postbag and my colleagues' postbags have been pretty much empty of complaints about switchover is a tribute to how much you have achieved.*

John Whittingdale, Chair, Culture, Media and Sport Select Committee

*My early fears about the risks around the switchover project haven't been borne out...what we see is a major national project that has gone...very successfully.*

Colette Bowe, Chairman, OFCOM

The power of communication to provide help and reassurance has overcome digital resistance to transform a potentially negative situation into a 'non-story'.

The digital switchover 'balance sheet' is very much in profit, not just from the effective delivery of a change with large net benefits, but also by the return of considerable funds to government based on implementation efficiencies delivering switchover well below budget (Table 5).

Vulnerable people have been protected and well-served, with the approach of providing help and reassurance via communications and outreach producing further savings in terms of the numbers actually needing to take up the assistance package.

**Table 5: The Digital Switchover balance sheet**

**Initial net benefit estimate**
DTI/ DCMS 2005 – central estimate of £1.7 billion, net of all anticipated costs incl. marketing

**Incremental benefits – revenues**

- delivered without delays – worth c.£300m pa
- likely additional revenues (in the billions) from auction of spectrum to mobile networks

**Dependent on:**

- effective protgramme delivery (across all aspects)
- 100% readiness via communications
- the vulnerable protected and last 10% addressed

**Incremental benefits – cost savings**

- projected savings on the Digital UK budget of c.£60m (30%+)
- projected savings on the Help Scheme budget of c.£300m (50%)

**Dependent on:**

- relentless focus on cost
- communications efficiencies demonstrated
- reassurance and choice contributing to lower than projected take up of the Help Scheme (high cost impact as c.75% of costs relate to assistance package delivery)

**Total projected DUK and Switchover Help Scheme costs** (already accounted for in initial net benefit above)
Digital UK c.£140m + Help Scheme c.£300m = c.£440m (projected costs at completion, end 2012)
**This equates to a *minimum* return on investment (inc. Help Scheme) of 4.7/1**
(but in practice likely to be much more due to sale of spectrum)

## Notes

1 Digital Switchover was under close review by the Culture, Media and Sport Commons Select Committee.
2 No similar switchovers have been completed elsewhere in the world when we commenced the process (see section entitled 'Could we have done this differently for less?').
3 DTI/DCMS Cost Benefit Analysis, covered later – part of benefit is sale of frequencies for mobile network use.
4 66% of the UK completed by end 2011, the four remaining areas including London complete switchover during 2012 – although we obviously don't have final results for the 2012 areas, we do have, and include, final projections on total scheme costs.
5 Attitudes to Digital Switchover – The Generics Group with Ipsos, for the DTI, March 2004.
6 It is currently projected that over £300m will be returned, and used to extend national broadband availability.
7 Nielsen gives total category media spend on 'Digital TV' as £711m for the period January 2007–December 2001.
8 Research and consultations were extensive – Figure 5 gives a small taste of this. More on our research – and learnings on understanding and reaching vulnerable groups – can be found at http://www.helpscheme.co.uk/en/research and www.digitaluk.co.uk/reports.
9 Areas switched up to 2011. £40m includes media and DM, inc. postage and printing for both DUK and the Help Scheme; costs for Roadshows and Outreach add c.£8m to this.
10 See 'Marketing in the Era of Accountability', IPA/WARC, 2007; pp. 103–105.
11 This is covered extensively in Digital UK legacy documents available at www.digitaluk.co.uk/reports.
12 As already noted, Nielsen gives total category media spend on 'Digital TV' as £711m for the period January 2007–December 2001.
13 DTI/DCMS February 2005 – The quantifiable (net) benefits of switchover compared with dual transmission were estimated as to be in the region of £1 to £2.9bn in NPV terms with a central estimate of £1.7bn. The central case shows a loss of NPV for every year of any delay in switchover from 2012 of around £250 to £300m a year. This did not include costs of the Help Scheme (decided on later), but because this essentially transfers costs from consumers to the scheme, it has little net effect on these initial estimates.
14 Source: Ipsos; main set readiness at switchover within statistical error margin of 3.5% (tracking is run in each transmitter area from at least 12 months before switchover).
15 With switchover in the final 2012 areas nearing completion we are confident in these projections, which also have been shared with government.
16 This includes agency and production fees, substantial call centre costs, events, roadshows, PR, research and outreach – paid-for media, direct and production will account for c.50% of this.
17 £603m was budgeted in January 2007, ring-fenced within the current licence fee settlement to deliver the Switchover Help Scheme – the great majority of this for the subsidised, physical delivery of assistance. That figure was based on research by the DCMS to assess people's likelihood to take up the Scheme, but it was always understood that the eventual cost would depend largely on take-up. These estimates proved high, and also a very effective procurement exercise by the BBC reduced the cost of the Scheme by £100m, and ensured that it would reflect the actual level of take-up (which, in part due to effective communication relating to Switchover, has been lower than initially projected). Over one million people have had help from the Scheme so far – DCMS and the Help Scheme now expect the underspend to be at least £300m.
18 Circa 75% of the Help Scheme budget spent relates to the in-home services and assistance package provided; the remainder relates to Call Centre, DM, Outreach, Media, PR and associated costs.

## Chapter 13

# Dove

## Dove winning in China

**By Tim Broadbent, Anthony Wong and Geoffrey Ogay, Ogilvy & Mather Shanghai**
Contributing authors: Lizzy Chen, Gilberto Pires, Judy Zu and Shannon Ye, Unilever (China) Limited; Kate Yung, Ogilvy & Mather Shanghai
Credited companies: Creative Agency: Ogilvy & Mather Shanghai; Digital Agency: OgilvyOne; Media Agency: PHD China; Client: Dove, Unilever China

### Editor's summary

This case shows how Dove transformed from a small, declining player in a large market into a leading shower gel brand. It is a great paper for anyone wanting to learn about differentiating a brand where the product was undifferentiated and the price at a premium. Dove got under the skin of Chinese women to produce a campaign that went against the grain of communications norms. Through the proposition that Dove's new shower gel nourished skin better than bathing in milk, it repositioned the brand for women who wanted 'healthy, wholesome protection' for their beauty. This was an impressive insight that was rooted firmly in a real understanding of the needs of Chinese women. The campaign propelled market share from 2.1% to 8.8% in 16 months, delivering incremental sales of £25.5m and a ROMI of 1:1.5.

## Introduction

This case shows how Dove transformed from a small, declining player in a large market into a leading shower gel brand.

Dove got under the skin of Chinese women's insights, and produced a campaign that went against the grain of communications norms, to propel market share from 2.1% to 8.8% in 16 months. For the first time in Chinese history, Dove was bigger than Olay.

This case demonstrates how Dove's marcomms were the winning factor across its marketing mix. Marcomms per se delivered incremental sales of RMB 255m (or £25.5m) with a ROMI of 1:1.5.

## August 2010: the decline

### *Dove was a very small and rapidly declining brand*

In the gigantic Chinese market where 85% of urban women used a shower gel,[1] Dove's sales declined while its key competitor Olay and the category grew (see Figure 1). Out of 18 tracked brands Dove was the only one that had declined in sales in the previous six months.[2]

Figure 1: Shower gel monthly value sales percentage growth August vs. March 2010

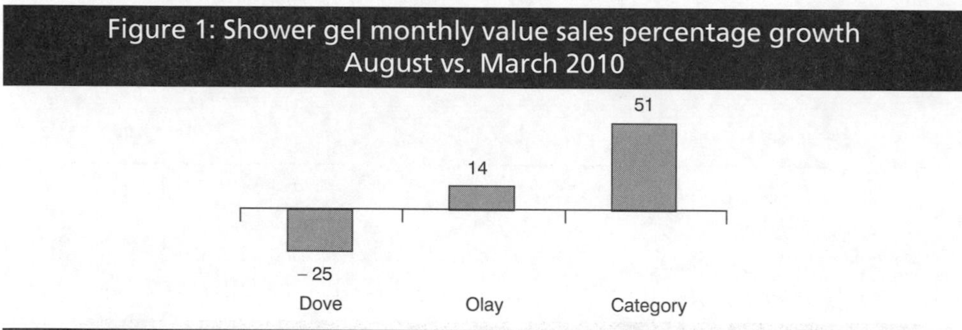


Source: Research International H&A Study 2008

Dove's rapid sales decline resulted in losing half its market share in six months.[3] At 2%, Dove became a fraction of the size of the top five brands, each of which commanded 8–11% respectively (see Figure 2).

Figure 2: August 2010 China shower gel percentage value share

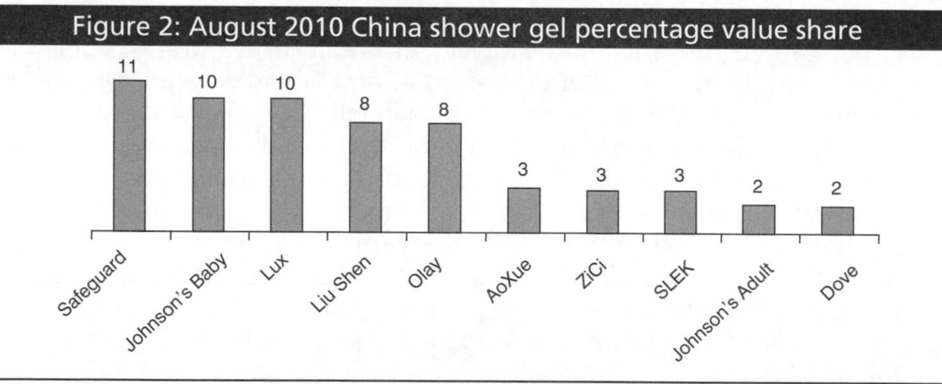


Source: AC Nielsen 2010–2011, Ogilvy analysis

### *Dove's enemy: Olay*

Across China's top five shower gel brands, Dove's immediate enemy – our focus – was Olay, as germ-killing Safeguard and Johnson's Baby were not beauty brands, and Lux (a Unilever brand like Dove) or Liu Shen was not premium-priced.[4]

### *Marketing challenges*

#### 1. Dove lost among 261 variants

Dove was lost among 261 variants of shower gels offered by 86 brands,[5] with seemingly all possible combinations of benefits (e.g. moisturising, whitening, nourishing, energizing, calming…) and flavours (e.g. green tea, milk, lemon, honey, mint…) available for sale. Dove sold moisturisation; so did competitors.

#### 2. Dove mute in a noisy category shouting with RMB 1bn[6]

Along with this cacophony of products came a noisy media environment. Annual estimated actual media spend in shower gel in China was to the tune of RMB 1bn.[7]

And to consumers, Dove had been mute. Its key competitor Olay spent RMB 99m (or £9.9m) more on media than Dove in six months alone – Dove spent only six (see Figure 3).

Figure 3: March–August 2010 China shower gel estimated actual media spend (RMB million)

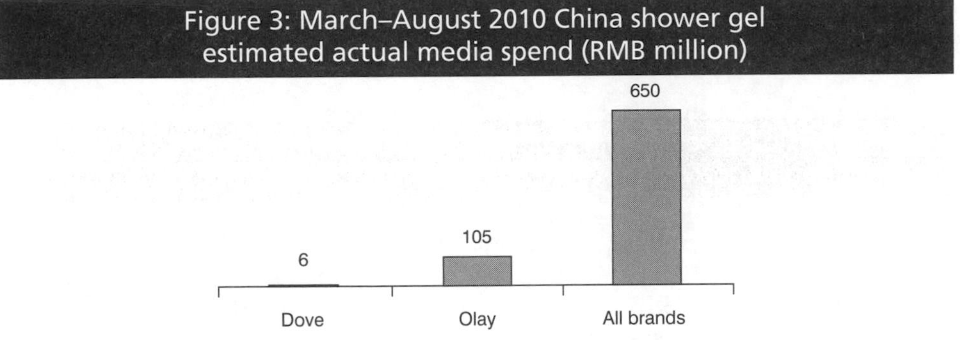


Source: Adquest (TV, print & radio), iADtracker (internet), Zhongtianxinghe (OOH), PHD analysis

#### 3. Dove was not well distributed

To compound the challenge, Dove shower gels were also harder to find than key competitor Olay, whose weighted distribution was 22% broader.[8] For every five outlets, one would carry Olay and other brands but just not Dove.

#### 4. Dove was expensive

Chinese women had 261 choices and what did not help Dove in growing was that it cost 53% more than the category average and 12% more than Olay.[9]

#### 5. Olay was better than Dove

Olay was most often chosen over Dove because Chinese women believed Olay was better at nourishing skin and making them look and feel beautiful (see Figure 4).

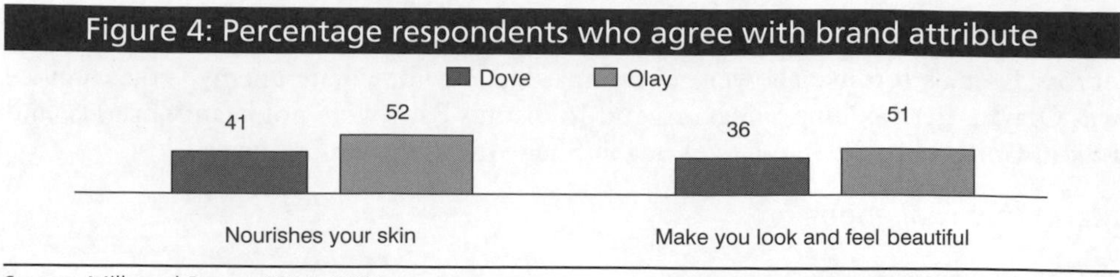


Source: Millward Brown 2010, 2011

Olay's strength in shower gel enjoyed a beauty halo from its number one position in facial moisturizers such as whitening and anti-aging, where approximately one out of four jars of such products sold in China were Olay's,[10] supported by an RMB 800m annual media budget.[11] While all Dove had in China, other than its shower gel, was a bar soap with a tiny 0.5% market share and zero media spend before, during and after Dove's new shower gel re-launch campaign.[12]

### *Key objectives*

With a declining and small market share, the high costs of maintaining the brand on shelves in vast China did not make business sense unless sales grew significantly and quickly.

Unilever made one 'last bet' with an increased media budget to deliver the following objectives:

1. Expand market share from 2.1% to 3.4% by December 2010.
2. Demonstrably increase 'nourishment' brand perception.
3. Demonstrably increase 'beauty' brand perception.

Although Unilever planned to increase Dove's media spend from RMB 4m in 2009 to RMB 77m in 2010, Dove would probably still be spending sizeably less than key competitors. Olay (RMB 114m spend in 2009), Safeguard (RMB 112m) and Lux (RMB 93m) were all likely to outspend Dove significantly.[13]

The long result short: by December 2010, Dove stood at 7.3%, not just 3.4%. One year later, Dove maintained and exceeded this growth to 8.8%, overtaking Olay for the first time in history.

## September 2010–January 2011: the re-launch

Here we describe the activities for Dove's four-month re-launch starting in September 2010.

During the re-launch, one new product was introduced, which moisturised skin better than previous variants and Olay. That said, moisturisation was a ten-year-old benefit offered by multiple brands. It was by no means news to Chinese women.

To compound the challenge, Dove's average distribution immediately before/after the campaign was essentially flat and significantly lagged behind Olay (see Figure 5).

Figure 5: Percentage distribution index

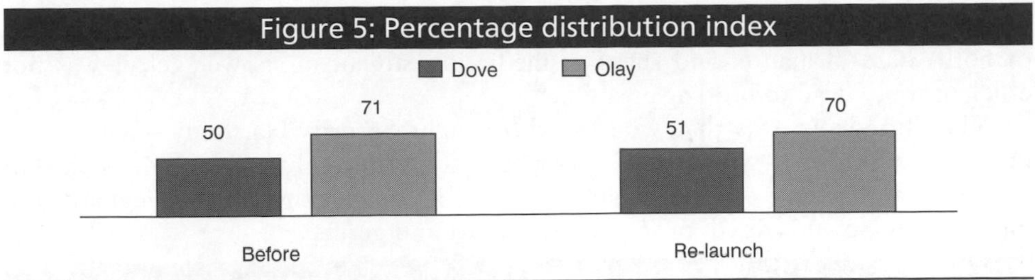


Source: AC Nielsen 2010–2011, Ogilvy analysis

To improve Dove's pricing appeal, average price was reduced by RMB 3 per kilo during the campaign period. When it was implemented, Dove realized it merely matched Olay's decrease, thus still maintaining a similar 10% premium over Olay (see Figure 6).

Figure 6: Percentage pricing (RMB/Kg)

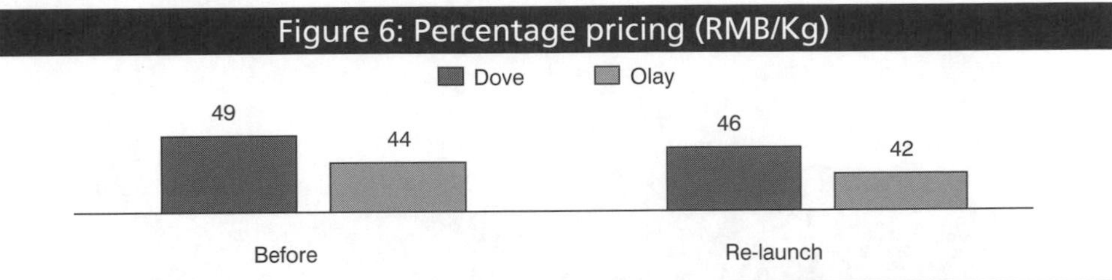


Source: AC Nielsen 2010–2011, Ogilvy analysis

Media investment was significantly increased during the re-launch period (see Figure 7), but taking into account what happened six months prior, Olay's total spend up to the point of Dove's re-launch had been RMB 99m higher, as established earlier.

Figure 7: Dove re-launch period estimated actual media spend (RMB million)

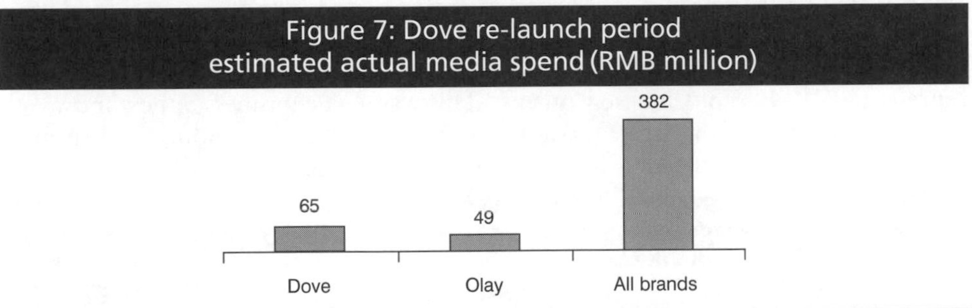


Source: Adquest (TV, Print & Radio), iADtracker (internet), Zhongtianxinghe (OOH), PHD analysis

As such, during the re-launch, more media investment was the only significantly improved variable. The crux of the re-launch was to change perceptions of the Dove brand with marcomms.

### *Repositioning brand from 'Admiration' to 'Security'*

We first went back to the human basics: what does a Chinese woman need?

There were six types of beauty needs: Admiration, Attraction, Fun, Control, Security and Harmony. Among these needs, Chinese women saw Dove as similar to Olay, that was about Admiration/Control, for women who desired to render themselves 'flawless' and 'elegant', so as to be 'admired'.

Was that a good position for Dove to be in? No. Given Olay's dominance in terms of both share of market and share of media investment in shower gel, it was not efficient to go head to head against Olay.

What stood out was that women who sought Security/Harmony – who were looking for 'healthy', 'wholesome' personal wash products that 'protected' their skin and delivered beauty – did not have much of a choice other than Safeguard (see Figure 8), which promised 'protection from dirt and germs'.

**Figure 8: Repositioning brand from 'Admiration' to 'Security**



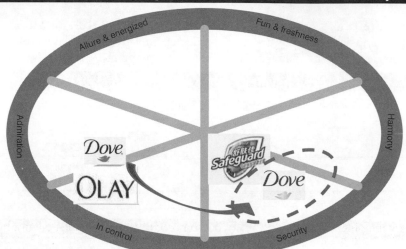

Source: Needscope 2008, Ogilvy analysis

Were other big brands not fulfilling this need, because it was small? No. This segment represented 30–40% of Chinese women.[14] This was a true business opportunity.

The implication of this strategy was that there would be no glamour, head-turning, heavily Photoshopped beauty or celebrities – all of which were norms that beauty marketers considered essential (see Figure 9).

**Figure 9: Beauty advertising norms in China**

### *Real beauty for real women*

After eliminating what Dove would not do, the logical conclusion was that Dove was to only use real women and show their real beauty, conveniently coinciding with Dove's famed global positioning. But would it work?

We first studied Chinese women's unique history. The Mao-era, hailing 'women can hold up half the sky' (see Figure 10), and the subsequent opening of the economy had led Chinese women to boast the highest female workforce participation in the world.[15]

Figure 10: 'Women can hold up half the sky'

That said, 3,000 years of Confucian culture was hard to silence. When a high-profile, wealthy female entrepreneur was interviewed, the journalist noted: 'When people ask which title she likes most, wife, President, or female elite, she always answers without any hesitation: "wife".'

The tension between career success, as exemplified by popular books with titles such as *Just be a Rich Woman: What Women Need is Money* (see Figure 11), and the fear of becoming a 'Shengnu' ('left-over girl') was rife in China among women and their dominating parents.

This tension sounded similar to that in the West, but it was not. It was much more severe. In China, daughters were considered inferior to sons, even in 2010. Employers could discriminate against 'unattractive' women – given China's vast lands and immature legal system, women relied on themselves to avoid such issues.

At the heart of how to resolve all this was beauty. Without a feminist or Christian history in China, beauty was not considered a sin of vanity, but essential to achieve the future Chinese women desired. There was never a 'beauty vs. brains' debate. Both were required. Thus being beautiful was not for the 'vain', but for every capable woman. This view could be best captured by what we heard real Chinese women say (which when repeated outside China, always raised eyebrows): 'There are no ugly women. Just lazy ones.'[16]

Figure 11: 'Just be a rich woman' and 'Here comes the left-over girl'

Source: Yiru Liu, 'Just be a rich woman'; Shan Lan, 'Here comes the left-over girl'

From these insights, Dove set its brand POV that every woman should unleash her beauty potential, and Dove shows this by only showcasing real women in its communications.

### *Establishing Dove's functional superiority: 'better than milk'*

Having established what the brand stood for and how to execute it, we then needed to establish that our product was superior, thus worth the premium price.

Given Dove's negligible presence in the Chinese market, we needed something hard-hitting to get the consumer's attention. What Dove really wanted to say was that its new shower gel was superior to Olay's in making one's skin softer and plumper, but advertising laws prohibited such messages.

We interrogated the shower gel until it confessed its strength, by asking Dove's product scientists to test its new product's nourishing functionality against anything one could think of. We tested milk after discovering select spas in China offered milk baths. From there came our proposition: Dove's new shower gel nourished skin better than bathing in milk.

With Dove, women who were not 'lazy' could unleash their beauty potential by doing the impossible for themselves – like bathing in milk, every day.

Milk proved to be an elegant solution on several fronts. It repositioned our brand for women who needed 'Security/Harmony', who wanted 'healthy' 'wholesome' 'protection' for their beauty – 'milk' telepathically did just that.

'Milk' also invoked an ancient myth – which every Chinese person knew – of how Empresses of old such as Yang Gui Fei, one of the 'Four Great Beauties', bathed in milk every day to have skin 'as fair and soft as snow' (see Figure 12).

Figure 12: Empress Yang Gui Fei bathing in milk

Source: 'Yang Gui Fei bathing in milk', by artist: Youhe Guo, born in 1963, Tangshan, Hebei Province

And to tell consumers Dove's new shower gel nourished better than Olay's, we raised the hard-hitting comparison to an even higher order: milk. This amplified the product's functional superiority with a rich cultural and emotional context that had never been done before in China.

### *Channel evaluation and implementation*

Here we describe how the new brand positioning and product proposition were implemented.

Recognizing that there were many channels to choose from, and that every channel did multiple jobs, it was up to us to decide which channel primarily did what, in isolation and together.

First, we selected the 'twin peaks' of Chinese women's media habits of TV and Internet – she spends approximately three hours on TV and three hours on the Internet every day.[17] For beauty-related news, she also reads magazines weekly to update herself on how to be more beautiful.[18]

While the above may not be news to global marketers, the following may be: a woman in London spent 75 seconds to browse and buy a skin-related product; a woman in Shanghai spent 246 seconds.[19] In China, selecting a shower gel was not as low involvement as in the West. The four long minutes of in-store browsing was a key channel in which Dove selected to invest marcomms funds.

### *Hear on Internet, see on TV, buy in store*

So TV, Internet, magazine and in-store were our chosen ones. How did we decide which does what, in isolation and together? Several women told us what we needed to do: 'I hear new things on the Internet. I see new things on TV. I browse and buy new things in store.'[20]

We realized the first day Dove launched its TVC wouldn't be seen by a Chinese woman until the evening, so TV was not the best place for 'awareness', as conventional channel thinking would perhaps wrongly suggest.

What was her first media touch point in a day? As women told us: 'Killing time on the Internet.'[21] We reached out to Chinese women through QQ, China's largest social media portal with 145 million daily users, with a video content-based 'Dove vs. Milk' game (see Figure 13), where women can invite friends and virtually play the game together. Dove used active, fun, social engagements online to create what's usually considered passive awareness.

Figure 13: 'Dove vs. milk' social media game

When she went home from work in the evening, watching her favourite TV drama, Dove then convinced Chinese women with its 'Milk bath test' TVC of how using Dove was better than bathing oneself in milk every day (see Figure 14).

Figure 14: Dove 'Milk bath test' TVC

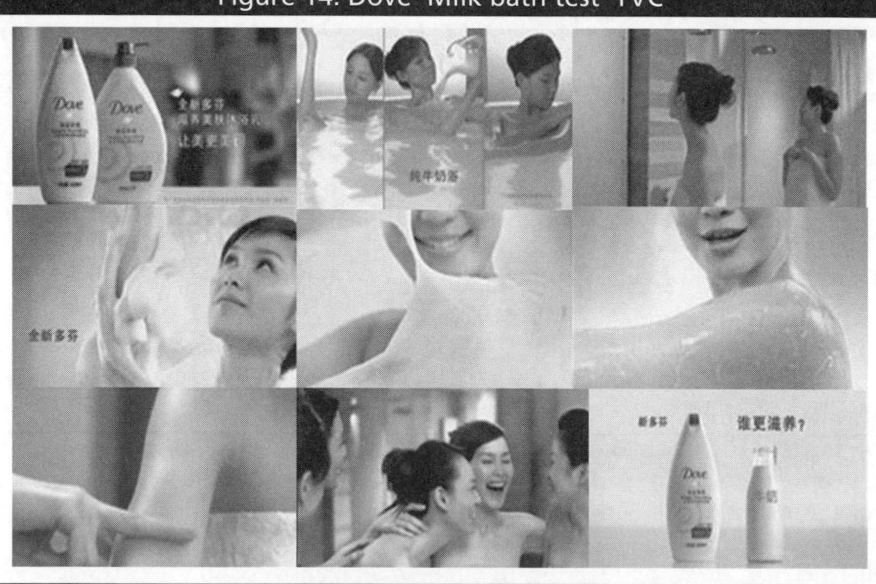

When she went online that evening at home or the following morning at work, she would 'hear' through her weibo (China's Twitter) from 'strangers with experience': Dove engaged key opinion leaders with millions of online fans, and seeded videos on major video portals and blogs to further spread the convincing objective proof about its new product (see Figure 15).

**Figure 15: Key opinion leader blog content seeding**

Source: www.dove.com.cn/MedicalClub

Later in the week, when browsing her favourite style magazine, she would see Dove's advertorials featuring dermatologists and other experts, to add even more credibility to our beauty claim (see Figure 16). She would become more convinced that Dove's new product indeed did work as promised.

**Figure 16: Dove 'Milk' search optimisation and advertorial**

Source: magazines: *Lifestyle*, 9 December 2011; *Fashion Weekly*, 'Beauty', 30 December 2010; *The Bund*, 'Life', 23 December 2010; *Oggi*, January 2011; *Women's Day*, January 2011

Our in-store execution was about a 'four-minute' product interaction, through demos, sampling, road shows and Dove Beauty Ambassadors (see Figure 17), to close the deal.

Figure 17: Dove activation

Shortly after Dove's 'Milk' campaign launched, we heard two rumours that reassured us that Dove would win in China. First, research agencies immediately tested the campaign for our competitors. Second, competitors were complaining to government censors about the comparative nature of Dove's campaign, suggesting the TVC should be withheld from airing.

Dove really hit a nerve. The brand's market share rapidly soared from 2% to 7%, and proceeded to almost 9% to overtake Olay by the end of 2011.

## February–December 2011: overtaking Olay

Here we describe what Dove did for the rest of 2011.

Riding on its surge in market share, Dove increased its distribution throughout 2011 to 59% in Q4 (though still lower than Olay's 70%).[22] Retailers were happily stocking Dove at better terms.

To further take advantage of retailers' receptivity, four additional variants were introduced in April 2011.[23]

As the volume manufactured increased dramatically, improved efficiencies allowed Dove to gradually reduce price further to RMB 43/kg by Q4 (below Olay's RMB 46).[24]

Dove also had the confidence to hold media investment at a similar level as Olay's in 2011 (see Figure 18) throughout the year.

Figure 18: Dove Feb–Dec 2011 estimated actual media spend (RMB million)

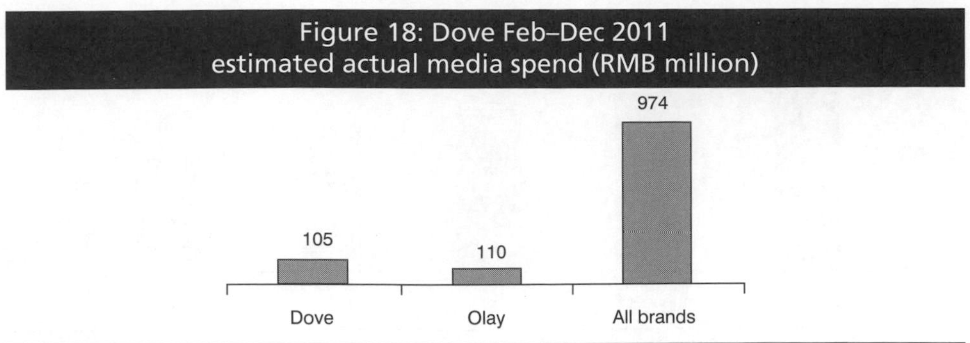


Source: Adquest (TV, print & radio), iADtracker (Internet), Zhongtianxinghe (OOH), PHD analysis

This investment sustained the 'Milk' campaign and the new positioning, such as by creating a social media event in Q2: 'every woman is a beauty story'. Dove invited real women to share their real beauty stories online – 2.4 million did, resulting in the largest single collection of beauty stories in world history (see Figure 19).

Figure 19: 'You are a beauty story' social media campaign

And Dove proceeded to grow its market share to 8.8% by December 2011, overtaking Olay.

## Effectiveness and payback

### *The campaign worked: rapid share rise*

Recall our first objective, to increase share from 2.1% to 3.4%. By January 2011, Dove propelled from number ten in China with 2% share before the campaign to number five with 7% share (see Figure 20).

Figure 20: January 2011 China shower gel percentage value share

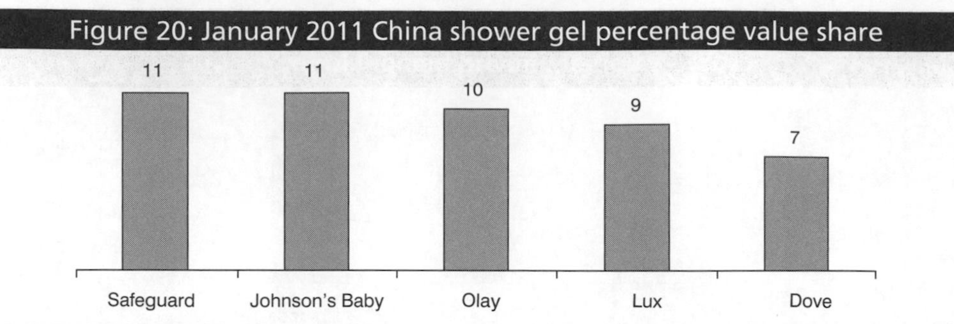


Source: AC Nielsen 2010–2011, Ogilvy analysis

This was not a case of 'everyone grew so should Dove'. Post-campaign, Dove's sales grew 111% as Olay and the category declined (see Figure 21).

Figure 21: Shower gel monthly value sales percentage growth pre- vs. post-campaign

111
–22
–38
Dove
Olay
Category

Source: AC Nielsen 2010–2011, Ogilvy analysis

And by December 2011, Dove sustained and exceeded this growth to an all-time high of 8.8%, overtaking Olay for the first time in history (see Figure 22).

Figure 22: December 2011 China shower gel percentage value share

11
10
9
8
7
Safeguard
Lux
Dove
Olay
Johnson's Baby

Source: AC Nielsen 2010–2011, Ogilvy analysis

### *How it worked*

The Dove campaign better fit the brand and was more persuasive to drive usage interest than competitors (see Table 1).

## Table 1: Better branding and higher persuasion for Dove 'Milk' campaign

| | Dove 'Milk' | Industry average | Dove 'Milk' higher by |
|---|---|---|---|
| 'Fits brand very well' | 29 | 16 | +81% |
| 'Strongly increased interest in using' | 33 | 23 | +43% |

Source: Millward Brown 2010, Ogilvy analysis

It had an immediate effect on consumers' perceptions of the brand. Recall our second and third objectives of improving Dove's nourishment and beauty equities. Both were achieved. Before the campaign, Dove was seen as less nourishing than Olay. However, now they saw it as better than Olay (see Figure 23), placing Dove as best at skin nourishment in China.[25]

## Figure 23: 'Nourishes your skin' brand image

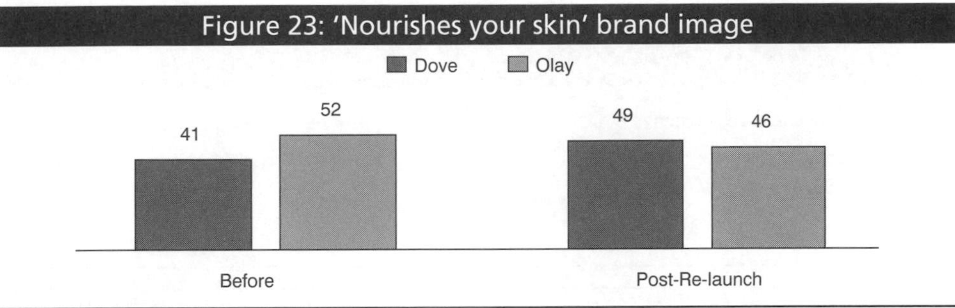


Source: Millward Brown 2010, 2011

More women also believed that Dove delivered beauty, while Olay's beauty image declined (see Figure 24).

## Figure 24: 'Makes you look and feel beautiful' brand image

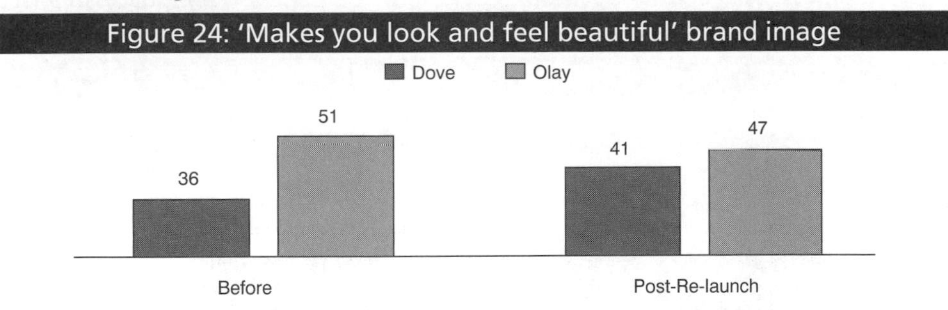


Source: Millward Brown 2010, 2011

Dove's newfound skin nourishment leadership, a key driver of the 'Security' need, did re-position Dove away from Olay's space of 'Admiration' according to our original strategic intent. Dove's sales share of 'Security' tripled from 15% pre-campaign to 44% by the end of 2011.[26]

This perception growth doubled penetration, adding an estimated 6 million new Dove users.[27] Not only were there more, they used more: heavy users doubled to 20% of Dove's newly expanded user base (see Figure 25).

Figure 25: Heavy/medium/light user percentage

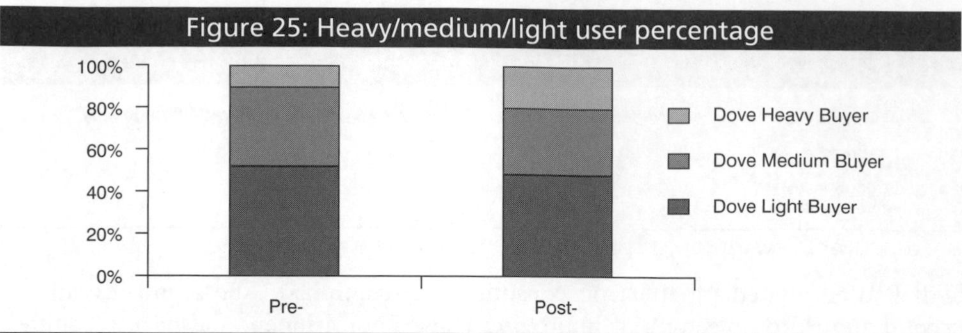


Source: AC Nielsen 2010–2011, Ogilvy analysis

### *Marcomms were the winning factor: discounting all other factors*

Dove did not win by shouting louder than competitors (see Table 2).

Table 2: Shower gel estimated actual media spend

| In RMB million | 2009 | 2010 | 2011 |
|---|---|---|---|
| Safeguard | 112 | 206 | 187 |
| Lux | 93 | 102 | 159 |
| Olay | 114 | 146 | 130 |
| Dove | 4 | 77 | 106 |

Source: Adquest (TV, print & radio), iADtracker (Internet), Zhongtianxinghe (OOH), PHD analysis

### Could it have been innovative packaging that drove purchase?

No. The newly launched product looked virtually the same as its predecessors (see Figure 26).

Figure 26: Old Dove packaging vs. new

### Could it have been the product benefit?

While the product did moisturise better than before, moisturisation was a ten-year-old benefit in China, thus not true new news to consumers.

### Could it have been Dove's bar soap?

No. It maintained a zero media budget and nothing about it changed before, during or after the campaign.

### Was it the distribution?

Highly unlikely. Consider the fact that when Dove increased distribution for nine months prior to the new campaign, its share declined by half (see Table 3).

**Table 3: Dove market share vs. distribution**

| | 9 months pre-campaign | 1 month pre-campaign | Variance |
|---|---|---|---|
| Market share % | 4.2 | 2.1 | -2.1 |
| Distribution % | 42 | 51 | +9 |

Source: AC Nielsen 2010–2011, Ogilvy analysis

### Was it the price reduction?

Arguably no. Between September 2010 and January 2011, Dove reduced its price by RMB 3/kg, while Olay reduced by RMB 2/kg, yet Dove grew sales by 111%, Olay's declined by 22% during the same period.[28] If price reduction could drive sales, Olay should have grown too, but it declined instead.

By process of elimination, if Dove's significant share growth was not by spending more than competitors on media, not by cutting price or expanding distribution, not by an innovative product benefit and not by packaging innovation – then we can reasonably conclude that Dove's marcomms *per se* were *the* winning factor driving its substantial business growth.

## *Evidence of payback*

Here we use three methods – ROMI, regional test and econometrics – to prove that marcomms generated significant business payback.

### Results from IPA's recommended 'return on marketing investment calculations' method[29]

Dove's average monthly sales prior to the re-launch were approximately RMB 12m.[30] This can fairly be assumed as the 'base sales' which would have happened, even if marcomms had not run.

On this basis, we estimate that Dove's campaign generated incremental sales of RMB 277m.

Thus, using the ROMI method we estimate that Dove's incremental sales ROMI was 1:1.6 and profit ROMI was 1:1.5. (see Table 4).

**Table 4: Incremental sales and profit ROI estimation**

| (In RMB million) | Sep 2010–Dec 2011 |
|---|---|
| Est. base sales | 192 |
| Actual sales | 469 |
| Incremental sales | 277 |
| Est. campaign investment | 170 |
| Incremental sales ROI | 63% |
| Est. incremental profit margin | 75% |
| Incremental profit ROI | 47% |

After reviewing 880 prize-winning papers in the IPA Effectiveness Databank, the advice for measuring payback was simple: 'use econometrics'.[31]

The IPA review also favoured regional weight tests, 'which can show the effect of the campaign quite clearly' (unlike simplistic advertised vs. non-advertised regional tests, which are 'fairly unreliable').

We also found clear campaign effects using both methods.

### Results from regional tests

We compared Dove user penetration vs. media weight in two Chinas, the South/East region and the North/West region.

Dove had 88% more marcomms in the South/East than in the North/West during the re-launch. Penetration growth in the South/East ended up 107% higher.

Even after taking into account Dove's higher distribution width in the South/East, penetration growth in the South/East was still significantly higher at 80% (see Table 5).

**Table 5: More TV weight resulted in higher penetration growth**

| | South/East | North/West |
|---|---|---|
| Est. population proportion | 50% | 50% |
| Average no. of bodywash brands used | 2 | 2 |
| Dove 'Milk' TV GRP's weight | 3.2 – 88% higher than the North/West | 1.7 |
| Penetration change | From 3.2% to 6.3% | From 1.0% to 2.5% |
| Gross penetration growth % | +3.1 – 107% higher than the North/West | +1.5 |
| Est. Dove distribution | 57% | 43% |
| Adjusted penetration increase % | +2.7* – 80% higher than the North/West | +1.5 |

Source: AC Nielsen 2010–2011, Ogilvy analysis; Adquest (TV, print & radio), iADtracker (Internet), Zhongtianxinghe (OOH), PHD analysis

The evidence could not be clearer: more marcomms equalled more consumers buying Dove.

## Results from econometric models

The Effectiveness Partnership developed econometrics models to isolate the specific impact of Dove's marcomms relative to other pieces of the marketing mix such as pricing, distribution or number of products.

Figure 27 illustrates the accuracy of the model. Dove's model picked up just over 96.6% of total variation with a standard error of 11.8%.

Figure 27: Actual vs. fitted model

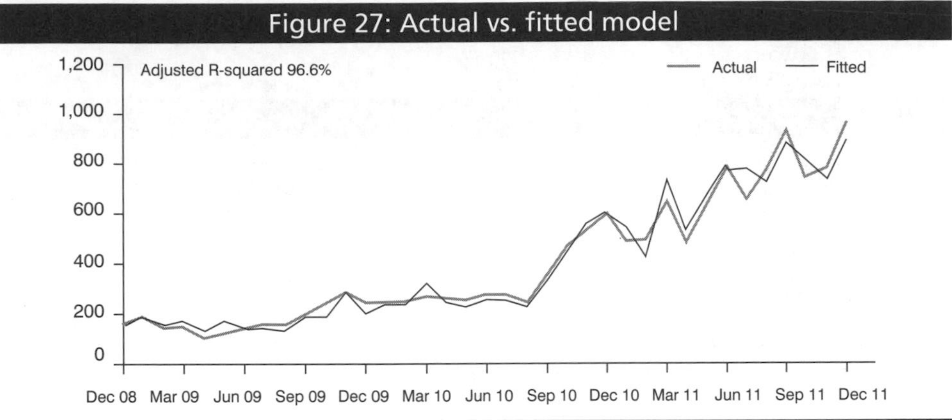


Source: Econometric models

We found clear campaign effects (see Figure 28) from the model, when comparing Dove's sales with vs. without marcomms.

Figure 28: Dove sales with vs. without marcomms

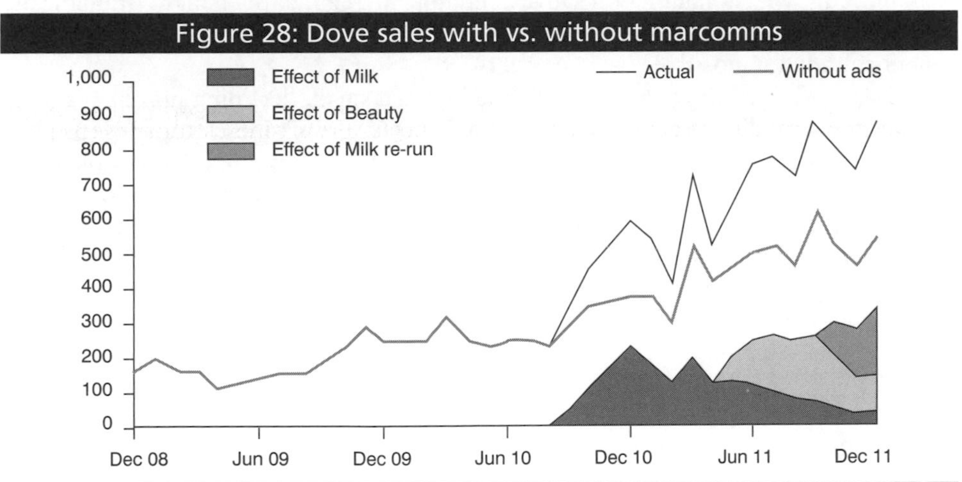


Source: Econometric models

The model suggests that the Dove campaign delivered incremental sales ROMI of 1:1.4, the highest single contributing factor across the marketing mix.[32]

As spend was RMB 170m, the incremental sales marcomms generated was approximately RMB 238m.

### *Payback summary*

Based on the range of payback results above, we conclude that Dove's marcomms in 2010–11, which grew share from 2.1% to 8.8%, generated the following payback (see Table 6):

- Sales ROMI: 1:1.5 – for every 100 dollars spent, est. 152 dollars in incremental sales were generated.
- Profit ROMI: 1:1.4 – for every 100 dollars spent, est. 139 dollars in incremental profits were generated.

**Table 6: Average ROI based on various methods**

| (In RMB million) | Sep 2010–Dec 2011 |
|---|---|
| Est. sales ROI from ROMI calculations | 63% |
| Est. sales ROMI from econometric modelling | 40% |
| Average sales ROMI from two methods | 52% |
| Est. incremental profit margin[33] | 75% |
| Est. profit ROMI | 39% |

## Summary

Back in 2009, while planning for Dove's re-launch in China, the goal to dramatically increase share as product number 262nd in China with no innovative packaging or benefit sounded impossible.

This case showed how Dove transformed from a small, declining player in a large market into a leading brand. Dove got under the skin of Chinese women's insights, produced a campaign that went against the grain of communications norms, to propel market share from 2.1% to 8.8% in 16 months. For the first time in Chinese history, Dove was bigger than Olay.

This case demonstrated how Dove's marcomms were *the* winning factor across its marketing mix. Marcomms *per se* delivered incremental sales of RMB 255m (or £25.5m) with a ROMI of 1:1.5 (on media spend of RMB 170m).

### *A new learning on winning in China*

Some say the Chinese consumer market changes so rapidly that rigorous, detailed strategic thinking on marketing communications is not meaningful. That was true perhaps, when the market was in its infancy, which was China's very recent past.

From our experience, we believe the days of 'putting something in the market and it will sell' are arguably over. As China matures, sophisticated, fact-based strategic choices are needed to win. This helped transform the Dove brand in China and sold very, very hard indeed.

## Notes

1 Research International H&A Study 2008.
2 AC Nielsen 2010–2011, Ogilvy analysis.
3 Ibid.
4 Ibid.
5 Ibid.
6 1 GBP = 10 RMB.
7 Adquest (TV, print & radio), iADtracker (Internet), Zhongtianxinghe (OOH), PHD analysis.
8 AC Nielsen 2010–2011, Ogilvy analysis.
9 Ibid.
10 Ibid.
11 PHD, Ogilvy estimate.
12 AC Nielsen 2010–2011, Ogilvy analysis. Adquest (TV, print & radio), iADtracker (Internet), Zhongtianxinghe (OOH), PHD analysis.
13 Adquest (TV, print & radio), iADtracker (Internet), Zhongtianxinghe (OOH), PHD analysis.
14 Needscope 2008, Ogilvy analysis.
15 Global Demographics Ltd., 2009.
16 Ogilvy focus groups.
17 CMMS 2009, Ogilvy analysis.
18 OgilvyAction 2009 Shopper Research.
19 Ibid.
20 Ogilvy shopper interviews 2010.
21 Millward Brown 2010, Ogilvy analysis.
22 AC Nielsen 2010–2011, Ogilvy analysis.
23 Ibid.
24 Ibid.
25 Millward Brown 2010, 2011.
26 AC Nielsen 2010–2011, Ogilvy analysis.
27 Ibid.
28 Ibid.
29 http://www.ipaeffectivenessawards.co.uk/ROMI
30 AC Nielsen 2010–2011, Ogilvy analysis.
31 Binet, L. & Field, P. (2007) *Marketing in the Era of Accountability.* WARC, p. 77.
32 The Effectiveness Partnership 2012.
33 Estimate from interviews with industry and financial analysts.

## Chapter 14

# Health Promotion Board Singapore

## I Quit: from anti-smoking to pro-quitting

**By Sonal Narain, Ogilvy & Mather Singapore**
Contributing authors: Benoit Wiesser, Tim Broadbent, Steve Back, Dan Gibson, Shirley Tay, Troy Lim, Jon Loke, Tania Chan, Huiwen Tow, Jamie Tang and Ng Hui Min, Ogilvy & Mather Singapore
Credited companies: Ogilvy & Mather Singapore; Vocanic Pte Ltd; Waggener Edstrom Worldwide; Flamingo International; Media Agency: OMD; Client: Health Promotion Board Singapore

**Editor's summary**

Smoking was on the rise in Singapore with tough measures such as fear campaigns, taxation and legislation proving ineffective and resulting in smokers feeling marginalised and smoking more, not less. Instead of an anti-smoking campaign that would marginalise them further, a pro-quitting campaign was created to help contemplators quit. The campaign spanned various touchpoints creating an environment conducive to quitting, inspiring quitting, and creating support through tools, resources and quit clubs. The results showed that every second smoker moved one step closer to quitting; the quitting success rate was three times the international average; and it achieved a payback of 15.7.

This paper is not only insightful about the power of addiction and the social willpower required to support quitters, it is also a good example of leveraging online channels to great effect.

## The model state and smoking

To many countries around the world, Singapore, a small and highly prosperous country is a model state, often serving as an inspiration, prototype and testing ground for the implementation of policies and measures, for a whole host of things – clean and efficient public transport, greener city living, safety, and especially public health policy.

It has for a long time prided itself on one of the lowest rates of smoking in the world, leading the worldwide effort to curb smoking both in terms of the extent of measures and communications, as well as their effectiveness.

Often called 'a police state', Singapore has some of the strictest anti-smoking laws in the world. Increasingly restrictive bans on public smoking, high taxation, scary imagery on packs and staggering fines make smoking almost impossible.

This reputation, however, is at risk. In a shock reversal, smoking in Singapore is on the rise despite this.

Not only was it on the rise, but in 2007, it had been rising at an alarming rate of 8% every three years.

## Its impact

Seven premature deaths result from smoking-related diseases each day in Singapore.[1] The result – not simply death and the concomitant personal and emotional loss; it also implies a staggering financial/economic loss to the public exchequer.

A 1997 study by Quah, Tan, Saw and Yong of the Department of Economics, of the National University of Singapore estimated the social cost of smoking to be around US$600m which at today's rates would amount to more than US$800m of state money (somewhere between a half to a third of the government's total spending on health in 2010).[2]

It was with a view to reducing this that the Health Promotion Board of Singapore (HPB) approached us for a campaign in late 2010.

## Why this was tough

There were several reasons why reversing this rise would not just be challenging, it would be next to impossible.

### *An irreversible youth culture phenomenon*

1. In line with the growing sense of dissatisfaction and rebellion in the city,[3] young people were beginning to smoke much earlier than the previous generation had. Over the last six years, the age at which 18–24 year olds first started smoking had gone down by one whole year (Figure 1).[4] The rise in smoking came from them.

Figure 1: Age of smoking experimentation

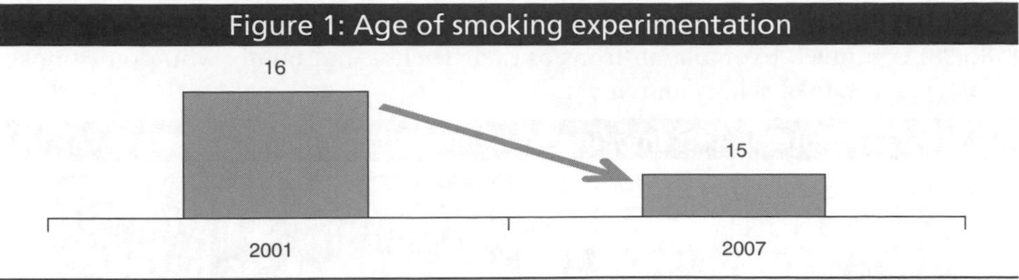


2. Youthful foolhardiness and a blinkered optimism made them believe that the things that anti-smoking communications warned of (cancer, etc.) could not happen to them or that they were not addicted and could quit whenever they wanted.
3. Popular culture was creating normalization for what had previously been considered unattractive and unhealthy by society (Figure 2).

*With Korean drama series showing their actresses lighting up, I worry about such unhealthy influences.*

Khaw Boon Wan (former Health Minister, Singapore)

Figure 2: Visual from Korean drama

### *An audience hardened and fatigued by years of scare tactics*

Constant campaigning against societal evils, such as smoking, gambling, substance abuse, etc., is something that Singapore specialises in. Smoking, particularly, is an act that has been heavily campaigned against, using fear as a tactic for discouragement and disincentivisation for over 30 years. Everything has been tried, from heavy taxation, bans on public smoking, to graphic imagery on cigarette packs (Figure 3). Despite increasingly tightening legislation, smoking was still on the rise.

A recent Singapore poll showed that smokers are unconcerned about the negative health impact of smoking on others around them.[5] Of the 243 smokers polled, almost all (97.1%) were aware of the harms of second-hand smoke to others, yet most (58.8%) continued to smoke in front of their friends and family who don't smoke, displaying a state of selfish inurement.

**Figure 3: Anti-smoking communications in Singapore**

SAMPLE REPRESENTATION - FOR REFERENCE ONLY
WARNINGS FOR SMOKED TOBACCO PRODUCTS 2006

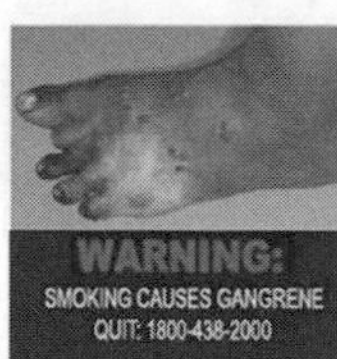

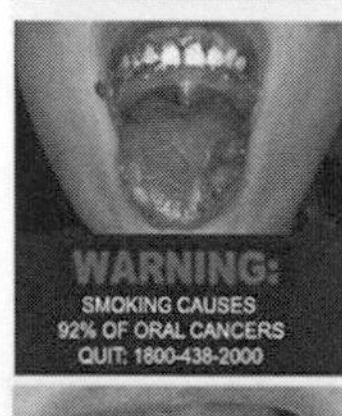


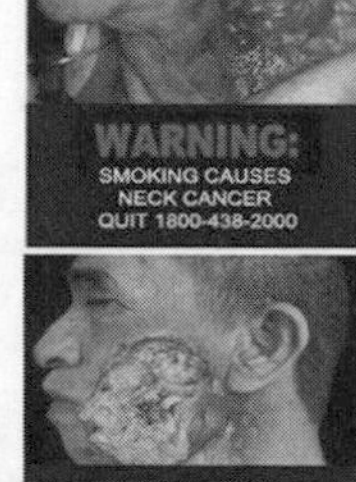


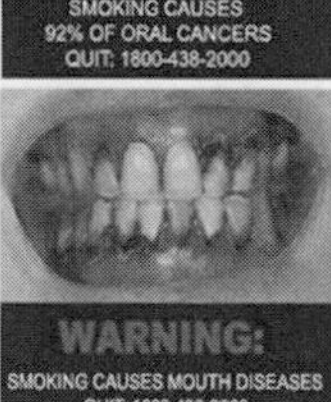


WARNING:
SMOKING CAUSES
92% OF ORAL CANCERS
QUIT: 1800-438-2000

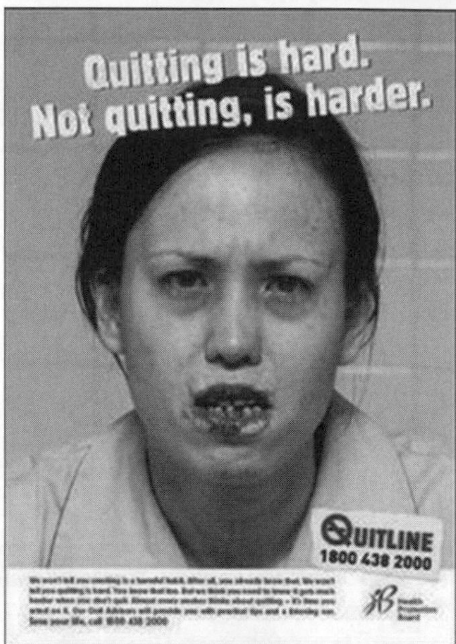


*'Campaign' based thinking and budgets*

Typical government health communications spending patterns and budgets decreed that a public service campaign could only last three months. We were attempting to undo something that had happened over three years with a campaign that could only last three months.

How could we, with a four- to five-month campaign:

- reverse a cultural phenomenon and physical addiction that were the result of bigger forces;
- do what legislation over years had not been able to, especially when the tried and tested approach of education on its ill effects was not working anymore;
- all amongst a deeply hardened audience?

Government communications that spoke of the harmful effects of smoking barked up the wrong tree... these people already knew smoking was bad, and yet they continued to smoke in defiance of it. We were not going to be able to stem the rise with just one campaign.

It was very clear that we needed a radically new and more efficient approach – in terms of who we spoke to, what we said and how we did it. And we needed something that could sustain itself beyond the four to five months of advertising spending.

## A new problem in a new target audience

We couldn't speak to all smokers; we had to segment smokers to find an audience amongst which we could make a real and discernible difference.

A deeper dive into the data revealed a significant but overlooked problem. Sixty-five per cent of all smokers intended to quit sometime in the future. But only 12.6% had any serious intentions of doing so in the next six months (Figure 4). Action was even lower; only 60 people were calling HPB's QuitLine every month.[6]

Figure 4: Intention to quit amongst smokers

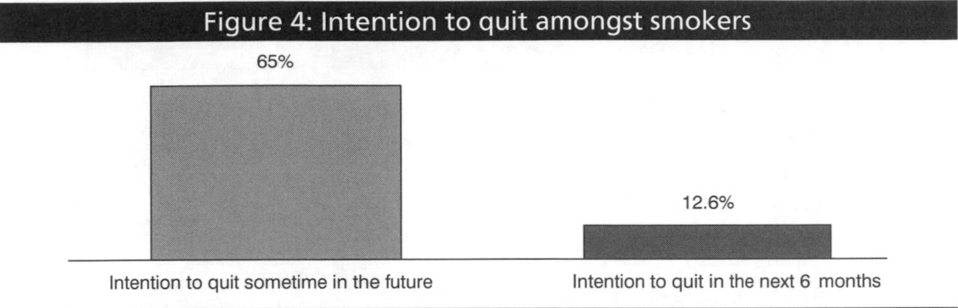


Source: National Health Surveillance Survey 2007

The problem: a gap between intention and commitment
The audience: smokers contemplating quitting

### *The barriers standing in the way of quitting amongst contemplators*

#### Attitudinal – increasing isolation of smokers

An increasingly trenchant and isolationist discourse had emerged recently against this already heavily targeted category. 2010 had seen the rise of almost militant anti-smoking activist groups rallying to kick smokers out of public areas and ban tobacco completely.[7] At the same time, simplistic fear-based anti-smoking communication assumed they didn't already know smoking was bad. Its top-down tonality made smokers feel like an unhealthy taint on an otherwise clean and healthy state (Figure 5).

The above two factors were making smokers feel hemmed in by an unsupportive and hostile environment, and actually compounding the problem instead of helping it.[8]

Communications trying to convince smokers to quit could actually do more harm than good as it did not factor in how they felt about smoking already, and their right to their own lives and decisions. They felt isolated, preached to, and outcast by the mainstream, when all they needed was guidance towards the right methods and support.

In this environment, telling people to quit using negative or fear messaging ran the risk of making smokers even more resistant to 'oversimplified propaganda'; it ran the risk of turning them off.

## Figure 5: Perceptions of smokers in Singapore

**However, the broad social views about *female* smokers in Singapore are**

| | |
|---|---|
| Sarong Party Girl/Ah Lians | Bad family background |
| Girls with a loose lifestyle – pubs, hookers | Sad, tense, suffering emotions |

**Almost no sense of positive female smoking icons in Singapore**

**The prevailing social view is reinforced by the local media too.**

**Teenage girls openly smoke and litter outside Woodlands swimming complex**

stomp .com.sg

STOMPer TL was disgusted to see these two girls openly smoking outside Woodlands swimming complex. They even littered the floor with their cigarette butts and left, says TL.

TL elaborates:

"What sort of teenagers is Singapore bringing up?

"Found these two wanton teenagers puffing profusely outside Woodlands swimming complex.

"They then littered the floor with their cigarette butts and went into the swimming pool.

"Their behaviour is so ugly."

Source: http://bit.ly/dwo2h7

### Behavioural – the difficulty of quitting, lack of confidence, usage of wrong methods

Amazingly, 60% of smokers had tried quitting before and failed. Thirty-seven per cent of smokers were unaware of any of the quit resources available, 41% had tried quitting on their own without any help, only 25% were confident about quitting.[9]

Most smokers wanted to quit, but weren't taking any concrete steps towards it because they lacked the knowledge and confidence to do so.

> *Giving up smoking is the easiest thing in the world. I know because I've done it thousands of times.*
>
> Mark Twain

We were amazed that what seemed to be the biggest problem had been ignored by most anti-smoking communication around the world.

It takes any smoker an average of six to seven attempts to quit smoking. The barriers to quitting are tremendous: not just emotional but also physiological. Few anti-smoking campaigns, if any, had even acknowledged, much less helped people through, the difficulties of quitting.

## A new role for communications

Our sweet spot was clear – we needed to bridge this gap between intention and commitment amongst quitting contemplators to get them to quit.

But, we couldn't scare them. Communications that tried to scare them into giving it up would turn them off.

The decisive insight came from the study, 'the process of smoking cessation – implications for clinicians' by Prochaska and Goldstein, which had concluded that 'helping patients progress just one stage can double their chances of not smoking six months later.'[10] We knew what we had to do.

We had to help contemplators quit, by overcoming the barriers that stood in the way of them quitting successfully.

## Our solution: from anti-smoking to pro-quitting

Instead of blanket bombing all smokers with a 'don't smoke' message, or trying to reverse the pickup of smoking amongst the youth, we had to approach smoking from the other end and help contemplators quit.

Our communications objectives were:

1. help contemplators move one step closer to quitting;
   - move intention to quit from a vague 'sometime in the future' to 'the next six months'
   - take the first active step towards quitting
2. increase success rate of actual quitting efforts;
3. slow down the rate of rise in smoking.

Through the following communications tasks:

- by building knowledge of the right methods;
- by creating a supportive environment conducive to quitting;
- by starting a movement that had the ability to sustain itself, instead of a one burst campaign.

### *The insight*

Qualitative research amongst entrenched and ex-smokers had revealed a powerful truth.[11] Smokers quit for very personal reasons, each one of these being personal watershed moments, such as discovering a patch on your lungs, or realising that your dependence on it was desperate (see Figure 6). There was no way communications could trigger these, through 'reprimanding delinquents into quitting'.

**Figure 6: Motivations for quitting**

**The strongest motives to quit are when you are hit with a moment of realisation – awareness that cigarettes have taken over your life and sense of self**

*I realised that it was getting too much when one day, I didn't have money to buy cigarettes and my boy friend and I actually picked up a used cigarette from the bin and smoked it. We tried to 'sterilise' it as much as we could*
***Hidayah, 22 y.o, non-contemplator***

**However, it is important for them to come to this realisation on their own terms for it to be truly effective – implications for anti-smoking communication!**

Conversely, each successful journey through the quitting process also revealed a huge sense of gratification and achievement.

We also knew that instead of a traditional message in which the government diminished the physical value of smoking, we needed to get *people or society* to enhance the social and personal value of quitting. This meant that the community would have to do it, not us.

## The idea

A social movement to salute quitters and their heroic accomplishment. A movement that got the larger public supporting them and talking about it.

I Quit was created as a statement and symbol that elevated quitters to the status of national heroes because it signified quitting as a heroic act and quitters as heroes (Figure 7).

To make it a bottom-up community movement, instead of a top down campaign, we chose real life ex-smokers as its heroes, and involved the community through a social media-based nationwide movement of support for quitters, which guided them to the right methods and resources.

Figure 7: The campaign symbol

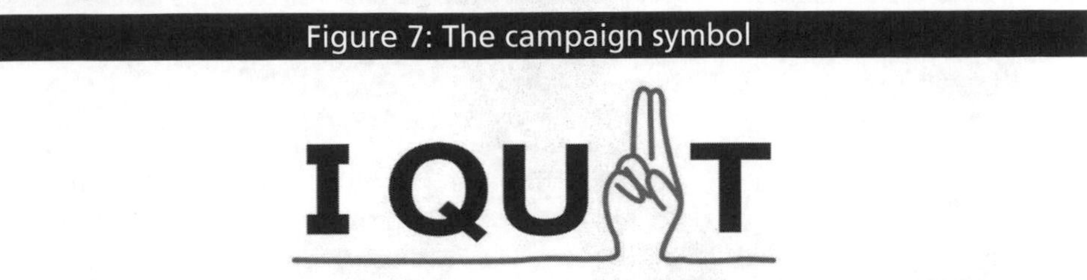


## A new channel strategy

We designed a messaging architecture and channel strategy that was aimed at starting a movement, and it drove people from taking the pledge to quit to actually quitting. To create a new large scale public discourse around quitters, and to make a big public statement around them we used ATL. But while ATL advertising was critical to amplifying our message, to reaching as many people as we could and for elevating this movement into national consciousness, social media was necessary for galvanising real social support. Social media had to be the heart of our campaign (Figure 8).

Figure 8: Media phasing plan

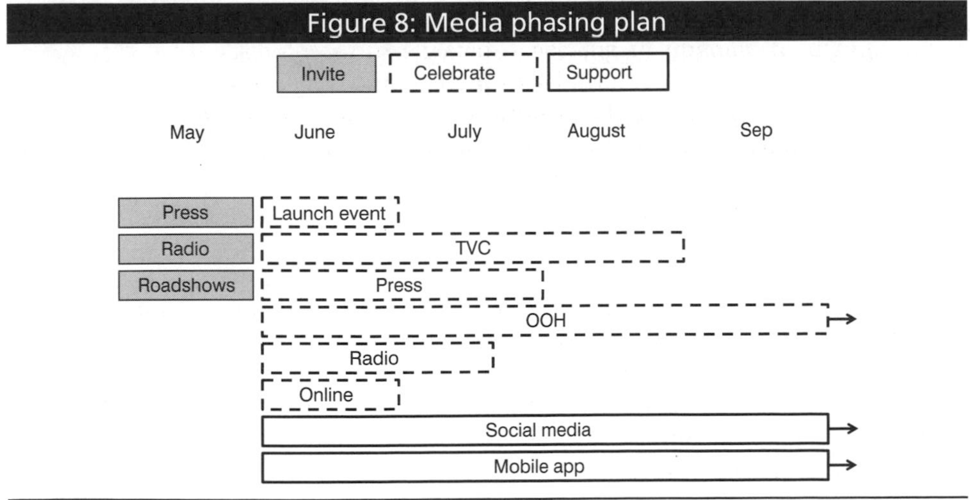

### *Phase 1: Inspired and rallied contemplators to take the first active step towards quitting*

Roadshows and mobile quit studios were set up and roamed the island, asking smokers to come forward and take the pledge to quit. Popular radio DJs from Class 95 FM egged on smokers to flock to these (Figure 9).

The pledges could also be taken online on the Facebook page. All their stories were recorded, and their queries answered. Each one of these was contacted by HPB's QuitLine consultants, and invited to join a cessation programme, which offered individually tailored quit strategies.

Figure 9: Recruitment and filming at the roadshows

### *Phase 2: Celebrate and support these individuals in order to overcome 'smoker isolation'*

Instead of using models or celebrities, we took the people who came forward in phase 1 and made them the heroes of our campaign. A moving TVC was created featuring ordinary quitters stepping forward to take the pledge to quit. Each hero told us a powerful story, which was then written in their own handwriting on T-shirts in the form of a pledge. 'I Quit because…'. Smokers of all ages, races, shapes and sizes came forward as a truly representative cross section of Singapore.

Their stories were broadcast using ATL (TV, Print, OOH and Radio), and on social media, inspiring more people to quit, and creating a groundswell of positive support (Figures 10 and 11). An online app allowed smokers to create their own customised I Quit poster.

Figure 10: TVC

Figure 11: Launch event on World No Tobacco Day (WNTD)

*Phase 3: Provide these quitters with necessary resources to kick the habit for good*

Support was critical from friends and families, or ex-smokers. In order to give smokers the support they needed, we created virtual and physical I Quit Clubs, inspired by Alcoholics Anonymous. The I Quit Club Facebook page provided community support, serving as the nerve centre for the campaign. Smokers could pledge here, interact with other quitters, share their experiences and offer/receive support. For those seeking to quit on their own, the page provided easy access to tools and resources, counselling at pharmacies and hospitals. The mobile app allowed people to get access to all of the above on the go, as well as track their progress (Figure 12). The movement was amplified across the public and private sector, with organisations lending their support to us. Volunteer ambassadors received training in the various modules of the I Quit Club.

Figure 12: I Quit Club sign up page and I Quit mobile app

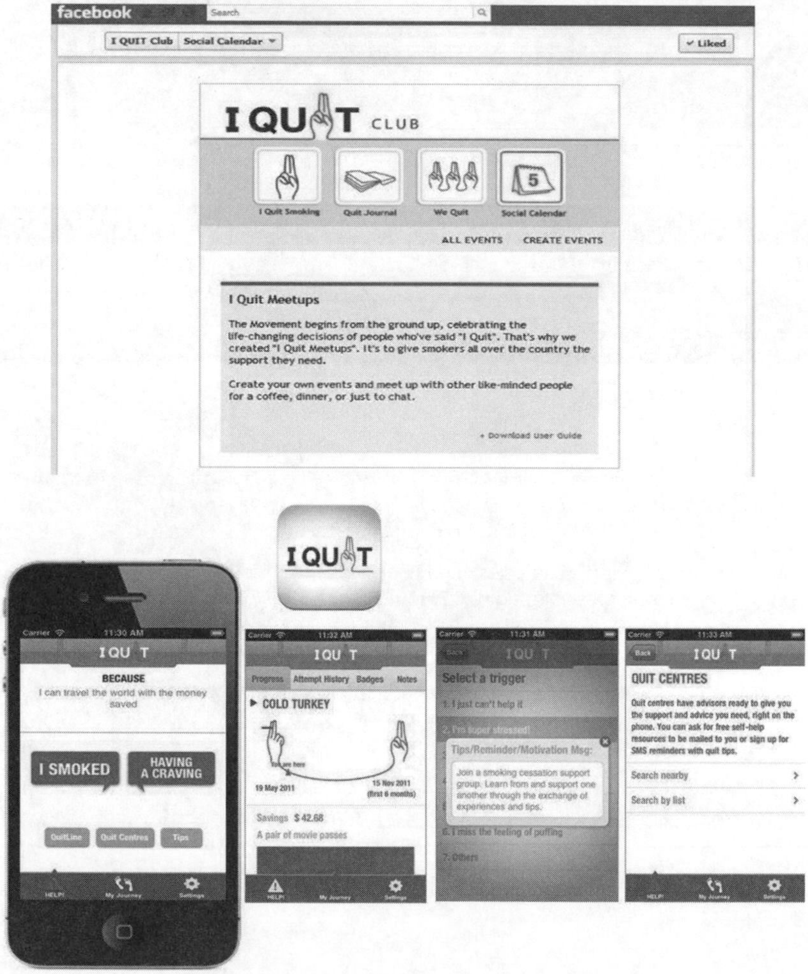

The cumulative effect of all these diverse activities? A feeling of being surrounded by quitting activity and support, in stark contrast to the previous hostile and isolationist discourse.

## How we know this has worked

Our change of approach is one with long-term implications, and hence does not work to reverse the rise in smoking. We cannot and should not prove effectiveness in the manner that previous short-term focused anti-smoking campaigns have (through a reduction in smoking prevalence). This is a new approach that aims at helping smokers quit successfully, through creating facilitative environments, through the creation of social value, through knowledge and empowerment. We must, therefore, in this section, first prove that this new strategy has worked how it was intended amongst this audience, and then by achieving the objectives it had set out to achieve.

We will, in this section, be laying out the journey from campaign impact to the achievement of campaign objectives (Figure 13).

**Figure 13: The campaign's effect – from communication tasks to commercial objectives**

1. It has created a supportive environment towards smokers

2. It has resonated and struck home with the new target audience of contemplators

3. It has generated greater awareness of quit methods amongst our target audience of contemplators

4. It has moved nearly every second smoker (almost 50% of all smokers) one step closer to quitting

5. It has increased the success rate of actual quitting efforts

6. This has slowed down the rate of rise of smoking

7. The slow down in the rate of smoking prevalence rise has given us an ROI of 15.7 on the campaign investment

8. Finally, it has started a movement that has the ability to sustain itself, by getting the community involved

9. I Quit has been widely recognized as a 'first of its kind' positive departure from typical anti-smoking communication

### 1. It has created a supportive environment towards smokers

Conversations about smoking have shifted to quitting and become positive,[12] creating an environment of support; a huge shift from the earlier hostile environment that focused on health risks associated with smoking (Figure 14).

**Figure 14: Sentiment analysis**

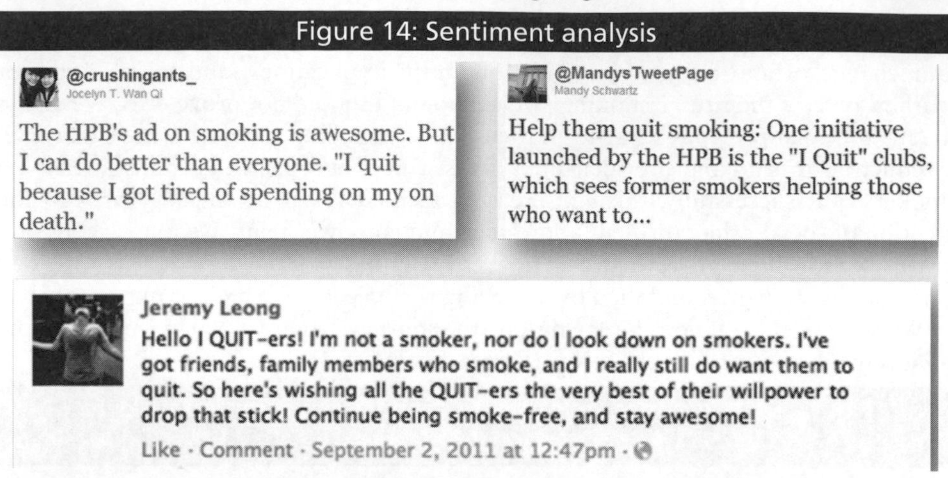

@crushingants_
Jocelyn T. Wan Qi
The HPB's ad on smoking is awesome. But I can do better than everyone. "I quit because I got tired of spending on my on death."
@MandysTweetPage
Mandy Schwartz
Help them quit smoking: One initiative launched by the HPB is the "I Quit" clubs, which sees former smokers helping those who want to...
Jeremy Leong
Hello I QUIT-ers! I'm not a smoker, nor do I look down on smokers. I've got friends, family members who smoke, and I really still do want them to quit. So here's wishing all the QUIT-ers the very best of their willpower to drop that stick! Continue being smoke-free, and stay awesome!
Like · Comment · September 2, 2011 at 12:47pm ·


Nearly 87% of all non-smokers who know a smoker say they have greater regard for people who quit, as a result of the campaign, while 75.6% non-smokers say they will talk to smokers about quitting after seeing the campaign.[13]

This support is overwhelmingly evident on the Facebook page. A total of 67,919 interactions have built a sense of community and solidarity.[14] The engagement on the page exceeds that of other current Facebook-based campaigns such as 'NYC Quits', and is three times the engagement of other longer running government initiatives with more investment behind them.

It has successfully shifted what used to be a hostile discourse to a more positive one, removing the sense of marginalisation smokers once felt.

### 2. It has resonated and struck home with the new target audience of contemplators

They have noticed it more, found it more unique and relevant to them, and been impacted by it more as well. Figure 15, from the post campaign research, shows a uniformly higher gravitation towards and engagement with this campaign among this target group.[15]

### 3. It has increased awareness of quit methods amongst our target audience of contemplators

Post campaign research indicates 73% of all intenders are aware of at least one more quit method, as a result of this campaign.[16]

Figure 15: Post-campaign diagnostics

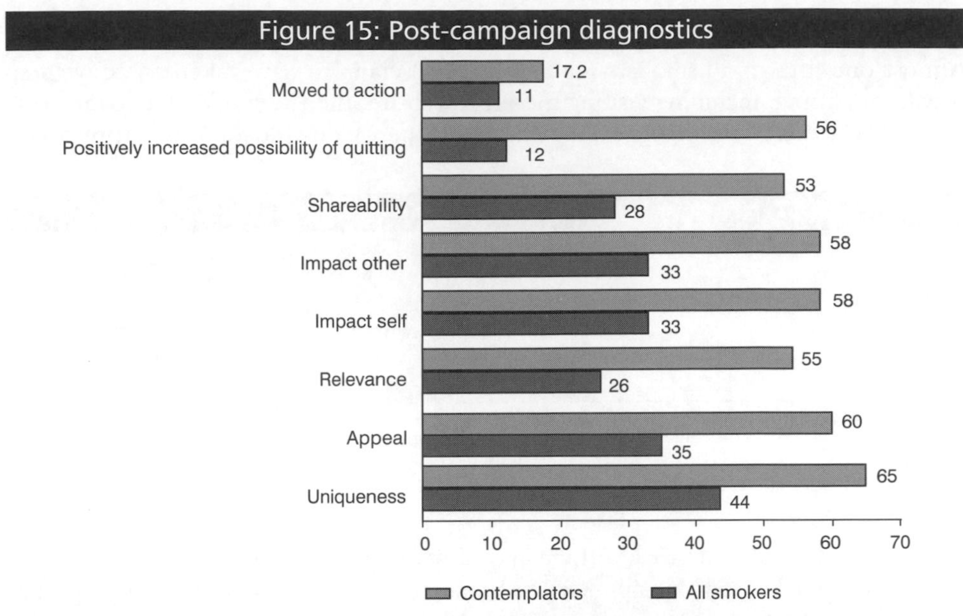


Source: Summary of campaign diagnostics, HPB commissioned post-campaign research (N=823), 2011

### *4. It has moved nearly every other smoker (almost 50% of all smokers) one step closer to quitting*

This breaks up into the following statistics/sub-objectives:

### Moving intention to quit from a vague 'sometime in the future' to the 'next six months'

Twenty-eight per cent of smokers (43.4% of contemplators) are likely to quit sooner after watching the campaign.[17] This translates to roughly five times more contemplators being likely to quit in the next six months, as compared to 2007, as a direct result of the campaign (Figure 16).[18]

Figure 16: Intention to quit in the near future among contemplators

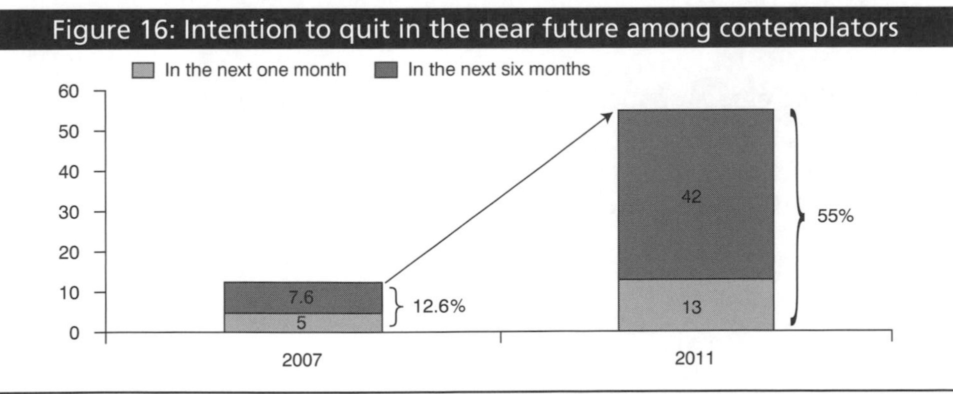

### Take the first active step towards quitting

Almost one fifth of all smokers (or nearly 20%) claim to have taken an active step towards quitting, including visiting the HPB website, the Facebook page, contacting an HPB certified consultant, calling the QuitLine or downloading the application (Figure 17).

**Figure 17: Action taken upon seeing the campaign (2007 to 2011)**

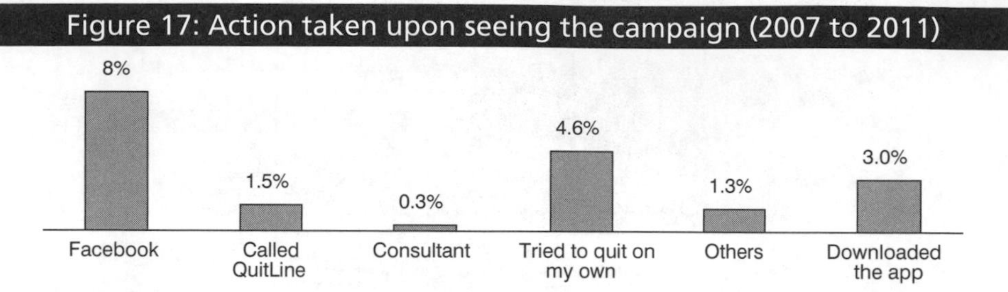


Source: Post campaign research among 823 smokers Q. After viewing the advertisement, did you do any of the following?

The number of calls to QuitLine has shot up by more than 300% since the campaign launch. And this number continues to rise, even after the campaign has ended, indicating long-term impact (Figure 18).

**Figure 18: Calls to QuitLine against media spend (Jun 2011 to Feb 2012)**

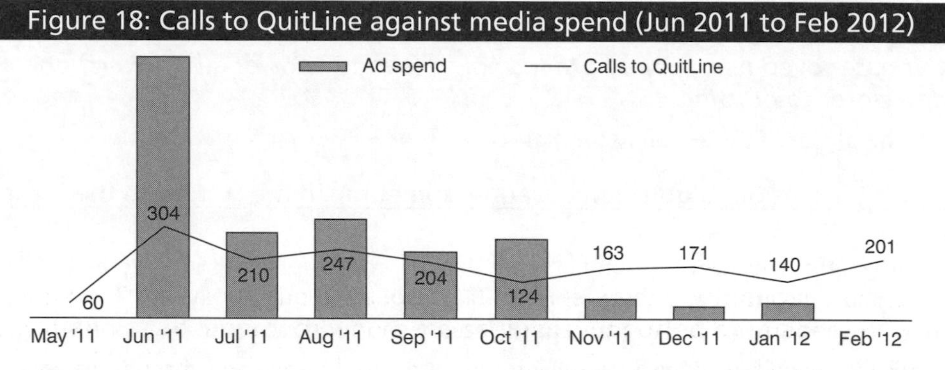


Source: Client data

### *5. This has increased the success rate of actual quitting efforts*

The success rate of those who signed up for the I Quit Club cessation programme is 31.5%, three times the average international success rate of smoking cessation programmes (10%, as estimated by Mayo Clinic Health Solutions) (Figure 19).[19]

Figure 19: Quitting success rate comparison with I Quit

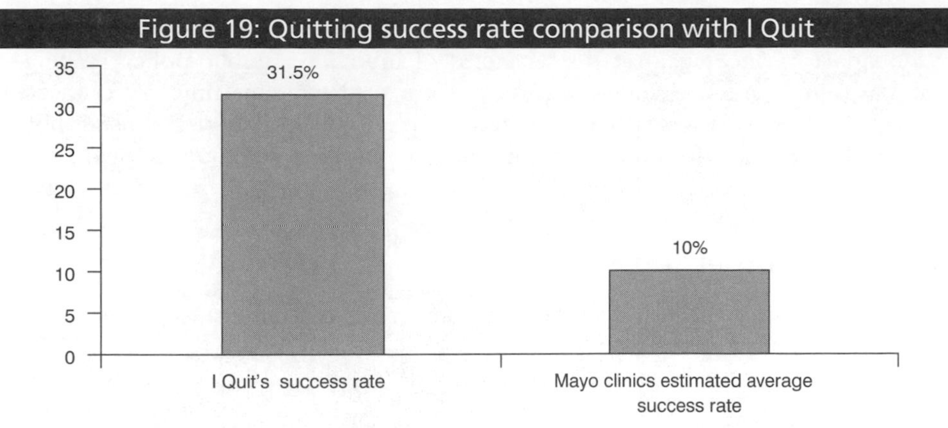


Source: Comparison between I Quit Club cessation rate (source: client data) and Mayo Clinic Health Solutions – Tobacco Quitline: Reports and Outcomes

### *6. This has slowed down the rate of rise in smoking*

From an 8% rise in smoking between 2004 to 2007, the rate at which smoking is increasing has currently slowed down to 5%.[20]

### *7. The slowdown in the rate of smoking prevalence rise implies an ROI of 15.7 on the campaign investment*

The slowdown implies 14,550 fewer smokers.

In 1997, the cost of smoking was estimated to be at around US$600m, or US$1,432 per smoker. This at today's rates (after applying CPI) would amount to US$1,564 per smoker. 14,550 fewer smokers implies the state can save US$1,566 × 14,550 = nearly US$23m.

With campaign spends under US$1.5m, this is an ROI of 15.7.[21]

### *8. Finally, it has started a movement that has the ability to sustain itself, by getting the community involved*

Smokers are taking up the cause themselves and are volunteering to be the face of the campaign. The positive nature of the campaign has also started a movement of sorts; 33 ex-smokers have volunteered to be ambassadors of I Quit. They are being trained in the White Belt training programme to become I Quit champions and will run more I Quit Clubs in their districts.

Meanwhile, the calls to QuitLine continue to increase despite media spending having stopped (refer to Figure 18).

### *9. I Quit has been widely recognised as a 'first of its kind' positive departure from typical anti-smoking communication*

The campaign has been showcased at the World Conference for Tobacco or Health 2012, as an example of an innovative anti-smoking communications that has relied on and involved the community to take it forward.

HPB have received accolades, praise and congratulations for the same.

Singapore is once again at the vanguard of innovative public policy making. I Quit has found supporters and praise, even from academics and universities that are at the cutting edge of social marketing theory development, who recognise it for its empowering and participatory approach to anti-smoking communications, and its innovative use of social media for social marketing.[22]

## Eliminating other factors

In this section we will illustrate how other factors/legislation against smoking have not contributed to the aforementioned results.

### *Health warnings*

Picture warnings on packs have been around since before the campaign.

### *Taxation*

Tobacco taxes were last raised in 2005 from S$293 to S$352 for every 1,000 cigarettes imported. This raised the price of a pack of cigarettes to the current average of S$12, making Singapore one of the world's most expensive places to light up. Since then there has been no other increase in taxation.

### *Anti-smoking bans*

The ban on outdoor smoking was introduced in 2007, when the intention to quit amongst contemplators was last measured.

### *Other communications*

The last mass anti-smoking campaign in Singapore was run in 2007, amidst huge controversy over the graphic imagery used in it. There has been no other mass-based campaign against smoking since then to 2011.

### *Citizen activism*

On 22 November 2010, citizens of Singapore supported the Towards Tobacco-Free Singapore online campaign. The campaign promotes a proposal (which was published in the *British Medical Journal*, 'Tobacco Control') to prevent the supply of tobacco to Singaporeans born from the year 2000 which would result in a gradual phasing-out of tobacco in Singapore. We know, however, that this has resulted in making smokers defiant instead of making them want to quit.[23]

With all the above factors we can reasonably conclude that the current results are from the campaign effects and not the result of the above measures.

## Learnings and conclusions

While benefit-based communication may be a cliché in the commercial marketing world, it is a novelty in the social marketing world, especially in the encouragement of healthy/safe behaviour. As social marketers, we need to open our eyes to what is a fundamental truth of behavioural psychology – that we cannot make people change behaviour with threats; we need to motivate them with incentives. It validates again, the power of tapping into positive motivations, positive ideals and self-identification as the most effective in driving behaviour change. People will do better if you tell them they can.

Social media is not just desirable but an imperative for social marketing campaigns. Much has been said about the ability of social media to increase the efficiency of campaigns through the compounding effects of amplification and tacit endorsement. But what this paper proves is that in the case of government/ social change communications, social media has a more transformational effect. As a medium, it is intrinsically 'of the people/by the people' (dare we say 'for the people'), hence allowing communicators to truly transcend older top-down models. It results in an appropriation of the message, and more importantly of the intent by your audience, making it hugely more effective, and even more so in highly socially affiliative societies in Asia. This has an important implication even for commercial brands. Participation in this day and age needs to go beyond allowing consumers to like and interact with you/your brand. It means allowing them to be the face of your brand/cause and driving it.

What this paper also proves is the power of smart integration in translating attitudinal change into real action and behavioural change. Adopting a 'CRM' approach, converting people one step at a time and hand-holding them from attitude change towards action and conversion will disproportionately impact the effectiveness of campaigns.

In these financially-challenged times, all these are lessons that governments around the world would do well to heed, as they seek to balance their budgets, and optimise the effectiveness of their healthcare and social communications investments to do ever more with ever less.

## Notes

1 http://www.hpb.gov.sg/smokefree/article.aspx?id=432
2 Source: Quah, E., Tan, K.C., Saw, K.L. & Yong, J.S. (2002) The social cost of smoking in Singapore. *Singapore Medical Journal,* **43**, 7, pp. 340–344. Department of Economics, National University of Singapore.
3 http://www.pressrun.net/weblog/2011/05/the-prophetic-singapore-poll-predictions.html
4 National Health Surveillance Survey 2007.
5 http://www.pfizer.com.sg/sites/sg/news_and_media/Pages/news_article9.aspx, sample size: 450 smokers and non-smokers combined.
6 Client data.
7 http://www.tobaccofreesingapore.info/
8 Research amongst entrenched smokers conducted by Flamingo International 2010.
9 Client commissioned research on attitudes to smoking amongst smokers, 2011.
10 Source: Prochaska, J.O. & Goldstein, M.G. (1991) Process of smoking cessation: implications for clinicians. *Clinics in Chest Medicine*, **12**, 4, pp. 727–735. Behaviour Change Institute, University of Rhode Island, Kingston.
11 Research amongst entrenched smokers conducted by Flamingo International 2010.
12 Social media sentiment analysis carried out by Waggener Edstrom Worldwide.
13 HPB commissioned post campaign research among non-smokers. Q: Please rate your views on the following statements on a scale of 1 to 5. 'I have greater respect for smokers who have decided to quit', 'I would talk to smokers about quitting but leave the choice on how to quit to them'.
14 We Are Social Facebook page analysis.
15 HPB commissioned post campaign research among non-smokers.

16 Post campaign research among 823 smokers. Q: Which one of the following methods were you aware of before the campaign?
17 HPB commissioned post campaign research among 823 smokers. Q: Overall, which of the following statements best describes how much this advertising campaign affects your attitude towards smoking? Answer options: 'Plan to quit in the next six months', 'Plan to quit in the next one month'.
18 The comparisons here are to 2007, since that was when the last mass state sponsored conventional anti-smoking campaign was run.
19 www.mayoclinic.com
20 Source: National Health Surveillance Surveys 2004, 2007, 2010 and client data 2011.
21 Calculations based on National Health Surveillance Study conducted once every three years and client data supplemented in 2011.
22 Dr Gerard Hastings, Faculty of Social Marketing, University of Stirling.
23 Post campaign research amongst smokers.

## Chapter 15

# McDonald's

## Getting Britain lovin' it once again

**By Tom Roach, Leo Burnett London and Alistair Macrow, McDonald's Restaurants**
Contributing authors: Beate Lettmann, Mindshare ATG; Mike Treharne, Leo Burnett London
Credited companies: Creative Agency: Leo Burnett; Digital Agency: Razorfish; Media Agency: OMD; Others: The Marketing Store; Client: McDonald's Restaurants

**Editor's summary**

The judges felt this paper was an incredibly inspiring story about a business that achieved an impressive turnaround of consumer opinion. It shows how advertising helped McDonald's achieve five successive record-breaking sales years since its turnaround. In 2007, McDonald's was back in growth after four years of stagnation, but it had yet to regain the trust and love of its customers. Two complementary brand advertising campaigns, 'Trust' and 'Favourites', rolled out over a number of platforms, including TV, press, in store, outdoor and digital, worked in harmony to get people to trust and love the brand again through celebrating its role in modern British life. They delivered £349m in short-term sales in addition to the £460m delivered by promotional advertising and a near fourfold increase in payback of £9.79. A clear demonstration of the power of both product and communications strategy working together to generate great results.

## Introduction

Turning McDonald's around in 2007 after four years of stagnation has been widely celebrated as a remarkable business achievement.

This is about what happened next: how advertising helped accelerate McDonald's growth in the next four years, helping take the business from recovery to resurgence.

In 2007 customers had begun to return in sufficient numbers for the business to register positive growth. But for millions of customers, McDonald's had yet to regain its shine – we'd lost their trust, and their love for the brand was a distant memory.

By 2011 McDonald's had achieved five successive record-breaking sales years.[1]

We will prove and quantify the considerable contribution that brand advertising made to this success, showing how two distinct brand campaigns worked simultaneously to regain people's trust and love for the brand. We will quantify the contribution advertising made to improving brand image and show that this drove millions of new customer visits. We will show the considerable and increasing sales impact these campaigns have had and the near four-fold increase in ROI they delivered.

But before we tell the resurgence story, here's a reminder of the recovery story.

## Background: 2002–2006, the wilderness years

From 2002–2006 McDonald's suffered at the hands of a perfect storm of issues which took a considerable toll on the brand and the business.

These issues included the McLibel trial, the obesity debate, the legacy of health scares such as foot-and-mouth, the book *Fast Food Nation* and the movie *Supersize Me*. The brand was fashionable to attack and appeared out of step with the mood of Britain, with media commentators, celebrity chefs and politicians all taking turns to score easy points (Figure 1).

Figure 1: Negative media coverage

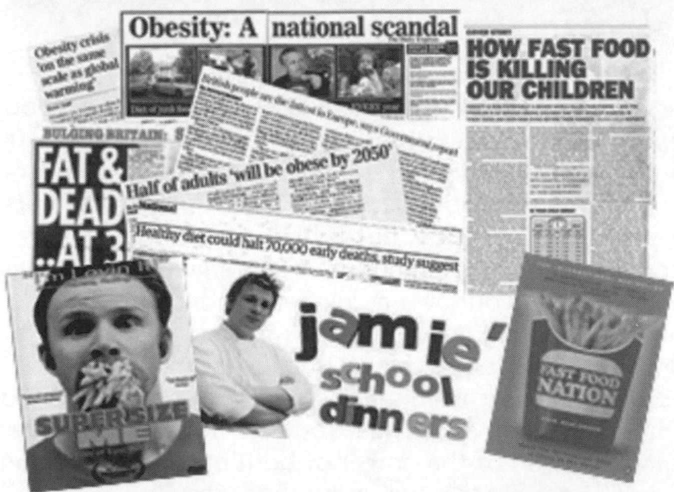

Unsurprisingly, people's trust in the brand suffered at the hands of this criticism (Figure 2).[2]

Figure 2: Decline in trust in McDonald's 2003–2006

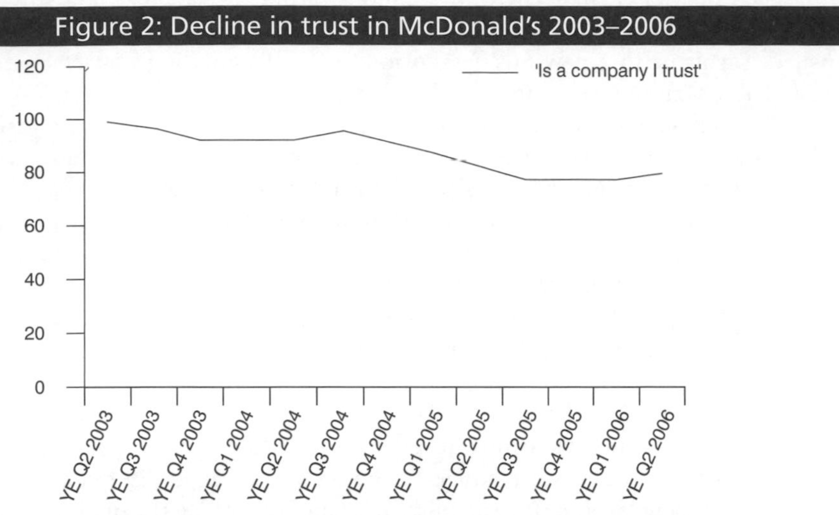


Source: TNS FastTrack brand tracker. Base: last 4-week IEO users

Alongside this brand image decline came a decline in visitor traffic[3] and sales (Figure 3).

Figure 3: McDonald's UK visitor traffic 1998–2006

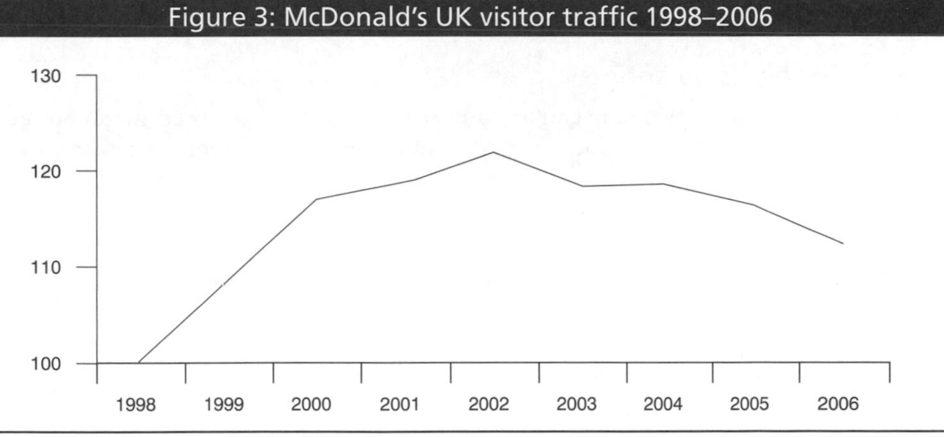


Source: McDonald's UK

Since the brand's arrival in the UK in 1974, McDonald's had only ever known sales growth. So to see stagnation from 2002–2006 understandably caused anxiety within the business.

## 2006–2007: re-building the business

The seeds of McDonald's UK's now famous business recovery were sown in 2006, with the appointment of a new CEO, Steve Easterbrook. A period of soul-searching ensued, resulting in a new business vision, an understanding that change would be needed across the entire business and an acceptance of a home truth: many customers no longer felt so good about coming to McDonald's so were coming a little less.

The new business vision was to be a 'modern progressive burger company': all the changes that were made from this point on sprang from this.

First, the business sought to fix the fundamentals: introducing more balanced choices to the menu, improving the nutritional profile of the food, increasing investment in crew training and redesigning the restaurants.

Only once these changes were in place did we adopt a new approach to managing external brand perceptions. Our principle was 'act first, talk later'.

### *Changes to the food*

New premium products were introduced including Rainforest Alliance certified coffee, and porridge and bagels were added to the breakfast range. Product reformulations included reducing levels of fat, salt and sugar and improving the quality of ingredients such as only using 100% chicken breast from approved poultry farms, free range eggs and organic milk.

Changes to Happy Meals included adding fibre to buns, serving unsalted fries, organic milk and fresh orange juice, and the nutritional content was managed to ensure that 79% of the Happy Meal is classified as not high in fat, salt and sugar.

### *Changes to the restaurants*

The restaurant re-designs that began in 2006 completely changed their look and feel. Out went the bright red and yellow plastic and in came softer greens, purples, wood and contemporary furniture.

### *Communications*

We adopted a transparent approach to managing external relationships, firstly with stakeholders and later the public. After years of being more defensive, the company now regularly met government bodies and NGOs and became a willing participant in public debates. The change programme was also openly shared with the media.

The only customer-facing communications at this time were the launch of a website, makeupyourownmind.co.uk, inviting people to ask us any questions they wanted, and a small burst of magazine advertising announcing improvements to ingredients in Happy Meals to parents.

Apart from this, the vast majority of our media spend continued to focus on driving footfall from frequent customers by promoting our Saver menu and promotional food.

With a wide range of business issues addressed, customers began to return in sufficient numbers to make 2007 the year of the first upturn in footfall since 2002 (Figure 4).[4]

Figure 4: McDonald's UK visitor traffic 1998–2007

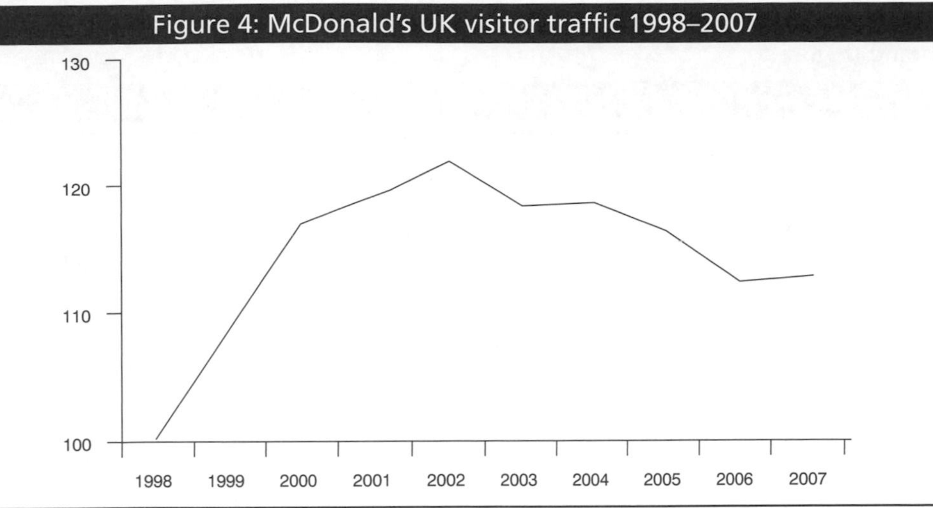


Source: McDonald's UK

These changes combined to make the turnaround possible. We can't reveal the contributions of all the changes, but restaurant refurbishments accounted for around a 6% sales increase per store.[5]

McDonald's had achieved its turnaround. But for millions of customers, McDonald's had yet to regain its shine – what follows is the story of how communications helped achieve this.

## 2008: re-building our marketing strategy

The decline in trust in the brand was by now well-known to us as a key factor in the poor sales performance,[6] and we already believed driving trust would unlock future growth.

But in exploring this problem more deeply, we uncovered another one: McDonald's also had a brand 'affinity' problem.

We undertook a range of research initiatives to help us understand how to re-build the brand – co-creation weekends with groups of customers, employees and franchisees, a bespoke 4,000 sample 'Usage & Attitude' study and mining the data from our tracking tools.[7]

Our U&A study, conducted in early 2008, shed new light on the problems, highlighting a need to rekindle the emotional bond with our customers.

It revealed that a significant proportion of customers had fallen into a functional relationship with the brand, visiting McDonald's purely for its convenience and value: a surprising 44% of visits came from customers critical of or neutral towards McDonald's.[8] And it revealed that increasing these customers' brand advocacy would increase their frequency.

The data also showed that McDonald's brand performance was weak on the most important drivers of brand advocacy in the 'Informal Eating Out' (IEO) category. McDonald's worst performing brand attributes were the most important category drivers – perceptions of our food quality and integrity, and customers' affinity for the brand (Figure 5).

Figure 5: McDonald's performance-importance matrix 2008

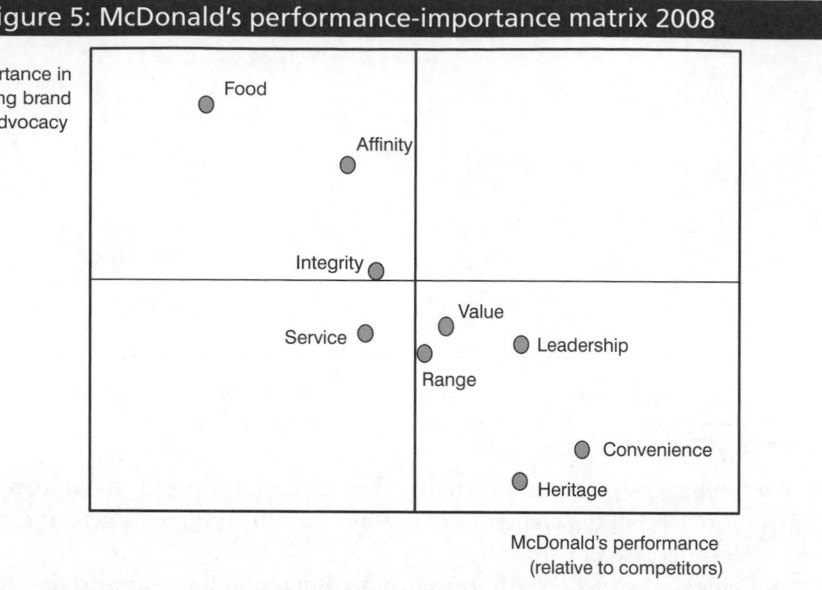


Source: U&A 2008

To bring the brand back to health we would not only need to increase people's trust in it (via the quality of our food and our integrity as a business), but we would also need to get people to feel a close affinity or love for it once again.

Relationships between people are built on trust. And whilst trust is a pre-condition of a loving relationship, on its own it is not enough. Trust means you *can* love someone, but is not the *reason* you do. And the same is of course true of brands.

We would need two complementary brand campaigns working in harmony: one to regain customers' trust in the brand, another to re-ignite their once strong love for it. And doing both together would get customers coming back a little more often.

## Two new roles for brand communication

Alongside our two existing promotional communication strands that drive sales by 1) communicating our great value menu items and promotions and 2) launching new products and temporary food events, we now needed to commit significant spend to brand communication to drive both trust and affinity.

Our two existing roles for promotional communications were defined as follows:

1. *Reward* customers with affordable prices and generous promotions.
2. *Stimulate* them with exciting new products.

To these we added two new roles for brand communications:

1. *Enlighten* them about our food and behaviour as a company.
2. *Remind* them why they once fell in love with McDonald's.

With a growing array of communications tasks we needed a simple marketing framework. So we brought everything together into a model we call our 'marketing pillars', each pillar defining the details of the communications strategy to achieve one of our key objectives. The 'Trust' pillar aims to drive brand trust, the 'Favourites' pillar aims to drive brand affinity.[9] Figure 6 is a simplified version of our marketing pillars.

Figure 6: McDonald's communications framework

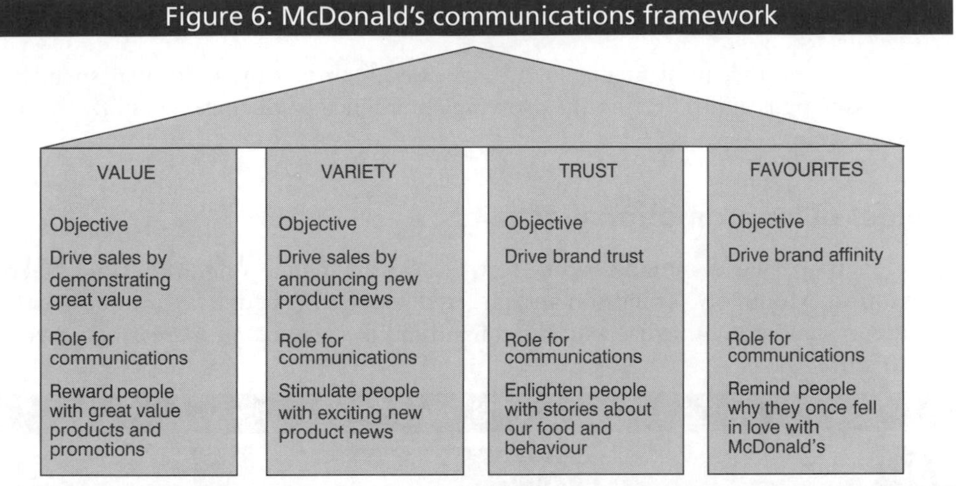

VALUE
Objective
Drive sales by demonstrating great value
Role for communications
Reward people with great value products and promotions
VARIETY
Objective
Drive sales by announcing new product news
Role for communications
Stimulate people with exciting new product news
TRUST
Objective
Drive brand trust
Role for communications
Enlighten people with stories about our food and behaviour
FAVOURITES
Objective
Drive brand affinity
Role for communications
Remind people why they once fell in love with McDonald's


All of our marketing since 2008 has been driven by these pillars. They structure and simplify a complex marketing programme, help deliver long-term creative consistency with creative freedom and balance our promotional and our brand activities.

Persuading the business that we needed to fundamentally change how we used advertising was a major challenge. Previously McDonald's advertising had been a promotional not a brand-building tool, a series of ad hoc and unconnected campaigns, each one expected to deliver strong year-on-year comparative sales. Brand campaigns played a minimal role, the belief being that they weren't able to drive sufficient short-term sales.

Persuading internal stakeholders was hard. Finally they agreed, but on one condition: our new brand advertising had to match the short-term sales performance of promotional campaigns.

## Re-balancing our communications spend

The new marketing strategy required us to balance our predominantly promotional spend more evenly across our four pillars. Trust spend was introduced from June 2008 and Favourites from October 2009 (Table 1).

Table 1: Media spend by communications pillar

| | 2007 | 2008 | 2009 | 2010 | 2011 |
|---|---|---|---|---|---|
| Total McDonald's advertising spend (Nielsen) | £30.24m | £36.35m | £44.99m | £52.55m | £53.28m |
| % of total spend on Value pillar activity | 33% | 20% | 37% | 25% | 29% |
| % of total spend on Variety pillar activity | 67% | 70% | 41% | 46% | 43% |
| % of total spend on Trust pillar activity | 0% | 11% | 12% | 12% | 11% |
| % of total spend on Favourites pillar activity | 0% | 0% | 10% | 17% | 17% |

Over the period, total media spend increased,[10] driven by additional spend on brand campaigns and reflecting the growing confidence of the business in the results we were seeing.

## 'Value' pillar promotional activity

This encompasses communications for the Saver menu, our free Coke Glass promotion, Monopoly promotion and targeted vouchering activity. Outdoor and TV are the primary Value media, with digital and mobile playing an increasingly strong role (Figure 7).

Figure 7: Value pillar outdoor examples

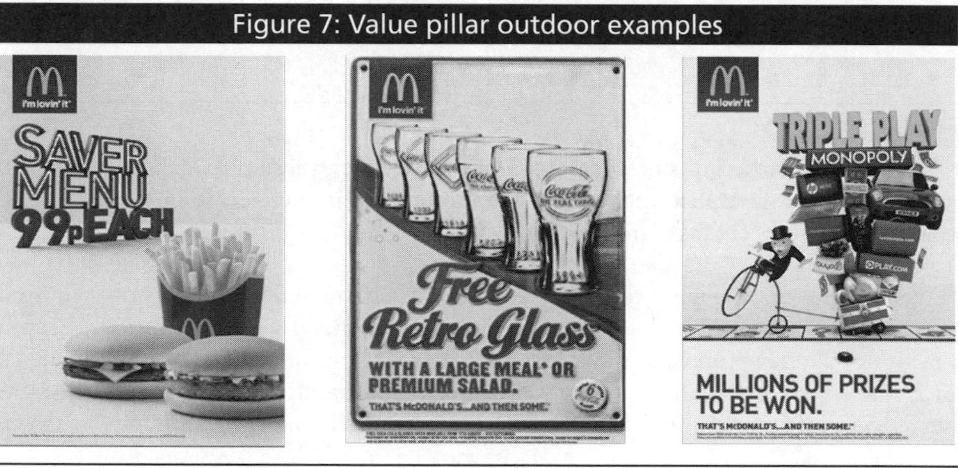


## 'Variety' pillar promotional activity

This encompasses limited time food promotions (such as the Festive menu and 1955 burger) and permanent product launches such as 2010's launch of a new wraps range. TV and Outdoor are the primary media, with social media playing supporting roles (Figure 8).

Figure 8: Variety outdoor examples

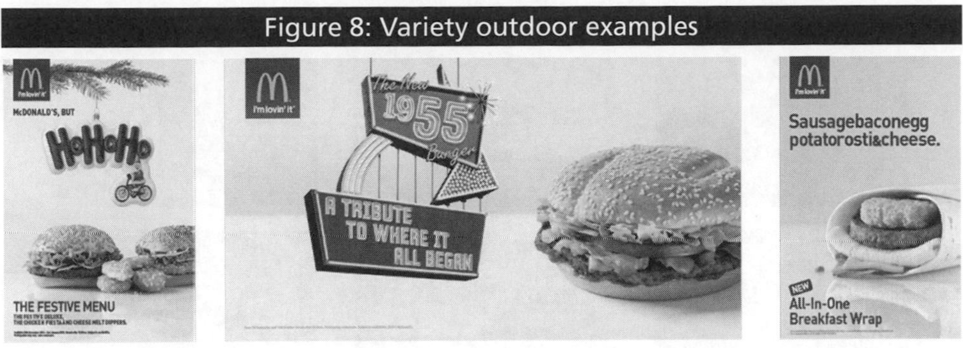


## 'Trust' pillar brand activity

Trust advertising aims to enlighten people with surprising stories about the quality, nutrition and sourcing of our food, our positive impact on communities, our pride in developing our people and how we limit our impact on the planet.

A combination of quantitative[11] and qualitative[12] research helped us understand the most powerful stories to communicate, for example that our burgers are made only from whole cuts of 100% British and Irish beef and our chicken products are made only with breast meat from approved farms.

Television is Trust's primary medium, with press, in-store and digital display used in support. Media is bought against parents, who research identified as the most in need of reassurance about food quality given their role as both customers and gatekeepers to children's visits.[13]

Our first three Trust campaigns (2008–2009's 'Planting', 2009–2010's 'Big Nothing' and 2010's 'Weather') aimed to enlighten parents about our sourcing of great quality, British ingredients (Figure 9).

2011–2012's Trust campaign, 'The A-Z of M', broadened the campaign out to encompass the full range of stories, including facts such as our use of the oil from our fryers as bio-diesel in our trucks, our litter patrols and the educational qualifications crew members can earn (Figure 10).

Creatively we convey the facts with charm and humility, never being worthy or chest-beating. Trust campaigns all feature the end line *'That's what makes McDonald's'*.

## 'Favourites' pillar brand activity

This aims to remind people why they once fell in love with McDonald's.

Qualitative research[14] uncovered a range of brand truths to help us create resonant advertising that could re-ignite people's latent love of the brand: it's welcoming, inclusive, consistent, always there for you, part of the fabric of British life, everyone has their favourite products and their own quirky ways of eating them.

Figure 9: TV stills from 'Planting', 'Big Nothing' and 'Weather'

Figure 10: TV stills from 'A-Z' and 'A-Z' press examples

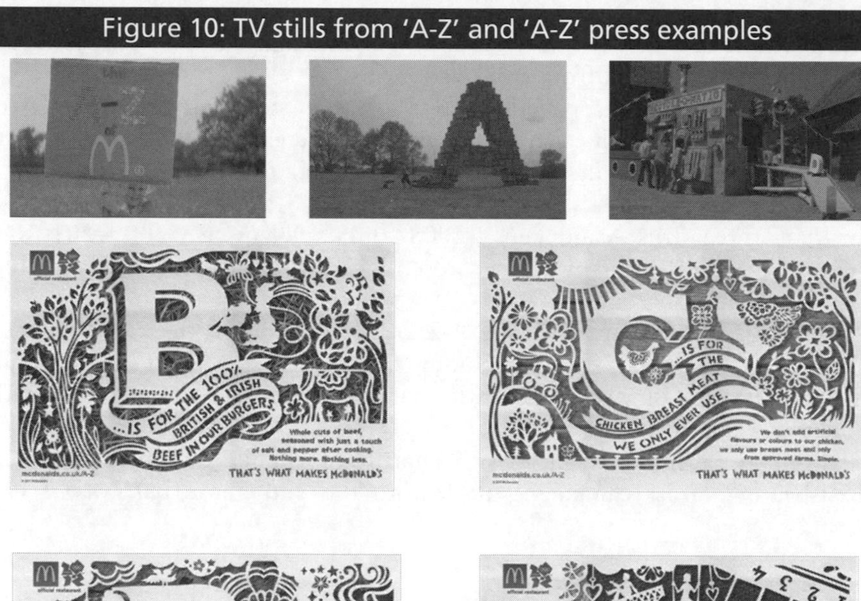

These truths inform all our Favourites creative briefs. For the initial campaigns we brought them together into one proposition, celebrating the brand's role in modern British life:

McDonald's is the People's Restaurant

So far we've created six Favourites campaigns. The first four (2009's 'Just Passing By', 2010's 'World Cup', 2010's 'Golden Arches Beacon' and 2011's 'Symphony' campaign) highlighted that McDonald's is welcoming, inclusive and always there for you, all featuring the end line *'There's a McDonald's for everyone'*.

Television is the lead medium for Favourites, supported by outdoor focusing on people's relationships with their favourite food (Figure 11).

Figure 11: TV stills from 'Just Passing By'

Favourites outdoor shows glorious close-ups of our food alongside insightful headlines about what makes these iconic products so special (Figure 12).

The most recent campaigns (2011's 'He's Happy' and 2012's 'First Day') focus on the fact that McDonald's is a welcoming, familiar haven for people (Figure 13).

Figure 12: Favourites outdoor examples

Figure 13: TV stills from 'He's Happy' and 'First Day'

## 2007–2011: market context

Before sharing the results, the tough market conditions we faced in achieving our objectives are worth outlining.

Once 2007's turnaround had been achieved, the economy worsened. Retail footfall, which correlates strongly to traffic in our market, fell dramatically[15] and traffic in the informal eating out market was mostly negative or flat (Figure 14).[16]

Figure 14: Retail and IEO market footfall 2007–2011

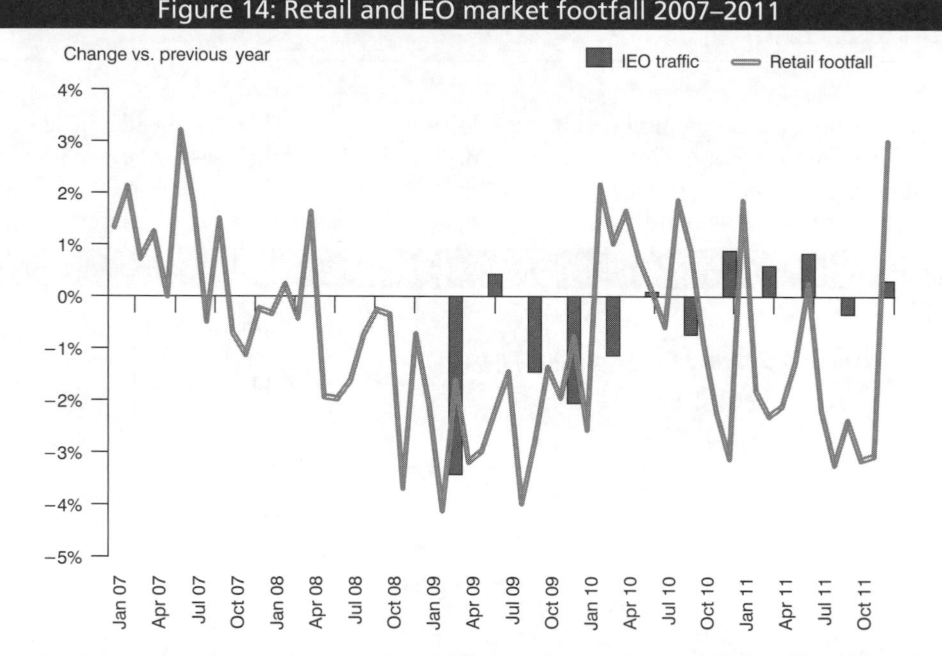


Source: NPD Group; IEO traffic: visits to informal eating out places (quarterly, change vs. last year). Source: Experion; retail footfall: visitor traffic to UK retail outlets (monthly, change vs. last year)

Figure 15 shows that sales growth in the IEO market was correspondingly flat 2008–2011:[17] it is a misperception that our market benefits from recession. To grow in this period, McDonald's needed to either grow the market or increase share.

Figure 15: IEO market value growth (excluding McDonald's) 2008–2011

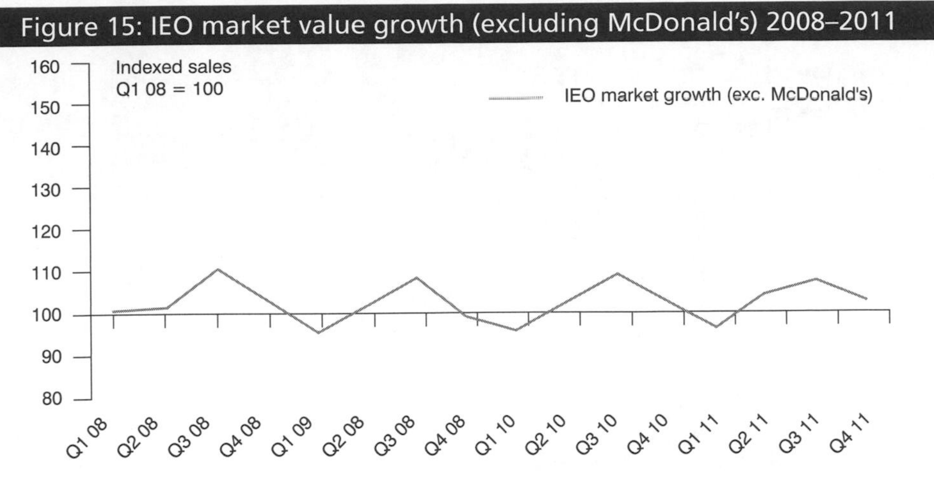


Source: NPD Group

## The impact of our new brand communications approach

### *1. The impact on advertising tracking measures*

Our two new brand advertising strands delivered a step-change in key ad tracking metrics. Our brand advertising was more enjoyable, more motivating and much more likely to make people feel good about McDonald's than our previous campaigns.

We saw remarkable 74% and 84% uplifts for 2009–2011's brand campaigns on the measures 'talking to people like me' and 'makes me feel good about McDonald's'. These scores are especially worth noting as these statements are close to the brand image measures in our separate brand tracker for affinity and trust ('a place for someone like me' and 'a company I trust'). Figures 16 and 17 show the dramatic increases in key tracking measures from 2009–2011 vs. 2006–2008 caused by our new brand campaigns.[18]

Figure 16: Percentage increase in average tracking scores for key metrics 2009–2011 (brand ads) vs. 2006–2008 (all ads)

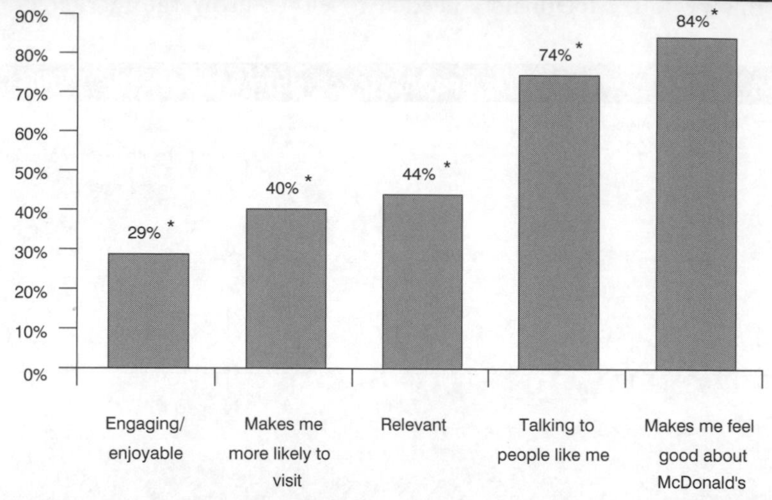


Source: HPI advertising tracking

Figure 17: Percentage increase in average tracking scores for key metrics 2009–2011 (all ads) vs. 2006–2008 (all ads)

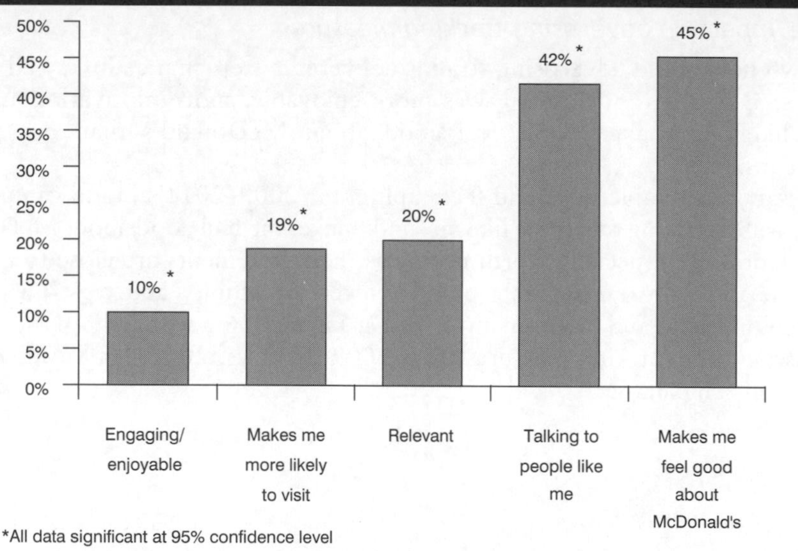


Source: HPI advertising tracking

Also worth noting is the 40% uplift in motivation to visit for 2009–2011's brand campaigns vs. 2006–2008's promotional advertising, given McDonald's fears about the sales-driving ability of brand advertising.

And it wasn't just customers who noticed a step-change in the quality of our advertising: our brand campaigns impressed awards juries too, with 31 major creative awards from 2009 onwards,[19] including a Cannes Creative Effectiveness Lion.[20]

### *2. The impact on brand image*

Since the introduction of our brand advertising, we have seen dramatic shifts in all our key brand image measures, but most importantly from the two key brand image measures our two brand advertising strands were designed to influence.

We've seen remarkable shifts in our Trust and Affinity image statements, the Trust measure appearing to improve from around 2007, the time of the initial recovery, with the rate of increase in both measures accelerating from 2008–2010 when we embarked on our new communications approach (Figure 18).[21]

Figure 18: Trust and affinity brand image measures 2003–2011

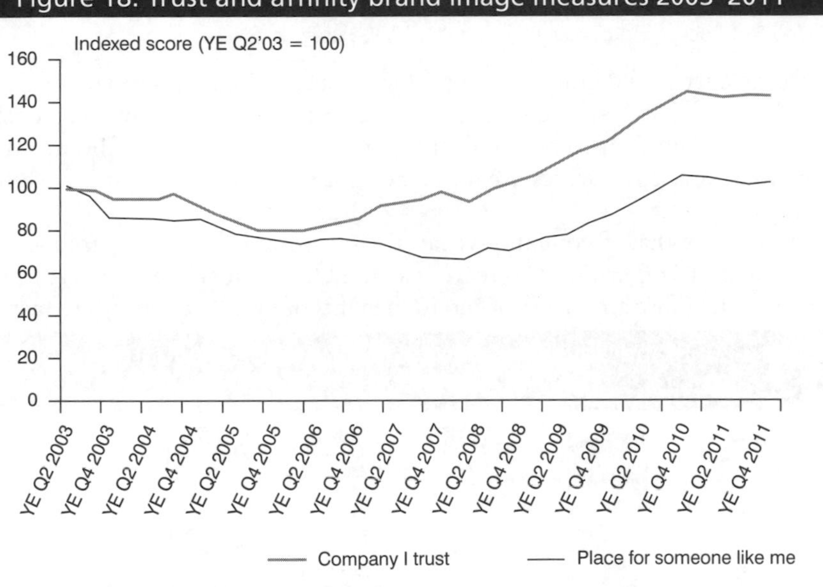


Source: TNS Fast Track brand tracker. Base: last 4-week IEO users

Importantly, the measures we sought to drive experienced disproportionate increases. On average these two statements increased +51% and +50% from 2007 whilst the other 24 image measures we track rose on average +33% over the period (Figure 19).

Figure 19: Percentage increases in McDonald's brand image scores 2007–2011

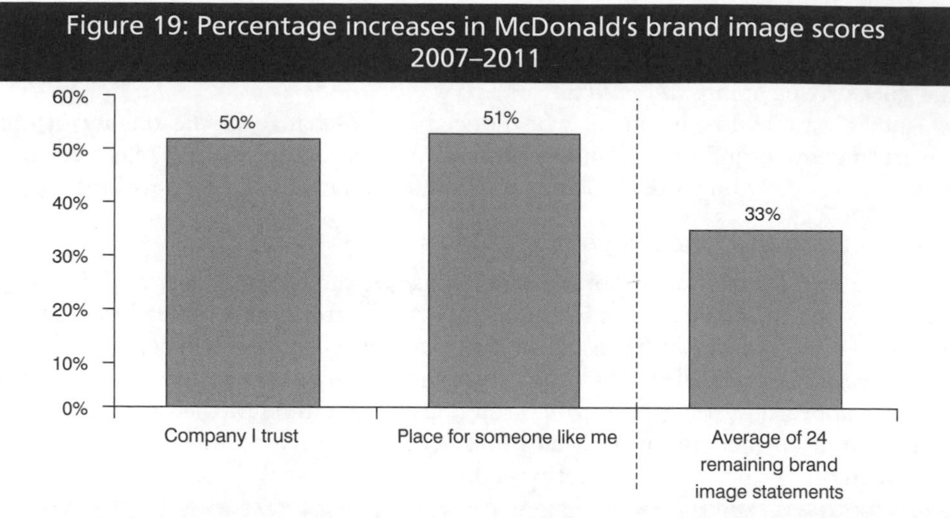


Source: TNS Fast Track brand tracker. Base: last 4-week IEO users

A consequence of the brand image problem was our high number of 'critics'[22] and 'neutrals',[23] even amongst frequent customers.[24] Since 2007 we have seen declines in the number of neutral customers and strong increases in numbers of brand advocates (Figure 20).[25] Hardened critics are a tougher nut to crack and we still have work to do here.

We now know that 'frequent advocates' visit around 50% more frequently than frequent 'neutrals' or 'critics'[26] so there is a tangible business benefit in creating more advocates even before any word-of-mouth benefits of brand advocacy are factored in.

Figure 20: Brand advocacy amongst McDonald's frequent customers 2007–2011

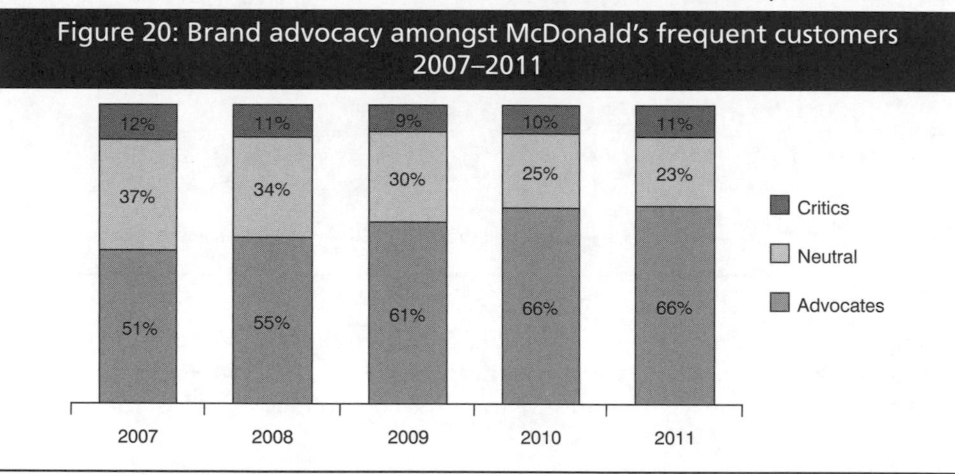


Source: TNS Fast Track. Base: McDonald's frequent customers

## Proving the advertising impact on brand image

Of course it is not enough to observe improvements in brand measures and suggest advertising was responsible. So in addition to our rigorous econometrics analysis, evaluating the sales impact of our campaigns, we have gone further and used econometric modelling to prove the contribution made by media in driving our brand image measures and then linking these improvements in brand image to sales.

To do this we built a range of new regression models to investigate whether the factors driving sales (such as restaurant refurbishments, PR and media investment) also drive brand metrics, establish which campaigns do this, and to what extent. We then explored the sales impact of improving brand metrics by evaluating the impact on customer visits.

The results show our brand media investment has a strong impact on key brand metrics, and that without it, agreement with key brand measures would have been much lower. So without brand media, 'company I trust' would have grown much more gradually. As soon as Trust media was introduced, improvements in this statement are evident (Figure 21).

Figure 21: Brand media contribution to McDonald's 'company I trust' metric 2007–2011

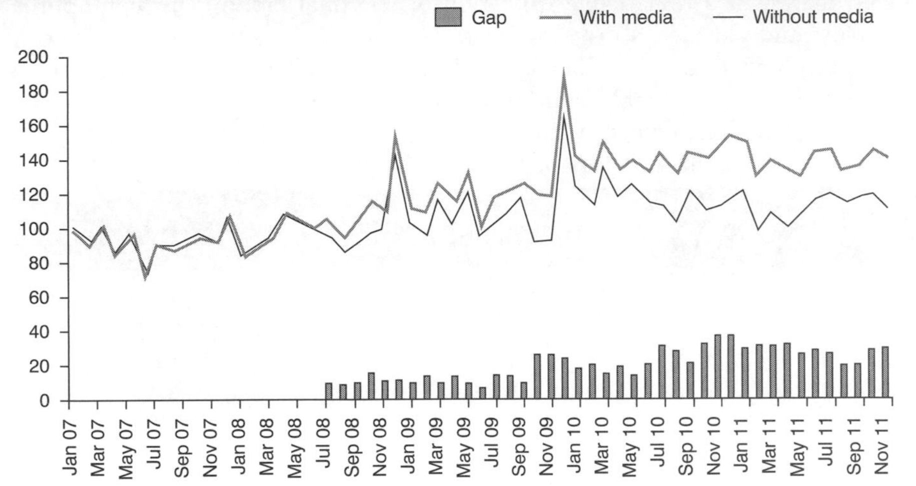


Source: Fast Track/Mindshare ATG. Base: last 4-week IEO users

Similarly, without brand media, agreement with 'place for someone like me' would have been much lower and we see strong improvements as soon as our Favourites campaign began in October 2009 (Figure 22), with a smaller impact evident before this when our Trust campaign began in June 2008.

Figure 22: Brand media contribution to McDonald's 'place for someone like me' metric 2007–2011

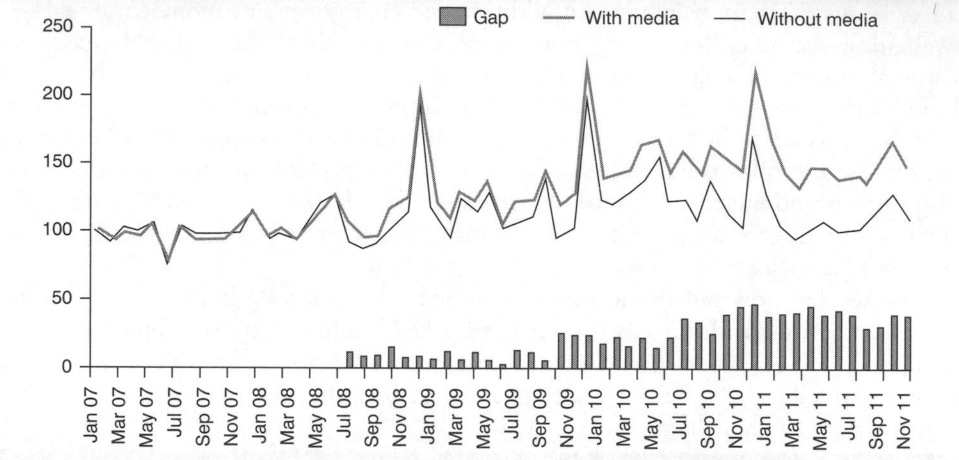

Source: Fast Track/Mindshare ATG. Base: last 4-week IEO users

This analysis is a remarkable validation of our dual brand campaign approach: both Trust and Favourites drive their primary brand measures, whilst also having a secondary impact on the other key brand measure (Figure 23). Our two brand campaigns work in a highly complementary way, together being responsible for 16.8% of the total agreement with 'company I trust' and 17.9% of agreement with 'place for someone like me' (average from 2009–2011).

Figure 23: Contribution of brand media investment to key brand metrics

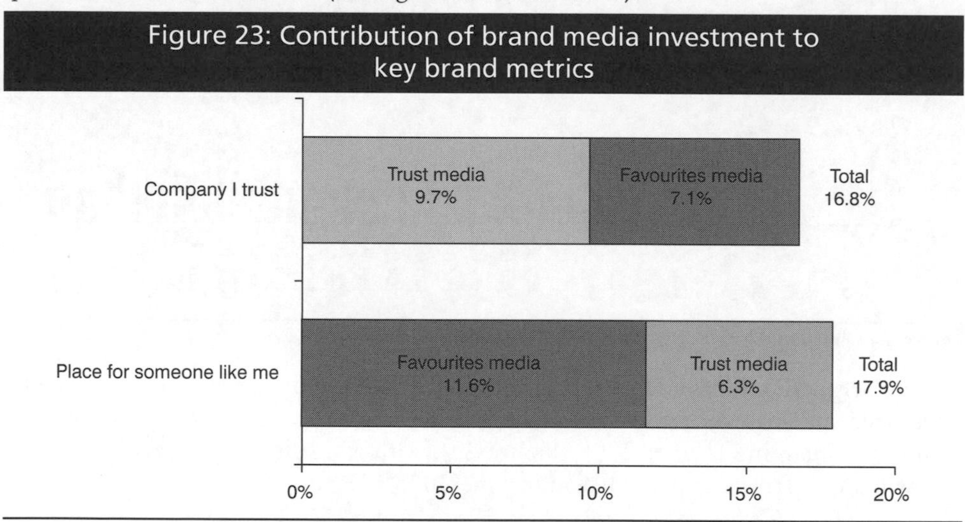


Source: Fast Track/Mindshare ATG. Base: last 4-week IEO users

Our models show that whilst Trust media is the strongest *advertising* factor driving 'company I trust', positive PR also has a strong impact on this measure. And they show that whilst Favourites media spend is the strongest driver of 'a place for someone like me', accounting for 11.6% of total agreement with this image statement on average from 2009–2011, our three other communications strands (Variety, Value and Trust) have a lesser, but still important, impact (Figure 24).

**Figure 24: Percentage contribution of all drivers to total agreement with key brand metrics**

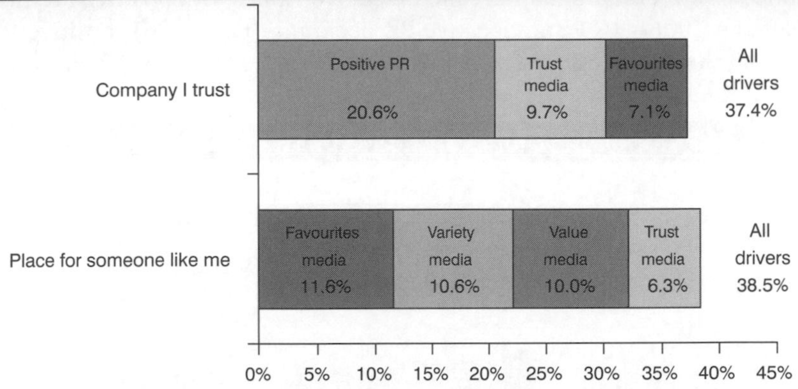

Source: Fast Track/Mindshare ATG. Base: last 4-week IEO users

It is also worth noting the greater increase in 'company I trust' amongst parents vs. non-parents, given Trust media is bought against the former (Figure 25).

**Figure 25: Average percentage increase in agreement with 'company I trust' with media spend by audience**

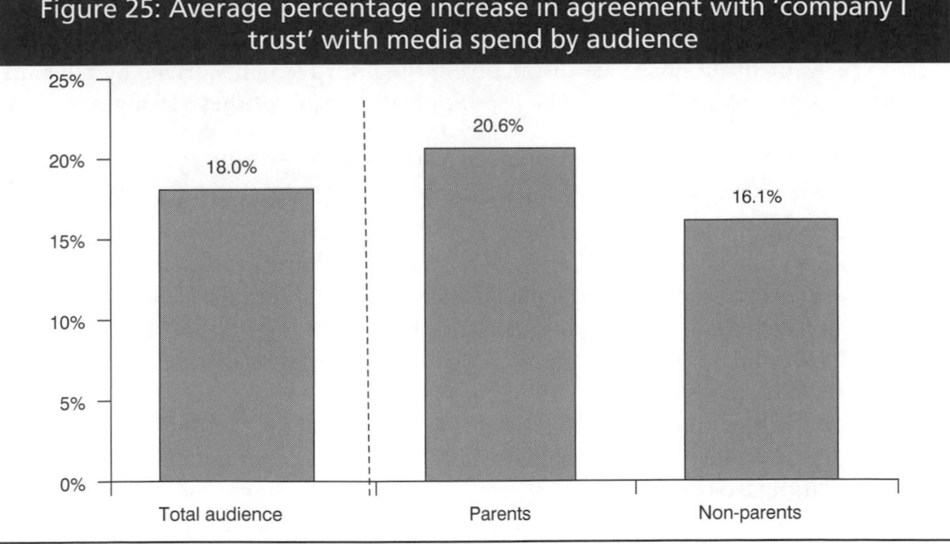


Source: Fast Track/Mindshare ATG. Base: last 4-week IEO users

### 3. *The impact of 'free' communications channels on brand image*

Using econometrics to evaluate the factors driving brand measures has given us useful learnings not only about how our paid-for channels work but also how they work in combination with 'free' channels – in this case PR and refurbished restaurants.

Positive PR, as we have seen, is the strongest driver of 'company I trust'. And we also found that refurbished restaurants are not a driver of our Trust or Affinity measures, but are the strongest driver of 'my favourite informal eating out place to visit'.

The impact of PR on brand image increased over time, with positive PR more than doubling from 2006–2011 and negative PR declining (Figure 26): positive PR grew because of all the positive changes that were made in the business which were shared openly with the media.

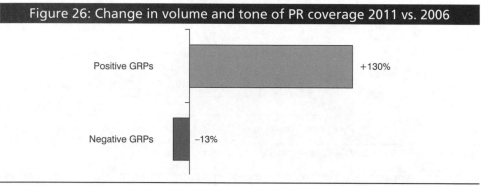

**Figure 26: Change in volume and tone of PR coverage 2011 vs. 2006**

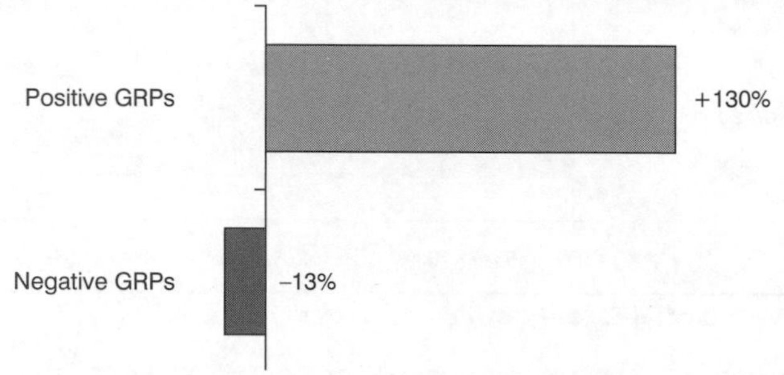

| | |
|---|---|
| Positive GRPs | +130% |
| Negative GRPs | −13% |

Source: Mindshare ATG

So from our analysis of 'free' channels we see that changes to our food and restaurants helped improve brand image. And importantly for this paper, we see that these improvements in image are distinct from the improvements driven by the paid-for communications that, from 2008, *communicated* many of these changes.

### 4. *The impact on customer frequency of improving brand image*

We have seen that media investment drives key brand measures and that specific campaigns drive the measures they were intended to drive.

In addition, our new econometric models also demonstrate how improving key brand measures increases the frequency of visit to our restaurants.

Driving agreement with 'company I trust' or 'place for someone like me' delivers an additional 0.81 and 0.95 visits a month respectively amongst McDonald's customers, a 36% or 40% increase in average frequency.[27]

Our models show that purely due to our brand campaigns, 1.8 million additional McDonald's customers now agree that McDonald's is 'a company I trust' and 2.3 million additional customers now agree it's 'a place for someone like me'.[28] We know they are now visiting nearly once a month more often as a result, so are worth millions of incremental sales each month.

So we see a significant but indirect benefit for the business in driving these brand metrics, in addition to any direct sales impact measurable via our standard econometrics (Figure 27).

**Figure 27: The impact of brand communication on McDonald's business**

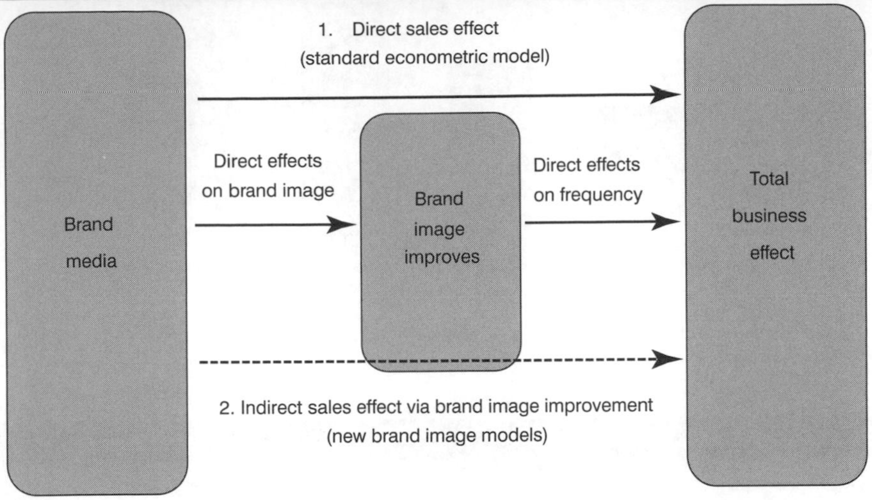

### *5. The impact on sales and ROI*

When we began investing in brand advertising from 2008, we were challenged not only with driving brand image, but also with driving short-term sales. The consequence of our campaigns not achieving both was that this kind of advertising would cease: an outcome we self-evidently avoided.

Mindshare ATG's econometric modelling proves that our brand campaigns drive both brand image and sales, and also deliver much stronger ROIs than our promotional campaigns.[29]

We have seen a stronger total sales impact every year, with brand campaigns responsible for an incredible £349m in incremental sales over and above the £460m sales driven by existing promotional campaigns since 2007. Brand campaigns account for a growing and now dominant share of the sales impact of our media (Figure 28), despite promotional advertising still receiving 72% of the total spend (see Table 1).

The ROI from both our total media investment and from brand media has seen strong increases every year since 2007, the short-term sales ROI[30] of our brand advertising spend in 2011 being, at £9.79, nearly four times 2007's total ROI (Figure 29).

Figure 28: Incremental sales from brand vs. non-brand media £m, 2007–2011

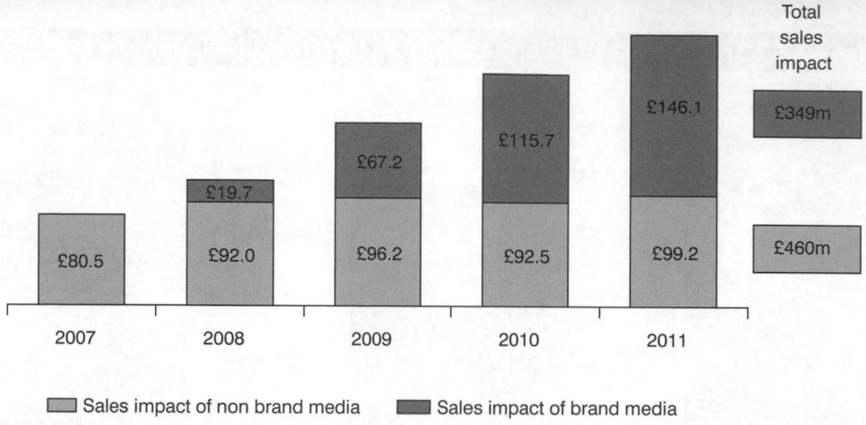

| | 2007 | 2008 | 2009 | 2010 | 2011 | Total sales impact |
|---|---|---|---|---|---|---|
| Sales impact of brand media | | £19.7 | £67.2 | £115.7 | £146.1 | £349m |
| Sales impact of non brand media | £80.5 | £92.0 | £96.2 | £92.5 | £99.2 | £460m |

Source: Mindshare ATG

Figure 29: Short-term sales ROI of all media vs. brand media

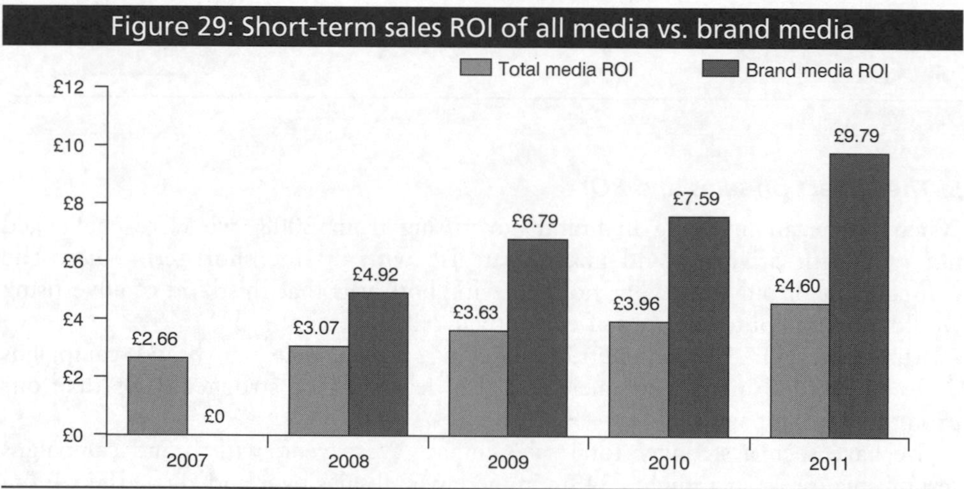


Source: Mindshare ATG

Trust campaigns deliver our strongest returns. 2011's Trust campaigns delivered a short-term ROI of £12.40, or £24.80 over the long term.[31] And our best performing individual Trust campaign, 'Big Nothing', achieved a short-term ROI of £15.41 in 2010, or a phenomenal £30.82 in the long term (Table 2).

Table 2: Media spend and ROI

| | 2007 | 2008 | 2009 | 2010 | 2011 |
|---|---|---|---|---|---|
| Total media spend (Nielsen) | £30.24m | £36.35m | £44.99m | £52.55m | £53.28m |
| Sales impact of total media | £80.53m | £111.7m | £163.4m | £208.2m | £245.2m |
| Sales impact of 'brand' media | n/a | £19.7m | £67.2m | £115.7m | £146.1m |
| Short-term ROI of total media | £2.66 | £3.07 | £3.63 | £3.96 | £4.60 |
| Short-term ROI of 'brand' media | n/a | £4.92 | £6.79 | £7.59 | £9.79 |
| Short-term ROI of Trust media | n/a | £4.92 | £9.53 | £10.79 | £12.40 |
| Short-term ROI of Favourites media | n/a | n/a | £4.50 | £5.34 | £8.10 |

## *6. The impact of advertising on the success of the business 2007–2011*

Recent business success has been remarkable. Each of the five successive years from 2007 onwards was a record-breaking sales year, and McDonald's growth far exceeded that of the market, which was mostly flat over this period (Figure 30).[32] We have now experienced 24 consecutive quarters of growth, in stark relief to the stagnation of 2002–2006. And 2011 capped it all with an incredible 48 million more customers served vs. 2010. Remarkably, this was all achieved without increasing store numbers (Figure 31).[33]

Figure 30: IEO market value growth (exc. McDonald's) vs. McDonald's value growth 2008–2011

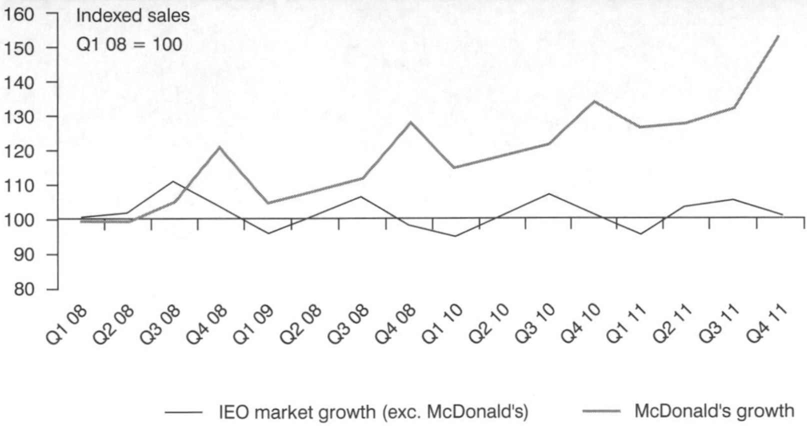


Source: NPD Group

This success came as a result of a wide range of business and communications factors all working together in harmony.

We saw the initial turnaround in 2007 before any significant paid-for media intervention. This was fuelled by a renewed clarity of vision and a range of changes to the business.

Our two new brand campaigns built on this change, working cleverly together to regain trust and re-ignite love for the brand. They accelerated improvements in brand image which we have shown improves customer frequency, so have an indirect sales impact in addition to their remarkable direct sales impact which has been growing stronger every year.

Brand advertising has made a significant and growing contribution to the dramatic growth in the business,[34] helping to accelerate growth in the UK (Figure 31).

Figure 31: McDonald's UK sales history 1974–2011

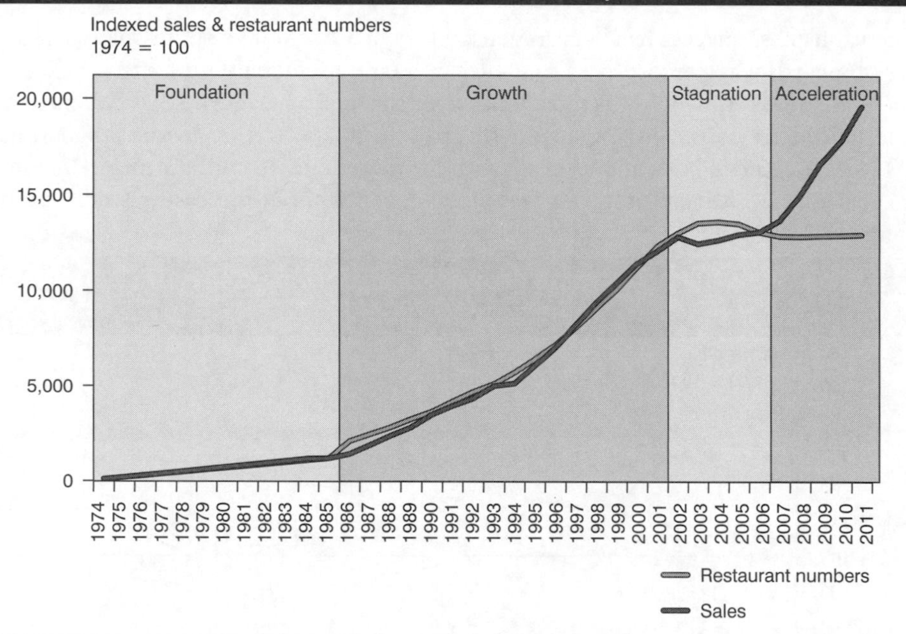


Source: McDonald's UK

## The lessons we have learnt

The journey from recovery to resurgence has taught us invaluable lessons: about when to act and when to talk; about balancing complex marketing programmes; about television's enduring ability to simultaneously drive sales and brand image better than any other channel ever invented; about using complementary brand campaigns to solve different problems; and, an IPA Effectiveness case first, about using econometrics to evaluate the brand image impact on sales of not one, but two campaigns, each driving different image measures.

## In summary

2007–2011 saw the UK business enter a new phase. A phase in which it has seen stronger, faster growth than at any other time in its 37-year history. And brand advertising had a huge part to play: because of it, millions of people trust and love McDonald's more, are coming back a little more often and feeling good about it.

## Notes

1 McDonald's Corporation does not publish total sales or profits, % sales or profit growth, profit margins or customer numbers for individual markets so it is not possible to disclose this data anywhere in this paper. Where possible we have indexed or hidden data to disguise it.
2 Source: TNS Fast Track brand tracker, data indexed for confidentiality, IEO = 'Informal eating out' market.
3 Source: McDonald's UK, data indexed for confidentiality.
4 Source: McDonald's UK, data indexed for confidentiality.
5 Source: McDonald's UK.
6 TNS Fast Track brand image tracking, McDonald's UK sales data.
7 HPI Advertising tracking, TNS Fast Track brand image tracking, NPD Group's Crest customer share data, Mindshare ATG econometric modelling, McDonald's sales data.
8 Leo Burnett Usage and Attitude Study, April 2008.
9 'Favourites' was so called because it focused on people's favourite aspects of the brand such as their favourite food.
10 Nielsen media spend data.
11 PSB Research.
12 Davies + McKerr Research.
13 Ibid.
14 Ibid.
15 Source: Experian; 'retail footfall' = visitor traffic to UK retail outlets (monthly, change vs. last year).
16 Source: NPD Group; 'IEO traffic'= visits to informal eating out places (quarterly, change vs. last year). YOY data only available from Q1 2009 onwards.
17 Source: NPD Group, IEO market growth, data indexed to disguise confidential McDonald's data shown later.
18 HPI advertising tracking data. 2006–2008 all campaign average includes 36 campaigns; 2009–2011 brand campaign average includes six waves of Favourites activity and nine waves of Trust activity; 2009–2011 all campaigns average includes 42 campaigns including both our new brand campaigns and our promotional campaigns.
19 Including Creative Circle, Kinsale, British Television Awards, D&AD, One Show, Cannes Lions, Campaign Big Awards.
20 'Just Passing By' was awarded one of the first ever Cannes Creative Effectiveness Lions in 2011, the first year this category was introduced, to add to its two silver Lions from 2010.
21 All brand image data in this paper is indexed against 2007 levels for confidentiality reasons.
22 Source: TNS Fast Track; critics agree that 'I would be critical of them if someone asked/without being asked'.
23 Source: TNS Fast Track; neutrals agree that 'I would be neutral about them if someone asked'.
24 'Frequent' customers are those visiting McDonald's once a week or more.
25 Source: TNS Fast Track; advocates agree 'I think so much of them that I would speak highly of them without being asked/if someone asked'.
26 Leo Burnett/McDonald's U&A Study 2010 (a re-run of 2008's U&A study).
27 TNS Fast Track brand image tracker and Mindshare ATG econometrics.
28 The number of additional McDonald's customers agreeing with each brand image statement as a result of media was calculated by taking an average agreement score for 2011 with and without the impact of media. The difference between the two scores was multiplied by 43.5 million (the number of UK adults who visit IEO at least monthly) and then multiplied by 0.64 to reflect McDonald's monthly penetration.
29 Mindshare ATG tested hundreds of variables and the model includes nearly 100 variables from over 30 categories of drivers of the McDonald's business.
30 McDonald's UK does not publish profit margins so all ROIs quoted are calculated using £ sales revenue rather than £ profit. We have calculated our ROIs by taking the sales impact of our media

spend and dividing it by the total media spend on that activity (see Table 1 for the % of media spent on Trust and Favourites activity each year). McDonald's Corporation's 2011 financial statement published profit margins for the global business of 31.6%.

31 Mindshare ATG calculate McDonald's long-term ROI using a multiple of 2–2.5 times the short-term ROI. For the purposes of this paper we have taken the conservative view and used a multiple of 2.

32 Source: NPD Group, IEO market growth vs. McDonald's growth, actual data disguised for confidentiality purposes.

33 Total store numbers actually saw slight declines from 2006–2011 to around 1,200.

34 McDonald's Corporation does not publish total sales or £ sales growth for individual markets so it is not possible to reveal the proportion of total UK sales or the contribution to UK sales growth driven by advertising.

GOLD AWARD: BEST DEMONSTRATION OF CONSUMER PARTICIPATION, THE CHANNON PRIZE FOR BEST NEW LEARNING

## Chapter 16

# Metropolitan Police Service

## The case in defence of Deon

**By Ila De Mello Kamath, Abbott Mead Vickers BBDO**

Contributing authors: Craig Mawdsley and Amy Witter, Abbott Mead Vickers BBDO

Credited companies: Creative Agency: Abbott Mead Vickers BBDO; Media Agency: MediaCom; Others: MadCow; Research Agency: Cello MRUK; Client: Metropolitan Police Service

**Editor's summary**

This paper was regarded with much excitement and enthusiasm over its fantastic use of social media to engage with a difficult target audience and unlock the key insight to shaping the solution. 'Who killed Deon?' was designed to help tackle youth violence by educating disenfranchised teenagers about a legal principle known as Joint Enterprise. The idea was an interactive murder mystery hosted on Facebook, a 'whodunnit' about a boy called Deon. It embraced a teenage audience by enlisting them as co-creators and collaborators. The campaign was 4.5 times more efficient than budgeted, but its intention was also to prevent young people entering a life of crime in the future. It is predicted the campaign will generate a payback of £8.50 for every £1 spent. The fact it is now used as a piece of stimulus in schools is testament to its effectiveness to affect behaviour and help educate on youth crime.

The Metropolitan Police Service's 'Who killed Deon?' campaign was designed to help tackle youth violence by educating disenfranchised teenagers about a complicated legal principle known as Joint Enterprise. We needed to communicate a highly sensitive and complex message to an extremely niche audience, on a modest budget. To this end we hope to show that it was a success.

However, there is also a longer term effect intended by educating young people about Joint Enterprise. Commander Simon Foy, head of the MPS Homicide and Serious Crime Command, said: 'The hope is that once young people appreciate the way the law operates, they will think twice about their involvement with groups and gangs and walk away before any trouble starts.'[1] Tackling complex social issues often requires pre-empting behaviour and stopping something before it even starts, which makes the precise scale of the effect difficult to quantify; a fact that meant this paper nearly didn't get written. And yet communications can play a vital role in helping do just this, even on modest budgets. We therefore felt it was important to try and find a way to prove the future-facing effect of this campaign, not just because it is a long-term intention of the campaign but because if we do, we can show that communications can be a vital and effective tool in preventing violent crime, a problem that affects society and us all, financially and emotionally.

Seeing as this campaign is about a legal principle, we have turned to legal protocol to help establish our case. In a court of law, barristers use two types of evidence to convince judge and jury that they have the 'burden of proof' behind their argument: direct evidence and circumstantial evidence. We will use direct evidence to prove awareness, understanding and behavioural intention; but circumstantial evidence in the form of personal testimony from key witnesses to help qualify the actual behavioural impact of this campaign. And for precedent, we'd like to refer you to the recent convictions in the Damilola Taylor trial, which were achieved with predominantly circumstantial evidence to build up an overwhelming 'burden of proof'; likewise, we hope to convince the judges of this paper that 'beyond reasonable doubt' this campaign has played a part in reducing the probability that young people in London will unwittingly be involved in Joint Enterprise prosecutions.

## A complex challenge

Youth violence is a serious issue. Between January and September 2010 there were 14 teenage murders in London, including four shootings. To help the Metropolitan Police Service tackle this problem we needed to explain the little known, complex legal principle of Joint Enterprise – that if you are connected to or have knowledge of a crime you can be charged for it – to 13–15-year-old Londoners on the periphery of crime.

Briefs like this are usually a welcome challenge, but this one was frankly daunting. Our message was complicated, our audience were disenfranchised and hard to reach, and we had a societal responsibility to get it right. This was exacerbated by a modest budget and tight timescale – six weeks to launch in time for the summer holidays when incidents of youth violence traditionally peaked.

## A complicated crime

There had been a number of high profile murders in which youths had been charged under Joint Enterprise, such as the Victoria Station stabbing involving over 20 teenagers and the so-called honey-trap girl who lured Shakilus Townsend to his death.

The operational officers who deal with gun and knife crime explained that violent crimes among young people are often not down to the actions of a single perpetrator but can involve multiple people who each play a role. These crimes weren't usually gang-related but minor arguments that start off as banter, but escalate into a fatal incident because more and more people get involved, with each person playing a small but significant role. This is why, under Joint Enterprise, each person involved is deemed as responsible as the person pulling the trigger.

A typical scenario could be:

- Girl A brags to a friend about sleeping with girl B's boyfriend X.
- B finds out, gets angry and tells her brother Y.
- Y decides his sister has been disrespected, and asks friend Z to bring the weapon he's been storing.
- B is asked to call X to a meet at which Y and his friends are waiting.
- A fight breaks out and X gets stabbed.

Both Joint Enterprise and these crimes seemed extremely complicated and if trained planners were struggling to understand this, how would we get 13–15-year-olds to?

## A disenfranchised audience

We needed to understand more about this teenage 'pack mentality' so we spoke to an ex-con-turned-mentor called Twilight, who worked with youths on West London estates. He explained these 'packs' were just ordinary school kids who, through circumstances beyond their control were surrounded by crime. They played the same games we used to: forming clubs, stealing friends' girl/boyfriends, getting into fights through boredom. The difference was they had access to weapons, so playground disputes that escalated could become fatal. His view was that this was going to be a difficult message to convey to teenagers without alienating them, because it essentially branded them guilty for a crime they didn't physically commit. Our other problem in trying to educate them about a point of law was that the message could be extremely dull to them.

## An unconventional process

It seemed that if we were going to get to an idea that not only explained Joint Enterprise to teenagers, but also engaged them sufficiently without disenfranchising or boring them, we needed a different approach. With agreement from the creative team, media agency and client we embarked on a process of co-creation with the target audience themselves. Our plan was to get to an idea organically. It could be risky, but on the other hand having our audience to bounce ideas off could get us all to a more interesting and effective answer.

## Co-creation

Through the work the police do with schools, we had access to 'typical' London schools with 'typical' 13–15-year-olds on the periphery of crime. These boys and girls became our collaborators. They were frank and surprisingly willing to help, but shocked us by their in-depth knowledge about guns and knives. When we explained Joint Enterprise, their first reaction, as we suspected, was anger at how unfair it was. *'How could you get charged with murder for making a phone call?'*, one girl asked. But they were also genuinely alarmed that if you were connected to a crime, in any way, you could be charged for it. The thought about connections was interesting. For our message to be understood and not dismissed we would need to show how the role each person played was connected to the end crime.

We asked the youngsters for examples of other types of roles that might lead to guilt – shockingly they all had some experience to recount. They explained how social media was instrumental in organising and stirring situations; how roles played by girls and boys differed; the nicknames these roles had, e.g. Miss Chinese Whispers (the stirrer), the Link (main co-ordinator), the Transporter (weapon carrier). They revealed a fascinating sub-culture and language associated with these crimes, unknown to us.

## The idea

This gave the creative team an idea: what if we created an interactive murder-mystery for Facebook, a Whodunnit about the murder of a boy called Deon? We could create six short films, each featuring a different role, that lead to the murder. A trailer could set up the six characters and Deon's murder, and we'd challenge viewers to work out 'Who killed Deon?'. On guessing a suspect the viewer would get to watch that character's film and see what role he or she played. The films would end by explaining that your character did not kill Deon, but was charged with murder under Joint Enterprise because of the role they had played. Viewers would then be asked to guess again by clicking on another character's film. It sounded like an interesting way to explain Joint Enterprise in a way that could show how an individual action was connected to and played a role in the end crime. For a fresh perspective, we decided to run our idea past different young people from the after-school club that Twilight ran. They loved it and even suggested one new character, an 'Elder', who could try and intervene to stop it and not be guilty.

## Crafting

To get the details of the story right we asked our teenage collaborators to help us create a scenario that might escalate into a stabbing or shooting, one which they and their friends could relate to. They didn't want to use a real crime, even if we changed the names, because everyone would know who it was about. Instead they helped map out a fictional but believable scenario, suggesting names for our characters and helping us work out the details of the story (Figure 1).

Figure 1: Story planning from the workshop with after-school group

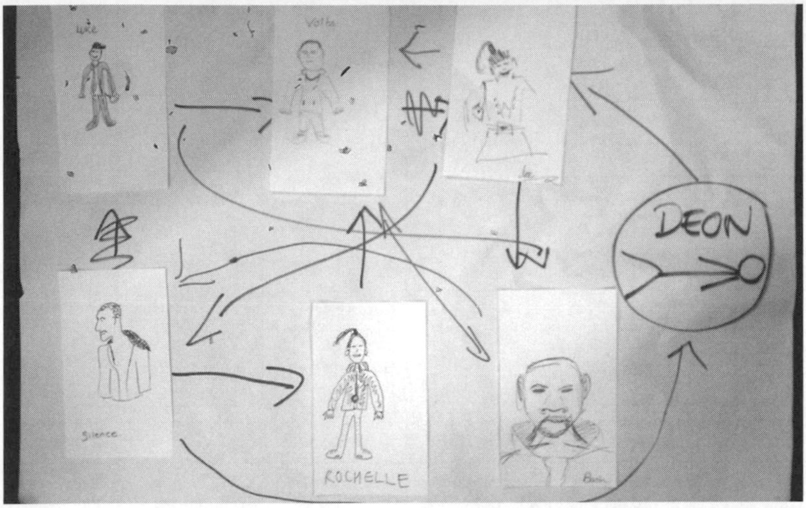

Their story was about Miss Chinese Whispers (Rochelle) who starts a rumour about Deon flirting with Bash's girlfriend. In their story, the link (Bash) sets up the meet at a party, the honey-trap (Dee) lures the intended victim (Deon), the weapon-storer (Voltz) tries to provide a gun, but when that fails, the transporter (Silence) takes a knife to the party, and an elder (Luke) tries to calm the situation before it escalates, and our victim (Deon) gets stabbed.

To ensure each character's story was correct we carefully mapped out a timeline for each so that we had the correct structure to form the basis of each film (Table 1).

We now had to get the execution right. The teenagers were clear on what they liked: big budget, glossy blockbusters! Unrealistic with £300k for media and production. Fortunately they had another suggestion; it could be real-life, like Kidulthood, but needed to be a spot-on representation of their world, otherwise they'd know it was a fake. It's easy to think you know what 'youf' are into, but after our humiliation at thinking Dizzee Rascal was cool and gangsta bling was in, we knew getting the subtleties right was essential to capturing life as they saw it and to engage and not alienate them.

## Co-starring

And the collaboration didn't stop there. To make it feel as real as possible, the films were shot on a London estate, using a mix of normal teenagers and actors. The teenagers brought their own wardrobe and did their own styling. Instead of giving them a script, the creative team and director gave them key sentences to say and let them ad-lib the rest, so the dialogue was as natural as possible (Figure 2).

## Table 1: Character's timeline for film structure

<table>
<tr><th>Rochelle</th><th>Bash</th><th>Dee</th><th>Silence</th><th>Voltz</th><th>Luke</th></tr>
<tr><td>Is dismissed by Guy</td><td>Hanging at party</td><td rowspan="2">Flirts with Guy</td><td rowspan="5">At home getting ready for party</td><td rowspan="6">Plays video games</td><td rowspan="2">Hangs out with a girl</td></tr>
<tr><td>Takes and sends photo of Guy and Dee to Bash</td><td>Receives photo from Rochelle</td></tr>
<tr><td>Distracts Guy</td><td>Phones Dee</td><td>Ignores Bash's call</td><td rowspan="5">Sees Bash getting angry and planning something</td></tr>
<tr><td>Gets a call from Bash</td><td>Phones Rochelle</td><td>Flirts with Guy</td></tr>
<tr><td>Hands phone to Dee</td><td>Speaks to Dee</td><td>Speaks to Bash</td></tr>
<tr><td rowspan="3">Follows Dee and Guy to party</td><td>Phones Silence</td><td rowspan="3">Lures Guy to party</td><td>Gets a call from Bash</td></tr>
<tr><td>Phones Voltz</td><td rowspan="2">Goes and gets the knife</td><td>Gets a call from Bash</td></tr>
<tr><td>Speaks to Luke at party</td><td>Finds gun but broken</td><td>Tries to calm Bash down</td></tr>
<tr><td rowspan="2">Points out Guy to Bash</td><td rowspan="2">Rochelle points guy to him</td><td rowspan="4">Arrives at party and looks nervous</td><td>Picks up knife from Voltz's home</td><td>Gives knife to someone at door</td><td rowspan="4">Gives up and goes back to girl</td></tr>
<tr><td>Carries knife to party</td><td rowspan="6">Goes back to playing video games</td></tr>
<tr><td>Is joined by Silence</td><td>Is joined by Silence carrying the knife</td><td>Tries to give Bash the knife</td></tr>
<tr><td>Sees Silence is up for it</td><td>Puts pressure on Silence in front of Rochelle</td><td>Gets pressured by Bash in front of Rochelle</td></tr>
<tr><td>Hears confrontation</td><td>Confrontation</td><td>Sees confrontation</td><td>Confrontation</td><td>Sees fight break out</td></tr>
<tr><td>Sees commotion</td><td>Commotion</td><td>Sees commotion</td><td>Commotion</td><td>Tries to prevent commotion</td></tr>
<tr><td>Stays and looks on from afar</td><td>Runs from scene</td><td>Screams next to victim</td><td>Runs from scene</td><td>Stands over victim covered in blood</td></tr>
<tr><td>Gets arrested</td><td>Gets arrested</td><td>Gets arrested</td><td>Gets arrested</td><td>Gets arrested</td><td>Doesn't get arrested</td></tr>
<tr><td>Joint Enterprise message</td><td>Joint Enterprise message</td><td>Joint Enterprise message</td><td>Joint Enterprise message</td><td>Joint Enterprise message</td><td>Joint Enterprise message</td></tr>
</table>

They offered us styling hints, suggesting what the characters would wear, explained subtleties about carrying knives, and hints as to what music was cool – Dubstep if you didn't know.

Figure 2: On the shoot

With the films ready to go, we did one last check on message take-out and sent the final edit with a questionnaire to some new teenagers. It seemed they were clear on what Joint Enterprise was. Figure 3 is just one snippet.

Figure 3: Snippet from questionnaire.
Dharmi, age 13 years

The ad is telling you that if you get involved with knife crime you will be charged even if you never stabbed the person. What I found interesting is that one small thing turned into something big.

## The campaign launch

The campaign launched with an unbranded trailer to set up the six characters and Deon's murder encouraging the viewer to go to Facebook to work out Who Killed Deon? The trailer aired on Sky music channels including MTV, Viva, NME and Flava (Figure 4), and teaser radio spots ran on stations popular with a youth audience, Kiss FM and Choice FM, and on Spotify. Music channels are often viewed by young people with their friends and provided an outlet to encourage conversation.

Figure 4: 30" unbranded MTV trailer

To engage our target in a credible environment, the campaign was hosted on Facebook. There you could view the films of each of the six suspects' stories, discovering that the person had not committed the murder but had been charged for murder under Joint Enterprise (Figure 5). Using Facebook allowed us to reach teenagers where they were comfortable, which encouraged peer-to-peer debate and allowed them to discuss who they thought killed Deon, share the link with their friends and comment on aspects of what they had seen. Here are some examples (Figure 6).

Figure 5: Who killed Deon? Facebook page



Source: Facebook

Figure 6: Who Killed Deon? Facebook comments

**Aleigha Askingalexandria Fearon** can someone put up what happens coz i cant watch it im on me phone! thankz :)
December 16, 2010 at 12:46pm · Like · 1 person

**Emily Rose** why does it say silence killed deon?
den it says he wernt only charged wiv one murder?
whoo else did hee murderrr?
December 16, 2010 at 2:56pm · Like

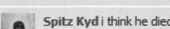

**Spitz Kyd** i think he died him self
December 17, 2010 at 8:30pm · Like

**Ryan TheLion Varatharajah** Luke seems like a safe man !
December 17, 2010 at 10:05pm · Like

**Reece Jordan Okugbeni** Silence Killed him
December 18, 2010 at 8:15am · Like · 3 people

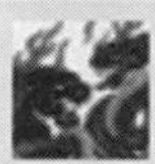
**Adam Collins** It was Silence who killed Deon u have to watch the videos to figure it out and how it was organised
December 18, 2010 at 11:16pm · Like

**Peter Kamara** Rochelle is bad, she got jealous and started the whole thing, you can even hear her shouting at bash to stab Deon.
December 19, 2010 at 11:21am · Like · 3 people

**Sam Richardson** i killed deonnn bluddd
December 19, 2010 at 11:46pm · Like · 1 person

**Eno Qekrezi** no
December 20, 2010 at 8:46am · Like

**Max Craig** Silence and bash
December 20, 2010 at 2:53pm · Like

**Ree' Huggs** bash or the white chick
December 20, 2010 at 5:32pm · Like · 1 person

**Asha Henry** im tellin u lot silence killed deon
December 20, 2010 at 7:07pm · Like · 3 people

**Allec Foley** Silence
December 20, 2010 at 7:31pm · Like · 3 people

Source: Facebook, snapshot of comments

The media strategy aimed to both engage but also educate our audience about Joint Enterprise. Mediacom worked with the Metropolitan Police Service to put in place a commentary matrix to help answer questions and deal with negativity around Joint Enterprise. A radio partnership with DJ advertorials was used to help explain Joint Enterprise credibly, driving people to the website for information and advice. We developed two further radio spots recounting accounts of the two characters charged under Joint Enterprise, to further educate our audience (Figure 7). The campaign was also provided as a DVD to be used as an educational resource by Safer Schools Officers who went into many London schools to talk to young people about Joint Enterprise in the context of gun and knife crime. This resource is still in use today, 18 months later.

After the launch phase, all the people who had 'liked' the film were re-contacted, and prompted with provocative questions about Joint Enterprise to keep the debate alive.

We also created a short 5-minute film that combined all the characters' points of view and ran in a small number of cinemas in South London. And as an ambient stunt, a teaser poster campaign appeared on the street (Figure 8).

The campaign ran from 16 August until 10 October.

## The case for success

As we said in our opening statement, proving the success of our campaign relies on both direct and circumstantial evidence. Our direct evidence will show the campaign reached the right people, that they understood what Joint Enterprise was, understood its implications and were not bored or alienated by it. But we also believe that we have enough circumstantial evidence to prove that understanding this law has made teenagers change their behaviour and, for a few, avoid getting into a life of crime, the cost of which is substantial to society.

But let's start with the former.

## Direct evidence

We reached our audience, achieving 135,371 unique visitors on our Facebook page, 4.5 times more than the 30,000 estimated (Figure 9) and at a cost per user of £1.33 vs. £6.04 as originally budgeted.[2] Nearly a half (45%) of our 13–15-year-old London target claim to have 'recognised at least one element of the campaign'.[3] And they liked the campaign; over 59% of our fans were 13–17 years old (89% 13–24 years old) (Figure 10).

## Figure 7: Radio scripts

| Client | Metropolitan Police | Date | |
|---|---|---|---|
| Title | Trailer | Timelength | A&L |

SFX: A fight and screaming

MVO: Who killed Deon?
A true-to-life, interactive story of murder in London now on Facebook
6 stories

SFX: (Rochelle) It's that guy in the yellow shirt
(Bash) He's a dead man
(Rochelle) He's all over her
(Bash) She's a snake man

MVO: 6 suspects

SFX: (Bash) Silence is going to handle this
(Dee) OK OK I'll bring him to the party
(Silence) Yeah I've got that wetter bro
(Rochelle) He deserves it

MVO: ... Follow them all to see if you can find the killer

Search for Who Killed Deon on Facebook

FVO: Here for London. The Metropolitan Police service

---

| Title | Chantelle | Timelength | A&L |
|---|---|---|---|

A girl angrily defends herself in a police cell

Chantelle: It's not my fault the guy fancied me
What can I do?
It's not my fault my boyfriend got jealous
I had nothing to do with it
It was all his idea
I can't help it if my boyfriend wanted to knife him
All I did was lead the guy to the park
Pause

SFX: We hear an officer putting someone in the cell next door
and slamming the door shut
(shouting) It's his fault

I'm not a killer
I'm not guilty

FVO: (holding line) If your presence, knowledge or actions
lead to a murder you'll be charged with murder
under the law of Joint Enterprise

Source: AMV BBDO

Figure 8: Ambient posters (before and after reveal)

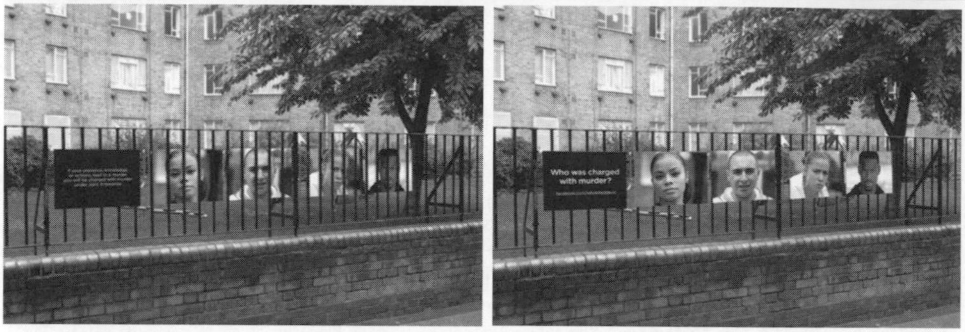

Figure 9: Online Information

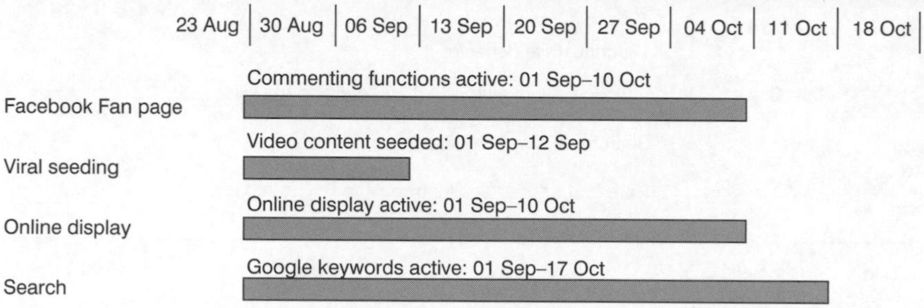

23 Aug | 30 Aug | 06 Sep | 13 Sep | 20 Sep | 27 Sep | 04 Oct | 11 Oct | 18 Oct

Facebook Fan page — Commenting functions active: 01 Sep–10 Oct

Viral seeding — Video content seeded: 01 Sep–12 Sep

Online display — Online display active: 01 Sep–10 Oct

Search — Google keywords active: 01 Sep–17 Oct

| | Estimated | Delivered | % Difference |
|---|---|---|---|
| Facebook | 30,000 uniques | 135,371 uniques | +451% |
| Viral Seeding | 141,023 views | 191,097 views | +35% |
| Display | 12,822 clicks | 49,217 clicks | +284% |
| Search | 1,796 clicks | TBC | TBC |

Source: Mediacom online review, November 2010

They understood the complex message about Joint Enterprise with 59% agreeing that *'You can be charged with murder even if you didn't actually kill someone'* (Figure 11). And in addition, 39% said 'If you are with someone and they commit a crime such as murder, you too could be arrested and charged.' It is worth mentioning that whilst we were not intending for people to remember the technical name of the law, Joint Enterprise, a surprising 28% were able to recall it.

Figure 10: Age and gender of fan base

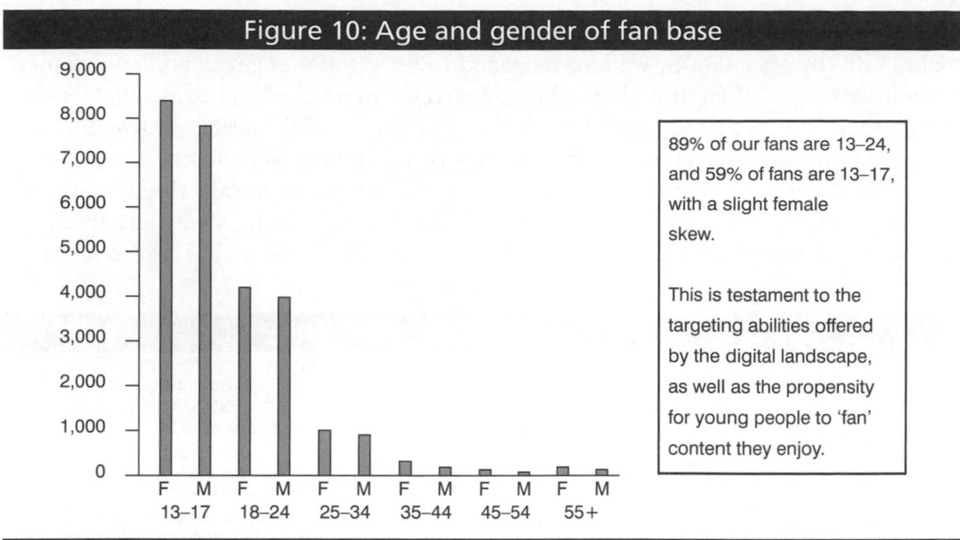
9,000
8,000
7,000
6,000
5,000
4,000
3,000
2,000
1,000
0
F M F M F M F M F M F M
13–17 18–24 25–34 35–44 45–54 55+
89% of our fans are 13–24, and 59% of fans are 13–17, with a slight female skew.
This is testament to the targeting abilities offered by the digital landscape, as well as the propensity for young people to 'fan' content they enjoy.

Source: Mediacom online review, November 2010

Figure 11: Key take out messages of advert

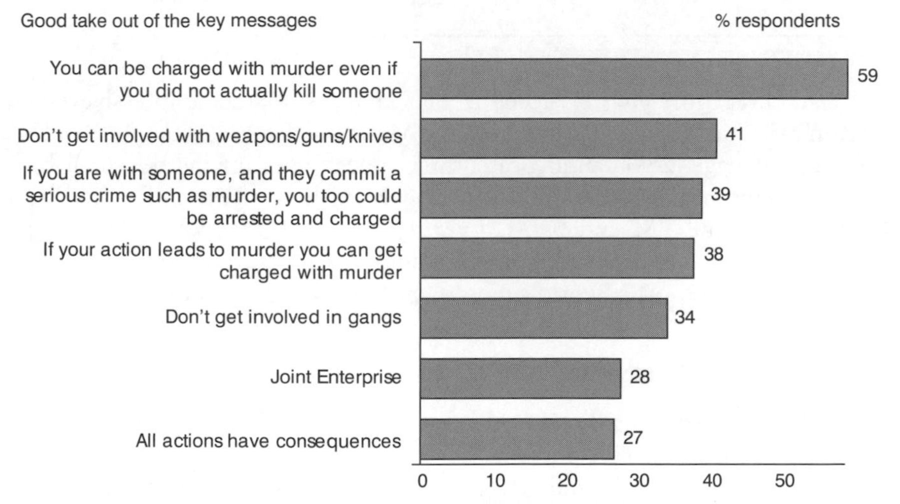
What were the main things the adverts you have seen today were trying to tell you?
Good take out of the key messages
% respondents
You can be charged with murder even if you did not actually kill someone
59
Don't get involved with weapons/guns/knives
41
If you are with someone, and they commit a serious crime such as murder, you too could be arrested and charged
39
If your action leads to murder you can get charged with murder
38
Don't get involved in gangs
34
Joint Enterprise
28
All actions have consequences
27
0 10 20 30 40 50

Source: CELLOmruk tracking, November 2010, base 350 13–15-year-old Londoners

But most reassuringly they understood the implications of this in terms of what they should not do. Our campaign put them off getting involved with weapons, with 41% of 13–15-year-olds agreeing *'Don't get involved with weapons/guns/knives.'* And over a third also agreed 'Don't get involved with gangs.' This is a staggering effect, not least because teenagers normally reject messages telling them to do anything, let alone something that they consider to be 'cool'. We succeeded because it was not an explicit part of the communication message, but implicit.

Considering the subject matter was a message about a legal principle that branded them guilty by association; we also managed to keep them engaged and entertained, without boring or alienating them. We achieved six times the level of engagement for the average Facebook campaign (1% Action Rate vs. 0.15% Facebook benchmark).[4] In fact, an average 3.5 videos (eight minutes of film) were watched before guessing 'Who killed Deon' correctly, delivering the Joint Enterprise message three times; and over 60% of the videos were viewed in full (Figure 12). And, as was intended, the Facebook campaign even got them chatting about the issue with 3,857 comments generated.[5]

Figure 12: Video views over time

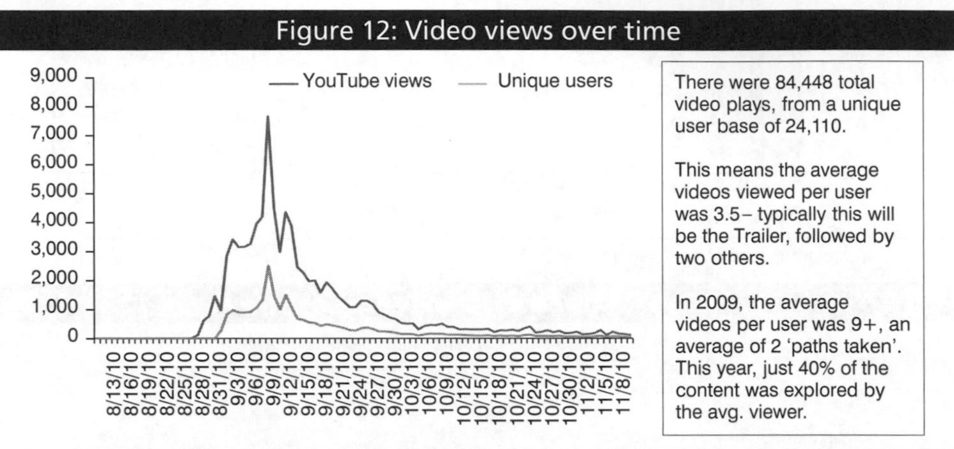
YouTube views
Unique users
9,000
8,000
7,000
6,000
5,000
4,000
3,000
2,000
1,000
0
8/13/10
8/16/10
8/19/10
8/22/10
8/25/10
8/28/10
8/31/10
9/3/10
9/6/10
9/9/10
9/12/10
9/15/10
9/18/10
9/21/10
9/24/10
9/27/10
9/30/10
10/3/10
10/6/10
10/9/10
10/12/10
10/15/10
10/18/10
10/21/10
10/24/10
10/27/10
10/30/10
11/2/10
11/5/10
11/8/10
There were 84,448 total video plays, from a unique user base of 24,110.
This means the average videos viewed per user was 3.5 – typically this will be the Trailer, followed by two others.
In 2009, the average videos per user was 9+, an average of 2 'paths taken'. This year, just 40% of the content was explored by the avg. viewer.

Source: Mediacom online review, November 2010

We had three times more Facebook fans than estimated, impressive given our subject matter and being a message from the Metropolitan Police Service; and 37,836 users liked the page (28% fanning rate, three times the estimated benchmark).

The campaign was covered on TV, national and local press and radio, including BBC News, Capital FM and XFM, *Evening Standard*, *Daily Mirror*; examples in Figure 13. And it has received creative plaudits from the industry, recently being named the Gunn Report's 'world's most awarded TV/video campaign' of 2011.

## Circumstantial evidence

We already know from the direct evidence that our complex message was seen, liked and understood by a high proportion of the target group, and that they claim to want to stay away from weapons and gangs. But we'd like to offer further circumstantial evidence that the campaign is working from the Metropolitan Police Service who are on the front line of tackling youth violence.

Firstly, the campaign is still being used by the Metropolitan Police Safer Schools Officers as an educational resource in schools today, 18 months later. According to one officer in Lewisham, 'Who Killed Deon?' is not only a very useful resource, but it has created unprecedented levels of engagement and interest, whereas the subject is normally met with boredom when it is discussed (Figure 14).

## Figure 13: Examples of news coverage

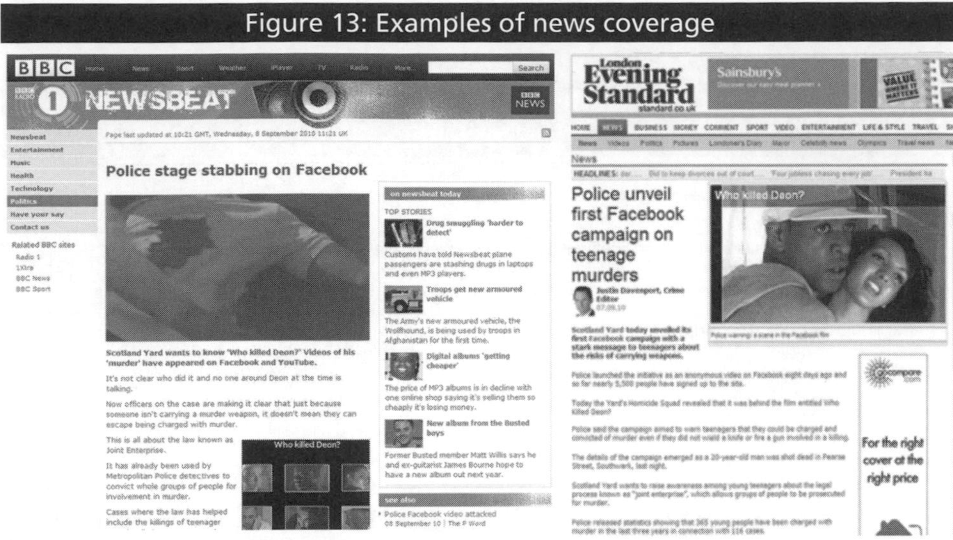

BBC Home News Sport Weather iPlayer TV Radio More... Search

NEWSBEAT

Newsbeat
Entertainment
Music
Health
Technology
Politics
Have your say
Contact us

Related BBC sites
Radio 1
1Xtra
BBC News
BBC Sport

Page last updated at 10:21 GMT, Wednesday, 8 September 2010 11:21 UK

**Police stage stabbing on Facebook**

**Scotland Yard wants to know 'Who killed Deon?' Videos of his 'murder' have appeared on Facebook and YouTube.**

It's not clear who did it and no one around Deon at the time is talking.

Now officers on the case are making it clear that just because someone isn't carrying a murder weapon, it doesn't mean they can escape being charged with murder.

This is all about the law known as Joint Enterprise.

It has already been used by Metropolitan Police detectives to convict whole groups of people for involvement in murder.

Cases where the law has helped include the killings of teenager

Who killed Deon?

on newsbeat today

TOP STORIES

**Drug smuggling 'harder to detect'**

Customs have told Newsbeat plane passengers are stashing drugs in laptops and even MP3 players.

**Troops get new armoured vehicle**

The Army's new armoured vehicle, the Wolfhound, is being used by troops in Afghanistan for the first time.

**Digital albums 'getting cheaper'**

The price of MP3 albums is in decline with one online shop saying it's selling them so cheaply it's losing money.

**New album from the Busted boys**

Former Busted member Matt Willis says he and ex-guitarist James Bourne hope to have a new album out next year.

see also

- Police Facebook video attacked
08 September 10 | The P Word

London Evening Standard
standard.co.uk

Sainsbury's

VALUE WHERE IT MATTERS

HOME NEWS BUSINESS MONEY COMMENT SPORT VIDEO ENTERTAINMENT LIFE & STYLE TRAVEL

News

**Police unveil first Facebook campaign on teenage murders**

Justin Davenport, Crime Editor

Who killed Deon?

**Scotland Yard today unveiled its first Facebook campaign with a stark message to teenagers about the risks of carrying weapons.**

Police launched the initiative as an anonymous video on Facebook eight days ago and so far nearly 5,500 people have signed up to the site.

Today the Yard's Homicide Squad revealed that it was behind the film entitled Who Killed Deon?

Police said the campaign aimed to warn teenagers that they could be charged and convicted of murder even if they did not wield a knife or fire a gun involved in a killing.

The details of the campaign emerged as a 20-year-old man was shot dead in Pearse Street, Southwark, last night.

Scotland Yard wants to raise awareness among young teenagers about the legal process known as "joint enterprise", which allows groups of people to be prosecuted for murder.

Police released statistics showing that 365 young people have been charged with murder in the last three years in connection with 116 cases.

gocompare.com

For the right cover at the right price

Source: www.bbc.co.uk; www.standard.co.uk

## Figure 14: Email campaign feedback to MPS from Safer School Officer, Lewisham

I thought it was a brilliant resource that captured the interests of the students and really made my message a lot easier to get across…

*Q. Did the response to the campaign stand out in any way?*

Absolutely – it was actually aimed at them, and they were engaged from the beginning.They were immediately hooked on the female who got snubbed by Deon in favour of her better looking mate – and from then on they really were transfixed.

*Q. Do you think the MPS Joint Enterprise campaign was successful?*

Yes, definitely successful. Talking about Joint Enterprise would have been really difficult without it. The students loved it. Several sessions overran because the students wanted to watch all of the clips, even after the discussion had finished and we had run out of time. A lot of them asked me how they can find it on YouTube to look at the bits they'd missed (our sessions were only 50 mins).

*Q. What sort of response would you normally expect from this age group to seeing a 'government' campaign telling them about a law?*

Boredom.

The officer also provided evidence that the teenagers were thinking and behaving differently as a result of seeing the campaign (Figure 15).

Figure 15: Email campaign feedback to MPS from Safer School Officer, Lewisham

*Q. What were the changes you noticed? Are you able to provide any specific examples?*

We spoke in the context of a school fight that had occurred a few weeks previously, and most of the students said they would have handled that differently because of what they had learnt about Joint Enterprise. The girls gave examples of carrying weapons for friends and they had no idea that they could also be dealt with under Joint Enterprise.

We also have direct evidence from the teenagers themselves, that they would now walk away from the wrong sort of situation or not even get involved in the first place.

*I wouldn't even be friends with them [bad people] in the first place. You're going to be seen with those people so if they do anything bad you're going to be seen as bad and accused of things you haven't done. That's because I now understand what the implications of that are.*

Yamman, age 15

*I have learnt that I shouldn't get involved with the wrong people. I could still hang around them but as soon as it gets to the bad parts I would move away from it.*

Rohanna, age 14

Additional proof that teenagers exposed to the campaign will now stay away from 'bad' situations and people comes from a feedback questionnaire at the end of the school Joint Enterprise session (Figure 16). Each quote is from an individual respondent, and therefore an individual testimony.

## Calculating the real value

However, the real worth of this campaign is its anticipated future effect. It will have started during the summer holidays of 2010, but the hope is that the teenagers influenced will carry the message forward and act on it in coming years. The effect we are dealing with is not a reduction of crime itself, but hopefully a reduction in the number of participants in a potential crime, as a result of the Joint Enterprise campaign convincing some teenagers to simply stay clear. Ultimately fewer people involved means there is less chance of a crime escalating into a serious crime. This could be measured by cost of lives saved, costs to the NHS, etc. Whilst these might be eventual impacts of the campaign it is not something we can ever hope to prove.

**Figure 16: Comments from questionnaires at the end of the Joint Enterprise session at a school in Lewisham**

*Q. What will you do differently now?*

'I will keep away from gangs.'

'Stay more alert at what my friends do and what they are capable of.'

'I will stay away from people into crimes because you could also be convicted.'

'Always make the right choice at all times.'

'I will talk my friends out of serious situations and be good.'

'Stay away from people into crimes because you could also be convicted.'

'If I know about a friend about to commit a crime I will actively tell them to stop so I don't get charged for joint enterprise.'

'Be careful who I'm friends with.'

'If I see or know something bad is going to happen I will tell someone e.g. the police, adult or try and stop it so that I don't get convicted.'

'I will think carefully.'

'Try and think of things that will help.'

'Watch who my friends are.'

'Take more care in life.'

'I will be careful about my friends.'

'Won't mess around with friends, won't be bad because I know what you go through now and what happens i.e. you are arrested.'

'Choose my friends wisely.'

Source: Feedback questionnaire provided by L. Bunting, PL

However, should a crime occur, fewer people being involved will mean fewer arrests made under Joint Enterprise, and this alone provides a substantial cost saving to society. We have shown through personal testimony and Officers' testimony that seeing the campaign has changed behaviour and convinced individual teenagers to stay away from crimes; so our question now is how many might our campaign have influenced?

## How many teenagers might we have affected?

We know that in a typical year 150,000 young people enter the young offenders system.[6] Of these, 2,070 are 13–15-year-olds from London, the target group on which we have attitude change evidence.[7]

Our data shows that 45% of this group recognised one element of the campaign = 932 people.

Of whom 59% understood *'You can be charged with murder even if you didn't actually kill someone'* = 549 people.

Therefore we can hope that as a consequence of our campaign, 549 fewer young people will enter the Youth Justice system as a result of seeing the campaign.

## So, what are the economics of this?

Four percent of all young offenders are given a custodial sentence.[8]

Therefore of our 549 fewer young people entering the Youth Justice system, 22 would normally have received a custodial sentence.

The average custodial sentence for a young person tried in the Crown Court is 25.1 months.[9] And it costs an average of £55,000 to hold a young offender in custody for a year.[10]

Therefore, if we stopped 22 people entering the Youth Justice system, that is a saving to society of £2.54m.[11]

So on a campaign budget of £300,000 this would generate an ROI of 1:8.5.

## Evidence from just one key witness

We know that this campaign has affected individuals. So looking back at the evidence we provided earlier, we would like to also show the potential ROI based on one testimony provided by a Safer Schools Officer: *'The girls gave examples of carrying weapons for friends and they had no idea that they could also be dealt with under Joint Enterprise.'*

From this testimony alone, we know that at least one girl who has carried a weapon will no longer do so as a result of the communication. This single change in behaviour, irrespective of hoped-for effect of the campaign presented above, is likely to have averted a crime.

A mandatory minimum custodial sentence for a young offender carrying a gun is five years.[12] A young offender's custodial sentence costs society £55,000 per year, rising to £200,000 for a secure training home.[13]

This anecdote alone will have covered at least 90% of the cost of the campaign; or at most delivered an ROI of 1:3.3, if it avoided a stay in a secure training home.

## Summing up

This case proposes a way to prove the effectiveness of small budget, digitally-led public information campaigns, the effectiveness of which relies on a tightly targeted message to eliminate wastage, and the real value of which is in the long-term future-facing effect of the communications. Whilst the numbers of people we are reaching are small, the potential effects of preventing even one person getting into a life of crime and becoming a disproportionate burden on the prison system and society are large. We hope this paper will be able to justify the vital role communications can play in tackling complex social issues on small budgets by preventing the inevitable rather than waiting until it is too late; and also the power of individual's testimony in proving effectiveness.

Having studied the evidence, we hope this is a compelling case to support the development of publically funded, pre-emptive behavioural reinforcement campaigns in the future.

We rest our case.

## Notes

1 Press release, The Metropolitan Police Service, 7 September 2010.
2 Source: Based on Mediacom online benchmarks.
3 Source: CELLOmruk tracking, November 2010, base 350 13–15-year-old Londoners.
4 Source: Mediacom online review, November 2010.
5 Source: Mediacom online review, November 2010.
6 www.education.gov.uk; Education of Young People Supervised by the Youth Justice Board, Background paper, 2005/6, para 1.1.
7 www.education.gov.uk; Education of Young People Supervised by the Youth Justice Board, Background paper, 2005/6. Calculation based on 46% 13–15-year-olds and 0.03% Londoners, Figs 1 and 4.
8 www.education.gov.uk; Education of Young People Supervised by the Youth Justice Board, Background paper, 2005/6, para 2.1. N.B. Young offenders can receive a DTO (Detention and Training Order) which is a combination of a community and custodial sentence. However, for most violent crimes they would be tried and sentenced in the Crown Court and if found guilty delivered a custodial sentence.
9 Ministry of Justice, Sentencing Statistics Quarterly briefing 2011. There has been little variation in average sentence lengths at the Crown Court since 2008.
10 The New Economics Foundation (NEF), *Punishing Costs*, 2010.
11 Based on 22 people × £115,000 (25.1 months at 55,000 for 12 months).
12 www.direct.gov.uk: Anyone who is found guilty of possessing an illegal firearm faces a minimum sentence of five years.
13 www.education.gov.uk; Education of Young People Supervised by the Youth Justice Board, Background paper, 2005/6, para 4.2.

## Chapter 17

# Snickers

## You're not you when you're hungry

**By Alex Lewis, Abbott Mead Vickers BBDO**
Contributing authors: Peter West, Mars Inc; James Miller, Abbott Mead Vickers BBDO
Credited companies: Integrated Agencies: BBDO New York and BBDO Worldwide; Client: Mars Inc

### Editor's summary

Snickers was losing market share to other global chocolate brands. This paper shows how Snickers' big global idea 'You're not you when you're hungry' delivered creative work that got people talking about the brand. Using celebrities and big media placements, a variety of television ads displayed iconic females embodying certain hunger traits set in male-focused settings. The campaign resulted in Snickers' most successful period of growth, increasing sales by 15.9% in one year, capturing market share in all but two of the 58 markets in which it ran, and growing global market share by US$376.3m. The judges loved this paper; it is a fantastic case of how an astonishing ambition to decentralise an approach and gain buy-in across so many markets, was realised with brilliant and quantifiable results.

## Section 1: Introduction

Creating global advertising ideas is tricky business. More often than not, the great global brands of our time have been born out of being great global products rather than big communications ideas. And a quick look at the IPA Effectiveness database would seem to confirm this; only 13 of the 526 winning papers represent global campaigns, and only one of these is a food brand, where the localised nature of culinary trends typically works against you.

What successful global ideas there are tend to stem from rigorous central control. But such an approach was never going to work for Mars, home of Snickers and perhaps the world's largest de-centralised company. So we needed to embrace this philosophy and give local markets an idea so exciting that they couldn't fail to execute it brilliantly themselves.

The 'You're Not You When You're Hungry' idea did just that, growing the value sales of this billion dollar, 80-year-old brand 15.9% in one year, capturing market share in all but two of the 58 markets within which it ran and ultimately growing global market share by US$ 376.3m.[1] In doing so it helped Snickers not just retain its position as the world's biggest chocolate bar, but pull away from the chasing pack.

## Section 2: A little context

### *Rewind to 1932*

When Mars decided to start selling their products in markets outside the US, the logical option was to simply export.[2] But Frank Mars and his son Forrest had very different ideas. Yes, they had proven US recipes, but they believed these needed to be combined with a strong local flavour. So in 1932, Forrest set up base in the UK, combining this knowledge with his own local understanding.

This philosophy of strong central guidance, aligned with a freedom to do what's right locally, formed the backbone of Mars's success across a further 70 markets.

### *Fast-forward to 2009*

It has remained that way in their marketing. Mars have never been the kind to export top-down global ideas, nor could they today.[3] Instead they've provided central 'recipes' as strategic guidance and let markets put them together in a way that will be right for local tastes. This yielded brands with a global footprint, rather than what you'd call global brands.

But by 2009 the global Snickers team asked whether such an approach was holding the brand back. We could see that this freedom had potentially gone too far, to the extent that you'd struggle to tell that much of the marketing was based off the same original recipe.

In 2009, Snickers communications was markedly varied in tone, message and quality (Figure 1).

## Figure 1: Snickers global campaigns by market 2009

| Market | Strategy | Target | Creative device | Campaign |
|---|---|---|---|---|
| North America | Reinforce the product's credentials | Those who get narrow, niche, quirky humour | The distinctive parallelogram font | 'Snacklish' |
| UK and Ireland | Stand up as the chocolate bar for 'real men' | Regular 'Blokes' | Mr T | 'Get some nuts' |
| China | Emphasise the energy properties of the bar | Young, dynamic Chinese males | Various | 'Game on' |
| Middle East | Act as the bar that brings mates together | Male youth | Football related activity | 'Don't stop' |
| Western Europe | Position Snickers as the bar for when you have a big task to accomplish | Everyone | Hyperbolic, filmic dramatisations of enormous tasks | 'Big Job' |
| Mexico | Align Snickers with street sports | Teens | Gritty, down-to-earth festivals | 'Urbania' |
| Russia | Position Snickers as the bar for lapses in energy | Cool, emerging Russian youth | Transformer style films | 'Don't stop' |
| Central and Eastern Europe | Reinforce the peanuts | Everyone | Flying peanuts | 'Peanut power' |

Source: Snickers campaigns from the UK, the US, China, Russia, Germany, South Korea, Gulf Coast Countries, Mexico

The brand was still growing, but not at the speed of the other global chocolate brands.

Between 2007–2009 Snickers growth lagged behind the other big global chocolate brands in both relative and absolute terms (Figure 2).

Figure 2: Global incremental value growth 2007–2009

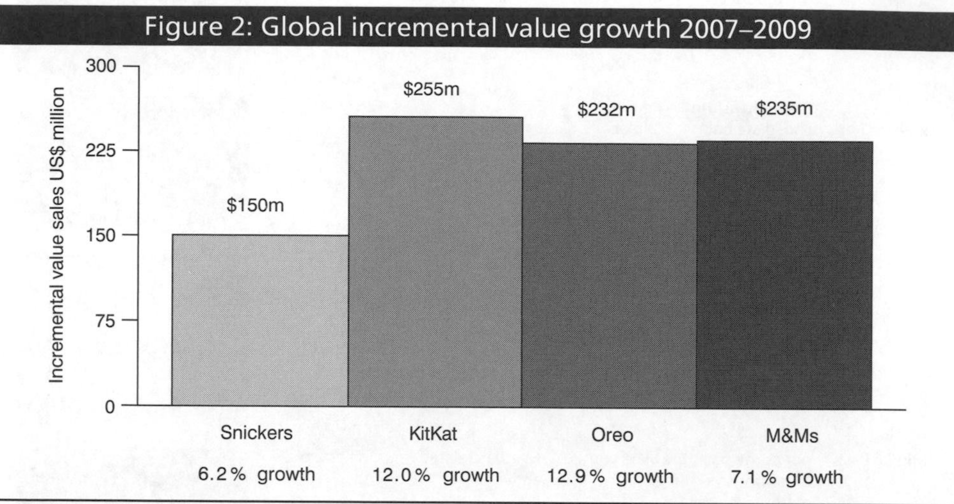


Source: Euromonitor

Consequently, Snickers was losing market share (Figure 3) and in the context of a US$ 85.5bn market the 0.26% drop represented some US$ 222m in value sales. The Snickers share of global value sales was in decline.

Figure 3: Snickers global value sales market share 2006–2009

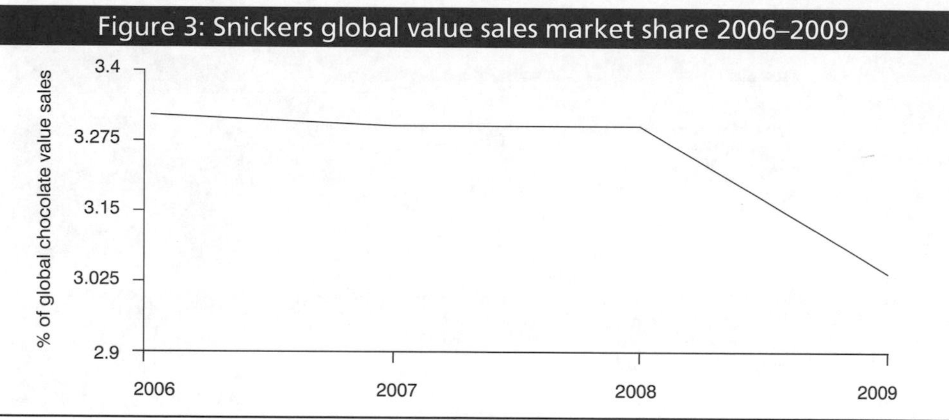


Source: Mars internal market share database based on Nielsen data

If the pattern continued, Snickers would lose its status as the world's biggest chocolate bar (Figure 4).

Figure 4: Projected value sales 2009–2013, based on 2007–2009 growth rates

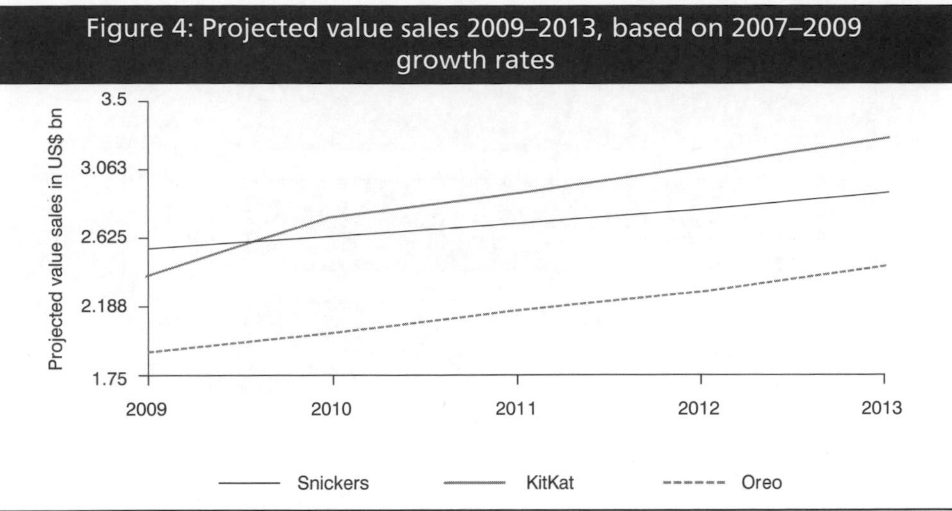


Source: Based on 2007–2009 growth rate provided by Euromonitor

## Section 3: Our challenge

Ask any local market brand manager why their brand is losing market share and it's unlikely they'll point to the lack of a global idea.[4] But it wasn't just a varied global reel and slowing sales that was putting pressure on this approach.

Firstly, given tough times, Mars were looking to realise efficiencies of scale and we could see the benefits others were enjoying from a more focused, global approach.[5] We sensed that it might be easier to get to a global idea than continually course correct individual markets. Secondly, we wanted better work in smaller markets to help drive healthier growth amongst our 'long tail'. Finally, we felt that if we all pulled in one direction we would start to assert ourselves as an iconic, global brand.[6]

This approach meant we needed to get local brand managers excited, providing them with an idea that acted as a recipe for their own success rather than the finished product. So we built a communications model that could accommodate these seemingly conflicting needs.

Our communications model centred around a creative device that could ultimately deliver local fame (Figure 5).

### *Increasing penetration*

We've already established that we needed to *drive sales* in order to regain market share. We also knew that achieving this in the chocolate category meant increasing *penetration.*[7] Analysis of the IPA databank also showed that campaigns targeting penetration were more likely to achieve our goals. Campaigns targeting penetration have a demonstrably bigger effect on both sales and market share (Table 1).

Figure 5: Snickers new communications model

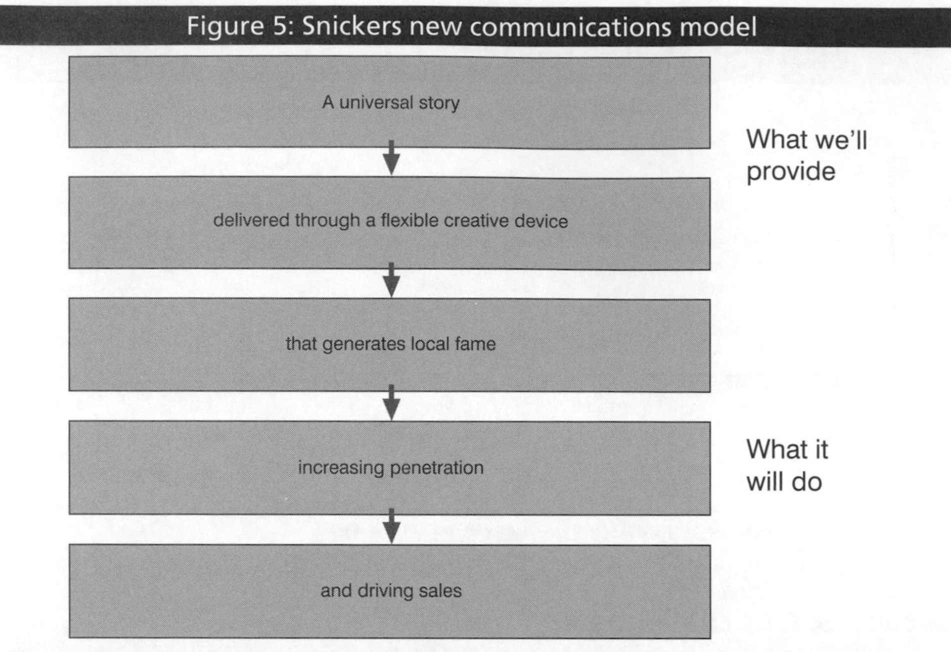
A universal story
delivered through a flexible creative device
that generates local fame
increasing penetration
and driving sales
What we'll provide
What it will do

Source: Schematic of the communications model employed for Snickers idea development, BBDO

Table 1: Impact on business measures arriving from different campaign objectives

| Percentage reporting very large business effect on: | Average of all campaigns reporting hard evidence | Campaigns aiming to increase penetration |
|---|---|---|
| Sales | 45% | 62% (+++) |
| Market share | 25% | 35% (+++) |
| Profit | 23% | 31% (++) |
| Penetration | 23% | 46% |
| Loyalty | 7% | 7% |
| Price sensitivity | 4% | 5% |
| Any measure | 55% | 77% (+++) |

Source: Field, P. (2007) *Marketing in the Era of Accountability*. London: WARC

### *Delivering local fame*

### Quote 1: Peter Field (2007) *Marketing in the Era of Accountability*. London: Warc

> *Fame is not simply about generating brand awareness (which turns out to have limited value for most established brands). It is about building word-of-mouth advocacy for the brand – getting it talked about, creating authority for the brand and the sense that it is making most of the running in the category.*

There are plenty of chocolate bars competing at the shelf so increasing penetration means being the most salient. Since everyone knows Snickers, the goal wasn't about brand awareness but about *delivering brand fame*. Being famous was our single most important metric as it meant being talked about by a higher proportion of those people who currently didn't care about us.

We knew this dynamic meant fame could deliver significantly and exponentially in terms of market share gains,[8] whilst evidence from previous Snickers campaigns (Figure 6) and further afield (Table 2) also suggested it would pay back.

Snickers's highest penetration and market share coincided with the brand's most famous period, when talk and publicity around the axed Speedwalker advert was at its highest.

Figure 6: UK penetration and value market share 2007–2008

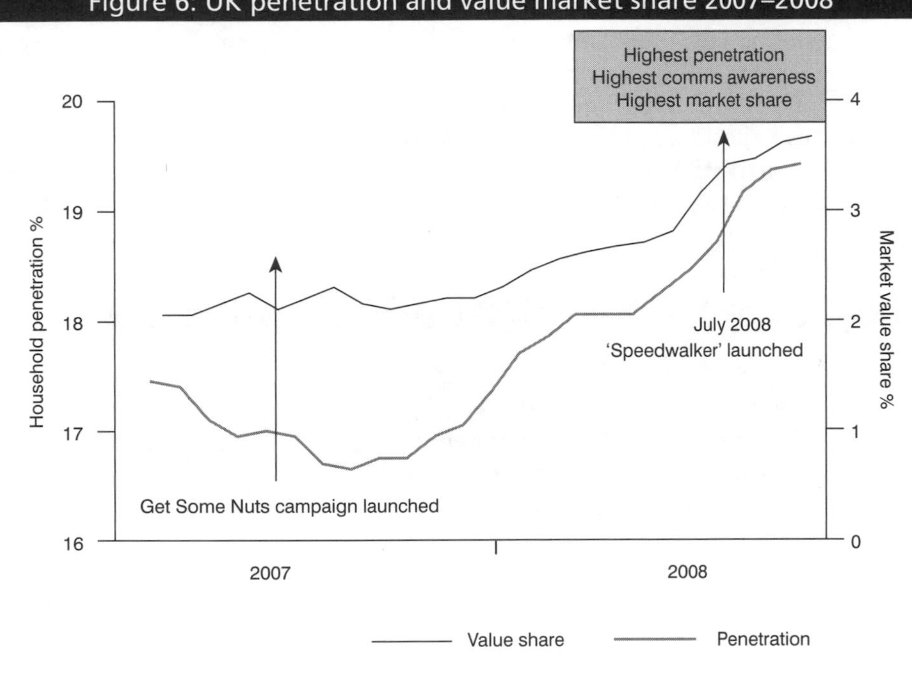


Source: Market share from Euromonitor, penetration from IRI HH panel, total UK all outlets

Fame is the most frequently observed intermediate objective in cases recording very large business uplifts (Table 2).

**Table 2: Success rate of intermediate objectives**

| | Effectiveness (percentage reporting very large business effects) |
|---|---|
| Fame | 78% (++) |
| Quality | 73% |
| Trust | 72% |
| Differentiation | 70% |
| Commitment | 70% |
| Image | 68% |
| Direct | 67% |

Source: IPA/Gunn Report (2011) The Link Between Creativity and Effectiveness

We found that the most important influence on driving fame was carrying universal meaning.[9] Whether it's X-Factor or Adele, the key to success is that everyone can connect to it. This seemed especially pertinent to us since just about everyone buys chocolate. The problem was that narrowcast targeting meant that in too many markets Snickers was highly salient amongst a niche audience, but not amongst the masses.[10] We were cool (for a chocolate bar), when we needed to be famous.[11] Being famous rather than cool meant exciting the broadest possible audience (Table 3).

**Table 3: Fundamental shifts of the new communications model**

| Where we were | Where we needed to be |
|---|---|
| Niche | Populist |
| Deep male insight | Deep human insight |
| Loved by a minority | Talked about by the masses |
| Targeting guys | Targeting everyone |
| Cool | Famous |

Source: Strategic changes needed to drive penetration, BBDO

## Section 4: Our solution

As discussed, our communications model called for a *universal insight* that could be delivered through a *flexible creative device.*

### *Our universal story*

We needed something that not only connected the broadest audience possible, but which could also do this in 58 markets.

We started with the Snickers DNA. There was a distinct male tonality defining much of the brand's past which we couldn't turn our back on. But whereas until now we'd been targeting blokes head-on, our new approach meant finding an insight about the guys' world that would be enjoyed by everyone. Turning to qualitative research, we found that there is always a universal code of conduct that needs to be abided by in order to stay part of the male pack. This felt globally consistent, but it was also something that everyone could recognise.

We then needed to marry this up to a role for the brand. Our connection came through the impact being hungry can have on your ability to actually abide by those typical male behaviours that keep you as 'one of the guys'. Whether you turn cranky and irritable, weak and lethargic, or dopey and slow, there are certain universal 'symptoms' of hunger that can stop a guy from keeping to that code of conduct. But of course you didn't need to be a bloke to recognise this.

Our big idea 'You're Not You When You're Hungry' was all about showcasing this story; that when guys get hungry, they're actually not themselves and their role in the pack is threatened. As a proper, nut-filled bar Snickers can sort out that hunger and restore your place. We then just needed a flexible creative device that could make this story famous in a diverse set of markets.

### *Our creative device*

To deliver that fame there appeared to be two options: go big and global, or go deep and local. The former was so clearly counter-cultural to the Mars way that we needed to find a way to deliver the latter, whilst still driving global scale.

We knew that in just about every market, TV would be our most important tool. It's still the best rocket launcher, reaching a higher proportion of light buyers than any other channel.[12] Starting here, we combined big celebrities with big media placements.[13]

The ads used the juxtaposition of iconic, often female, celebrities that embodied certain hunger traits set in male-focused settings (Figures 7a–e). This provided the flexibility to tailor specific executions to markets, improving our chances of fame but not at the expense of a consistent global story.

Our global pool of advertising shows how the same story is told but in such as way that it drives real local talk-value (see Figures 7a–e: five of the 20 new TV adverts created in the campaign).

**Figure 7a: Game – USA**

Opening shot – guys playing on the field

Betty White running towards the ball

Betty White gets tackled

Mike, you're playing like Betty White out there!

That's not what your girlfriend says!

Eat a Snickers! Better?

Better!

Source: Storyboard for TV advert from the US

## Figure 7b: Pushing Car – Gulf coast countries

Opening scene – group of guys pushing a car

The car is on fire! Push and stop being a diva!

I'm the one doing all the pushing!

Karim, have a Snickers!

Why? Because when you get hungry you turn into a drama queen!

Better?
Better!

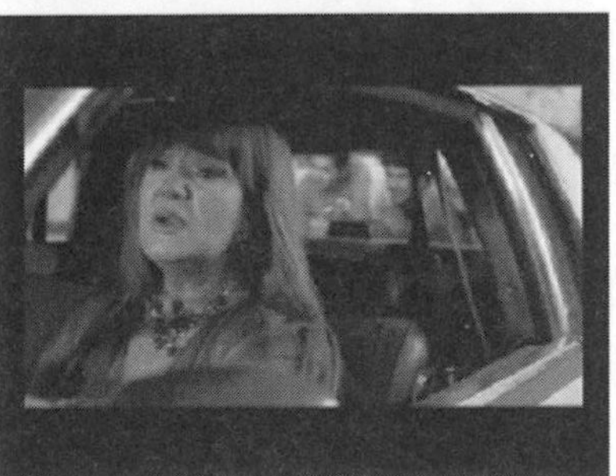

Come on! Push!

Snickers. Don't stop!

Source: Storyboard for TV adverts from the Gulf Coast countries

## Figure 7c: Streetball – Russia

Guys playing basketball

Ballerina appears in the background

She catches the ball and falls over

Play in a tougher way!
Kiss my tutu!

Snickers? When you're hungry you're not on your top form

Better? Better!

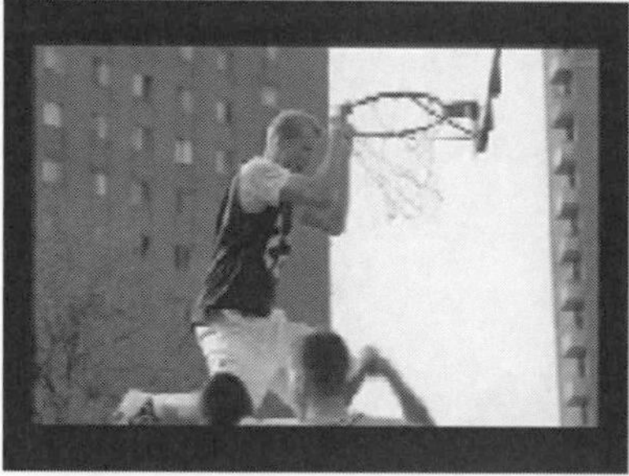

Don't stop! Grab a Snickers!

Source: Storyboard for TV advert from Russia

## Figure 7d: Goalkeeper – China

Crowd cheering

Hey Bro, can you get any worse than that?

You are as weak as Lin Daiyu when you're hungry

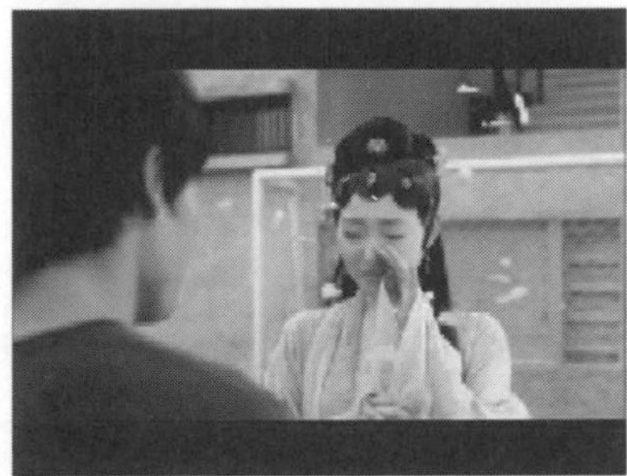

Why don't you do it then?

You can't even stand on your feet when you're hungry

Here, have a Snickers. Better?

Yep, I'm back!

Satisfy your hunger and be yourself again

Source: Storyboard for TV advert from China

### Figure 7e: Road trip – Germany

Opening shot – road trip

Can we turn the AC up? I'm dying back here!

It's on! Can't you feel it?
Can you feel that? (Slap)

Jeff, eat a Snickers! Every time you get hungry you turn into a diva. Just eat it.

Oooo, turning into a diva? (childish voice)

Better? Better!

Would you get your knees out of the back of my seat?!

Source: Storyboard for TV advert from Germany

The idea provided the simplest of recipes. Now in other media, lower production and media costs meant even more local flavour could be injected into it. Snickers could harness local insights to drive local brand fame whilst also benefiting from the scale and impact of a big, global idea. Local work all stemmed from the same simple idea, but leveraged local insights and creativity to drive fame for the brand locally (Figures 8a and 8b).

Figure 8a: Outdoor, Moscow (headline: You're not you when you're hungry); Print, Germany (bottom left); Outdoor, Australia (bottom right)

## Figure 8b: 'Mockumentary', US; Radio, Puerto Rica; Twitter, UK

A 'mockumentary' in the US told the unknown story of how NFL player Leon Lett made one of the game's most famous ever mistakes because he 'played hungry'.

In Puerto Rico, the island's most popular breakfast show DJs played out-of-character music, all on the same day. Hip Hop stations played opera, classic stations played hard rock... all until an announcement revealed that they were hungry and needed a Snickers.

In the UK, five celebrity Twitter users tweeted out of character until they revealed that they'd simply been hungry.

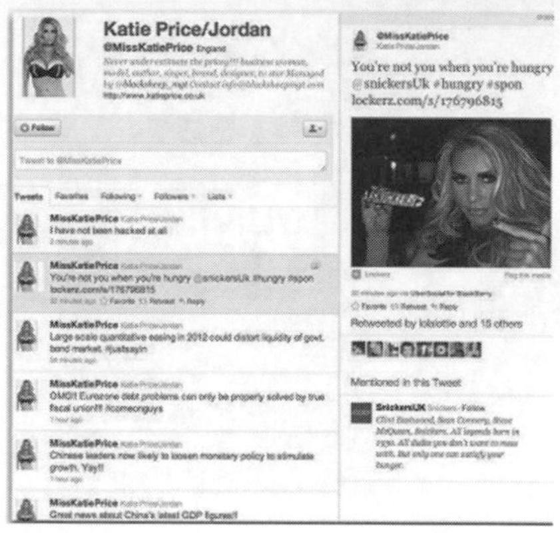

## Section 5: Our results

We will first examine the global picture before going deeper into a broad spectrum of markets and finally looking at the impact within the organisation.

### *The global impact*

Given that the campaign was taken up at different times around the globe, we will use three timelines to illustrate the influence over time as more global sales have been affected by the campaign.[14]

- Phase 1 – 0% of global value sales influenced by campaign *(no markets running the campaign)*
- Phase 2 – 49.17% influenced *(34 markets)*
- Phase 3 – 88.67% influenced *(54 markets)*

It's worth remembering that those not running the campaign were running other advertising, so the media spend is relatively consistent across each of these phases. Whilst advertising and media spend was up in 2010, this is attributable to the production cost of developing a new campaign rather than media spend and we can see that in 2011 (Phase 3) the spend was actually below 2009 levels (Figure 9).

Global advertising and media spend has remained steady for five years, with 2011's spend actually below pre-campaign levels.

Figure 9: Index of global Snickers advertising spend (media and production)

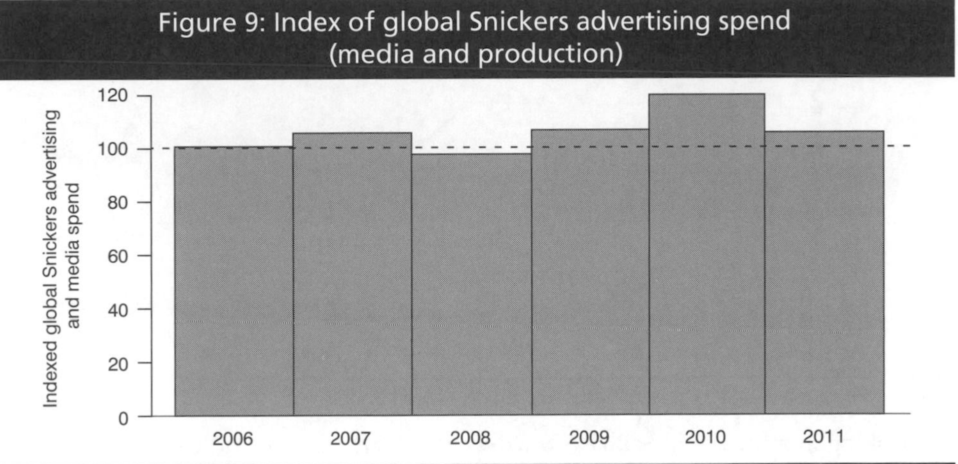


Source: Mars internal data

We can see how the impact on value sales has been significant as more markets have run the work (Figure 10).

As a higher proportion of markets have adopted the campaign, the rate of value sales growth has accelerated significantly.

This growth has been reflected by Snickers regaining global market share (Figure 11) equivalent to US$ 376.3m, helping it not just retain its status as the world's biggest bar but to also pull away from the chasing pack.

Snickers has regained and surpassed its previous value market share to strengthen its position as the world's biggest bar.

Figure 10: Global value sales growth 2009–2011

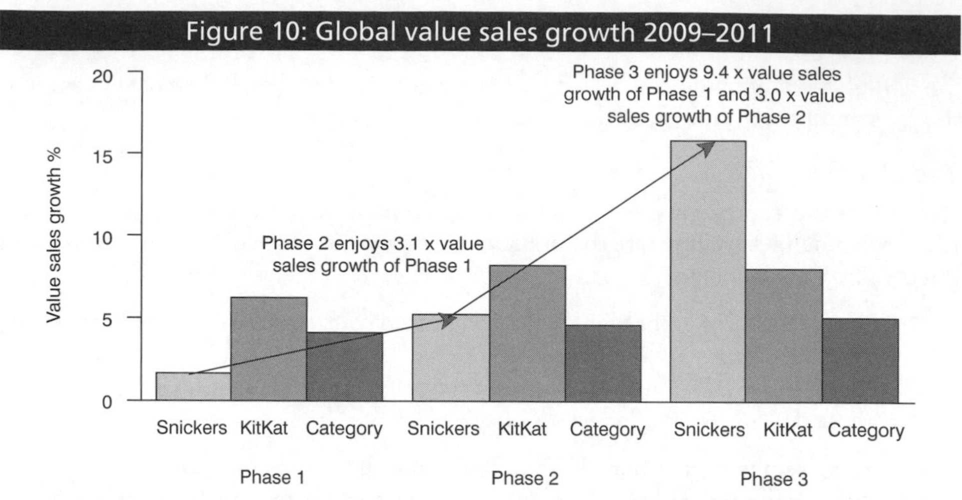


Source: Nielsen

Figure 11: Snickers global value market share 2006–2011

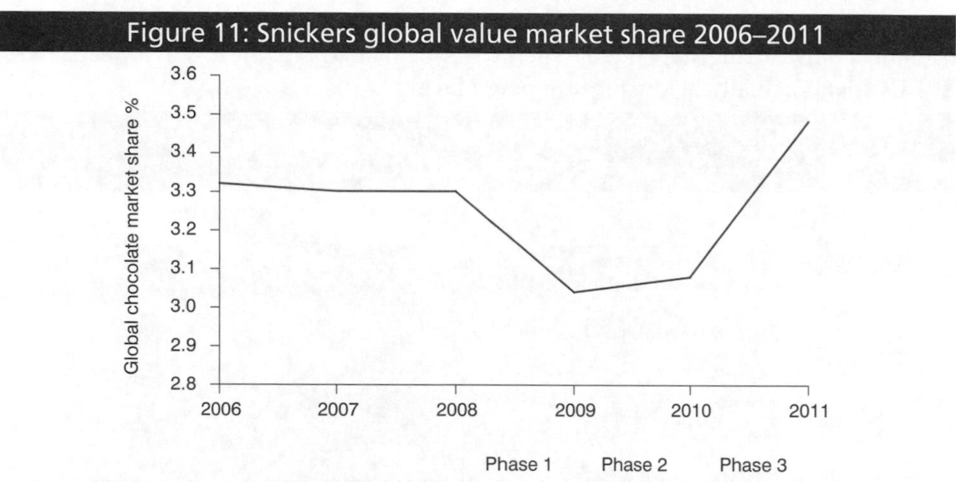


Source: Mars internal market share database based on Nielsen data

Looking in more detail at Phase 3, we see that only Mexico and UAE failed to gain market value share (Figure 12). Ninety-one per cent of those markets running the campaign grew value share in 2011.

This pattern is also reflected in volume growth, where Snickers grew in all but one market (Figure 13). Snickers outperformed the volume growth of the category in 17 out of the 22 markets running the campaign.

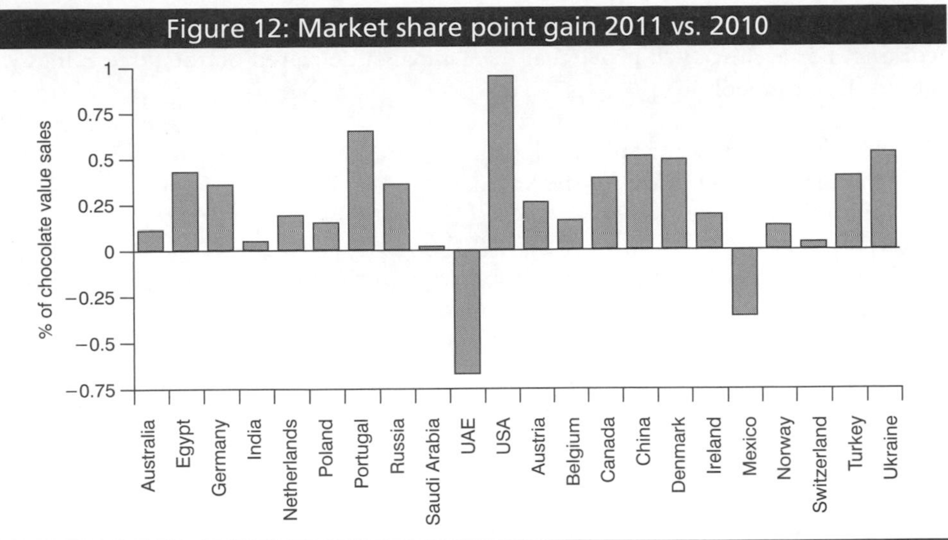


Figure 12: Market share point gain 2011 vs. 2010

Source: Mars internal market share database based on Nielsen data

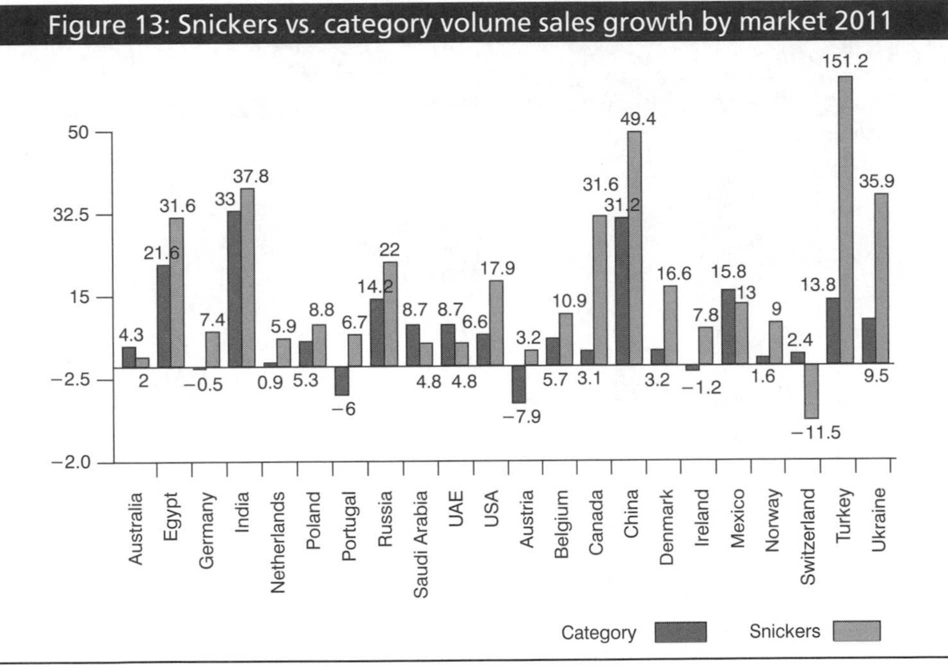


Figure 13: Snickers vs. category volume sales growth by market 2011

Source: Off-take growth vs. the market from Mars internal data

### *The local impact*

We've shown how a global turnaround in sales and market share began with the introduction of the idea and accelerated as more markets embraced it. But with little beyond sales data available at a global level, we'll now look more closely at four specific markets in order to get a deeper understanding of how the campaign was working. For each we will prove that the campaign delivered on the three things we set out in our model:

1. It delivered *fame* for Snickers locally;
2. that drove *penetration* for the brand;
3. and ultimately built *sales*.

The markets that follow represent a spectrum of the challenges we faced as well as a significant proportion of our global value sales.[15]

## The US

*Delivering fame*

The idea provided famous work that regained Snickers' place in popular culture. *Game*, the first ad in the campaign, was voted #1 Super Bowl ad, earning over 400 million incremental media impressions, with an equivalent media value of 11.4 times the initial investment (Figure 14).

*Game* earned over 400 million incremental and unpaid media impressions, with an equivalent media value of US$ 28.6m.

Figure 14: Earned media generated by Snickers Game following Super Bowl

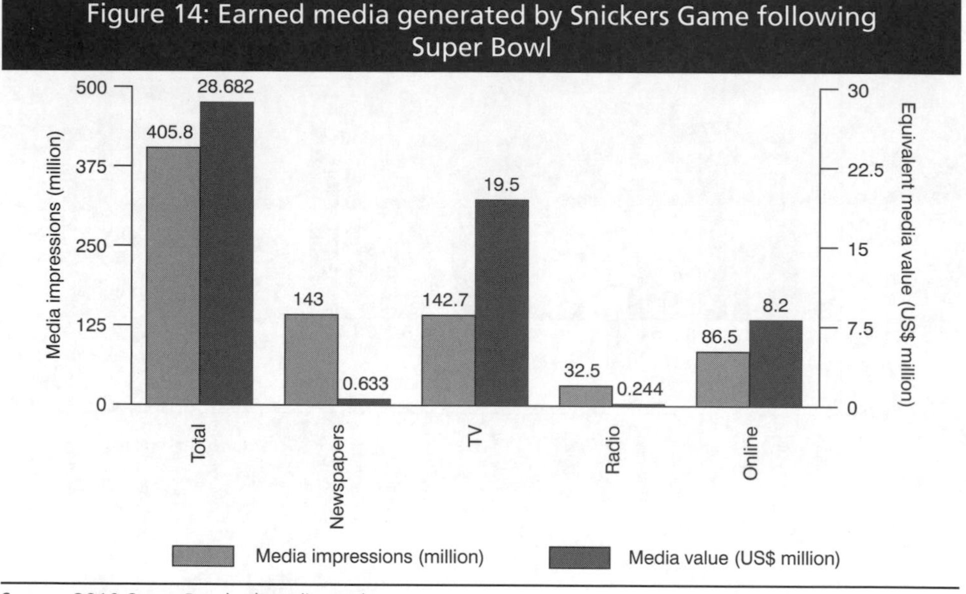


Source: 2010 Super Bowl ad media tracker

The sheer variety of this coverage also indicated that we'd driven fame, as popular with Oprah as it was with political satirists (Figure 15).

From Larry King to Jay Leno, ESPN to Ellen, the campaign delivered the 'rocket launch' fame we'd aspired to.

Figure 15: A selection of the PR generated by the campaign launch

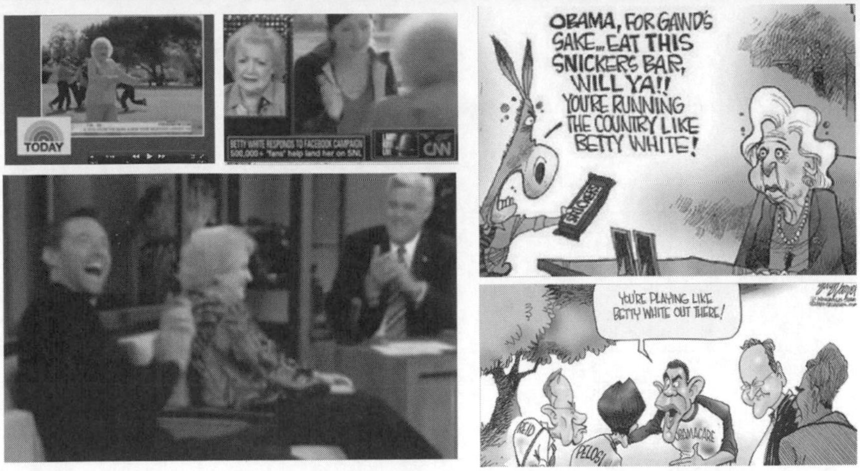

Source: Earned media in PR from Game and Road Trip adverts

The diagnostics revealed the reasons behind some of this, with *Game* three times more likely to get talked about (Figure 16).

It was its propensity to get talked about that was helping *Game* drive fame for Snickers.

Figure 16: IPSOS Super Bowl talk factor analysis

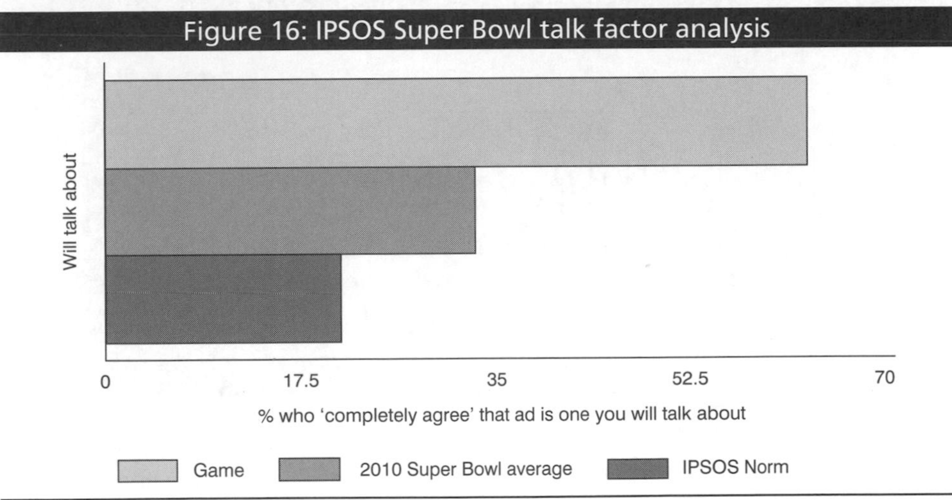


Source: IPSOS ASI

*Driving penetration*

Our rediscovered fame was helping to drive penetration gains, which were up 1.8% (Figure 17).

Whereas Snickers had been losing penetration, it experienced strong gains on the back of the campaign.

Figure 17: US household penetration

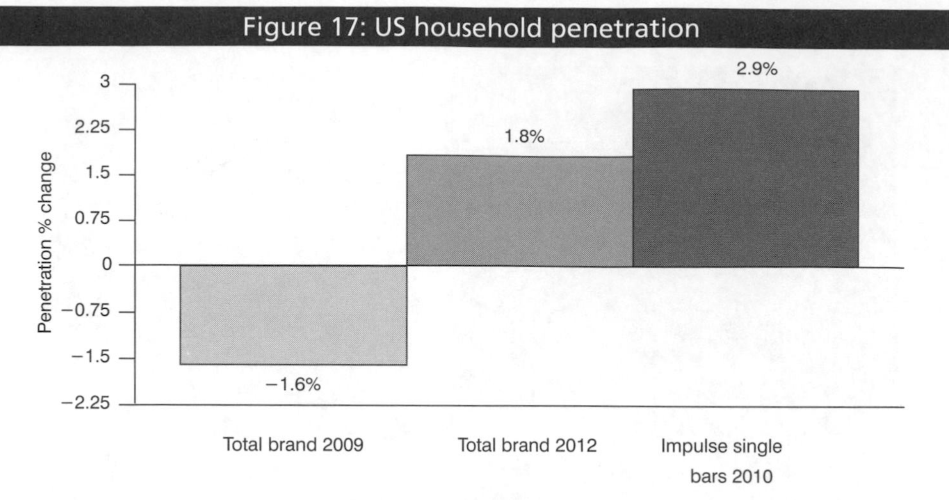


Source: IRI HH Panel, total US all outlets

This was driven by enjoying more populist appeal than the previous niche, male audience (Figure 18).

The campaign achieved its objective of carrying broad, populist appeal for everyone.

Figure 18: Game IPSOS Copy Effectiveness Index* score

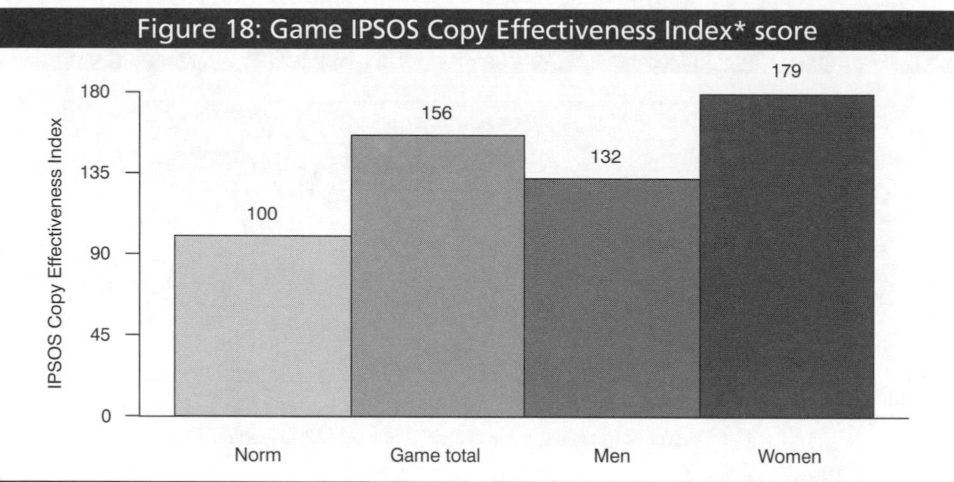


Source: IPSOS ASI. *The Copy Effect Index (CEI) is IPSOS ASI'S proprietary measure of in-market sales performance potential; a weighted combination of branded ad recall and ad persuasion

And when the second ad arrived we could see that we now enjoyed much broader relevance (Figure 19).

The new campaign's greater relevance was helping to broaden its populist appeal.

Figure 19: New vs. old campaign relevance

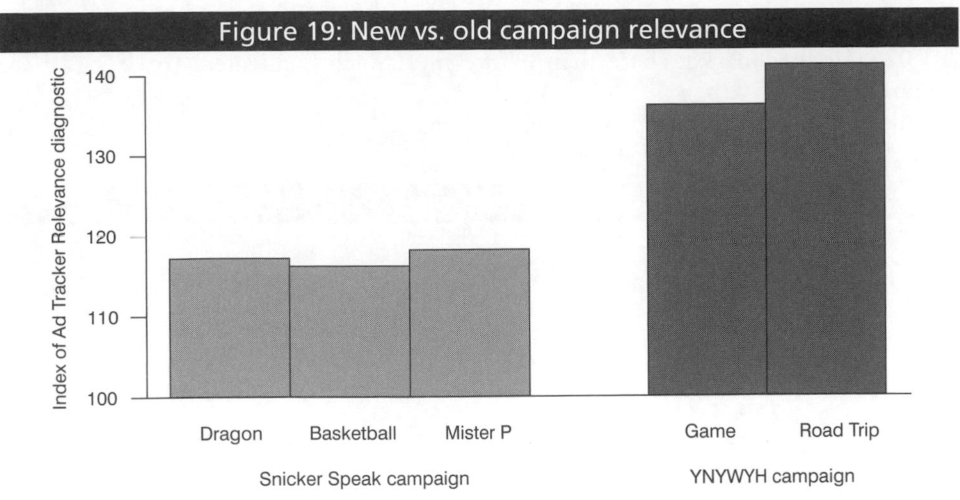


Source: Mars Ad Tracker tool

*Building sales*

After only three months in market, the brand not only reversed volume sales decline, but experienced growth, a trend that continued at a rate of over twice the category growth ever since (Figure 20).

Volume sales performance versus the category has improved ever since the campaign was introduced.

Figure 20: US volume sales growth

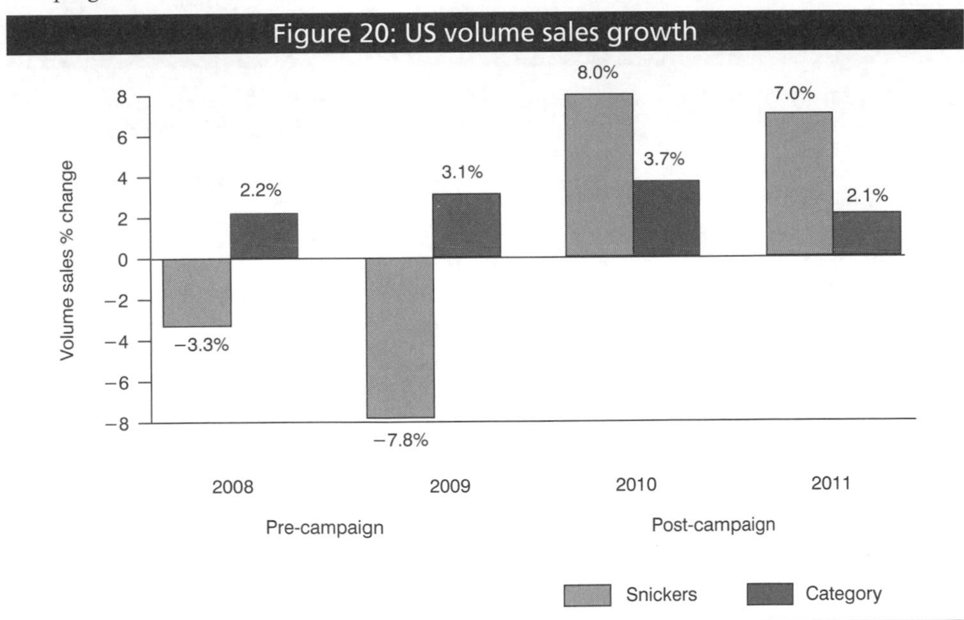


Source: Mars internal data, Nielsen

This has helped regain market value share to the extent that Snickers now enjoys a 1.02% greater market share than before the launch, equivalent to US$ 180.3m (Figure 21).

Snickers has regained and significantly surpassed its previous value market share in the US.

Figure 21: Snickers US market value share 2008–2011

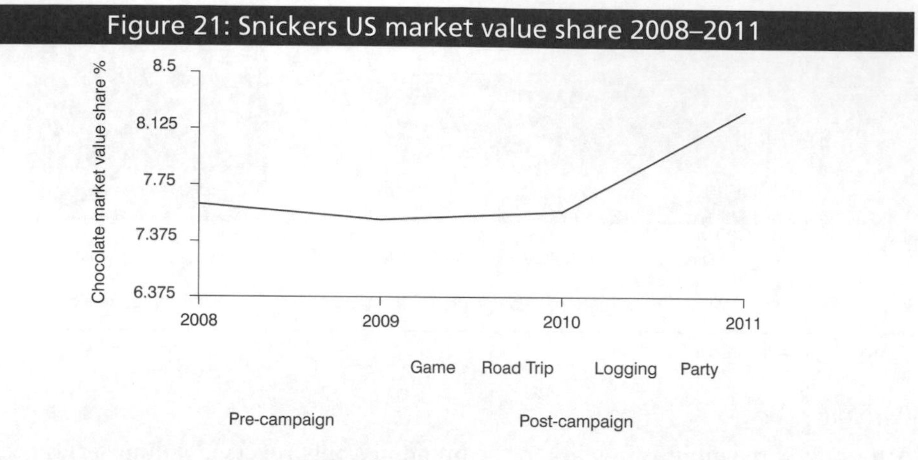


And whilst the campaign as a whole has been a success, the *Game* spot that launched the campaign has been singled out as the most effective Super Bowl commercial ever (Table 4).

Table 4: Most Effective Super Bowl ads

| **Commercial** | **Year** | **Likeability score** | **Share price change** | **Media mentions** | **Kellogg School of Management score** |
|---|---|---|---|---|---|
| | | USA Today AdMeter ratings | Friday before vs. one month after | Major US newspapers and cable channels | Based on attention, distinction, positioning, linkage, amplification and net equity |
| 1. Snickers Game | 2010 | 8.68 | +2.5%* | +100% | A |
| 2. Doritos – Dog Collar | 2010 | 8.27 | +3.3% | +142% | B |
| 3. Doritos – Crystal Ball | 2009 | 8.46 | +1.9% | +102% | A |
| 4. Pepsi Max – Stars | 2008 | 7.60 | +2.6% | +867% | B |
| 5. Budweiser – Young Clydesdale | 2006 | 8.18 | +0.8% | +138% | A |
| 6. Doritos – Crunch | 2009 | 7.79 | +1.9% | +102% | A |
| 7. Budweiser – Crabs | 2007 | 8.56 | +0.7% | +128% | A |
| 8. Budweiser – Stray | 2007 | 8.29 | +0.7% | +128% | A |
| 9. Budweiser – Sheep | 2006 | 7.81 | +0.8% | +138% | A |
| 10. Denny's – Nannerpuss | 2009 | 6.62 | +11.2% | +77% | A |

Source: an indexed equal ranking of likeability, impact on share price, media mentions and the Kellogg School of Management score on Super Bowl commercials. http://www.thedailybeast.com/articles/2012/01/31/the-20-most-effective-super-bowl-ads-from-doritos-to-Snickers.html

To find the most effective Super Bowl advertisements they measured the USA Today Ad Meter rankings for 2005–2011, the share price of the parent company for the Friday before the Super Bowl with the average price the month after (modelled after a Buffalo University study that found a correlation between Super Bowl ads and share prices), mentions of the product in major US newspapers and on cable news stations for the month before and after the ad aired, and scores from the annual Kellogg Super Bowl Advertising Review, which evaluates each brand based on marketing criteria that try to translate branding into sales. All factors were weighted equally.

*Could anything else be at play?*

A new peanut butter variant was launched in January 2011. Clearly these don't impact the sales growth in 2010, but in 2011 they accounted for 6.7% of value sales growth.[16] However, this still means core growth was above both the category and Snickers performance before the campaign.

## Germany

*Delivering fame*

Whilst no metrics are available for the off-line buzz the launch generated, we can see from the online search volume that interest peaked in conjunction with the start of the campaign (Figure 22). Comparisons over time and with a similar market that didn't support the campaign highlight this.[17]

In stark contrast to France where the campaign didn't run, a sudden surge in online interest around the brand indicates that the campaign was driving brand fame in Germany.

**Figure 22: German and French searches for 'Snickers' on Google**

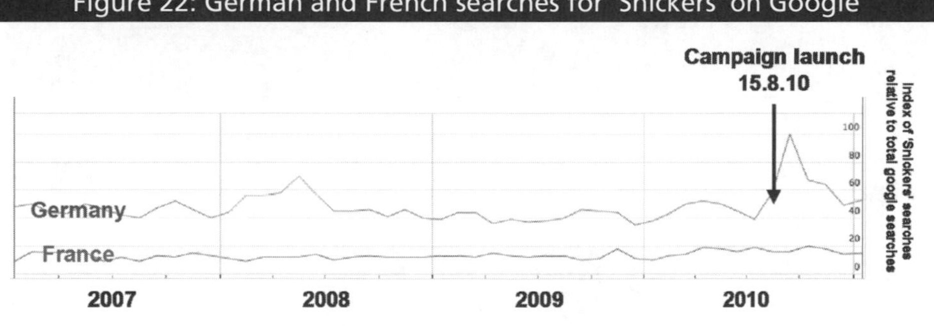


Source: Google Search Insights. The numbers on the graph reflect the number of searches that have been done for 'Snickers', relative to the total number of searches done on Google over time. They don't represent absolute search volume numbers, because the data is normalised and presented on a scale from 0–100.

*Driving penetration*

Within 12 months of the campaign launch, Snickers total household penetration was at an all-time high of 15.9%, driven by strong gains since the campaign launch (Figure 23). This helped it reach 1.24 million more households than the previous year.[18]

Figure 23: Germany household penetration

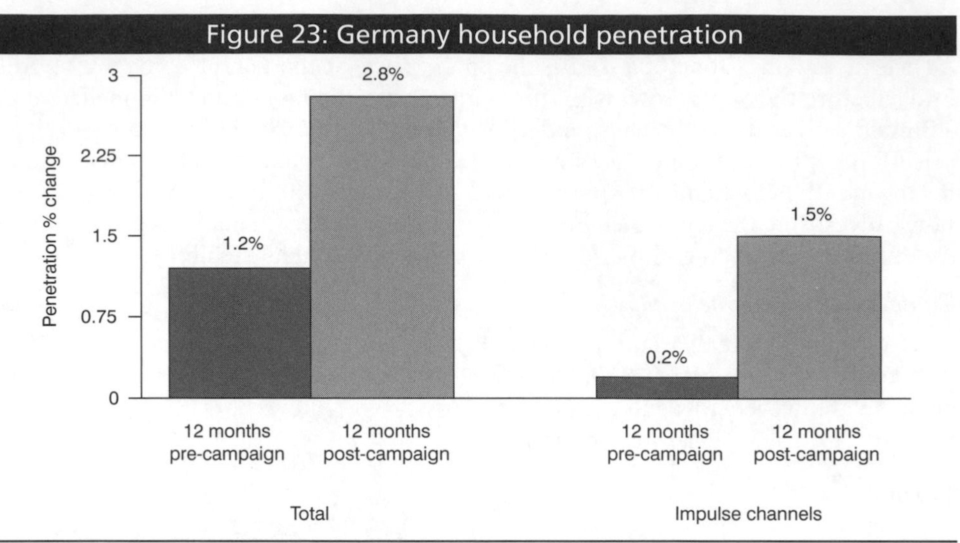


Source: IRI HH Panel, total German households all outlets

*Building sales*

The campaign ran for five months in 2010 during which time Snickers returned to value growth, outstripping the category and its two closest competitors (Figure 24).

Value sales performance versus both the category and major competitors has improved ever since the campaign was introduced.

Figure 24: Germany value sales growth

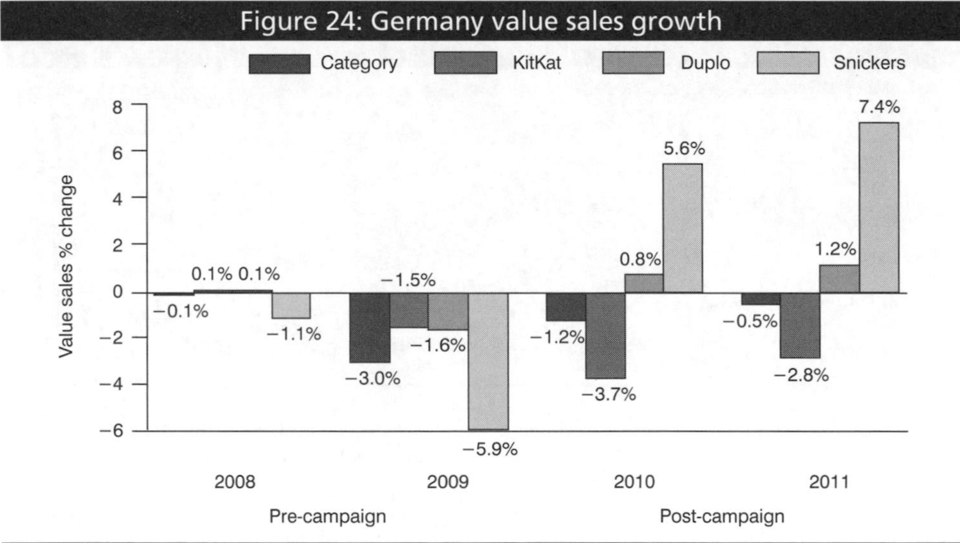


Source: Mars internal data, Nielsen

This has helped regain value market share to the extent that Snickers now enjoys a 0.55% greater market share than before the launch (Figure 25), equivalent to US$

43.2m. And whilst volume growth data is only available for 2010, this shows the brand has grown 8.4%, versus market leader Duplo's –0.2% decline.

The market share of value sales has grown consistently and considerably since the campaign's launch.

Figure 25: Snickers Germany market value share 2007–2011

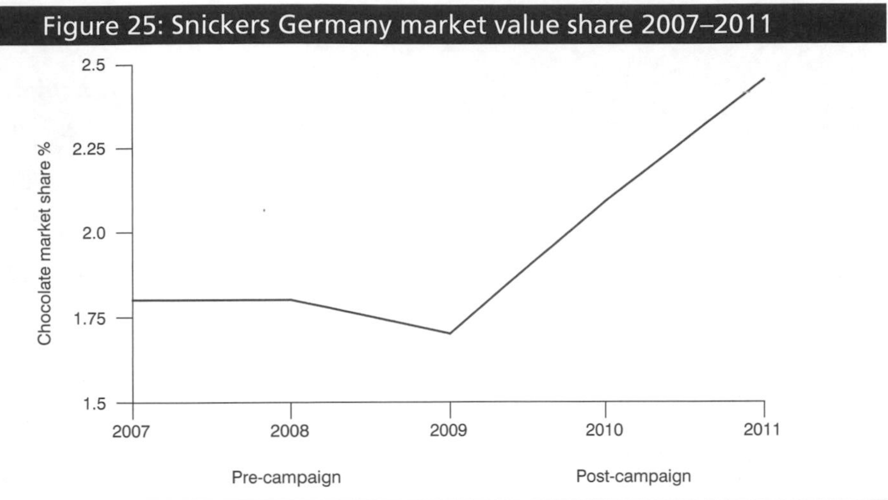


Source: Mars internal market share database based on Nielsen data

## Russia

### *Delivering fame*

Snickers was Russia's most famous chocolate brand before the campaign, so we had a greater challenge here than anywhere else. But real talk-value has helped drive an impressive amount of earned media (Figure 26).

There have been more than four times as many earned media placements than in the previous campaign.

Figure 26: Earned media generated by campaign in Russia

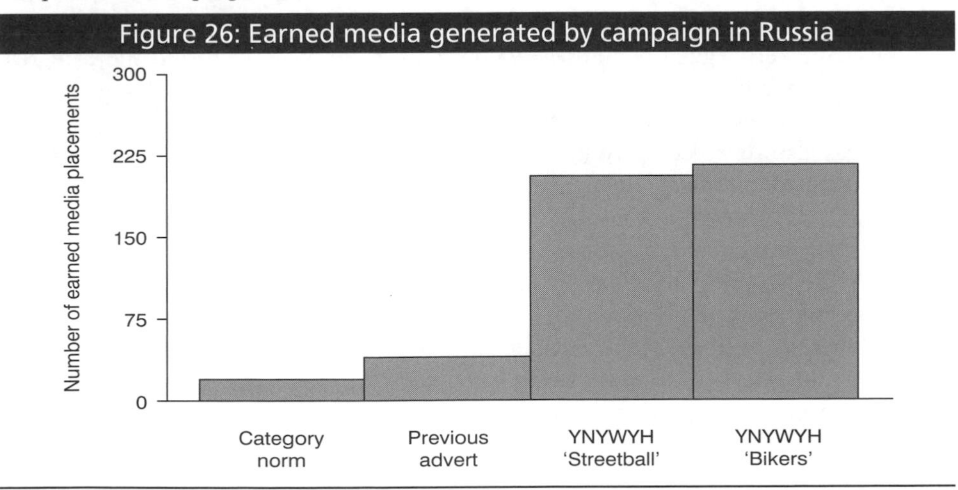


Source: BBDO Moscow ad media tracker tool

And whilst awareness isn't a true indicator of fame, it's still encouraging to see that the brand is once again growing spontaneous awareness (Figure 27).

A sharp rise in spontaneous awareness indicated that the brand was regaining some of its lost fame.

Figure 27: Russia spontaneous brand awareness

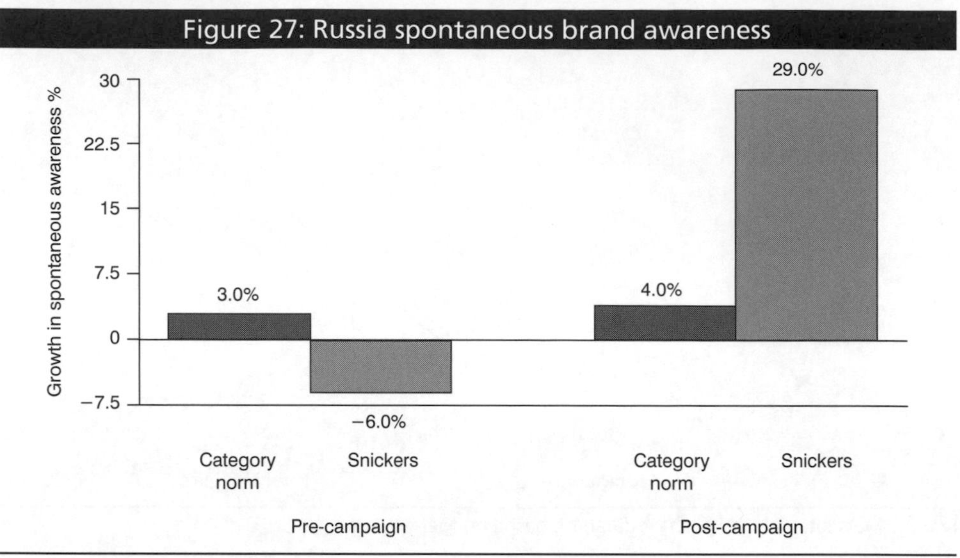


Source: IPSOS ASI

*Driving penetration*

At the time of writing the paper, no penetration data was available in Russia.

*Building sales*

Whilst in the 12 months prior to the campaign, Snickers's value growth lagged behind the category, in the 12 months following launch it was growing 44% faster (Figure 28). 2011 as a whole was even more impressive, thanks in part to a second, even more talked about ad within the campaign.

Whilst Snickers lagged behind the value sales growth of rivals and the category before the campaign, since launch it has overtaken them to the extent that growth in 2011 was 3.4 times more than the category.

This was also reflected by volume growth, which went from lagging behind rivals and the category to outstripping them (Figure 29).

Volume sales growth overtook that of the category and rivals in the 12 months following the launch and continued to grow faster in 2011.

This helped regain value market share to the extent that Snickers now enjoys a 0.47% greater share than before the launch, equivalent to US$ 33m and allowing it to strengthen its position as the number one Russian brand (Figure 30).

Whilst value market share was being lost before the campaign, it has steadily been regained since its introduction.

Figure 28: Russia value sales growth

Source: Mars internal data, Nielsen

Figure 29: Russia volume sales growth

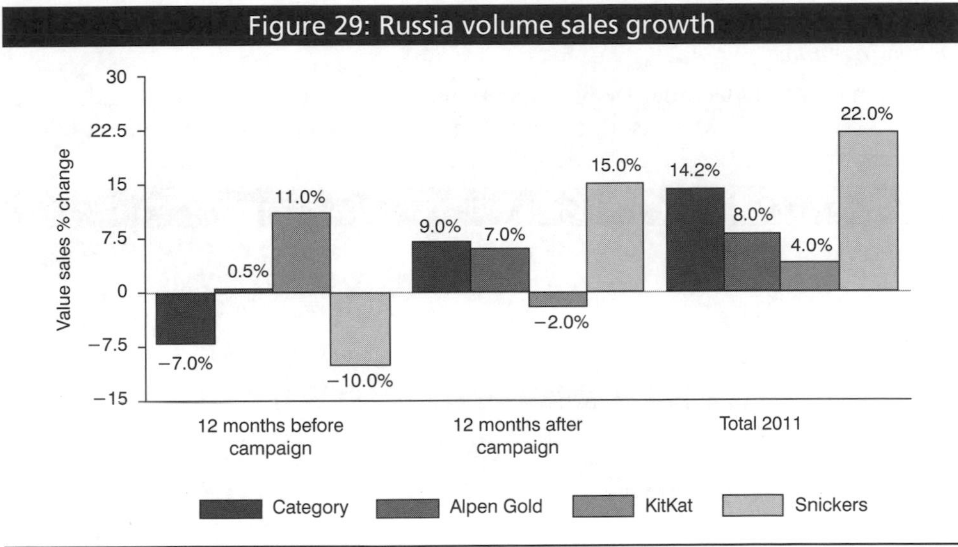


Source: Mars internal data from Nielsen

Figure 30: Snickers Russia market value share 2007–2011

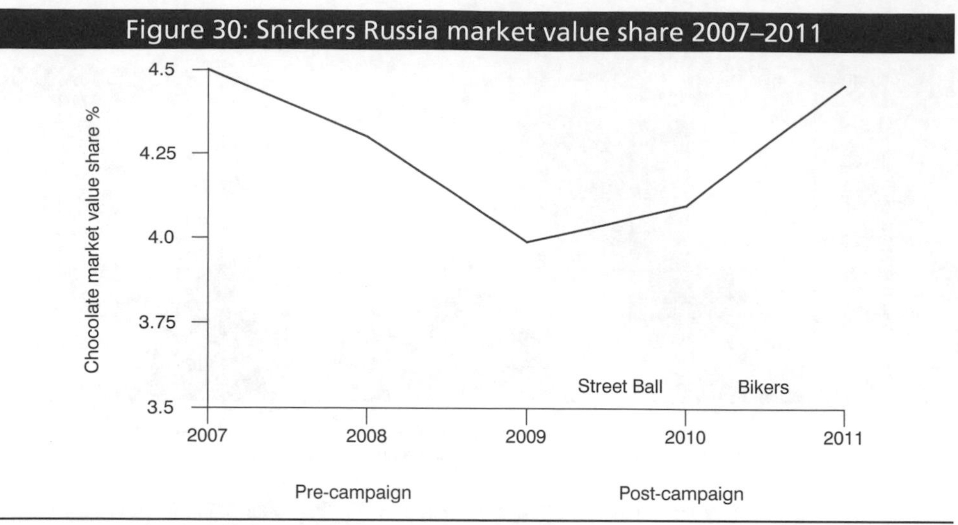


Source: Mars internal market share database based on Nielsen data

## China

### *Delivering fame*

Earned media included nine TV placements and equated to US$ 1.1m in total.[19] And, again, whilst awareness is just one facet of fame, we can take encouragement from a doubling of unaided brand awareness (Figure 31).

Figure 31: China unaided brand awareness

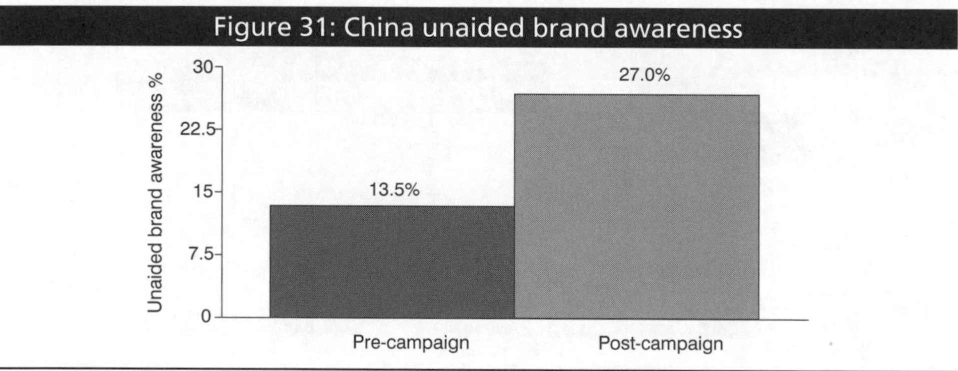


Source: IPSOS ASI

We saw its impact on popular Chinese culture when the advert was spoofed in consumers' video uploads and the mainstream media (Figure 32).

Consumers and comedians started to play with the formula of the advert for their own comedic effect.

Figure 32: Consumer-generated versions of the Chinese advertising

Source: Consumer-generated versions of the Chinese Goalie advert

*Driving penetration*

Within 12 months of the campaign launch, strong gains meant Snickers penetration was at an all-time high of 9.53% (Figure 33).

Following the campaign launch, Snickers total household penetration had grown nearly four times as much as in the previous 12 months.

Figure 33: China total household penetration

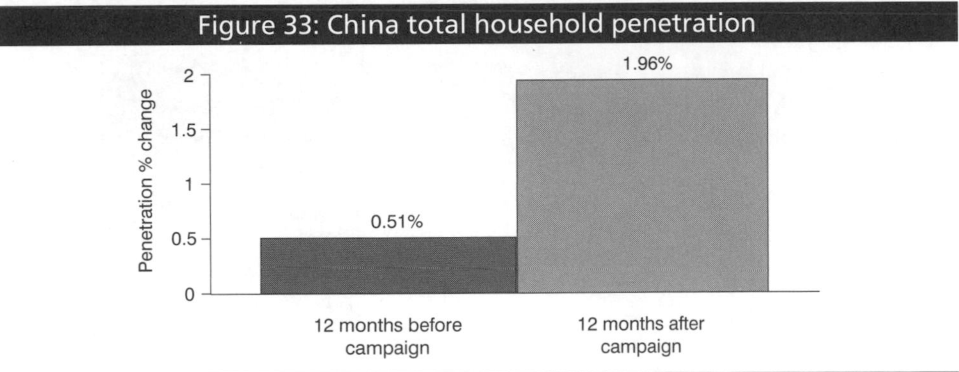


Source: IRI HH Panel

*Building sales*

China already enjoyed fantastic growth but the introduction of the campaign has accelerated it (Figure 34). This was reflected in a 0.51% value market share gain, equivalent to US$ 7m.[20]

Whilst Snickers value growth had begun to lag behind the category, following the campaign it has accelerated dramatically to 2.8 times the pre-campaign growth.

Figure 34: China value sales growth

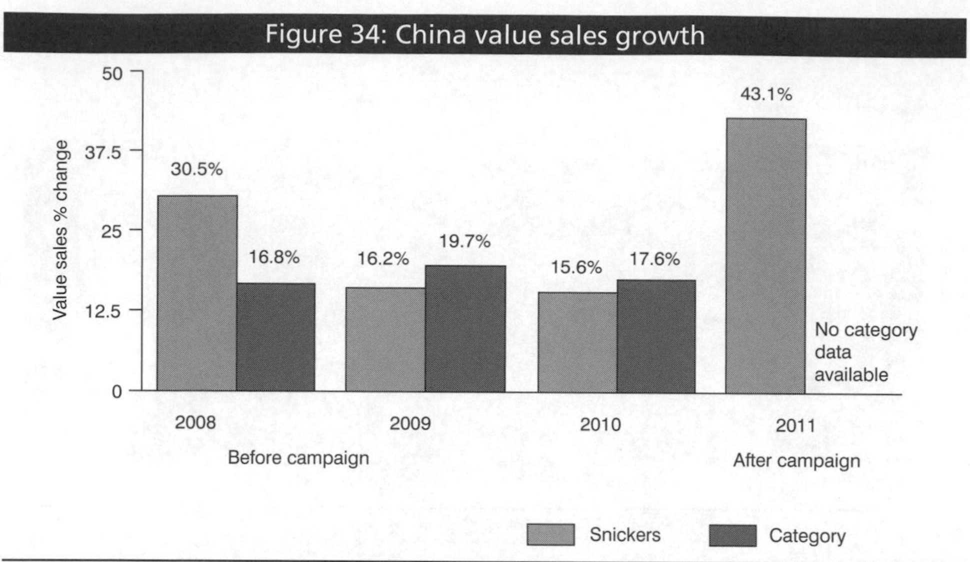


Source: Mars internal data, Nielsen

It also correlated with volume growth significantly higher than the category (Figure 35).

Volume sales growth also accelerated to stand at over twice the category growth.

Figure 35: China volume sales growth

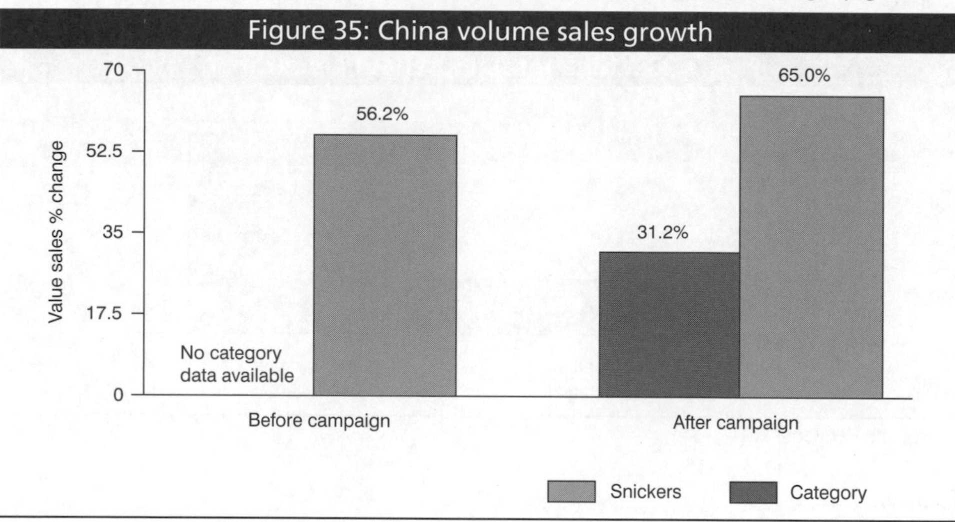


Source: Mars internal data from Nielsen

### *The organisational impact*

Knowing that organisational alignment would be crucial if we were to be successful, we anonymously surveyed those responsible for its marketing (Figures 36a and 36b). We will look at the impact on:

1. ways of working;
2. sales and confidence to invest;
3. alignment within the organisation.

The 36 Marketing Directors represented a broad spectrum of both regions and market size.

**Figure 36a: Market representation from the Snickers global marketing community survey**

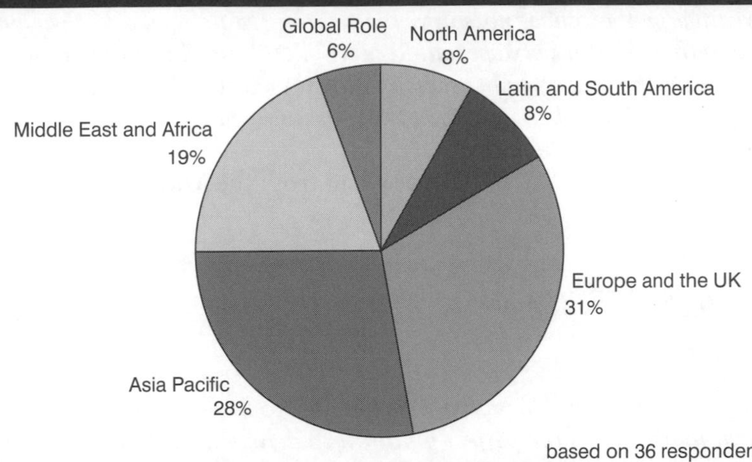


Source: Internal anonymous survey of 36 Marketing Directors responsible for marketing Snickers across the world

**Figure 36b: Market sales of the Snickers global marketing community survey**

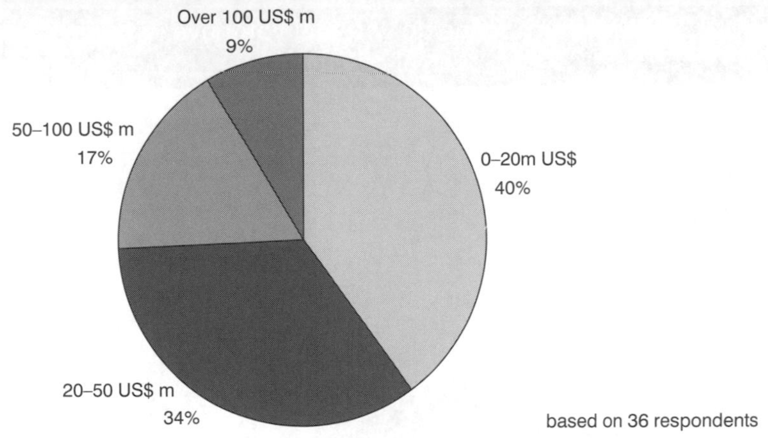


Source: Internal anonymous survey of 36 Marketing Directors responsible for marketing Snickers across the world

## Ways of working

Our model was designed to provide global scale whilst being sensitive to the need for local fame and the Mars culture. Responses indicated we had achieved this balance (Quote 2 and Figure 37).

The benefits of the new communications model have been felt throughout the business.

### Quote 2: A selection of quotes from the Snickers Marketing Director survey

*Every creative in the office, no sorry, the region, wants to work on it and be part of something that is very special. Recently P&G asked us in Egypt to give a presentation on the power and success of global creative ideas to their regional marketing team. Now when you have P&G asking you to come in and do that you must be doing something right!*

Respondent from the Middle East and Africa

*It's a big global idea but with real sense of local momentum – something that we can really get our teeth into and run with.*

Respondent from Europe and the UK

*I think the idea has shown Mars that it is possible to have a global idea executed in the local markets. It's the perfect platform to deliver all the benefits of global scale without sacrificing the local insight and creativity that can make Snickers famous at a local level.*

Respondent from Asia Pacific

78% of the marketers feel that the communications model is striking the right balance between being a global idea and scope for local creativity.

**Figure 37: How much scope do you feel you have within the idea for local creativity?**

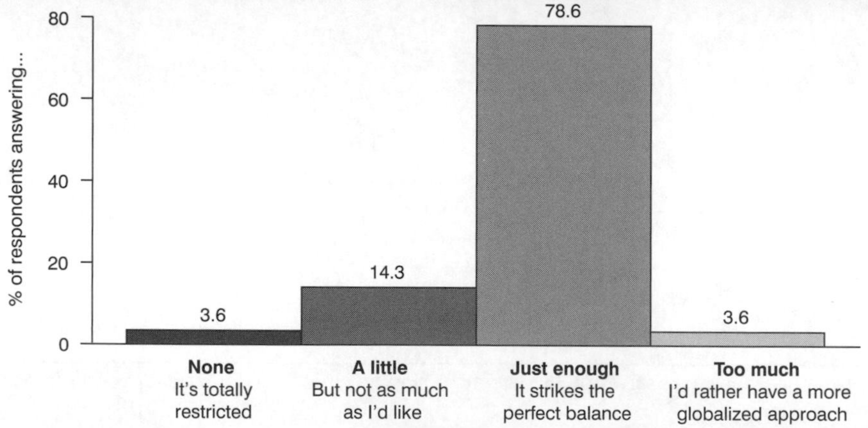

Source: Internal anonymous survey of 36 Marketing Directors responsible for marketing Snickers across the world

### Sales and confidence to invest

The idea has instilled a real sense of momentum amongst the marketers (Figure 38).

93% of those responsible for marketing Snickers think the brand has a real sense of momentum, whereas before the campaign only 43% did.

Figure 38: How much momentum would you say the Snickers brand has?

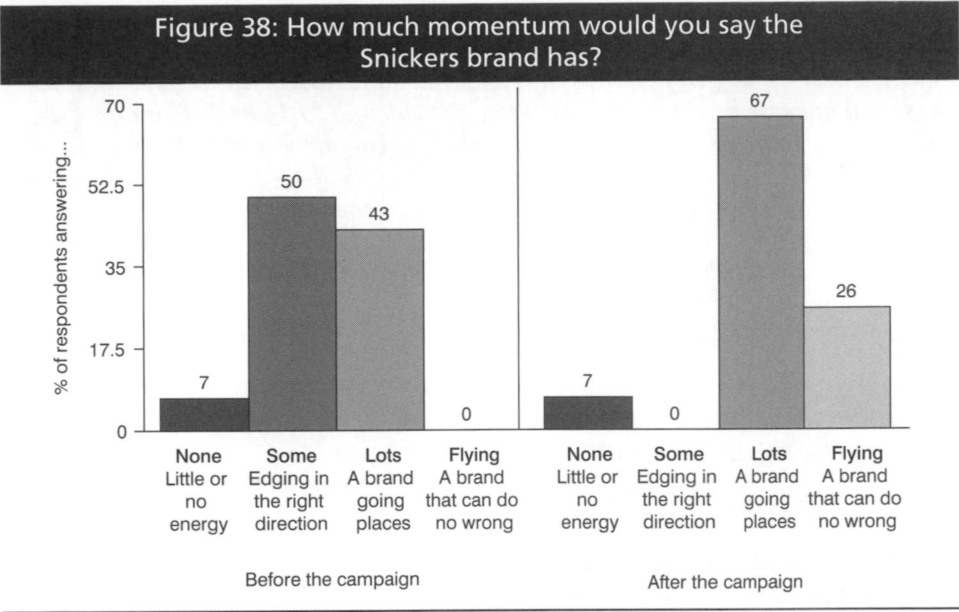


Source: Internal anonymous survey of 36 Marketing Directors responsible for marketing Snickers across the world

Whilst the majority think that the idea has been highly significant in terms of business performance (Figure 39 and Quote 3).

Over 96% feel that the idea has been significant in driving business performance.

Figure 39: How important do you think the idea has been in terms of your recent business performance?

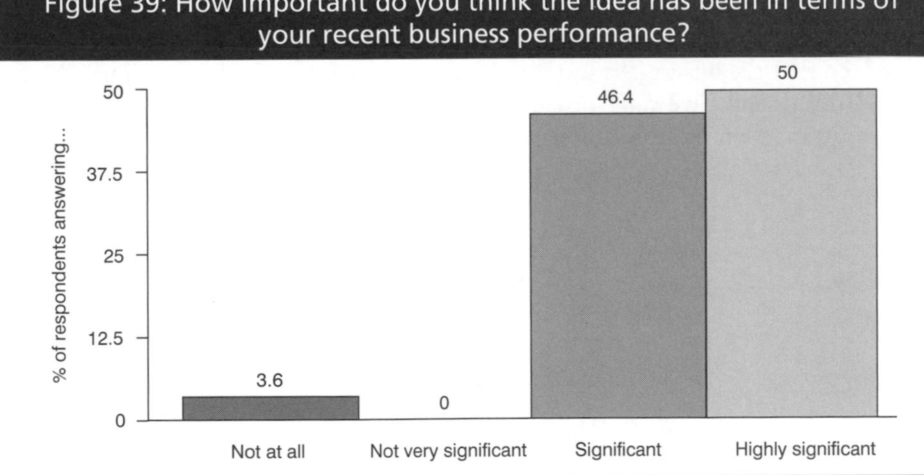


Source: Internal anonymous survey of 36 Marketing Directors responsible for marketing Snickers across the world

Marketers place real emphasis on the role of the idea in driving recent business performance.

### Quote 3: A selection of quotes from the Snickers Marketing Director survey

*There is no doubt in my mind that You're Not You has played a significant role in terms of our global success. Don't forget that this is an 80 year old bar which hasn't changed its recipe once. We've had no distribution gains of note, no real increase in spend and yet we've grown close to 16% since most of the world has come on board with the campaign, gaining global market share as a result. What's more, it's energised everything we do – from promotions to POS. And freed us up to really commit focus on the other things that can help grow our business. Finally, I know that people now want to work on this brand and we're attracting a disproportionate share of the talent from an agency and Mars POV.*

Respondent from Global

*The idea is amazing, a touch of genius. I think the sales results we've seen tell the success.*

Respondent from Asia Pacific

*At the moment, Snickers is the only candy bar in my region still growing in the impulse segment! Both the commercials we've used have been rewarded for being some of the most talked about advertising in market.*

Respondent from Europe

This then translated into a real confidence to invest. Over 96% also feel confident or highly confident investing in marketing support for the brand, with 3.5 times as many now highly confident (Figure 40).

### Alignment within the organisation

We've seen that the business is more aligned thanks to the campaign (Figure 41 and Quote 4). And whilst we can't disclose specific details, an auxiliary benefit has been the extraordinary amount of time and money saved as a result.

## Figure 40: How confident are you investing in supporting Snickers?

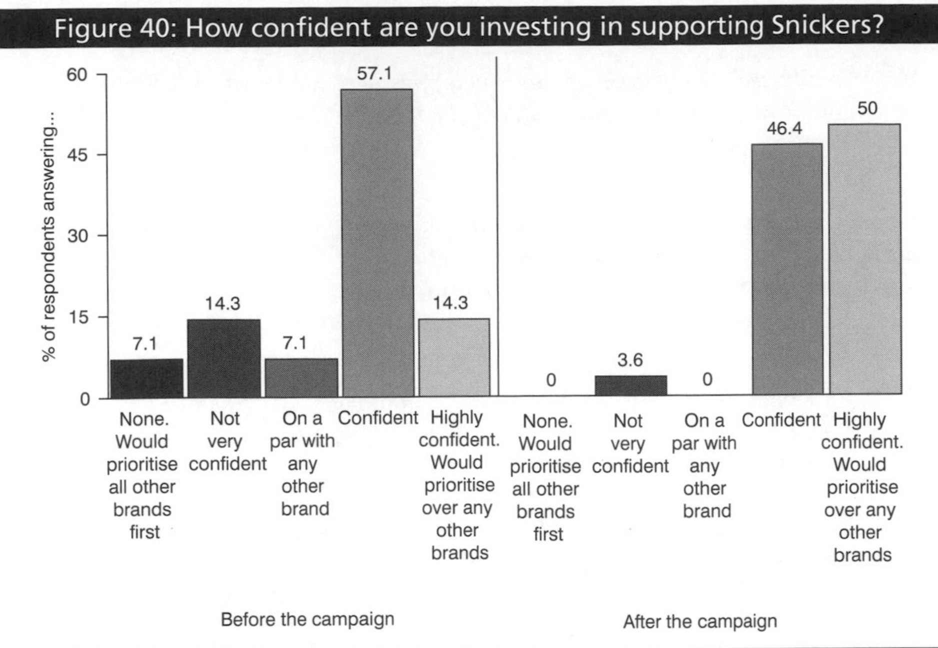


Source: Internal anonymous survey of 36 Marketing Directors responsible for marketing SNICKERS across the world

## Figure 41: How aligned would you say the Snickers brand is?

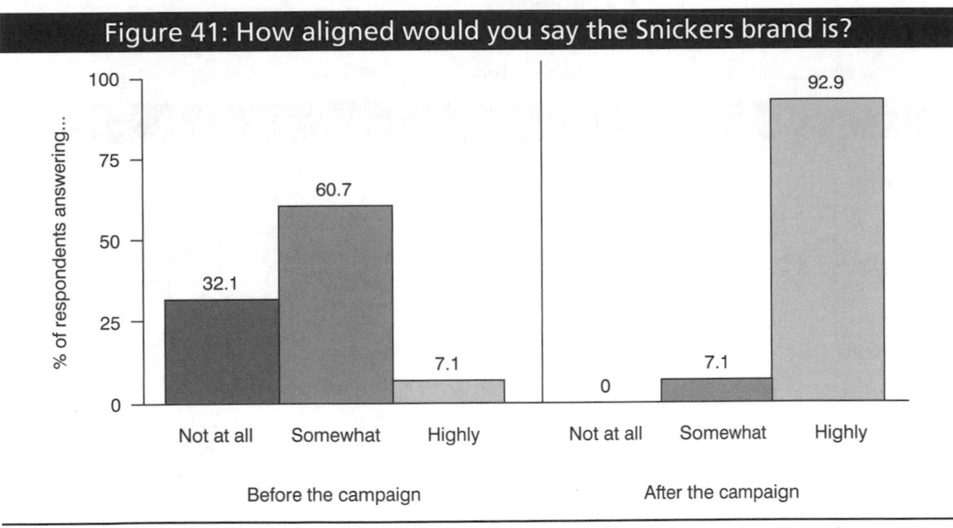


Source: Internal anonymous survey of 36 Marketing Directors responsible for marketing Snickers across the world

Those working on the brand have seen real benefits from the more aligned approach.

## Quote 4: A selection of quotes from the Snickers Marketing Director survey

*We've really seen the power of one single message; we learn as a global team and avoid losing time trying to reinvent the wheel in every country every time.*

Respondent from Latin America

*Before the campaign Snickers was disjointed, misaligned, and inconsistent. Now we're consistent, aligned and have meaningful communication that is worthy of the biggest chocolate bar brand in the world.*

Respondent from North America

*Without a big idea to join up the disparate markets, Snickers didn't feel like a big, global brand. So it was difficult to get the sort of global focus that can drive a brand forward – you felt like we were treading water rather than building something with momentum. Now the idea has helped make the brand famous at a global and a local level. It feels like a global brand with big, powerful work. A brand that truly has a role in popular culture.*

Respondent from Europe

Furthermore, with the UK recently joining the campaign, it has achieved 100% market coverage within two years (Figure 42). With the decentralised nature of Mars meaning that markets are free to choose their own strategy, this is testament to both the excitement around the idea and the results it has driven.

Despite operating an 'opt-in' culture, all 58 markets supporting the brand were doing so through the campaign within two years.

### Figure 42: Speed of market uptake of the campaign

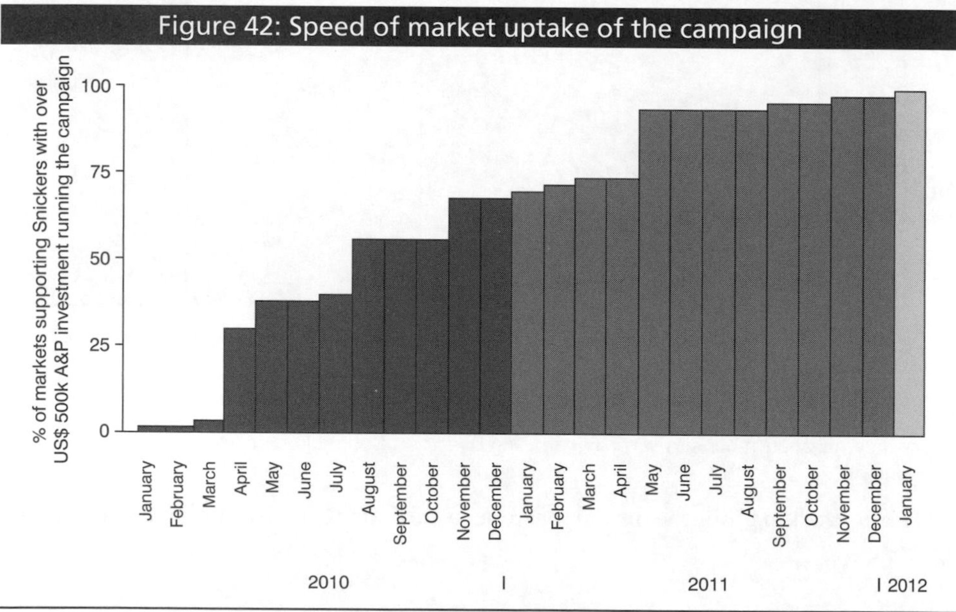


Source: Mars

## Attributing the impact to the campaign

We'll now show that the 'You're Not You When You're Hungry' idea was the key driver of this success by showing that:

1. Those markets running the campaign have been more successful than those that haven't.
2. The advertising is working as intended.
3. No other factors could have contributed to the sales effect.

*Those markets deploying 'You're Not You When You're Hungry' have been more successful than those that haven't.*

We've seen the global picture, and explored in more depth through markets that together account for 62.8% of global sales.[21] But what of the remaining markets?

Firstly, we have seen similar fame across the world (Figure 43).

In market after market, we've seen the campaign increase the fame of the brand.

**Figure 43: A selection of the buzz created by the campaign in the UAE, Japan, Mexico, the UK, Germany and the Ukraine**

Source: Earned media and PR from UAE, Japan, Mexico, the UK, Germany and the Ukraine

Secondly, those markets running the campaign contributed significantly more towards the 2010 value sales growth than those that didn't (Figure 44).

Whilst 75% of the global Snickers sales came from markets running the campaign, they contributed 94% of the value sales growth.

Figure 44: Value growth from those running the campaign vs. not running the campaign

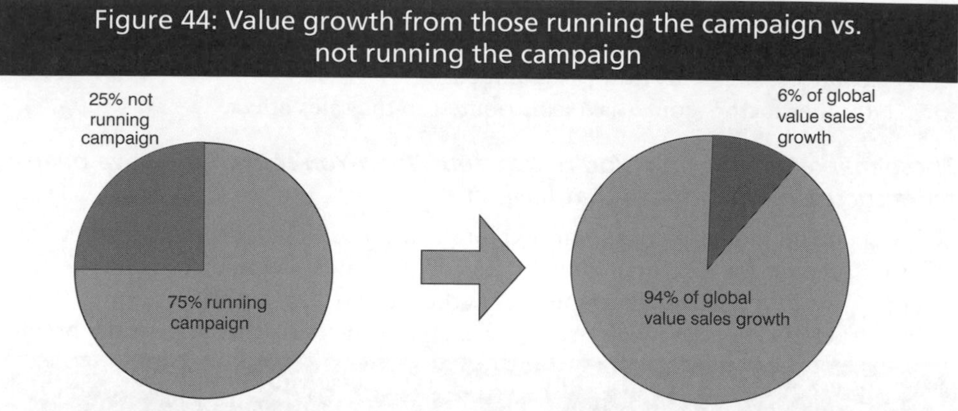


Source: Calculated from a market's % of global value sales from Nielsen data x the proportion of that phase in which the campaign ran. E.g. 5% of global sales for six months of Phase 2 = 2.5% of global sales influenced by the campaign

Taking the top 25 markets that have run the campaign, we see that those running the campaign in 2010 performed much more strongly in terms of value share gain than those that didn't (Table 5),[22] and that of those that adopted it only one didn't grow market share.[23]

Of the 11 markets not running the campaign in 2010, eight were losing market share yet everyone started to grow share once they had adopted it the following year.

### *Testing and in-market performance indicates that the campaign is working as intended*

Whilst globally there is large variation in the advertising tracking used for Snickers, the work of our research partners IPSOS has provided a comprehensive and valuable indication that the advertising is working as intended (Quote 5).

### Quote 5: Keith Glasspoole, Deputy Managing Director Ipsos ASI

> *The idea has certainly been proved to be big enough to travel. It travels because it is based on an insight which is relevant to a universal consumer need. This insight can be readily linked to the brand in an engaging and credible way. And when this is delivered with humour it heightens the opportunity for the brand message to be noticed and remembered.*

Through assessing 43 global executions from their database we can see that copy effectiveness of the work that has ultimately run has improved by 41%, and is 51.7% higher than the norm (Figure 45).[24]

Table 5: Global value market share point gain 2010 and 2011

| | Market share point gain 2010 vs. 2009 | Market share point gain 2011 vs. 2010 |
|---|---|---|
| **Running campaign in 2010 and 2011** | | |
| Australia | 0.18 | 0.11 |
| Egypt | 0.39 | 0.43 |
| Germany | 0.17 | 0.36 |
| India | 0.04 | 0.05 |
| Netherlands | 0.05 | 0.19 |
| Poland | 0.08 | 0.15 |
| Portugal | 0.21 | 0.65 |
| Russia | 0.11 | 0.36 |
| Saudi Arabia | -0.04 | 0.02 |
| UAE | 0.15 | -0.67 |
| USA | 0.07 | 0.95 |
| **Not running campaign in 2010, but running it in 2011** | | |
| Austria | -0.01 | 0.26 |
| Belgium | -0.14 | 0.16 |
| Canada | -0.06 | 0.39 |
| China | 0.63 | 0.51 |
| Denmark | -0.03 | 0.49 |
| Ireland | -0.06 | 0.19 |
| Mexico | 0.77 | -0.36 |
| Norway | -0.04 | 0.13 |
| Switzerland | -0.02 | 0.04 |
| Turkey | 0.01 | 0.40 |
| Ukraine | -0.61 | 0.53 |

Source: Mars internal market share database based on Nielsen data

The in-market sales performance potential for 'You're Not You When You're Hungry' is much more effective than previous campaigns.

Two other indicators show the advertising to be working as intended. Firstly, the flexible approach the model adopted to drive local fame has been validated since those using a local celebrity have enjoyed better performance than those 'importing' one (Figure 46).

Those markets that leveraged the flexibility of the creative device to use a local celebrity enjoyed better value sales growth and gained a higher percentage of value market share.

## Figure 45: Copy effectiveness testing before and after YNYWYH

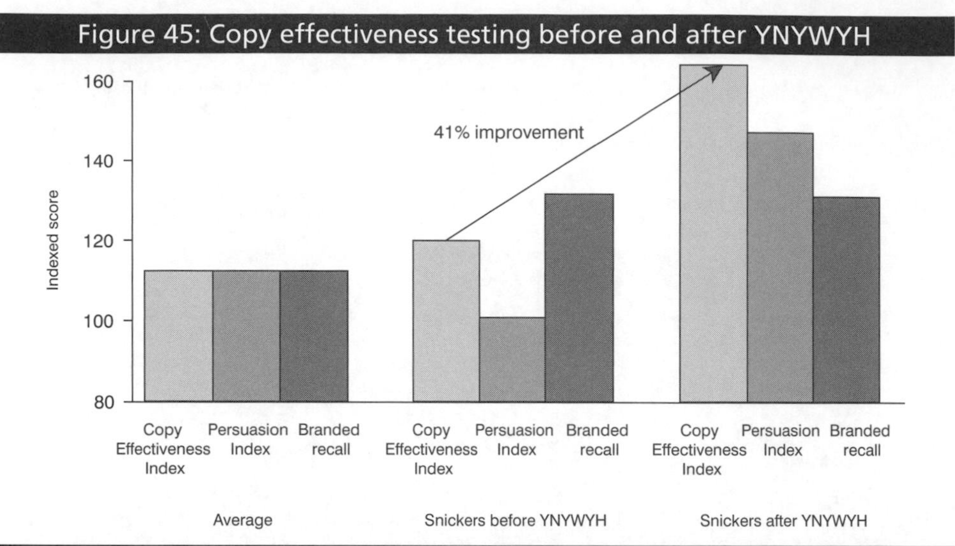


Source: IPSOS ASI. The Copy Effect Index (CEI) is IPSOS ASI's proprietary measure of in-market sales performance potential; a weighted combination of branded ad recall and ad persuasion

## Figure 46: Sales performance of local celebrities vs. non-local celebrities within the campaign

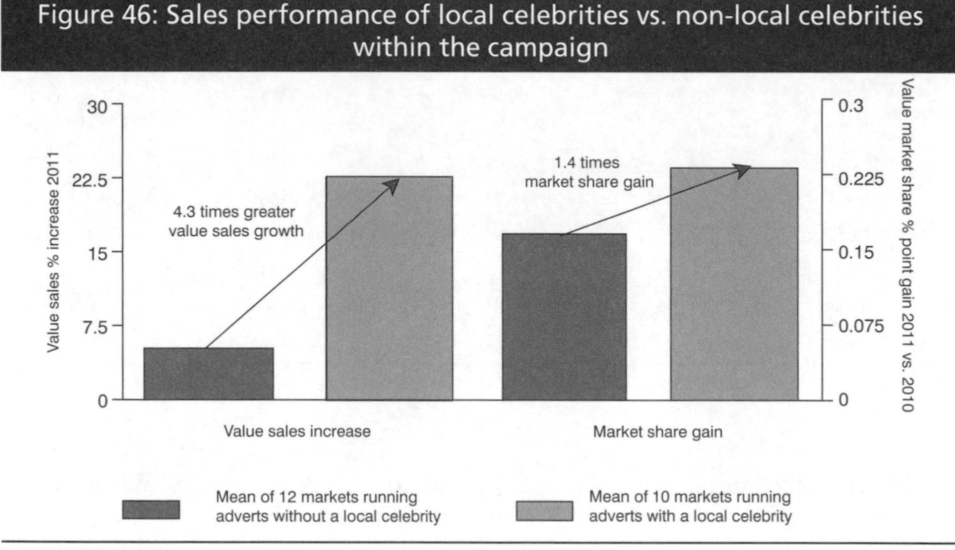


Source: IPSOS ASI

Looking at this on an individual basis, we can see the opportunity (Quote 6) of using localised executions on advertising impact alone (Figure 47).[25]

The finished film version of *Game* performed significantly better in testing in the US where Betty White was known versus the UK where she's not as well known.

Figure 47: Copy effectiveness of Game starring Betty White in the US vs. the UK

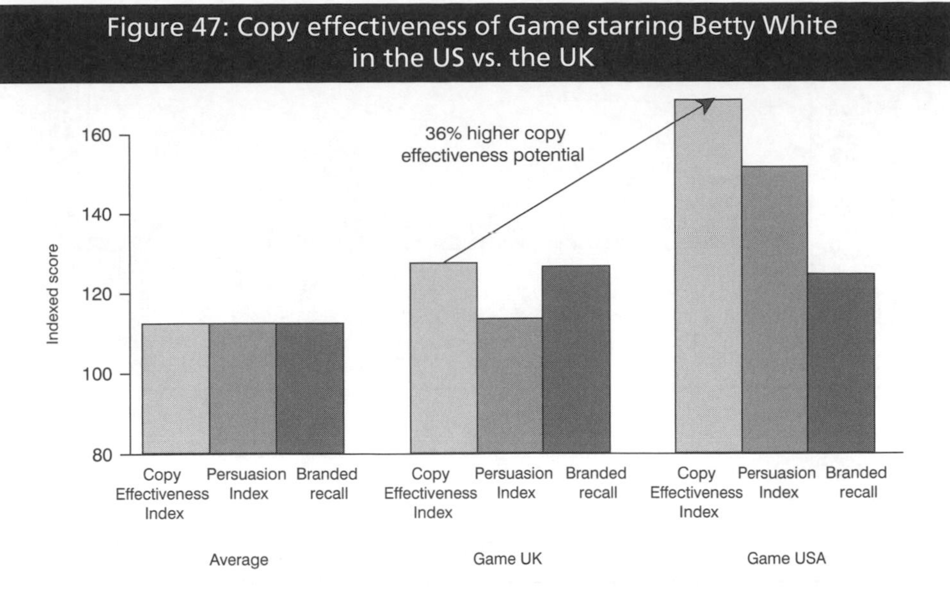


Source: IPSOS ASI. The Copy Effect Index (CEI) is IPSOS ASI's proprietary measure of in-market sales performance potential; a weighted combination of branded ad recall and ad persuasion

## Quote 6: Keith Glasspoole, Deputy Managing Director Ipsos ASI

> *It lacks simplicity relative to other 'global' ideas. And whilst this generates a risk it also generates an opportunity. A piece of humour might lose something in translation, or not be understood in the same way from market to market. However, create a local execution with humour that will resonate in a particular market then you combine thinking global (universal insight) with acting local (being sensitive to the cultural consonance of an individual market).*

Secondly, we know that unlike novelty, true fame isn't fleeting and we've seen that markets have tended to perform better in the second year of the campaign (Figure 48).

82% of markets that have deployed the campaign for two years enjoyed greater value market share gain in their second year of running it.

Figure 48: Market share point gain 2011 vs. 2010

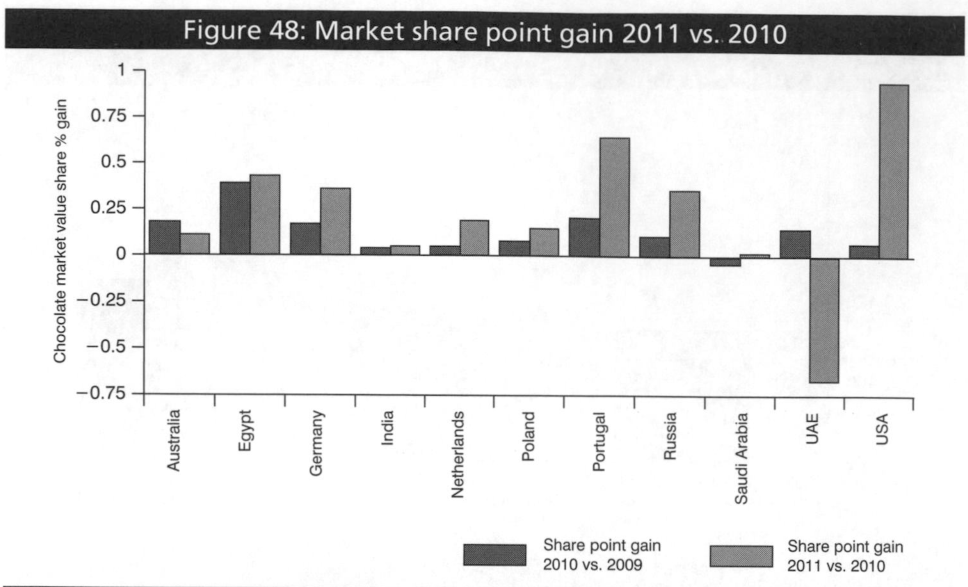


Source: Mars internal market share database based on Nielsen data

### *We can remove all other factors*

To put it beyond reasonable doubt that the campaign has contributed to this recent success we will finally rule out any other factors that could have impacted upon these results.

### Competition

Whilst any local market will have a certain amount of new entrants, globally the picture has been consistent for the past 20 years.

### Market factors

Whilst global economic or population growth could have impacted our growth, we have shown through our global market share that we can discount such category generic forces.

### Promotions

We've already seen that media spend wasn't a factor, whilst promotional spend has actually decreased through each year of the campaign (Figure 49).

Global promotional spend has actually been lower in 2010 and 2011 than pre-campaign levels.

### New variants

The only new permanent variant during the time of the campaign has been the peanut butter product, launched only in the US in 2011. We've already seen how despite this, US results exceeded the category and pre-campaign benchmarks. At a global level they are even less significant; with 5.03% of global value sales, they accounted for 5.8% of value sales growth, leaving Snickers growth at still over twice the category.

Figure 49: Snickers global promotional spend

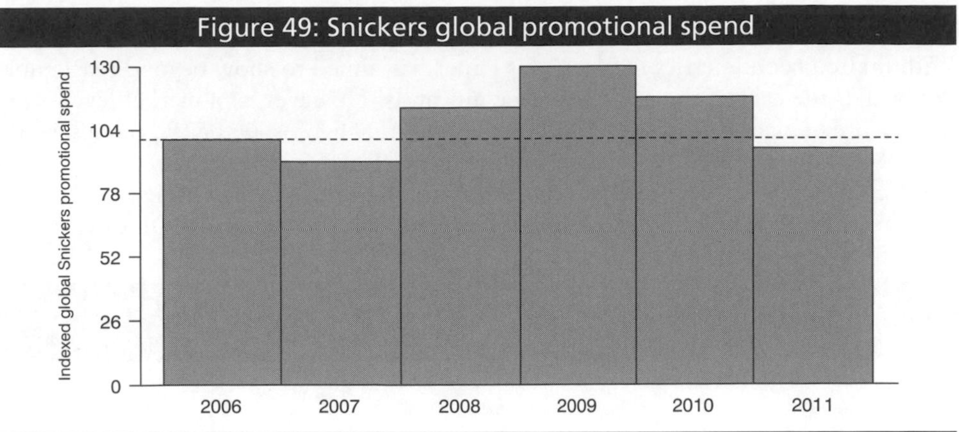


Source: Mars internal data

Some markets run specific limited editions and these have continued as per their previous calendar with similar (or often reduced) levels of spend. None can be considered large enough to be seen as a key driver of growth in any individual market.

### Distribution

Turkey represents the only significant launch during the timeframe of the campaign.[26] Whilst its growth is impressive, it has only risen from 0.11% of Snickers's global share to 0.24% so we can therefore exclude emerging market distribution as a driver of growth.[27]

### Mars Inc. performance

When we look at the other global brands in the Mars portfolio that typically enjoy shared display, pricing structures, distribution and geographical footprint we can see that Snickers has considerably outperformed their growth (Figure 50).

Snickers has grown significantly faster in terms of value sales than other global Mars brands.

Figure 50: 2011 values sales for Snickers, Dove/Galaxy, Twix and M&Ms

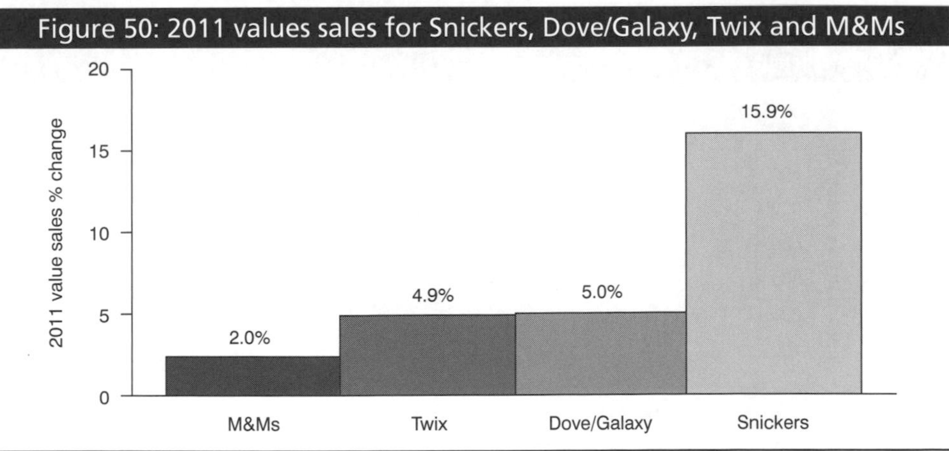


Source: Mars internal data, Nielsen

## Finally, a word on ROI

With limited econometrics in place, this paper has aimed to show beyond reasonable doubt that the campaign has delivered significantly. However, at a market level some metrics are in place.[28] Whilst we can't reveal the actual figures, in the US, econometrics has shown the total 2010 campaign to have an ROI of 1.26 times the return of 2009 and for Germany we can say that it is 2.86 times the return in 2009 (Figure 51).

Where available, econometric modelling has shown Snickers ROI to improve upon that of previous campaigns.

**Figure 51: Snickers campaign ROI of new and old campaigns in the US and Germany**

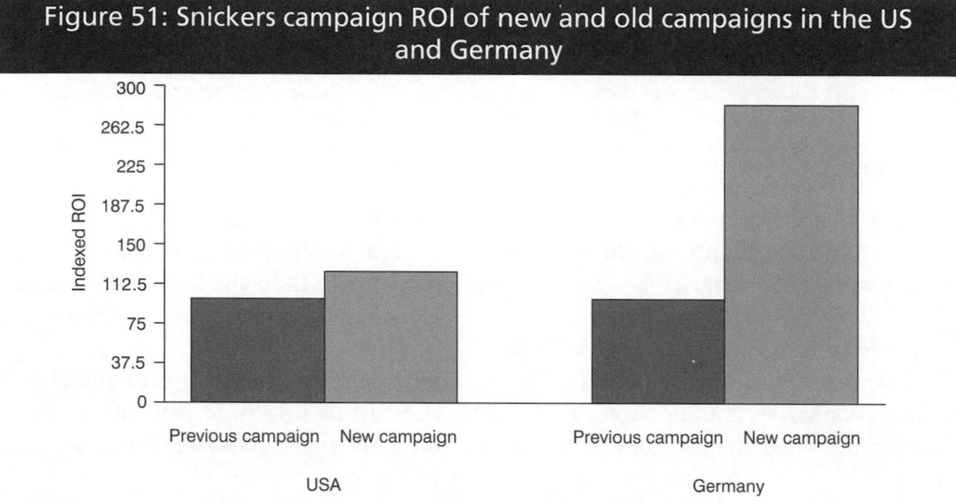


Source: Mars Germany GmbH and Analytic Partners North America

Furthermore, when indexed against the FMCG norm[29] we can see that both countries are performing significantly stronger than average (Figure 52). And with these representing two of our most developed, competitive markets we would expect to see even more impressive ROI in most of the others.

Indexed versus the FMCG norm, we can see that the USA delivers over five times the return whilst Germany enjoys nearly eight times the ROI.

**Figure 52: Snickers campaign ROI in the US and Germany**

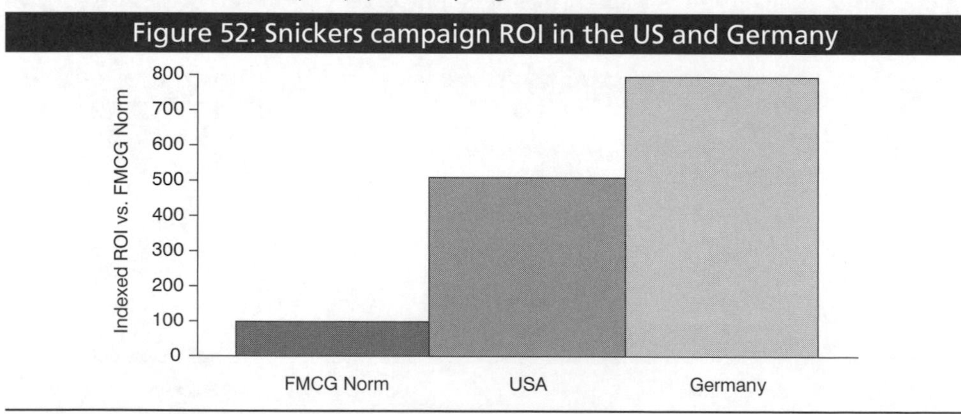


Source: Mars Germany GmbH and Analytic Partners North America

## Section 7: What we've learnt

We've seen through this paper how maintaining its position as the world's largest chocolate bar meant Snickers had to think big and act small.

A decentralised brand, led by a highly decentralised client wasn't suddenly going to become suited to the kind of top-down, autocratic tactics so typical of big, global ideas. Yet we knew a global approach was needed, and we knew that this approach needed to make Snickers famous everywhere it ran.

Our answer was to create a communications model that started big; finding a universal story that anyone in any market could connect with. Then to go small; delivering creative work rich in local flavour so that it got people talking about the brand.

In doing so, 'You're Not You When You're Hungry' has led Snickers into its most successful ever period of growth,[30] growing global market share by US$ 376.3m. We've seen how much of this success has been driven by the commitment to the campaign from the Mars marketing community. This data, combined with the fact that the idea is now running in every one of the 58 markets that support Snickers, suggests that it's a success that shows no signs of abating.

## Notes

1 Snickers organic growth excluding ice cream, Mars Chocolate financial reporting.

2 After all, they'd just built a new factory with massively increased capacity in Chicago and knew very little about setting up abroad.

3 The Mars global HQ in McLean is 60 times smaller than P&G and eight times smaller than Nestlé.

4 When brands are in trouble, the inclination is to go more local, developing solutions that are even more suited to a specific market's unique challenges. Similarly, ask any local brand manager whose brand is flying to move over to a global idea and you're likely to be met with short shrift. This was the reality of our situation, with markets like Korea losing share through a series of failed campaigns, and markets like the UK very happy with their successful Mr T-led 'Get Some Nuts' idea.

5 Oreo had begun airing global copy in a number of markets and between 2007–2009 was growing 12.9% globally, versus Snickers at 6.2% (source: Euromonitor).

6 According to Heskett, Sasser and Schlesinger (2003) *The Value Profit Chain* (London: Free Press), an aligned organisation will typically outperform a non-aligned one by four times in revenue generation; the time was nigh to unlock some of Snickers's latent potential.

7 'The main driver of market share is not consumer loyalty but large differences in market penetration – the sheer number of consumers each brand has.' Andrew Ehrenberg, Ehrenberg-Bass Institute.

8 OMDMetrics, PIMS and Pravda (2005) Fame Metrics have shown that a 10% rise in the fame of a brand will increase market share by 20%.

9 Sampson, J. (2005) How much is fame worth to the bottom line? *Market Leader Journal*, winter.

10 From qualitative research in the UK, the US, Mexico, Russia, UAE and Argentina.

11 As Creative Director David Lubars put it: 'Snickers should be part of American pop culture, on a par with Budweiser and baseball'.

12 Byron Sharp speaking at *Fads, Fashions and Effectiveness: How Brands Grow*, Thinkbox, 2012.

13 In the US we used Super Bowl, in Mexico we bought out all the terrestrial channels consecutively, in Germany we used Champions League football.

14 Calculated from a market's % of global value sales x the proportion of that phase in which the campaign ran. E.g. 5% of global sales for six months of Phase 2 = 2.5% of global sales influenced by the campaign.

15 The US represents the brand's spiritual home and 40.3% of global sales, whilst Germany is the most important European market with 5.2% of global sales. Russia and China represent two of the most important emerging markets, with Russia the second largest Snickers market globally with 13.8% of sales and China one of the fastest growing and 2.5% of sales. Based on 2010 value sales data from Nielsen.

16 Snickers franchise value sales from Nielsen.

17 France's market is 73% the size of Germany, but similar in history, brands in the market and communications development.
18 Gfk Consumer tracking.
19 BBDO China media analytics.
20 Mars internal market share database based on Nielsen data.
21 Based on 2010 global value sales, Euromonitor.
22 This trend is all the more apparent when you consider that China and Turkey's growth can be attributed to distribution gains and Mexico's to a new 5 Peso product launch.
23 Mexico suffered from a Mars-wide distribution issue with one of the market's major retailers in 2011.
24 From across Europe, the UK, Russia, China, the US and the Gulf Coast countries.
25 This doesn't take into account the arguably more significant impact of the fame it creates from earned media, buzz and talk.
26 Based on 2011 value sales data from Nielsen.
27 151.2% value sales growth vs. 13.8% category growth.
28 Mars employ ROI assessment in the US, Germany, France and the UK. In a Snickers context, France doesn't support the brand, whilst the UK has not yet run the campaign.
29 Average ROIs from Equity database in the Thinkbox Payback 3 Study.
30 Based on total value sales from Mars historical sales data.

## Chapter 18

# Virgin Atlantic

## Taking on the world with a dash of 'je ne sais quoi'

**By Jeremy Poole, RKCR/Y&R; Lee Moran, OMD International; Tyler Schultz, Hall & Partners and Rebecca Bourdon, Gyro**
Contributing author: Tosin Osho, Brand Science
Credited companies: JointEntrants: Gyro; OMD International and Hall & Partners; Client: Virgin Atlantic

**Editor's summary**

Mass consolidation in the industry left Virgin Atlantic facing a new breed of global competitor. With a historical reliance on the UK to drive growth, it was crucial that other markets of Virgin Atlantic's route network were working equally hard to deliver incremental revenue. 'Your airline's either got it or it hasn't', the first global campaign for a Virgin brand, used TV, press, poster and digital support across Upper Class and Economy cabins to capture the unique values of Virgin, showing the glamour, fun and comfort of the flying experience. It has outperformed previous Virgin Atlantic campaigns in the UK, and delivered significant growth across the rest of the world. The estimated global ROMI is £15.66 per £1 spent.

It is notoriously difficult to write IPA Effectiveness papers for the airline industry given the complexity of the market and the limited availability of data. However, the judges felt that this paper overcame these hurdles delivering a clearly written paper, beautifully presented, with very detailed modelling results. The paper demonstrates how Virgin spent their money wisely on this multi-media campaign, with TV and virally amplified work.

## Authors' summary

Mass consolidation in the industry left Virgin Atlantic facing a new breed of global competitor.

With a historical reliance on the UK to drive growth, it was crucial that both ends of Virgin Atlantic's route network were working equally hard to deliver incremental revenue.

'Your airline's either got it or it hasn't' is the first ever global campaign for a Virgin brand. Not only has it outperformed previous Virgin Atlantic campaigns in the UK, including Still Red Hot, but delivered significant growth across the rest of the world.

The global return on marketing investment is estimated at £15.66 per £1 spent.

## A global minnow

Virgin Atlantic is an airline industry anomaly.

With 38 aircraft servicing 30 routes, all out of London, Atlantic is the only major long haul airline in the world that isn't a national flag carrier.

But in airline terms Atlantic is anything but big. At London Heathrow, Virgin Atlantic's main global hub, the business holds only 3% of the total take off/landing slots and supplies 5% of total seat capacity. Albeit these slots are very valuable, this is well behind British Airways with 42%[1] of slots and 39% of seats (see Figure 1).

Virgin Atlantic is also the only Heathrow-based airline that is neither part of a larger group nor even of an alliance.[2]

Figure 1: London Heathrow capacity by carrier

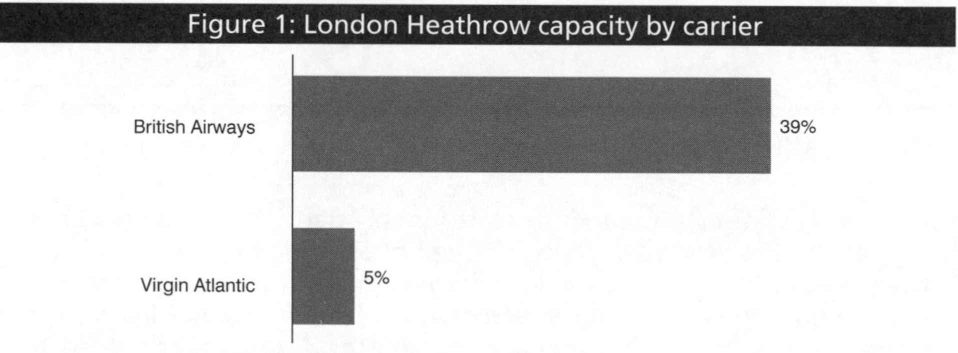


Source: Centre for Asia Pacific Aviation and Innovata

## Big is beautiful

The last decade has been a turbulent one for the airline industry.

With escalating fuel costs, taxes rocketing, increasing security costs, coupled with stalling global economies it's easy to see why it's not a great time to be running an airline.

Upwards of 50 airlines have gone under since 2001 and all the major US airlines have filed for Chapter 11 bankruptcy protection. British Airways made a loss of

£401m in 2008–2009 and £531m in 2009–2010 – successively BA's biggest losses since privatisation in 1987.

To counter the storm, airline industry wisdom is to seek success in size.

In the last few years, regulators have approved a succession of mega tie-ups. Air France and KLM merged in 2004. British Airways and Iberia merged to become the International Airlines Group in 2010. They've subsequently added bmi to their stable and then tied up with American Airlines to create a dominating force across the Atlantic.

In the US, Delta merged with Northwest. Then in 2010 United and Continental trumped Delta/Northwest to create the world's largest carrier by passenger traffic.

All benefit from a series of structural advantages acknowledged by industry experts.

> *The linking of networks has produced increased traffic volumes and revenues... all of which have helped the allied airlines improve their efficiency and reduce costs.*
>
> Airline choices for the future – Iatrou & Oretti

But the most notable benefit of size is the strength of your feeder network – crucial in maximising 'bums on seats'.

## Virgin Atlantic under significant threat

The effect of this industry consolidation leaves Virgin Atlantic highly vulnerable.

Consider a flight from London Heathrow to New York JFK. Atlantic's catchment area covers around 30 million people, whereas BA's European network feeds in some 711 million potential passengers. Add in Iberia, bmi and American Airline's networks and the scale of the threat is clear.

Not only is Virgin Atlantic dwarfed by this new breed of global giant, it also has a disproportionate reliance on the UK for passengers and revenue.

In 2009, 68% of Virgin Atlantic revenue was delivered by the UK, with just 32% coming from the markets at the other end of Virgin Atlantic's routes. The UK also accounted for the majority of growth with 81% of incremental revenue being delivered by the UK versus just 19% by the rest of the world (RoW) (Figure 2).

**Figure 2: Contribution of UK and RoW to incremental revenue growth**

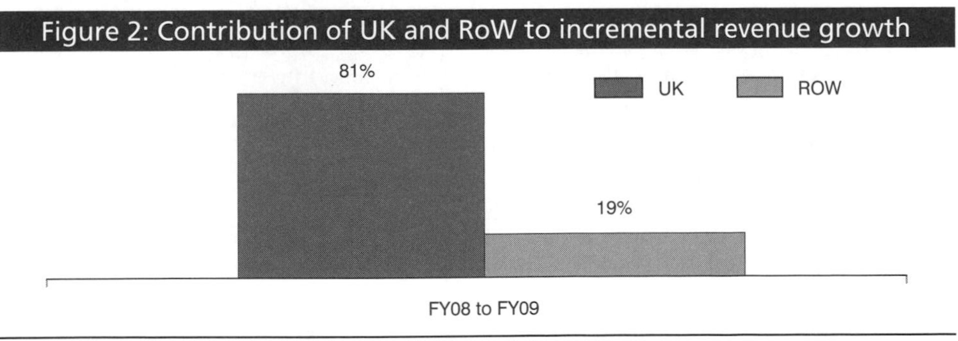


Source: Virgin Atlantic Commercial

To stand a chance against the new breed of consolidated global giants it was imperative that both ends of Virgin Atlantic's route network were working hard to deliver passengers and revenue. In other words, the UK had to keep growing, but the RoW had to grow even faster and increase its contribution to incremental revenue.

## The role of the brand and communications

As a UK-based business it's no surprise that Virgin Atlantic is a stronger brand at home than abroad. But the dominance of the UK in strength and stature is considerable as can be seen in Figure 3.

**Figure 3: 2008 status of the Virgin Atlantic brand in the UK vs. the rest of the world**

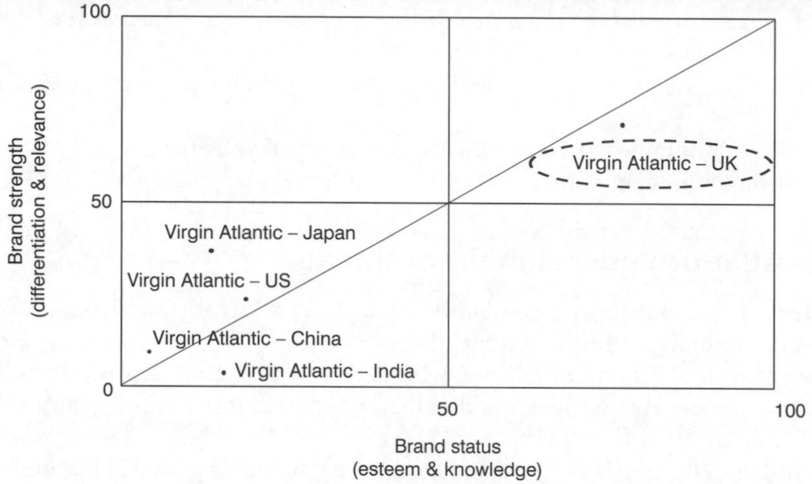

Source: BAV 2008. Base: all adults

The success of the brand in the UK can, in part, be attributed to the communications that have helped it grow from a maverick upstart in 1984 to the UK's second largest airline as it is today.

Two IPA papers have documented the story of Virgin Atlantic's communications, with a 15-year historical case in 2008 and the Still Red Hot campaign in 2010.

Both papers demonstrated that building an understanding of 'Virginness' led to an increase in brand commitment, the measure that most closely correlates with revenue growth. This model is summarised in Figure 4.

The key to fuelling demand at both ends of the Virgin Atlantic route network would lie in taking what we'd learnt over many years in the UK and applying it to a global communications campaign that would be relevant in every market.

This would not only increase demand at the other end of each route but align the brand globally to maximise synergy for our audience (who since they were flying, were always exposed to the brand in more than one market).

Until this point, communications outside the UK had been largely tactical with different positionings and values being expressed around the globe (Figure 5).

**Figure 4: Communications model**

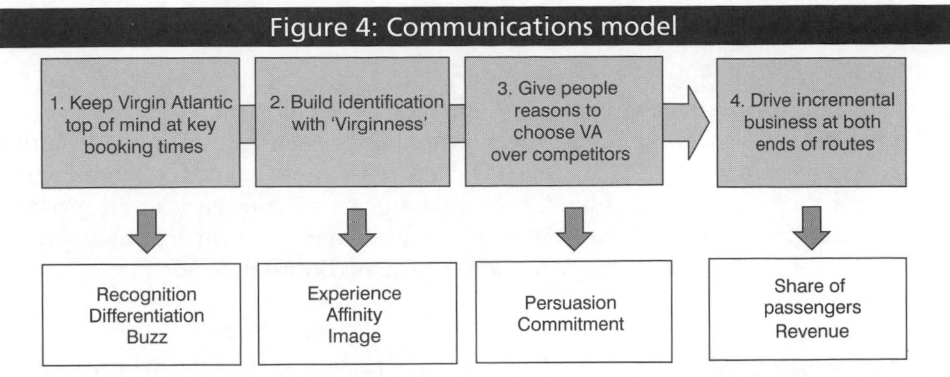


**Figure 5: Example Virgin Atlantic communications outside the UK 2007–2009**

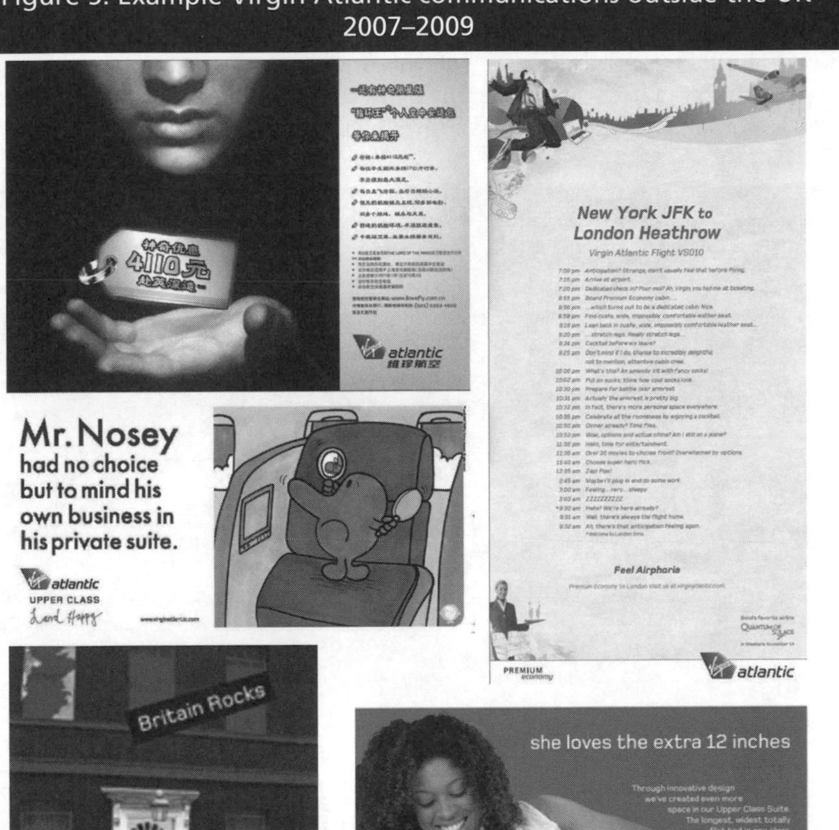

## The creative challenge

With a legacy of highly effective communications in the UK, it was critical that the move to a global approach didn't compromise its impact at home.

So the wit, style, audacity and irreverent humour (essentially what made Virgin Virgin) would need to stay. But to make it globally relevant we needed a unifying truth. Something that could act as a hook for communications and work in all markets, where more often than not British Airways was no longer our primary competitor.

The answer to this challenge lay in the very reason Branson decided to launch an airline in the first place.

> *I was fed up with identical seats, identical food, identical service and extortionate fares. I decided to create an airline that I wanted to fly myself.*
>
> Sir Richard Branson

Virgin Atlantic was built from a passion for a better flying experience – a belief that flying should be a pleasure, not a chore. And that passion is still evident in every touch-point today. The flying experience is second to none and the way the brand behaves is fun, glamorous, sexy and brings back a little of the golden age of flying (Figure 6).

Figure 6: Virgin Atlantic imagery

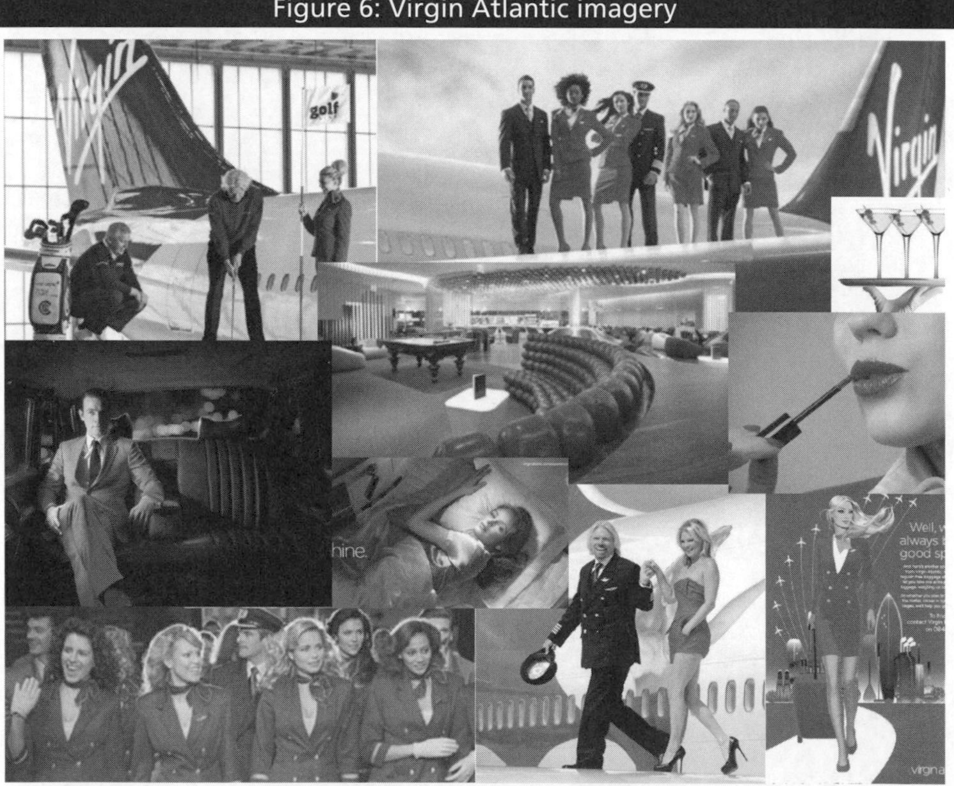

In contrast, national flag carriers the world over fly out of duty. Although, mercifully, service levels have improved significantly since 1984, the role of the flag-flying brand remains the same – to represent the nation – and with that comes a certain formality, seriousness and (often) stuffiness (Figure 7).

Figure 7: Flag carrier airline imagery

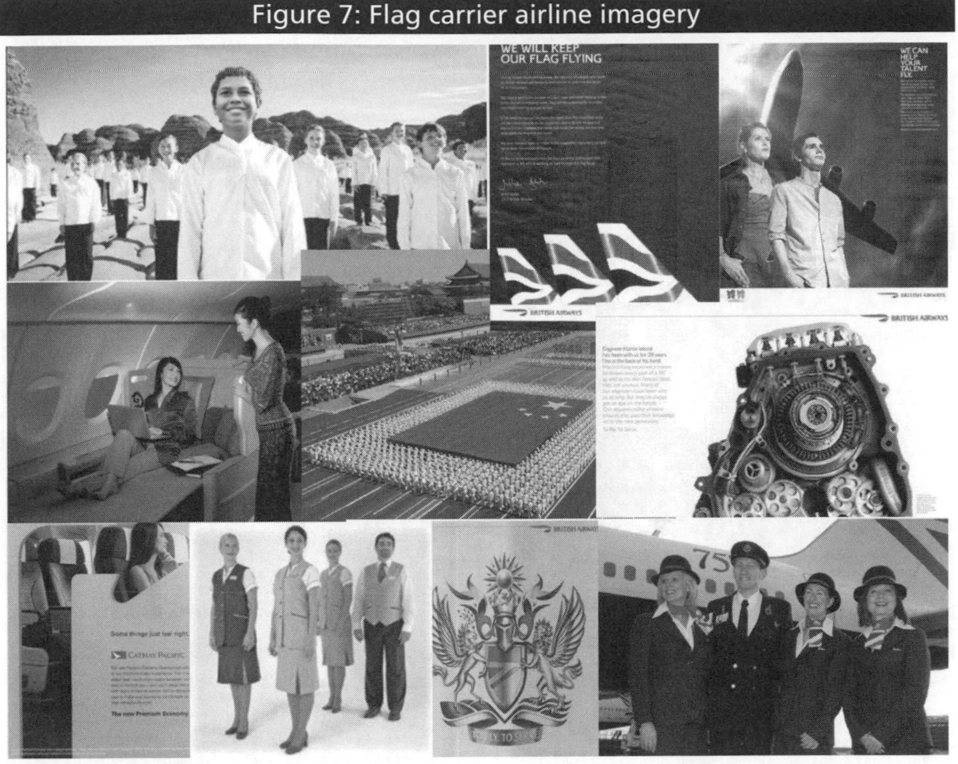


And the contrast of the Virgin experience versus the local flag carrier is evident time and time again in research all over the world:

> *There's just no comparison. Virgin is in a different league from Continental.*
>
> Business Traveller, USA 2009

> *Virgin have something extra – I don't quite know what – but it's the whole package.*
>
> Leisure Traveller, China 2009

So unlike flag carriers that fly out of duty, Virgin Atlantic flies for the love of it. This was a truth that was relevant in every market; an opportunity we could exploit globally.

We summed it up as 'Virgin Atlantic. Born to fly.'

## The creative idea

Our idea was to create advertising no other airline in the world would dare to and in doing so dramatise the totally different flying experience Virgin Atlantic offers.

Featuring the strap-line 'Your airline's either got it or it hasn't', the TV execution takes the viewer on a metaphorical flight with Virgin Atlantic (Figure 8).

Press, poster and digital support for the Upper Class and Economy cabins captured the unique values of Virgin, showing the glamour, fun and comfort of the flying experience (Figures 9 and 10).

And the idea was fully integrated across all touch points, from Flying Club communications, to credit card mailers, to trade advertising and point of sale (Figure 11).

Figure 8: TV and cinema execution, Title: 'Your airline's either got it or it hasn't'

Source: RKCR/Y&R; Music: Muse, 'Feeling good'

## Figure 9: Upper class press, poster and digital creative work

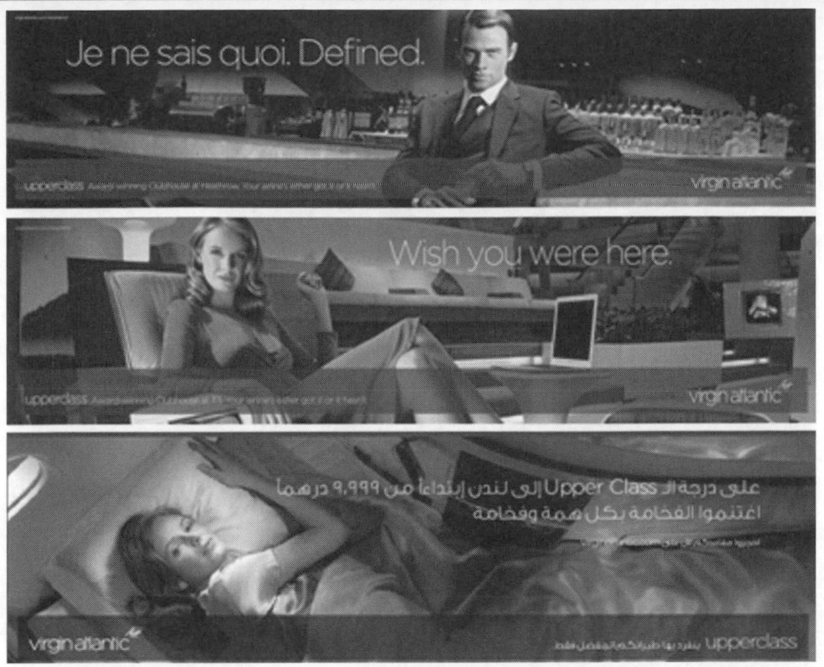


Source: RKCR/Y&R

## Figure 10: Economy press, digital and outdoor creative work

UK service & fares message

US digital banner

Hong Kong flight promotion

Ghana taxi wrap

Source: RKCR/Y&R

Figure 11: Integration across brand touch points

Flying club eDM & DM

Trade advertising

Credit card mailer

Source: Gyro

## Media strategy

Virgin Atlantic's media spend on a global basis was dwarfed by the global giants it was competing against. The total global budget for the first year FY10/11 was £15.2m.

Approximately half was allocated to the UK in reflection of its dominance in revenue generation. Although still a significant spend, this meant the UK budget was £2m lower than in the previous year with the Still Red Hot campaign.

The remaining £8m was allocated across the rest of the world. Given Virgin Atlantic's relatively low share of voice in each market, we had to be clever with how we spent it.

The media strategy around the world was one of key city domination according to the route network.

Highly targeted television in our two key markets (UK and US) plus cinema in Australia ensured we maintained/built a strong emotional relationship communicating 'Your airline's either got it or it hasn't'.

Print media was selected according to quality rather than quantity opportunities, using unusual formats and media firsts where possible, e.g. the first advertiser to wrap the business section of *The Times*; partnering with *The Daily* in the US – the first iPad publication.

Online worked alongside ATL to directly drive sales at key booking moments. And we leveraged Virgin Atlantic's entrepreneurial spirit to capitalise on tactical opportunities wherever possible, creating cut-through and a sense of scale: wrapping a London taxi in Ghana, creating giant shopping mall banners in India, even wrapping our own office building in Barbados.

The campaign first broke in March 2010 and ran in 13 markets (Figures 12 and 13).

## Figure 12: Virgin Atlantic FY 10/11 global media laydown

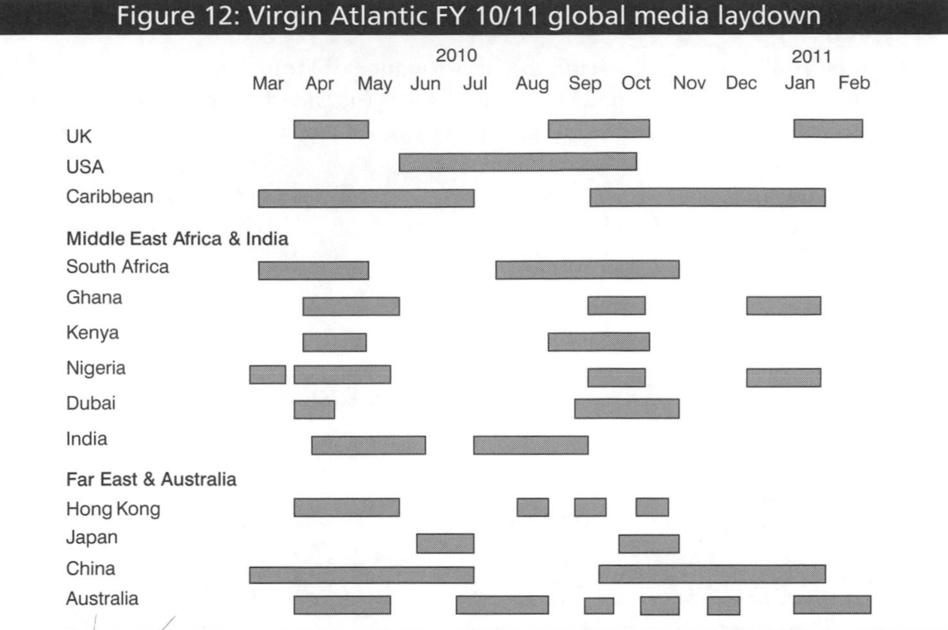


## Figure 13: Media-led amplification

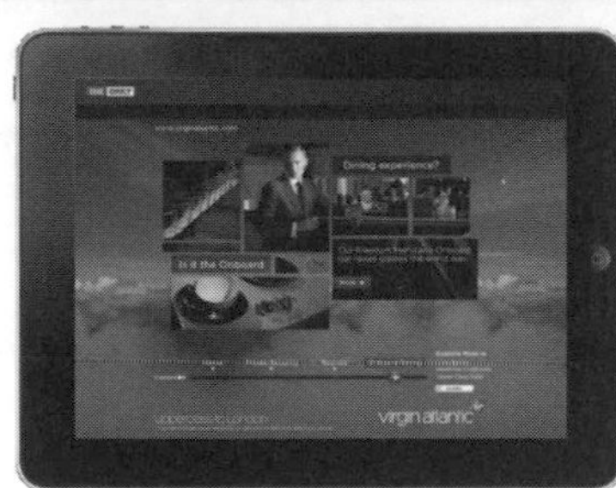


US: ipad creative

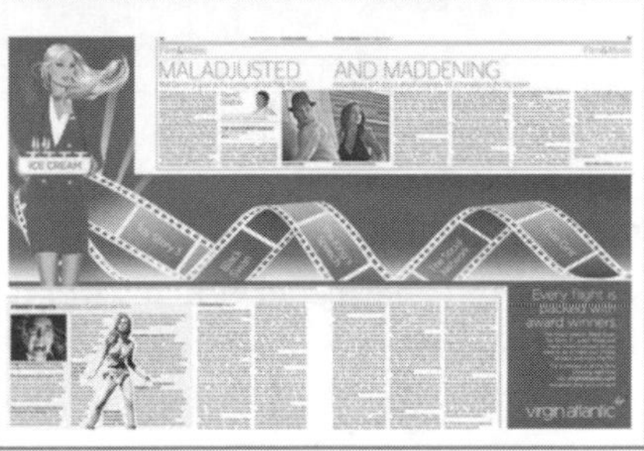


UK: Oscar night tactical ad

India: shopping mall domination

Kenya: Event invitation

## Demonstrating the impact of global communications

In this section we will demonstrate how the campaign worked:

- First in the UK – comparing the performance of 'Your airline's either…' with the previous UK campaign 'Still Red Hot' (heralded by Branson as the best Virgin campaign ever made and itself the subject of an award winning IPA paper in 2010).
- Second across the RoW – where we compare performance against a global norm constructed by Hall & Partners based on 23 airline brands around the world (there is no pre measure to compare against).

We will use the communications model referenced earlier in the paper to show how the campaign delivered at each stage (Figure 14).

Figure 14: Virgin Atlantic communications model

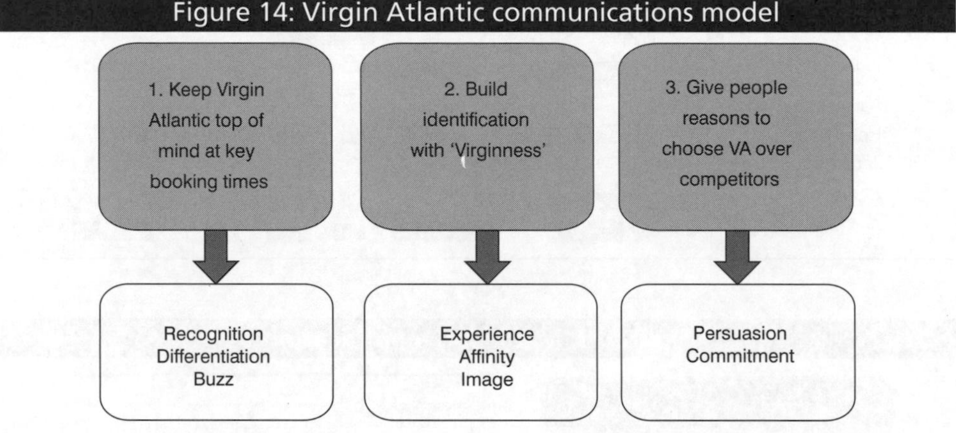


### *UK campaign performance*

As we can see in Table 1, despite an overall decrease in media spend of around £2m, 'Your airline's either got it or it hasn't' more than held the brand position in the UK. Across key elements of our communications model it actually strengthened our position.

### *Rest of World campaign performance*

In overseas markets the advertising worked as intended (Figure 15).

Cut-through for 'Your airline's either got it or it hasn't' was above norm in all markets for business and leisure passengers (Figure 16).

The creative approach universally stood out as different from other communications (Figure 17).

## Table 1: Stronger UK tracking results than 'Still Red Hot'

| | **Still Red Hot** | **Your airline's either got it or it hasn't** |
|---|---|---|
| 1) Keeping VAA top of mind | | |
| Cut through (% recognition per £ spent ) | 3.3 | 5.1 |
| Salience | 81% | 83% |
| 2) Build identification | | |
| Involvement | 67% | 73% |
| Made me feel flying with VAA would be a fantastic experience | 33% | 43% |
| 3) Give people reasons to choose | | |
| Persuasion | 76% | 78% |
| Brand commitment | 43% | 48% |
| Brand commitment vs. BA | + 8% pts | + 10% pts |

Source: Hall & Partners Brand Tracking, UK Jan 09 vs. Oct 2010, First/Business passengers

## Figure 15: Virgin Atlantic communications model

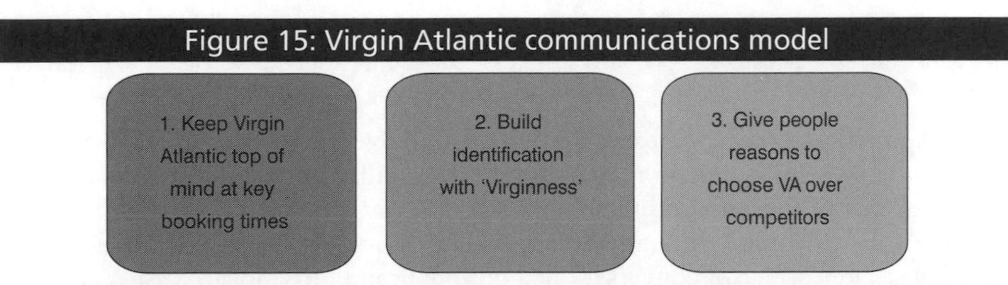


## Figure 16: Advertising recognition was above norm

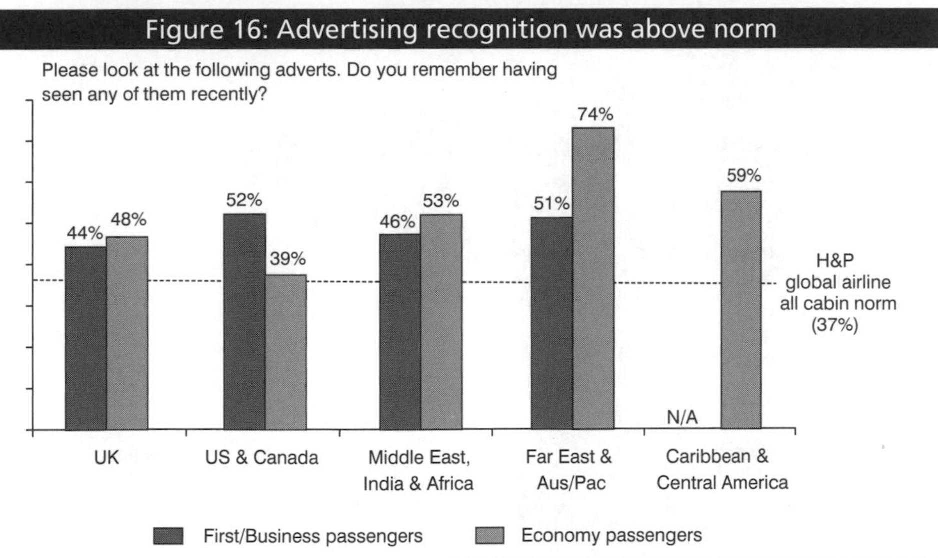


Source: Hall & Partners Brand Tracking, UK/US Oct/Nov 2010; Rest of World May/Jun 2011. US & Canada – New York, LA, San Francisco (base: 480); Middle East, India & Africa – India (base: 243/115); Far East & Aus Pac – China (base: 115/145); Caribbean & Central America – Barbados (base: 153, leisure sample only)

## Figure 17: The campaign stood out as different

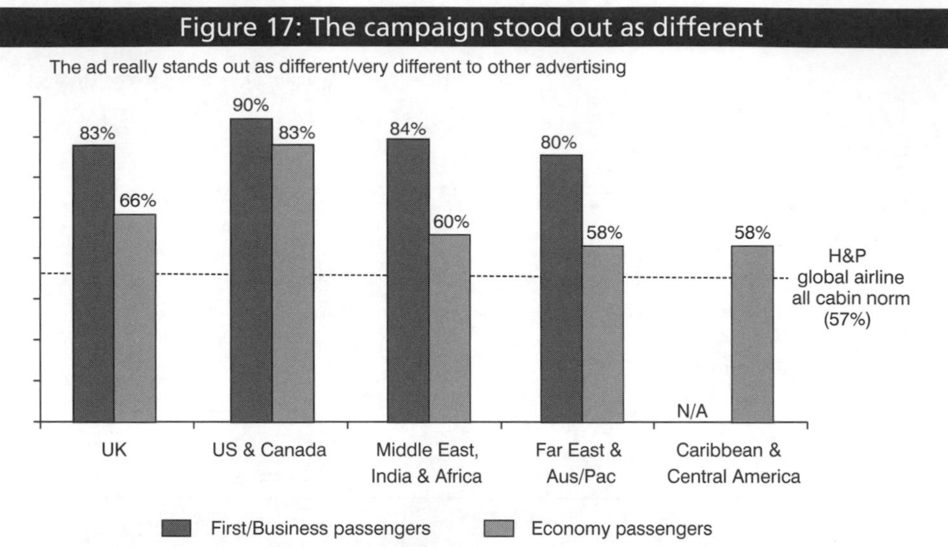


Source: Hall & Partners Brand Tracking, UK/US Oct/Nov 2010; Rest of World May/Jun 2011. US & Canada – New York, LA, San Francisco (base: 480); Middle East, India & Africa – India (base: 243/115); Far East & Aus Pac – China (base: 115/145); Caribbean & Central America – Barbados (base: 153, leisure sample only)

The launch sparked an increase in brand buzz all over the world. This is illustrated by the tangible increase in online brand sentiment, with positive sentiment increasing by 56.3% between August and October 2010.

Largely spread virally through Twitter, Facebook and on YouTube (Figure 18), the TV ad was a key driver of conversation about the brand, driving a 62.3% increase in general brand mentions.

## Figure 18: Facebook word cloud

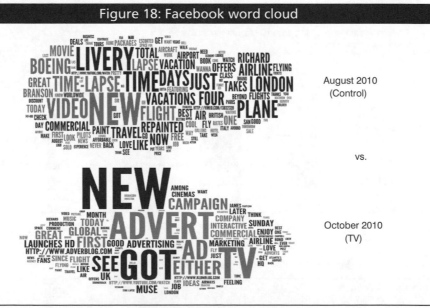

August 2010 (Control)

vs.

October 2010 (TV)

Source: MGM/OMD – Virgin Atlantic online influence monitor, August to November 2010

The campaign built identification with Virginness around the world – across all markets the takeout of the communication was aligned, with the flying experience and brand attitude coming through strongly (Figure 19).

**Figure 19: Verbatim comments about the advertising**

'It gives the feel of a 7 star hotel in a flight.'
Business traveller, China

'It says that passengers can travel with comfort and that travelling is a fantastic experience on Virgin Atlantic.'
Leisure traveller, Caribbean

'It is the way to go. They are always ready to serve you. When you think about flying, you think about Virgin. Virgin is the airline to travel on.'
Business traveller, India

'It's modern, up to date with excellent service.'
Leisure traveller, South Africa

'It gave me a best impression about their company. I would like to use their service as soon as possible.'
Leisure traveller, India

Source: Hall & Partners Global Tracking Study

The idea successfully conveyed how great the flying experience would be (Figure 20).

**Figure 20: The campaign communicated a great flying experience**

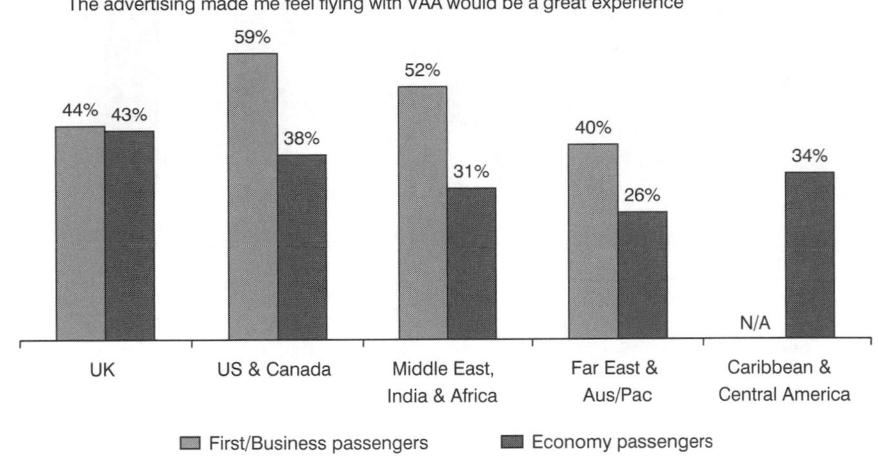


Source: Hall & Partners Brand Tracking, UK/US Oct/Nov 2010; Rest of World May/Jun 2011. US & Canada – New York, LA, San Francisco; Middle East, India & Africa – India; Far East & Aus Pac – China; Caribbean & Central America – Barbados (leisure sample only)

The campaign appeared to improve brand understanding (Figure 21) and affinity (Figure 22) across the board (but particularly in newer markets) with recognisers showing significantly higher understanding than non-recognisers.

Figure 21: Those who saw the campaign felt they understood the Virgin Atlantic brand better

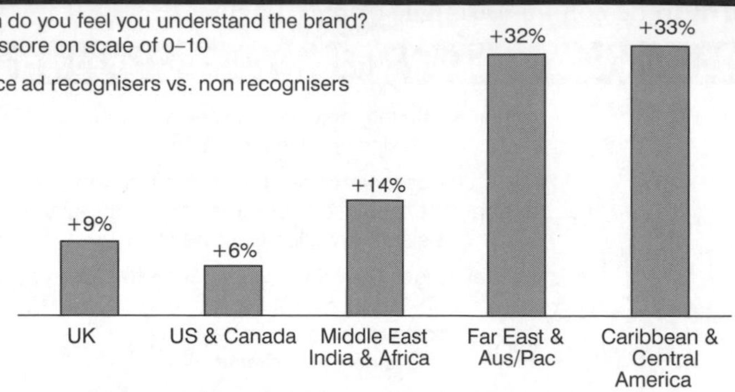


Source: Hall & Partners Brand Tracking, UK/US Oct/Nov 2010; Rest of World May/Jun 2011. US & Canada – New York, LA, San Francisco (base: 480); Middle East, India & Africa – India (base: 243/115); Far East & Aus Pac – China (base: 115/145); Caribbean & Central America – Barbados (base: 153, leisure sample only)

Figure 22: And felt more affinity for the brand

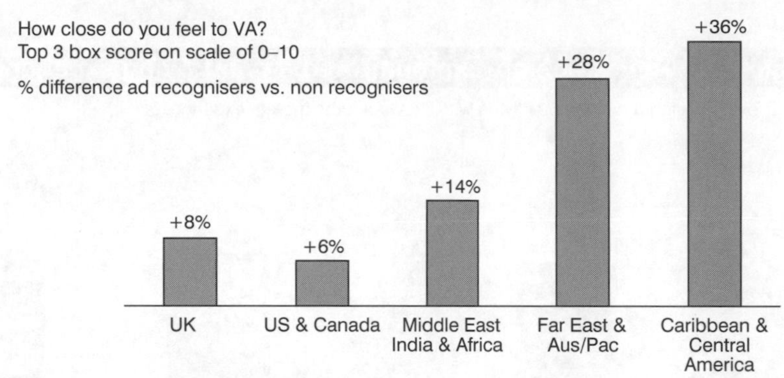


Source: Hall & Partners Brand Tracking, UK/US Oct/Nov 2010; Rest of World May/Jun 2011. US & Canada – New York, LA, San Francisco (base: 480); Middle East, India & Africa – India (base: 243/115); Far East & Aus Pac – China (base: 115/145); Caribbean & Central America – Barbados (base: 153, leisure sample only)

And local flag carriers were left seeming relatively staid and old fashioned as the campaign further reinforced Virgin's innovative and forward thinking positioning (Figure 23).

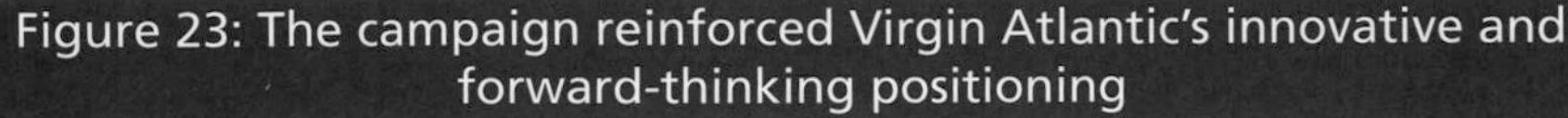

Figure 23: The campaign reinforced Virgin Atlantic's innovative and forward-thinking positioning

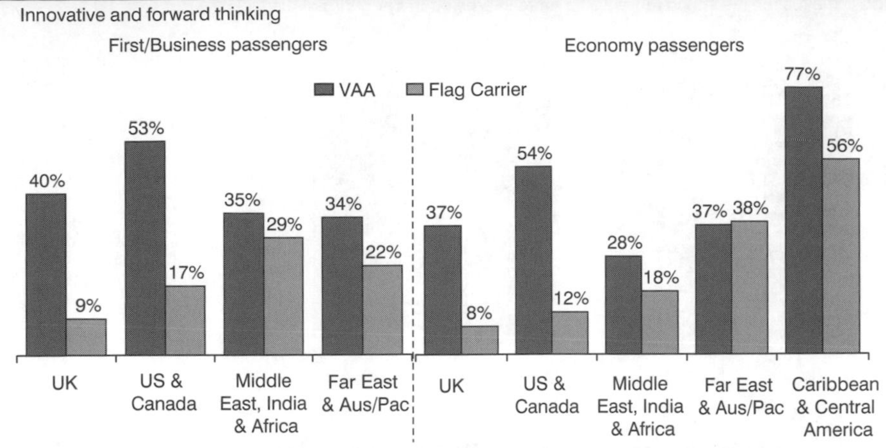


Source: Hall & Partners Brand Tracking, UK/US Oct/Nov 2010; Rest of World May/Jun 2011. US & Canada – New York, LA, San Francisco; Middle East, India & Africa – India; Far East & Aus Pac – China; Caribbean & Central America – Barbados (leisure sample only)

Similarly, Virgin was seen as worth paying more for than the flag carrier in almost all markets (Figure 24).

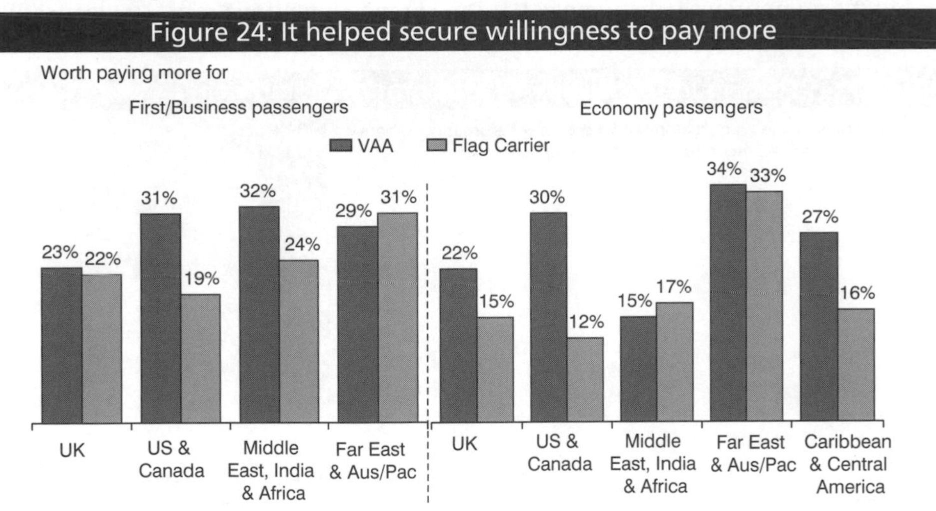


Source: Hall & Partners Brand Tracking, UK/US Oct/Nov 2010; Rest of World May/Jun 2011. US & Canada – New York, LA, San Francisco; Middle East, India & Africa – India; Far East & Aus Pac – China; Caribbean & Central America – Barbados (leisure sample only)

Consumers found the communications highly persuasive with above norm scores on 'makes me interested to fly Virgin' in all markets (Figure 25).

Figure 25: Persuasion was above the norm

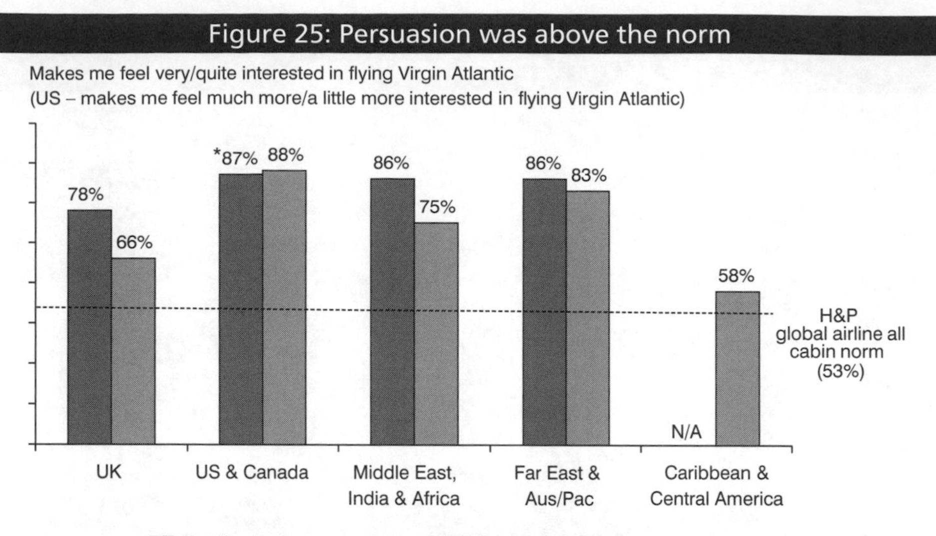


Source: Hall & Partners Brand Tracking, UK/US Oct/Nov 2010; Rest of World May/Jun 2011. US & Canada – New York, LA, San Francisco; Middle East, India & Africa – India; Far East & Aus Pac – China; Caribbean & Central America – Barbados (leisure sample only).

But most importantly the campaign shifted brand commitment, the single measure most closely correlated with sales, in all markets (Figure 26).

Figure 26: Virgin Atlantic brand commitment

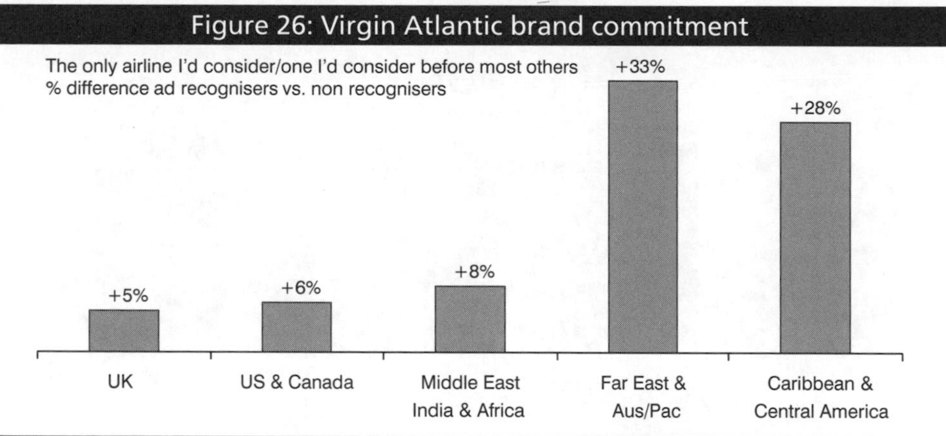


Source: Hall & Partners Brand Tracking, UK/US Oct/Nov 2010; Rest of World May/Jun 2011. US & Canada – New York, LA, San Francisco; Middle East, India & Africa – India; Far East & Aus Pac – China; Caribbean & Central America – Barbados (leisure sample only)

In summary, we have seen how the advertising worked as intended against our model.

We'll now illustrate the business results.

## Global business results

In FY10/11 (March 2010–February 2011), their first year of going global, Virgin Atlantic announced record results.

Seats filled per plane were up year-on-year (Figure 27). And Virgin Atlantic's lead on the market was further enhanced.

**Figure 27: Seats filled per plane increased, Virgin Atlantic passenger load factor vs. market average**

IATA mkt average
IATA European airline average
VAA
75.5%
74.6%
77.0%
73.0%
72.7%
+7.3% pts
80.0%
73.1%
72.6%
+9.4% pts
82.0%
FY 2009
FY 2010
FY 2011

Source: Virgin Atlantic Commercial/IATA

Virgin Atlantic share of passengers flown has grown across all routes (Figure 28).

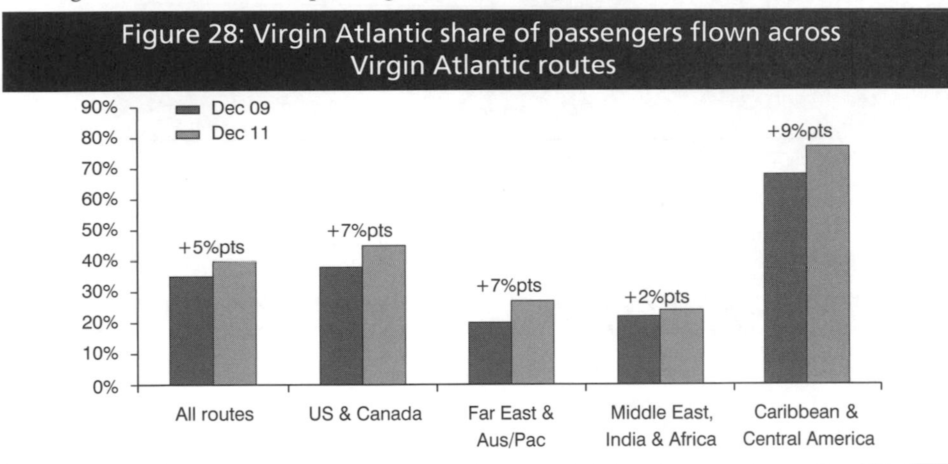


**Figure 28: Virgin Atlantic share of passengers flown across Virgin Atlantic routes**

Source: Virgin Atlantic Commercial/IATA data for overall number of passengers flown

Moreover they were spending more. Average price paid per ticket grew strongly after a number of years of decline (Figure 29).

Figure 29: Virgin Atlantic average yield, FY 2008–FY 2011

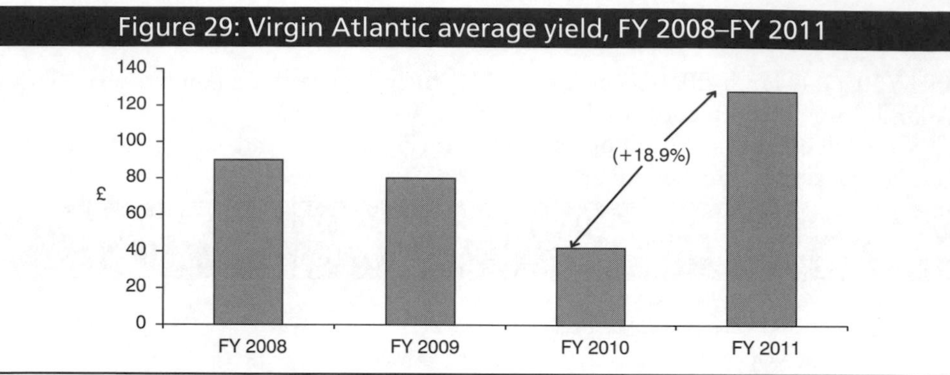


Source: Virgin Atlantic Commercial

The effect of increased loads and yields on the business was growth in passenger revenues of over £200m year-on-year (Figure 30).

Figure 30: Virgin Atlantic passenger revenue, FY 2010–FY 2011

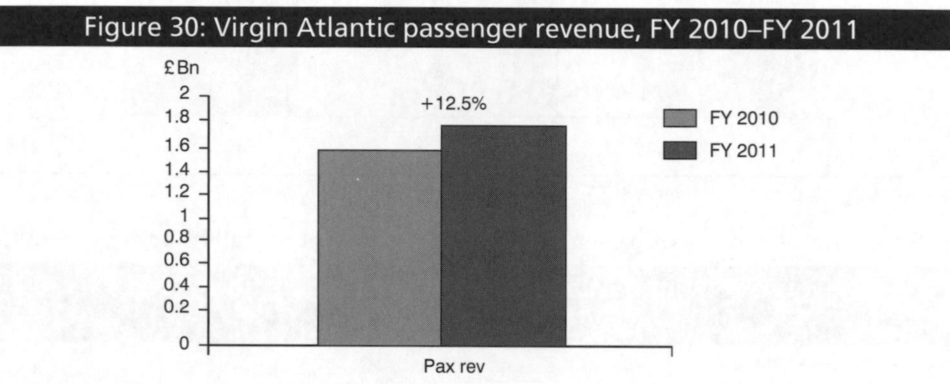


Source: Virgin Atlantic Commercial

Importantly, the strategy of growing the importance of overseas markets was working – revenue grew 8.7% in the UK and nearly 20% in the rest of the world (Figure 31).

Figure 31: Virgin Atlantic passenger revenue growth by UK and RoW

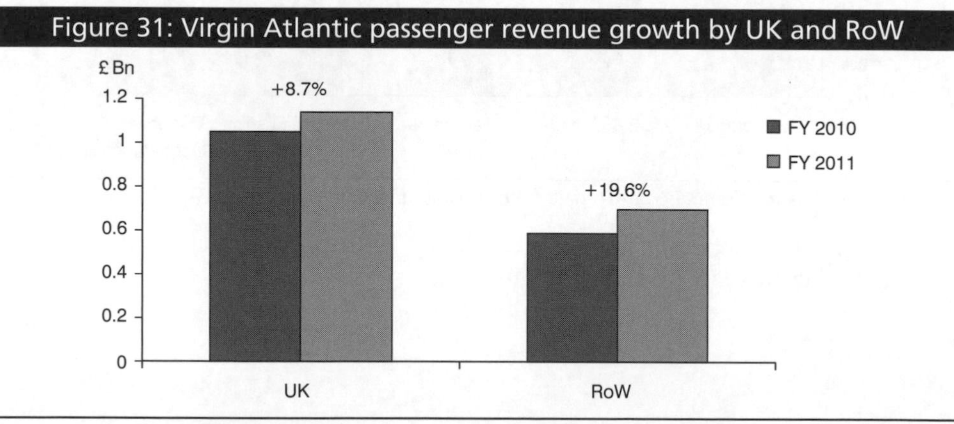


Source: Virgin Atlantic Commercial

And for the first time ever, overseas markets contributed the majority of passenger revenue growth – £108.8m in incremental revenue overseas versus £89.5m from the UK (Figure 32).

Figure 32: Contribution of UK and RoW to incremental passenger revenue

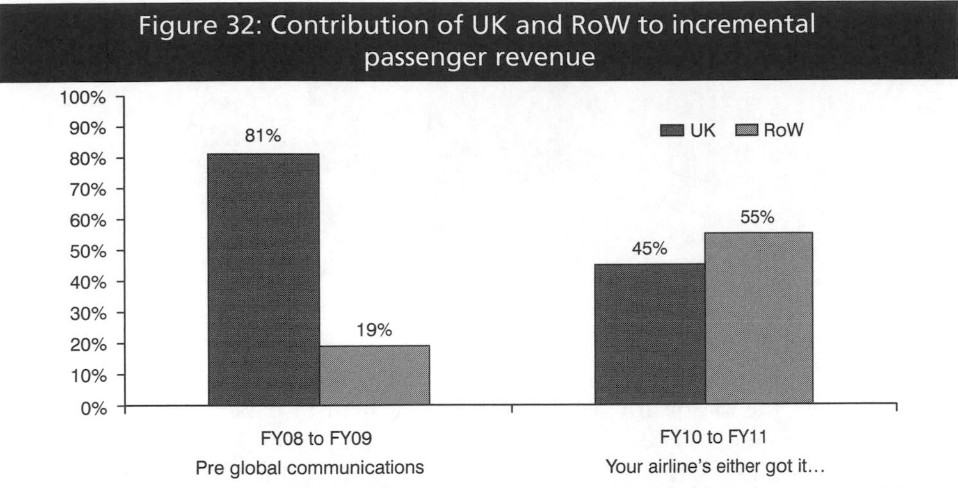


Source: Virgin Atlantic

This is particularly impressive considering the UK revenue base was twice the size of overseas in FY 2010.

Consequently Virgin Atlantic's overall revenue reliance on the UK reduced from 68% pre global campaign to 62.7% in FY 2011.

And the latest results for Q1 FY 2011/2012 indicate Virgin Atlantic's rise in passenger revenues continues, up 7.6% year-on-year.

Commenting on the results, Virgin Atlantic CEO, Steve Ridgway, said the carrier had 'demonstrated the resilience of our business by weathering the toughest economic period for aviation'.

While the campaign clearly can't claim all the credit for these results we do believe the communications had a key role to play.

## Isolating the communications effect

In the UK, Virgin Atlantic's lead market, we are fortunate enough to have econometric modelling to isolate the effect of communications from other factors that may have contributed to the record business performance coinciding with the campaign.

However, in other markets we have to draw on a range of evidence to quantify the influence of wider factors and isolate the communications impact. To illustrate this we will take each potentially influencing factor and quantify its effect.

### *1. Was the enhanced performance down to general growth in the market?*

International passenger traffic into and out of London Heathrow (Virgin Atlantic's main international hub) has been largely flat since 2007 with 2011 seeing a slight increase on passenger numbers – growth of 2.2% (Figure 33).

Figure 33: LHR international passenger traffic, inbound and outbound

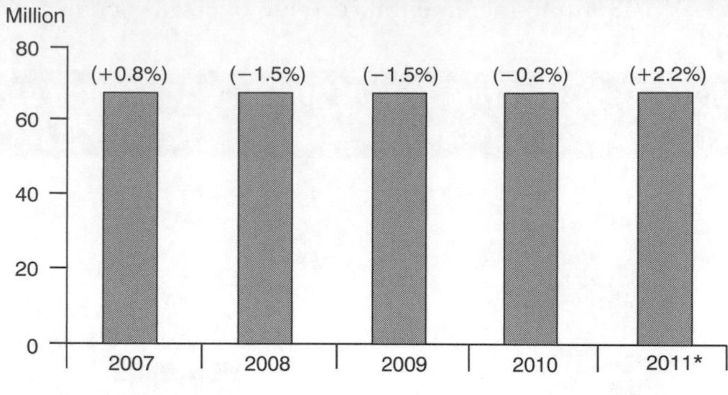


Source: Airports Council International

If this were the reason for Virgin Atlantic's growth in passengers and revenue, then Virgin Atlantic's share of the market would remain more or less stable. But Figure 34 shows how Virgin's share of the market grew significantly, coinciding with the campaign.

Based on this evidence we believe it's fair to discount market fluctuations from Virgin Atlantic's performance.

Figure 34: Virgin Atlantic market share pre–post campaign

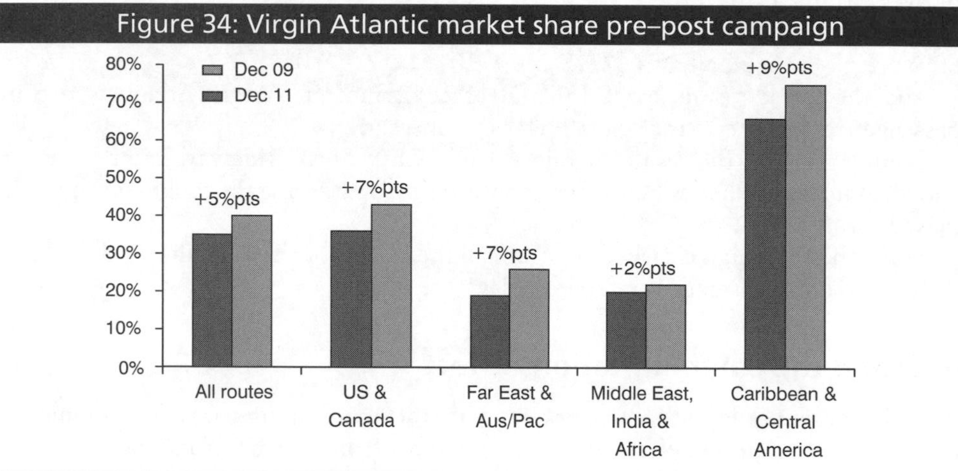


Source: Virgin Atlantic Commercial/IATA data for overall number of passengers flown

### *2. Might Virgin Atlantic's growth come from competitor airlines collapsing?*

There have been no major airline collapses since the campaign launched in 2010 and nothing on Virgin Atlantic's routes.

### 3. Did industrial action surrounding British Airways benefit Virgin Atlantic

Although Virgin Atlantic competes with carriers all over the world, its primary competitor is still British Airways because both airlines are based out of Heathrow. In fact over 90% of Virgin Atlantic's routes are also flown by BA.

BA's industrial dispute led to union Unite balloting cabin crew for strike action four times between December 2009 and March 2011 and 22 days of strikes in Spring 2010.

'Your airline's either got it or it hasn't' launched in April 2010 and this paper covers the period to December 2011. So clearly any BA losses during the latter part of that period of industrial action could have ended up as Virgin Atlantic's gains.

We've been able to use econometrics to quantify what impact the dispute had on Virgin Atlantic's business.

It can be seen in Table 2 that the total benefit to Virgin Atlantic of BA's industrial dispute was almost £32m. This has been discounted from the ROI of the campaign later in the paper.

Outside of the UK, the commercial benefit to Virgin Atlantic was negligible. Negative publicity, the main factor driving switching in bookings in the UK, was almost non-existent around the world. And anecdotal evidence suggests, if anything, BA passengers in other markets avoiding the strikes switched to local flag carriers.

**Table 2: Modelled increase in Virgin Atlantic booked revenue FY 2011**

| | BA cabin crew strike | As % of total booked revenue for each cabin |
|---|---|---|
| Upper Class cabin | £12.82 | 3% |
| Premium Economy cabin | £6.31 | 4% |
| Economy Cabin | £17.98 | 3% |
| Overall gain in revenue | £31.64m | 3% |

### 4. Was there a reduction in price that could explain increased passenger numbers?

No, in fact quite the contrary. During the campaign period yields went up 19%. This shows that average prices were increased rather than lowered once the campaign launched.

This, coupled with the fact that 'willingness to pay more' went up in response to the campaign, would suggest that activity helped support a crucial price premium during challenging market conditions.

### 5. Were there any Virgin Atlantic product innovations or enhancements that could explain the growth?

The last big investment Virgin Atlantic made in its aircraft fleet was with a Premium Economy cabin overhaul in 2005. Since then, and for the duration of this campaign, there were no changes to the inflight (or airport) experience.

Since 2005, BA have introduced a 6ft 6" flat bed in First class, completed the roll out of an upgraded Club World (business class) and rolled out video on demand in their economy cabin.

At the same time a number of competitors (Emirates, Qantas, Singapore Airlines, etc.) invested in the A380 super jumbo, benefitting from features such as onboard showers, private suites and a bar & lounge area.

So the fact that Virgin Atlantic stole share from these operators despite the relative erosion of the brand experience is all the more remarkable.

### *6. Might the growth have been a function of any other Virgin activity (across other categories) in any market?*

Virgin Group has interests across many of the markets in question, beyond the presence of Virgin Atlantic. During the campaign period, local markets would have undertaken marketing activity on a small and local scale across a variety of brands.

But to explain the uplift that was shown across all regions, any activity from elsewhere in the Virgin Group would have to have been coordinated and of some scale.

Given 'Your airline's either got it or it hasn't' is the first global initiative in Virgin's history, and investment across the rest of the portfolio remained stable, we believe this cannot explain an uplift in Virgin Atlantic's performance.

## Quantifying the effect of Virgin Atlantic's global communications

Revenue contribution is an appropriate measure of effectiveness for the airline industry because of the high level of fixed costs in the market (estimated at more than 90%). This precedent has been set by the British Airways paper in 2004 and Virgin Atlantic 2008 and 2010 effectiveness papers.

Virgin Atlantic has used econometric modelling in the UK for some years now, so we can be confident of the return of the campaign at home. But we don't have the benefit of econometrics in other markets, so need to use the data available to us to estimate the global return of the campaign.

In pursuit of thoroughness, we have calculated the global return on investment using two methodologies:

1. Using econometric modelling conducted in the UK and extrapolating the effect across other markets.
2. A form of regression analysis to determine what the financial implications would have been had we not moved to a global communications model.

We believe the first methodology delivers the most conservative estimate of the revenue return on investment at £10.76 for every £1 invested.

Based on the evidence presented in this section, it is the second methodology which we feel provides a more likely return at £15.66 for every £1 invested.

We will go on to explain both methodologies.

### *Methodology 1: econometric modelling extrapolated*

'Still Red Hot' was heralded by Sir Richard Branson as the best Virgin ad ever made; it achieved the highest overall payback of any Virgin Atlantic campaign in the UK since we began modelling and was itself the subject of a winning IPA paper in 2010.

Yet, the model estimates that the new global idea was significantly more efficient per pound spent, with a total ROI of £12.42 for every £1 spent in the UK (Table 3).

**Table 3: UK comparative return on investment per £ spent**

| | Still Red Hot | Your airline's either got it... | % difference |
|---|---|---|---|
| TV | £14.64 | £19.22 | +31% |
| Upper Class press/poster | £6.31 | £7.68 | +22% |
| Economy press | £17.98 | £20.64 | +15% |
| Overall campaign | £10.58 | £12.42 | +17% |

Source: BrandScience – Virgin Atlantic econometric model

N.B. the econometrics strips out other variables – economic recovery, the BA strike, etc. to make this a like for like comparison. Although there was a difference in media budget, FY09 £10m vs. FY10 £8.4m, the model doesn't indicate any diminishing returns in FY09.

Putting this is context, if they had enjoyed the same TV budget, 'Your airline's either got it or it hasn't' would deliver £20,602,238 *more* revenue in the UK for the business than the previous, highly successful campaign, 'Still Red Hot'.

However, based on the actual investment in the 'Your airline's either got it...' campaign, communications were responsible for delivering 10.4% of total UK revenue, equivalent to £116.4m.

Two factors have led us to conclude that the campaign would deliver *at least* the same proportion of revenue across other markets:

a. performance on key tracking measures was even more pronounced in markets outside the UK (Table 4).

**Table 4: Performance on key advertising metrics**

| | UK | Other global markets (average) |
|---|---|---|
| Ad recognition | 46% | 53% |
| Ad appeal | 67% | 79% |
| Flying with VAA is the way flying should be | 33% | 33% |
| Brand understanding (ad recognition vs. non recognition) | +8% | +21% |
| Brand commitment (ad recognition vs. non recognition) | +5% | +19% |

Source: Hall & Partners, total sample

b. the rest of the world contributed higher revenue growth than the UK (Figure 35).

Figure 35: Virgin Atlantic passenger revenue growth by UK and RoW

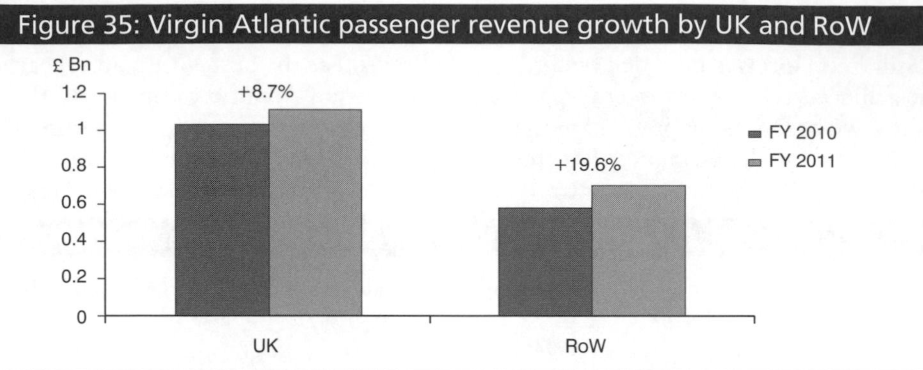


Source: Virgin Atlantic Commercial

So if you apply the UK's 10.4% figure to the total revenue generated in the rest of the world (£664m), it estimates the total revenue generated by the campaign outside the UK at £69m.

Adding the UK and RoW revenues together, the total revenue generated by the campaign was £185m. Based on a total spend (media and production) of £17.23m, this equates to a revenue ROI of £10.76 for every £1 spent.

### *Methodology 2: base level sales analysis*

The second methodology calculates the value to the business of the global brand model by identifying the base level of sales we might have expected by continuing with our historic approach of building the brand in the UK and using tactical campaigns overseas.

The market/capacity share quotient is an airline industry measure that strips out the underlying effect of increasing capacity (i.e. number of available seats) by dividing your market share by capacity share.

Like sales per point of distribution for FMCG brands it can be thought of as a long-term comparative measure of how hard your brand is working for the business (because the quotient is based on share of passenger flown, it strips out economic or market effects to give us a pure like for like measure of brand performance).

In theory, all things being equal, your market/capacity quotient should be 1 – indicative of taking your fair or expected share of the market according to availability.

Prior to the global campaign, Virgin Atlantic's quotient ran at 1.346 (i.e. 34.6% more market share than share of capacity), indicative of the power of the brand in the UK.

In the 21 months post launch of 'Your airline's either got it or it hasn't' (that we have data for), Virgin Atlantic's quotient was 1.586. This means, since going global, Virgin Atlantic have taken 58.6% more market share than capacity over the routes they fly (Figure 36).

So what we can see is by using one powerful, well executed globally consistent idea, the Virgin Atlantic brand has worked 18% harder for the business (1.586 divided by 1.346).

Nothing else has changed – the only thing that could have influenced the in-market performance of the brand is communications.

Figure 36: Virgin Atlantic market/capacity share quotient (share of passengers flown divided by capacity share on Virgin Atlantic routes)

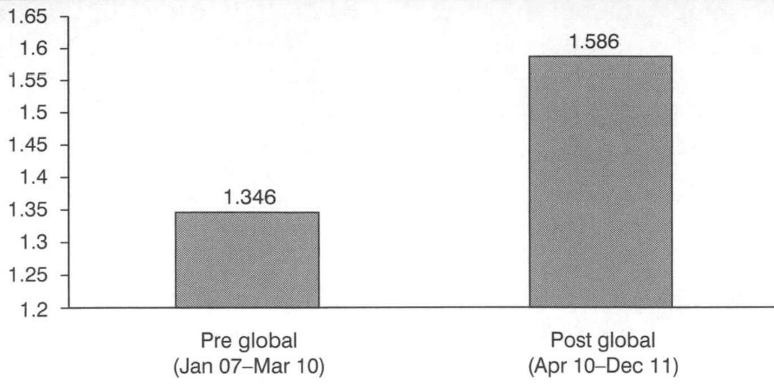


Source: Virgin Atlantic Commercial

The market/capacity share quotient enables us to estimate what the commercial impact would have been had we continued with a local model of marketing.

We know that with the global campaign our total passenger revenues in FY 2011 were £1,783.3m with our quotient running at 1.586 (or 58.6% more market share of passengers flown than our share of available capacity).

If we hadn't run the global campaign, it's reasonable to expect our quotient would be the same as for the previous 38 months:1.346. If we apply the difference in brand performance to our total revenue figures we get a projected total passenger revenue figure if we hadn't run the global campaign of £1,513.5m (Table 5).

Table 5: Overall global return on marketing investment

| | With global campaign | Without global campaign | Difference |
|---|---|---|---|
| Market/capacity share quotient (measure of brand performance for the business) | 1.586 | 1.346 | 0.24 |
| Total passenger revenue | £1,783.3m | £1,513.3m | £269.8m |
| Media spend FY11 (including production & usage) | – | | £17.23m |
| ROMI | – | | £15.66 |

Source: Virgin Atlantic Commercial/BrandScience – Virgin Atlantic Econometric model

This gives us a calculation of the financial value the global brand campaign unlocked for the business of £269.8m – a UK campaign revenue derived from econometrics of £116.4m and an overseas campaign revenue of £153.4m.

Based on the total spend (media and production) of £17.2m this gives a revenue ROI of £15.66 for every £1 spent.

We believe this is a more realistic calculation of value to the business of the global brand campaign 'Your airline's either got it or it hasn't'.

## What have we learnt in this paper?

This paper tells the story of how one of the UK's most loved brands adopted a global communications model to help combat the threat of a new breed of global competitor.

We took learning gathered over many years on how communications worked in the UK and applied it to other markets around the world, while at the same time finding a universal truth that made the campaign relevant to each local market.

'Your airline's either got it or it hasn't' worked as intended across all markets and even outperformed the acclaimed 'Still Red Hot' campaign in the UK, despite the lower budget.

We believe it's a case study in creating global communications that don't compromise on local relevance.

It's also an example of capitalising on the scale of production that a global budget affords, to help give the brand stature and stand out in markets where it's still relatively small.

And ultimately it's an illustration of how global communications can deliver business results to help drive a longer-term strategy.

In the year after launch, Virgin Atlantic achieved record results and made good progress on ensuring both ends of the route network were delivering growth.

The global return on marketing investment is estimated at £15.66 per £1 spent.

As they say, your airline brand's either got it, or it hasn't.

## Notes

1 The merger with bmi will give BA 51% of take-off and landing slots at London Heathrow.
2 49% of Virgin Atlantic is owned by Singapore Airlines but this is purely an investment. Other than allowing customers to spend frequent flyer points on the other airline, there are no further alignments or benefits.

Chapter 19

# Walkers

## Going from good to great

**By Adam Glasner, Abbott Mead Vickers BBDO**
Contributing authors: Serge Vaezi, Freud; Bridget Angear, Sarah Sternberg and Tom White, Abbott Mead Vickers BBDO; Tim Warner, PepsiCo UK; Mike Cross, Ninah Consulting; Ruth Taylor, Millward Brown; Kate Osborne, OMD
Credited companies: Creative Agency: Abbott Mead Vickers BBDO; Media Agency: OMD UK; PR Agency: Freud; Research Agency: Millward Brown; Marketing Services: Ninah; Client: PepsiCo Walkers

### Editor's summary

While the years preceding 2008 had provided strong return on marketing investment for Walkers, produced from well-loved, famous advertising, Walkers were dissatisfied with just being good; they wanted to be great. A model for communications was developed that sought to achieve higher levels of consumer engagement, that would spark greater buzz and excitement around the brand and that in turn would lead to improved marketing return on investment. Through the six campaigns that followed this model's development, the return on investment for Walkers communication increased by 62% in four years.

This paper is a must read for anyone whose clients want to build deeper relationships with consumers. It is not clear how Walkers use their database of captured names yet but it is abundantly clear that strong campaign ideas and a sustained strategy for actively involving customers has resulted in a successful campaign which genuinely integrates and leverages paid, earned and owned media.

## A few words to begin

Good is the enemy of great.

While the years preceding 2008 had provided strong return on marketing investment for Walkers, produced from famous advertising, we were dissatisfied with just being good; we wanted to be great.

We developed a model for communications that sought to achieve high levels of consumer engagement, that would spark greater buzz and excitement around the brand and that in turn would lead to improved marketing return on investment.

Through the six campaigns that followed this model's development, we have increased the return on investment for Walkers communication by 62%.

This paper demonstrates that in the space of four years, Walkers went from being good, to being great.

## You can always do better

Throughout the 50-year history of Walkers crisps, and present within all their product innovation and marketing activity, there has always been a focus on the key drivers in the crisp category, namely taste (which is highly correlated to flavour) and quality (Figure 1).

Figure 1: Taste and quality are key category drivers

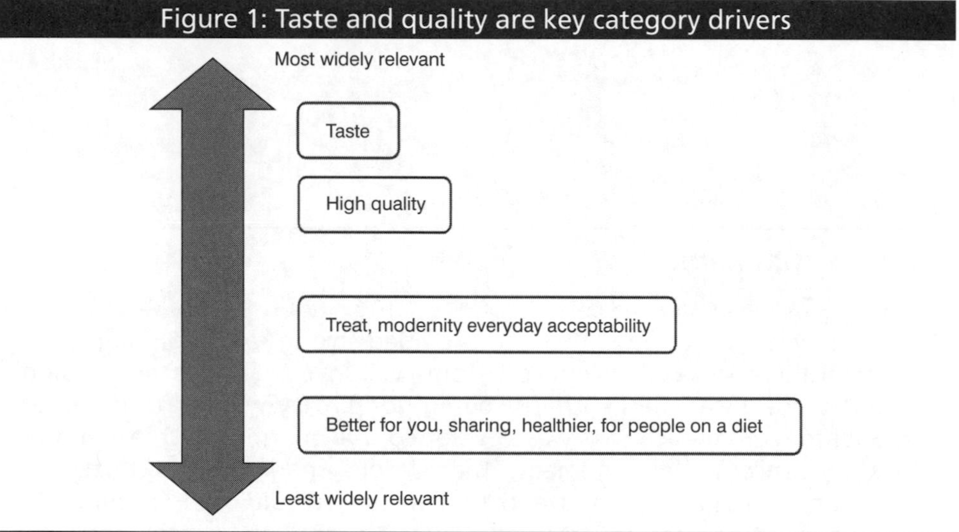


Source: Millward Brown, July 2007

The marketing campaigns centring on Walkers' great new flavours and quality messages were famous. The Gary Lineker advertising had formed an iconic part of British advertising lore. The campaigns were big, fun, and very successful (Figure 2).

As reported in the 2002 IPA paper 'Staying loyal to Lineker', campaigns in the early 2000s were achieving impressive return on investment.[1]

Looking more recently from 2006–2008, the marketing returns on investment for Walkers campaigns were still doing consistently well. The average TV profit return

Figure 2: Classic Walkers advertising, the 1995 'Welcome home' TV ad

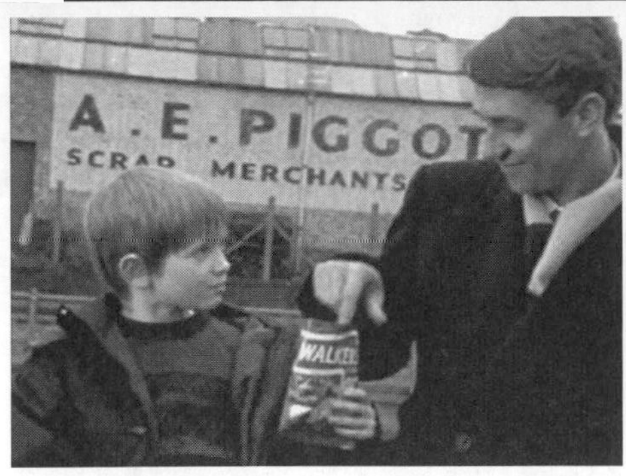

on investment was in line with other FMCG brands, paying back at average levels for a brand of its size (over £500m in annual brand value) (Figure 3).

Figure 3: Walkers campaigns 2006–2008 TV profit ROI at expected levels

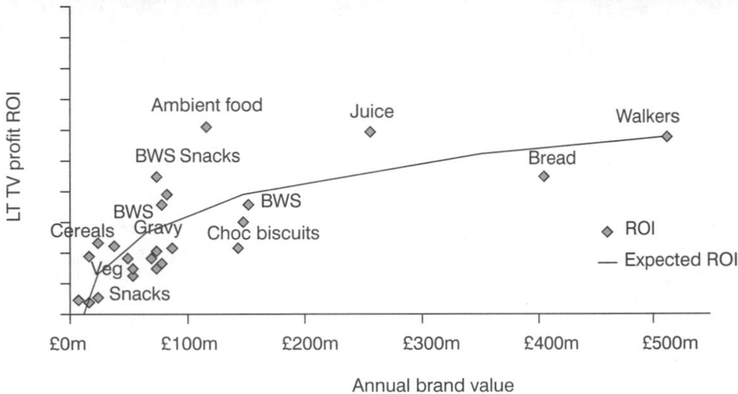


Source: Ninah[2]

So we were doing well.

But believed we could do better.

Having seen the success of the early Gary campaigns, neither PepsiCo UK nor the agencies who worked on the advertising and marketing were content.

None of us were satisfied with being average.

## Looking beyond the surface

We needed to find out why we were only performing averagely.

With such a popular, well-known, long running advertising campaign, we thought that consumers would love us just as much as they always had done.

But our research suggested something quite different.

Consumers did still love Walkers, but they had grown *too* familiar with us. We were no longer the exciting lover – we were the taken-for-granted long-term married partner. We were seen as predictable. We had become a bit stale (Figure 4).

Figure 4: Qualitative research which showed Walkers had become 'predictable'

**Walkers is still loved but is more long term married partner than exciting lover!**

*Taken for granted*
*Comfortable familiarity*
*Stopped noticing the great things about them*

And there are temptations out there!

I don't really eat them, the flavours don't appeal to me.
Female rejecter

Walkers are my usual choice, but sometimes I like the more adventurous crisps.
Female in repertoire

I like to have Kettle chips nowadays, I put them in a bowl, they just look and taste a little different to normal crisps.
Female lapsed

If you walked into a newsagent and they didn't have cheese and onion Walkers it wouldn't be right.
Female in repertoire

Walkers just haven't changed for years. There are more modern, stronger flavours now.
Male lapsed

I prefer more exciting crisps, but you couldn't not have them as you would be bored with the alternatives.
Female in repertoire

I was an addict but I'm growing out of them, I moved on and they're not enticing me back.
Male lapsed

Source: Flamingo 2007

## All about us

This finding led to one of those observations that can be hard to face up to: we had become a bit too fond of our own voice.

Through the Gary Lineker TV campaign we had created our own world of Walkers. It was a colourful, funny and entertaining world, and we invited TV viewers to visit. But the invitation was only for 30 seconds at a time, just enough time to tell them what we wanted to tell them.

We had become predictable. We had become a little too wrapped up in ourselves. We had avoided the simple truth that to sustain any good relationship, you need not only to do the talking, but must let the other person speak once in a while.

It was this realisation that helped us develop our communications challenge: to make consumers feel like they wanted to become involved with Walkers.

## Opening up

By opening up our brand to involve consumers, we believed we could re-excite the British public and we could set the conditions for growing sales.

A joint piece of research by Harvard Business School and Yale School of Management shows that if a brand is able to create word of mouth or 'buzz' among consumers, it can in turn lead to improved sales returns.

> *Using field data, we empirically demonstrate for the first time, to our knowledge that [a] firm can create WOM [word of mouth] that drives sales.*
>
> Godes and Mayzlin, 'Firm-Created Word of Mouth Communication: Evidence from a Field Test', 2007

With this in mind, our first step was to get a quantitative read on the buzz generated by the Walkers brand. We added a new tracking metric to PepsiCo's monthly tracking study, which would provide a reading on the buzz and excitement consumers attributed to the brand.

The results chimed with the qualitative findings; only 7% of people (who had heard of Walkers) agreed that Walkers had a buzz or excitement about them. This was a sobering thought (Table 1).

**Table 1: Brand tracking metric: 'Have a buzz or excitement about them'**

| Millward Brown image statements (monthly) | Jan 08 |
|---|---|
| Have a buzz or excitement about them | 7% |

Source: Millward Brown monthly tracker, image statement 'Have a buzz or excitement about them'.
Base: 280

## Our goal

*To improve marketing and advertising return on investment – to go from good to great.*

And we believed that if we could foster a better relationship with consumers, involving them in a surprising and exciting way, this would lead to buzz around the brand (no more 'Mr Predictable'), and that through this combination we would achieve improved marketing return on investment for Walkers (no more 'Mr Average').

This was our model (Figure 5).

**Figure 5: Model for communication**

Participation → Buzz → Sales return

While the idea of participation was an emerging trend of the time, we were determined to do it in a uniquely Walkers way. We would engage the masses, not the niche, and use that engagement to drive return on investment, rather than simply for engagement's sake.

We embarked on a new model of communications that was to guide subsequent campaigns. Each was engineered to drive participation in different ways and each had its own internal dynamics. Taken as a whole, they have transformed Walkers' return on investment.

In the following sections of the paper, we will go on to explain how each of the campaigns worked to meet these objectives and utilised this new model for communication. However, due to reasons of confidentiality we will not be able to release individual sales results or return on investment figures for each campaign; rather we will show the overall effect that this shift in communications has had on Walkers' marketing and advertising return on investment over the course of four years.

The six campaigns that were responsible for driving the increase in return on investment, each built on the previous idea, each including Gary Lineker TV ads, but each went much further in inviting mass participation (Table 2).

**Table 2: The six campaigns**

| Phases | Date | Campaigns |
|---|---|---|
| 1 | July 2008 | Do us a flavour – engage the nation in creating a new Walkers flavour |
| 2 | March 2010 | Sandwich – engage the nation in choosing Walkers for lunch |
| 3 | May 2010 | Flavour Cup – engage the nation in crowning the world champion flavour |
| 4 | October 2010 | Rainy Day – engage the nation in Walkers British potato provenance |
| 5 | February 2011 | Clash of the comics – engage the nation in Walkers support of Comic Relief |
| 6 | February 2012 | What's that flavour? – engage the nation in guessing Walkers' mystery flavours |

The combined effect of the shift, based on the Walkers campaigns outlined in this paper, has been an increase in the average return on investment from Walkers communication by 62%, taking an already successful and profitable advertising model into best in class (Figure 6).

Figure 6: Walkers' ROI increased by 62% (excluding production costs) post 'Do us a flavour'

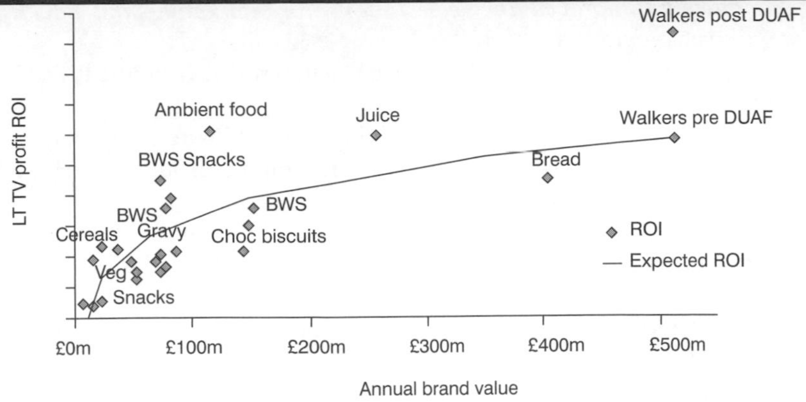

Source: Walkers post DUAF (including Do us a flavour, Sandwich, Flavour Cup, Rainy Day, Clash of the Comics, What's that flavour) vs. pre DUAF (Walkers campaigns 2006–2008) (Ninah)

## The moment of truth

In 2008, we received a brief to talk about Walkers' great flavours.

At first, we were somewhat despondent; this was a brief like so many from Walkers advertising gone by. Back in the old days, the campaign would have been relatively straightforward, most likely 30 seconds of Gary magic, but from everything we had learned, while that might have produced good results, we were looking for great.

So we challenged ourselves to produce something different, something that would respond to the brief (to excite the public about Walkers' flavour), but importantly, that utilised our new model and spoke to people in a way that they wouldn't expect.

Our solution was the 'Do us a flavour' campaign (Figure 7).

## Phase one: July 2008

Figure 7: 'Do us a flavour'

*The 'Do us a flavour' marketing, advertising and PR, reflects a big turning point for Walkers, one that has influenced the last four years of our marketing model and dramatically improved the expectations for marketing and advertising return on investment.*

Tim Warner, Director of Insights, PepsiCo UK

For the first time in the brand's history, Walkers would invite consumers to be part of its business. In this instance, to be part of the brand's product development, to help create the next great Walkers flavour.

'Do us a flavour' was brought to life in three simple phases and ended with one lucky winner who would take home £50,000 and 1% future sales of their winning flavour (Figure 8).

Figure 8: 'Do us a flavour' campaign phasing

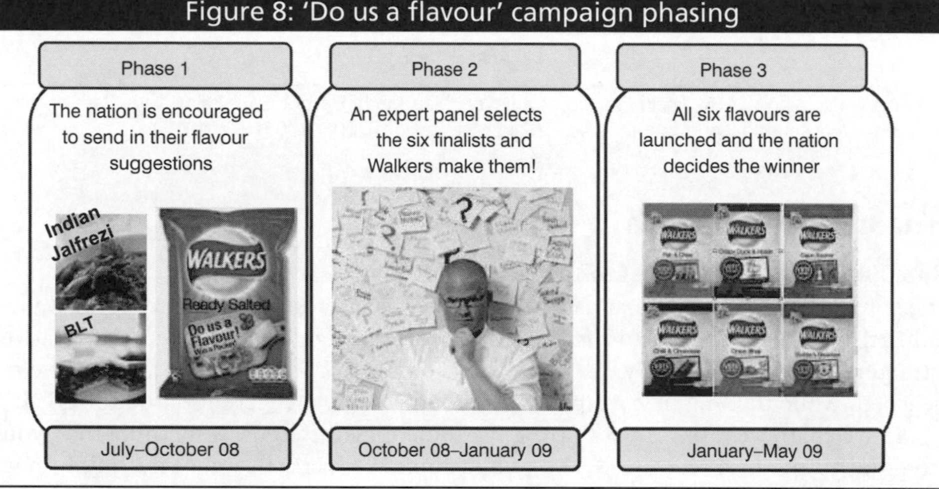
Phase 1
The nation is encouraged to send in their flavour suggestions
Indian Jalfrezi
BLT
WALKERS
Ready Salted
Do us a Flavour!
July–October 08
Phase 2
An expert panel selects the six finalists and Walkers make them!
October 08–January 09
Phase 3
All six flavours are launched and the nation decides the winner
January–May 09

In order for these phases to be followed, PepsiCo factories had to create quick turnaround new flavours, which brought the public's suggestions to life. This was a novel exercise for PepsiCo and one not to be underestimated for its complexity. It usually takes six to nine months to develop a new flavour, but for this campaign the factories made the six limited edition flavours in three months.

The 'Do us a flavour' idea was designed to engage consumers over a period of months, with a simplistic structure and a realistic expectation of consumer participation. At each stage, participation was encouraged with a combination of multiple media touch points, advertising and PR. At first this occurred when people created and sent in their flavour suggestions, then secondly, when the public purchased the new varieties and voted for their favourite finalist (Figure 9).

Figure 9: 'Do us a flavour' media mix

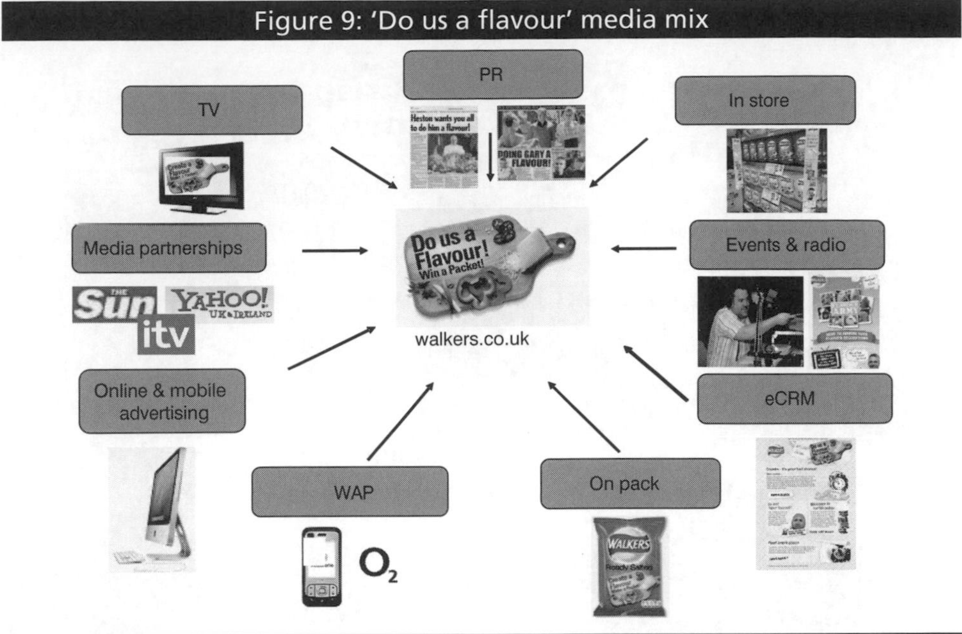


*Results*

## Participation

We had challenged ourselves to communicate flavour in an exciting, surprising way, and for the first time, to encourage consumer participation within Walkers' business.

The public's response surpassed all expectations. While consumer involvement was not new to advertising, we had achieved something that few brands had in 2008, a *mass* engagement campaign (Table 3).

Table 3: 'Do us a flavour' key participation results, 2008/2009

| Key participation metric | 'Do us a flavour' result |
|---|---|
| Flavour entries | 1,200,000 |
| Votes | 1,100,000 |
| Site views | 4,300,000 |

Source: PepsiCo UK

## Buzz

The extremely positive PR results for the campaign indicate that we had gone some way to create buzz for Walkers (Figure 10 and Table 4).

Figure 10: 'Do us a flavour' press cuttings

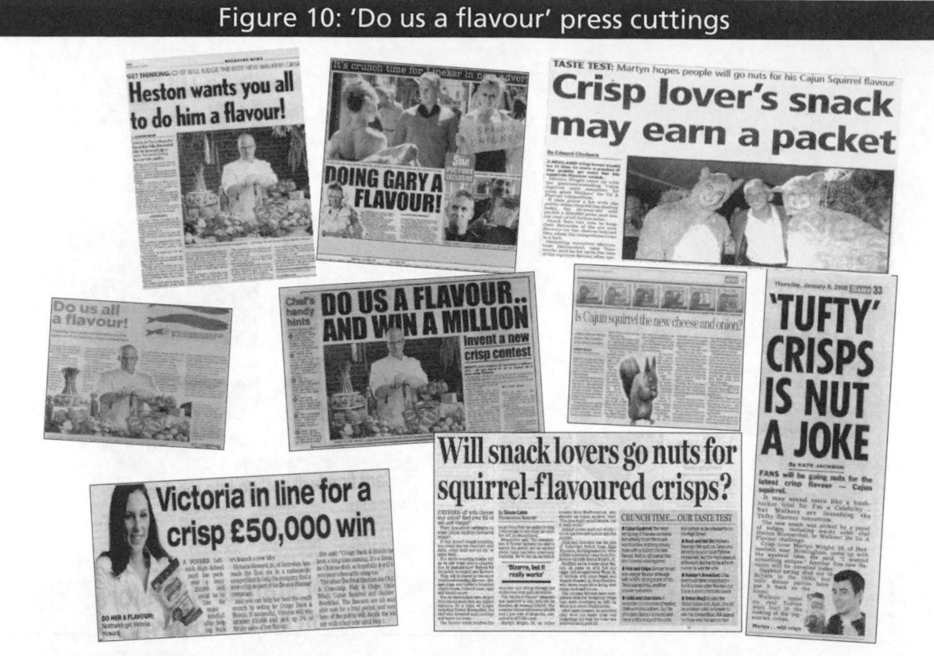
Heston wants you all to do him a flavour!

DOING GARY A FLAVOUR!

TASTE TEST: Martyn hopes people will go nuts for his Cajun Squirrel flavour

Crisp lover's snack may earn a packet

Do us all a flavour!

DO US A FLAVOUR.. AND WIN A MILLION

Invent a new crisp contest

Is Cajun squirrel the new cheese and onion?

'TUFTY' CRISPS IS NUT A JOKE

Will snack lovers go nuts for squirrel-flavoured crisps?

Victoria in line for a crisp £50,000 win

Table 4: 'Do us a flavour' key PR results, 2008/2009

| Key PR metric | 'Do us a flavour' result |
|---|---|
| Pieces of coverage | 724 |
| Opportunity to see | 432,000,000 |
| PR value | £6,500,000 |

Source: Freud

The 'Do us a flavour' campaign has had success not only in the UK, but it has gone on to be replicated with 14 global iterations and two more in progress. Imposed on none, the campaign has been sought out by PepsiCo marketing teams worldwide. Individual campaign results have been very positive, and an indication of the overall success that the communications model developed by Walkers has had are the total levels of consumer participation achieved from the numerous campaigns around the world (Figure 11).

## Phase two: March 2010

The 'Sandwich' campaign, which launched in March 2010, centred on communicating a taste message tied to the lunchtime occasion (Figure 12).

Figure 11: Total number of entries (7,295,042) and votes (18,857,111) from 14 countries running 'Do us a flavour' campaign, 2008–2012

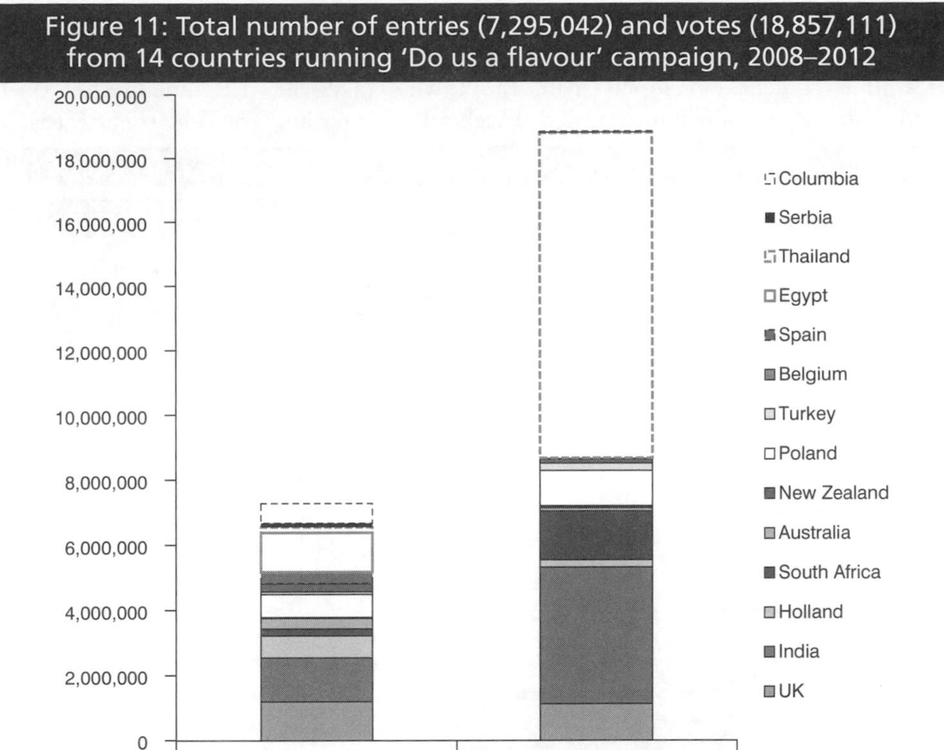


Source: PepsiCo

Figure 12: 'Sandwich'

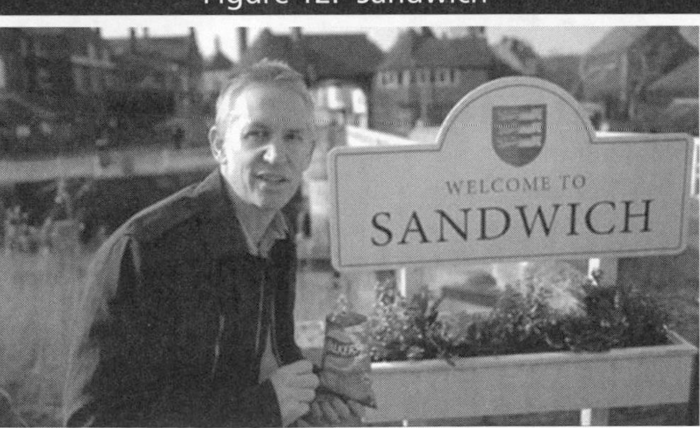


The idea was to prove Walkers can make *any* sandwich more exciting, even the town of Sandwich, Kent. Through a series of surprise celebrity-led events, we turned the sleepy town into the most exciting town in Britain. Timely distribution of content from the events then created a sustained buzz nationwide.

Consumer participation here involved the Sandwich locals posting user-generated content, and chiefly encouraging the wider public to interact with the vast amount of online content developed from the town's takeover. This manifested itself predominantly via social media, with Facebook, Twitter and YouTube (Figure 13).

Figure 13: 'Sandwich' campaign phasing

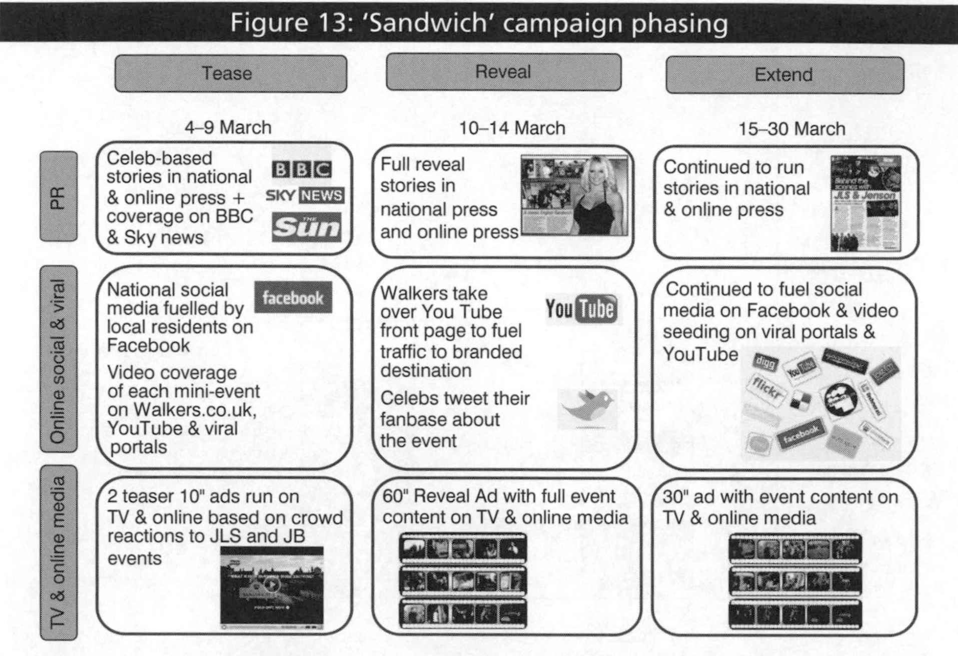


## *Results*

### Participation

The key metrics measuring the levels of consumer engagement for the campaign were extremely positive. With the majority of the content viewed on YouTube, there was in total 1.7 million video views. Furthermore, the 'walkerssandwich' YouTube channel became the #1 most viewed sponsored channel in the UK in March (Table 5).

Table 5: 'Sandwich' key participation results, 2010

| Key participation metric | 'Sandwich' result |
|---|---|
| Video views | 1,700,000 |
| Social media mentions | 2,641 |
| Site views | 285,000 |

Source: PepsiCo UK

Buzz

Of key importance for the activity was for the campaign to be picked up by journalists, which would in turn help influence retailers and sales teams. The campaign worked as intended with hundreds of pieces of PR coverage which equated to £2.7m in value (Figure 14 and Table 6).

Figure 14: 'Sandwich' press cuttings

Table 6: 'Sandwich' key PR results, 2010

| Key PR metric | 'Sandwich' result |
|---|---|
| Pieces of coverage | 302 |
| Opportunity to see | 80,999,000 |
| PR value | £2,776,209 |

Source: Freud

## Phase three: May 2010

It was a daunting task following the success of 'Do us a flavour' with our next flavour campaign, yet with the knowledge we had learned and the results we had garnered, we felt we were in a strong position to create a successful sequel.

In May 2010, the 'Flavour Cup' launched. The campaign was inspired by the approaching World Cup and again had consumer participation at its heart. The idea was to find the world's greatest crisp flavour by staging the Walkers Flavour Cup in which 15 flavours competed to be crowned the world champion crisp (Figure 15).

The campaign involved the creation of 15 new flavours; this was more than double the number launched under 'Do us a flavour', and the biggest ever in the category's history.

Consumer engagement was encouraged via the campaign's two phases (Figure 16).

Figure 15: 'Flavour Cup'

Figure 16: 'Flavour cup' campaign phasing

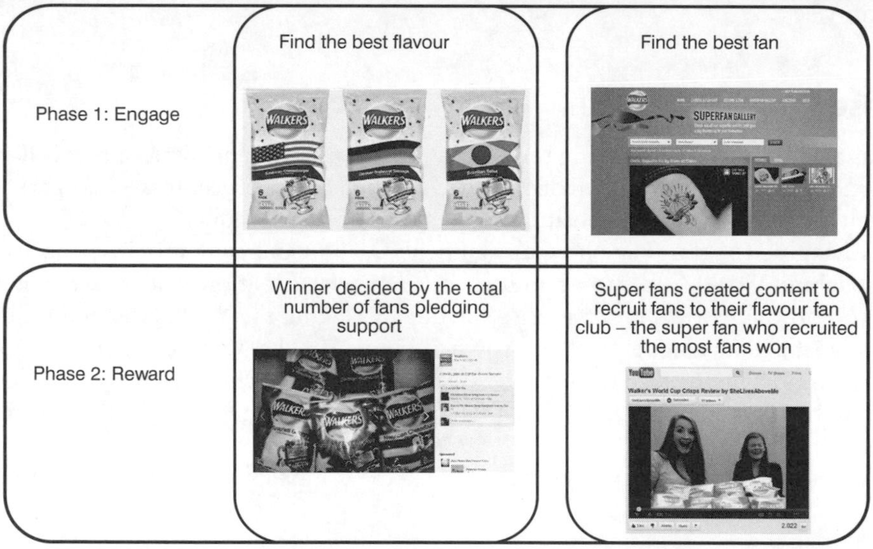

| | | |
|---|---|---|
| Phase 1: Engage | Find the best flavour | Find the best fan |
| Phase 2: Reward | Winner decided by the total number of fans pledging support | Super fans created content to recruit fans to their flavour fan club – the super fan who recruited the most fans won |

## *Results*

### Participation

While we may have been competing with the Fifa football World Cup, Walkers' 'Flavour Cup' held its own in terms of engagement. With no entries or votes, the currency of the participation here was primarily recruiting fans, but also user-generated content posts and views of the campaign website (Table 7).

**Table 7: 'Flavour cup' key participation results, 2010**

| Key participation metric | 'Flavour Cup' result |
|---|---|
| Flavour fans | 667,829 |
| User-generated content | 7,300 |
| Site views | 1,058,732 |

Source: PepsiCo UK

### Buzz

PR played a pivotal role in the campaign, firstly, by setting up the launch of the competition and then, secondly, revealing the results (Figure 17 and Table 8).

**Figure 17: 'Flavour cup' press cuttings**

Table 8: 'Flavour cup' key PR results, 2010

| Key PR metric | 'Flavour Cup' result |
|---|---|
| Pieces of coverage | 230 |
| Opportunity to see | 212,573,000 |
| PR value | £3,059,334 |

Source: Freud

## Phase four: October 2010

Walkers 'Rainy Day', which launched in October 2010, represented a different take on consumer participation than the preceding campaigns. The brief for the campaign was also a departure from the previous communications; rather than flavour, there was need to deliver against the other key driver in the category: 'quality'. Specifically, we needed to communicate the fact that Walkers use only British potatoes in their crisps.

This key message, while we knew to be motivating with regard to the product, was not the most exciting, so again we challenged ourselves to create a mass engagement campaign that brought excitement and surprise to the British public.

Based on the old insight, that Brits are obsessed with the weather, the idea was to invite consumers to play a game with us, to bet on the rain. 'Rainy Day' encouraged people to tell us where they thought it was next going to rain, and if they were right, Walkers would give them a tenner (Figure 18).

Figure 18: 'Rainy day'

It involved a three-stage process (Figure 19).

Figure 19: 'Rainy day' campaign mechanic

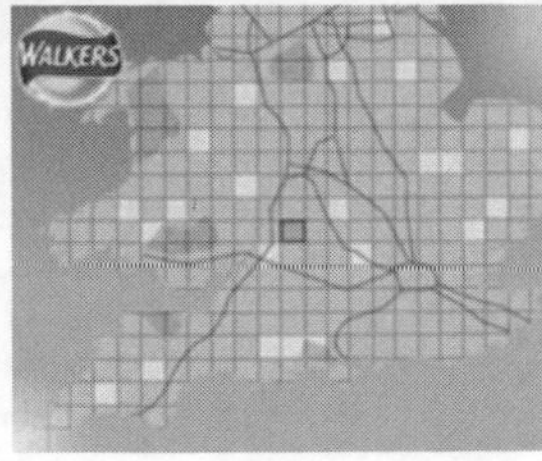

| | | |
|---|---|---|
| 1. Go to walkers.co.uk and input a code from any pack of Walkers. | 2. Get one prediction on where and when in Britain you think it's going to rain. Pick a square. Every square is unique; once that square is 'taken' for that day (say, West St Albans on 14 October) it's yours. | 3. Come back in a couple of days and check if you predicted correctly. The results are verified by the Met office data and winners receive a £10 cheque through the post from Walkers (signed by Gary Lineker!). |

## *Results*

### Participation

The unique consumer proposition that had been created for 'Rainy Day', encouraging people to bet on the rain, proved extremely popular; so much so, that the campaign took more bets than the Grand National that year (Table 9).

Table 9: 'Rainy day' key participation results, 2010

| Key participation metric | 'Rainy Day' result |
|---|---|
| Rain predictions | 828,000 |
| Registered accounts | 65,000 |
| Site views | 2,500,000 |

Source: PepsiCo UK

### Buzz

Betting on the rain seemed to have become a national craze. The campaign featured on the BBC's Watchdog programme, and the website moneysavingexpert.com advised its readers to act quickly and pick their square before they all ran out. The campaign was even the subject of articles by Cambridge University professors advising readers about how to improve their chances of winning (Figure 20 and Table 10).

Figure 20: 'Rainy day' press cuttings

Brand in the news Walkers

STRICTLY DUMB DANCING GARY

IT'S GARY LINEDANCER

Gary puts vest foot forward

With odds like these the money's in the bag

MoneySavingExpert.com

Gary's smoky Bacon

Table 10: 'Rainy day' key participation results, 2010

| Key PR metric | 'Rainy Day' result |
|---|---|
| Pieces of coverage | 402 |
| Opportunity to see | 103,431,000 |
| PR value | £1,444,333 |

Source: Freud

## Phase five: February 2011

To support Comic Relief's Red Nose Day and produce a campaign that would communicate Walkers' great flavours, 'Clash of the Comics' was developed in February 2011. It was a new flavour promotion that saw four of Britain's best loved comedians, Stephen Fry, Jimmy Carr, Al Murray and Frank Skinner go head to head in a comedic battle to ensure their limited edition Walkers flavour became the bestseller (Figure 21).

The focus of the idea went a step further than previous engagement efforts. For this campaign consumers could vote for their comedian of choice by buying a pack, and then get behind their favourite by showing their support online via social media. Consumers could watch content from the comedic quartet and, finally, see the forfeits of the unlucky runners-up on Comic Relief night via a podcast (Figure 22).

Figure 21: 'Clash of the comics'

Figure 22: 'Clash of the comics' campaign phasing

LAUNCH  ENGAGE  REVEAL

| LAUNCH | ENGAGE | REVEAL |
|---|---|---|
| Launched 4 new flavours backed by Britain's favourite comedians to raise money for Comic Relief | As the comedians battled it out, consumers supported their favourites and sabotaged the competition | It all culminated with three embarrassing public forfeits on Comic Relief night |

## *Results*

### Participation

As well as generating over 250,000 views on YouTube and over 200,000 podcast downloads, the campaign also raised over a £1m for Comic Relief (Table 11).

Table 11: 'Clash of the comics' key participation results, 2011

| Key participation metric | 'Clash of the comics' result |
|---|---|
| YouTube views | 263,055 |
| Podcast downloads | 207,341 |
| Site views | 341,212 |

Source: PepsiCo UK

### Buzz

With nearly 250 million opportunities to see, the campaign produced the largest PR value of all the Walkers campaigns in recent years with a worth of just under £5.3m (Figure 23 and Table 12).

Figure 23: 'Clash of the comics' press cuttings

Walkers holds comedian battle for Comic Relief

Mail Online

Do they taste funny? Jimmy Carr

STEAK & AL CRISPS

Comic flavours are a

Mirror 3am

Comics' Crisp Clash For Comic Relief

Jimmy Carr, Al Murray and Frank Skinner get waxed as Stephen Fry is crowned King of Crisps - pictures

Table 12: 'Clash of the comics' key PR results, 2011

| Key PR metric | 'Clash of the comics' result |
|---|---|
| Pieces of coverage | 932 |
| Opportunity to see | 248,511,010 |
| PR value | £5,295,923 |

Source: Freud

## Phase six: February 2012

The most recent campaign to benefit from the communications model developed with 'Do us a flavour' was 'What's that flavour'. The campaign, which launched in February 2012, was designed to spark a national flavour debate with the launch of three new mystery flavours inspired by ingredients and recipes loved by the Great British public.

Consumers were given the chance to bag three £50,000 prizes if they correctly identified the mystery flavour names. They were launched as Mystery Flavour A (Sour Cream and Spring Onion), Mystery Flavour B (Lincolnshire Sausage and Brown Sauce) and Mystery Flavour C (Birmingham Chicken Balti), with the real flavours revealed at a later date (Figure 24).

Figure 24: 'What's this flavour?'

The public's debate itself took place online via Facebook, Twitter, blogs and the campaign's microsite (Figure 25).

Figure 25: 'What's that flavour' campaign phasing

| 1 Buy & Try | 2 Guess & join the flavour conversation | 3 The flavours are revealed |
|---|---|---|
|  |  |  |
| | - Through mobile or online<br>- No code required<br>- Unlimited entries | - Revealed packs released<br>- Prize draw for each flavour<br>- Each winner drawn wins £50K |



*Results*

## Participation

Only running for 11 weeks, 'What's that flavour' achieved consumer engagement figures that outperformed any other Walkers campaign over a comparable period. The campaign recorded nearly 800,000 guesses and over 1.8 million web sessions (Table 13).

| Key participation metric | 'What's that flavour' result |
|---|---|
| Flavour guesses | 793, 011 |
| Likes on Facebook | +127,597 |
| Site views | 1,812,417 |

Table 13: 'What's that flavour' key participation results, 2012

Source: PepsiCo UK

## Buzz

The challenge of uncovering the three different flavours generated a lot of excitement among the British public; then with clues being leaked out and the winners revealed, the campaign was able to generate strong PR results (Figure 26 and Table 14).

Figure 26: 'What's that flavour' press cuttings

DAILY STAR

NEWS SPORT BABES CELEBRITY TV LIVING REVIEW

A SPICY MOMENT FOR GARY LINEKER

A spicy moment for Gaz

What's That Flavour

LOTTO WINNER GIVES MATE £1MILLION

A fam bid in a box when I was moving!

10 METRO Friday, January 20, 2012

Lineker is flavour of the month

GARY LINEKER has always had a cheesy grin – now here's the proof. A gastronomic portrait of the former footballer, 51, has been made from 72 pieces of cheese, 31 packets of mushrooms, 16 aubergines and 28 blueberry punnets. Prudence Staite's work of art helped to launch a new 'mystery flavour' campaign for Walkers crisps.

| Key PR metric | 'What's that flavour' result |
|---|---|
| Pieces of coverage | 168 |
| Opportunity to see | 104,028,000 |
| PR value | £2, 067,436 |

Table 14: 'What's that flavour' key PR results, 2012

Source: Freud

## The long-term effect

At the beginning of this paper we outlined our goal, namely:

To improve marketing and advertising return on investment – to go from good to great.

We set out to achieve this by nurturing a more involving relationship with consumers; to generate participation and create buzz around the brand.

Through our explanations of the individual campaigns, we have provided some evidence of success against these aims, but in the next section of the paper we will go on to prove the long-term effects which have arisen from the shift in communications that took place with the 'Do us a flavour' campaign.

### *1. To nurture a more involving relationship with consumers – to generate participation*

For the years up to 2008, aside from the promotional mechanics of some campaigns, we had created 'push' style communications.

To readdress this focus, we created a new communications model that set about to engage and involve consumers with Walkers in an unexpected way and, importantly, on a mass scale.

Since 2008, millions of people have been involved in Walkers campaigns; they've chosen new crisp recipes, viewed the takeover of an entire town, uploaded content to garner support for their favourite world flavour, bet on the rain, supported a British comic and guessed a mystery. In the last four years we have exceeded our expectations for creating mass engagement.

While it is not possible to quantify the varying engagement metrics for the campaigns, as each idea had differing ways to encourage participation, we are able to provide an indication of the cumulative results with one measure. In total, for the six campaigns, Walkers have had over 10,000,000 views of the campaigns' online destination (e.g. site, microsite, branded social media page) (Table 15).[3]

**Table 15: Campaign online destination views, 2008–2012**

| | Do us a flavour | Sandwich | Flavour Cup | Rainy Day | Clash of the comics | What's that flavour | Total |
|---|---|---|---|---|---|---|---|
| Views | 4,300,000 | 285,000 | 1,058,732 | 2,500,000 | 341,212 | 1,812,417 | 10,297,361 |

Source: PepsiCo UK

### *To create buzz around the brand*

We had become increasingly aware of the importance of being able to create buzz and excitement with our campaigns, to firmly distance ourselves from being predictable and dull.

PR has helped deliver this. In total, for the six campaigns, there have been nearly 3,000 pieces of content, over a billion opportunities to see and a total PR value of over £20m (Table 16).

Table 16: Campaigns 2008–2012 key PR results

| Campaign | PR value | OTS | Pieces of coverage |
|---|---|---|---|
| 'Do us a flavour' | £6,500,000 | 432,000,000 | 724 |
| 'Sandwich' | £2,776,209 | 80,999,000 | 302 |
| 'Flavour Cup' | £3,059,334 | 212,573,000 | 230 |
| 'Rainy Day' | £1,444,333 | 103,431,000 | 402 |
| 'Clash of the comics' | £5,295,923 | 248,511,010 | 932 |
| 'Mystery flavour' | £2,067,436 | 104,028,000 | 168 |
| Total | £21,143,235 | 1,181,542,010 | 2758 |

Source: Freud

The result of campaigns with such high levels of involvement and impressive PR results has meant dramatic improvements in consumer perceptions of the brand.

From the time the metric 'Have a buzz or excitement about them' was introduced in January 2008 and looking at the data on a monthly basis up until March 2012, there has been a vast improvement, a 114% increase in just over four years, with scores rising from 7% to 15% (Figure 27).

Figure 27: Brand tracking metric: 'Have a buzz or excitement about them'

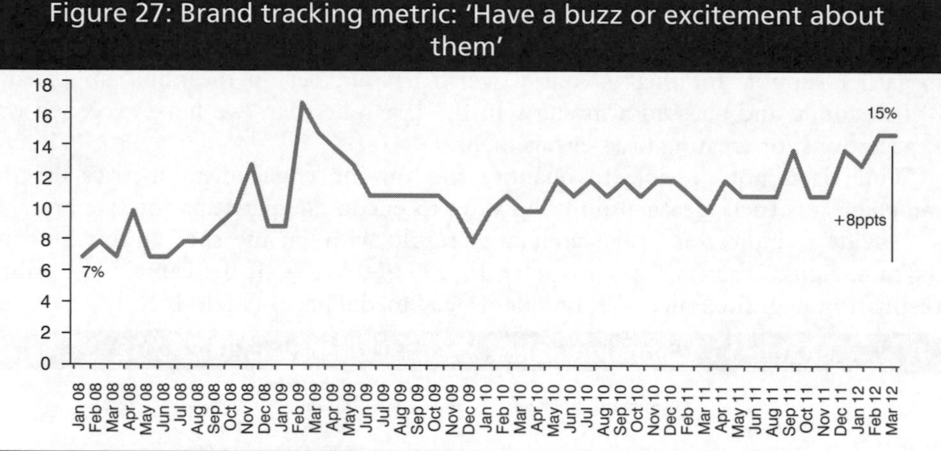


Source: Millward Brown monthly tracking data 2008-2012 'Have a buzz or excitement about them'

In fact, according to TalkTrack/Keller Fay data, Walkers remains the most talked about crisp brand in the UK. On an average day, Walkers is mentioned 173 times with 123 comments being positive (71%); this equates to 500% more mentions than Pringles.

Looking at BrandIndex data, online buzz (where 'buzz' is defined as 'hearing something positive/negative about the brand, whether in the news, through advertising, or talking to friends and family') for Walkers has also grown since 2008, with the overall number of positive Walkers mentions vs. 2008 increasing.

Table 17 displays this improvement, yet due to a methodology change in 2009 there is a jump in figures from 2009–2010. This has been normalised to allow for a comparison between the years.

Table 17: Online buzz for Walkers vs. category 2007–2011

Normalised for change

| | 2007 | 2008 | 2009 | 2010 | 2011 |
|---|---|---|---|---|---|
| Standard index score (annual avg.) | 27 | 28 | 33 | 40 | 39 |
| Category positive buzz | | 12,132 | 11,969 | 19,543 | 18,973 |
| | | | | 63% | |
| Walkers positive buzz (old methodology) | | 3,238 | 3,406 | | |
| Walkers positive buzz (2010 normalised for methodology change) | | | | 3,396 | 3,363 |
| Walkers positive buzz (new methodology) | | | | 5,390 | 5,338 |
| Year-on-year change % vs. 2008 | | | 5.17% | 4.86% | 3.84% |
| Share of category buzz | | 27% | 28% | 28% | 28% |

Source: BrandIndex[4]

The qualitative research which has taken place throughout the last four years has suggested Walkers has become anything but predictable.

> *It's clear from consumer responses in our research that the Walkers brand is now viewed as one that brings enjoyable, surprising and rewarding communication ideas to life on a regular basis. Consumers have grown to think of it not just as their staple brand of everyday crisps, but almost as a contemporary entertainment brand in its own right.*
>
> Roger McKerr, Qualitative Researcher for Walkers for five years, davies+mckerr

### *2. To improve marketing and advertising return on investment – to go from good to great*

As we have mentioned earlier in this paper, taste (correlated to flavour) and quality are key drivers of sales. Brand tracking measures, including those which relate to these drivers, have all seen significant increases since 2008 (Figure 28).

As was visible in the years leading up to the 'Do us a flavour' campaign, marketing and advertising return on investment was at average levels for a brand of its size compared to other FMCG brands, and while this was a good performance, we wanted to do better.

In order to judge accurately the true impact that the shift in the Walkers' communications model has had, it is necessary to evaluate those campaigns pre 'Do us a flavour' (2006–2008) with those post (2008–2012: 'Do us a flavour', 'Sandwich', 'Flavour Cup', 'Rainy Day', 'Clash of the Comics', 'What's that flavour'). The econometric modelling that has been completed by Ninah Consulting reveals an impressive increase in return on investment for Walkers advertising and marketing post 'Do us a flavour'.

Looking at TV profit ROI excluding production costs for the six campaigns that occurred including and post 'Do us a flavour', the increase in ROI is 62%. When production costs are included, the ROI is up by 42% (Figure 29).

Figure 28: Key brand tracking metrics

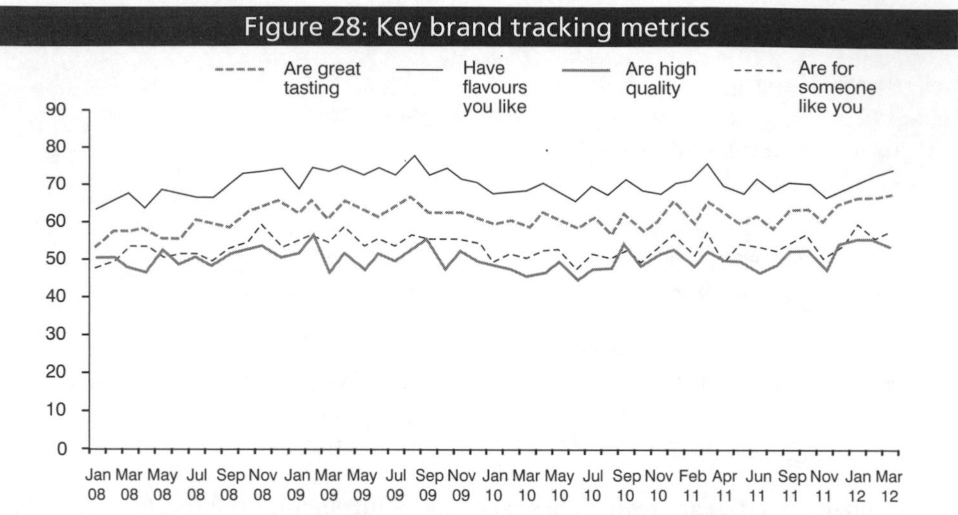


Source: Millward Brown. 'Are great tasting' (53% Jan 08–68% Mar 12). 'Have flavours you like' (63% Jan 08–74% Mar 12). 'Are high quality' (50% Jan 08–54% Mar 12). 'Are for someone like you' (48% Jan 08–57% Mar 12)

Figure 29: Walkers ROI increased by 62% (excluding production costs) post 'Do us a flavour'

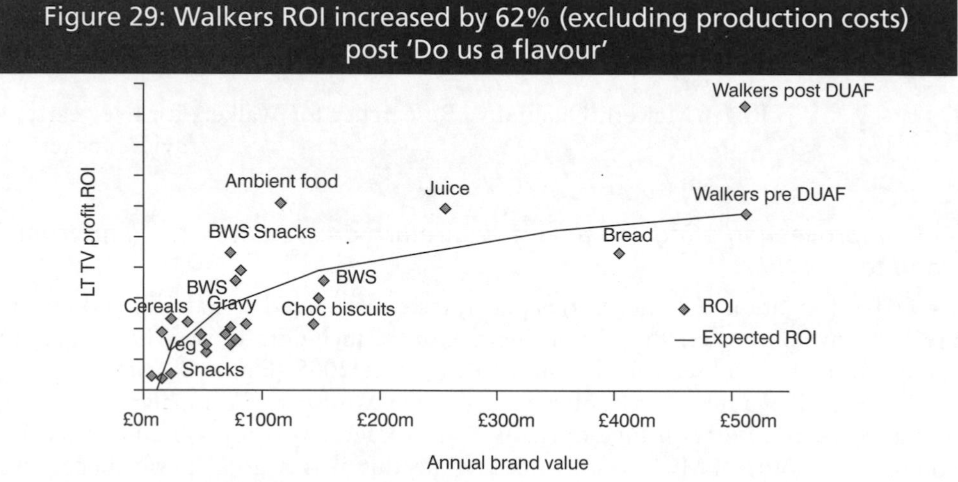


Source: Ninah. Walkers post DUAF (including Do us a flavour, Sandwich, Flavour Cup, Rainy Day, Clash of the Comics, What's that flavour) vs. pre DUAF (Walkers campaigns 2006–2008)

> *The Walkers campaign profit ROIs include the highest I have seen for an FMCG brand in my 14 years of econometric modelling.*
>
> Michael Cross, Director, Ninah Consulting

The greatly improved return on investment figures, with media spend paying back considerably better post 2008, has meant that it has been possible to reduce the average campaign budget and GRPs for the subsequent years after 'Do us a flavour'.

As well as this, the average spend per campaign has never been as high as in the first year of 'Do us a flavour' (Table 18).

**Table 18: Spend and GRPs for Walkers 2008–2011**

| Average campaign | 2008 | 2009 | 2010 | 2011 |
|---|---|---|---|---|
| GRPs | 765 | 927 | 490 | 686 |
| Spend (£000) | £1,641 | £1,469 | £1,546 | £1,555 |

Source: OMD

## Eliminating other factors

### *Was it price?*

No. During the last four years, Walkers' average price per unit actually increased. Given what we have shown in terms of the increase in marketing return on investment, it appears that advertising has more than supported this increase. This is visible in Figure 30.

### *Promotional activity?*

No. This is accounted for in the average price per unit data.

### *Was it distribution?*

No. In quantity terms, distribution has remained flat during the evaluation period. This is visible in Figure 30.

**Figure 30: Walkers core volume, price and distribution 7 July–January 2012**

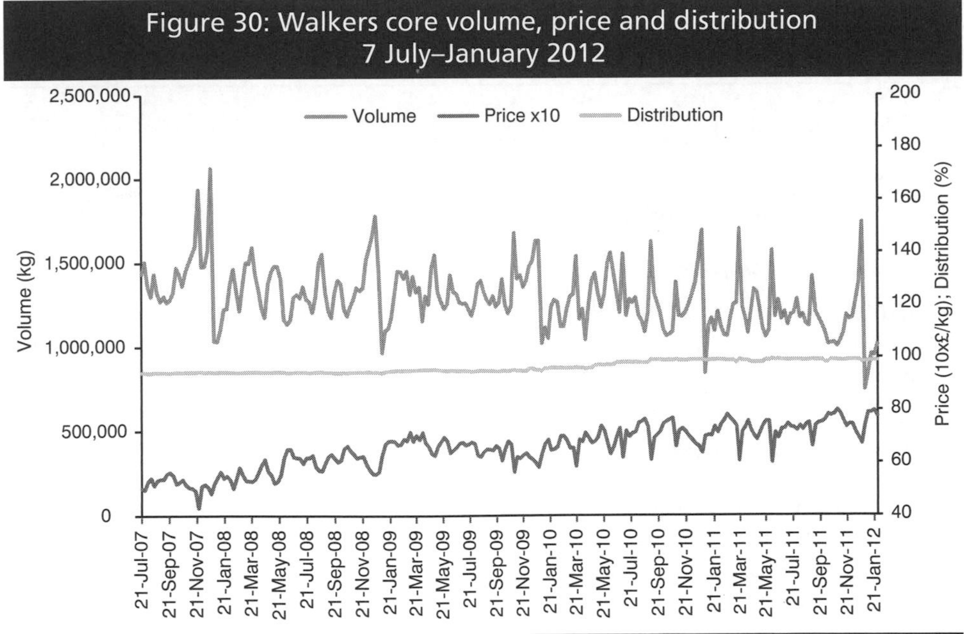


Source: Ninah

*Did Walkers benefit from weak competition?*

No. The campaigns have produced success even with the influx of numerous new competitors that have entered the market in the last four years (Figure 31).

Figure 31: Selection of the new competitors to Walkers in the snack category 2008–2012

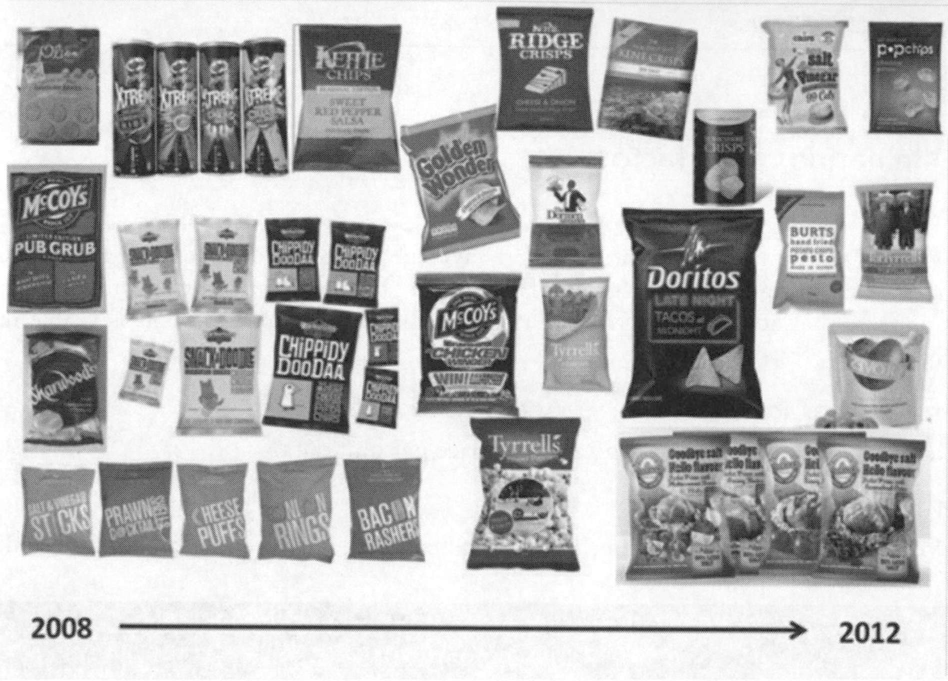


*The season?*

No. The period of measurement has been four years.

*Other Walkers campaigns?*

No. Ninah's econometric modelling has been able to strip out the impact of other successful Walkers campaigns ('Gary's Great Trips' and '3 Simple Things') that have occurred during the time of the six campaigns included in this paper.

## A few words to finish

In the run up to 2008, Walkers was in good shape with strong return on marketing investment produced from famous advertising.

Yet, we were dissatisfied with just being good; we wanted more, and after delving deeper into our understanding of the brand, we were able to find further ways to improve.

We realised that one-way communication was outdated, that engagement with consumers was far richer. That being seen as predictable was not satisfactory, that generating buzz was essential. That being at average levels for return on investment was decent, but that the brand could achieve much more.

We developed a model for communications that represented this; achieving high levels of consumer engagement would spark greater buzz and excitement around the brand and that in turn would lead to improved marketing return on investment.

In the years that followed this model's development, we have seen it put to use in several countries around the world, with the iterations of 'Do us a flavour'. We have seen it engage the British public in numerous ways, with each of the six campaigns building on the previous call for mass participation. And most importantly, we have seen it produce an increase of return on investment for Walkers communication by 62%.

## Notes

1 For details on the mentioned campaigns please refer to the 2002 IPA paper 'Walkers Crisps – Staying loyal to Lineker' by John McDonald, Bridget Angear and Peter Knowland. Institute of Practitioners in Advertising: Silver Medal, IPA Effectiveness Awards 2002.
2 The profit return on investment data in the chart exclude production costs; this has been done so it is possible to compare across other FMCG brands.
3 'Do us a flavour' achieved very high site views due to the campaign's length, around 18 months; this is considerably more than the other campaigns, such as Sandwich which ran for only one month.
4 Index = combination of all buzz metrics (buzz, reputation, quality, value, satisfaction, recommend, impression). Standard = positive minus negative excluding neutral divided by total number of responses. Brand Index category = Doritos, Kettle, Hula Hoop, McCoys, Pringle, Walkers.

## Chapter 20

# Which?

## Which? Subscriber recruitment

**By Mike Colling, Mike Colling & Co.**
Credited companies: Creative Agencies: Dare, Tangent Snowball and Watson Phillips Norman; Media Agency: Mike Colling & Co.; Marketing Agency: Summit Media; Client: Which?

**Editor's summary**

In the ten years prior to 2005, Which? had seen declining subscriber numbers. Over a six-year period, Mike Colling & Co. and Watson Phillips Norman led a three-stage interactive process, from initial direct response subscriber recruitment, to a brand uplift model, to the current fully integrated activity. Their insights drove a better understanding of the audience, a more motivating and engaging proposition, a more effective and responsive media schedule, and a more efficient journey from response to paid subscription. The campaign grew the magazine and online circulation by 52% over the six-year period, increased subscription numbers from 831,000 to more than 1.33 million in June 2011, and drove more than £64m in incremental profit.

Whilst this paper left some judges feeling that Which? were a little slow off the mark in understanding the power of the internet to disrupt their business model, the approach to this campaign is rigorous, insightful and believable. The DM rigour adds good learnings to the EASE database.

## Introduction

This is the story of rebuilding a subscriber base and defying market trends. It's a journey that has taken six years to date, and has at its heart direct marketing discipline and data insights, using advertising tools to achieve success.

In the ten years prior to 2005, Which? had seen declining subscriber numbers each year. Since then subscription numbers climbed from 831,000 to more than 1,330,000 in June 2011. Costs of acquiring a new subscriber have fallen by 44%. True return on investment has risen from 8% to an eye watering 176%.

There has been no one Damascene moment that solved all the issues facing Which?. Rather, this has been a six-year iterative process, driven by consumer insights and from the rich data sets that a direct sale brand provides.

It's not been easy. The decline of magazine circulations is well documented, but ours are up by 52% over six years. The challenge of getting consumers to pay for online content is equally well known. We have more than 250,000 paying £9.75 each month for content they use and value.

Mr Murdoch eat your heart out!

## Background

Which? is the UK's leading consumer organisation. Funding comes solely from members' paying circa £10 per month to subscribe to magazines, website and advice lines.

Which? offers reviews of products and services, providing advice on how consumers can obtain best value. Reviews are based on rigorous, independent research. Advice is truly independent, impartial and provided in a straightforward and easy to understand way.

Which? is only available via direct subscription – it's not in any retail outlets – so is totally dependent upon advertising to drive sales.

All subscriber recruitment activity is meticulously tracked and measured. The key performance metric is not cost per subscriber, but five-year net ROI, calculated as *Discounted 5 Year Expected Net Revenue – Total Recruitment Cost* divided by total recruitment costs.

Which? currently use a discount rate of 6% per annum.

## The initial challenge

In 2005 Which? recruited subscribers only via a prize draw mechanic, only communicated in direct mail, with some five million mailings each year. Response rates, ROIs and subscriber numbers had fallen from 1988 onwards.

Reliance on direct mail to a small group of prospects had caused the brand to disappear from public view.

Research highlighted that the magazine was not seen as contemporary and seen to review mostly white goods. Potential subscribers thought they could either live without the information or find it elsewhere.

Which? appointed Mike Colling & Co. and creative agency Watson Phillips Norman to turn this business performance around.

## Phase one: return to growth

### *Simple brief: reverse the long-term decline in subscribers*

Within this were three other key asks:

- Get consumers who knew the Which? brand but thought it wasn't relevant to them to reappraise it.
- Radically change the main marketing message from prize draw and replace it with brand-led messages.
- Improve marketing returns on investment.

## The initial solution

### *Four stages, each informing the next*

1. Understand who might become subscribers, and their needs and attitudes towards product research.
2. Create a new proposition, motivating enough to stimulate huge volumes of response, based on a central brand thought so that responders would stay.
3. Change the media schedule to reflect audience behaviour.
4. Change the way that consumers interact with the brand, ensuring that for as many as possible their first encounter with Which? was through a telephone conversation.

### *Step one: target market and targeting*

Which? had traditionally targeted either the profile of their current subscribers (older, male, upmarket and educated) or responders to prize draw mailings.

We set out to discover the key variables that would predict an individual's potential as a Which? subscriber.

We used TGI to identify the variables most associated with Which? subscription and found two key axes (Figure 1):

- first, a tendency to research a product/service before making a purchase;
- second, a lack of confidence in one's own research abilities.

We used these variables to create a cluster analysis, segmenting the UK adult population into eight groups.

We focused on four key groups, circa 40% of the population.

Each group had a common tendency to research products/services before buying them, and responded to Which?'s values of:

- independence;
- integrity;
- thoroughness of research.

Figure 1: Identifying a target audience

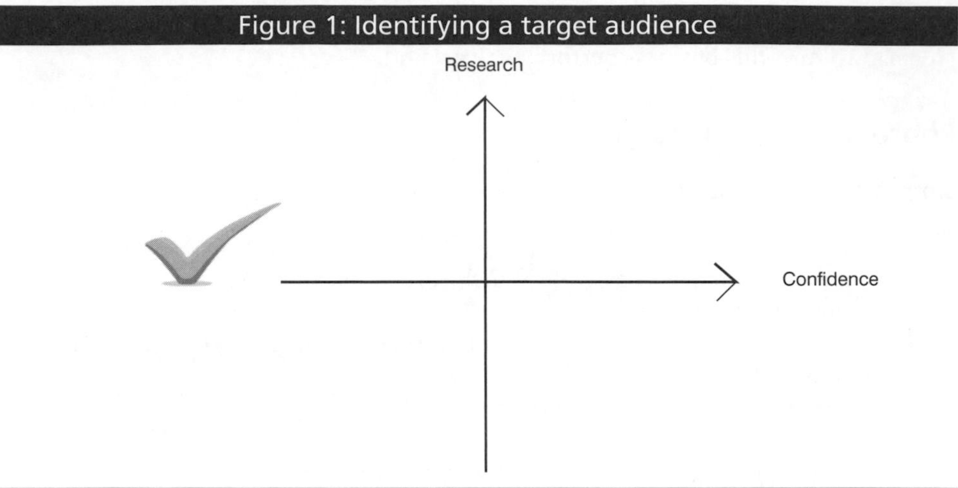


Source: Which? research

We took the learning into the field. Members of each cluster were recruited, and variables were confirmed/elaborated – building a pen portrait of each segment.

We then carried out bespoke qualitative research and re-segmented the base to identify our four target groups. This segmentation was enhanced with media consumption and attitudinal data to inform creative and media planning.

### *Step two: developing a new consumer proposition*

Being good direct marketers we know 'free' is the strongest offer!

At the heart of Which's? offer are the 'best buys': the product/service that offers best value for the consumer. These are our crown jewels and we didn't want to give them away. So we created a new set of information – 'how to get the most out of products and services guides'. These crucially do not tell consumers *what* products to buy, but rather how to go about buying them.

Our free guides provide independent and impartial advice – in areas of mass consumer confusion – e.g. changes in technology (Figure 2).

This 'free guide' offer has been sustained as a proposition for the last six years. It has appeared in more than 50 different guises, covering topics from laptops to smart phones to vegetables.

It does a number of remarkable things.

First, it creates huge levels of consumer response. The attraction of free advice creates response rates typically ten times higher than for a comparable paid offer.

Second, it generates qualified response. Many 'free' offers (think free Parker pen) create response from offer hunters, who then do not convert to sale.

The offer here is research. It only appeals to consumers who are researchers, and thus likely to find Which? of value.

Third, it creates reciprocity. Because our first engagement with consumers is us giving them something they value, they are far more likely to convert to a trial and then a full subscription.

Figure 2: Our consumer offer

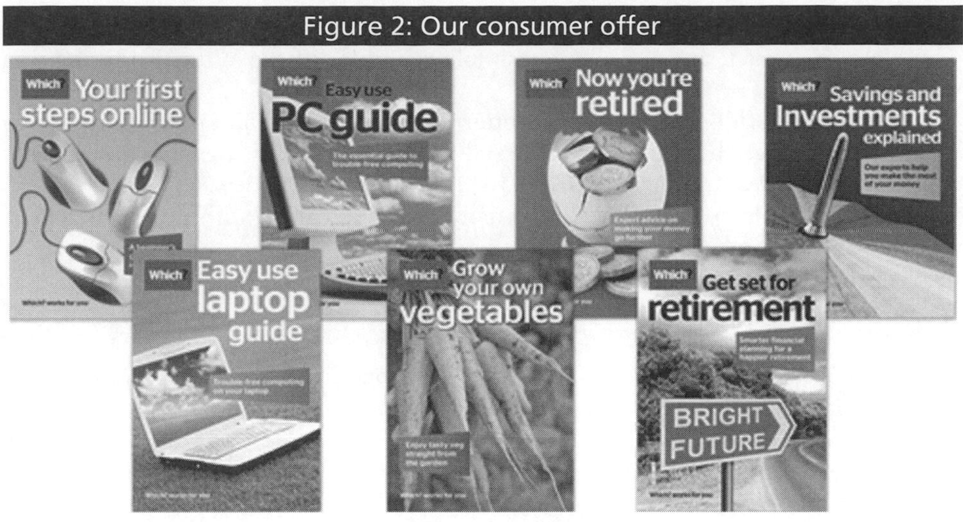


Source: Which? Guides

And finally, the presence of a wide range of free guides in public media, even if they are not immediately relevant for a consumer, starts to restore the saliency and modernity of the Which? brand. They don't just test washing machines, but products and services that I buy every day.

### *Step three: delivering a media schedule that reflected the new strategy and began to revitalise the brand*

Our objective was two-fold:

- first, to reach our new target audience when they were considering purchasing a new product/service;
- second, to reach more people than via direct mail, and put Which? back in the public eye.

Identifying when a consumer would research a product was impossible so we had to be present as often as possible to catch prospects when they were in consideration mode. We moved our funds into 'broadcast' media: DRTV, newspaper and inserts.

Each channel was chosen on three criteria:

- its efficiency at reaching our target audiences;
- its efficiency in generating response;
- its cost per contact and thus resultant cost per subscriber.

All of these media schedules were planned, bought and evaluated as pure 'direct response' schedules. Our primary benchmarks were five-year ROI and volumes of new subscribers. The only business case for investment was five-year ROI for the organisation.

Our key objective at this stage was to maximise reach against, or one plus cover of an audience of researchers, *who were in the initial stages of a research project at the time.*

This stage of pure direct response activity essentially harvested those consumers who were in market, and for whom a simple reminder of the Which? offering was sufficient.

The tripartite offline schedule was supported with heavy weight paid search. Up to 350,000 terms were bid on – not just brand names, but specific product models that consumers were researching, e.g. aeg f65011vi dishwasher review.

Our new schedule took Which? to a daily communication with prospects with a reach of 25 million adults via public media. The odds of being in the right place at the right time astronomically improved.

### *Step four: changing the consumer experience*

To fulfil our strategy of offering free guides we replaced mail with phone response, inviting consumers to call for a free guide. Historically consumers responded by clipping a coupon and posting it off. A month later, when the magazine arrived they had completely forgotten they had ordered it. Their first reaction was often to cancel their subscription!

We hired call centres that employed intelligent operators who could follow guidelines. The operators were asked to chat to callers and discover what they were researching. During this conversation we offered a three month trial of Which? at a reduced price. If the subscriber continued with the magazine after three months it reverted to full price (Figure 3).

Figure 3: Consumer journey to trial: offline

Source: MC&C/Which?

The paid search journey was very different. Consumers wanted specific information, so search copy deep-linked to a sector review landing page, limited free content, and then a paid trial offer.

## The result of phase one

Response rates to trial soared, and conversion to fully paid subscribers held. Within 18 months we doubled the number of trialists from 170,000 to 337,000.

Those callers who only took the guide and didn't subscribe straight away had a positive experience and real added value from Which? and were therefore much more predisposed to say 'yes' when offered a subscription later.

Return on investment rose by 91% within a year, reaching circa 86% true ROI.

This 'business as usual' direct response campaign continues to this day. It has evolved to include large amounts of paid and natural search, and affiliates, as well as the original core media channels, with continuous high reach of those actively in market as its key goal.

## Phase two: return the brand to health

After two years' rapidly growing investment in pure direct response we saw a ceiling. Whilst we had recruited many new researchers we found a hard core rump of our audience whose needs were not met by our current messaging.

Two specific objections to subscribing were identified:

- an emotional objection: Which? is an old fashioned brand – not for me;
- a rational objection: Which? just tests washing machines.

So we proposed a 'brand uplift' campaign with two key objectives:

- change and update the image of Which? amongst core audiences;
- and by doing so, predispose a larger group to respond to the direct response subscriber recruitment campaign.

The business case: uplift the excellent direct response results.

### *Creative messaging*

This has evolved through several iterations of brand uplift activity. At the heart of all of the work are two central thoughts:

- Which? tests a range of products and services that are relevant to consumers;
- Which? tests with an unrivalled thoroughness.

The brand uplift creative work from Dare illustrates this well (Figures 4 and 5).

From each commercial three key messages emerge:

- Which? test rigorously: e.g. using a range of pet odours on washing to ensure machines can cope.
- Which? test relevantly: e.g. they test things the way you (mis)use them, like dropping cameras downstairs to see they work afterwards.
- Which? test responsibly: e.g. they test for things that matter, like crash testing baby seats, which no one else does.

The commercials use actual testing methods, but dramatise them using humour and perceived hyperbole to communicate the value of the brand.

The end line 'Which? works for you' reflects the rigour of testing, but also emphasises the value that the organisation creates for consumers.

Online display builds on and amplifies these themes, but uses the 'lean forward' behaviour of consumers in the medium to provide more detail to the argument. Lower costs of production allowed us to show a wider range of testing examples, amplifying the rational argument.

Figure 4: Brand TV commercial 2011

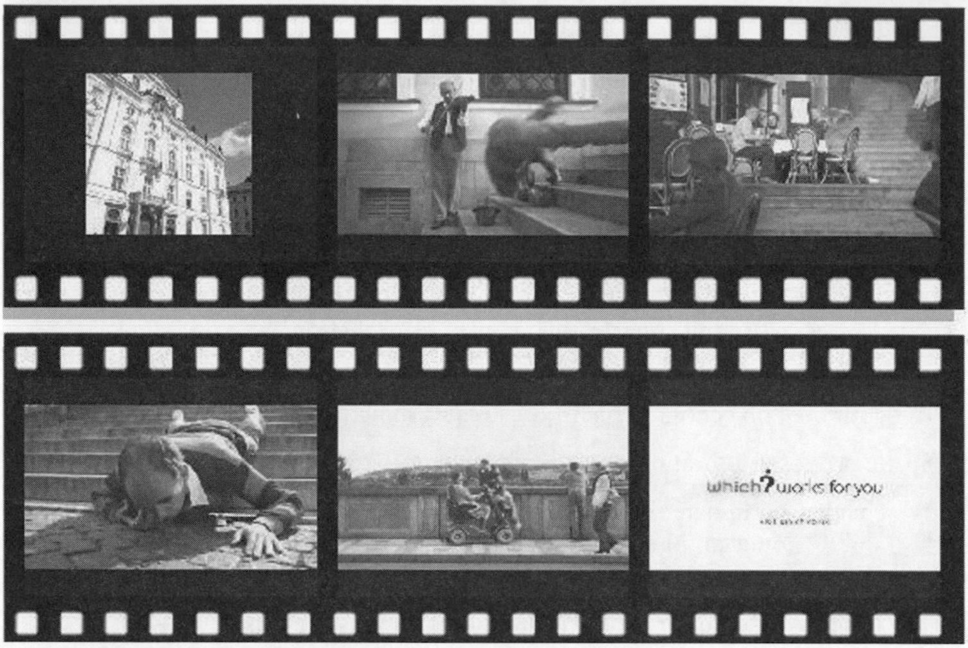

Source: Which? TV commercial stills by Dare

Figure 5: Brand digital display ad

Source: Which? banner ad by Tangent One

*The media mix*

This has evolved over the last four years. As support media we have used magazines, radio, online display, online video, but our lead medium has always been television. But television used in a very different way to the direct response advertising.

For DRTV we seek to maximise cover, and limit frequency. We run lowish weight, continual drip activity, with programming selected for lower attention to view. This maximises immediate response, to both off and online channels.

Brand uplift TV uses very different schedules. We maximise cover again, but also focus on frequency. We initially maximised 4+ frequency, but this has evolved as our understanding of the campaign dynamics has built. We select very different airtime, seeking high attention to view and dwell time programming for our core audiences. We seek a long-term attitudinal change, not just immediate behaviour change. This element of activity is not merely harvesting researchers in market, but seeking to predispose the behaviour of future researchers as they come into market.

## Results of phase two: business payback with the brand overlay

From the initial uplift campaign, Which? recruited 145,000 new trialists in 12 weeks. That's as many as were recruited in the whole of 2004, and at more than three times the ROI of 2004.

Integration of the media, timing and creative gave significant uplift to the business as usual direct response.

Uplift was measured on a channel by channel basis, and for the campaign as a whole. We created control cells and measured uplift vs. those cells. Uplift reached its peak towards the end of the burst, but was sustained, albeit at lower levels, for some time after the campaign ended.

This brand uplift activity has been repeated several times, with the most recent national campaign running December 2010–February 2011. (We have run regional activity since then, and we will be running at the end of April 2012.)

In every case we have seen significant (circa 30%+) uplifts to the response rates of our underlying subscriber recruitment activity. This translates into positive five-year net ROI's for the brand uplift activity.

## Phase three: integration and optimisation

During 2007 and 2008 strong growth continued, and ROI's improved, albeit more slowly. Gains were incremental – not transformational. In 2009 the challenge went out again: discover the new step change.

*The insight*

Once again, the breakthrough came from a research-led insight. In a qualitative group consumers described their research journey, from first contemplating if they needed to purchase goods or services, through active research at category and product level, to finally arriving at price and supplier choices.

They described the journey we show in Figure 6.

Figure 6: Consumer research journey

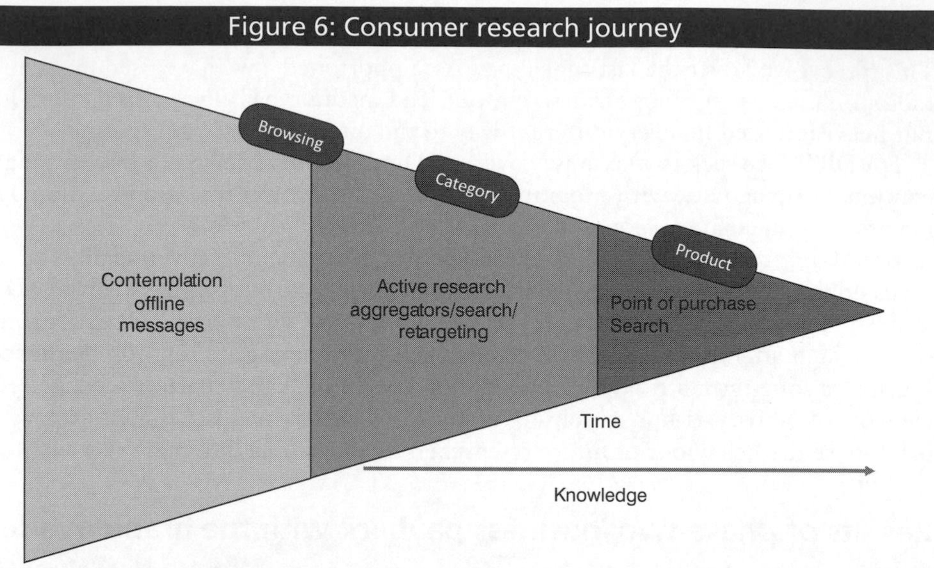


Source: MC&C customer journey process

The journey begins with large numbers of consumers contemplating a purchase. It ends with one consumer making one purchase.

Our first interaction is an emotional DRTV message, nudging them into the start of their research.

From contemplation our target consumers move to active research: investigating at the product or service sector level.

Here rational messaging is more important. Historically this would have been the sole domain of print media, but online research is increasingly important, and the sole channel for many groups. Press and inserts are effective, but even more so search, affiliates and display activity on aggregator sites.

The completion of the majority of research journeys was described by the groups as ending with a search result. We do not subscribe to any 'last click wins' view of the world, but we do recognise that this is the last point where Which? can offer to add value to a consumer's purchase.

From a media planning viewpoint this was a description of a world where consumers were influenced all along their journey of discovery. This made sound sense and reinforced our multichannel media schedule.

The insight came when we realised that we might have a mulitmedia schedule, but we neither planned, bought, nor evaluated our media choices as a journey. Instead we had fallen into the oldest direct marketing trap of all: optimising our activity by silos. DRTV campaigns were perfectly planned, but took little notice of the equally perfectly, but separately planned, paid search activity.

### *Acting on the insight*

Historically we optimised each media channel on a stand alone basis, typically maximising one plus cover for each channel each month.

In any one month, around 60% (see Figure 7) of our target audience saw our TV, our print media and our search. Eighty-four per cent saw at least one of our messages. But nowhere near this figure saw at least one TV, print *and* search message.

Figure 7: Silo optimised media schedule monthly reach by channel

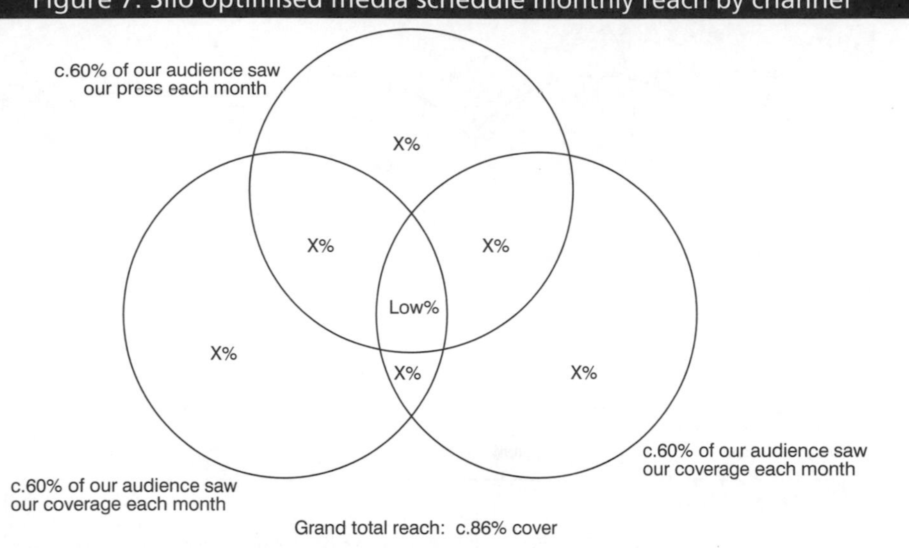
c.60% of our audience saw our press each month
X%
X%
X%
Low%
X%
X%
X%
c.60% of our audience saw our coverage each month
c.60% of our audience saw our coverage each month
Grand total reach: c.86% cover

Source: IPA Touchpoints

From the research findings we hypothesised that, given consumers took input from all three channels, if we exposed them to messages from all three channels during their journey we might expect better results.

So we did. Using the second iteration of the Touchpoints tool we replanned our media schedules to maximise the number of our target audience seeing at least one TV, print and search message within a month.

(For those not familiar with Touchpoints it is the world's first consumer-centric multi-media dataset. Conventional media research tells us who saw our messages in any *one* media channel. Touchpoints allows a media planner to understand and measure how a sequence of messages delivered by separate media channels is seen by their target audience. Without Touchpoints the work in this third phase of growth for Which? would not have been possible. We would have had insight, but no means of acting on that insight.)

The biggest practical step in this third phase was evolving the TV schedule. The nature of print is that one quickly reaches maximum effective cover and then builds ineffective (for direct response) frequency. The nature of search is that it is a reactive medium. So that left television. Judicious movement of channel, daypart and programme selection left us with an evolved DRTV schedule.

## Phase three: the results

The results of Phase three are summarised in Figure 8.

Figure 8: Integrated journey optimised media schedule monthly reach by channel

c.60% of our audience saw our press each month
X%
X%
X%
X+50%
X%
X%
X%
c.60% of our audience saw our coverage each month
c.60% of our audience saw our coverage each month
Response +44%
ROI +51%

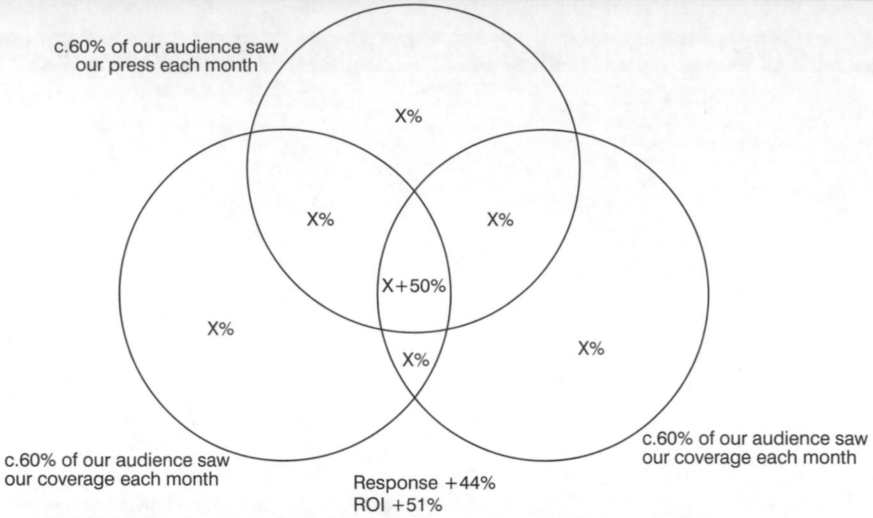

Source: IPA Touchpoints

The results were dramatic. Forty-four per cent more response, and a 51% improvement to our five-year ROI. We did spend a little more (some 8% more impacts) but mostly we rearranged the TV schedule.

## What have we achieved, what have we learned?

In six years Which? has completely transformed its marketing activity.

Following ten years of decline, the total number of subscriptions has reached 1,331,000, and annual revenue £74.6m. We have seen growth year-on-year every year since we started.

The first phase of pure direct marketing activity doubled response and increased ROI by 91% within a year.

The second phase of brand uplift activity improved response rates and ROIs by circa 30% on a sustained basis.

Driven by phase three integrated insights, 2010/2011 saw record numbers of new trialists and new subscribers – the latter up by 38% on the previous year.

All of this activity has been driven by brand-led consumer insights, not a prize draw in sight.

## New learning

The challenges we faced are common to many advertisers. How does one:

- Balance the need for a tightly defined target audience (to avoid wastage) with the requirement to maintain the fame of the brand?

- Balance the short-term efficacy of a pure promotional message with the instinctively 'higher value' benefits of brand-centric messaging?
- Place a value on each element of an integrated schedule beyond just TV and search, and avoid the absurdity of 'last click wins' measurement?

## Our answers

1. Understand and quantify your target audience, not just in terms of who is in market immediately, but who might be predisposed to subscribe once they are in market for your service. Amongst whom should your brand be famous?
2. One can reconcile both long-term brand growth with short-term sales impact within one message. Most brands have at their heart a motivating truth that will spur consumers into action. The free guide unlocked this for Which?.
3. Understanding the whole journey that a consumer takes from first engagement to final click to buy is vital. Don't just focus on the obvious money from search. Last click can't win on its own, only as the last baton holder in a relay.

## Payback

As a direct sales organisation, Which? measure and monitor payback each and every week.

Figure 9 shows the number of subscriptions each year since we started this journey in 2005.

Figure 9: Subscriptions

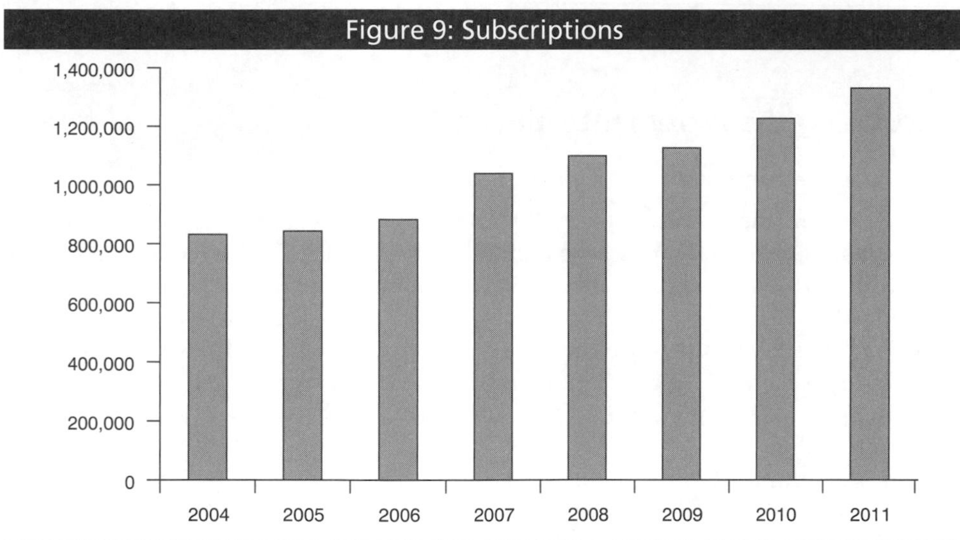


Source: Which? marketing performance analysis

Figure 10 shows the true return on investment for subscribers acquired in each year from 2004 onwards.

Figure 10: ROI

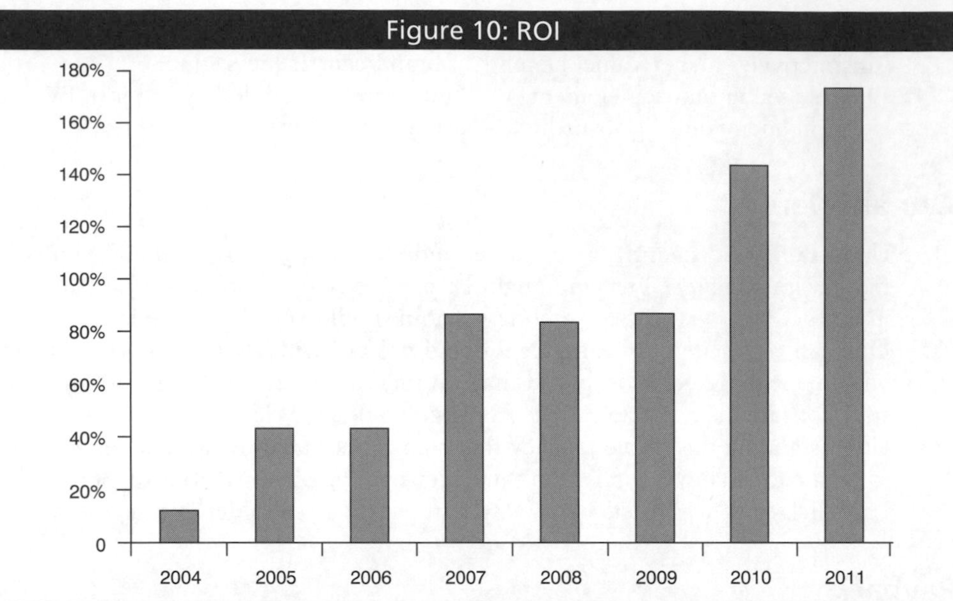


Source: ROI data from Which?

NB. Which? calculate return on investment as being the net profit per subscriber after deducting all costs of both acquiring and servicing (i.e. producing and sending magazines, producing websites and acquiring a new subscriber) vs. the cost of acquiring a new subscriber. It is truly the net incremental profit gained vs. the capital risked in gaining that profit.

## Calculating the incremental payback

### *What was the net incremental profit at discounted value?*

We have taken the financial year 2003/2004 as the benchmark year before this campaign commenced. During that year Which? spent £8,371,000 as a total cost of recruiting 101,000 paying subscribers, at a discounted true ROI of 8.1%, i.e. a profit of £681,000.

Across the six years that are the subject of this paper (from FY 2005/2006 until 2010/2011) Which? spent £60,359,000 as a total cost of recruiting 1,149,000 paying subscribers, at a discounted true ROI of 107%, i.e a profit of £64,317,000 at current discounted value.

Had we continued with the strategy and performance seen in 2003/2004 (8% margin on marketing spend) we would have generated only £4,828,746 profit (£60,359,000 marketing spend x 8% [the original ROI]).

Therefore the true net incremental profit generated by this new strategy is £59,488,254 (£64,317,000 minus £4,828,746) profit generated by this activity over the six years in question.

In other words, for every £1 of marketing money we spent we generated an additional incremental profit of 99 pence compared with the 2003/2004 results.

### *And it gets better*

The £60,359,000 spent on marketing to acquire new subscribers during these six years covers all marketing costs, not just advertising but the costs of staffing call centres, sending out trial magazines and data capture. We only spent £34,758,000 on activities that the jury would recognise as advertising.

Using that number as a base, our true absolute ROI becomes 185%.

### *Distribution*

This classic and powerful marketing lever is not relevant to Which?

Subscriptions are only available direct from Which? via either telephone or web. No retail distribution exists.

### *Pricing*

We have not achieved subscriber growth by discounting pricing. Figure 11 shows that across the six years of this entry the price of Which? rose faster than RPI.

Figure 11: Monthly price of Which? subscription by year

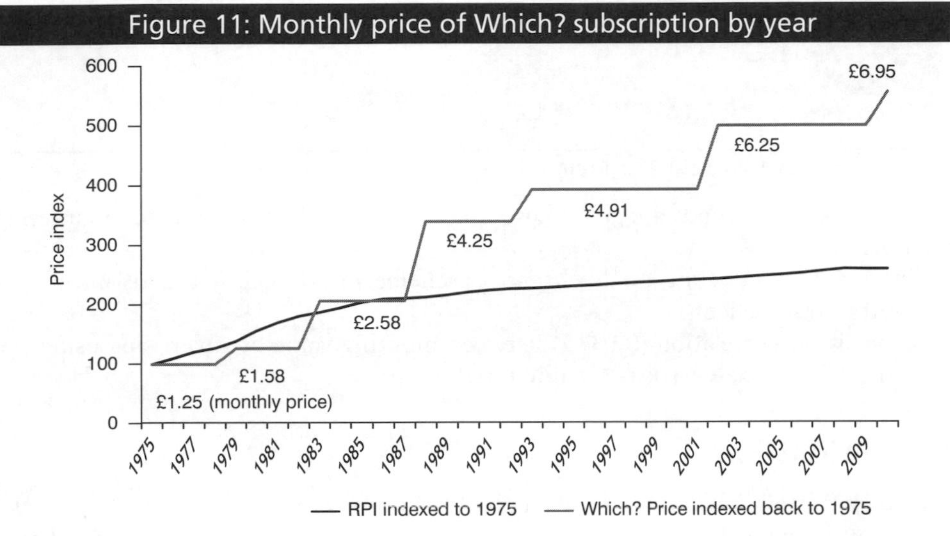


Source: Which? Annual Report

### *PR*

Which? are regularly asked to comment on consumer affairs, across national and regional media.

There is a very weak negative correlation of -0.197 between monthly PR exposure and new trialists recruited each month.

### *Other promotions*

Which? licence the use of the 'Best buy' icon to brands awarded 'Best buy status' (Figure 12).

Figure 12: Examples of Which? 'Best Buy' logo license usage

Source: Which? External Affairs Department

The 'Best buy' brands are able to use that icon in their advertising and marketing materials.

Since the introduction of this licencing scheme in 2006, 264 brands have been licensed to use the icon.

There is no correlation (0.0315) between monthly value of advertising using the icon and Which? new trialists recruited each month.

## Conclusions

Which? has been the consumer's champion for more than 50 years, seeking to make each of us individually as powerful as the organisations we deal with on a daily basis.

It relies on insights into consumer needs and rigorous data collection and analytics to provide that advice.

It seems only fitting that a revitalised advertising effectiveness that has generated the highest subscription numbers and revenues for more than 20 years, is also based on those two core disciplines: consumer insight and rigorous data collection and analytics.

SECTION 4

# Silver winners

## Chapter 21

# Art Fund

## Never without art

**By Laurence Green, 101**
Contributing author: Luke Tipping, 101
Credited companies: Creative Agency: 101; Media Agency: Hypernaked; PR Agency: Sputnik; Client: Art Fund

### Editor's summary

The Art Fund is a small British charity that funds the acquisition of art for the enjoyment of future generations. By re-launching its member benefits in the guise of the National ArtPass, communications drove a 16% surge in memberships, its fastest growth in 20 years, and recruited a new generation of members who were on average 21 years younger than its existing members. Payback has indicated that the campaign generated £3.5m of incremental revenue for the charity against a media investment of £745,000.

The Art Fund paper highlights the importance of genuine consumer insight in creating a stepchange in communications for brands which have become a little bit 'stuck in a rut'. The brand had for too long depended on Accomplishment and Philanthropy needstates amongst older audiences as the core of its revenue base but needed to get to grips with the social needs of younger consumers in order to win new members.

The Art Fund is a small but precious British charity that funds the acquisition of art for the enjoyment of future generations.

By relaunching its member benefits in the guise of the National Art Pass, communications drove a 16% surge in memberships (its fastest growth in 20 years) and recruited a new generation of members (on average 21 years younger than existing members, see Figure 1).

Even our most conservative estimates of payback suggest our campaign will crystallise £5.5m of incremental revenue for the charity against a media investment of £745,000: a revenue return of £4.70 per £1 spent.

**Figure 1: Art Fund membership up 15% despite downturn**

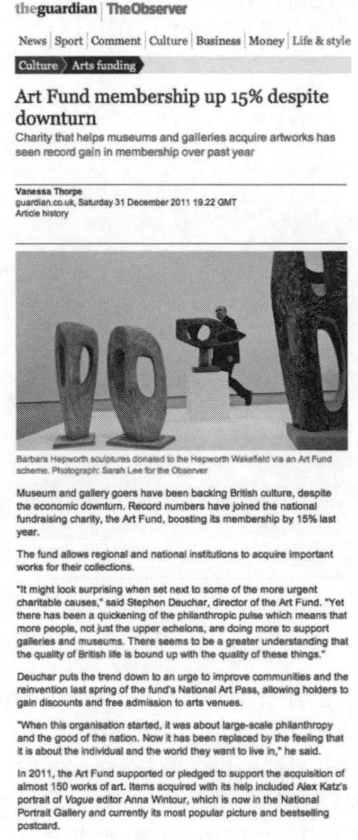

theguardian | TheObserver

News | Sport | Comment | Culture | Business | Money | Life & style

Culture > Arts funding

**Art Fund membership up 15% despite downturn**

Charity that helps museums and galleries acquire artworks has seen record gain in membership over past year

Vanessa Thorpe
guardian.co.uk, Saturday 31 December 2011 19.22 GMT
Article history

Barbara Hepworth sculptures donated to the Hepworth Wakefield via an Art Fund scheme. Photograph: Sarah Lee for the Observer

Museum and gallery goers have been backing British culture, despite the economic downturn. Record numbers have joined the national fundraising charity, the Art Fund, boosting its membership by 15% last year.

The fund allows regional and national institutions to acquire important works for their collections.

"It might look surprising when set next to some of the more urgent charitable causes," said Stephen Deuchar, director of the Art Fund. "Yet there has been a quickening of the philanthropic pulse which means that more people, not just the upper echelons, are doing more to support galleries and museums. There seems to be a greater understanding that the quality of British life is bound up with the quality of these things."

Deuchar puts the trend down to an urge to improve communities and the reinvention last spring of the fund's National Art Pass, allowing holders to gain discounts and free admission to arts venues.

"When this organisation started, it was about large-scale philanthropy and the good of the nation. Now it has been replaced by the feeling that it is about the individual and the world they want to live in," he said.

In 2011, the Art Fund supported or pledged to support the acquisition of almost 150 works of art. Items acquired with its help included Alex Katz's portrait of *Vogue* editor Anna Wintour, which is now in the National Portrait Gallery and currently its most popular picture and bestselling postcard.

Source: www.guardian.co.uk

## Introduction

This is an unusual effectiveness paper, especially for a small budget marketer. It describes a moment of marketing-inspired reinvention and a radically reimagined comms campaign that have delivered a short-term 'sales' surge for the charity in question and established not just a new long-term platform for it to trade from but also a new level of base sales.

One of the UK's best kept cultural secrets, the Art Fund exists to secure great art for museums and galleries all across the UK for everyone to enjoy. But at the end of 2010 it was stuck between a rock and a hard place: determined to increase its funding of British art at a time when the government was reducing its commitments, but with a static and ageing membership base, unsustainably high member acquisition costs and a philanthropic proposition arguably ill-suited to the belt-tightening going on all around it.

This paper demonstrates how in the course of just a year, the reinvention of the Art Fund brand's acquisition marketing efforts and, more specifically, its consumer proposition (but not, note well, its product) served to drive record new membership numbers and lay the platform for continued growth.

Those new members come chiefly from a new, younger and previously unpenetrated cohort. Better still, their recruitment has been accompanied by an appreciable hike in awareness and understanding of the Art Fund, and improved perception of the organisation amongst the art galleries and museums that deliver its 'product'.

It is an unusually straightforward case study of the returns to an organisation of marketing at its best and its simplest: the pivoting of a proposition around what the consumer wants, rather than what it currently has for sale. In the interest of completeness we will describe the consumer insight that served to reframe the opportunity; the subtle repositioning of the organisation and its proposition; the 'organising idea' that populated its comms; and the effects that followed. (All in the space of a year.)

It's a story that we hope provides generalisable learnings for anyone trying to advance a charity's cause, make a difference on a small budget or, more generally, undertake marketing-led reinvention.

## About the Art Fund, and its problems

The Art Fund charity was established in 1903 to help secure works of art for the nation and is still dedicated to that mission 110 years on.

Its funds help museums and art galleries of all shapes and sizes to buy, show and share art of all ages and all kinds. (Over 860,000 extraordinary artefacts have been acquired with the Art Fund's help over its long history.)

The Art Fund receives no government financial support and is funded entirely by the public, with the majority of its income coming from membership subscriptions. (The annual membership fee is £50 single; £70 double.)

In essence, its 80,000 members help buy works of art for everyone to enjoy. In turn, they enjoy free entry to over 200 museums, galleries and historic houses across the country, as well as reduced price admission to major exhibitions and other member privileges.

But membership numbers had long stalled, with expensively acquired new members simply replacing those lapsed or lost. Even a major rebrand in 2006 – accompanied by a significant upweight in marketing against the campaign thought, 'If you love art, help us save it' – had no effect on overall membership numbers.

In addition, that membership base was ageing steadily: 56% of Art Fund members are over the age of 65; their average age is 69.

Awareness and understanding was low amongst non-members (and even amongst members) and the effectiveness of the Art Fund's marketing had diminished markedly, as judged by ever-escalating – indeed unsustainable – costs per acquisition. (Costs per response from the Art Fund's direct response advertising efforts were often running into the hundreds of pounds, and sometimes even thousands.)[1]

Equally critically, the world of giving is a tough place to be in an age of austerity. Overall charitable giving in the UK had begun to creep back upwards after a sharp drop.[2] But research suggested that the Art Fund would struggle to command its 'market share' versus other so-called 'harder' charities: those with a humanitarian mission such as Amnesty or Oxfam; or those single issue charities such as Cancer Research or the NSPCC.[3]

All this at a time when government funding of the arts, and specifically of museums and galleries, was in retreat for exactly the same reason (government arts funding is to be cut by around 30% overall, and funding to national museums by 15%, over the period to 2014–15).

## The task

In line with its mission, the Art Fund was keen to bridge the funding gap for the arts (as documented in their 2011–14 plan, the Art Fund's strategic vision envisaged a 50% growth in their charitable programme, aiming to distribute £7m per annum by 2014).

But to do so it would need to catalyse its funding by dramatically growing its membership base:

*In order to achieve our fundraising and income ambitions within the 2014 plan, we need to broaden the supporter demographic and reach.*[4]

While this all looked plausible enough on paper this was something the Art Fund had not managed since the early 1990s.

## The solution

### Proposition

Strategic research was conducted amongst Art Fund members and prospects in late 2010. Initially conceived to investigate a shift of platform from 'saving art' to 'buying art' (and any consequent impact on the organisation's 'hierarchy of benefits') the research in fact reached a more profound conclusion.

Even among its current members (who you might expect to be motivated by philanthropic zeal), the primary impulse for Art Fund membership was in fact to save money on gallery and museum visits:

*The members...hold their benefits in exceptionally high regard.*[5]

Indeed, most chose to describe the Art Fund as more of a cultural membership scheme than a charitable organisation:

> *Whilst they fully support the cause, engage and believe in it, this element is an important secondary benefit.*[6]

Non-members, meanwhile...

> *Consider the benefits to represent exceptional value for money ... many are bewildered as to why they are unaware of the offering as they are incredibly predisposed to it ... the 50% offer plus the free entry to other galleries is very appealing for all.*[7]

Our research suggested that the modern 'giver' wants to receive as well. That member benefits rather than the Art Fund's philanthropic mission should be placed front and centre in the marketing mix. Rather than 'doing their bit' to help keep British art for the nation, prospects would be invited to join a cultural membership scheme granting them free or reduced entry to a range of galleries and museums.

A previously hidden benefit would be made public. (And the 'mission' would take a back seat, for now.)

### *Audience*

In line with this thinking, our understanding of our target audience also changed fundamentally. The Art Fund had previously targeted prospects who resembled their current member base: (older) art lovers with a philanthropic bent.

Repositioning the Art Fund as more of a cultural membership scheme, and one with hard benefits in terms of museum and gallery discounts (especially so for urban- and suburban-ites) drew us to two new 'psychographic' target audience segments: so called 'Liberal Opinions' (young, professional, urban-dwelling *Guardian* readers) and 'Professional Rewards' (successful folk with busy lives and expensive leisure interests).[8]

The idea of branding Art Fund membership as a kind of national 'art passport' for this new audience soon crystallised, and 101 was briefed to develop an organising idea, identity and promotional plan for this art passport. The objective: to deliver 10,000 new members in 2011.

That target represented a 12% uplift on its current base of 80,000 members: an especially ambitious target in the context of Austerity Britain and three previous years of marketing activity, at similar budget levels, that had served to keep the charity at 'steady state' membership levels, but no better.[9]

### *The National ArtPass*

In response to the brief, 101 designed the National ArtPass (deliberately styled to complement the Art Fund 'parent brand') and the banner thought of 'Never Without Art': the product's ultimate benefit to members, an echo of the Fund's overall mission and a flattering sentiment for art lovers everywhere.

It is worth stressing that no change was made to the Art Fund's product benefits or member privileges. The 'new' National ArtPass and the comms that followed simply re-presented the organisation's benefits in a more galvanising and desirable form.

101 and the Art Fund worked together to design the pass itself, membership pack, and launch materials that included digital and print advertising (Figure 2). It would be disingenuous, indeed impossible, to try to tease all of these apart and we will not attempt to do so; to the consumer they are all 'comms'.

**Figure 2: Member cards and membership packs**

## Media activity

Our reinvention of the Art Fund, and the invention of the National ArtPass, meant that we could (and should) behave more like a retailer with a product to sell rather than a charity with a cause to promote.

There were two main waves of activity supporting the new National ArtPass: a spring launch followed by a burst in the autumn.

Wave 1 began with a launch event on 13 April at London's Foundling Museum, attended and endorsed by Culture Secretary Jeremy Hunt, the Tate's Nicholas Serota and the artist Grayson Perry, and supported by a PR push.

Launch advertising in outdoor, press and digital then drove awareness of the National ArtPass under the umbrella of our organising idea, Never Without Art (Figure 3).

**Figure 3: Media activity**

6 sheet posters

X-track posters

48 sheet posters

We devised a weekend-long promotion with *The Guardian* and *The Observer*, our prospects' newspaper brands of choice. This centred around a weekend promotion offering a free three-month 'trial version' of the Pass. (Our common expectation – based on *Guardian* precedent – was that approximately 2,000 people might take up this offer. As you will see we were only 70,000 or so out...)

Consumer PR amplified the idea that a life lived 'Never without art' was good for you. We also ran the organising idea across all third-party materials: on t-shirts, badges and bags for gallery staff, for example (see Figure 4).

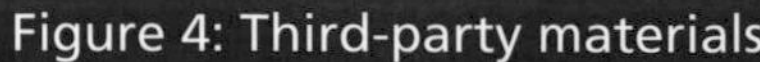

Figure 4: Third-party materials

Wave 2 followed in October and was designed to squeeze the maximum return from remaining media monies by concentrating activity in London, Bath and Edinburgh: those conurbations with the highest concentrations of both prospects and participating galleries and museums (see Figure 5).

Figure 5: Wave 2 advertising

6 Sheet posters

Ad gates

48 sheet posters

Our total media budget for the year was £745,000 across all media (Table 1).

**Table 1: Media budget**

| | Launch | Autumn |
|---|---|---|
| Outdoor | £135,000 | £80,000 |
| Press | £50,000 | £80,000 |
| Digital | £70,000 | £45,000 |
| Partnerships | | £80,000 |
| PR | £45,000 | £20,000 |
| Direct marketing | £60,000 | £80,000 |
| Total | £360,000 | £385,000 |
| | | |
| Total spend | | £745,000 |

Source: Art Fund

## Results and payback

The launch of the National ArtPass has surpassed all expectations, despite its modest media budget.

It has created both a surge of new memberships and a large pool of ongoing prospects. Along the way it has established a new and better-understood platform for the Art Fund: as a cultural membership scheme, in addition to its ongoing and fundamental role as a philanthropic arts organisation.

We will look first at the results for 2011 (the Art Fund's financial year) before briefly turning to some apparently persistent campaign effects that have 'carried over' in to the first few months of 2012.

The Art Fund's limited resources mean that we can only report occasional and topline 'brand tracking' and cannot provide finely nuanced econometric analysis.

Happily our 'sales' results, their magnitude and timing, we hope brook little argument.

### *2011 results*

Within six weeks of launch, awareness of the National ArtPass had already grown as high as 31% among the prospect base.[10]

Prompted awareness of the Art Fund had leapt by 21%, and understanding of it as a cultural membership organisation by 11%.[11]

The autumn activity in London, Bath and Edinburgh not only doubled advertising awareness and 'intention to join' but also drove further advances in ArtPass awareness and understanding (Table 2).

Table 2: National ArtPass product understanding

| National ArtPass product understanding | Wave 1 | Wave 2 |
|---|---|---|
| | % | % |
| 'The National ArtPass means you will never miss out on the art you enjoy' | 18 | 30 |
| 'A card that gives you unlimited access to art' | 7 | 12 |

Source: Muse tracking, November 2011

Much more importantly, sales ticked up *immediately* after launch, as we shall see. (And in addition to those permanent new members coming 'direct', we would attract 70,000 temporary members as a result of the *Guardian* promotion.)

By the year-end we had secured 13,374 permanent new memberships and a total of 18,558 new members (since some of those memberships were double), thus outperforming our target by 80% (Table 3 and Figure 6).

Table 3: Memberships

| | |
|---|---|
| New member target | 10,000 |
| New memberships achieved | 13,374 |
| New members acquired | 18,558 |
| Over-delivery against target | +86% |

Source: Art Fund

A recruitment rate that vastly outperformed previous years on the same budget, and brought an immediate revenue upside of £735,000, matching our media spend virtually pound for pound.[12]

Figure 6: New Art Fund memberships, 2008–2011

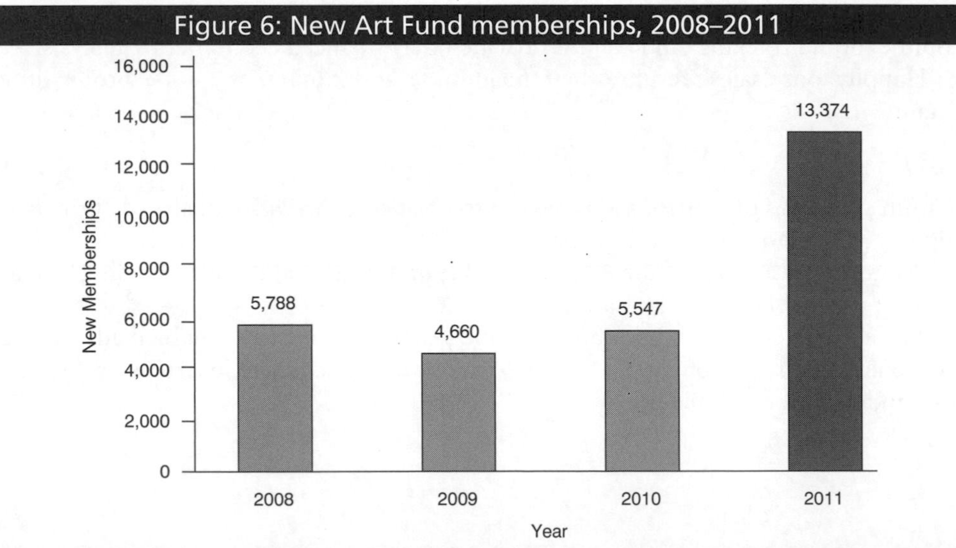


Source: Art Fund

The Art Fund's calculation of lifetime value is no speculative IPA-friendly figure but based on actual precedent and indeed the 'actuarial' basis on which they advance funds for marketing. The average £55 membership fee is payable annually and members tend to remain so for at least five years, hence a lifetime value confidently (and conservatively) assigned per new member of £261.65.[13]

Since our new members are demonstrably younger than previous recruits, this figure is more likely to be an underestimate than an overestimate.

Our 13,374 new memberships therefore equate to a revenue upswing of £3,499,307.10. That's a revenue return of £4.70 for each £1 spent on media in 2011.

Note that this is in large part pure 'profit' for the organisation as the cost of a new member to the organisation (and participating galleries and museums) is marginal.

The upswing coincides perfectly with our two waves of media activity. The Art Fund's internal marketing metric and 'measure of success' is cumulative new memberships, compared each month against the previous year. So that's what we show here.

Our 'sales' figures accelerate away from trend from launch in April. They spike in August as temporary *Guardian* passes are upgraded into permanent passes as they expire. (They are arguably 'lagged' sales from May.) They kick up again as the Autumn campaign gets under way (Figure 7).[14]

Figure 7: 'Sales' figures

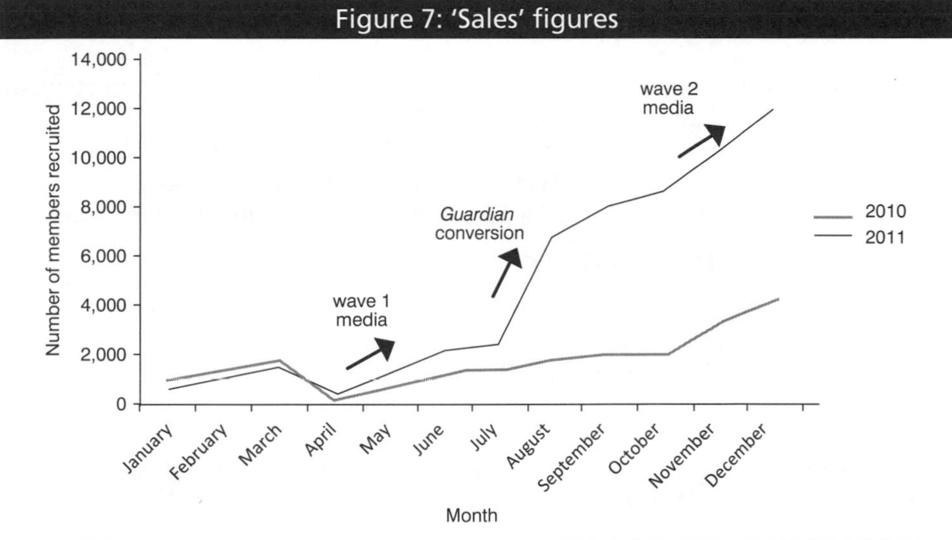


Source: Art Fund

There is no other explanation for this sudden upswing in memberships apart from the launch of the National ArtPass and the media investment behind it (in fact, as we have seen, the prevailing winds were against improved business performance).

Recruitment from traditional sources such as museum and gallery leaflets, or from face-to-face volunteer efforts, remain in the low single digits for example.

There was no change in product, price or distribution nor any change in competitive context; or any sudden upswing in art attendance.

The launch has also left us with a large pool of identifiable 'hot prospects' thanks to the *Guardian* promotion: those who signed up for a temporary membership but have not yet 'traded up' to permanent. (The activity was responsible for 4,490 of our new memberships by year-end.)

At the time of writing we have 59,213 interested art lovers remaining to segment, mine and hopefully convert.

The launch of the Pass has demonstrably recruited a new generation of Art Fund members, with new members three times as likely to be under the age of 35 as existing members (Table 4).

**Table 4: Art Fund membership by age**

| Age | All members | New members | Index |
|---|---|---|---|
| | % | % | % |
| 0–25 | 5 | 16 | 320 |
| 25–35 | 5 | 13 | 260 |
| 35–55 | 15 | 21 | 140 |
| 55–65 | 19 | 23 | 121 |
| 65+ | 56 | 27 | 48 |
| | 100 | 100 | |

Source: Art Fund

Indeed the average age of a new recruit in 2011 was just 48, 21 *years* younger than the current member equivalent.

Meanwhile – although it was not an explicit objective of the campaign – the Art Fund also credits the activity with achieving record retention rates of *current* members: 91.6% of members were retained through 2011, compared with an average of 85%.

### *2012: A higher level of base sales?*

The first few months of 2012 have not featured any comms activity, but already suggest that our National ArtPass campaign has not just grown sales when 'on air' but also served to establish a higher running rate of ongoing sales.

Monthly recruitment in the first quarter is running at a rate of roughly twice that of previous years (Table 5).

**Table 5: New Art Fund memberships (Jan–March, 2010–2012)**

| | Jan | Feb | March | First Qtr total | % Change vs. previous year |
|---|---|---|---|---|---|
| 2010 | 842 | 429 | 370 | 1,641 | * |
| 2011 | 631 | 462 | 430 | 1,523 | -7 % |
| 2012 | 1,122 | 892 | 1,039 | 3,053 | +100 % |

Source: Art Fund

Using our lifetime value calculation from earlier, those extra 500 base sales each month achieved *in the absence of advertising* equate to an incremental revenue return of £130,825 per month (or £1.57m over the course of a year).

Again, there is no other explanation for the Art Fund's improved recruitment in the first quarter of 2012 versus previous years, other than some kind of 'ad stock' or 'brand stock' created by our 2011 activity.

### *Broader effects*

Lining marketing efforts up against the National ArtPass – against seeing rather than saving art, if you like – has opened up other opportunities for the Art Fund, all of which bring a revenue as well as reputational upside.

Tying our *Guardian* 'sales promotion' in with editorial activity not only catalysed our promotion but led to the creation of a new editorial section on the *Guardian*'s website, 'Art Weekly', from which click-through rates to the National ArtPass landing page are four times higher than average.[15]

Crystallising member benefits in the form of the ArtPass also encouraged the Art Fund to launch a physical 'gifting' version, trialled in Waterstone's at Christmas and rolling out into galleries shortly – an entirely new form of distribution for the charity.

Its new, higher profile and more obvious role as a cultural membership organisation has helped the brand's Twitter followers to increase six-fold from 2,000 to over 12,578 and laid the basis for the successful launch of the Art Guide app in April 2012: a 'what's on' art guide that shouts out ArtPass discounts and that has already enjoyed 16,515 downloads.

Initiatives like these have helped to advance the Art Fund's reputation as an arts marketing and funding 'force for good' amongst both government and the arts community generally, and amongst its partner galleries and museums specifically.

The revenue upside to the Art Fund from the launch of the ArtPass is also part of a broader piece of value creation in the arts, above and beyond its enhanced ability to fund more acquisitions for the nation.

Fifty per cent of Art Fund members say that since buying the pass, they visit museums and galleries more than they did before, of whom 90% 'always or nearly always' visit the museum café or the shop. In this way the National ArtPass also brings incremental revenue for participating venues in exhibition ticket income and secondary visitor spend (i.e. in shop or café).

In short, the Art Fund's ongoing reinvention as a cultural membership organisation, and the re-presentation of its member privileges in the form of the National ArtPass, have enabled it to make great business strides in a short period of time, and primed it and its partners for further growth.

## Notes

1 Art Fund internal data.
2 Charitable giving in the UK had fallen by 10% in 2008/09. Source: Marie Curie Cancer Care (2011) IPA Effectiveness Paper. *Advertising Works 20*. London: Warc.
3 Source: Muse Membership Qualitative Debrief, 2010.
4 Source: Art Fund Strategic Plan 2011–2014.
5 Source: Muse Membership Research Qualitative Debrief, 2010.
6 Source: Muse Membership Research Qualitative Debrief, 2010.
7 Source: Muse Membership Research Qualitative Debrief, 2010.
8 Source: Muse Segmentation.
9 Source: Art Fund internal data.
10 Source: Muse Tracking, June 2011.

11 Source: Muse Tracking, June 2011.
12 13,374 new memberships x £55 'blended' membership fee = £735,570. £55 is a blended rate of single membership fees (£50) and double (£70).
13 £55 is a blended rate of single membership fees (£50) and double (£70). A 25% discount is offered in the first year to secure payment by direct debit, which is more likely to recur. Lifetime value is therefore calculated as (£55 – 25%) + (£55 x 4).
14 Postcode analysis of autumn results shows Bath up 120% and Edinburgh up 57%, albeit from small bases. Source: Art Fund internal data.
15 Source: *Guardian* data.

Chapter 22

# Danone Activia

## How a little bit of T.L.C. made a market leader

**By Rowenna Prest and Alice Huntley, RKCR/Y&R**
Contributing authors: Alan Bloodworth, Benjamin Morgan, OHAL; Beatrice Boue, MEC; Shawn Pitt, Millward Brown
Credited companies: Creative Agency: RKCR/Y&R; Client: Danone

**Editor's summary**

In 2009 Activia was the major challenger within the chilled yoghurt and dessert market; but its positioning, a solution to the problem of bloating, had finite relevance preventing it from taking the top spot. To rectify this, RKCR/Y&R developed a powerful new brand platform moving Activia from the problem of bloating to the positively framed space of maintaining happy tummies; the rational message of improving digestive transit to the emotional space of feeling better inside and out. The resulting creative idea, 'Give yourself some tummy loving care' or 'T.L.C.', made Activia the market leader, delivered £58.6m incremental sales, £3.6m incremental net profit and a payback of £1:1.23. In this overcrowded category the judges couldn't deny the fantastic achievement of reaching the number one brand and generating a 73% share of voice.

## Introduction: the payback of thinking big

This is a story of how a challenger brand became leader in an especially competitive market.[1]

How a brand built on a functional claim to be the solution to a particular kind of problem found a way to engage an even wider group of consumers who didn't identify with that problem.

How a small pot of yoghurt gave over 10 million people a simple way to give themselves a little bit of T.L.C.[2]

How a new brand platform delivered incremental sales of £58.6m, a net profit of £3.6m and an ROI of 23%.[3]

This is the story of Activia.

## Activia to 2009

Activia is a range of yoghurts that contain pro-biotic culture that aid your digestive system.

It's part of the Chilled Yoghurts and Desserts (CYD) market which by 2009 was worth over £2.2bn.[4] This category is tough, dominated by high-spending brands.[5] And as a discretionary part of the shopping basket, a constant stream of new products are launched, competing to keep consumers interested.

Launched in 1999, Activia's fortunes really took off in 2004 with a campaign that focused on the relief it gave to women who suffered from a 'digestive disorder'.[6] The campaign engaged millions by referencing these disorders in a way women could identify, 'bloating'; presenting it in a believable way, using real women testimonials.

This functional health claim was highly differentiated from the market leader.[7] And, as our 2008 IPA paper demonstrated, it was a powerful challenger-brand strategy.[8] Activia grew exponentially in value from 16th in 2004 to 2nd by 2007. There it stayed vying with, but never overtaking, the market leader Müller Corner.

## Activia's ambition for 2010

Activia UK is extremely important for Danone.

The UK isn't just one of the most valuable markets,[9] it's a barometer for the business globally, where new products and communications are trialled.

So, Activia UK had to be a true talisman for success: being second wasn't good enough. In 2010 we were tasked to make Activia number one.

To achieve this, Activia needed to grow faster than Müller Corner, which meant we had to grow our value by 7%, equating to over £13m value sales.[10]

## What communications had to do

Activia is a strong product with a high repeat purchase rate: in 2009 70% who bought Activia did so more than once (Figure 1). Once hooked, the frequency of purchase is high: 6.6/year versus 4.6/year for Müller Corner.[11]

Figure 1: 1+ Repeat purchase rate for Activia in 2009

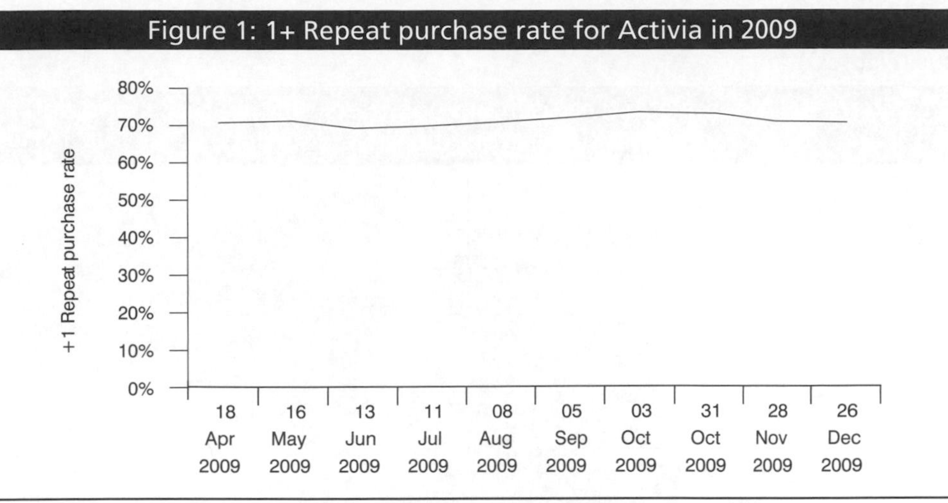


Source: Nielsen Scantrack

So, we knew trial would deliver more growth than frequency of purchase amongst an already loyal customer base. To meet the 2010 target of 7% value growth we needed to increase household penetration by 3.5 points to 38%, in other words add 900,000 new consumers (Figure 2).[12]

Figure 2: Activia's role for communications

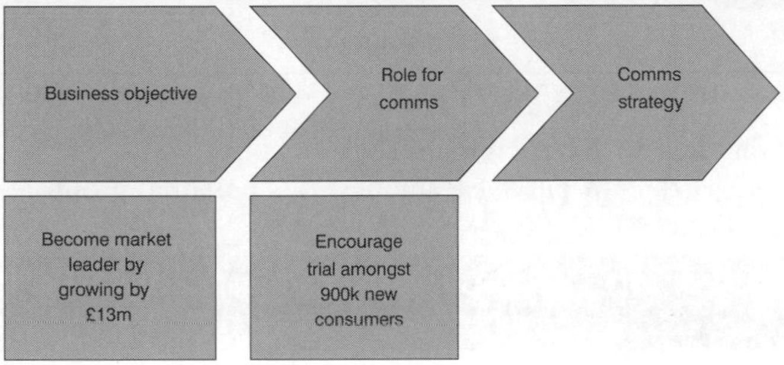

Business objective

Role for comms

Comms strategy

Become market leader by growing by £13m

Encourage trial amongst 900k new consumers

Source: RKCR/Y&R

## The challenges

To encourage trial, there seemed no reason why we couldn't continue with our existing approach.

Yoghurt is a healthy category, and Activia had a health claim: being a solution to the problem of 'digestive disorders'. This refers to a broad set of self-reported issues which the Activia U&A study demonstrated were experienced by 57.7% of women.[13] By December 2009, household penetration of Activia was 34.5%, two-thirds of whom (i.e. the 21% segment in Figure 3) reported digestive disorders. If growth was solely being driven by solving digestive disorders, as the success of the testimonial campaign suggested, there should have been an additional 36.7% penetration to play for (Figure 3).

**Figure 3: UK female Activia user and non-users, split by those who do and don't suffer from digestive disorders**

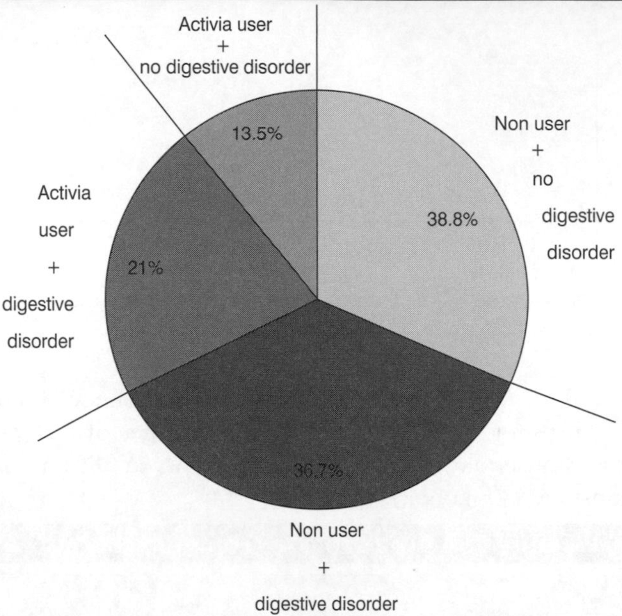


Source: Activia U&A, TNS, June 2008. Base: 610 women aged 18–70 years old, nationally representative

But why hadn't this 36.7% tried it already?

The top three barriers to purchase amongst this potential group were relevance, price, and taste (Figure 4).

**Figure 4: Top 3 barriers to trial amongst non-users with digestive disorders**

Relevance
Price
Taste
0 5 10 15 20 25

Source: Activia U&A, TNS, June 2008. Base: 224 women aged 18–70 years old, who have a digestive disorder but don't use Activia

*Barrier 1: Lack of relevance*

Lack of relevance amongst people with digestive disorders seemed peculiar. Activia had been successfully marketed on the basis of a widespread problem, so people with that problem should be open to trying it.

Qualitative research showed that, however convincing our consumer testimonials had been for many, there were many others who, even if they said they sometimes experienced the symptoms on the U&A survey, didn't think they had a digestive 'problem'.[14] Simply, it wasn't for them, it was for 'others'.

> *I just don't suffer from that bloated stomach thing and that's what those ads say.*
>
> *I've seen that ad before and I thought it looked really good, but it isn't for me because I don't have that problem.*
>
> *It doesn't interest me one iota because I don't have that bloated thing.*
>
> Source: IPSOS, May 2008

Looking at frequency of suffering from digestive disorders revealed that two-thirds didn't experience them often enough to feel they had a problem (Figure 5).

**Figure 5: Frequency at which women claimed to suffer from digestive issues**

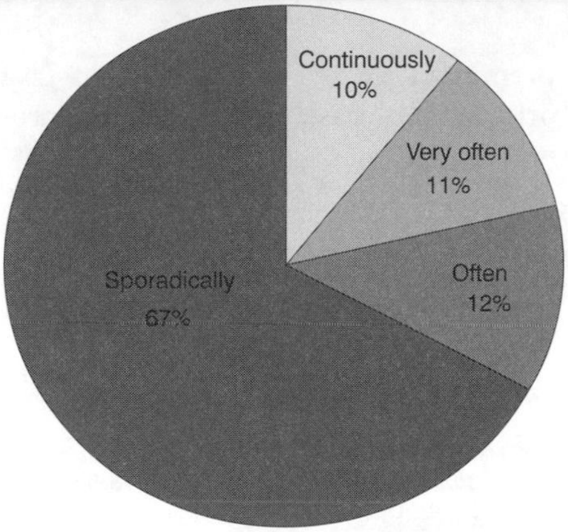

Source: Activia U&A, TNS, June 2008. Base: 352 women aged 18–70 years old, who have a digestive disorder

It was clear that to continue increasing penetration we needed an idea that would move beyond the 'problem' and make the benefit of Activia more relevant to more women.

However, we were mindful that broadening relevance couldn't be at the expense of differentiation. BrandAsset Valuator[15] (which measures brand perceptions, linking them to commercial performance) demonstrated that both were important to build brand strength and a market leading position (Figure 6).

**Figure 6: BAV Powergrid: In 2008 Activia had to increase relevance and differentiation**

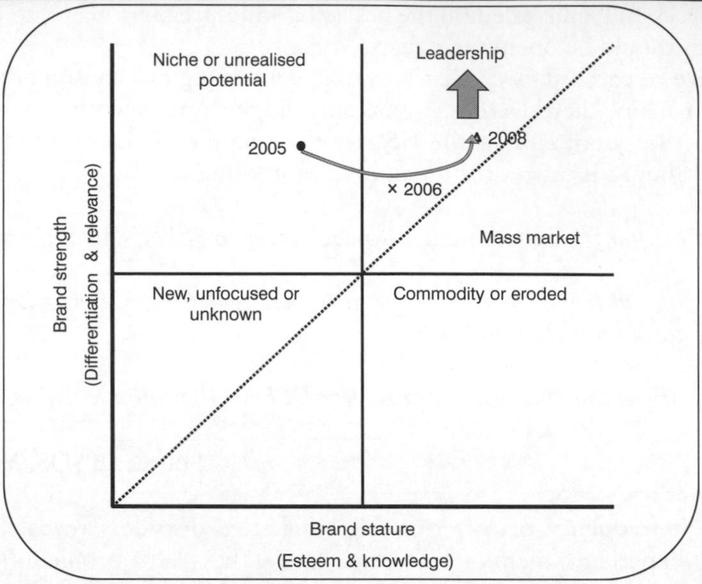

Source: BAV, RKCR/Y&R UK. Base: 1,856 British women, nationally representative

### *Barrier 2: Price*

Activia was sold at a premium. We felt confident that if we could fix relevance and taste perceptions, price would cease to be a barrier, proved by the high repeat purchase rate amongst existing users.

### *Barrier 3: Taste*

Taste was an essential driver in the category.

> *Health looks set to remain on the nation's long-term food agenda, but taste is still the top factor in consumers' choice of snacks. Against these often contradictory demands facing snacks, the majority view of yoghurt as a healthy but tasty snack and a popular alternative to chocolate or desserts puts it in a rare, strong position for long-term growth.*
>
> Source: Kiti Soininen, Senior Food Analyst, Mintel

It was all about the lick shot (Figure 7).

Figure 7: Taste category conventions

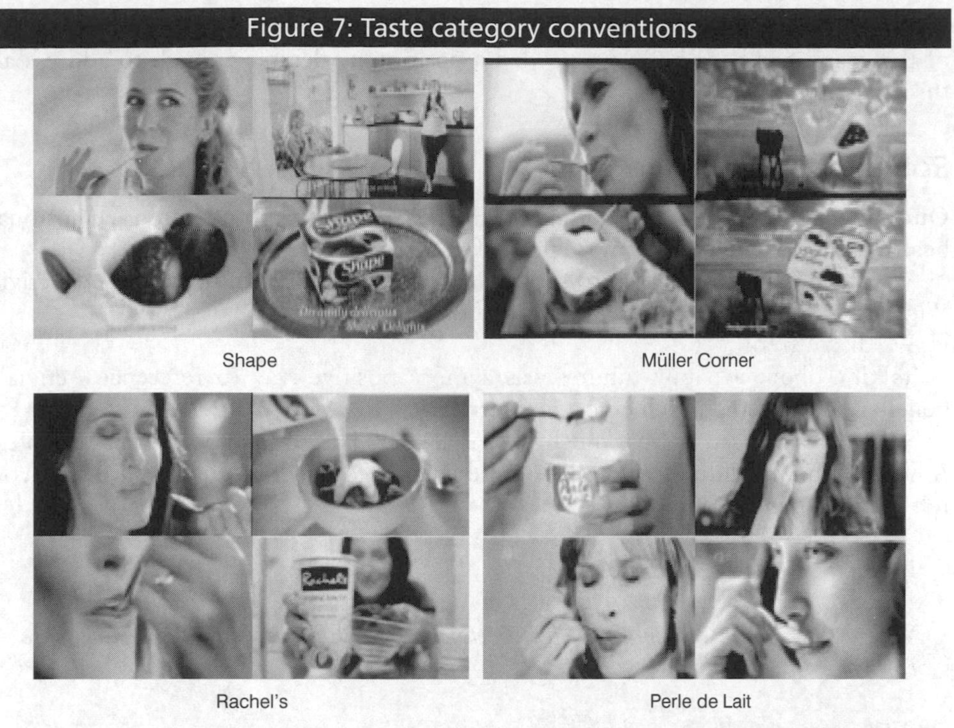


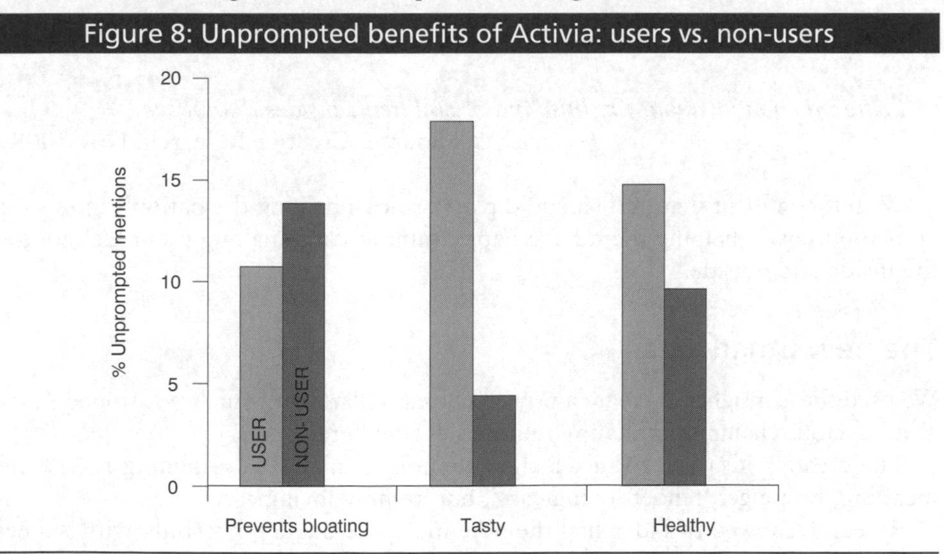


Fortunately, Activia was very tasty.

Users see Activia's taste as even more of a benefit than its ability to reduce bloating, impacting more on its repeat purchase rate. But for non-users, the problem of bloating obscured taste, leading to low taste expectations (Figure 8).

Figure 8: Unprompted benefits of Activia: users vs. non-users



Source: Activia U&A, TNS, June 2008. Base: 610 women aged 18–70 years old, nationally representative

Whilst Activia's positioning had to centre on health, as this was where the equity of the brand had been built, we needed a positioning flexible enough to address all three barriers.

## Solving the challenge

Our hunch, backed up by the findings of the IPA, was that a broader, more emotional health positioning would be more powerful.[16]

We commissioned research to see what would happen if we repositioned Activia (Figure 9).

We discovered:

Talking about a happy tummy was a more positive way to reference Activia's benefit and delivered a rich emotional territory.

We were surprised at how much potential users had to say about their tummies. A healthy tummy didn't just mean you didn't have to linger in the loo; it meant you felt great too, inside and out.

> *If you are healthy you are happier.*
>
> *When your tummy is right you feel better, more confident, better able to tackle things.*
>
> *When your tummy is working you are happy.*
>
> Source: Cre8tive Research, Nov 2008

The bigger emotional need was for a bit of T.L.C., not just a remedy for tummies.

The mums we spoke to were facing endless and exhausting multitasking, resulting in little time to care for themselves:

> *We're usually bottom of the pile.*
>
> *I care much more about my husband or children's insides than mine.*
>
> Source: Cre8tive Research, Nov 2008

We felt confident that Activia could play a role in helping the nation's mums look after themselves, helping them have happy tummies and making them feel good on the inside and outside.

## The new brand idea

We used these insights to create a powerful brand platform, which positioned Activia as a delicious champion of happy tummies everywhere.

The creative idea was to hijack the common term 'T.L.C.', imbuing it with new meaning, no longer 'tender loving care', but 'tummy loving care'.

Research showed this idea had the potential to resonate powerfully with women:

Figure 9: Hypothesis on how Activia's positioning ought to shift

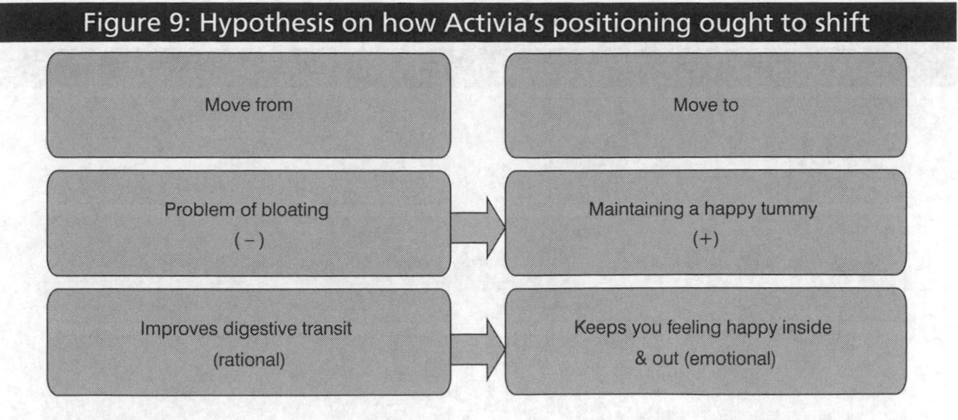
Move from
Move to
Problem of bloating
(−)
Maintaining a happy tummy
(+)
Improves digestive transit
(rational)
Keeps you feeling happy inside
& out (emotional)

Source: RKCR/Y&R

*It pricks your conscience that you should think about yourself more*

*It made me feel better – because it's moved me away from the bloated thing*

*It's quite caring and warm in a way*

*People will remember T.L.C. – tummy loving care.*

Source: Cre8tive Research, Nov 2008

Importantly, given the competitive nature of the market, it still felt distinctive – no other brand owned this emotional territory.

## Communications strategy

We now had a clear communications strategy (Figure 10).

Figure 10: Activia's 2010 communications strategy

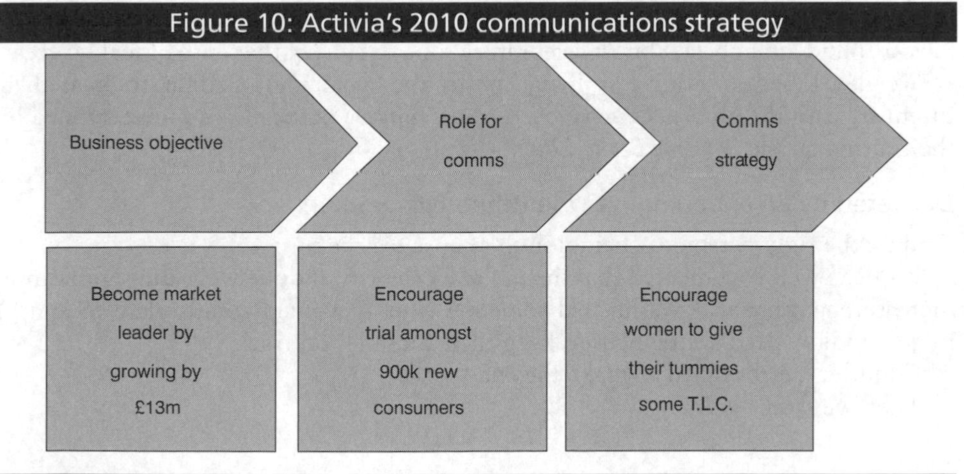
Business objective
Role for comms
Comms strategy
Become market leader by growing by £13m
Encourage trial amongst 900k new consumers
Encourage women to give their tummies some T.L.C.

Source: RKCR/Y&R

Communications needed to deliver four attitudinal shifts (Figure 11).

Figure 11: How the communications strategy had to work

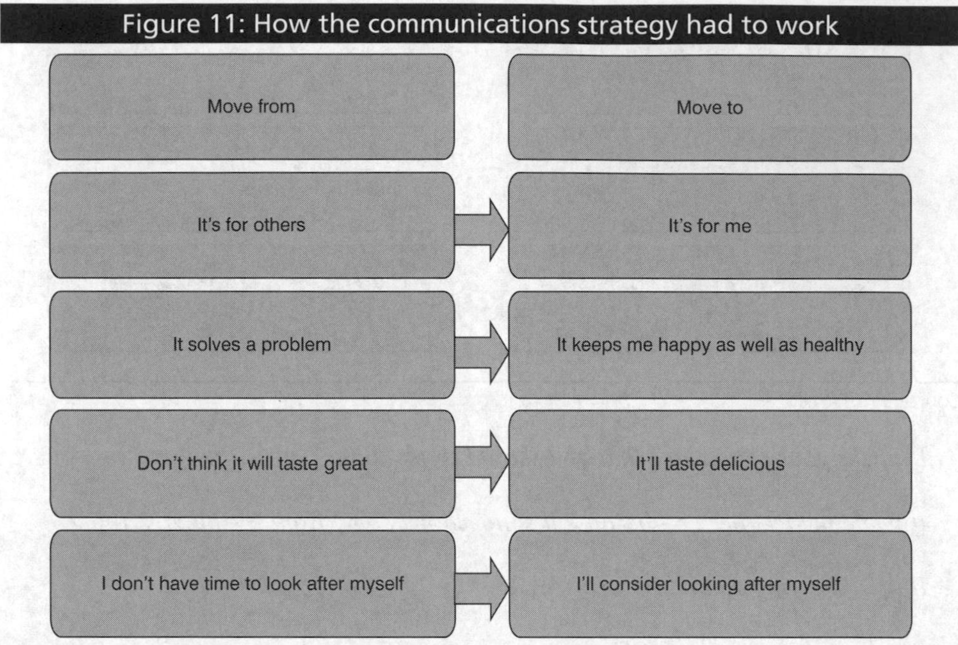
Move from
Move to
It's for others
It's for me
It solves a problem
It keeps me happy as well as healthy
Don't think it will taste great
It'll taste delicious
I don't have time to look after myself
I'll consider looking after myself

Source: RKCR/Y&R

## A new communications approach

### *1. Creative vehicle*

### Championing women's right to T.L.C.

We wanted to motivate women that they had the right to a little T.L.C., a much bigger message than normally delivered by CYD brands. So, communications had to have a confident, upbeat, almost celebratory tone to convey the sense of feeling great.

We developed a positive rallying cry to the women of Britain to love their tummies, with the phrase *'Give yourself some Tummy Loving Care'*, underpinned by the rousing classic, *Gimme Some Lovin'*.[17]

### Delivered by an engaging, yet identifiable champion

Finding the right person to champion this cause was key.

It's been well documented that the use of a celebrity, if done well, can significantly increase engagement.[18] We needed someone who a) women could relate to and b) might credibly need a little help to keep their tummies on track.

Countless celebs failed to make the cut.

Then we struck gold.

We found the nation's typical 'girl next door': Martine McCutcheon (Figure 12).

Figure 12: Martine McCutcheon

Her appeal was strong, having starred in big heart of the nation entertainment such as *Eastenders* and *Love Actually*. Yet, in spite of her success, research found that our audience could still identify with her:

*I like Martine McCutcheon she is a real woman – not all skin and bone like some.*

*You can imagine her shopping in Tesco's like we do.*
Source: Movement, T.L.C. Creative Development, 2008

And the audience believed that Martine, unlike most skinny celebs, might need a little help to keep her digestive health on track:

*She'd have eaten like a pig like the rest of us.*
Source: Movement, T.L.C. Creative Development, 2008

### Looking like a market leader

We wanted Activia to feel like a brand for everyone. But we also wanted Activia to feel like a leader, building an iconic image in consumers' minds. So, we developed a strong visual for Activia T.L.C. (Figure 13) which ran as posters, a medium rarely used by other CYD brands.

This image was then successfully taken across other media, such as the Activia website (Figure 14).

Figure 13: Activia launch poster & key visual

Figure 14: Activia's website with key visual

## 2. Media and messaging

### Delivering taste: the flexibility of the creative thought and vehicle

The testimonial approach made delivering non-health messages difficult. However, because 'T.L.C.' was a clear idea with more flex, it could carry a range of messages, including taste. After all, as the previous quote indicated, people believed Martine wouldn't be shy indulging her taste buds.

The media plan (Figure 15) demonstrates the range of messaging delivered with T.L.C.

Figure 15: Activia's 2010 communications plan

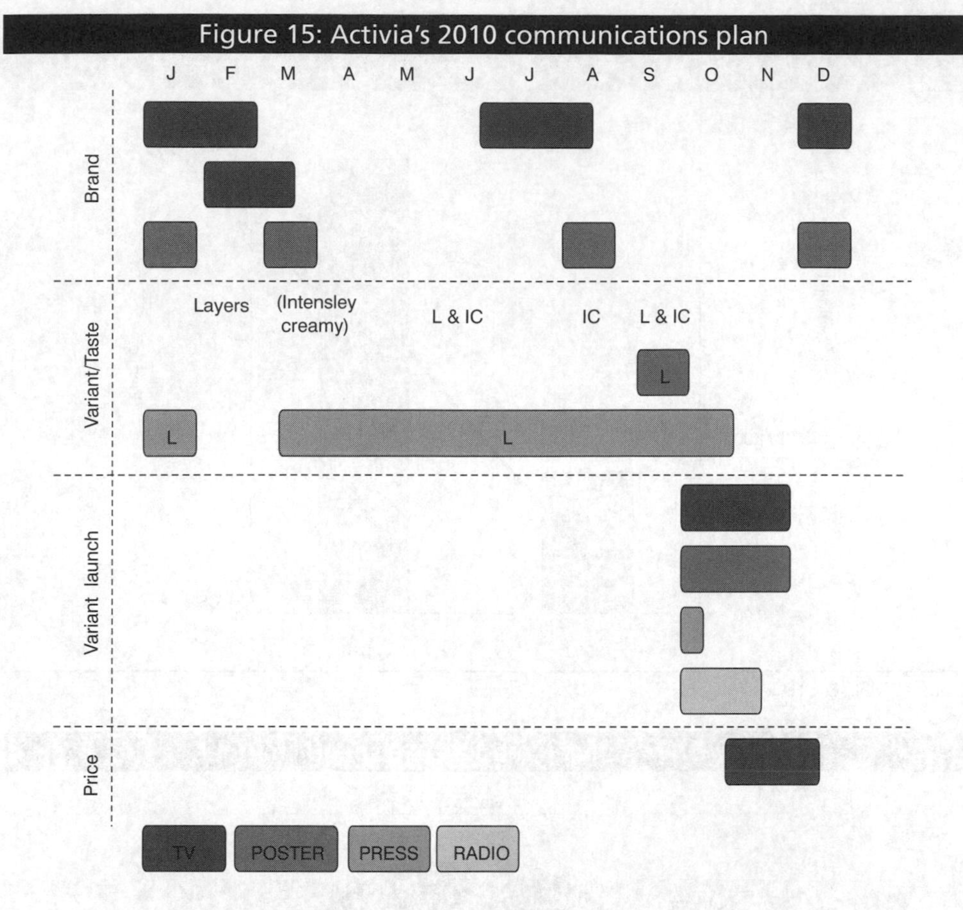


Source: MEC and RKCR/Y&R

## Market-leading media behaviour

Activia acted like a market leader, increasing its media investment by 17% and share-of-voice by 8% (Figure 16).[19]

TV predominantly delivered this (Figure 17) because it was excellent at provoking an emotional response, and econometrics had proved its ability to payback for Activia previously.[20] Outdoor was the key secondary media, delivering the brand stature worthy of a market leader.

Media placements built relevance. TV was placed in key 'talkable' slots and strong daytime programming. Posters were placed where busy women were most likely to be, i.e. train stations, bus stops and in proximity to supermarkets.

## Maximising the relevance of T.L.C.

We were confident we had a strong, engaging creative vehicle and were working off a strong insight which would deliver the necessary relevance to a broader audience.

Figure 16: Activia media spend and share of voice: 2009 vs. 2010

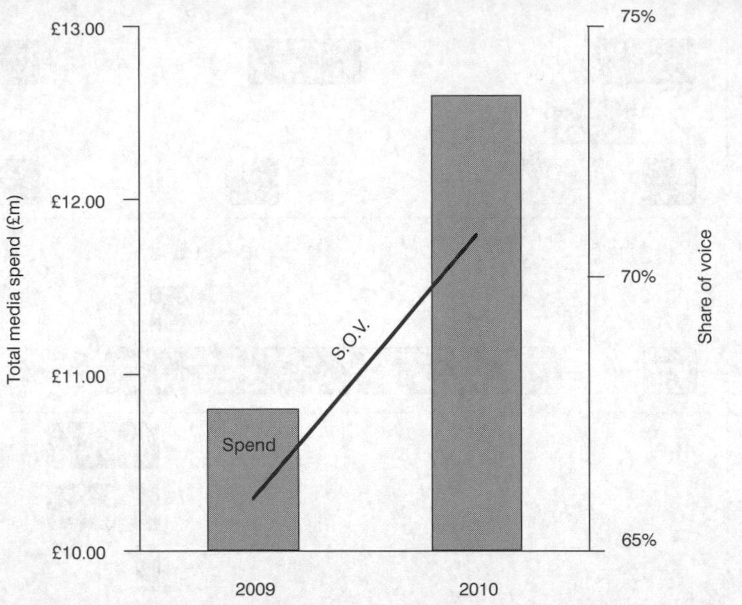


Source: MEC & OHAL

Figure 17: Activia's media 2010 spend/channel

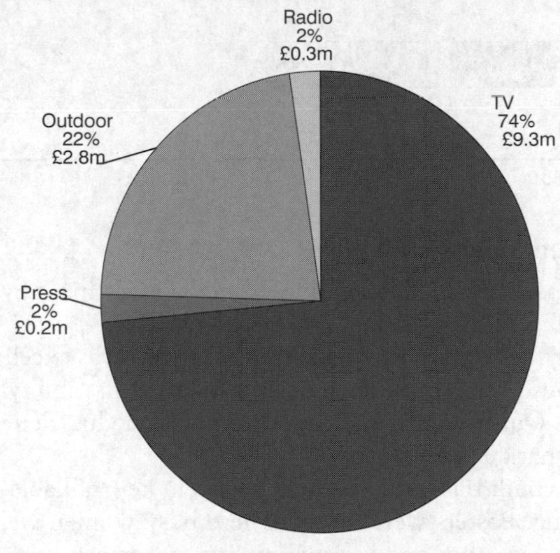


Source: MEC

However, we knew we could increase relevance further by launching the campaign at a time when more tummies were gurgling for T.L.C., and when women were most likely to be considering their future health and happiness…

…New Year.

This contextual insight was confirmed by research:

*I always think, new year, new start.*

*By New Year I'm thinking about sorting myself out.*

Source: Movement TLC Creative Development Research, 2008

So New Year was when we launched T.L.C. (Figure 18).

**Figure 18: Activia TLC Launch**

OK, we're done with those Christmas indulgences. It's a brand new year and time for a fresh start. And Britain, you better watch out 'cause I'm on a mission. Because 2010 is officially the Year of T.L.C.

That's Tummy. Loving. Care.

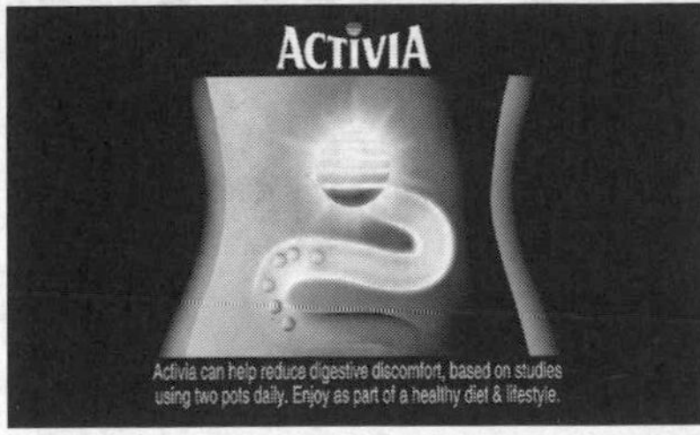

You see, eating Activia every day is a great way to help your digestive health.

And when you feel happier on the inside, you're happier on the outside

It's easy. So what are you waiting for? Get stuck into a pot of New Year's resolution.

And start giving your tummy some lovin'. Activia. Isn't it time you gave yourself some T.L.C?

Figure 19 presents an example of creative flexibility, delivering a variant and taste message.

**Figure 19: Activia Intensely Creamy (variant and taste)**

Activia Intensely Creamy. Available in seven gorgeous flavours.

My personal favourite? Peaches and Cream. Deliciously indulgent. Wonderfully creamy…

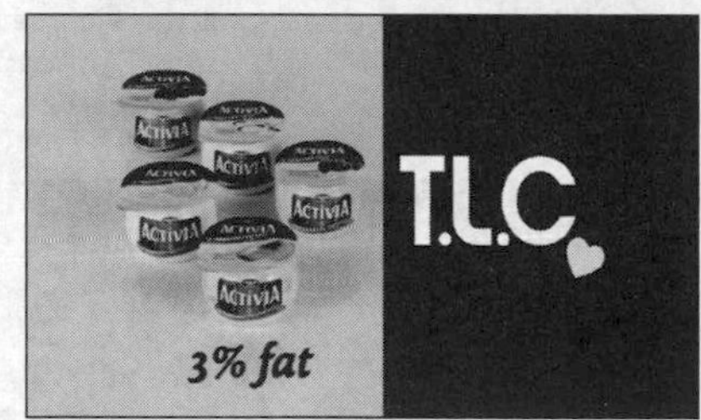


…and only 3% fat.

Now that's what I call T.L.C.

Activia. Isn't it time you gave yourself some T.L.C?

By Summer 2010 we had successfully overtaken Müller Corner. Acting as market leader, we encouraged consumers to make this the 'Summer of T.L.C' and were confident enough to make great taste our lead message (Figure 20).

Figure 21 presents a summary of the comms approach.

Figure 20: Activia Summer Gathering

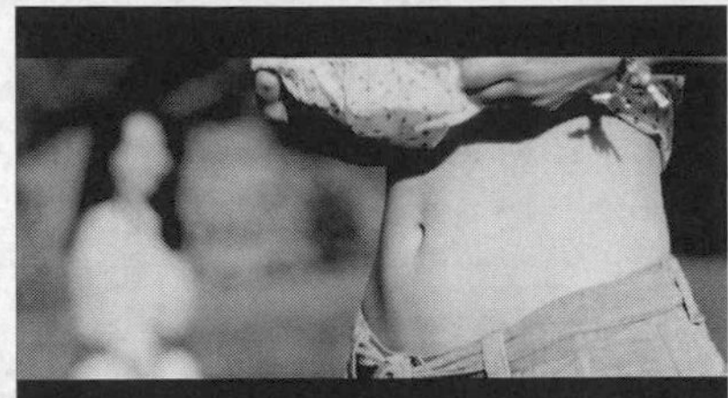

Activia, you might think you know all about it,...

...but c'mon, there's got to be more than one reason why it's Britain's best selling yoghurt brand.

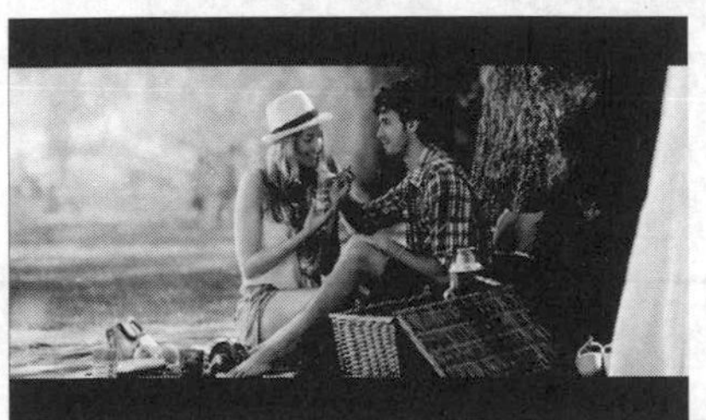

Well, it turns out that millions of you buy Activia, simply because it tastes absolutely delicious.

So, it's Britain's best selling yoghurt brand. But, just how tasty is it? Well, you'll just have to find out for yourself, won't you?

Activia. Make this the summer of T.L.C.

## Business results

We had been tasked to grow Activia to number one in market. We needed to achieve a minimum value growth of 7%, worth an incremental £13m, by driving penetration 3.5 points to 38%, equating to 900,000 new customers.

After the launch of the T.L.C. campaign, penetration significantly increased (Figure 22).

Figure 21: Activia's 2010 communications approach

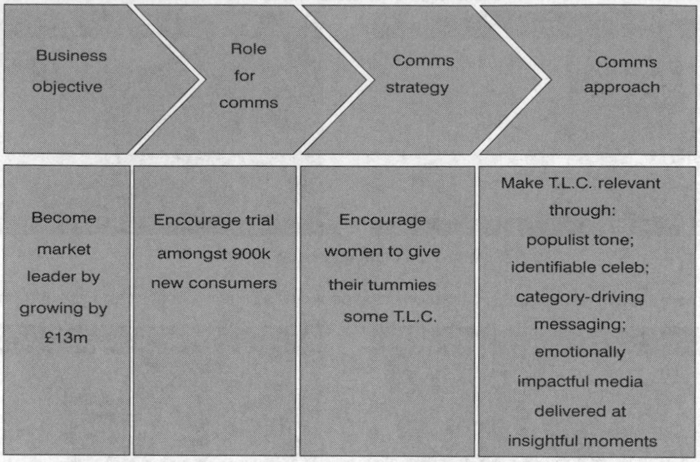

| Business objective | Role for comms | Comms strategy | Comms approach |
|---|---|---|---|
| Become market leader by growing by £13m | Encourage trial amongst 900k new consumers | Encourage women to give their tummies some T.L.C. | Make T.L.C. relevant through: populist tone; identifiable celeb; category-driving messaging; emotionally impactful media delivered at insightful moments |

Source: RKCR/Y&R

Figure 22: Activia's household penetration vs. actual TVRs in 6-month increments

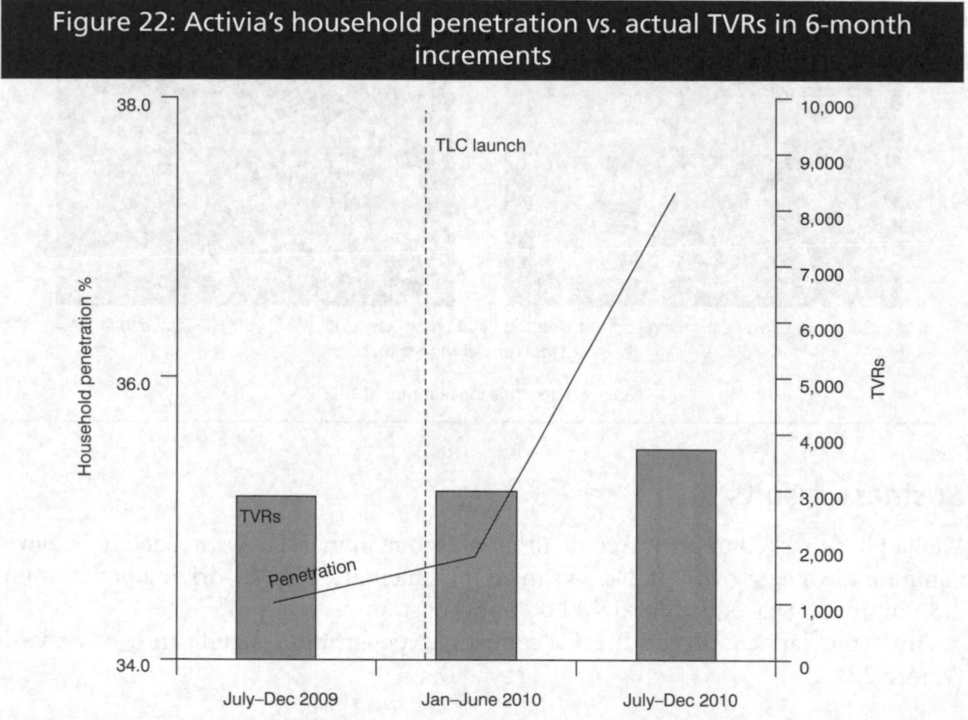


Source: AC Nielsen, April 2009–January 2011, 52wk rolling data; MEC actual TVRs. (Note: Activia only buy data for the past 3 years which is why a 12-month pre comparison could not be made)

A more granular look (Figure 23) shows we met the 38% target two months ahead of plan, finishing the year a point ahead, attracting 1.2 million new customers (versus 900k target).

Figure 23: Activia's household penetration vs. actual TVRs

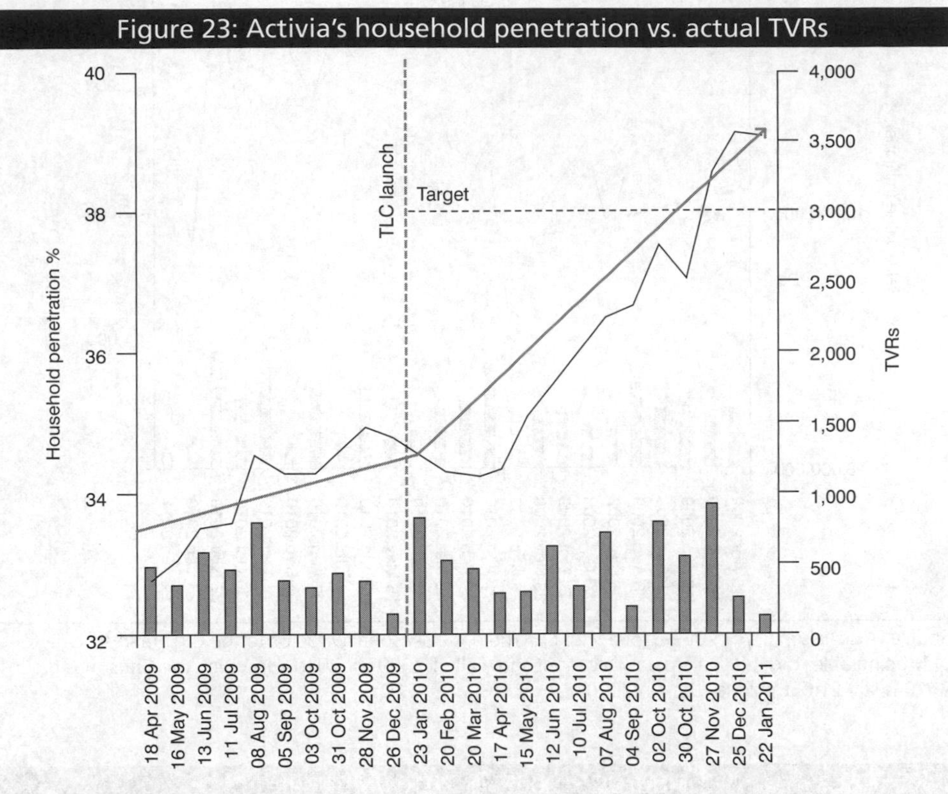


Source: AC Nielsen, April 2009–January 2011, 52wk rolling data; MEC actual TVRs.

As a result, value sales (Figure 24) also saw a significant rise.

Activia beat its 7% increase in value sales target by 1.9 points, delivering incremental sales of £20.1m (£7.1m above target). Müller Corner performed less strongly than expected, but even if it had grown at its 2008–2009 rate, Activia would have still edged ahead (Figure 25).

The increase in value sales meant Activia increased its value share by 7% whereas Müller Corner remained static; this enabled it to take its position as market leader (Figure 26).

Figure 24: Activia's total market value sales (4 weekly rolling)

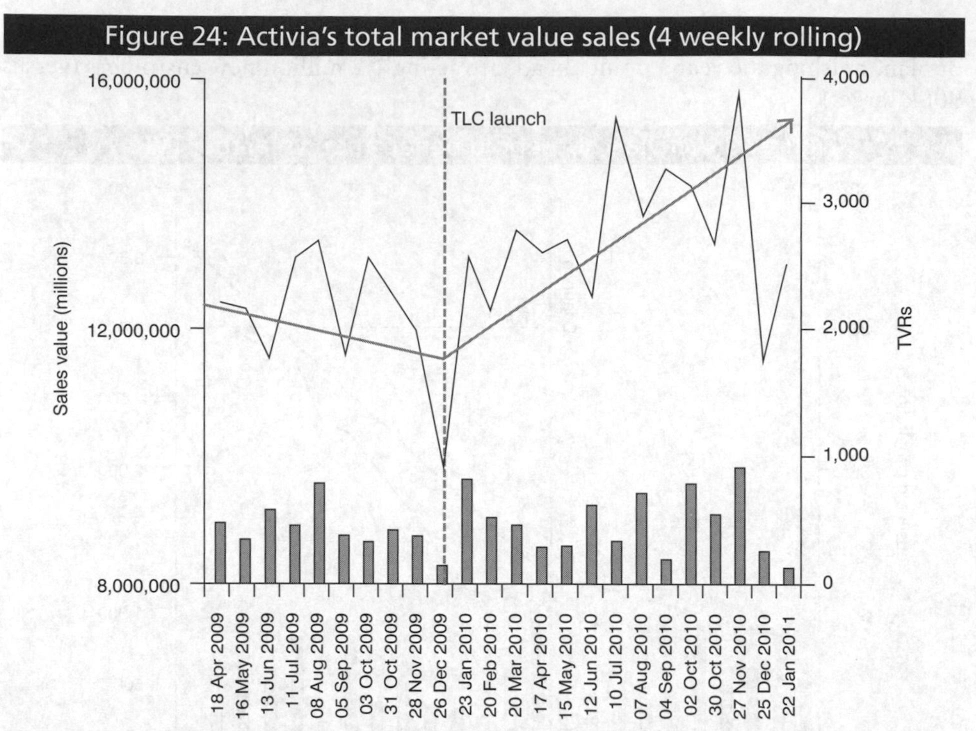


Source: AC Nielsen, April 2009–January 2011. (There is a seasonality factor to the CYD market. Due to only being able to get 3 years data we cannot show all of 2009 vs. 2010. However, the Christmas dip in 2010 is still £1.65m higher than in 2010)

Figure 25: 2009 vs. 2010 value sales

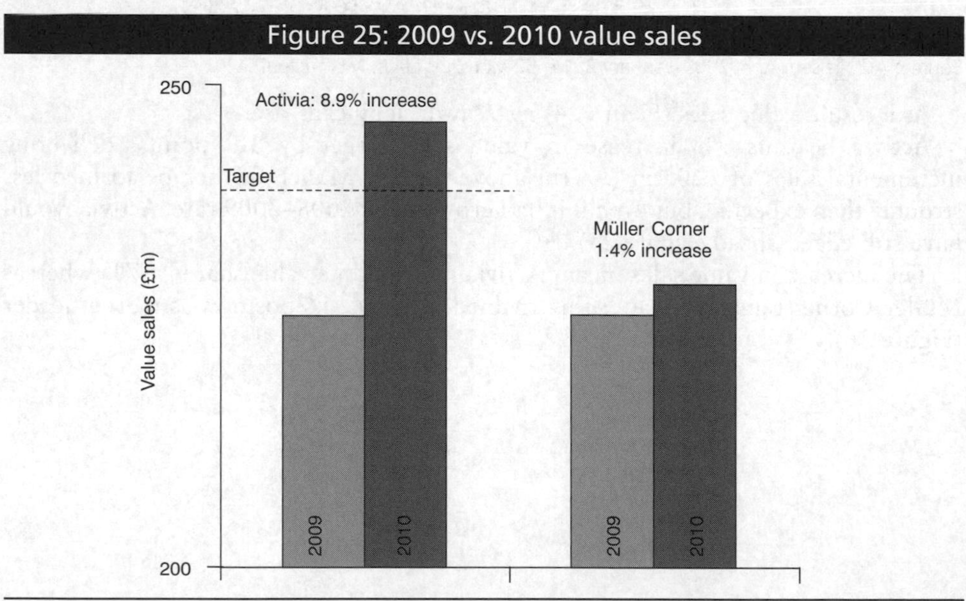


Source: Nielsen

Figure 26: Value share of Chilled Yoghurt & Dessert market 2009 vs. 2010

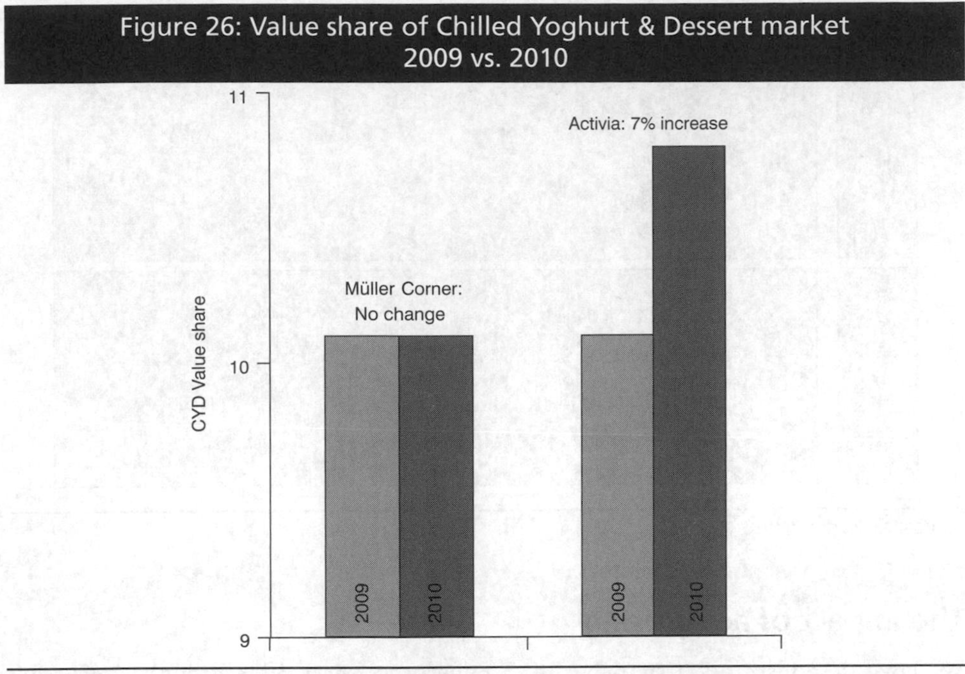


Source: Nielsen

Activia's growth outperformed the market, even though it grew by 1.7%, instead of a projected 1%. (Figure 27).

Figure 27: CYD value sales 2009 vs. 2010

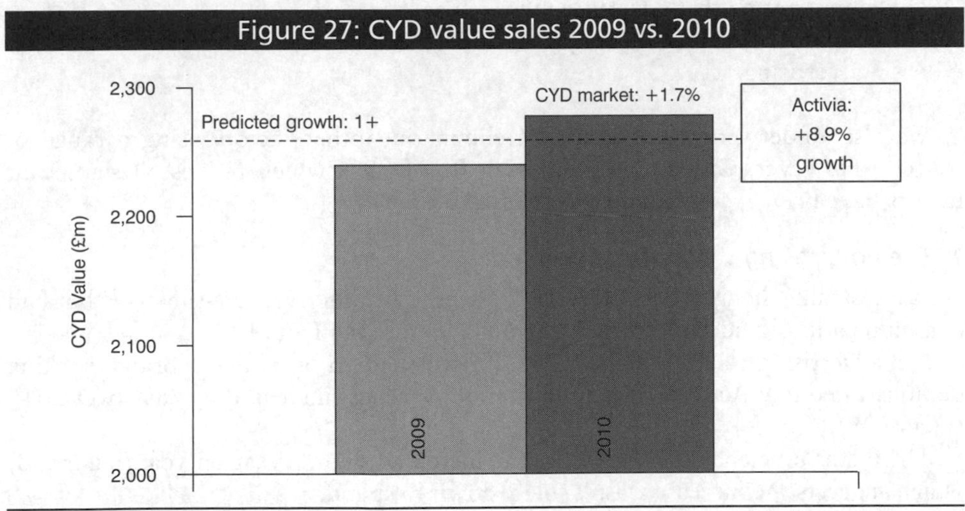


Source: Nielsen

Figure 28 presents a summary of the business results.

Figure 28: Summary of Activia's 2010 business results

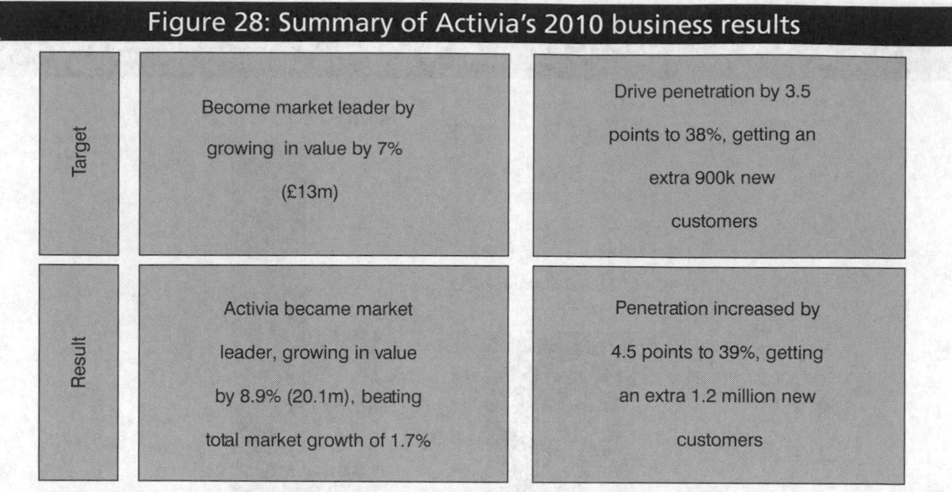

Target
Become market leader by growing in value by 7% (£13m)
Drive penetration by 3.5 points to 38%, getting an extra 900k new customers
Result
Activia became market leader, growing in value by 8.9% (20.1m), beating total market growth of 1.7%
Penetration increased by 4.5 points to 39%, getting an extra 1.2 million new customers


Source: Nielsen and RKCR

## The impact of advertising

We have demonstrated a step-change in penetration and value growth concurrent with the launch of T.L.C.

We will now prove that advertising was the key driver of this change by:

1. Demonstrating that advertising worked as intended
2. Using econometric modelling from OHAL to precisely identify the contribution of advertising.

We also underwent the exercise of eliminating other factors using a range of sources. However, OHAL's model has an $R^2$ of 99% which proves all significant factors have been accounted for.

### *1. The advertising worked as intended*

We successfully changed the behaviour of over 1.2 million UK consumers,[21] but had communications made the attitudinal shifts identified in Figure 11?

For advertising to have made these shifts, it had to be noticed. Brand tracking demonstrated that Activia's communications awareness increased by 28% over 2010 (Figure 29).

The media efficiency (spend/awareness) increased slightly year-on-year (Figure 30) which suggests the increase wasn't solely down to spend.

Figure 29: Percentage of women who were aware of Activia advertising

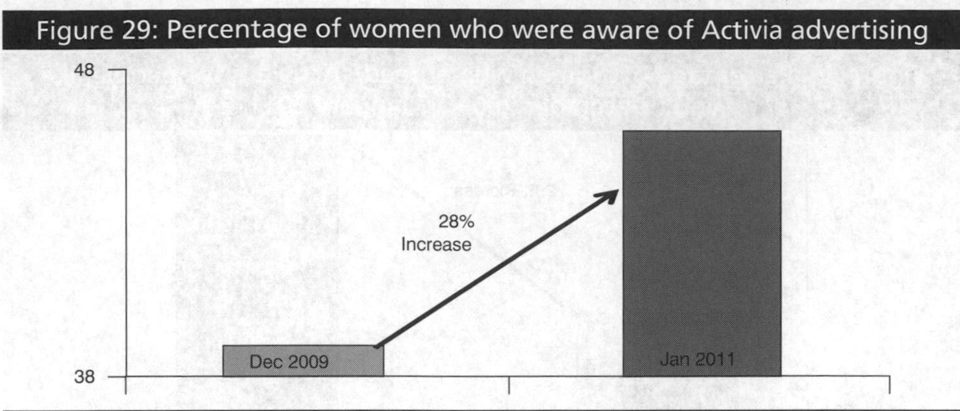


Source: Millward Brown. Base: 320 women. Statistically significant to 95% confidence level

Figure 30: Media efficiency 2009 vs. 2010

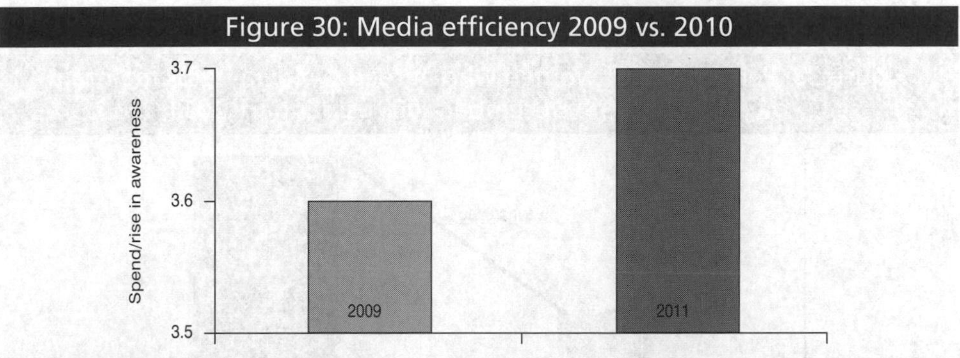


Source: Millward Brown and MEC

Whereas the previous testimonial campaign struggled to engage consumers, the T.L.C. campaign had no problem, performing 29% better (Figure 31).

Figure 31: Average Activia engagement score 2009 vs. 2010

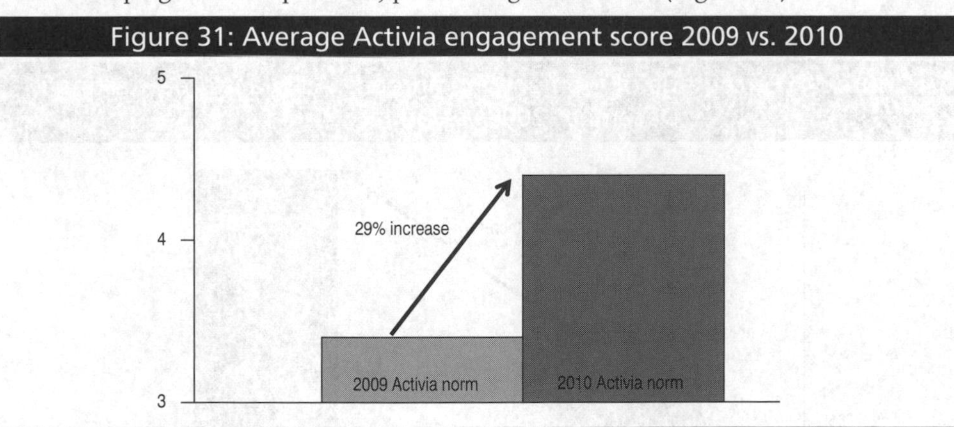


Source: Millward Brown. Base: 320 women

Engagement and awareness of T.L.C. helped drive relevance by 26% (Figure 32).

**Figure 32: Percentage of women who agreed, 'Activia is for people like you': December 2009 vs. January 2011**

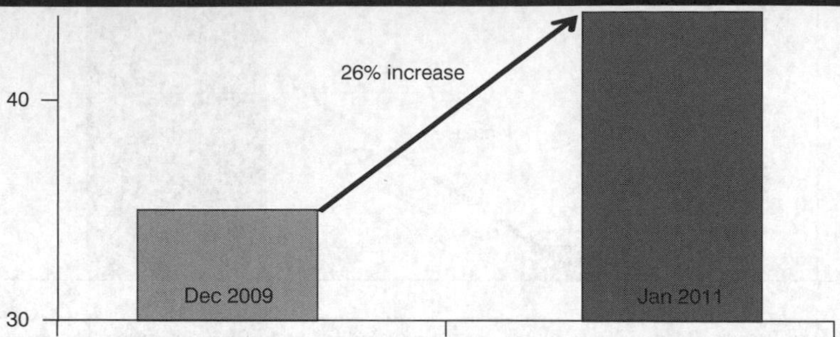


Source: Millward Brown. Base: 320 women. Statistically significant to 95% confidence level

Perceptions that Activia maintained digestive health also increased (Figure 33).

**Figure 33: Percentage of women who agreed, 'Activia helps maintain digestive health': December 2009 vs. January 2011**

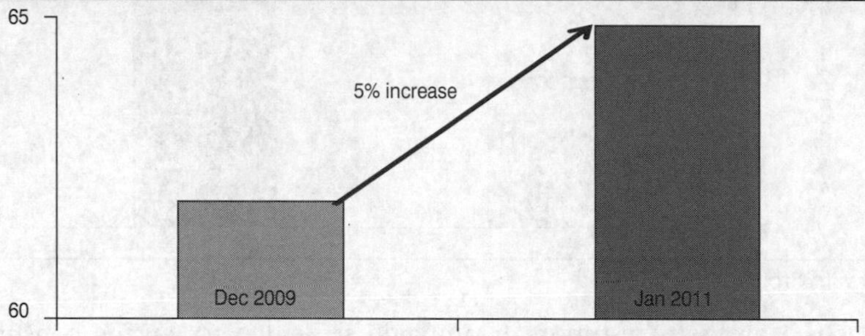


Source: Millward Brown. Base: 320 women. Statistically significant to 85% confidence level

Taste perceptions improved by 8% (Figure 34).

**Figure 34: Percentage of women who agreed, 'Activia is great tasting': December 2009 vs. January 2011**

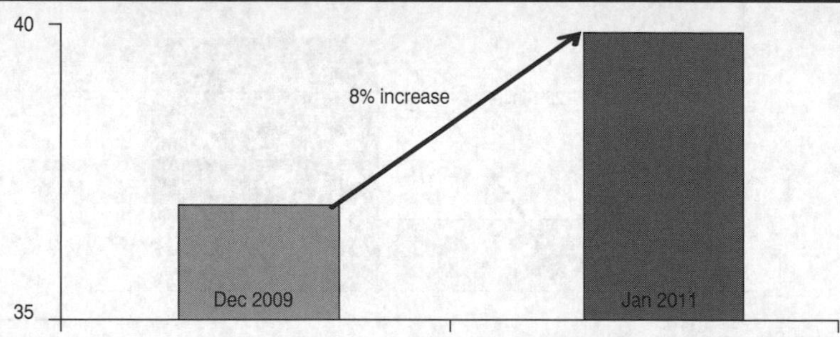


Source: Millward Brown. Base: 320 women. Statistically significant to 85% confidence level

A key aim of the campaign had been to increase the number of women who'd consider giving themselves some T.L.C. Consideration over the period increased by 27% (Figure 35).

**Figure 35: Percentage of women who agreed, 'I would consider Activia': December 2009 vs. January 2011**

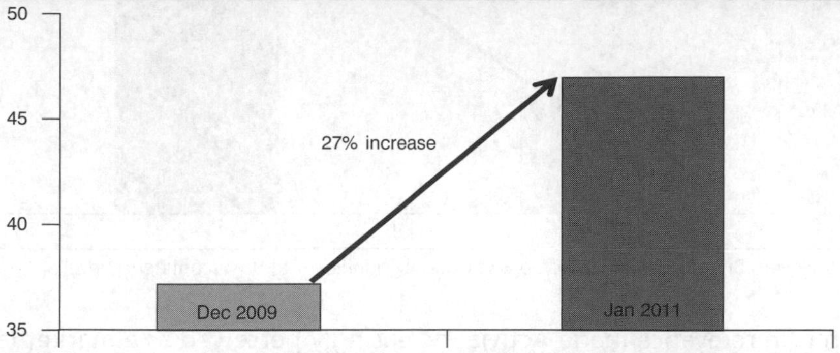

50
45
40
35
27% increase
Dec 2009
Jan 2011

Source: Millward Brown. Base: 320 women. Statistically significant to 95% confidence level

In summary, all our attitudinal measures improved over the T.L.C. campaign period (Figure 36).

**Figure 36: Summary of attitudinal shifts towards Activia**

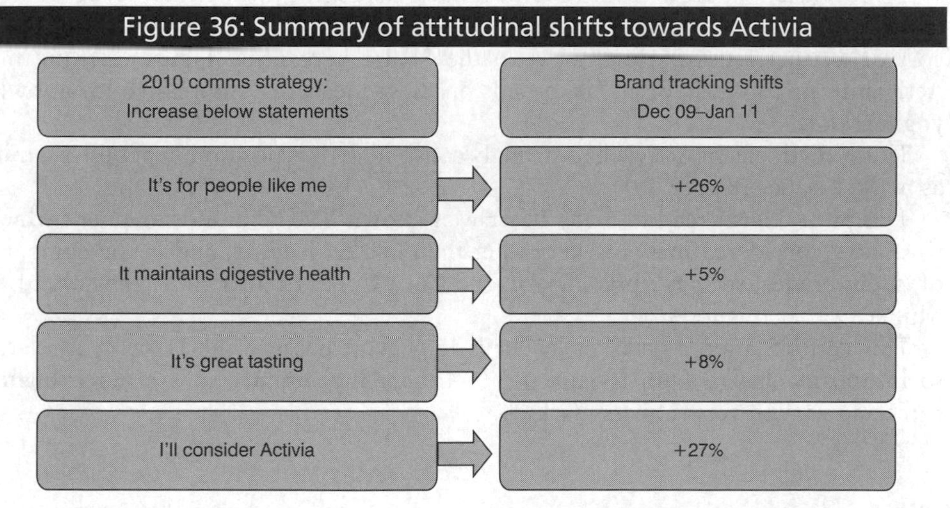


Source: Millward Brown and RKCR/Y&R

Penetration increase is the best proof of actual trial but claimed trial also increased, with an uplift of 17% (Figure 37).

Figure 37: Percentage of women who agreed, 'I have tried Activia': December 2009 vs. January 2011

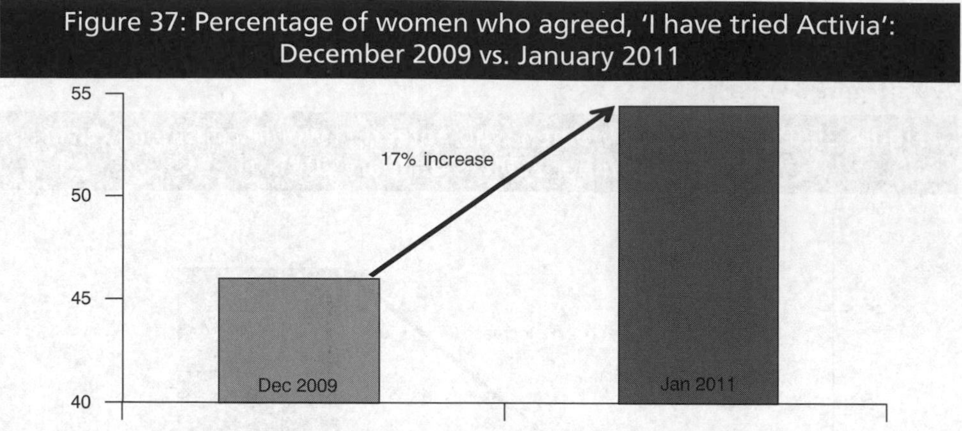


Source: Millward Brown. Base: 320 women. Statistically significant to 95% confidence level

## The shift in relevance made Activia increasingly perceived as a market leader

Significant improvement in relevance is corroborated by BAV.

Due to the survey's scale it is not run every year, but we have data from 2008 vs. 2011 which provides a good indicator of campaign impact.

It shows Activia grew from 64.2nd ranked percentile to the impressive 80.4th percentile out of 1,500 brands. Importantly, broadening relevance wasn't at the cost of distinctiveness, which grew to the 86.1st percentile (Figure 38), putting Activia in the top 20% of all UK brands on these measures. Impressive for a lowly yoghurt pot.

This growth meant Activia had strongly consolidated its position in people's minds as market leader (Figure 39).

This put Activia ahead of many other well known FMCG brands, many of which were now considered mass market rather than market leading, and in the company of 'super brands' such as Apple, Dyson and Coca-Cola.[22] It also put Activia ahead of Müller Corner (Figure 40).

This consolidation as market leader is important because the Powergrid relates to future financial growth (Figure 41).[23] 'Leadership' brands have a much higher projected growth versus 'mass market'.

## Figure 38: How UK female perceptions have shifted across four key brand health measures

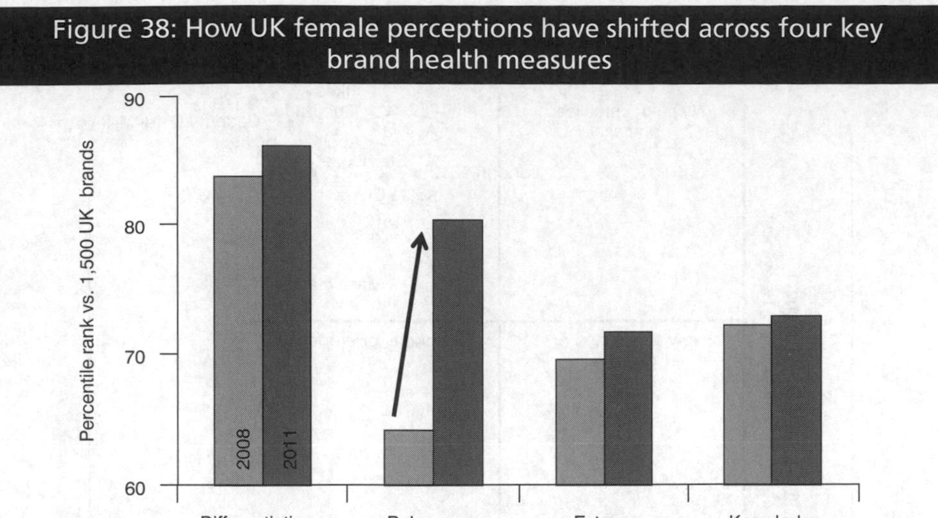


Source: Y&R UK. Base: 1,856 women in 2008, 815 women in 2011. Statistically significant to 99% confidence. Note: Due to the scale of the study it isn't run every year, but the 2008–2011 time frame gives us an idea of perception shifts during the campaign

## Figure 39: BAV Power Grid showing Activia increasing in market leader perceptions

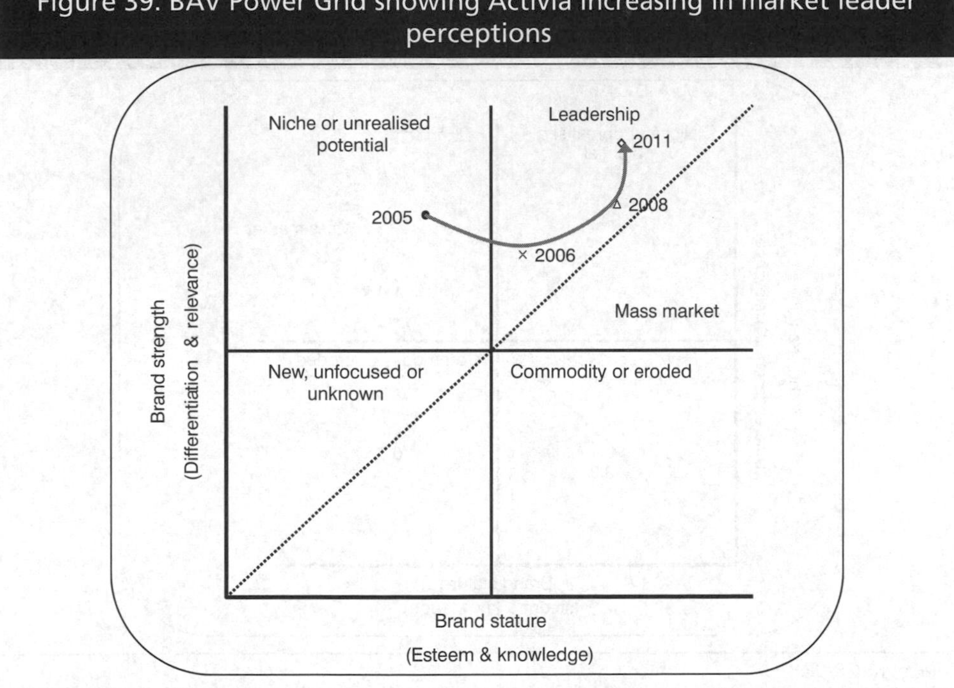


Source: Y&R UK. Base: 1,856 women in 2008, 815 women in 2011

### Figure 40: Perceptions of Activia vs. other market leaders

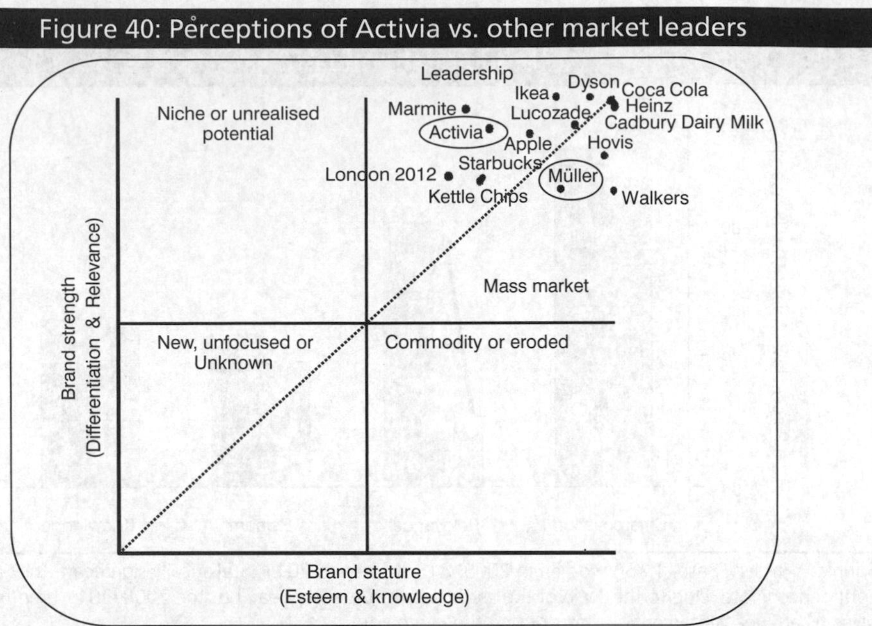


Source: RKCR/Y&R UK. Base: 1,856 women in 2008, 815 women in 2011

### Figure 41: Multiple of intangible value per unit sale

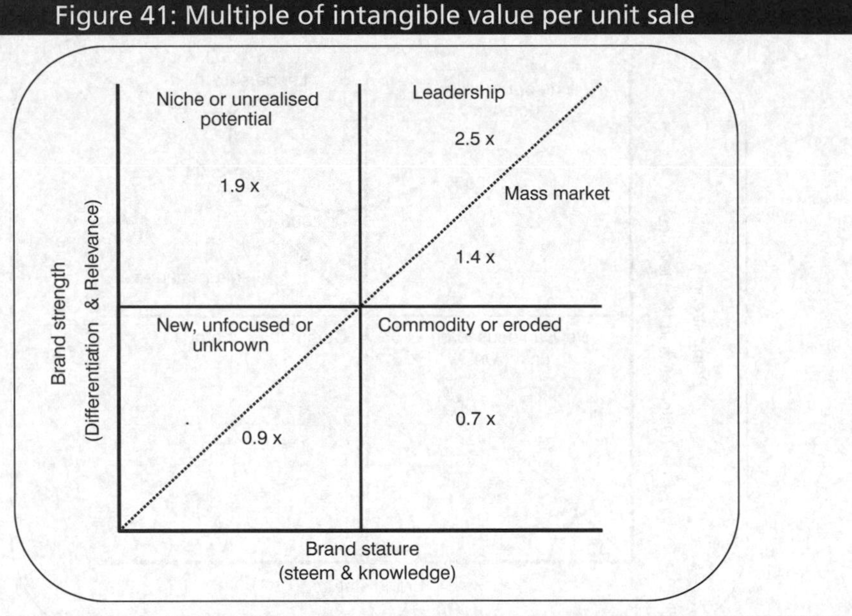


Source: RKCR/Y&R

### *2. Econometrics*

Econometric modelling has been used to identify and accurately quantify the effect of advertising and other relevant factors on Activia's sales.

The fit of the model is very strong with an $R^2$ of >99%.

OHAL have supplied us with the incremental uplift figures which take into account the full impact of advertising. It looks at the campaign period, but also includes the longer term impact of the advertising with a cut-off period of 52 weeks.

The model demonstrates that the 2010 T.L.C. campaign drove an incremental uplift of £58.6m revenue from sales of Activia.

Confidentiality prevents us from publishing actual gross profit. So, as in the previous 2008 IPA paper, we have used an average margin for this category as a proxy to help us establish whether the advertising was profitable for Danone. OHAL's experience in this category indicates that it is reasonable to assume a gross profit margin of 33% which gives us an incremental profit of £19.5m.

Minus the total marketing cost (production, media spend and agency fees) of £15.9m, the end campaign had generated £3.6m incremental profit.

So, for every pound spent, advertising generated a profit of £1.23 (Table 1).

**Table 1: T.L.C.'s 2010 Return on marketing investment**

ROMI = (Net profit)/(cost of campaign) x 100

| | |
|---|---|
| Incremental sales generated by advertising | £58,600,000 |
| Incremental profit generated by advertising | £19,533,333.33 |
| Marketing costs | £15,885,982.77 |
| Incremental net profit generated by advertising | £3,647,350.56 |

Return on marketing investment:

£3,647,350.56/£15,885,982.77 x 100 = 23%

Source: OHAL and RKCR/Y&R

## Conclusions and wider learnings

### *1. Market leaders differentiate themselves both emotionally and functionally*

This case shows how it is possible to develop powerful emotional platforms that resonate widely with consumers, but still retain the functional product truth that is at the heart of a brand's original differentiation. For Activia, this ensured a solid platform for continued growth and market leadership. As the client commented:

> *Launching the T.L.C. campaign successfully ensured Activia's position as market leader and gave us a great platform to build from for the future.*
>
> Corinne Chant, Marketing Director of Danone UK

### *2. Behaving like a leader can make you a leader*

Activia were ambitious enough to go for the number one slot, and brave enough to move on from a highly successful but ultimately limiting functional communications approach. Like a leader they adopted a more emotional platform, and they supported that platform with the media investment and behaviour of a leader.

### *3. Driving trial with new users is a powerful engine of growth for high-quality products*

When you know you have a product that performs very well for people, sometimes all you have to do is overcome the barriers that prevent new people from trying it.

## Notes

1 The competitive nature of the category Activia operates in can be seen from Mintel's adspend:sales ratio. Yoghurt remains high (3.5%) compared to most food categories, reflecting the intense competition amongst numerous large operators. The ratio in cakes and desserts is much lower (0.9%), as expected given the fragmented market and the strong position of Own Label (Mintel, *Yoghurt and Desserts UK,* June 2011).

2 By 25 December 2010, Activia had 10,074,812 buyers (Nielsen).

3 Activia Econometric Model, OHAL.

4 The market is Chilled Yoghurts and Desserts which includes everything from luxury organic yoghurt to children's gooey desserts. Value provided by Nielsen data.

5 In 2009 brands made up 84% of market value, and spent £54m in media (Mintel, *Yoghurt and Desserts UK,* June 2011).

6 Digestive disorders is a broad catch-all phrase for any issue caused by poor digestion, i.e. heaviness, acidity, constipation, diarrhoea or flatulence.

7 Market leader was Müller Corner, who was positioned around a key, but generic, category driver: taste.

8 Bamford, J. & Poole, J. (2008) *Danone Activia: The value of letting the product shine.* IPA.

9 Activia was in 71 markets and the UK was the 5th most valuable in 2009.

10 An increase of 7% value from 2009 was £13,370.8m because Activia was worth £191,011m.

11 Nielsen data April–December 2009.

12 Nielsen shows that a point of household penetration = 258,049 people. On that basis, increasing penetration by 3.5 points means attracting 903,172.

13 The full question on the U&A study is 'to begin with, can you please let me know with which frequency do you experience digestive disorders like bloatedness, heaviness, acidity, constipation or diarrhoea.'

14 Ibid.

15 BAV is the world's largest brand database and model for managing brand equity. It has over 750,000 consumers, 45,000+ brands, across 51 countries, and 18 years worth of data. This data has empirically evidenced that all brands are built on four key pillars: differentiation and relevance (which indicate brand strength) and esteem and knowledge (which indicate brand stature). Brand strength and brand stature are then plotted on a x/y graph called the 'Powergrid' which shows the health of the brand and enables one to plot its lifecycle: new/unknown; niche/unrealised potential; a leader; mass market; a commodity or eroded (Figure 42).

## Figure 42: Y&R Powergrid

The 'Powergrid' is a diagnostic tool in the BrandAsset® Valuator that can summarise the strength and development of a brand, as well as the associated level of consumer attraction.

The strongest brands are in the top right hand quadrant (above the diagonal), while the weakest brands have low 'Brand strength'.

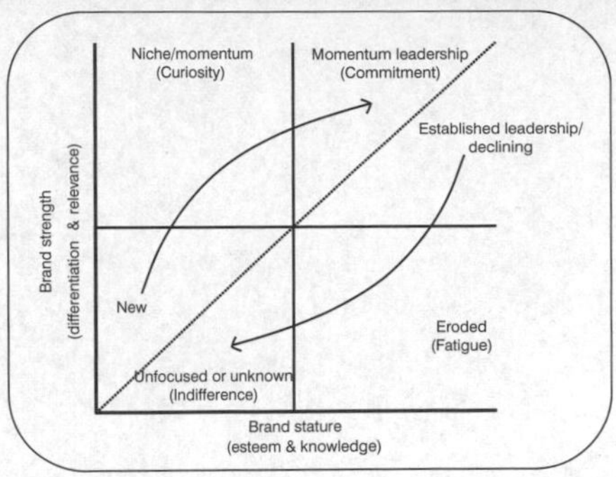


16 Binet, L. & Field, P. (2007) *Marketing in the Era of Accountability*. IPA/WARC.
17 Sung by The Spencer Davis Group and reaching number 2 in the UK charts in 1966.
18 Pringle, H. (2012) *How to Use Celebrity in Brand Building*. Warc, March.
19 MEC.
20 The previous campaign paid back £1:£3.03 – Bamford, J. & Poole, J. (3008) *Danone Activia: The value of letting the product shine*. IPA.
21 Campaign period saw an increase of 1,232,006 buyers (Nielsen).
22 Consumer Superbrands, 2011.
23 Y&R. Data modeling using 400 observations for companies 1993–2001.

## Chapter 23

# IBM

## Watson

**By Magnus Blair, Ogilvy & Mather New York**
Contributing authors: Ashley Wood and Kenan Ali, Ogilvy & Mather New York
Credited companies: Creative Agency: Ogilvy & Mather New York; Design Agency: VSA Partners; Digital Agency: Neo@Ogilvy; Direct Marketing Agency: OgilvyOne Worldwide; Client: IBM

**Editor's summary**

IBM had developed a computer capable of understanding human language, but the technology was hard to explain to the average human. The answer to this challenge and the key to a successful launch was the ultimate head-to-head competitive product demonstration: combat between human champions and the computer on the US TV quiz show *Jeopardy!* A fully integrated campaign was employed to drive awareness to 70% of Americans, showing them why they should root for the machine, not against it. The campaign generated $250m in immediate revenue.

Judges loved the bravery of this campaign, the use of consumer channels to answer a B2B brief and also the partnership demonstrated between IBM, their agencies and the team behind *Jeopardy!* A wonderfully focused solution to what could have been considered a complex brief.

## Background

In February 2011, on a three-night special edition of the US TV quiz show *Jeopardy!*, an IBM computer named Watson took on the two finest human players ever to play the game.[1]

It won.[2]

Yet the real victory wasn't of a computer over humans. It was a computer over *language*. Because while many TV quizzes just test general knowledge, *Jeopardy!* challenges contestants with wordplay. As an example, given a category ('Let's have a ball') and a clue ('Sink it and you've scratched'), your answer (phrased as a question) would be 'What is a cueball?' – assuming you'd pressed the buzzer fast enough to beat out your competitors.[3]

A magazine execution we ran in the lead-up explained the rationale for the competition – and what was at stake (Figure 1).

**Figure 1: Magazine ad**

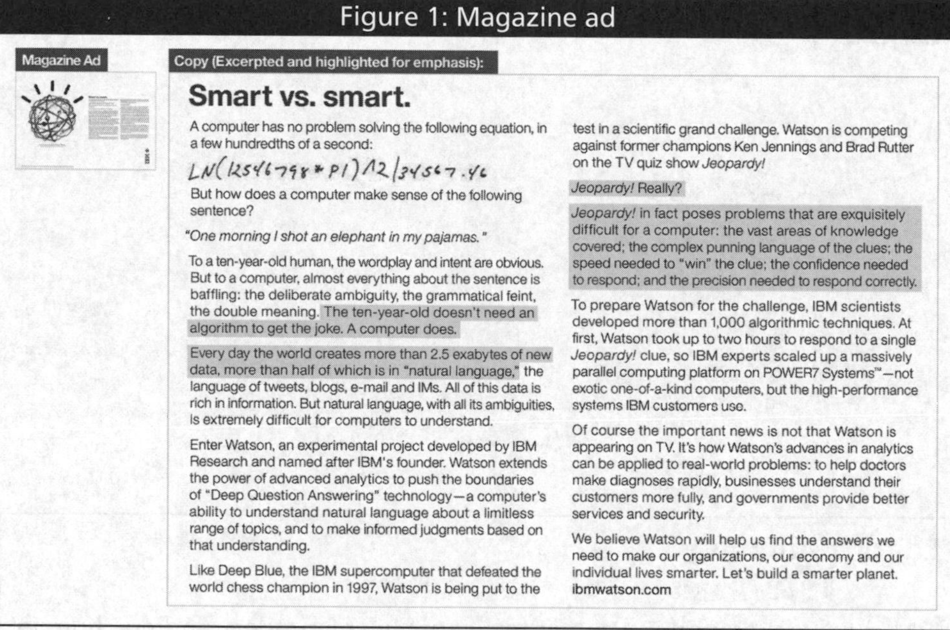

Magazine Ad
Copy (Excerpted and highlighted for emphasis):
Smart vs. smart.
A computer has no problem solving the following equation, in a few hundredths of a second:
LN(12546798*PI)^2/34567.46
But how does a computer make sense of the following sentence?
"One morning I shot an elephant in my pajamas."
To a ten-year-old human, the wordplay and intent are obvious. But to a computer, almost everything about the sentence is baffling: the deliberate ambiguity, the grammatical feint, the double meaning. The ten-year-old doesn't need an algorithm to get the joke. A computer does.
Every day the world creates more than 2.5 exabytes of new data, more than half of which is in "natural language," the language of tweets, blogs, e-mail and IMs. All of this data is rich in information. But natural language, with all its ambiguities, is extremely difficult for computers to understand.
Enter Watson, an experimental project developed by IBM Research and named after IBM's founder. Watson extends the power of advanced analytics to push the boundaries of "Deep Question Answering" technology—a computer's ability to understand natural language about a limitless range of topics, and to make informed judgments based on that understanding.
Like Deep Blue, the IBM supercomputer that defeated the world chess champion in 1997, Watson is being put to the test in a scientific grand challenge. Watson is competing against former champions Ken Jennings and Brad Rutter on the TV quiz show Jeopardy!
Jeopardy! Really?
Jeopardy! in fact poses problems that are exquisitely difficult for a computer: the vast areas of knowledge covered; the complex punning language of the clues; the speed needed to "win" the clue; the confidence needed to respond; and the precision needed to respond correctly.
To prepare Watson for the challenge, IBM scientists developed more than 1,000 algorithmic techniques. At first, Watson took up to two hours to respond to a single Jeopardy! clue, so IBM experts scaled up a massively parallel computing platform on POWER7 Systems™—not exotic one-of-a-kind computers, but the high-performance systems IBM customers use.
Of course the important news is not that Watson is appearing on TV. It's how Watson's advances in analytics can be applied to real-world problems: to help doctors make diagnoses rapidly, businesses understand their customers more fully, and governments provide better services and security.
We believe Watson will help us find the answers we need to make our organizations, our economy and our individual lives smarter. Let's build a smarter planet.
ibmwatson.com


## Objective: turn a game into serious commercial payback

Beyond the spectacle, *Jeopardy!* represented an extremely important launch for IBM: the first public view of its *DeepQA* 'Natural Language Processing' analytics technology, on which it had been working for over five years. IBM knew that a computer capable of 'NLP' would have huge commercial value in fields as diverse as medicine (where published knowledge doubles every seven to eight years, faster than any doctor can read), law, customer service or pharmaceutical patent research. But to create this market and capture its value, the technology would need to be launched. And launching a technology that's hard to explain and understand isn't easy.

*Jeopardy!* offered a perfect launch platform, serving both to demonstrate the new technology and to make it highly visible. But the broadcast itself would only go so far; a fully-integrated campaign was needed to translate visibility into tangible results.

We defined three stages of objectives for this campaign (Figure 2).

Figure 2: 3 stages of objectives

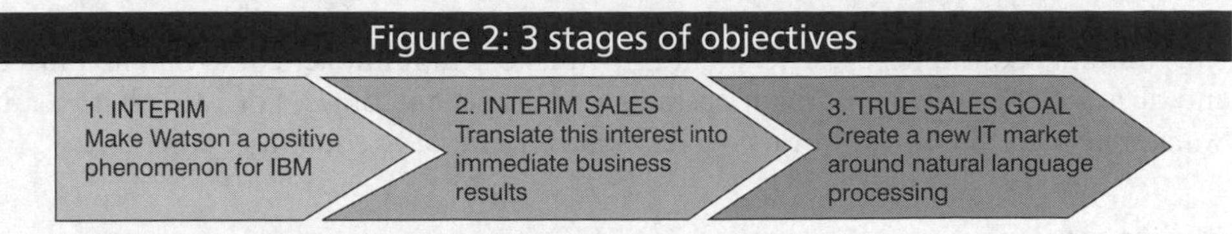
1. INTERIM
Make Watson a positive phenomenon for IBM
2. INTERIM SALES
Translate this interest into immediate business results
3. TRUE SALES GOAL
Create a new IT market around natural language processing

A number of KPIs were identified to assess success in delivering on each of these objectives:

### *1. Interim: Make Watson a positive phenomenon for IBM*

- Ensure viewership of the *Jeopardy!* event itself.
- Ensure magnification of event in 'Earned Media'.
- Ensure deeper engagement with the Watson story in IBM 'Owned Media'.
- Ensure magnification in social media.
- Create mass awareness and interest, drive positive perceptions of IBM.

### *2. Interim sales: translate this interest into immediate business results*

There were effectively two parts to Watson, (a) the new-to-market Natural Language Processing software and (b) the 90 currently-available IBM POWER servers and middleware it ran on. While commercialising NLP is the focus of our third objective, in the meantime there was money to be made selling the underlying hardware, broader analytics software and consultancy: demand-generation programs would quantify exactly which leads and sales came uniquely from Watson activities. In addition, we hoped for 'halo' effects on IBM's POWER server business. Our objectives were:

- Drive potential client attendance at Watson events.
- Generate qualified response through demand generation tactics.
- Generate resulting sales leads and the potential revenue these represent.
- Capture 'Win Revenue' from resulting confirmed engagements.
- Drive a 'Halo' effect on POWER factory sales.

### *3. True sales goal: create a new IT market around Natural Language Processing*

This is the ultimate potential of Watson and is obviously a multi-year effort. Thus it's (mostly) beyond the scope of this paper. But it's worth remembering as our true commercial goal.

Other than the humans Jennings and Rutter, Watson has no real competitors (yet). But IBM does, ranging from IT players like HP, Microsoft and Dell to the infrastructure providers GE and Siemens to consulting outfits like Accenture and

McKinsey – most of whom outspend it.[4] R&D has always been a core source of differentiation – for 18 years straight, IBM has filed more US patents per year than any other company.[5]

Watson provided an important opportunity to leverage that R&D investment to drive perceptions amongst a broad audience (important for a B2B company now with minimal consumer presence), but only if its cultural impact could be maximised and directed towards the optimal business and brand outcomes. For IBM that meant Watson needed to be proof of its overall *Smarter Planet* agenda in action.

## Strategy

To ensure we accomplished our objectives, we defined three negative scenarios to avoid:

### *A failure to capture public attention*

Beloved cultural institution it may be, but *Jeopardy!* is hardly watched by everyone. Nielsen ratings showed an average 8.4 million viewers in 2010.[6] Of these, over half are not employed, and under 1% fall within IBM's optimum 'C-Suite' target.[7] Communications would need to extend the impact of the broadcast, driving additional viewers to the show and driving cultural presence beyond actual viewership.

### *Interest, but the wrong kind*

Here, IBM history was instructive. As mentioned, in 1997 IBM's Deep Blue defeated the world chess champion, Garry Kasparov. While the story was front page news, the tone of the coverage left something to be desired: it was presented almost as an Alamo of the mind, with Kasparov as John Connor against the terminating rooks of Skynet.[8]

The communications and communications persona of Watson would need to minimise the chance of negative perceptions.

### *Cultural but not business impact*

Deep Blue had no effect on IBM's hardware business in the 90s, and it was playing the 'game of kings'.[9] Now IBM was playing a less serious game, and one harder to link to commercial applications than the well-worn metaphors of business = war, war = chess, chess = brains. Plus its technology would take time to commercialise. Communications needed to make the relevance and benefits clear, and exploit this not-yet-released technology to drive sales of currently-available IBM hardware, software and services.

As a first priority, we sought to understand the extent of potential negative sentiment, even fear. Instinctively, no one wants a computer to beat a human at anything. We might see antipathy either at a cultural 'killer-robot' level (the trap Deep Blue had fallen into; the name sounds cold, contemplative and probably not to be trusted with podbay doors),[10] or an economic one – with unemployment at 9%, fear of robots moving in to white-collar cubicles as they'd done blue-collar factories was not to be provoked.

Qualitative research confirmed the potential for fear, but led to the insight to neutralise it. This couldn't be about machines displacing humans. It had to be about humans achieving a feat for the benefit of humankind.

If we could make people feel this, they'd get involved and we'd generate the scale we needed. And if we could make people understand this, they'd grasp the technical challenge solved and the benefits achieved, which would be critical to driving short- and long-term commercial impact.

We set out to *Make Humanity the Winner.*

This strategy led us to play up two key human dimensions in the campaign:

### *A human team embarked on a classic 'quest'*

Focusing on a colourful cast of scientists (including project lead Dr David Ferrucci) and the technical challenges they overcame would make Watson itself part of the team and a human triumph in its own right.

### *Focus on defining the clear human value proposition of Watson*

It's not replacing or threatening anyone – it's here to help. And once it's done with *Jeopardy!* we'll use it to solve many of our most pressing human challenges.

## Creative work

As we began to develop communications, IBM's system was getting better at *Jeopardy!*, but had an image problem: it resembled a PowerPoint slide and didn't have a name. To achieve the impact we needed, this needed to change: a key first deliverable was a public face and stage persona.

Research helped us choose the name Watson: yes, a homage to IBM's first president Thomas J. Watson in the year of the company's Centennial, but also – for those who knew their Sherlock Holmes – a solid and reliable assistant to discovery.[11]

Then we designed Watson's identity. Heeding the concept of the 'Uncanny Valley', we realised one thing we shouldn't humanise was Watson itself.[12] Instead – and to link the activity to the overall IBM brand – we evolved IBM's Smarter Planet icon into a dynamic 'Avatar'. We set out to visualise Watson's 'thoughts', using shapes, colour and speed to show its experience of the game, its confidence in answers, and perhaps even hint at emotions (Figure 3).

Figure 3: Watson's 'Avatar' at different confidence states

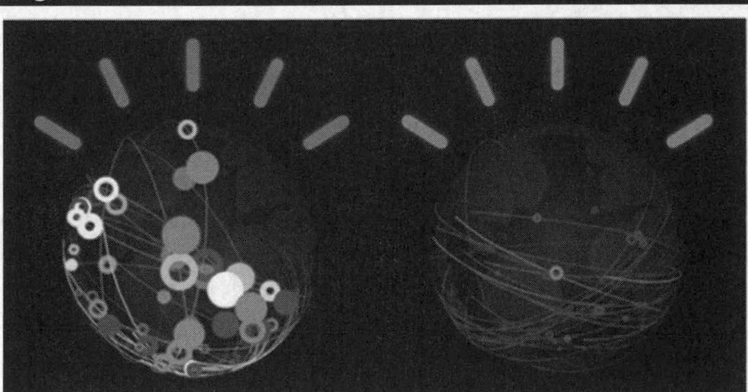

This was no small design challenge: we needed something dynamic enough to hold attention for 90 minutes over three nights, but we needed Watson to look friendly and approachable to neutralise any possible fear. We had to give a computer a personality.

The design ethos extended to the creation of Watson's speech-synthesised voice (avoiding cultural 'HAL' pitfalls) and the design of the set, which we partnered with *Jeopardy!* to create at IBM's T.J. Watson Research Center in Yorktown Heights, NY (Figure 4).

Figure 4: IBM *Jeopardy!* challenge set

While the set was recognisably *Jeopardy!*, we embedded significant IBM iconography, including the brand's Smarter Planet icon on the floor, and the IBM mantra 'THINK' in various languages on the walls.

While the design was ongoing, our embedded team spent two years documenting the quest to build Watson, capturing hundreds of hours of footage of highs, lows, but always progress. We created 22 videos chronicling the human story and exploring the human possibilities of the technology. Importantly, we often showed Watson failing – which removed the feeling of computers en route to domination.

In the run-up to the challenge we ran a carefully orchestrated three-month Owned-and-Earned media-centric campaign to tell the Watson story on our terms, position it prominently in culture and extend its impact:[13]

### *Phase 1: Set the stage*

- We released our video series through IBM owned media channels, and embarked on a large scale PR campaign. To seed conversation and curiosity about Watson, we worked to feed online conversations with posts highlighting events, press and provocative thoughts on technology. We offered access to the researchers through live web-casts, e.g. on InformationWeek.com.
- We launched a dedicated website filled with Watson content: videos, infographics, tutorials, white papers, etc.

### *Phase 2: Promoting the event*

- We partnered with *Jeopardy!* to shape the three nights of the broadcast (aired 14–16 February 2011), creating branded videos constituting 20% of screen-time to promote Watson's technology, the hardware it ran on and future human implications. The show was merchandised further with watching events around the country where IBM clients and prospects could watch the broadcast alongside IBMers – with the intention of lead capture and sales-force engagement.
- We drove interest in the show through advertising with TV, print, banners, pre-roll, and promos airing on *Jeopardy!*. A 'Let's Go Humans' full-page ad even ran in the *Wall Street Journal* on the day of the broadcast.

### *Phase 3: Seed and exploit the future implications*

- People had to understand that a win for Watson was a win for the world. So in the days after the event we ran a print and online campaign explaining why 'Humans Win!'. We also had IBM project lead Dr David Ferrucci give a TED live talk, broadcast online the week after the event.
- To translate public focus into real results we rolled out advertising, events, white papers and demand-gen activities focusing on both the future commercial applications and the currently available technology of Watson. We created sales-force enablement kits for IBM's sales function, which broke all records for downloads and deployment (Figures 5 and 6).

Figure 5: A selection of campaign materials including TVCs, films, 'Op-Ad' print insertions and Demand-Gen

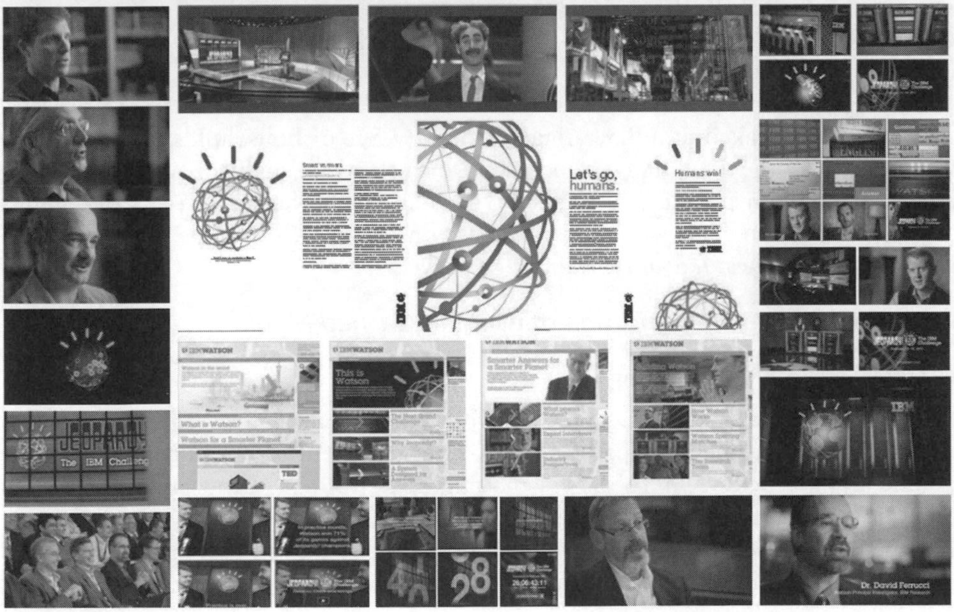

Figure 6: An outline flow of the campaign

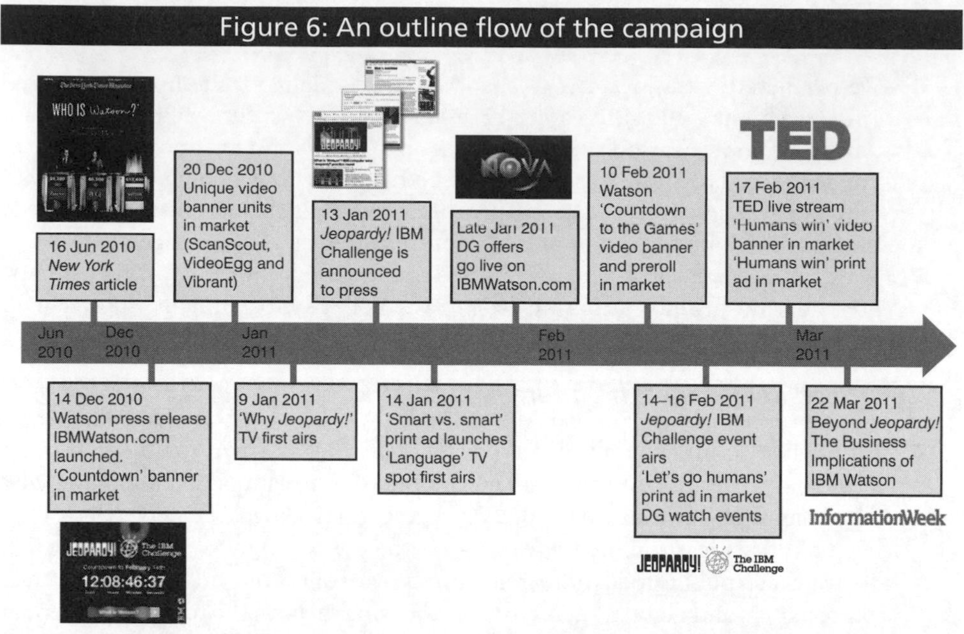


## Campaign results

Watson achieved incredible results across all three stages of our objectives:

*Objective: Ensure viewership of the Jeopardy! event itself*

### The *Jeopardy!* broadcast seized public attention

The broadcast peaked at a 9.5 rating/17 share (9.5% of households, 17% of those watching TV at the time). It averaged 9.1/17 over the three nights. Each ratings point equals 1.2 million people; we totalled 31.5 million viewers over the three nights of the competition. This was a 30% increase on *Jeopardy!*'s average February 2010 viewing – the highest *Jeopardy!* ratings for six years.[14]

*Objective: Ensure magnification of event in 'Earned Media'*

### Watson was a PR phenomenon

Watson was featured in a ten-page *New York Times Magazine* cover story, and was an A1 exclusive in the daily paper the day after the event – overall generating over 10,000 news articles. On TV, it was the talk of Letterman, Leno and Conan each night, and was featured in everything from *SNL* to *The Daily Show* to a full episode of PBS' *Nova to the View* – 5,700 TV mentions in all, yielding an estimated additional 808 million viewers. The overall value of coverage is assessed at over $50m.[15]

### *Objective: Ensure deeper engagement with the story in IBM 'Owned Media'*

### Owned media captivated the public

860,000 unique visitors visited the Watson microsite in the campaign period: 45% more visitors than the whole of IBM.com managed in its best quarter of 2010. Our videos have been watched 1.77 million times.[16]

### *Objective: Ensure magnification in social media*

### Watson became a star: Webby 'Person of the Year'

Watson was the top trending term on Twitter on all three nights, and 2nd highest during the follow-up TED broadcast. Bloggers wrote 12,000 posts, user-generated videos garnered 2.3 million views. 3.6 million people visited Watson's Facebook page in three months, and it attracted over 15,000 Twitter followers. A measure of Watson's popularity was that it was named 'Person of the Year' at the 15th Annual Webby awards in June 2011.[17]

### *Objective: Create mass awareness and interest, drive positive perceptions of IBM*

### Watson had huge positive cultural impact

A nationally weighted survey of 1,026 respondents two weeks after the event showed that:[18]

70% of Americans were aware a computer had competed on *Jeopardy!*, versus 48% aware of the week's top news, the unrest in Egypt: Watson got huge visibility (Figure 7).[19]

Figure 7: Total awareness

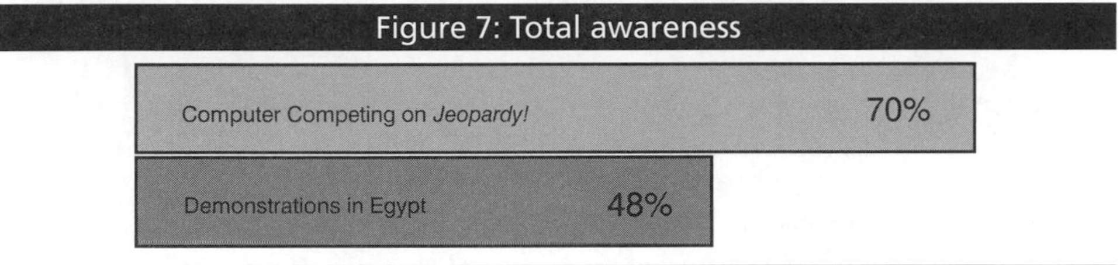


73% of those aware knew the computer was called Watson, 52% that IBM designed it. There was very low misattribution to other brands: Watson was very strongly branded to IBM (Figure 8).[20]

Figure 8: Name awareness and brand attribution

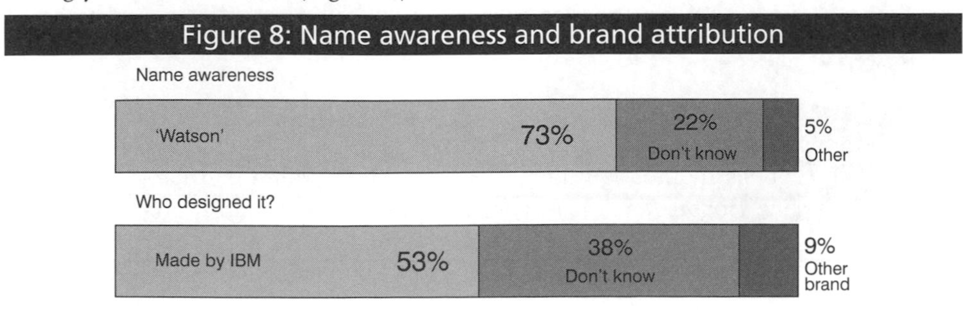

57% of those aware were impressed/interested; only 9% concerned. 40% said they thought more positively of IBM, with just 1% claiming it hurt their impression: we had positioned Watson correctly (Figure 9).

Figure 9: Watson awareness and perceptions

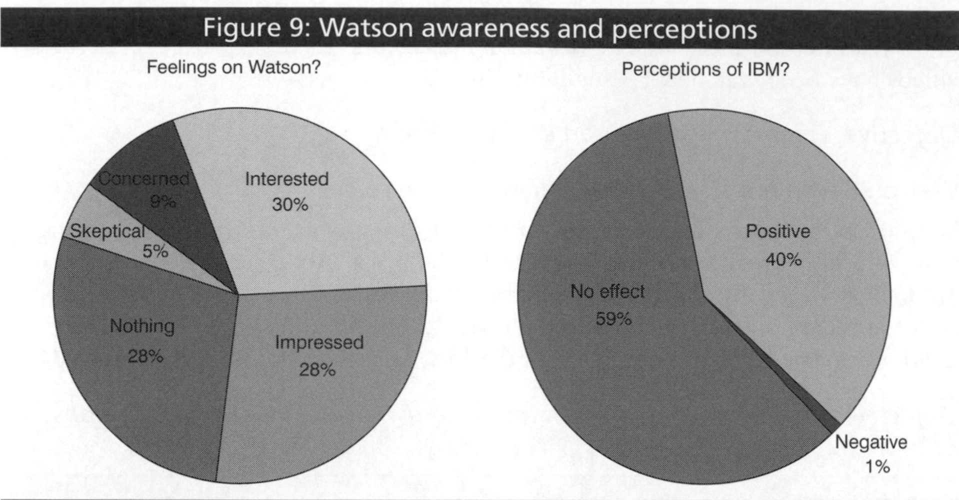


Amongst the 7% of the survey sample representing IBM's 'Forward Thinker' attitudinal target,[21] these numbers were even stronger: 100% were aware, 70% impressed/interested, 57% thought better of IBM: Watson connected even better with IBM's true target (Figure 10).

Figure 10: 'Forward thinker' awareness and perceptions

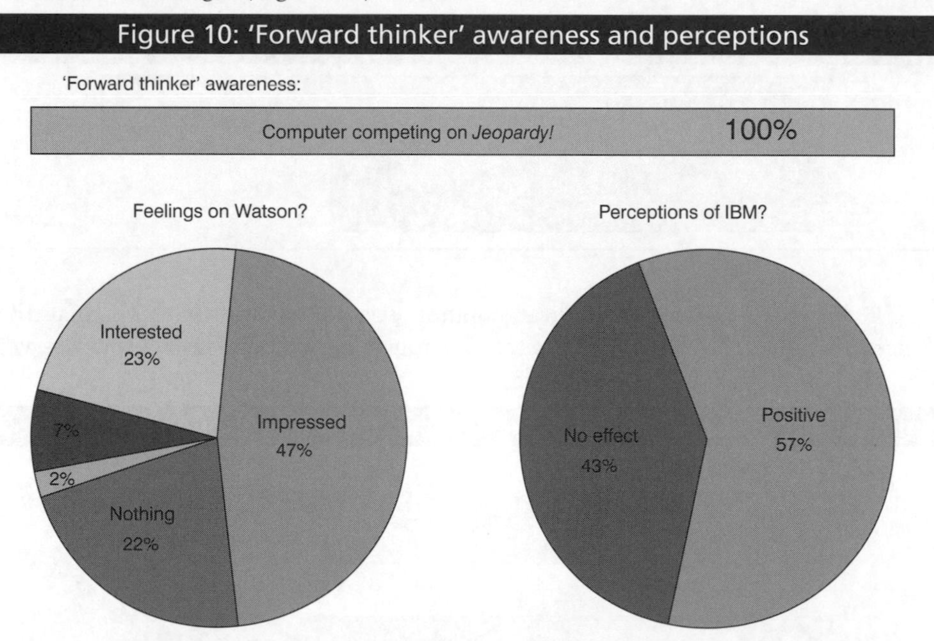

### Watson drove exceptional revenue through IBM's 'demand system'

IBM goes to market via its sales force, with money made through client engagements. These come in as 'Qualified Responders', progressing to 'Validated Leads'. 'Validated Lead Revenue' (VLR) is a measure of potential pipeline revenue (leads multiplied by budgets). 'Win Revenue' is then what is actually booked (Figure 11). IBM is rigorous about tracking how engagements enter and progress through the demand system, especially with regard to which activity drove them there. The following numbers are for North America and are specifically tracked directly to the Watson campaign.

Importantly, these are engagements for currently available hardware, services and software, not 'Watson-like' engagements (next section).

Figure 11: Schematic IBM 'demand system' sales funnel

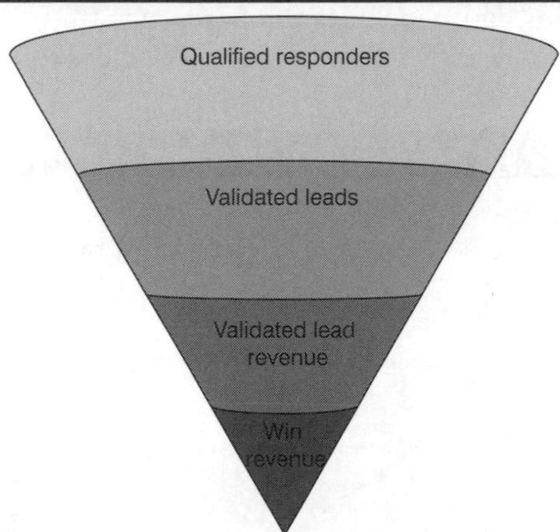


*Objective: Drive potential client attendance at Watson events*

### 12,400 people attended Watson events

At 68%, registration to attendance ratios were twice IBM's average. *Information Week*'s *Jeopardy!* webcast was its highest-ever attended.[22]

*Objective: Generate qualified response through demand generation tactics*

### Watson drove huge interest in IBM analytics solutions

Watson 'DG' tactics (events, white papers, sales kits, emails, etc.) drove over 18,400 responses, 2,350 of which have been 'Qualified'.[23]

*Objective: Generate resulting sales leads and potential revenue*

### Watson has created $712m in potential pipeline revenue

1,100 responders have been nurtured to become 'Validated Leads'. These serious potential engagements represent $712m in 'Validated Lead Revenue', which IBM is now working on converting.

*Objective: Capture 'Win Revenue' from resulting confirmed engagements*

### Watson activities have directly led to $254m in confirmed, booked revenue

Of this $712m, $254m has already been converted and booked, with more to come. $76m was sales of POWER systems (the machine Watson ran on and featured heavily in the campaign).

*Objective: 'Halo' effect on POWER factory sales*

### Watson made a big contribution to a turnaround in POWER sales

IDC Quarterly Server Tracker data shows sales in long-term decline pre-Watson, despite a refresh of the line in February 2010. Post-Watson we see strong growth. The most recent Q3 2011 data show sales up 9.1% (+$209m) on MAT versus their low point in Q4 2010.[24] This figure includes the $76m we can track directly to Watson, but indicates an additional effect (Figure 12). We will explore how much can be attributed to Watson on page 507.

Figure 12: IBM POWER $ factory sales North America MAT

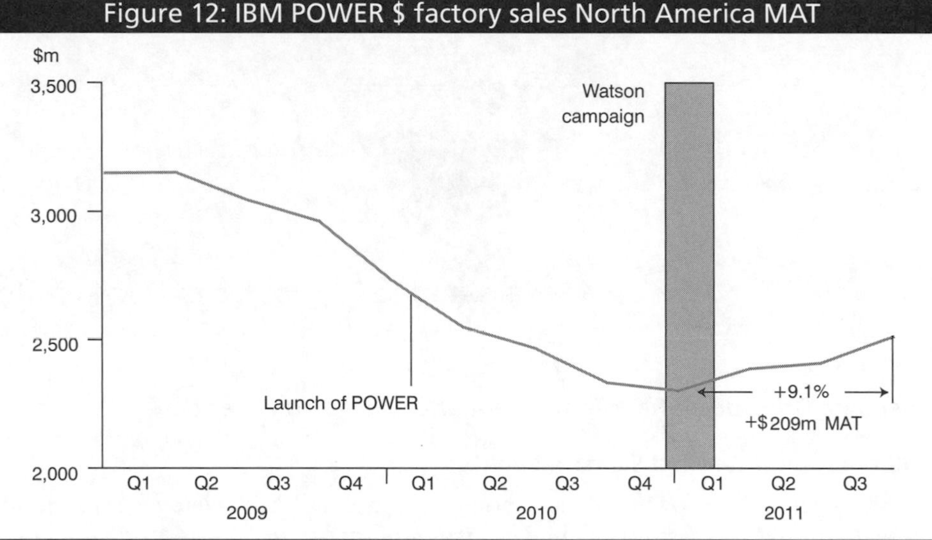


Source: IDC Worldwide Quarterly Server Tracker

IBM has disclosed predictions that they expect the DeepQA analytics technology launched by Watson to grow into a $1bn a year business.[25]

The first commercial engagement was announced in September 2011 with health insurer WellPoint, to provide care to its 34 million members. The value of the engagement is confidential, but highly significant. Subsequently IBM has announced a second deal with Seton Healthcare.[26]

As a result of the launch, over 180 clients have approached IBM about potential Watson-like implementations, with 30 top opportunities prioritised for commercialisation. IBM will be announcing several deals in the coming months, and has teased (as of 8 February 2012) an upcoming financial sector implementation.[27]

Although we cannot release financial details, this has been a hugely successful launch. Manoj Saxena, IBM's general manager for IBM Watson Solutions, was recently quoted talking about 'huge' interest.[28]

## Proving our campaign's effectiveness

We will return to our objective stages to discount other factors to prove Watson's success:

1. INTERIM: Make Watson a positive phenomenon for IBM

*All Watson awareness stemmed from Jeopardy! and our campaign*

### Watson was created ex-nihilo by marketing

Google Trends shows no mention of 'IBM Watson' prior to April 2009, our first PR release.[29] Buzz was low until the *NYT Magazine*'s 20 June cover story. Things only built with our full programme (Figure 13).

Figure 13: Google Trends: IBM Watson

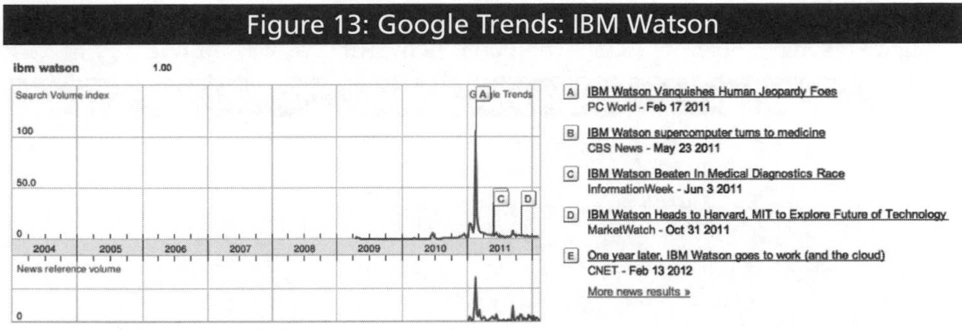


Source: Google Trends

### We peaked above ambient 'Watson' buzz

There's a base level of 'Watson' buzz (driven by golfers), but IBM (point E) peaked above (Figure 14).

Figure 14: Google Trends: Watson

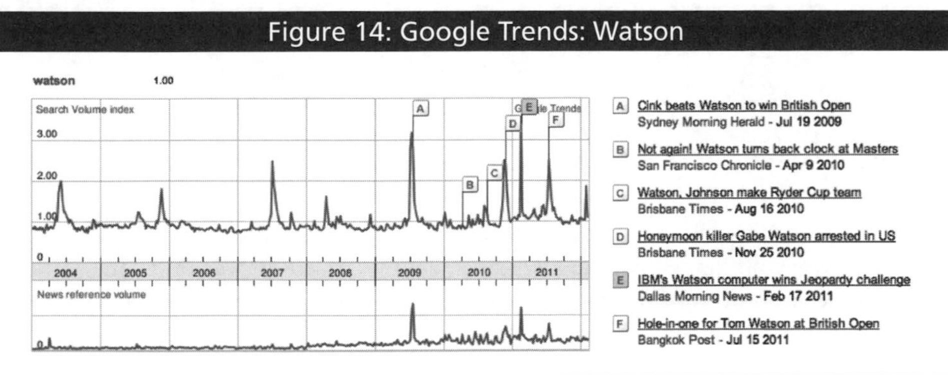


Source: Google Trends

## We didn't draft off *Jeopardy!* popularity

*'Jeopardy!'* buzz was flat/declining until being revitalised by the IBM Challenge (Figure 15).

Figure 15: Google Trends: *Jeopardy!*

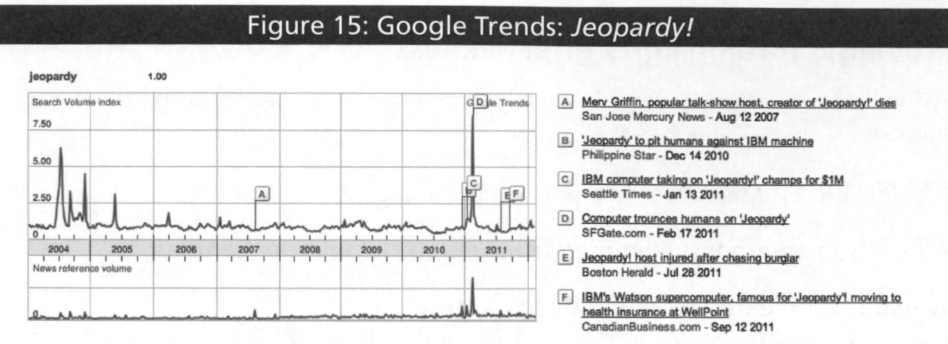


Source: Google Trends

## *Jeopardy!* ratings were also in decline

Though seasonal, *Jeopardy!* ratings trended downwards pre-Watson (Figure 16).[30]

Figure 16: *Jeopardy!* TV ratings FY 2009, 2010

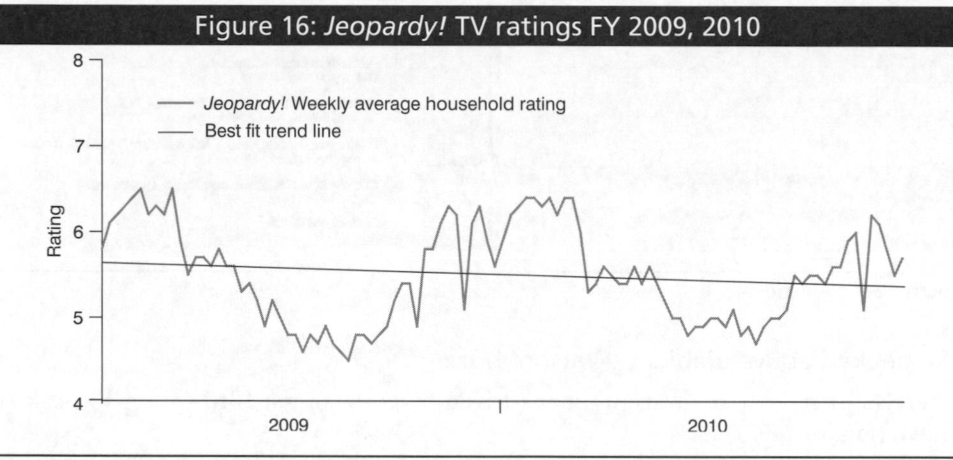


Source: Nielsen

2. INTERIM SALES: Translate this interest into immediate business results

### *Our 'demand system' results are tracked uniquely and specifically to the Watson campaign*

Every response which became a lead which became revenue was specifically captured by Watson demand-gen activity: engagements commenced at Watson events, or via lead capture around Watson materials. This isn't to say Watson didn't drive other leads, just those aren't the leads we're reporting here.

### What about price? promotions? distribution?

These factors work differently in IBM's high-ticket B2B space. Price/promotions are important, but apply after lead capture, effecting lead conversion to wins during negotiations. They don't affect whether the Watson campaign initially captured the lead. You also don't get to be a *validated* lead unless you're serious about spending six figures with IBM.[31]

IBM's sales force structure removes distribution as a factor. The only partial analog is the size of the sales force. IBM only reports headcount globally, but we can confirm the US sales force did not increase in size in 2011.[32]

### Would IBM have got this business anyway (without Watson)?

While this is a valid question, it doesn't reflect how IBM evaluates campaign success. What we can do is look at IDC data for IBM's three lines of servers (POWER, Z, and X). These represent the majority of Watson revenue (we do not have accurate third party tracking for the rest: Storage, Software, Services). IBM's revenue rose through/ post campaign, implying this was likely incremental volume (Figure 17).

Figure 17: IBM server factory sales – North America MAT

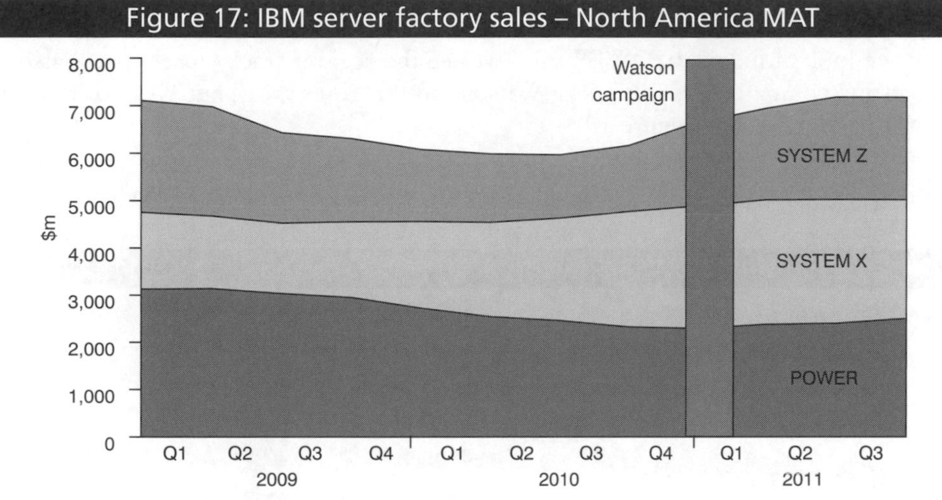


Source: IDC Worldwide Quarterly Server Tracker

### Was it just the market?

No, IBM was gaining share, especially in POWER and Z (Figure 18).

### How big was the 'halo' effect on POWER servers?

On page 504 we showed POWER revenue +9.1% ($209m). $76m of this is tracked directly to Watson, but how much of the rest might have been driven indirectly (via making IT deciders more disposed to POWER systems)?

By comparing North America figures to those from Western Europe, we can partially isolate a Watson effect: North America was heavily Watson-exposed, Europe to a lesser extent.[33] Otherwise, though, these are the most similar IT marketplaces we can compare in tracking.[34]

Figure 18: IBM server market share – North America MAT

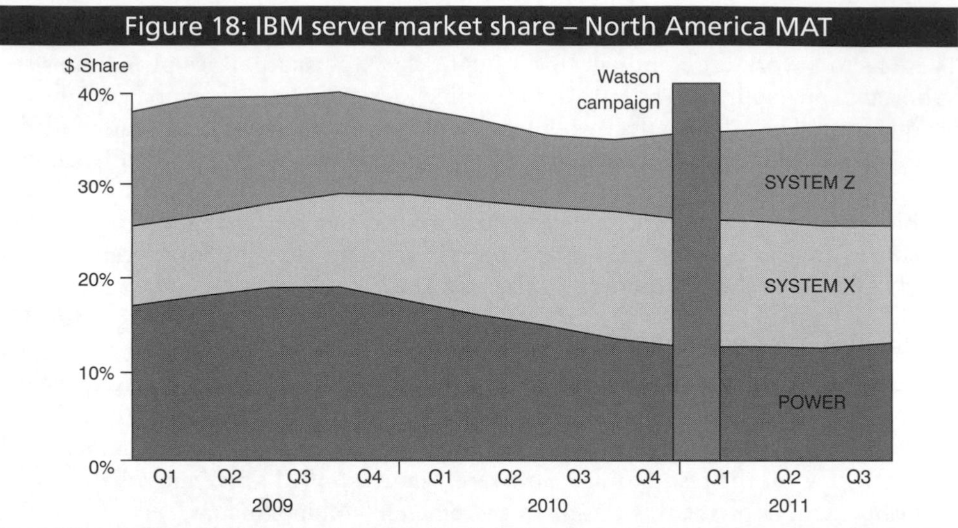


Source: IDC Worldwide Quarterly Server Tracker

If we look at indexed POWER sales we see the regions track closely pre-Watson, suggesting comparison is valid. Post-Watson, both regions grow, but Western Europe lags at 7.5% vs. 9.1% (Figure 19).

The 7.5% growth, though, includes currency effects: IDC reports in $, thus falling € exchange rates inflate the growth. Factoring this in, growth is 2.9% in real terms.

Figure 19: POWER $ factory sales MAT, indexed vs. Q1 2011

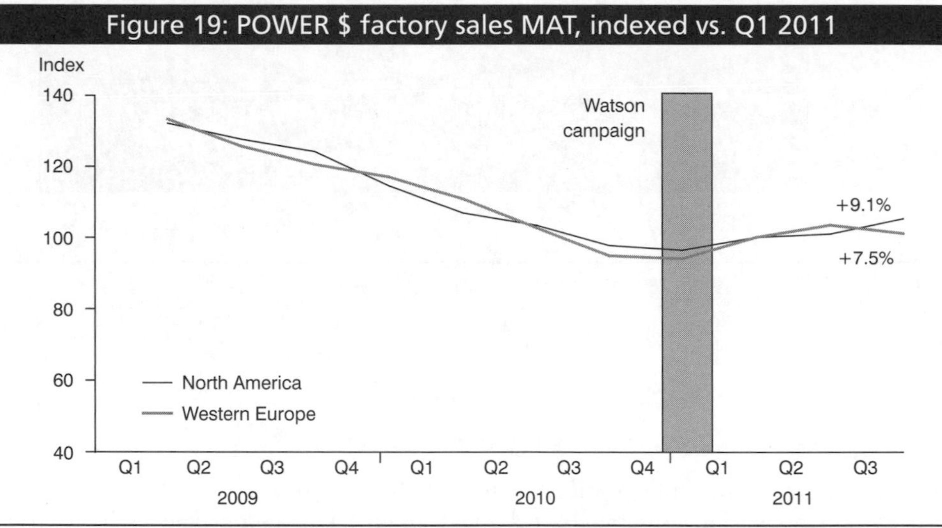


Source: IDC Quarterly Server Tracker

Of the 9.1% growth in North America, $76m is already tracked to Watson, leaving 5.8% (or $131m) yet to explain. The difference between this and Western Europe represents the upper limit for our Watson 'halo' effect: +2.95% ($68m revenue).

It's an upper limit as other factors in which Western Europe and North America differed will be involved, including the relative economic situation in the first three quarters of 2011. That said, the economic picture was arguably equally bad in both areas in this period, and both tracked closely together pre-Watson (Figure 20).

Figure 20: POWER $ factory sales MAT growth, Q3 2011 vs. Q4 2010

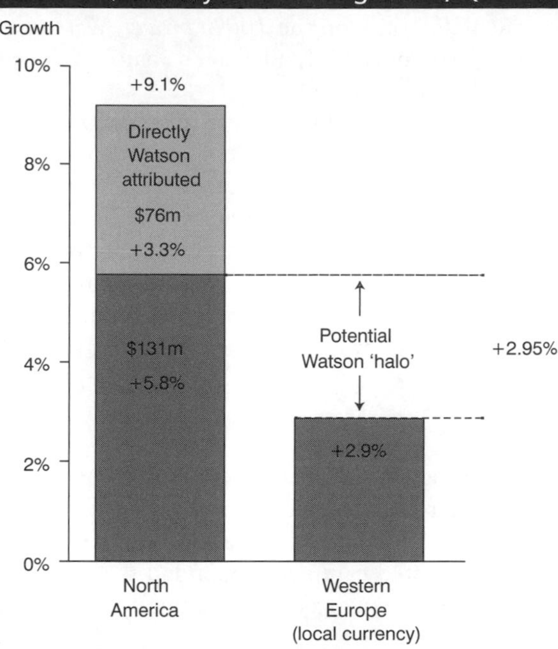


Source: IDC Quarterly Server Tracker

## What about new product effects?

Here we're reporting sales of previously available products/services. They may have been marketed by a new product, but they themselves were unchanged.

3. TRUE SALES GOAL: Create a new IT market around natural language processing

## New product effects? Yes, but created by our campaign

New product effects are difficult to control for. And with a revolutionary technology like Watson, they were clearly highly significant: Wellpoint wouldn't have signed up if this wasn't brand new.

That said, we believe that Watson's new product effects were in large part created by marketing. Had we not launched IBM's DeepQA technology in this visible way, and had we not made the human value proposition clear, this launch would have been of minor interest outside highly technical communities.

In these circumstances, it's meaningless to control for new product effects: our job was to produce them.

## Payback

Return on investment (i.e. incremental revenue/expenditure) is at least 23 times.

Return on marketing investment (incremental profit/expenditure) is at least 2.4 times.

Both of these figures are based only on interim sales of existing hardware, software and services, and are calculated only on the *100% proven Watson-generated revenue* – i.e. we are not including the previously identified 'halo' effect on POWER sales, because its exact magnitude is unclear.

When Watson attains its predicted $bn per year revenue, our ROI will be 91 times and our ROMI 18 times. Per year.

This is not to mention additional gains via Watson's effect on IBM's stock price: it rose 14% during the campaign and 28% through the end of 2011.[35] Or the fact IBM confirmed its status in 2011 as the second most valuable brand in the world, rising 8% to almost catch Coca-Cola as number one, despite being 'only' B2B.[36] Or one other additional benefit: visits to ibm.com/employment almost doubled during the campaign, and 'careers' was the number one search term on IBM.com.[37]

## Summary

IBM had a brilliant technological advance: a computer capable of understanding natural language. For all its genius, the technology was hard to explain. So we created the ultimate product demo: head-to-head competition on the US's most popular quiz show, *Jeopardy!*. A fully integrated campaign extended the impact of the broadcast, creating a billion dollar category, a quarter billion in immediate revenue, and proving these two points:

### *a) B2B doesn't have to 'B2Boring'*

No consumer is ever going to buy a DeepQA system – or even a POWER box. But by building presence at a mass level, we created excitement and energy to drive response amongst our smaller 'true' target. We also helped the internal sell at client companies, enabling CTOs and CIOs to convince now more educated C-Suite colleagues: *'Boss, I think we need a Watson.'*

### *b) Can you monetise a media idea? Yes*

As we enter a post TV-advertising world, a key question in marketing relates to the business effectiveness of sponsored and branded content. Watson proves these effects can be huge: when Paid, Owned and Earned channels work perfectly together.

## Notes

1 Brad Rutter, the show's all-time biggest money winner, and Ken Jennings, the record holder for most consecutive wins (74).

2 Final score: Watson $77,147, Jennings $24,000, Rutter $21,600. Watson (or rather, IBM) donated the $1m prize to charity.

3 This particular question was asked in show #3662, first aired on 4 July 2000.

4 Kantar Media figures for the year to Q4 2010 show IBM US SOV at 11%, behind Microsoft (32%), HP (15%), Dell (14%) and GE (13%).
5 c.f. Forbes (2011) 'IBM and its stranglehold on patent leadership', 'For 18 straight years, IBM has... [been] granted more U.S. patents than any other company on the planet', 13 September.
6 Source: Nielsen Ratings.
7 Source: MRI 2010 Doublebase.
8 Typical was *The New York Times* writing of a 'brutal unseating of humanity', a 'blow to the collective ego of the human race' and bemoaning 'the coming days of ascendant computers'. NYT (1997) 'Inscrutable Conqueror', 'Computer topples Kasparov', 12 May.
9 According to IDC's Worldwide Quarterly Server Tracker, IBM Systems revenue actually fell from 1997 through until 2003.
10 It's worth noting that 2001: A Space Odyssey's 'HAL' is just a very small alphabetic shift from IBM.
11 IBM was founded as the Computing Tabulating Recording Corporation on 16 June 1911.
12 A hypothesis (especially in robotics and computer animation) holding that humans are repulsed by not-quite-perfect human imitations.
13 A brief schematic of the campaign is on the next page.
14 Source: CBS Television Distribution, Nielsen Ratings.
15 Source: IBM Media Monitoring, Critical Mention.
16 Source: IBM Web Metrics.
17 Source: IBM Social Media Metrics.
18 Our seven question survey was carried out by IPSOS the week of 28 February 2011.
19 Egyptian President Hosni Mubarak resigned on 11 February, three days before the *Jeopardy!* Challenge.
20 The 10% misattribution broke down as Microsoft 4%, Google 2%, Apple 2%, Dell 1%, HP 1%.
21 Our base of 'Forward Thinkers' (defined as agreeing to five attitudinal statements) was 69, so these numbers are still relatively robust.
22 Source: IBM, Information Week.
23 All data for this and subsequent sections: source, IBM internal figures.
24 Source: IDC Worldwide Quarterly Server Tracker. At the time of writing, Q4 2011 data are not yet released
25 c.f. *Wall Street Journal* (2011) 'WellPoint's new hire. What is Watson?', 'Steven A. Mills, the IBM senior vice president... believes the Watson technology carries the potential to grow into a business generating $1 billion of annual revenue', 12 September.
26 c.f. MIT Technology Review (2012) 'Watson's new job: IBM salesman', 'Seton Healthcare, which operates hospitals and clinics serving 1.8 million people in central Texas, recently signed up for a system branded "Ready for Watson"', 8 February.
27 Ibid.
28 c.f. Forbes (2012) 'IBM's Watson, Cedars-Sinai and WellPoint take on cancer", 1 February.
29 c.f. Press Release (2009) 'IBM developing computing system to challenge humans on America's favorite quiz show, *Jeopardy!*', 27 April.
30 Source: Nielsen Ratings.
31 Our figures show 1,100 Validated Leads, $712m of Validated Lead revenue. Average lead was for $650K project (= $712m/1,100).
32 c.f. ComputerWorld (2010) 'IBM stops disclosing U.S. headcount data', 12 March.
33 IBM did not market around Watson in Europe, nor was the event televised, though of course news of it spread through other channels.
34 IDC publishes their Server Tracker data at broad regional levels (e.g. Western Europe, CEE, Japan, Asia, etc.). Given the earthquake in Japan, it is an unsuitable point of comparison, thus Western Europe is the most similarly developed market to the US in the dataset. Forrester estimates 2011 IT industry growth to be similar in both regions.
35 Campaign period defined as 1 December 2010–1 April 2011. IBM rose 14%, versus e.g. Microsoft +1%, Google +0.3%, HP -5%.
36 c.f. Interbrand 'Best Global Brands 2011'. IBM rose 8% to a value of $70bn, behind only Coca-Cola on $72bn (which rose just 2%).
37 For more on this, c.f. Tech Jobs Watch (2011) 'IBM's Watson becomes big man on campus with *Jeopardy!* win'. 'By raising IBM's profile among students at technology programs at universities such as MIT and CalTech, Watson will likely help IBM better compete for talent against the Silicon Valley companies that are at the top of the list for engineering graduates', 17 February.

## Chapter 24

# Magnum Gold?!

## How one golden integrated idea sold 130 million ice creams

**By Erwin Flores, Lola Madrid; Jane Dorsett and Mihir Warty, Lowe and Partners**
Credited companies: Creative Agencies: Lola Madrid, Lowe Brindfors; Media Agency: Mindshare; PR Agency: Golin Harris; Client: Unilever

**Editor's summary**

To launch Magnum Gold?! as a global product, this fully integrated campaign engaged consumers in a product launch that leveraged celebrities in a fresh new way, from a spoof trailer of an action Hollywood blockbuster to ground breaking face-texturing techniques allowing consumers to star in their own Hollywood heist videos. The judges were very excited by the way the campaign blurred the lines between cinematic content, advertising, experiential marketing and digital, and delivered record brand growth. In total it sold 130 million Magnums globally, which was 55 million ahead of target, delivering incremental revenue of €37.9m and payback of €1.41 for every €1 invested. This is a great paper for a lesson on learning how to achieve global success with a new product without cannibalising the others in the portfolio.

## Introduction

This is the story of Magnum's biggest ever global product launch for the first ever golden ice cream on a stick: 'Magnum Gold?!'.

Based around one integrated idea: 'The Heist', the campaign aligned Magnum Gold?!, with the prestige of gold, and the concept of stealing gold.

The main piece of the communications architecture was a commercial that wasn't a commercial but the spoof trailer of an action Hollywood blockbuster: the story of a super heist. A big Hollywood star and his partner played the roles of a duo of high-profile pros who planned to break into a high-security vault and steal a cargo of gold. This initial teaser blurred the boundaries that separate advertising and cinematic content.

Supported by TV, outdoor and digital, the campaign included a viral campaign which used ground breaking face-texturing techniques to enable consumers to star in their own Hollywood heist online video movies and posters. Soon even US President Barack Obama was starring alongside Benicio Del Toro.

Magnum's challenge in 2010 was to sell 75 million pieces of Magnum Gold?! ice cream. The outstanding success of the campaign meant that we had to extend the 'limited' edition and revise the industrial plan in order to deliver what turned out to be 130 million Magnums sold globally, 55 million more than the original objective (+73%). Consequently, the brand delivered incremental revenue of €39.7m, a payback of €1.41 for every €1 invested.[1]

## New learning

### *Integrating outside the box*

At its heart, this campaign was about taking a very simple insight – the appeal and prestige of gold – as far as possible. Integration typically means combining across above-the-line, online and through-the-line. By creating the integrated idea of 'The Heist' we took this integration one step further. We aligned all of the campaign material, from the spoof trailer of an action Hollywood blockbuster, to the high security 'Gold' vaults and armoured trucks that appeared in cities worldwide, to enabling consumers to star in their own blockbuster films online, to blur the lines between advertising, cinematic content, experiential marketing and digital.

## Magnum – the story so far

Since launching in 1987, Magnum has become a world icon of adult ice cream pleasure. The brand has been continuously refreshed and repositioned through new product launches and variants. However, by 2009 this had to increasingly be done in a competitive context crowded with similar products, both from formidable blue-chip competitors as well as aggressive retailer own brands. Consumers needed reassuring of what was so special about Magnum.

Unilever was seeking a product and a campaign that would genuinely stand out in the category. In particular they wanted to promote the brand's credentials in two ways:

- with never-seen-before ice cream innovation; and
- an unconventional communication campaign.

## Objectives and strategic challenge

### *An international challenge*

Magnum is truly global. The Magnum Gold?! campaign launch is the biggest in Magnum's history, both in terms of ambition, spend and geography, covering 30 countries (Figure 1):

**Figure 1: Magnum Gold?! countries**

**Europe:** UK, Ireland, Germany, Belgium, Netherlands, France, Italy, Spain, Portugal, Austria, Switzerland, Poland, Czech Republic, Slovakia, Hungary, Croatia, Slovenia, Montenegro, Macedonia, Sweden, Denmark, Finland;

**AMET:** Turkey, Israel, South Africa;

**Asia:** Australia/New Zealand, Singapore;

**Latin America:** Mexico

### *Four big national stories*

Whilst we will demonstrate the success of the campaign globally, we will also illustrate our international story with findings for four of the 30 countries in which this campaign ran.[2] We hope doing so will:

- bring the campaign even more to life; and
- illustrate advertising effect by comparing high investment/implementation countries to the global outcome.

The countries selected had high levels of campaign implementation and investment (an average €2.3m per country vs. a global average of €1.2m) and whilst they cover a range of developed and developing countries, they demonstrate the universal challenge of selling more ice cream (Figure 2).

**Figure 2: Magnum Gold?! national stories**

- **France:** as one of Magnum's historical territories the market is a good test bed when trying to gauge future success for any new launch or initiative by the brand. There had recently been drops in brand equity attributes, particularly regarding quality and value for money;
- **Germany:** a very tough target audience to crack with a rational and sceptical consumer base. In this market, we needed to maintain brand awareness despite a drop in communications;
- **Turkey:** a highly seasonal market with the particular forthcoming challenge of Ramadan occurring in ice cream season which was likely to depress sales; and
- **Australia/New Zealand:** where Magnum is heavily outspent by competitors who had also been more innovative in product development

*Strategic challenges*

## Global business challenge

Magnum's challenge in 2010 was to sell 75 million pieces of Magnum Gold?!. This target was set with the objective of returning Magnum to double-digit yearly growth and as such was very stretching (Figure 3).

Figure 3: Target market

**Target market**

Both men and women, 21 to 35, who believe that pleasure is their birthright. They do not seek guilt-based pleasure, nor is pleasure merely a reward. They seek stimulation, rather than permission. The world is their playground and theirs to enjoy.

They feel entitled to pleasure.

For them pleasure is when something ordinary is transformed into something extraordinary. They measure their lives not by the number of breaths they take, but rather, by the number of times their breath is taken away.

## Individual market business challenges

A third of the 75 million units to be sold were to come from the four markets used to illustrate our case (Table 1).

Table 1: Sales targets for France, Germany, Turkey and Australia/New Zealand

| Country | Sales volume targets million pieces | Sales revenue targets €m |
|---|---|---|
| France | 3.1 | 1.6 |
| Germany | 15.4 | 6.7 |
| Turkey | 4.9 | 2.7 |
| Australia & New Zealand | 2.5 | 1.5 |
| Total | 25.9 | 12.5 |

## Perceptual/attitudinal objectives

The campaign would need to surprise and generate *talkability*, to give consumers a new and unique experience in the universe of ice cream. Equally, the campaign needed to build the perception of Magnum as the unbeatable leader in the ice cream category and as the undisputed authority in adult ice cream pleasure.

## The solution

### *Creating a new product*

Unilever had developed ground-breaking technology which enabled them to make ice cream any colour. In a joint client and agency collaboration, we developed the idea of the world's first golden ice cream on a stick, Magnum Gold?! (Figure 4).

Figure 4: Magnum Gold?!, the world's first ice cream on a stick

Source: Unilever

This was no regular ice cream, and it certainly couldn't go with a regular campaign. The launch pad would be fully focused on the inimitable product and its key distinctive characteristic: the colour gold.

### *The client brief*

The client brief was clear that the campaign had to position Magnum Gold?! as a superior product and maximise its unique 'gold' facet. The campaign had to succeed at retail keeping the new Magnum Gold?! top of mind in a crowded summer promotions market. It also needed a different approach in terms of channel strategy and delivery to geographies in five different regions.

### *The big idea*

From soundings with potential international consumers, the concept of aligning the product Magnum Gold?! with the prestige of gold was a powerful and attractive proposition. The research also showed that the concept of stealing gold, at a time when its value was sky-rocketing, was a common, international currency. Even more so than, say, gold medals. From these insights a global idea was born:

*'The Heist – Magnum Gold?!. An ice cream as good as gold.'*

## The activity

*Overview: 'The Heist – Magnum Gold?! An ice cream as good as gold.'*

The campaign was conceived to create maximum resonance around the product concept – the golden ice cream – and from there, to generate maximum impact and talkability. This was achieved by creating a 'story' based on the confusion between the product, Magnum Gold?!, and the precious metal. The campaign was implemented through a multi-channel approach, built around a core creative idea and commercial (Figure 5).

Figure 5: The Magnum Gold?! campaign

Source: Unilever

*'Universal trailer' and TV*

The main piece of the communications architecture was a commercial that wasn't a commercial but the spoof trailer of an action Hollywood blockbuster: the story of a super heist. A big Hollywood star and his partner would play a duo of high-profile pros who have planned to break into a high-security vault and steal a cargo of gold.

The initial teaser phase would generate enormous impact given the unusual format. It would blur the boundaries that separate advertising and cinematic content. Stopping-power would also be guaranteed by the use of a real Hollywood celebrity that would make the ensuing muddle believable.

The agency teamed up with A-list director Bryan Singer from the Hollywood blockbusters *Usual Suspects* and *X-Men* and created a story of a heist in *Mr. and Mrs. Smith* style, in which celebrity Benicio Del Toro and his partner Caroline Correa attempt to steal 75 million pieces of gold from a bank vault. Del Toro thinks he's actually stealing real gold but his beautiful wife is playing him to get to the coveted Magnum Gold?! ice creams (Figure 6). The theme played to the Pleasure Authority master brand idea and, at the same time, launched a new product with unequalled attributes.

The movie-like trailer film was 2min 30seconds long and was seeded on entertainment sites and blogs as a prequel to our launch TV (Figure 7).

Figure 6: Magnum Gold?! TV campaign

Source: Unilever

Figure 7: Magnum Gold?! seeded on entertainment sites and blogs

Source: Unilever

Two traditional TV ads were also developed to build up the excitement by showing different sides of the star couple and the Magnum portfolio. Consumers related to the couple's chemistry and enjoyed finding out that they too were being played by Magnum, i.e. that no film was being released and that it was 'only' an amazing new product being launched.

### *Outdoor*

For the launch, cities were filled with high security vaults and armoured trucks. We also covered major cities with giant movie outdoor billboards and ads. The way the local markets brought this to life was bold and unprecedented (Figure 8).

Figure 8: Gold vaults in Rome and armoured trucks and giant movie billboards in UK Waterloo IMAX, London and Turkey

Source: Unilever

### *Digital*

Online we engaged consumers by letting them star in their own blockbuster and create movie posters they could share by taking face-texturing techniques to a different level. With the consumer him or herself playing the part of a criminal mastermind, the outcome is not what Benicio intended. Soon, even President Obama appeared alongside Del Toro in our viral campaign (Figure 9).

Figure 9: Magnum Gold?! viral campaign and online face-texturing techniques

Source: Unilever

High quality and user-friendly tools make it easy to share the customised videos with friends via email and social networks (Figure 10).

Figure 10: Social networks (left) and email (right)

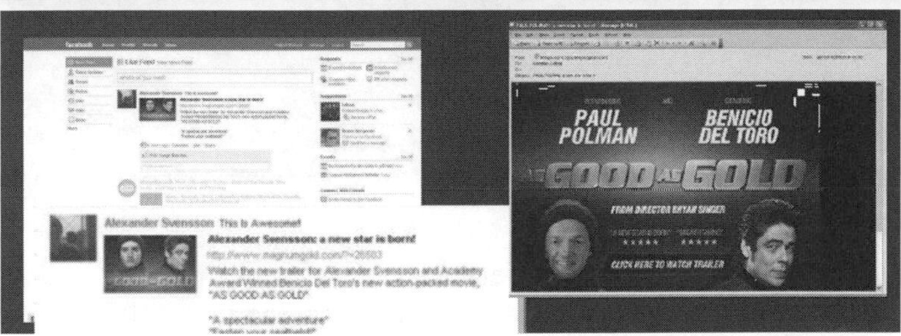


Source: Unilever

We also created high quality video content (click to play banner) (Figure 11). Targeting relevant environments was crucial: movie, celebrity, lifestyle sites, entertainment, news and TV websites: Imdb.com, virginmedia.com, digitalspy.co.uk, odeon.co.uk, guardian.co.uk, channel4.com, ivillage.co.uk.

### *PR*

On the PR front, we couldn't miss inviting the press. On 8 April 2010, at a secret location in the heart of Barcelona, the new Magnum Gold?! was unveiled by the most glamorous couple of thieves of the year!

Figure 11: Magnum Gold?! online video content

Source: Unilever

Reporters from 18 countries, and a few lucky consumers, partnered up with Benicio and Caroline in dodging laser beams and blowing up safes at the VIP event. Attendants got to take home their very own piece of film acting next to Del Toro dressed up as thieves (Figure 12).

Figure 12: Magnum Gold?! PR launch

Source: Unilever

We also developed a consumer PR event giving 15 lucky competition consumers from around the world, the winners from local competitions, the opportunity to 'Star in your own heist movie!' with the once-in-a-lifetime trip to Barcelona to star in the ultimate movie heist scene alongside Benicio del Toro (Figure 13).

### *Retail*

On the retail front, the campaign had to reach over five million retailers globally. To simplify the implementation, the agency created a retail toolkit that individual markets then localised. The launch landed in convenience stores, supermarkets, hypermarkets and summer-strong leisure outlets such as cinemas and theme parks.

The In-Home consumption challenge also required Magnum Gold?! to break through the clutter of the supermarket. The challenge was to lead buyers to the freezer section, too often buried at the back of the store (Figure 14).

Figure 13: Magnum Gold?! consumer PR competition

Source: Unilever

Figure 14: Magnum Gold?! in-store retail campaign

Source: Unilever

We also developed 'Crack the code with your Magnum stick', an on-pack sales promotion, in 12 European markets. By purchasing their promotional Magnum Classics they were given the opportunity to win top of the range, gold-coloured, Sony products (Figure 15). Pan-European promotions are a challenge to plan and execute as legislation varies greatly within the European Union.

Figure 15: Magnum Gold?! on pack sales promotion

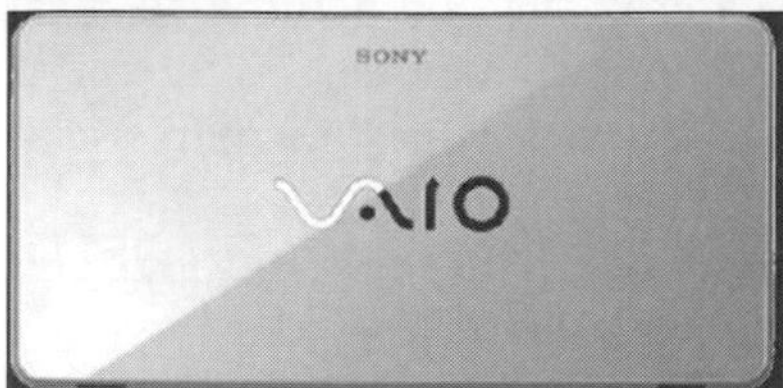

Source: Unilever

### *Media plan*

Table 2 presents the Magnum Gold?! media plan.

**Table 2: Integrated media plan**

| GOLD?! | Jan | Feb | Mar | Apr | May | Jun | Jul | Aug | Sep | Oct | Nov |
|---|---|---|---|---|---|---|---|---|---|---|---|
| Online seeding | | | | | | | | | | | |
| PR | | | | | | | | | | | |
| Online awareness | | | | | | | | | | | |
| Search | | | | | | | | | | | |
| Activation | | | | | | | | | | | |
| In-store | | | | | | | | | | | |
| Cinema (45" launch) | | | | Launch | | | | | | | |
| TV (30" launch; 20" chase) | | | | Launch | Launch & chase (1:1) | | | Chase | | | |
| TV promo (10", 5") | | | | Promo | | | | | | | |
| OOH (6-sheets) | | | | | | | | | | | |

Source: Mindshare

Total global media spend for 2010 was €26.9m, with a typical country split of circa 60% TV, circa 10% outdoor, and circa 20% online.[3] Media spend across our four countries was €9.3m, 35% of the total, in line with sales expectations.

## What happened?

### *Global ambitions were more than fulfilled*

Magnum Gold?! has been the biggest launch by the brand ever. The first to launch on such a massive scale, following a single concept consistently across all regions and markets. Results have far exceeded expectations and objectives.

### 1. Magnum Gold?! engaged consumers across the world

- Our universal trailer, the movie-like 2min 30sec trailer film which was seeded on entertainment sites and blogs as a prequel to our launch TV (1,318 seeded sites), was seen by over 1.9 million people worldwide, +129% vs. plan.
- Our online viral campaign, where we invited consumers to use face-texturing techniques to let them star in their own blockbuster and create movie posters, delivered 15 million page views, with 387,151 videos created and 410,464 visitors coming from shared videos.
- Over 2 million people globally entered the competition to make a real life video heist film with Benicio Del Toro in Barcelona.
- Our pack promotion 'Crack the code with your Magnum stick' saw over 2 million entries.
- The website http://mymagnum.com saw 3,848,060 visits, 3.2 million unique.
- Our banner ads saw UK click-through of 0.52%, the highest rate on any Unilever campaign in 2010.

## 2. The Magnum Gold?! campaign effect was magnified virally around the world

Our unconventional PR launch in Barcelona delivered 450 pieces of global coverage. Magnum Gold?! appeared in 42 TV programmes around the world, and circa 240 pieces of online coverage have been generated (Figures 16a–c). Total reach/ impressions achieved: 235 million; advertising equivalent of coverage achieved: €3m.

Figure 16a: TV coverage

Figure 16b: Press coverage

Benicio,
Barcelona

Eiskalt erwischt

Benicio Del Toro
COMMENT J'AI PARTAGÉ UNE GLACE AVEC LUI
Quand la nouvelle égérie de la marque Magnum m'invite à Barcelone pour le goûter, je fonce ! Et je raconte tout.

UN SPOT CLASSÉ X

Source: Unilever

Figure 16c: Online coverage

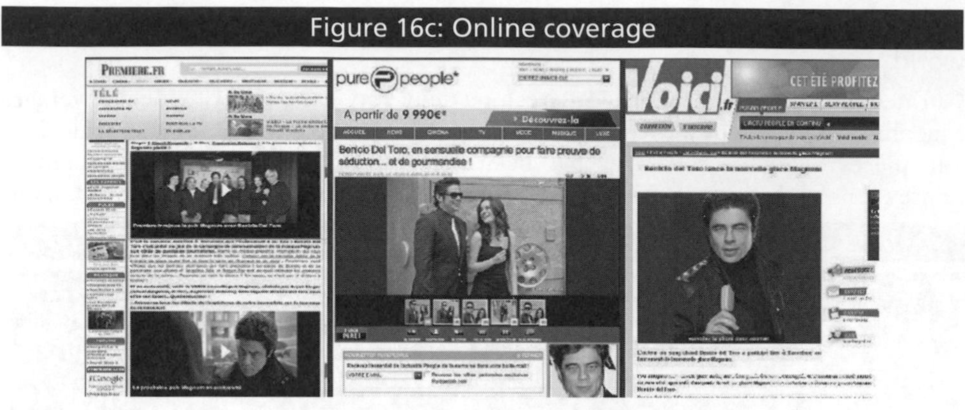

### 3. Magnum Gold?! sold 130 million pieces worldwide

Did we sell the fabled, ambitious 75 million ice creams, our global business challenge?

No, in the end we had to extend the 'limited' edition and revise the industrial plan in order to deliver what turned out to be 130 million Magnums sold globally, 55 million more than the original objective (+73%) (Figure 17). And the counter is still ticking as Magnum Gold?! continued to roll out in the rest of Asia and Latin America in 2011/12.

### 4. Magnum Gold?! delivered €80m in revenue globally, 50% ahead of target

The campaign saw sales revenue of €80m, €26.5m ahead of the €53.5m target (+50%) (Figure 18).

### 5. Magnum Gold?! saw fastest ever sales growth

The Magnum brand registered its fastest growth rate since 1997, up 13% year-on-year in 2010 vs. a global market average of 3.8% CAGR;[4] driving market share to 12.2% (up from 11.1%) and value share to 11.1% (up from 9.9%).[5]

Figure 17: Magnum Gold?! sold 130 million pieces, 73% ahead of target

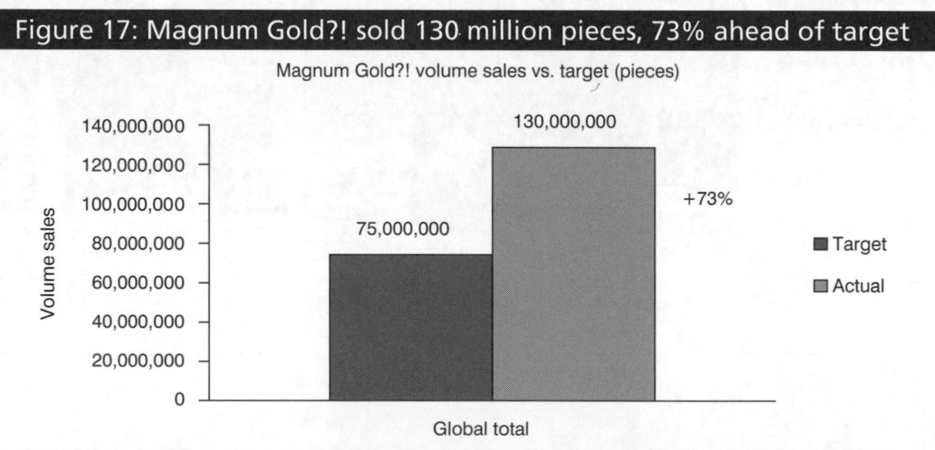


Source: Unilever, March to October 2010

Figure 18: Magnum Gold?! delivers €80m in revenue, 50% ahead of target

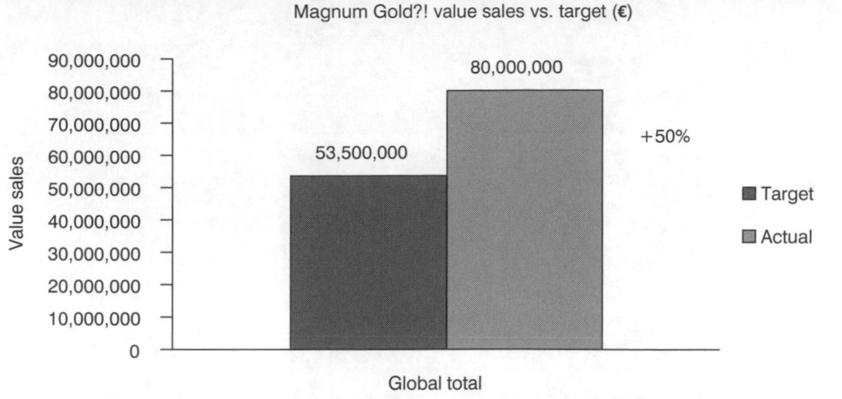

Source: Unilever, March to October 2010

### *Country-by-country deeper dive*

Above we presented results at a global level. In order to demonstrate the efficacy of the Magnum Gold?! campaign and the correlation between campaign investment and performance, we revert to our four countries chosen for their high levels of campaign implementation and media investment (average €2.3m per country).

We will show:

1. How we delivered an 'outstanding' campaign with Magnum Gold?!.
2. How the campaign met perceptual/attitudinal objectives of generating talkability, and positioning Magnum as the unbeatable leader in the ice cream category and as the undisputed authority in adult ice cream pleasure.
3. How the Magnum Gold?! campaign impacted on sales and market share.
4. Using our high investment/integration countries as a regional 'test and control' we will demonstrate that there were significant differences between these markets who utilised the Magnum Gold?! campaign extensively vs. globally where effect was diluted by lower investment/integration.

### 1. Across all four selected markets the Magnum Gold?! campaign was 'outstanding', outperforming previous Magnum campaigns

The Magnum Gold?! TV execution delivered an 'outstanding' result from Millward Brown PreView, which meant that the ad scored in the top 30% for both awareness and persuasion (Figure 19).

Strong Preview results were replicated in market, amongst our four countries. PostView results for Magnum Gold?! were in the top 30% across KPIs such as Enjoyment, Engagement, Branding, Differentiation, Brand Appeal and Persuasion (Figure 20).

The Magnum Gold?! campaign outperformed Magnum campaigns for early years, particularly against Engagement, Branding, Differentiation, Brand Appeal and Persuasion (Figure 21).

## Figure 19: Millward Brown PreView results show Magnum Gold?! as 'outstanding'

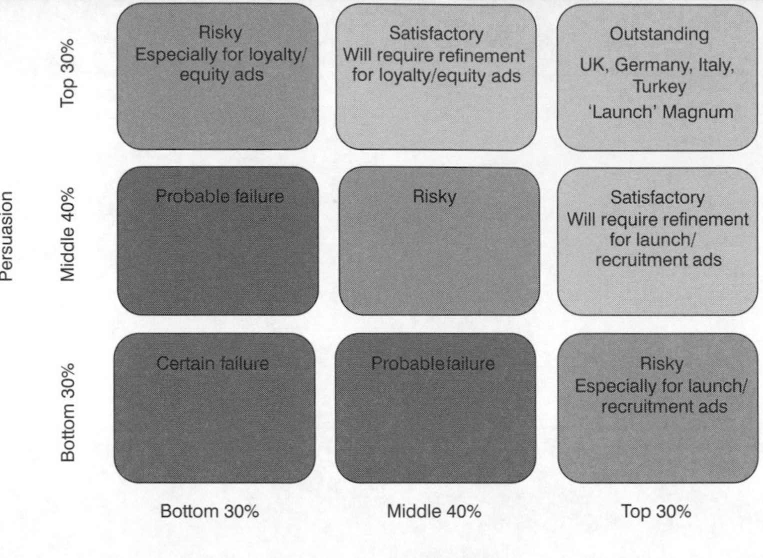


Awareness Index

**Magnum Gold?!**

'A copy strongly grabbing attention thanks to strong enthusiasm generated by the entertaining and distinctive story. A strong focus on Magnum Gold?! put at the core of the story providing strong linkage. Information focused the new Magnum Gold?! launch, generally perceived as different, raising interest towards the product.'

Source: Millward Brown; Communication Effectiveness Matrix: 'Gold' 45 seconds finished film; online: UK, Germany, Italy; offline: Turkey

## Figure 20: Excellent Millward Brown PostView results in France, Germany, Turkey and Australia

| | France | Germany | Turkey | Australia |
|---|---|---|---|---|
| Enjoyment | ● | ● | ● | ● |
| Engagement | ● | ● | ● | ● |
| Parent branding | ● | ● | ● | ● |
| Persuasion | ● | ● | ● | ● |
| Differentiation | ● | ● | ● | ● |
| Brand appeal | ● | ● | ● | ● |

Source: Millward Brown PostView (grey signifies top 30%)

Figure 21: Magnum Gold?! out-performed previous Magnum campaigns

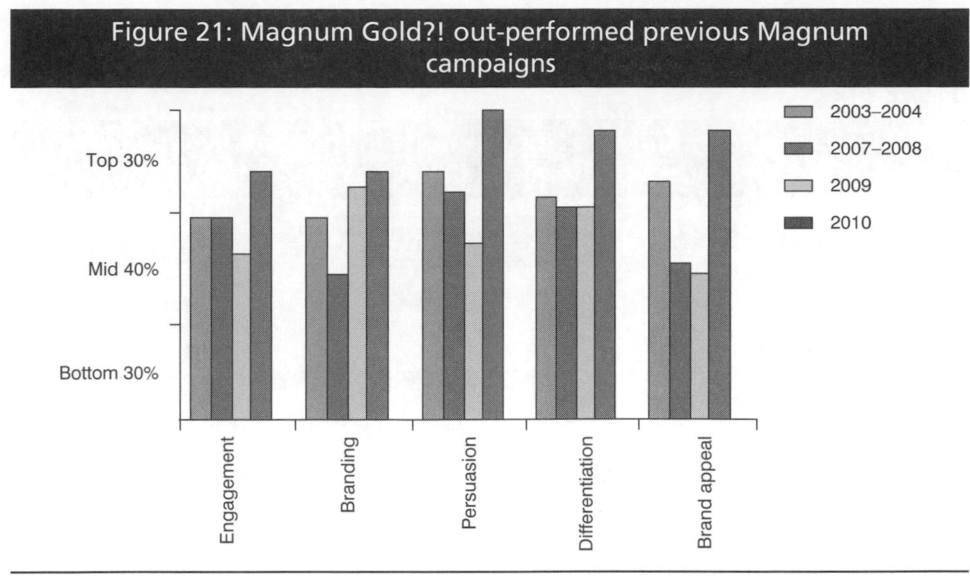


Source: Millward Brown

## Magnum Gold?! met our perceptual/attitudinal objectives

*a) Magnum Gold?! enhanced brand perceptions of Magnum as the undisputed authority in adult ice cream pleasure*

The objective was to build the perception of Magnum as the unbeatable leader in the ice cream category and as the undisputed authority in adult ice cream pleasure. Magnum Gold?! saw high levels of endorsement against 'are chocolate experts', 'indulgent', 'more for adults' and 'are for your personal moment of pleasure' across Germany, France and Australia (Figure 22).

Figure 22: Magnum perceived as the authority in chocolate and ice cream pleasure

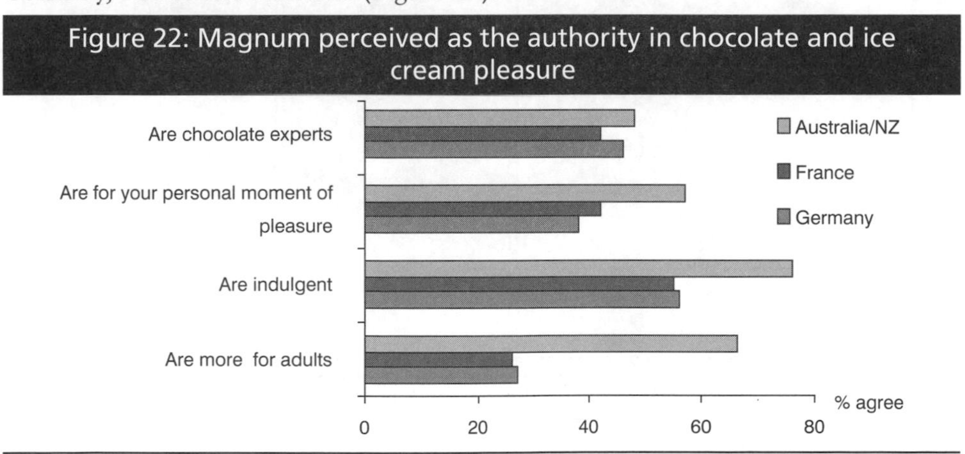


Source: Millward Brown Dynamic Tracker Apr–Oct 2010; absolute scores; comparable results not available for Turkey

Endorsement against key objectives can be seen more clearly when considering the same measures relative to competitors – we consistently outperformed (Figure 23).

Figure 23: Magnum Gold?! as the authority in chocolate and ice cream pleasure outperformed relative to competitors

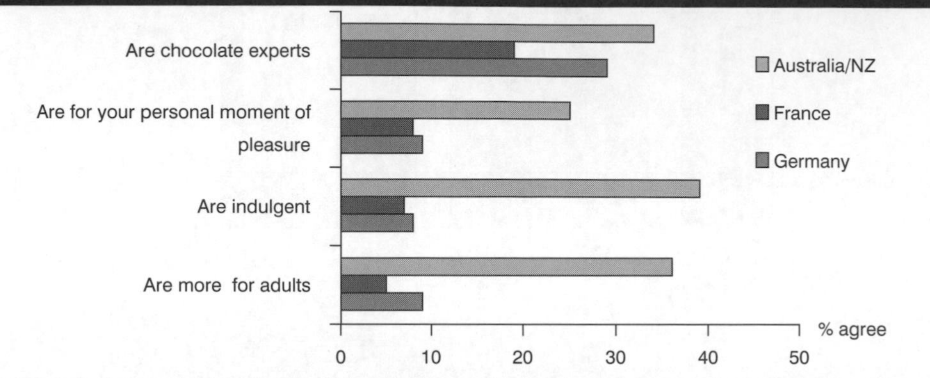


Source: Millward Brown Dynamic Tracker Apr–Oct 2010; relative scores; comparable results not available for Turkey

*b) Magnum Gold?! generated buzz and advocacy*

The campaign was also designed to surprise and generate talkability, to give consumers a new and unique experience in the universe of ice cream. We see high levels of endorsement against 'people talk a lot about' across Germany, France and Australia. Advocacy and recommendation are also consistently high (Figure 24).

Figure 24: Magnum Gold?! delivers 'buzz' and strong advocacy

| | Germany % | France % | Australia/NZ % |
|---|---|---|---|
| Would recommend to others | 50 | 45 | 56 |
| Would advise others not to try | 4 | 1 | 2 |
| Net advocacy (recommend/ advise not to try) | 46 | 44 | 54 |
| People talk a lot about | 44 | 59 | 35 |

Source: Millward Brown Dynamic Tracking; comparable results not available for Turkey

## 3. Magnum Gold?! campaign delivered sales and market share gains

*a) Magnum Gold?! more than doubled sales targets in our high investment countries*

In market, performance of our four countries confounded expectations; the original ambition across France, Germany, Turkey and Australia/New Zealand of 26 million units sold was nearly doubled with 51 million pieces sold (+97%). And Magnum Gold?! sales revenue, at €27m, was more than double the €12.6m target (+116%) (Figure 25).

**Figure 25: Magnum Gold?! sales double targets in high investment four countries**

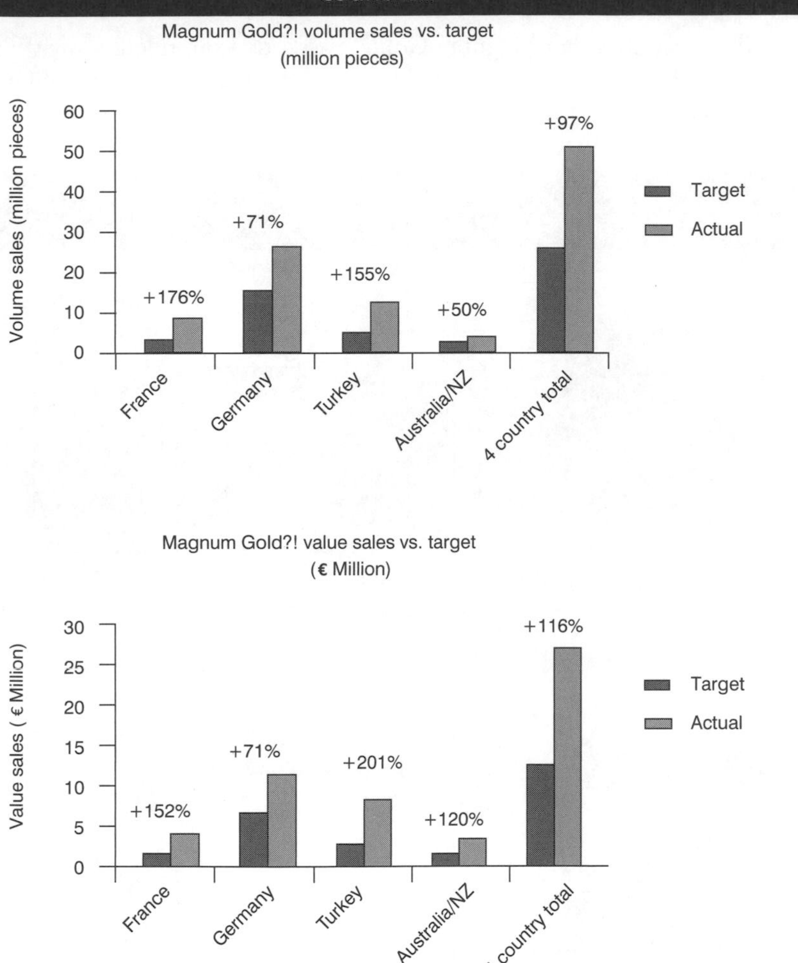


Source: Unilever, March to October 2010

*b) Diving even deeper into France and Germany we can see that Magnum Gold?! increased market share*

We saw 1.8 percentage point (ppt) and 1.0 ppt market share gains in Germany and France. These gains are incremental to the business (Figure 26).

*c) Magnum Gold?! sales growth is incremental to the business*

In Germany, 90% of the Magnum Gold?! growth was incremental to the business, 75% incremental to Unilever; 41% came from competitors and own label, 27% came from increased ice cream consumption, and 5% were new ice cream buyers (Figure 27).

## 4. High investment Magnum Gold?! market analysis shows enhanced effect

We have demonstrated that Magnum Gold?! worked as intended, to drive talkability and position Magnum as the unbeatable leader in the ice cream category and as the undisputed authority in adult ice cream pleasure. It seems reasonable to expect

Figure 26: Sales growth delivers incremental market share in Germany and France

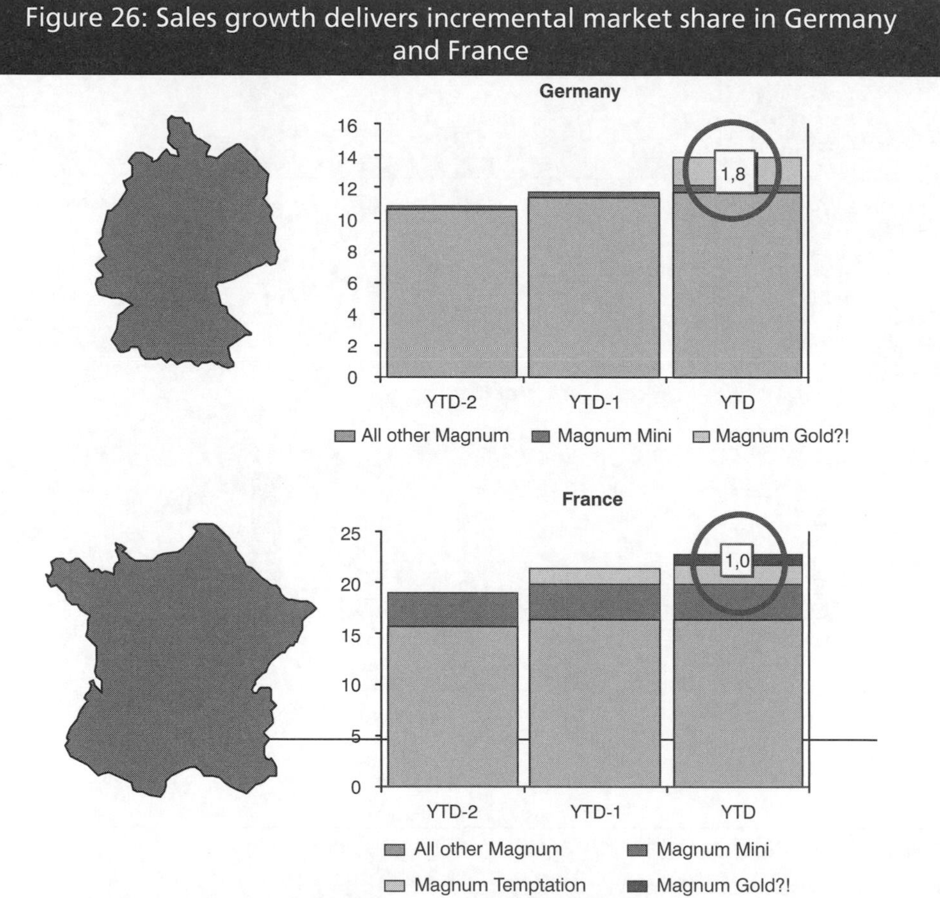


Source: Nielsen (Germany), IRI (France)

Figure 27: 90% of the Magnum Gold?! growth was incremental to the business in Germany

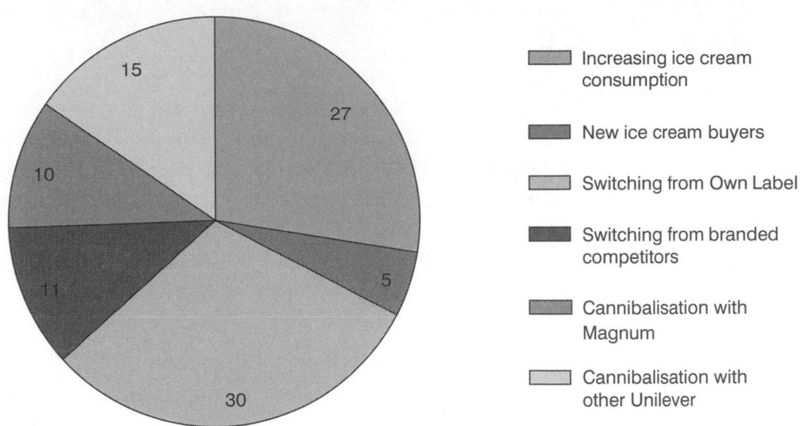


Source: Europanel; based on gains and loss analysis March–August 2010 vs. 2009

that this would have an impact on buying behaviour; persuasion measures would certainly suggest so.

Here we give additional evidence suggesting that Magnum Gold?! had a significant effect on sales by comparing sales in those markets that invested most heavily in the campaign, our four countries versus the global outcome.

As we have seen amongst the four countries with high investment/integration, incremental sales growth was +116% vs. the 50% uplift seen globally.

And whilst only 35% of media spend went behind our four countries (share of voice), they generated 55% of incremental revenue (share of market) (Figure 28).

Figure 28: High investment countries share of voice vs. Magnum Gold?! share of market

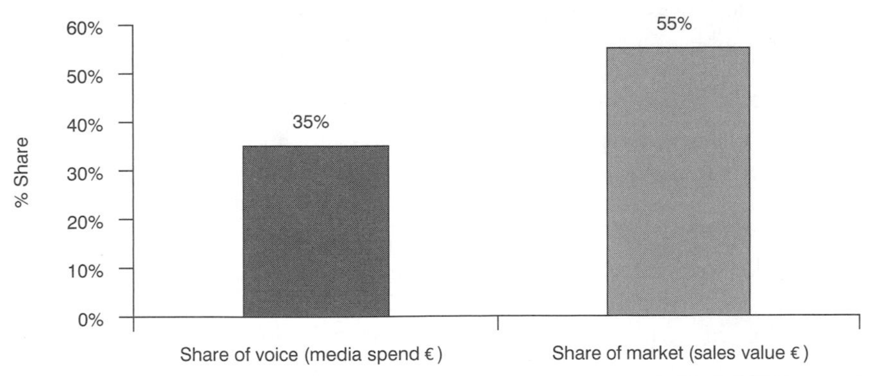


Source: Unilever, March–October 2010

## Eliminating other factors

Whilst there are factors that may influence campaign performance at a country level, none of Magnum Gold?!'s markets account for a large enough proportion to influence sales at a top line global level. We therefore exclude potential factors that might impact at a global level:

### *1. There was no underlying growth in the sector*

The global ice cream market generated total revenues of $55.4bn in 2010, representing a compound annual growth rate (CAGR) of 3.8% for the period spanning 2006–2010.[6] As we have seen, Magnum Gold?! out-performed this with its fastest brand growth rate since 1997, up 13% year-on-year in 2010. However, we will discount for the 3.8% CAGR in our payback calculations.

### *2. Competitor pressures were sustained*

Competitor marketing activity broadly stayed at similar levels and followed a consistent pattern of activity. There were no other major product launches or withdrawals.

### *3. Changes in Magnum spend were marginal*

Overall marketing spend remained flat from 2008 to 2010. Spend was diverted from previous variants into Magnum Gold?!

### *4. Magnum Gold?! did not benefit from a lower price*

Magnum Gold?! retails at an average price index of 130 vs. a Magnum standard. Magnum standard is priced in line with the competition so Magnum Gold?! operates at a price premium to both Magnum standard and competitors. Therefore, we did not benefit from a lower price: the 130 million pieces sold are not driven by consumers trading down to Magnum Gold?!

### *5. Promotions were sustained at previous levels with negligible impact at a global level*

Local levels activity focused on supermarket and out of home, point of sales promotions. There was no increase on previous years and any local activity would have been negligible at a global level.

### *6. No change in distribution*

There was no change in distribution at a global level and we did not enter any new markets with Magnum Gold?!

### *7. Seasonal factors were not a factor*

In many markets ice cream is a seasonal purchase. There was no major change in overall global weather patterns during this period, and whilst there may have been variance within countries, this is averaged out when looking across 30 countries.

## Calculating payback

We have already eliminated possible global factors that might have delivered the exceptional sales growth seen for Magnum Gold?!. We now go on to consider the financial impact of the Magnum Gold?! campaign. In the absence of econometric modelling, we consider an analysis of sales to calculate payback and return on investment.

We will consider two approaches:

1. Payback derived from total revenue across the global campaign.
2. Payback derived from incremental revenue vs. target.

### *A note on Unilever payback expectations*

Before we consider payback, it is worth highlighting that the initial outlay in terms of media spend was very high. The ratio of media spend to target revenue was 50%, with Magnum Gold?! media investment at €26m, and target revenue at €53.5m. This high ratio reflects the cost of entry for launching a new variant.

As a result, Unilever did not expect the campaign to deliver payback in its first year on air. Incremental revenue and profits would be generated in subsequent years.

So even though the targets of 75 million pieces of gold/€53.5m revenue was a stretch target to deliver double digit growth to the brand, it wasn't expected to pay back until the second year.

### *1. Payback from total revenue*

We consider the total global revenue delivered of €80m. We will discount this figure by 3.8% to discount market growth: €76.9m.

### Longer-term impact

As we have stated, the Magnum Gold?! campaign was not expected to deliver incremental revenue until year two. In order to consider the longer-term impact we turn to the latest (2011) IPA/Gunn Report, 'The link between creativity and effectiveness, the growing imperative to embrace creativity'.[7] This asserts that a major study by PricewaterhouseCoopers has demonstrated that 45% of the return on investment of brand-building TV advertising comes through more than 12 months after the campaign runs.

We therefore apply a 45% weighting to determine the longer-term impact of the campaign.[8] This shows the Magnum Gold?! campaign delivered €114.6m in total revenue over two years.

### Total payback

With Magnum Gold?! campaign costs of €26.8m, this shows our campaign as having a return on marketing investment (ROMI) of €4.27 for every €1 invested (Table 3).

**Table 3: The Magnum Gold?! campaign delivered a total ROMI of €4.27**

| | € Sales (March–October 2010) |
|---|---|
| Payback Year 1<br>Total revenue | €80,000,000 |
| Payback Year 1<br>Total revenue discounted for 3.8% market growth | €76,960,000 |
| Payback Year 2<br>45% of Year 1 | €34,632,000 |
| Total 2 year payback | €114,632,000 |
| Media costs | €26,861,033 |
| **ROMI** | **€4.27** |

Source: Unilever, Lowe & Partners calculations

### Profitability

With a revenue return of €4.27, the gross profit made on Magnum Gold?! would need to be 31% or higher for the campaign to be considered profitable. Unilever's confidentiality policy prohibits the release of profit margins; however, we can confirm that their actual gross profit margin is above 31%, meaning Magnum Gold?! has been a profitable campaign for Unilever.

Whilst we could refine our payback calculations above to account for the German experience which showed that 90% of sales were incremental to the business and only 10% were due to cannibalisation from Magnum, we consider a more robust analysis is derived from considering Magnum Gold?! performance against the pre-campaign target that was set.

#### *2. Payback from incremental revenue*

Our stretch campaign target was to deliver total global revenue of €53.5m. The Magnum Gold?! campaign exceeded this target by 50%, delivering a total of €80m in revenue, of which €26.5m was incremental revenue. This is discounted by 3.8% to account for market growth: €25.5m.

### Longer-term impact

Applying our 45% weighting to determine the longer-term impact of the campaign shows the Magnum Gold?! campaign delivered €37.9m in incremental revenue.

### Total payback

With Magnum Gold?! campaign costs of €26.8m, this shows our campaign as having a return on marketing investment (ROMI) of €1.41 for every €1 invested (Table 4).

### Benchmarking payback

There are only four ice cream papers in the IPA Effectiveness databank[9] and only two detail campaign payback; both are UK-only campaigns. The Haagen-Dazs 'Dedicated to Pleasure' campaign used econometrics to show a 'sales uplift due to advertising within the first year of nearly two times actual negotiated media spend'.[10] The Lyons Maid 'Favourite Centres' campaign showed that 'the one-year break-even point was

Table 4: The Magnum Gold?! campaign delivered an incremental ROMI of €1.41

| | € Sales vs. target (March–October 2010) |
|---|---|
| Payback Year 1<br>Incremental revenue vs. target | €26,500,000 |
| Payback Year 1<br>Total revenue discounted for 3.8% market growth | €25,493,000 |
| Payback Year 2<br>45% of Year 1 | €11,471,850 |
| Total 2 year payback | €37,971,850 |
| Media costs | €26,861,033 |
| **ROMI** | **€1.41** |

Source: Unilever, Lowe & Partners calculations

not reached'.[11] Our two-year payback of between €4.27 and €1.41 seems favourable compared to the available benchmarks.

## Conclusion

This paper is about Magnum's biggest ever global product launch: 'Magnum Gold?!'.

How a fully integrated campaign, 'The Heist', broke the rules of ice cream marketing and sold 130 million Magnums globally: 55 million ahead of target, delivering incremental revenue of €37.9m, and payback of €1.41 for every €1 invested.

The campaign had consumers participating in a product launch that leveraged celebrities in a fresh new way, from a spoof trailer of an action Hollywood blockbuster to ground breaking face-texturing techniques allowing consumers to star in their own Hollywood heist videos. The campaign blurred the lines between cinematic content, advertising, experiential marketing and digital, and delivered record brand growth.

## Notes

1 We will show the payback calculations later in the paper.
2 Data variability precludes a full 30 country analysis. Countries were selected based on high investment and campaign integration, and where a comprehensive set of effectiveness metrics were available.
3 Source: Mindshare.
4 Source: www.marketresearch.com. The global ice cream market generated total revenues of $55.4bn in 2010, representing a compound annual growth rate (CAGR) of 3.8% for the period spanning 2006–2010.
5 Source: Unilever Global Marketing Forum, Euro Panel.
6 Source: www.marketresearch.com.
7 Source: Field, P. (2011) The link between creativity and effectiveness. The growing imperative to embrace creativity. IPA/Gunn Report, 16 June. More findings from The Gunn Report and the IPA Databank 2011: 'It is over the longer term (weeks, months and years rather than hours or days) that the vast majority of the commercial benefit of a successful brand campaign is achieved (a major study by consultants PricewaterhouseCoopers demonstrated that 45% of the return on investment of brand-building TV advertising comes through more than 12 months after the campaign runs).'
8 Magnum brand products have been on sale in the 30 markets since the campaign ran in 2010, so the ongoing benefits of the high-impact campaign continue to be reaped.
9 1. Europe campaign – 'Magnum 7 Sins – Driving women to sin across Europe', IPA 2004; 2. UK campaign – 'How advertising has helped Wall's Viennetta establish a new sector in a mature market',

IPA 1984; 3. UK campaign – Haagen-Dazs: 'Dedicated to pleasure', IPA 1992; 4. UK campaign – 'How advertising licked Lyons Maid favourite centres into shape', IPA 1988.

10 Source: Haagen-Dazs: 'Dedicated to pleasure', IPA 1992.

11 Source: 'How advertising licked Lyons Maid favourite centres into shape', IPA 1988: 'the entire cost of the TV production and the additional point-of-sale material are included, the one-year break-even point was not reached. (Of course it is almost certainly more appropriate to amortise the costs of production and point-of-sale over a longer period.)'

## Chapter 25

# Nikon

## I AM Nikon

**By Louisa von Reumont and Julia Peuckert,**
**Jung von Matt AG**
Contributing authors: Birgitta Olson, Klaas Abreu Miedema,
Nikon Europe BV; Sean Fellows, Nikon UK
Credited companies: Creative Agency: Jung von Matt AG; Media Agency: Mediacom; Event Agency: JvM/relations; Adapting Agency: Doner; Brand and advertising tracking: Icon; Client: Nikon Europe BV

### Editor's summary

Nikon has a long history as a premium camera manufacturer and is strongly associated with professional photography. However, being perceived as 'pro' was alienating broader target groups, rather than being an attraction. To address this, the campaign needed to raise awareness of Nikon, making it a more approachable and relevant player in the compact segment. Within two years of the campaign launch, Nikon had created an emotional brand and communications platform, which increased sales dramatically and elevated Nikon from an insignificant market position to market leader in January 2012. For every €1 spent, the campaign yielded a €5.76 profit. The judges found this paper to be a very compelling story of the way Nikon demonstrated a real understanding of the brand positioning, using consumer interaction to penetrate the youth market and raise awareness of its compact products, without affecting its high end 'halo' models.

## Introduction

Nikon has a long history as a premium camera manufacturer and is strongly associated with professional photography. However, being perceived as 'pro' alienates broader target groups, rather than being an attraction.

The challenges we faced were to raise awareness for Nikon, making the brand more approachable and a relevant player in the compact camera segment.

## Background/The situation

### *General situation*

For years, Nikon Europe has been following a decentralised marketing and communications strategy, where each country fought on its own.

This resulted in very different market positions across the European countries. While some markets were quite successful, Nikon was a rather small market player in the UK and in Germany.[1]

In order to boost its position on a European level, Nikon decided in 2010 to bundle its marketing, branding and communications activities to create a pan-European brand and communications platform with a special focus on the important markets, Germany and the UK.

At the beginning of 2010, the economic situation in the UK was strongly characterised by the recession of 2008–2009, which was the most severe since World War II. The unemployment level was at its highest since 1994, overall household income (and hence consumption levels) were incredibly low. Even though the economic situation in the UK recovered from the recession in 2010, people were still facing lower levels of income and were thus reluctant to spend money on items that were not absolutely necessary. Evidently, the population's consumption behaviour was a reflection of the demand for cameras, yielding a severe decline in sales volume on the overall camera market.[2, 3]

### *Market situation*

The overall camera market is characterised by its subdivision into the rather small yet very specialised market segment of single-lens reflex cameras and the highly fragmented mass market of compact cameras.

All over Europe, Nikon had to face a declining market share, especially in the compact camera market, which resulted in a declining overall market share.

In the UK, the compact camera market segment seemed to be a tough battlefield and Nikon's position was already considerably weak in this segment, but the situation became even worse. In 2009, Nikon's absolute sales dropped by 23%, resulting in an all-time market share low of 3.3%.[4]

It was crucial for Nikon to stop this decline and to gain a strong position within this highly important market instead.

### *Brand situation*

Nikon has had a long history as a premium camera manufacturer and has always been a traditional photography brand, which is why Nikon is strongly associated with professional photography.

Nikon is a pioneer for leading camera and lens technologies, and their innovations set standards among high-performance single-lens reflex cameras.

Unfortunately, these valuable brand assets strongly connect Nikon with professional premium photography, which alienates broader target groups rather than being an attraction, resulting in a low level of brand awareness on the mass market for everyday compact cameras.

Especially the young target group, which is a strategically important part of the lifestyle-orientated mass market of compact cameras, was not aware of Nikon. Only 2% of the 16–24-year-old purchase decision makers would consider buying a Nikon camera.[5]

## The challenges

### *General challenges*

The 2008–2009 recession, and also the recovery phase in 2010, was a highly challenging market environment, especially considering the fact that the overall camera market had been declining steadily. People in the UK were reluctant to spend money; evidently, they preferred to save and to keep all discretionary spending at a low level.[6]

### *Brand challenges*

The broad target group was not aware of Nikon as a compact camera manufacturer. Therefore, our main challenge was to raise awareness for Nikon within the broad target group in the compact camera market, where it was especially important to raise brand awareness among the younger target group.

Evidently, we needed to open up the brand, making it more relevant and accessible, always keeping in mind not to abandon the brand's heritage.

## Objectives

The set goals were considered to be long-term objectives; the overall situation of Nikon should be improved on a lasting, sustainable level.

### *Business objectives*

#### 1. Increase in sales volume

Nikon had a clear objective of increasing their sales volume within the UK market.

### 2. Increase market share in the compact camera market

We wanted to stop the declining volume market share and regain Nikon's volume market position of 2008, meaning that Nikon's compact camera market share should at least increase up to 4.1% at the beginning of the campaign, and reach at least 8% within a two-year range.

### 3. Increase in overall camera market share

Nikon's volume market share should increase for Nikon to regain a significant position within the overall camera market.

*Communicative objectives*

### 1. Increase brand awareness

Most important to us was an increase in brand awareness among the broader target group of compact camera users, especially among the younger population of 16–25-year-olds.

### 2. Increase relevance and accessibility

Secondly, we wanted to gain more relevance by opening up the brand and by embracing the broad target group of everyday photographers.

### 3. Communicate more efficiently than the main competitors

*Additional objectives*

1. Connect with and activate the broad target group through a Facebook application on a European level.
2. Improve in-store visibility.
3. Further strengthen brand awareness within the highly important target group of specialised journalists, dealers and the photo-inclined public via participation at important trade fairs.

## Campaign planning

The competition focused on 'loudly shouting' about their 'premium flagship products' and features like face recognition, touchscreen and super zoom, in an attempt to not only drive sales for the specific winning model, but to benefit from an overall brand technology halo for the entire product range. As a result, all competitors were fighting over the same slice of pie – the affluent, up-market adult audience.

We did not want to join that battle but rather chose to go another way by promoting, instead of a high-end camera, very well-equipped but affordable and thus volume-driving compact camera models, the Nikon COOLPIX S3000 (2010) and the Nikon COOLPIX S3100 (2011).

Corresponding to our promoted camera, we addressed a broad target group between the ages of 15 and 54, slightly skewed towards women.

An emotionally powerful message would therefore not only be most suitable for attracting a broader target group, but it would also be the best way to target the female demographic while still appealing to the volume-driving younger demographic as well.

### *Our mission*

We wanted to rely on what the brand already had to offer and simultaneously open it up by involving a broad customer basis.

To play a relevant role in people's lives, we needed to connect Nikon with the everyday use of photography and be warm and inviting.

Therefore, we first needed to understand how photography is being used today and which needs are connected with it. Therefore, we conducted a pan-European trend survey.

### *The insights to our conclusion*

Photography has become democratic: today, everyone is a photographer and has his or her own audience.

- Nikon needs to be for everyone who loves images.
  Photography is not about the single image anymore: today, a special moment is captured not by just one picture, but by thousands, or even by filmmaking.
- Nikon needs to be every aspect of imaging.
  Photography is about sharing: today, photos enrich relationships, bring people closer together, and give meaning and value to technology-based communication.
- Nikon needs to be a link to the world.
  Photography is about self-expression: photographs have always been a way to express emotions, impressions and observations. Sharing pictures has increasingly made them a form of self-expression.
- Nikon has to be an expression of life.

From these insights and conclusions, we derived our core message:
*Nikon enables everyone to capture, share and express the richness of life.*

## Creative strategy

### *Our creative twist: a change of perspective*

Starting with the insight of the democratisation of photography, we decided to change the perspective. Instead of talking about our brand and the well-equipped Nikon cameras, we wanted to make the Nikon user our campaign hero and explore how customers feel and what they do when using a Nikon.

In order to take Nikon's brand image down from its 'professional high horse' and to lower the entry barriers to the world of Nikon, we aimed for an authentic look and feel taking place in the centre of our customers' lives.

Our goal was to make people think: 'I could have taken this photo.' Therefore, our creative twist was to switch from a brand talking about itself to a brand talking from its customers' perspective.

*Our brand and communication platform*

I AM Nikon.

Who are you with Nikon? (Figure 1).

Figure 1: TVC 30 seconds

Source: Jung von Matt AG

### *Media strategy*

In 2009, Nikon's media budget for the compact camera segment ranked third in the field with a 16% share of spending, following Canon with 34% and Panasonic with 18.4%.[7]

Our goal was to reach our target group in the most efficient way, which is why we focused our media expenses on the second half of 2010 for the roll out of our campaign, resulting in a rather low media budget of approximately €2.8m. Evidently, in order to fully exploit all media channels, we needed to increase this budget in 2011 in order to gain a relevant share of voice and thus making Nikon more visible.

### *Media mix*

We allocated the media budget amongst all relevant media channels, with a focus on TV. In order to increase brand awareness and to reach our image goals most effectively, we chose the media channel with the farthest reach and greatest suitability for evoking emotions as our main carrier.

We made placements that were highly relevant, including high-affinity TV spots, bespoke TV sponsorship and print advertising (Figure 2). Furthermore, we made use of display ads and accompanying social media activities (Figure 3).

### *Hollyoaks sponsoring for accessing the younger target group*

The youthful users represent a hugely important strategic section of the compact camera mass market, which Nikon did not focus on in the past several years. As a result, the audience did not come into contact with the brand at all. For Nikon, however, the younger target group is integral in supporting the overall perception shift and necessary for bringing Nikon into the hearts and minds of the mainstream consumer.

An analysis of the TV habits of the 16–24-year-olds revealed that *Hollyoaks* is the strongest performing TV series within the UK,[8] which is why we decided to cooperate with the channels that were broadcasting *Hollyoaks* and integrate the Nikon sponsoring into the main time slots of the show (Figure 4).

Figure 2: Product ads, print

Source: Jung von Matt AG

Figure 3: Display ads

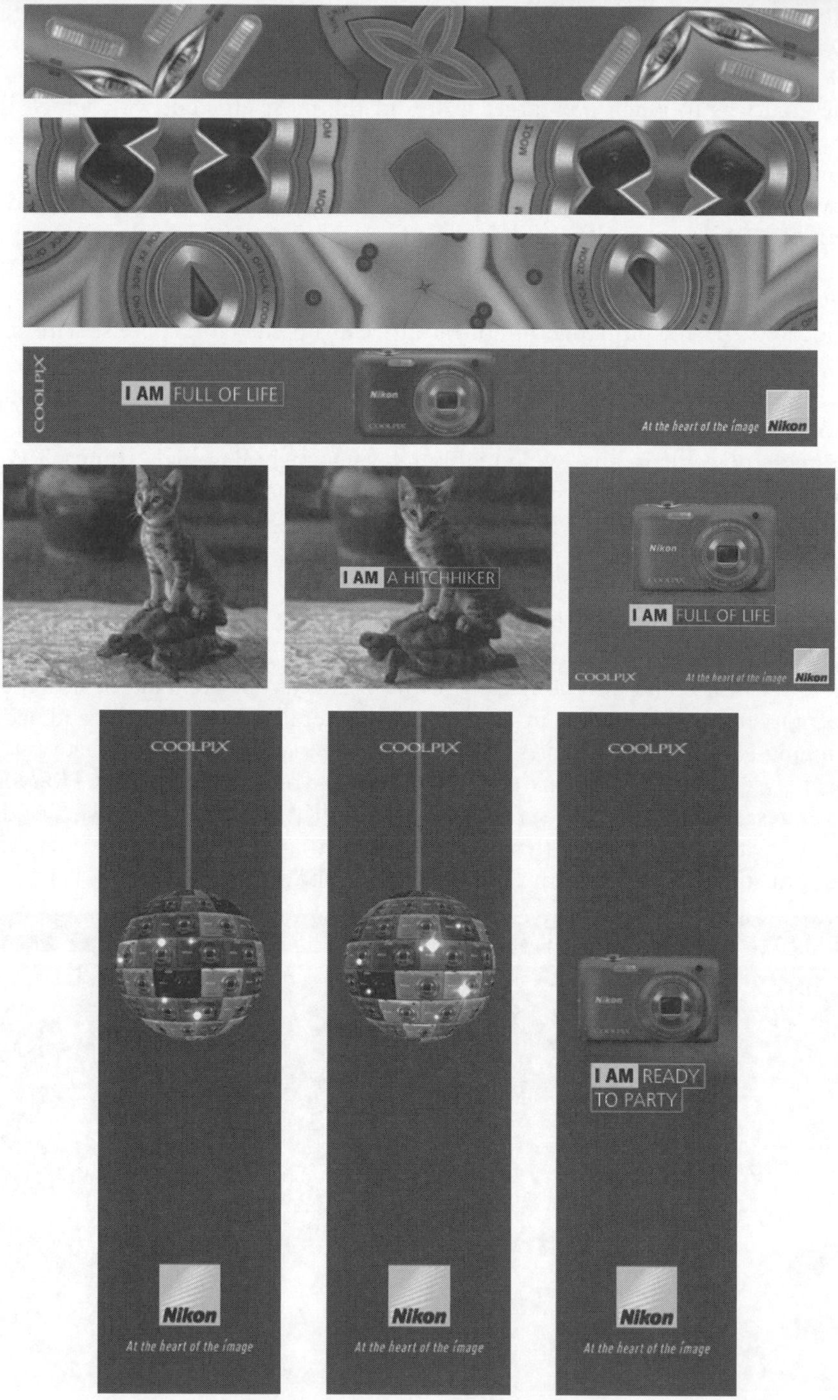

Source: Jung von Matt AG

Figure 4: *Hollyoaks* sponsoring:
programme presenting (left), 5-second ad (right)

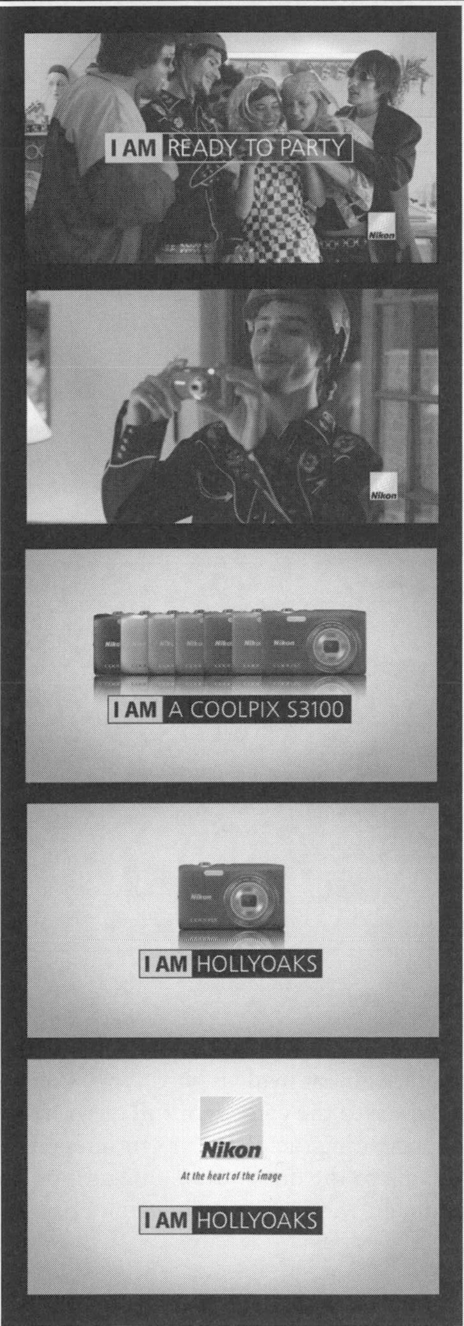


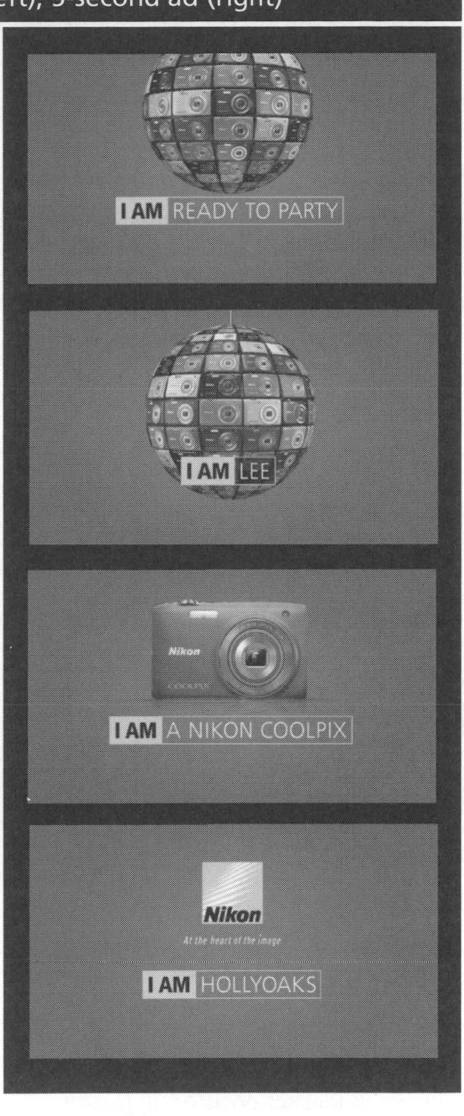


Source: Jung von Matt AG

## Further marketing strategies

### *Enhancing the relationship between Nikon and its consumers via a Facebook application*

To extend our campaign in the digital world and to truly activate and integrate our target group, we used 'Who are you with Nikon?' as our core message for the Facebook application and initiated a photo competition within the social media (Figure 5).

**Figure 5: Facebook App, 'Who are you with Nikon?'**

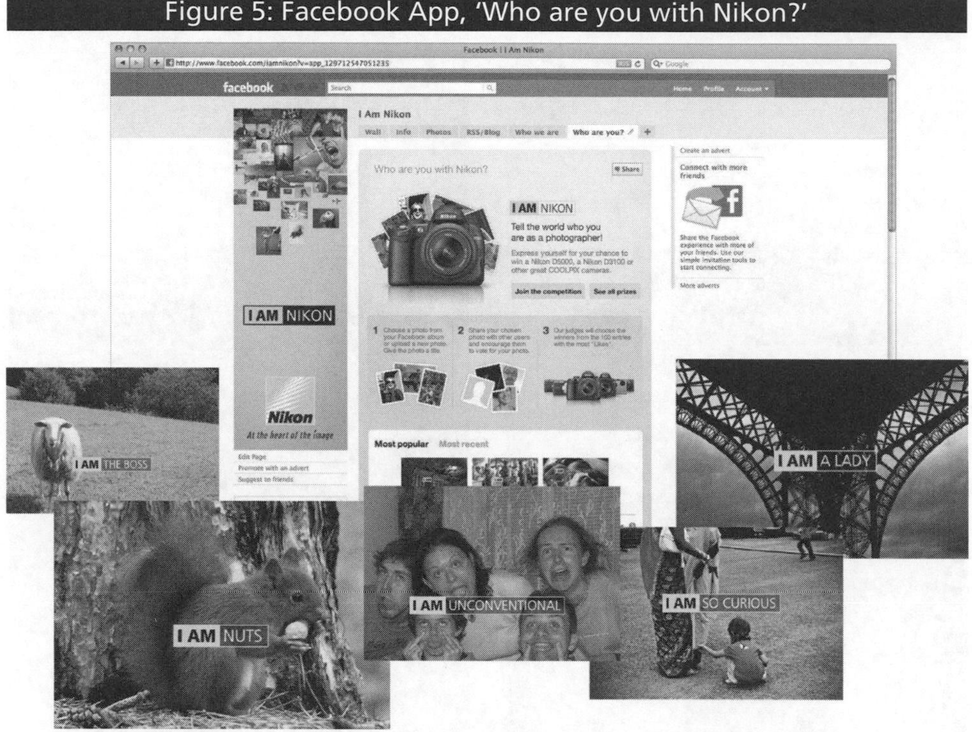


Source: Jung von Matt AG

### *Point of sale, increase in shelf space*

The weak market position in the compact camera segment made it hard for Nikon to sell-in their cameras. In the spring of 2010, previous to the campaign roll out, one of our first actions was to produce sales material, presenting the plans for our integrated campaign as a door opener for Nikon when talking to the distributors. In addition to the strong TV support, our most impactful argument was the new, campaign-adapted product packaging and the point of sale (PoS) material in line with our AtL-campaign (Figure 6).

Figure 6: PoS material

Source: Nikon Europe BV

### *Trade fairs*

We considered it highly important to introduce Nikon's new brand presence to the very significant target group of specialised journalists, dealers and the interested, photo-inclined public.

Therefore, we wanted to present Nikon as the leader of the imaging industry, always maintaining its approachability at Europe's most important biannual trade fair for photography, 'photokina', which took place in Cologne, Germany, in September 2010. The UK trade fair 'Focus-on-Imaging' was considered highly important as well. For both fairs, it was essential to carefully design and integrate all trade fair material, including an outstanding concept and design for the Nikon booth (Figure 7).

Figure 7: Presentation at 'photokina', booth (top) and 'Experience Cube' (bottom)

Source: Jung von Matt AG

## Evidence of results

*Business results*

Not only did we manage to reach those set business objectives but Nikon's 'I AM' campaign exceeded all expectations:

### 1. Increase sales volume

Within two years, Nikon managed to increase its sales volume by more than 200% from 187,216 sold units in 2009 to 568,811 units in 2011 (Figure 8).[9]

As a result, our promoted, volume-driving 'flagship' product, the Nikon COOLPIX S3100, became the best-selling camera in the UK in 2011.[10]

Figure 8: Nikon sales volume in units

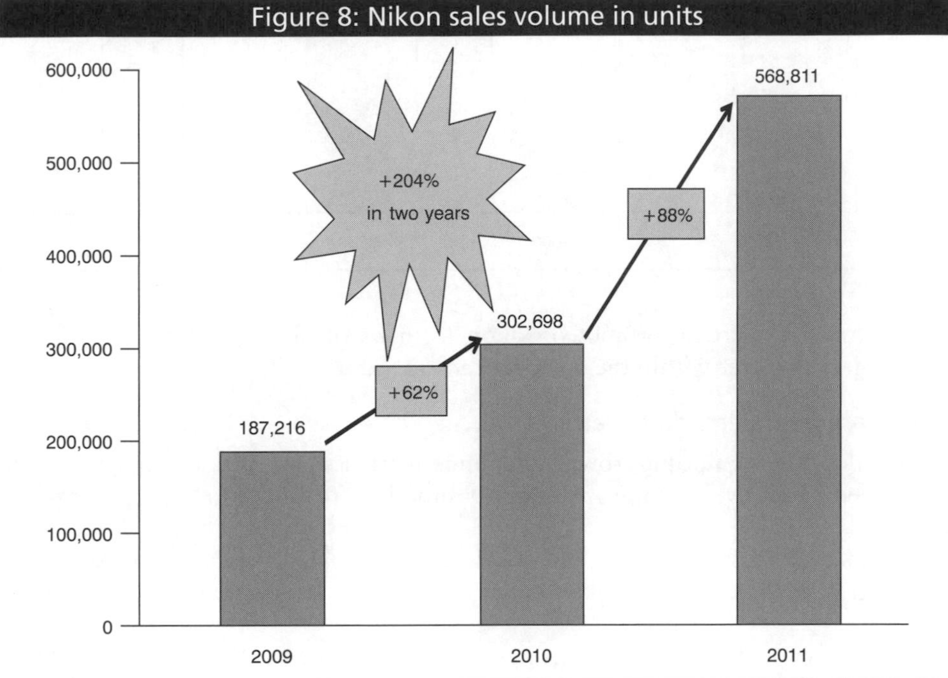


Source: GfK

### 2. Increase compact camera market share (from 3.3% to between 4.1% and 8%)

With the start of the 'I AM campaign' Nikon was not only able to stop the severe downward trend, but by the end of 2011, Nikon reached a volume market share of 11.7%, which is more than 250% above what we originally started with in 2009 (3.3%) and 46% above the 8% share Nikon had aimed for (Figure 9).[11]

Figure 9: Nikon compact market share

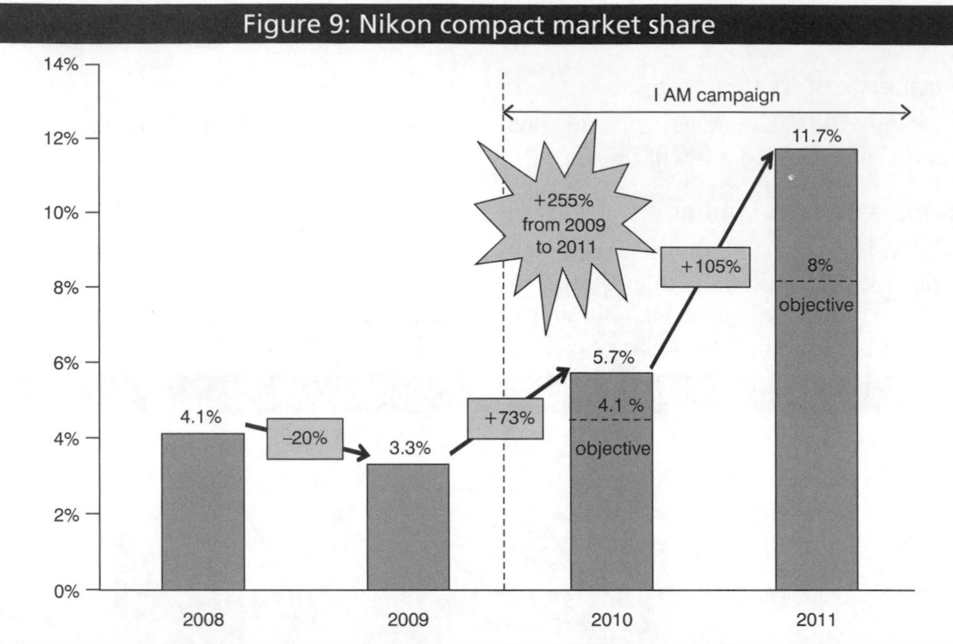


Source: GfK

This massive increase promoted Nikon from its outsider position to the third largest market player within the compact camera segment.[12]

### 3. Increase overall market share

As intended, the significant growth in volume market share of the compact camera market led to an overall improved market situation for Nikon in the total camera market.

Within two years, in 2010 and 2011, Nikon's overall volume market share increased by 83% to 13.9%. Nikon became the second largest market participant in the UK.[13]

And this is not all: the GfK market share figures for January 2012 show that Nikon became the UK market leader in both the compact and the overall market for the very first time.[14]

The outstanding results of the UK market also contributed to a dramatic improvement of Nikon's European market position in the compact camera market, resulting in the market leadership on a European level since the summer of 2011.

## *Communications results*

### 1. Increase brand awareness

From January 2011 until December 2011, brand awareness increased by 49% to 52%.

Similarly, when asked for a photography brand, 23% first mentioned Nikon, which constituted an increase of the 'first mention' value of more than 100% (Figure 10).[15]

**Figure 10: Total sample: unaided brand awareness (left) and first mention (right)**

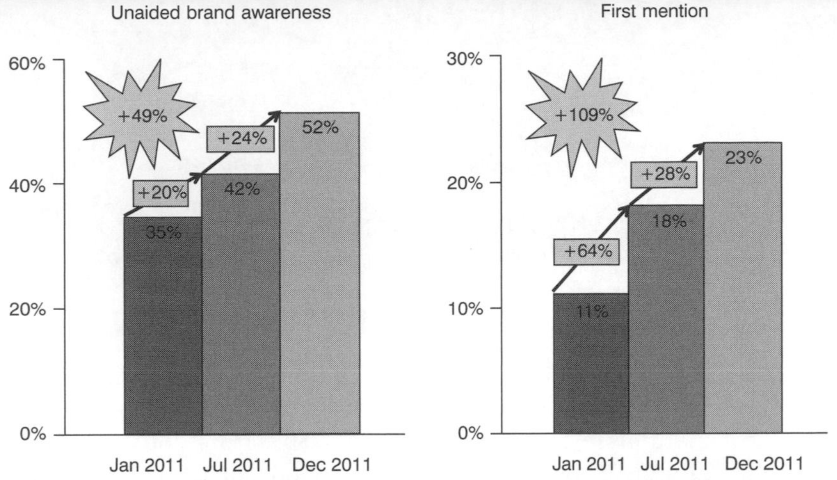

Source: Icon Added Value, Brand and Advertising Tracking UK

Since we were especially interested in the youth audience, we added a teen boost to our monthly tracking for six months. And these results even exceeded those of the 'total sample': within the shortened observation period of six months, Nikon's brand awareness among teens increased by 34% to 51%. Furthermore, the 'first mention' value increased by 80%, reaching 27% within six months of tracking (Figure 11).[16]

**Figure 11: Teen boost: unaided brand awareness (left) and first mention (right)**

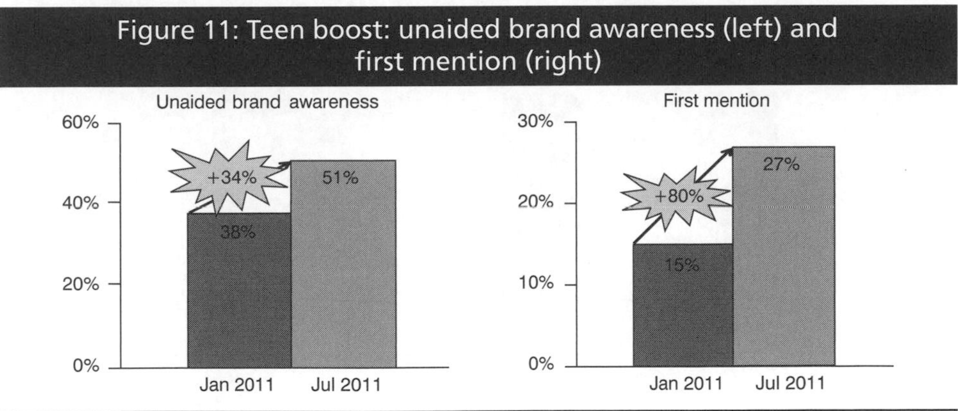


Source: Icon Added Value, Brand and Advertising Tracking UK

## 2. Increase the relevance and accessibility of the brand

Nikon managed to become an integral part of the consumers' relevant set; during 2011, this value increased by 31%, reaching 59% (Figure 12).[17]

Figure 12: Relevant set and first choice, total sample

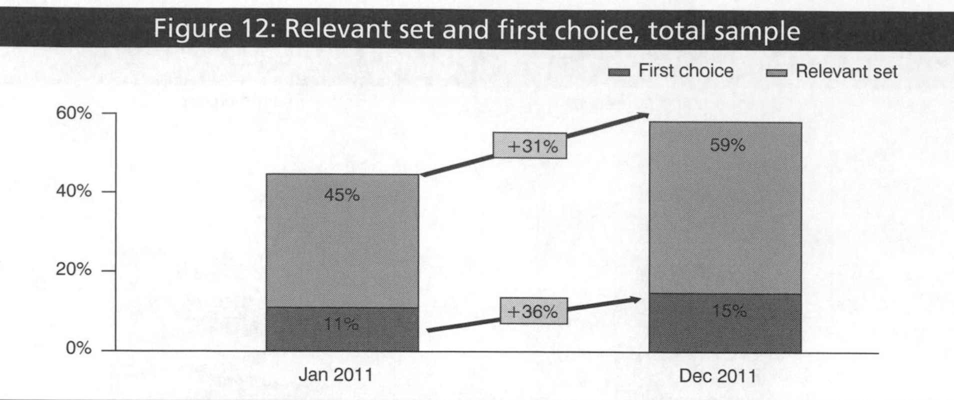


Source: Icon Added Value, Brand and Advertising Tracking UK

Since we had a special interest in Nikon's relevance for the youth audience, we examined the age groups of the purchase decision-makers and observed that Nikon was chosen far more often by young people in 2011: from 2009 until 2011, the group of 16- to 24-year-old decision-makers increased from 2% to 11%, whereas the share of this age group stagnated at 6% in the overall market – a sound indication that we successfully rejuvenated the brand appeal (Figure 13).[18]

Figure 13: Share of 16- to 24-year-old purchase decision-makers

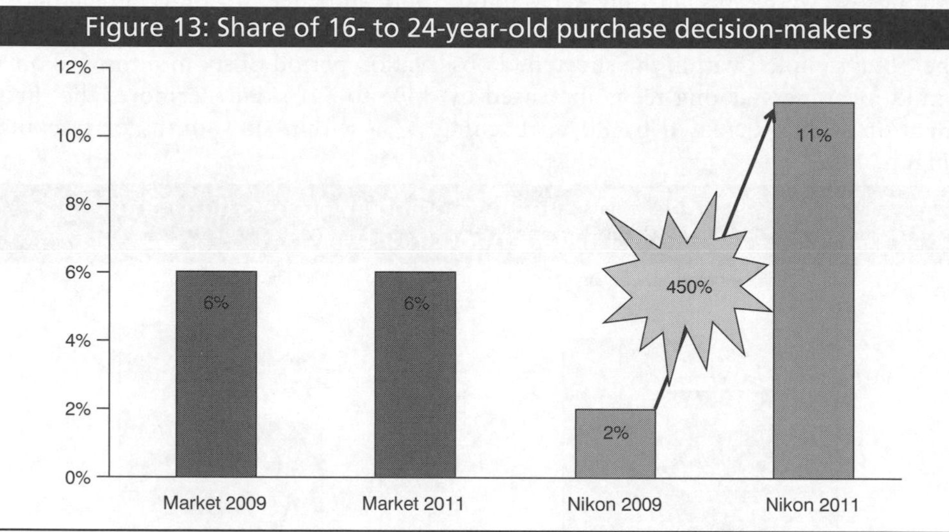


Source: GfK

Furthermore, the brand increased its accessibility because brand image dimensions, such as 'fun to use' or 'this brand is for people like me', increased throughout our campaign, whereas negative values, such as being perceived as 'conservative', decreased.[19]

## 3. Communicate more efficiently than the competition

Another objective was to communicate more efficiently than the heavily spending competitors.

With a lower share of voice referring to media spending of the compact segment in 2010 and 2011, Nikon managed to increase its sales volume.[20, 21]

However, the market share of Canon declined and Panasonic increased only slightly, even though their media spending, and hence share of voice, within this period of time was obviously higher (Figure 14).[22, 23]

Figure 14: Communication efficiency in a two-year period, SoV 2010 + 2011/sales volume 2009 vs. 2011

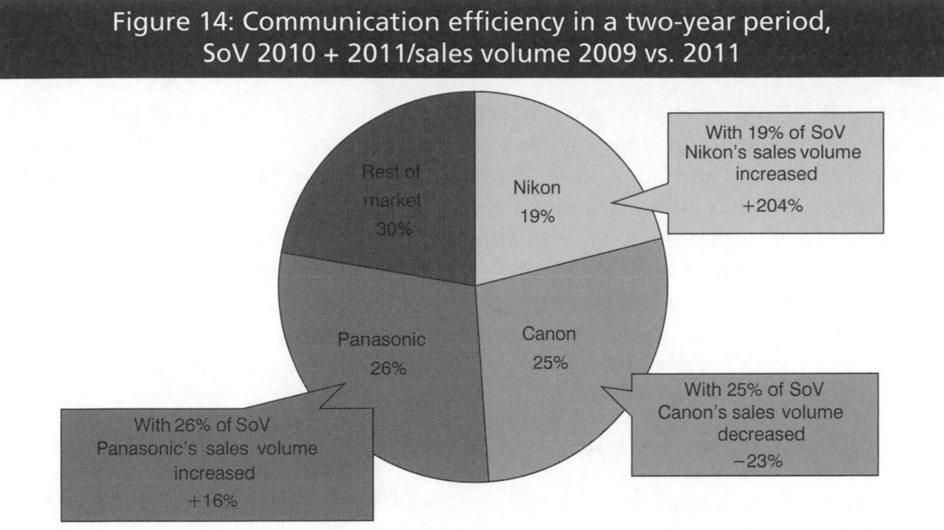


Source: GfK, Xtreme Spending

### *Additional results*

Last but not least, we exceeded our three additional marketing objectives.

Our additional objectives were:

### 1. Europe-wide Facebook activation

With our Nikon Facebook app, we created a unique interactive platform with the brand that activated many fans all over Europe in a very short period of time, and it has had a positive long-term impact on the brand.

We started our European Facebook application on 1 September 2010 with a total number of 60 fans. The competition lasted until 31 October 2010. All in all, we exceeded all expectations. Within two months, we reached the following figures: 80,000 page likes, over 40,000 picture uploads, around 260,000 photo likes, up to 40,000 visits per day, 560,000 unique visitors and over 1 million visits.

And the success did not end there. Even one and a half years later, the Facebook application is still a platform where Nikon fans from all over the world exchange their pictures and interact with the brand.

With this application, Nikon is demonstrating an interactive involvement with its target group that aligns with the core brand message.

### 2. Improve Nikon's visibility at the point of sale

Our thoroughly developed sales materials and the strategy of presenting our integrated campaign to the retailers before the actual launch of the campaign and the cameras was very successful. Compared to the time before the campaign, Nikon was much more visible in the retail area: Nikon's shelf space in our distribution channels almost doubled throughout our campaign.

### 3. Participate in trade fairs to strengthen brand awareness

As a result of our design of the Nikon booth at Europe's biggest photography trade fair, photokina, we not only managed to be perceived as the leading imaging company by 91% of all visitors, but 81% also found Nikon to be an accessible brand. Furthermore, 57% of all visitors rated our booth the most interesting one, far ahead of Canon (13%), Panasonic (7%) and Sony (2%).[24]

Moreover, the Nikon booth at the Focus Imaging Fair in Birmingham received the award for 'best booth' of the entire show.[25]

In addition to all previous results, we were delighted to receive such positive media feedback about our campaign.

## Exclusion of other factors

### *The growth in sales volume was not the result of an increase of overall market size or compact segment market size*

The sales units volume of the compact market segment decreased by 4% from 2009 to 2010 and by another 9% from 2010 to 2011.[26]

Hence, Nikon's overall growth in sales volume is not due to an increase in overall or segment-specific market size. On the contrary, Nikon managed to increase its sales volume despite the overall market trend (Figure 15).

Figure 15: Market development vs. Nikon development, sales volume

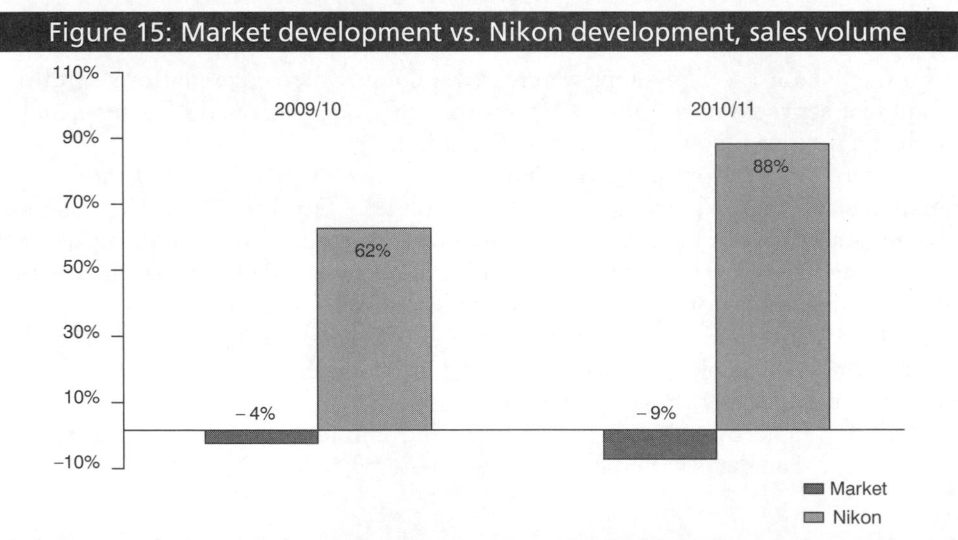


Source: GfK

### *Nikon's increase in market share was not the result of price dumping*

Despite some well-chosen periods of special offers, e.g. from Argos, Nikon maintained an average price premium compared to the rest of the market.

Thus, the increase in market share cannot be related to a decrease in Nikon's prices.[27]

### *Nikon's increase in market share was not the result of an expansion of distribution*

Nikon's increase in sales volume was not the result of an increase in distribution channels, but the result of our sell-in strategy, which brought the existing retailers to allocate more shelf space to Nikon. Hence, our activities before the product launch and the campaign start resulted in a more efficient use of our existing distributors: sales per shop increased by 150%, whereas the weighted distribution only increased by 4% (Figure 16).[28]

Figure 16: Increase in sales per shop

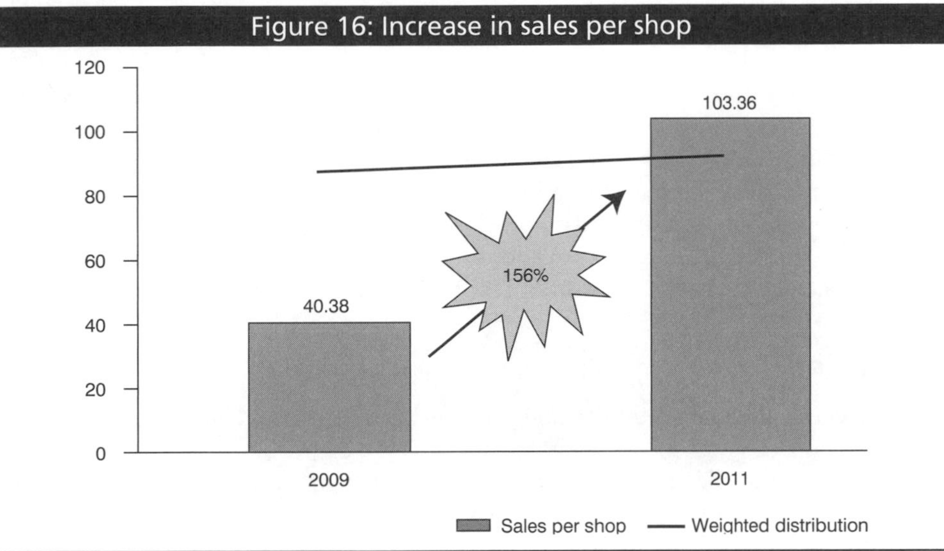


Source: GfK

## Communications payback

In order to calculate the ROI for the 'I AM Nikon' campaign, we compared the fiscal year of 2009/2010 before the campaign launch, with the fiscal year of 2011/2012, two years after the campaign launch (Table 1).

Table 1: Data summary before campaign launch

| **Before campaign**[29] (April 2009–March 2010) | |
|---|---|
| Market size units | 5,523,751 |
| Nikon GfK units | 194,898 |
| Nikon units market share | 3.5% |

In order to see what Nikon's market performance would have been without the 'I AM Nikon' campaign, we calculated a hypothetical market share development, based on Nikon's average compact camera unit market share over the past three fiscal years (April 2007 until March 2010), which resulted in a hypothetical market share of 4.2% (Table 2).

Table 2: Hypothetical development vs. actual development

| | **Nikon's hypothetical development without campaign** April 2011–Feb 2012 | **Nikon's actual development with campaign**[30] April 2011–Feb 2012 | **Additional development** (difference actual/ hypothetical development) |
|---|---|---|---|
| Market size units | 4,494,635 | 4,494,635 | |
| Nikon GfK units | 188,775 | 612,616 | 423,841 |
| Nikon units market share | 4.2% | 13.6% | 9.4% |

We are using these additional 9.4% in market share in order to calculate the additional return on investment of our marketing and communications expenses.

The additional investment to generate those 9.4% was €7,400,250.

The estimated profit per camera box is too sensitive to provide within this context but we calculated an additional ROI of €2,443,252 for this fiscal year.

For every €1 spent, we gained an additional €5.76 in profit – something we would not have been able to achieve without the 'I AM Nikon' campaign.

## Conclusion

Nikon successfully managed to establish a pan-European brand and communications platform.

Not only did the campaign meet all of the previously set business and communications objectives but it also exceeded them.

Within two years, Nikon advanced from a rather insignificant market position in the compact camera market to becoming one of the biggest market players. Nikon made itself accessible to broader and younger target groups, and its brand awareness and the level of compact camera sales increased dramatically.

The originally pan-European 'I AM Nikon' campaign was such a great success that meanwhile 133 countries worldwide have decided to adopt the campaign.

After two very successful years, we are looking forward to further evolutions of Nikon with the 'I AM' communication platform, not only in the UK and Europe but also beyond.

## Notes

1 GfK.
2 Wikipedia. Online at: http://en.wikipedia.org/wiki/List_of_recessions_in_the_United_Kingdom (accessed 15 April 2012).
3 Office for National Statistics (ONS) (2011) The impact of the recession on household income, expenditure and saving, October.

4 GfK.
5 GfK.
6 Office for National Statistics (ONS) (2012) Impact of the recession on household spending, February.
7 Xtreme Spending data.
8 Mediacom.
9 GfK.
10 Ibid.
11 Ibid.
12 Ibid.
13 Ibid.
14 Ibid.
15 Icon Added Value, Brand and Advertising Tracking UK.
16 Ibid.
17 Ibid.
18 GfK
19 Icon Added Value (2011) European Brand Track UK Report.
20 Xtreme Spending data.
21 GfK.
22 Xtreme Spending data.
23 GfK.
24 Icon Added Value (2011) Photokina research, November.
25 Nikon UK Ltd.
26 GfK.
27 Ibid.
28 Ibid.
29 Ibid.
30 Ibid.

## Chapter 26

# Nissan

## What is the most efficient path between two points?

**By Renata d'Ávila, Lew'Lara\TBWA**
Contributing authors: Felipe Senise and Rafael Prieto, Lew'Lara\TBWA
Credited companies: Creative Agency: Lew'Lara\TBWA; Client: Nissan Brazil

### Editor's summary

In early 2010 Nissan initiated an aggressive plan for Brazil: to be the first Japanese automaker in the sector with 5% market share. To help achieve this, Lew'Lara\TBWA established Nissan as a challenger brand. The campaign involved making direct comparisons between Nissan and its competitors, highlighting its positives over theirs; investing their media spend in television for peak reach in a short space of time; and creating fun and humorous content for execution via 30-second spots on television, with extended versions on YouTube. In two years the campaign has already generated 4% of market, despite investing three times less money than its competitors, and has yielded a projected marketing payback of over $41m. Many brands claim to have 'Challenger brand' status but fail to deliver this when you look deeper into their behaviours and communications activities. The judges felt that this paper genuinely has the ability to teach us some new tricks and to help clients who need to be extra smart in order to cut through from a low share of market. The learnings cut across category and could be just as relevant for cars to chocolate or cameras.

*The desire to acquire is truly something very natural and ordinary. When men can do it, they will always be lauded and not blamed. But when they cannot, and want to do it anyway, here is the mistake and the blame.*

Niccolo Machiavelli, *The Prince*

## What is this paper about?

It is said that the best path between two points is a straight line. However, when it comes to communications, nothing is done in a straight line. Nevertheless, one thing is certain: the path between two points may be more or less efficient.

This paper proposes a new way to assess effectiveness, by telling the story of two brands that started at the same point and reached the same point by very different paths.

We will show how Nissan and Hyundai went from 1% to 4% market share in Brazil, how communications influenced this, and how the path taken by Nissan was much more efficient.

## The starting point

The Brazilian auto market grows by leaps and bounds. Although it is now decelerating, growth in the sector was over 10% for more than five years (Figure 1).

Figure 1: Growth in the automotive market in Brazil

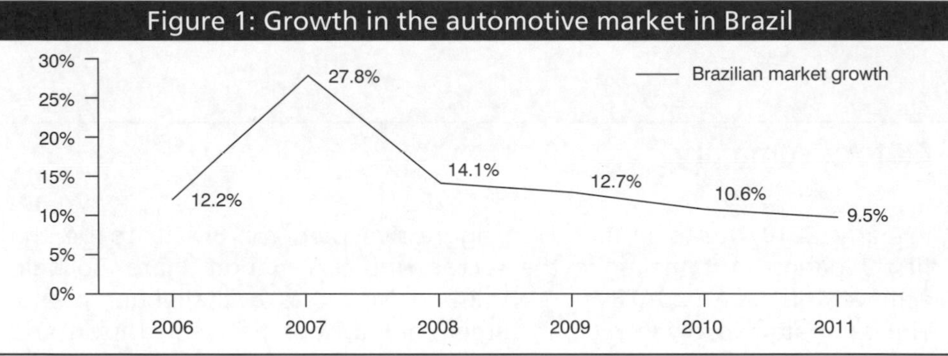


Source: Fenabrave[1]

This has been happening since the country opened up to imports in the early 90s, following which the auto market has become more and more competitive.

The market has always been dominated by what we call the 'big four': Fiat, VW, GM and Ford. Although these brands have been leading the market over the last two decades, the country saw the entry of a lot of new players, especially from the Asian continent.

The changes can be described as having two stages.

The 90s saw the arrival of the French and Japanese makers. Honda and Toyota quickly became successful. Today, they are references of strong brands and quality cars.

In the following decade the Koreans arrived, including Hyundai, which soon became perceived as a 'second division' of imported cars. Initially they were viewed with great suspicion by the Brazilian public and they had a lot of difficulty in establishing themselves.

Nissan arrived in Brazil precisely during this second phase. Although it is a Japanese brand and shares Honda and Toyota quality, the brand was grouped with the Koreans and suffered the same symptoms (Figures 2 and 3).

Figure 2: Historical ranking of automakers in Brazil

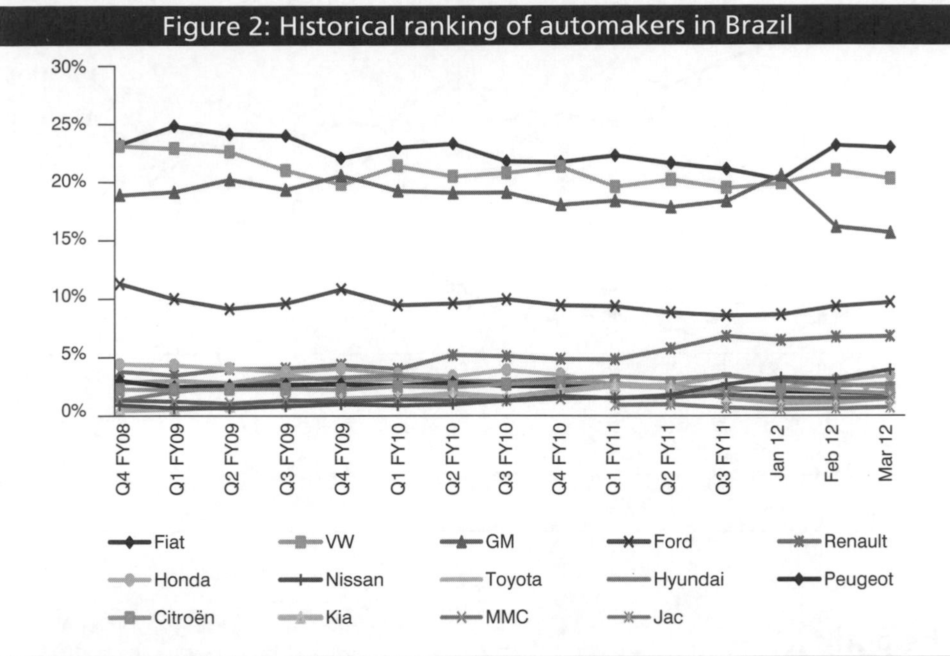


Source: Fenabrave

Figure 3: Grouping of brands by consumer perception

Source: Consumer focus group

## The point of arrival

Observing the significant economic growth in the country, and consequently the change in the consumption profile of the Brazilian public, Korean automakers decided to invest more heavily in Brazil. They've brought better products, practised better prices, opened more dealerships and increased investment in communications.

The result is that both Hyundai and Nissan have grown significantly, although in different periods, going from less than 1% to 4% market share and jumping by five or six positions in market ranking. Something that was unthinkable for most of the past decade. Today, these are the brands that most worry the big four (Figure 4).

Figure 4: Historical ranking of challenging automakers

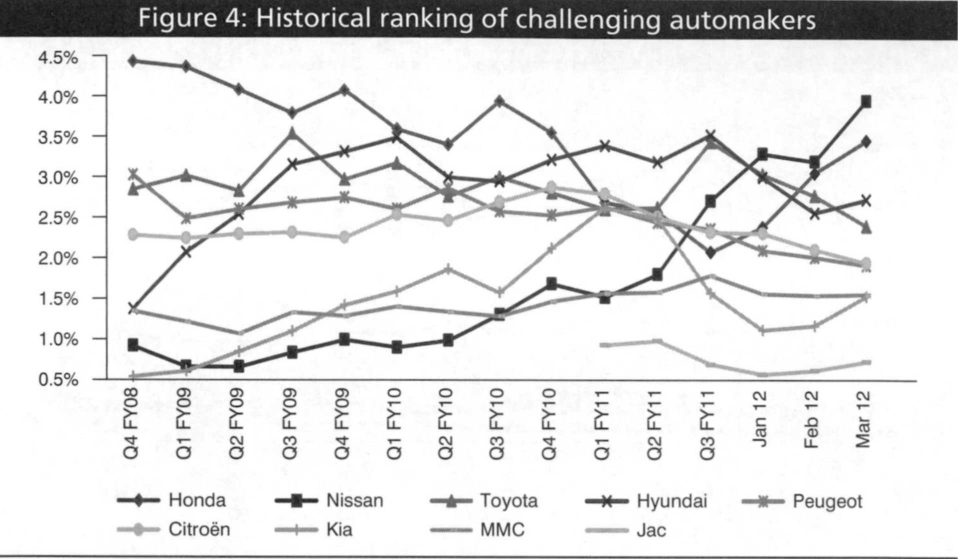


Source: Fenabrave

## The path

Up to now, we have two equal stories. Same starting point, same point of arrival. Now we will show why and how the two paths were so different. To demonstrate this, nothing better than to start by showing some results.

The first major difference in the paths is time. Hyundai took 49 months (from October 2007 to November 2010) to go from 1% to 4% market share, while Nissan took only 24 months (from March 2010 to March 2012) (Figure 5).

Our challenge here is analysing all the variables that may have contributed to growth and isolate the communications contribution, while respecting the different period of time shown above.

The first important variable is the growth of the automotive sector in Brazil. Could Brazilians have bought more cars in the period when Nissan had its biggest growth because of the economic scenario (more credit, less taxes, etc.)? The answer is no. Data show us that the sector had lower growth when Nissan had its biggest growth, as can be seen in Figure 6.

Figure 5: Change in market share Nissan vs. Hyundai

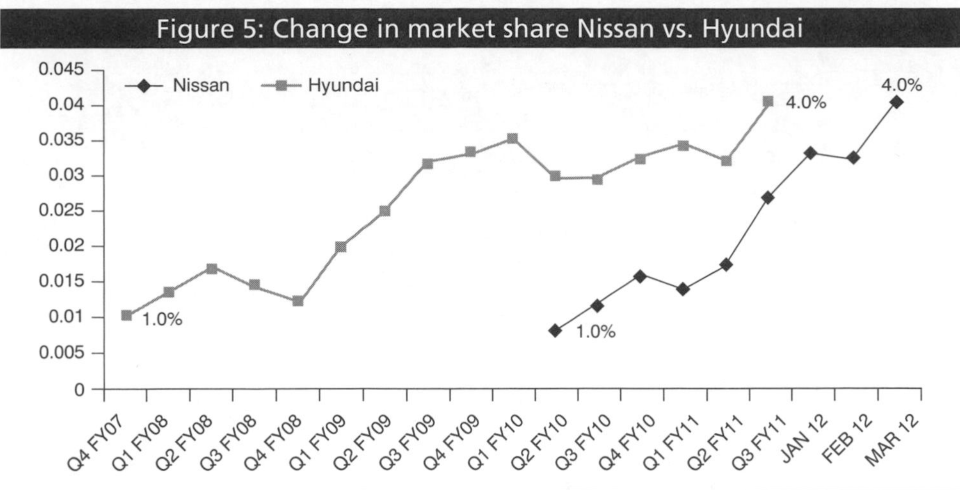


Source: Fenabrave

Figure 6: Market growth vs. Hyundai and Nissan growth

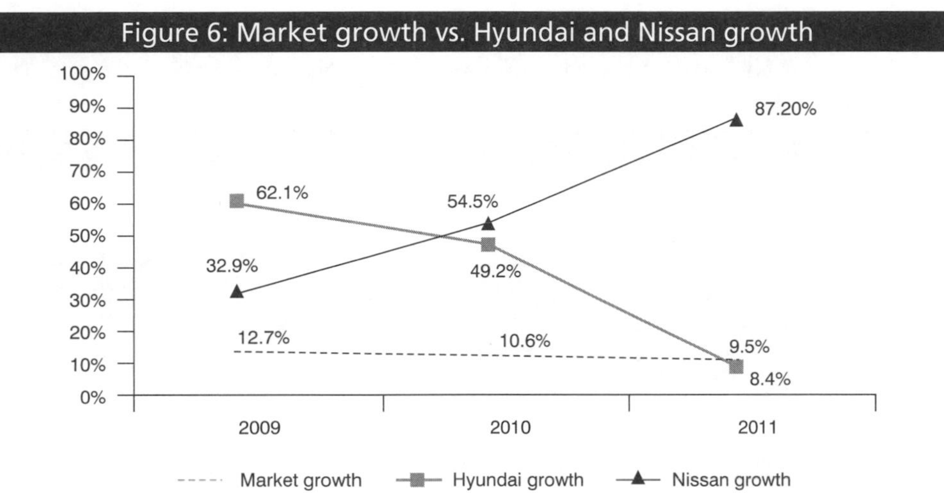


Source: Fenabrave

Another variable that did not influence our results was the number of dealerships in the country. During their respective growth periods Hyundai increased its number of dealerships by 248%, while Nissan increased dealerships by 38%. While Hyundai opened dealerships at the rate of almost three per month (2.83), Nissan opened a little over one per month (1.33) (Figure 7).

Figure 7: Number of dealerships Nissan vs. Hyundai

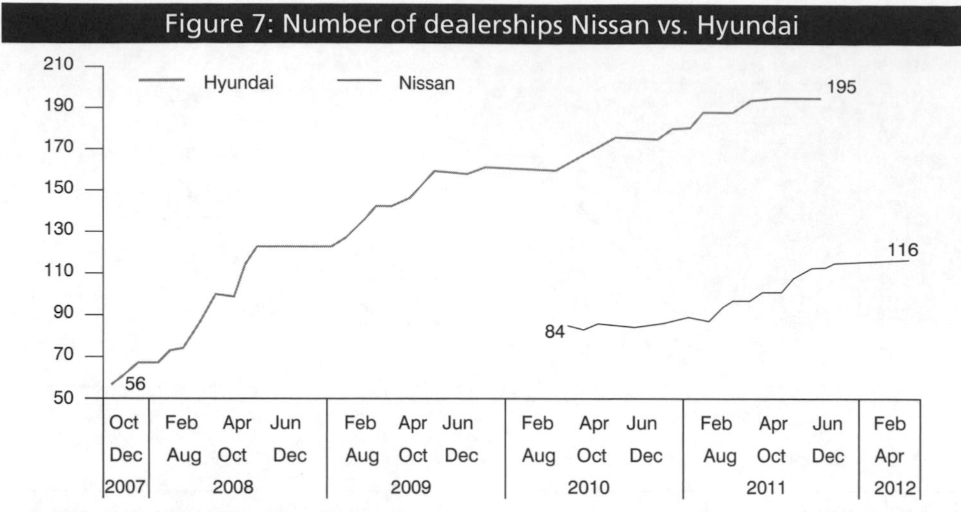


Source: Quatro Rodas magazine[2]

Another variable could have been the prices being practised. But while Hyundai had to decrease its average price by more than 20%, Nissan had no significant price variation in the period (Figure 8).

Figure 8: Hyundai line-up average price vs. Nissan

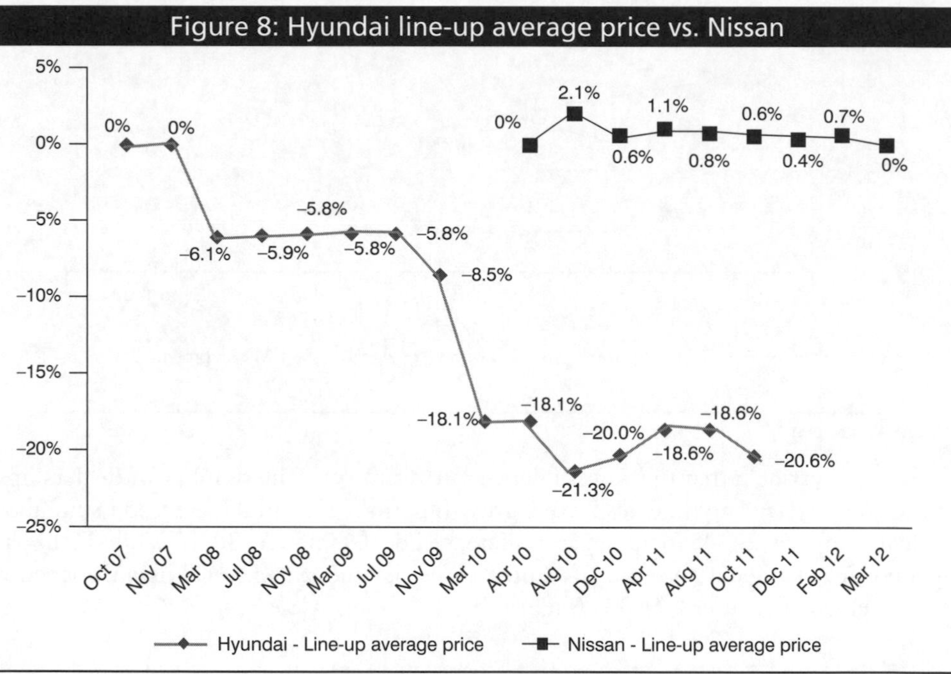


Source: Quatro Rodas magazine

Finally, product launches helped Hyundai much more than Nissan. During the analysis period, Hyundai launched six cars and started to produce its most popular car in Brazil. Meanwhile, Nissan launched just two cars and made no changes to its production.

As can be seen, it was not difficult to isolate variables other than communications without the need for econometric models. Now we can move on and see how communications influenced both results.

We can be certain that communications was the variable that made the most difference to the path of these two brands, but there is also a significant difference between them in this aspect.

In order to achieve its growth, Hyundai became the biggest communication spender in the Brazilian auto sector, even though it has a sales volume six times smaller than the leader, Fiat (Figure 9).

Figure 9: Communication investment evolution Hyundai, Fiat and Nissan

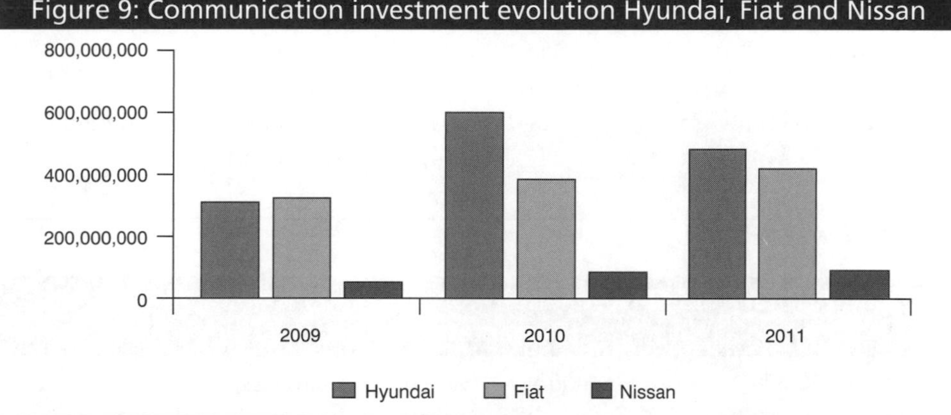


Source: Ibope Monitor[3]

During the period that it progressed from 1% to 4% market share, the brand spent US$ 877,801,030 (Table 1). Meanwhile, Nissan has remained one of the minor advertisers in the Brazilian auto sector, investing only US$ 149,642,660 in communication during its growth period (Table 2). Even proportionally to the time, period, and breaking out investment on a monthly basis, Hyundai spent around three times more than Nissan: US$ 18,287,521 against US$ 6,235,110.

That is a large number, and it shows us how a different strategy to reach a goal can be faster and less expensive to the company (Figure 10).

## Table 1: Total Hyundai investment in communications going from 1% to 4% market share

| | 2007 (US$) | 2008 (US$) | 2009 (US$) | 2010 (US$) | 2011 (US$) |
|---|---|---|---|---|---|
| **January** | | 5,072,090 | 5,253,530 | 19,848,010 | 10,148,290 |
| **February** | | 4,951,170 | 4,862,620 | 19,789,890 | 21,246,450 |
| **March** | | 7,870,760 | 6,170,340 | 27,954,430 | 16,432,080 |
| **April** | | 10,701,180 | 7,318,500 | 21,634,570 | 28,578,770 |
| **May** | | 10,175,140 | 11,791,850 | 28,246,050 | 35,311,460 |
| **June** | | 10,859,320 | 14,623,940 | 29,210,510 | 29,961,920 |
| **July** | | 12,996,060 | 15,355,890 | 28,942,080 | 28,451,190 |
| **August** | | 15,663,020 | 21,451,290 | 32,098,420 | 32,652,820 |
| **September** | | 11,179,250 | 21,400,320 | 27,358,620 | 27,549,520 |
| **October** | 4,614,070 | 8,875,890 | 21,627,410 | 33,743,720 | 24,219,210 |
| **November** | 4,133,620 | 5,263,170 | 21,747,480 | 32,947,280 | |
| **December** | 2,937,260 | 4,586,800 | 20,163,260 | 29,830,510 | |
| **Total** | 11,684,950 | 108,193,850 | 171,766,430 | 331,604,090 | 254,551,710 |
| | | | **All Hyundai investment (US$)** | | |
| | | | **877,801,030** | | |

Source: Ibope Monitor

## Table 2: Total Nissan investment in communications going from 1% to 4% market share

| | 2010 (US$) | 2011 (US$) | 2012 (US$) |
|---|---|---|---|
| **January** | | 4,800,340 | 8,240,760 |
| **February** | | 5,423,540 | 7,451,560 |
| **March** | | 4,395,080 | |
| **April** | 4,019,170 | 4,540,300 | |
| **May** | 3,728,590 | 7,472,490 | |
| **June** | 3,343,430 | 5,886,350 | |
| **July** | 2,625,150 | 6,709,520 | |
| **August** | 5,964,980 | 8,621,130 | |
| **September** | 7,798,860 | 7,809,130 | |
| **October** | 4,625,550 | 13,073,720 | |
| **November** | 5,294,990 | 11,365,700 | |
| **December** | 6,083,430 | 10,368,890 | |
| **Total** | 43,484,150 | 90,466,190 | 15,692,320 |
| | | **All Nissan investment (US$)** | |
| | | **149,642,660** | |

Source: Ibope Monitor

Figure 10: Hyundai vs. Nissan investment in communications going from 1% to 4% market share

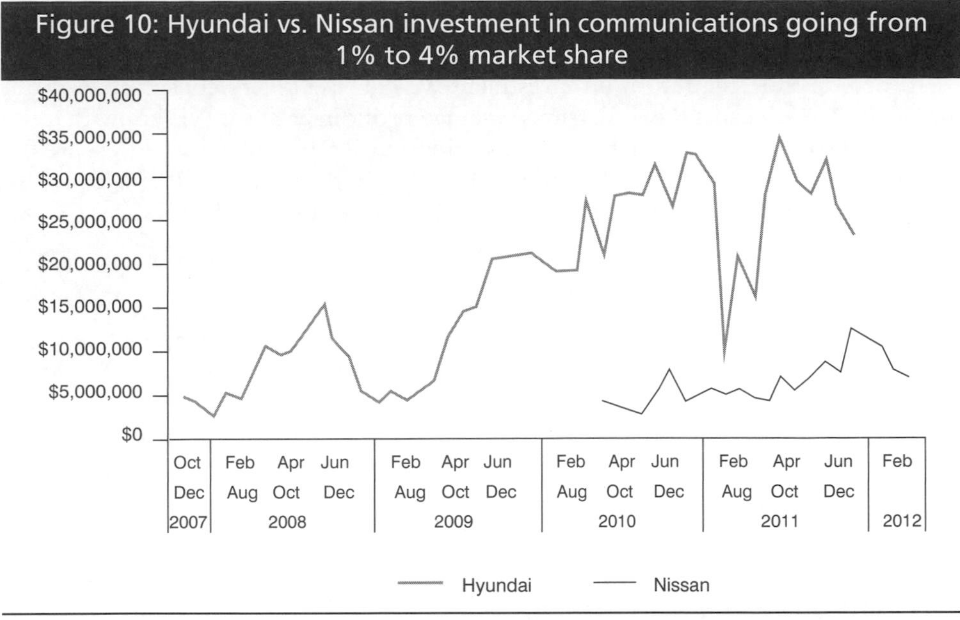


Source: Ibope Monitor

It can clearly be seen that Nissan's communications had greater efficiency than those of Hyundai. However, it is important to show how it was also efficient in absolute terms, providing return on investment.

### *Control region*

We will use the control region method to measure the contribution from communications. But first of all, paraphrasing the anthropologist Bronislaw Malinowski, to compare any two things we need to prove their comparability.

So we need to choose two places with similar contexts, like:

- national relevance;
- acceptance of the Nissan brand;
- number of dealerships;
- pricing;
- auto sector growth.

So we chose two important Brazilian cities (State capitals): Brasília and Florianópolis. The first one had communications investment. The second one didn't.

### *Local ROI*

During the period of analysis, Brasília (where Nissan had investment in communications) demonstrated an increase of 248% in the average monthly sales. In Florianópolis (control region) the same growth was 133% (Source: Fenabrave).

Considering that, we can attribute to communications the difference in growth, between the two cities, of 115%. In absolute terms it means that Nissan sold 2,539 extra units from communications.

When we combine these extra units with the mix of Nissan models and their respective prices, we arrive at a revenue of US$ 85,043,309.

To demonstrate the return on investment we will use a very conservative profit margin of 10%. That is the dealerships' average profit in each car. We know that the company profit margin is much bigger than this, but we are not allowed to share it.

Anyway, considering this 10% conservative margin, the profit was US$ 8,504,330. In a city where Nissan spent US$ 2,938,263 in communications, it had US$ 5,566,088 of return on investment.

### *National projection*

To make a national projection of this performance we need to apply the same methodology and a proportional sales growth attributed to communications, that is here 94.6% (on 204% national growth).

Doing that, Nissan sold 56,995 extra units from communications with a revenue of US$ 1,909,036,381. Using the same 10% profit margin and discounting the US$ 149,642,660 that Nissan spent on communications in Brazil, we have US$ 41,260,978 of national return on investment.

## Why Nissan was more efficient

At this point we are able to demonstrate how we were much more efficient that Hyundai and how we provided a very good return on our investment.

The question that remains is: why were we so much more efficient? Where was it that we made the difference, so that this communication effort was so effective?

Let's take this story from its very beginning.

## The task: massive growth

In early 2010, Nissan initiated a very aggressive plan for Brazil: to be the first Japanese automaker in the sector with 5% market share and an annual sales volume of 200,000 units sold. We had until 2014 to achieve this goal, and at that time we were the fourth Japanese brand, with only 0.9% of the market and 2,300 units sold (Figure 11).

Figure 11: Nissan goal triangle

Source: Nissan

## The role of communications: brand + sales

In order to support Nissan in achieving its goals, we established two main communication objectives:

1. Make a stronger brand, increasing awareness and overall opinion.
2. Put people in direct contact with our cars, increasing the show-room traffic.

With the first objective we would help Nissan to be the first Japanese brand in Brazil. With the second, we could work on sales growth.

## A tough decision: to become a challenger brand

The situation was this: an irrelevant brand with a highly pretentious ambition. It was necessary to establish a communications strategy as aggressive as the goal. It led us to take the most significant decision the company has taken in recent years, responsible for much of its recent success: take on the role of challenger in the market (Figure 12).

**Figure 12: Target of becoming a challenger brand**

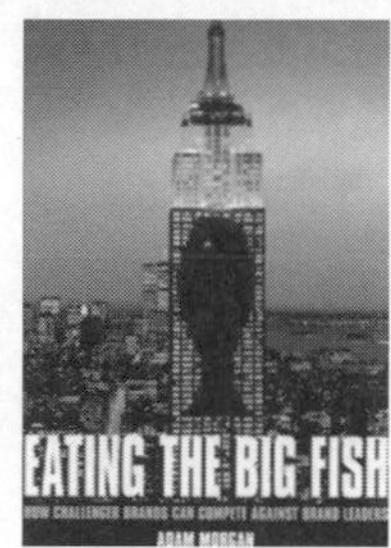


'The key failure for any company attempting to move up a gear in its performance is not the ability to define its intention, but the inability to translate intention into behaviour.'

Eating The Big Fish, Adam Morgan

We could not grow and set such a bold target without assuming the same boldness on our brand behaviour. Nissan had a good line-up and people needed to know that, they needed to pay attention to it.

Ok, looking at the scenario, this strategy seems to be the most obvious one. And it really is. The most obvious and the most correct. But it is far from being as simple as it seems.

Many brands have tried to become challengers in certain markets, but few have actually acted as such. Because it is not that easy. Putting it on a piece of paper is nice, it makes sense. In practice, it takes great courage and boldness to make it happen. Especially in Brazil.

This is because the advertising sector in Brazil operates in an environment with a series of unspoken agreements among its participants. Here, no one should be compared to another. Each agency speaks of itself, each one is looking out only for itself.

This situation of unspoken gentlemen's agreements is very comfortable for the leaders, who protect themselves from any attack by their competition, especially those who are at the bottom of the rankings.

Nissan broke that agreement and decided not to surrender to the will of the leaders. And that decision extrapolated to the corporate level. Every professional involved in this project had to have the courage to assume a posture that confronts so much of our culture. And we did it. And we take great pride in the results and of having created a precedent that allows new challengers to emerge with a bold posture in new markets outside the automobile sector.

## Impact, impact, impact

To take on the role of challenger, to take it to the streets and start fighting against our inexpressive position, we had to assume a mantra for ourselves: impact, impact, impact. This is for a very simple reason: Nissan needed a lot of visibility and attention with a very low investment compared to most of the players in the sector. If we did not ensure the impact of communications, neither would we ensure visibility nor attention (Figure 13).

Figure 13: Share of investment (automakers category): Apr 2010–Mar 2012

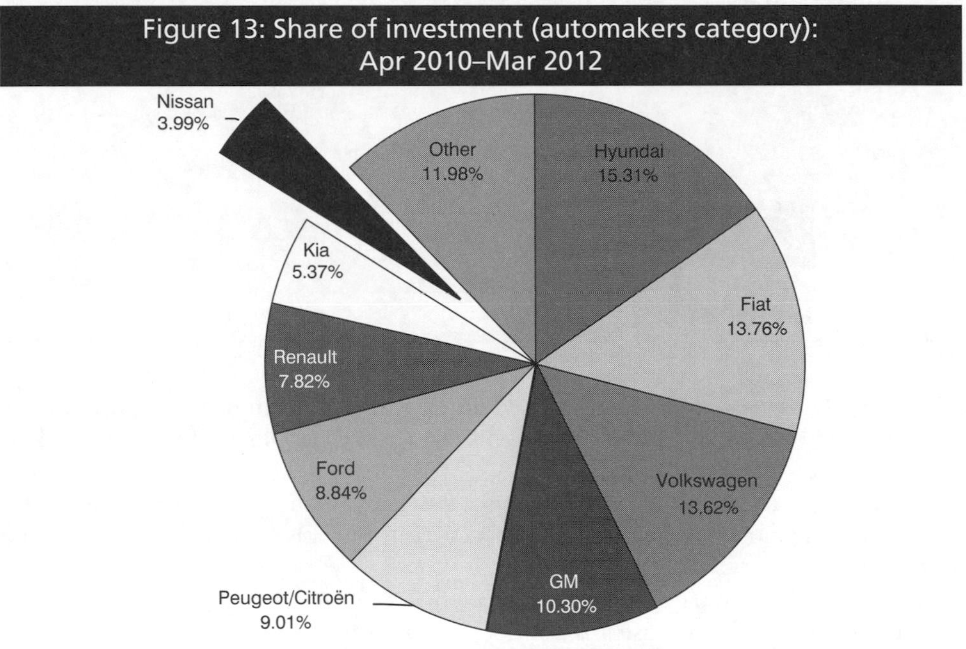


Source: Ibope Monitor

Our line of thinking on impact led to the three Cs, the basis for our strategy: clash, concentration, content (Figure 14).

Figure 14: Challenger three Cs chart

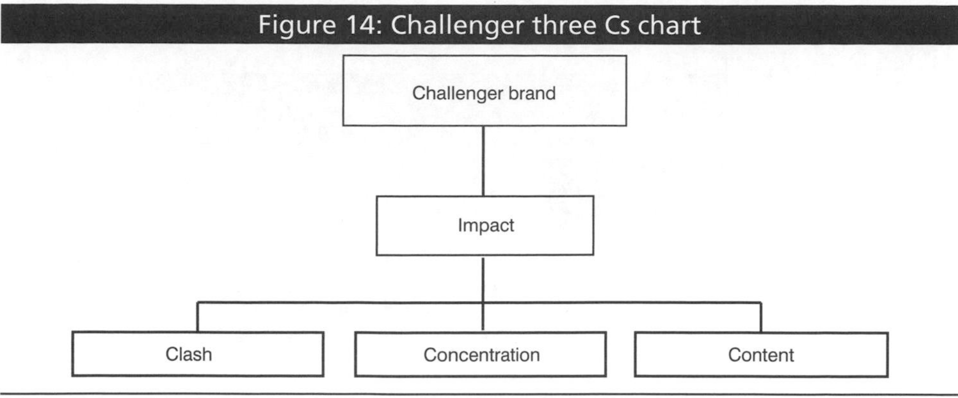


Source: Lew'Lara\TBWA

### *Clash*

A comparative strategy was our best alternative. Not just because it would ensure impact and visibility by being the opposite of what is done in communications in Brazil. This would be the most impactful way to show people the quality of our line-up. We do have products to compete with any automaker and Brazilians needed to know that.

Besides, strategically, it made sense for the brand to communicate their cars by placing them side-by-side with the leaders and references in each segment. If I need to communicate a car that people barely know, nothing better than placing it in the same context as another car that everyone already knows as a reference.

Therefore, it was crucial that we should define what our 'confrontation' was for each product, so we could find the best possible argument to win the dispute and call people's attention to that feature. We highlighted price at one moment, quality at another, sometimes some specific feature, always showing the advantage of our model compared to the main reference model for each market segment (Table 3).

Table 3: Nissan clash strategy

| Nissan core model | Main competitors | Clash |
|---|---|---|
| Nissan March | Fiat Palio | Brand new car against old cars with make-up |
| Nissan Livina | Fiat Idea<br>GM Meriva | Best choice endorsement against poor cost benefit |
| Nissan Tiida | Ford Focus | More performance against an overpriced car |
| Nissan Frontier | Toyota Hilux<br>VW Amarok | The strongest pick up against the wannabe 'off-roaders' |

Source: Lew'Lara\TBWA

This method allowed us to very quickly build a basic profile for every car of our line-up and it was our direct route to the first main communications objective: increase awareness and overall opinion (Figure 15).

Figure 15: Nissan – key brand indicators

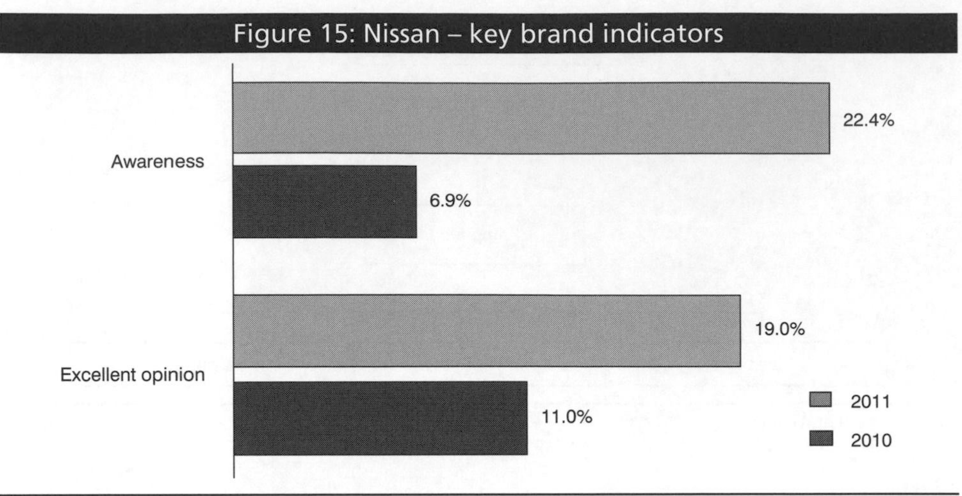


Source: GfK

Our search index on Google has also increased significantly, growing 200%. People were interested in learning more about the brand that nobody had heard of just a short while ago (Figure 16).

Figure 16: Nissan Google search growth vs. automakers average (index)

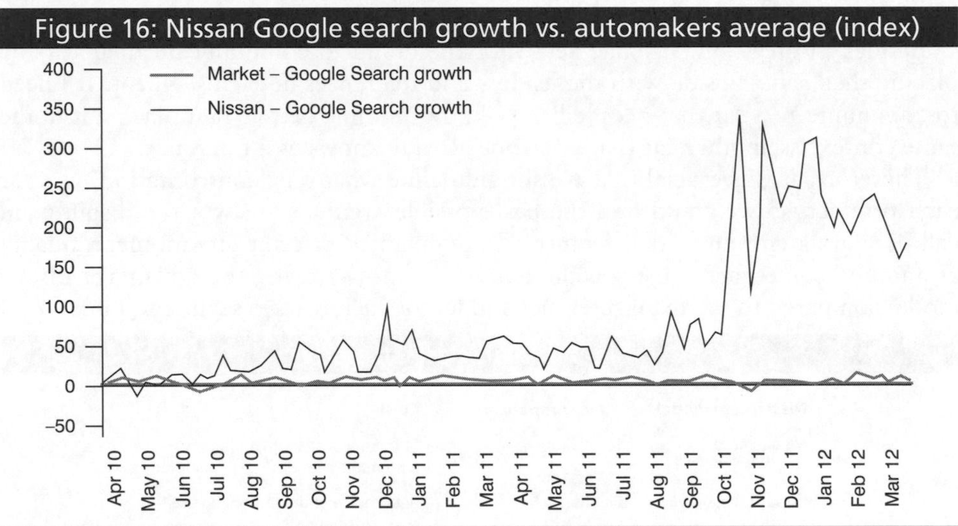


Source: Google Insights

This has a direct relationship with our investment in communications in mass media. Using the two areas of control available on Google, we see a significant difference in mentions of the brand in absolute terms (Figure 17).

Figure 17: 'Nissan' Google search in Brasília vs. Florianópolis (index)

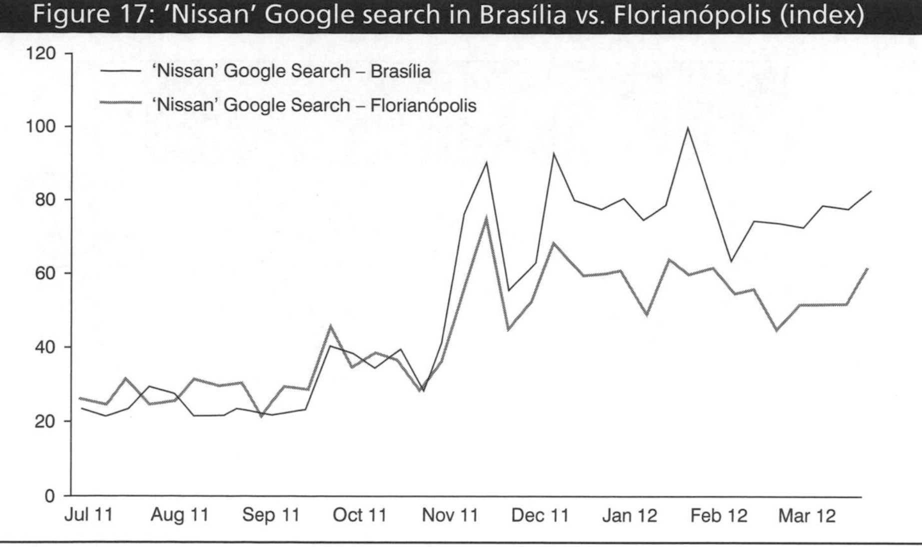


Source: Google Insights

### *Concentration*

Despite the impact of our confrontations, the main barrier remained: low resources for investment in communications.

This led us to adopt totally unorthodox thinking in terms of advertising, the basic rules of which seek a balance between coverage and frequency spread between different communications channels.

We completely abandoned the idea of frequency, investing all our efforts in coverage. We abandoned thoughts of other channels and placed everything in TV. That's because the entire media strategy was designed with the idea of *creating a peak of attention. So everybody would recognise and comment on our communications in a very short period of time.*

As a challenger brand with a low budget we cannot consider occupying a territory. We needed to make a loud single entry, provoke a reaction and move back. TV is the best way to do that, since in Brazil it is still the channel that guarantees visibility and talkability.

For this reason, the strategy was to run a flight that began on Friday night and ended on Monday morning, using every media resource available through this period. After all, it is during weekends that people are among friends and family looking for something to talk about.

Besides, the weekend is the moment in which we have the most traffic in our dealerships. People buy more cars during the weekend than during the week. And that was what led us to our second big communications objective: increase showroom traffic. And we did it. Today almost three times more people visit a Nissan dealership during a month than two years ago (Figure 18).

Figure 18: Nissan show-room traffic

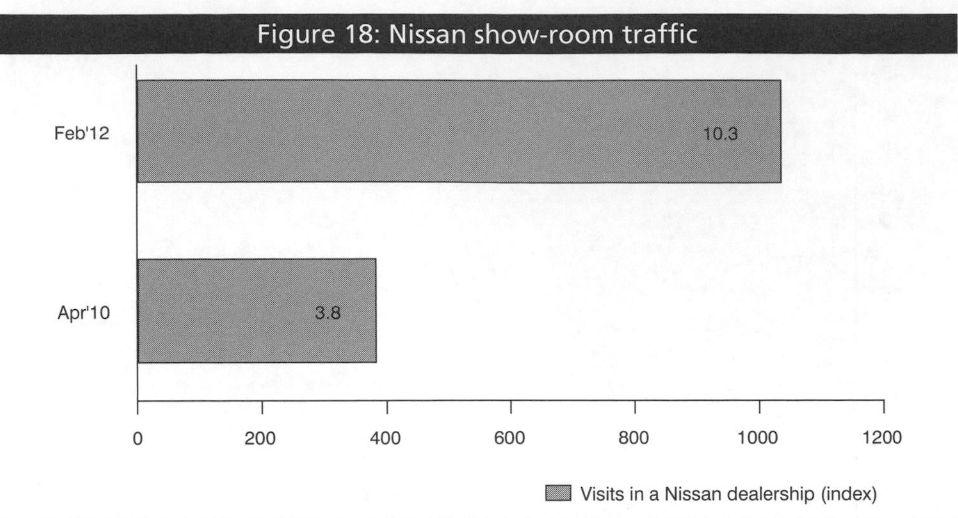


Source: Nissan

The traffic in our 'virtual showroom' also increased by a lot. Nissan's website has also received many more visits. People have wanted to know more about our cars. We have been generating a real interest for the brand (Figure 19).

Figure 19: Nissan site users

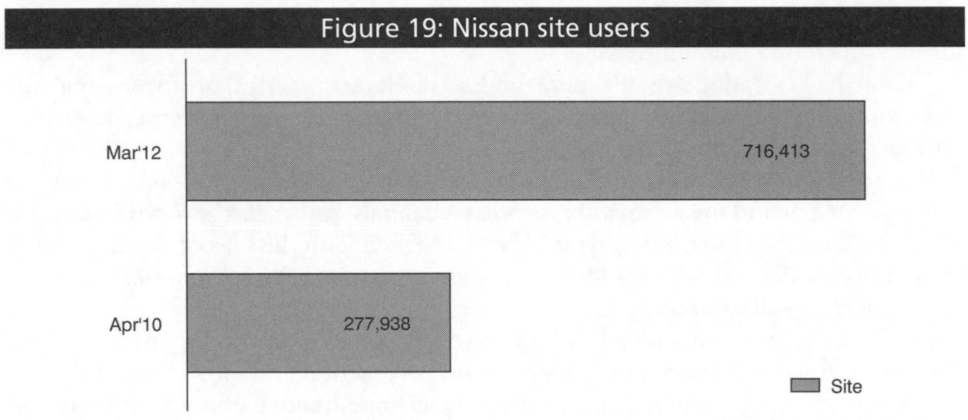


Source: Google Analytics

### *Content*

But all the impact depended a lot on the content we delivered to consumers. And content really is the best word to define the kind of campaign execution that we developed.

Going beyond an ordinary advertising campaign, the idea was to always provide a little entertainment for the public. Something fun and humorous, that they would want to see again, discuss with the person at their side, post on Facebook. That's why, many times, we used the strategy of running 30" spots on TV and extended versions on YouTube. It would create the peak of visibility and attention that we were trying to get.

Two years and many advertising campaigns later, we produced the most unusual types of content.

We made music video clips featuring the Frontier, to make fun of the 'wannabe' off-roaders, and the Tiida to show what happens when we pay more money for less performance (Figures 20 and 21).

**Figure 20: Frontier TV ad – 'Railuque e Maloque'**

The country singers that are not from the country side. "Really strong pickups get put through the mud"

Source: Lew'Lara\TBWA

**Figure 21: Tiida TV ad – 'Rappers'**

"Because you paid $3,000 more". "All this luxury is bought with your money"

Source: Lew'Lara\TBWA

We made fun of engineers from other automakers, showing how their lives are tough, because they do not work for Nissan (Figures 22 and 23).

**Figure 22: Livina TV ad – 'Target'**

"The Nissan Livina won the Best Buy from Quatro Rodas magazine". "The Nissan Livina was the choosen the best family car". "Can't you get anything right?"

Source: Lew'Lara\TBWA

**Figure 23: Frontier TV ad – 'Engineers'**

"Nissan made the Frontier the most powerful engine in its category". "Any other manufacturer would stop here". "Nissan has an innovative way of thinking about power".

Source: Lew'Lara\TBWA

We changed things at the PoS, challenging people to come to our dealerships not just to drive our car, but the competition's car as well (Figure 24).

**Figure 24: Livina TV ad – 'Livina challenge'**

"Which of these cars was voted Best Buy by Quatro Rodas Magazine?" "Which has the best conditions of payment?" "Go to a Nissan dealer and compare yourself Livina with Meriva and Idea"

Source: Lew'Lara\TBWA

We threw money up in the air in one of the country's main avenues, to show that those who purchase a Fiat people-carrier do exactly the same thing (Figure 25).

**Figure 25: Livina TV ad – 'Money'**

The crazy guy throwing money away . "More equipments for the best price"

Source: Lew'Lara\TBWA

To launch the Nissan March, we brought back an old toy to show an old industry practice: do a minor face-lift and say it's a new car (Figure 26).

Figure 26: March TV ad – 'Mr Zucchini head'

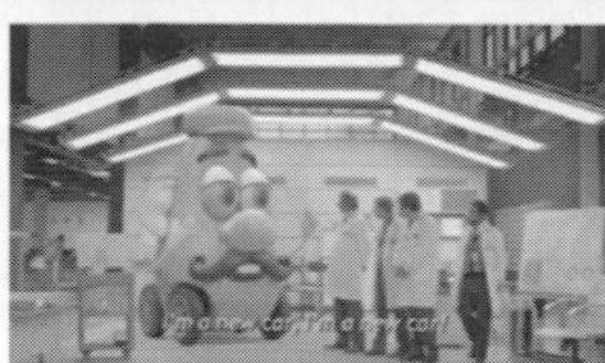

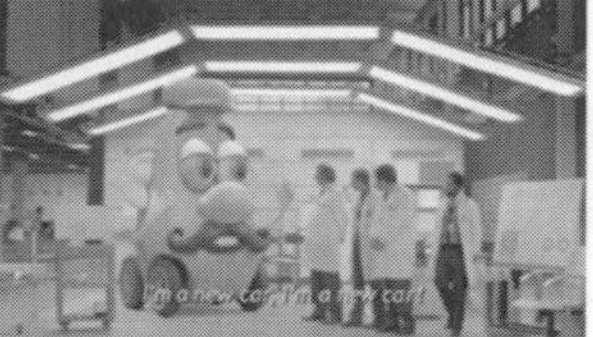

"What can we change in this car the the next year?" "What if we changed the front?"
"Why have a car that pretends to be new?"

Source: Lew'Lara\TBWA

After that, we presented our brand new car, tested 5,000 times to bring the best of Japanese quality to Brazil (Figure 27).

Figure 27: March TV ad – '5,000'

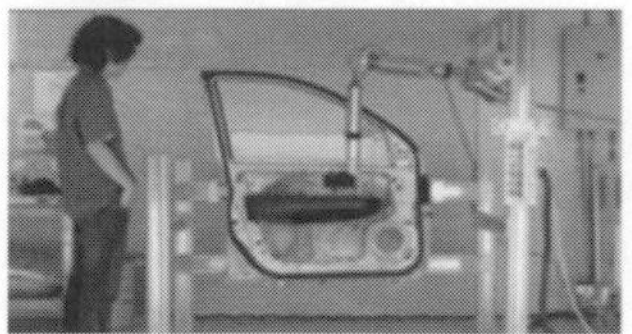

"The Nissan March went through more than 5000 tests, to be approved by you"

Source: Lew'Lara\TBWA

Finally, after so many successful productions, we scored the biggest hit of Brazilian advertising in 2011, showing what happens under the hood of a competitor pick-up when it gets stuck in the mud (Figure 28).

Figure 28: Frontier TV ad – 'Damn ponies'

"Do you want a pickup truck with horses or ponies?". "Choose a truly strong pickup truck"

Source: Lew'Lara\TBWA

This led us to make the most viewed clip on YouTube in the history of Brazilian advertising, with 14,590,215 views. It is the second most watched movie in the world in the automobiles category.

Not to mention the effect on popular culture spawned by the film. Even on YouTube we see a tremendous number of parodies made by users. There are more than 8,880 parodies, which generated more than 9 million views. There is no film by any Brazilian automaker that has had more views than the parodies of the 'Damn ponies'. The closest rival had to bring in Dustin Hoffman to feature in their commercial (Figure 29).

**Figure 29: Views of the second most popular ad vs. views of 'Damn ponies' parody**

| Fiat official ad: 500 "Casting" (w/ Dustin Hoffman) | Nissan parody: 'Damned Pony' song remix | Nissan parody: 'Damned Pony' w/ 10 minutes | Nissan parody: Soccer player blaming Ponies |
|---|---|---|---|
| | 2,167,222 views | 1,509,057 views | 831,229 views |
| **3,449,772 views** | **4,507,508 views** | | |

Source: YouTube

This is simply because we pursued this result since the beginning. We have always maintained our focus on bringing content and entertainment to the public.

Currently, on YouTube, Nissan is the automaker with (by far) the most views on its brand channel, with 55% more views than the second placed company. In addition, it is also the automaker brand channel with the most subscribers, almost double those of the second place (Table 4).

**Table 4: Views and subscribers – automakers brand channel**

| **Manufacturers** | **Brand channel** | |
|---|---|---|
| | **Views** | **Subscribes** |
| 1) Nissan | 25,179,652 | 7,933 |
| 2) Volkswagen | 16,239,463 | 4,399 |
| 3) Fiat | 12,426,724 | 3,992 |
| 4) Ford | 11,253,250 | 1,358 |
| 5) Renault | 3,916,805 | 1,010 |
| 6) Chevrolet | 3,713,467 | 2,542 |
| 7) Citroën | 1,580,444 | 551 |
| 8) Toyota | 255,390 | 120 |
| 9) Hyundai | 276,791 | 46 |

Source: YouTube

Even beyond the automotive market, we now rank among the most memorable advertising campaigns in Brazil, with an investment significantly smaller than that of the other brands sharing the ranking (Figure 30).

Figure 30: Brand preference in TV ads

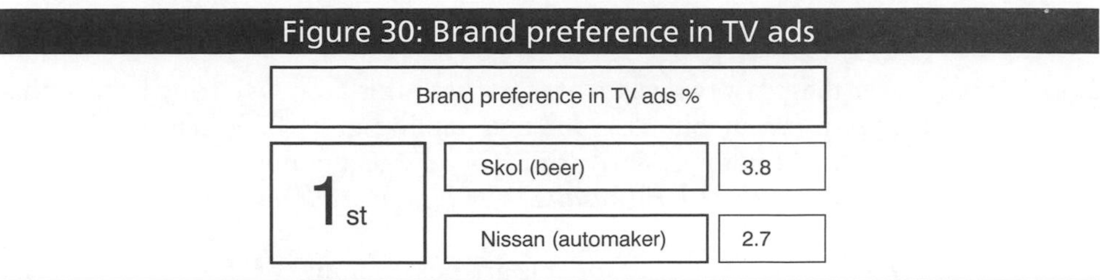

| Brand preference in TV ads % | | |
|---|---|---|
| 1 st | Skol (beer) | 3.8 |
| | Nissan (automaker) | 2.7 |

Source: Meio & Mensagem magazine[4]

All of these results signify that Nissan began to become relevant to the public in many ways. People wanted to relate to the brand. We can see this through the followers on our Facebook page, going from 77 to 106,893 people, an increase far above the market average (Figure 31).

Figure 31: Nissan Facebook growth

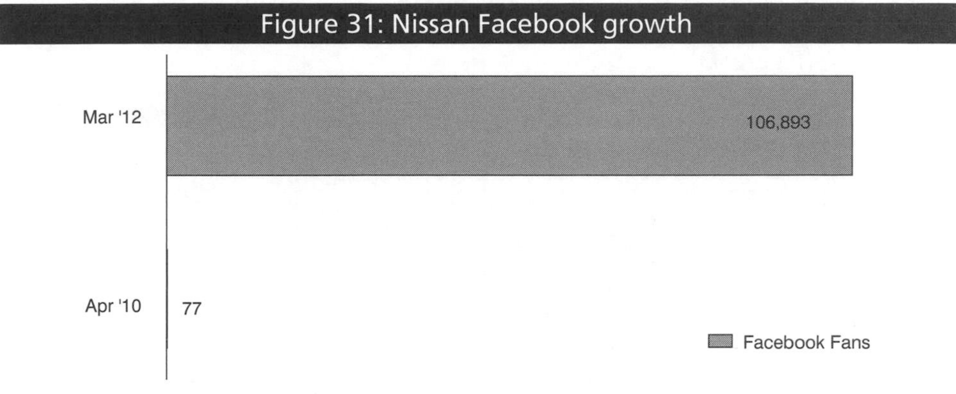


Source: Facebook

After all this, not even the market could close its eyes to the job we were doing. Even adopting a defiant stance that did not comply with the sector's unspoken non-aggression pact, we were voted advertisers of the year 2011 by two of the most important awards in Brazil (Figure 32).

Figure 32: Nissan 'Advertiser Of The Year' award

Prêmio Colunistas

PRÊMIO CABORÉ 2011

## What about the future?

Looking back over these last two years of work with this brand we truly believe that we have built a very favourable basis for maintaining growth. When we think of the long term we should not necessarily think of a large amount of time. *Long-term results are a sequence of short-term results. The last one allows the next one to be more efficient.*

As a result of our communications, people are now waiting for the next big Nissan advertising campaign. Each new commercial gives us more visibility and attention. In the near future it can allow us to spend less money on media, focusing our efforts on production of even better content.

In summary, it means that we have created room for more efficient and profitable communications investment.

We don't believe that it's just a coincidence that we've made 4% of market share in two years. It means we have achieved 75% of our goal (5%) in 50% of the time (four years) (Figure 33).

Figure 33: Results summary

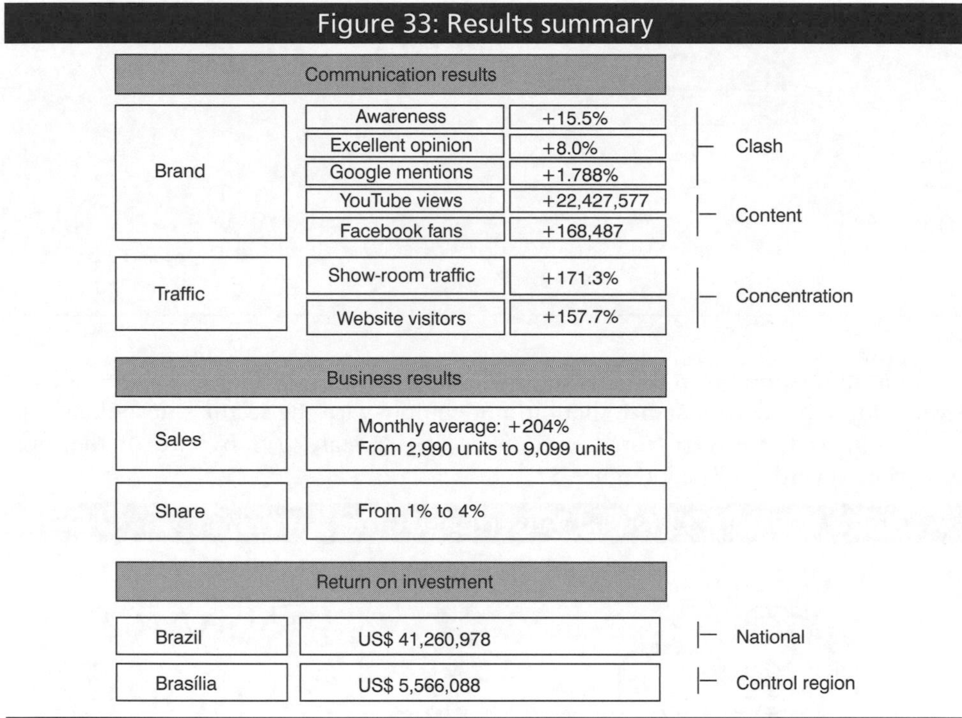

Communication results
Brand
Awareness
+15.5%
Excellent opinion
+8.0%
Google mentions
+1.788%
YouTube views
+22,427,577
Facebook fans
+168,487
Clash
Content
Traffic
Show-room traffic
+171.3%
Website visitors
+157.7%
Concentration
Business results
Sales
Monthly average: +204%
From 2,990 units to 9,099 units
Share
From 1% to 4%
Return on investment
Brazil
US$ 41,260,978
National
Brasília
US$ 5,566,088
Control region


## Finally, what is the most efficient path between two points?

In this paper we learned that courage can bring many rewards.

Courage from a company that did not identify with the lower places in sales rankings, but fully exposed itself to the general audience.

Courage from an agency that broke from common market practices because it believed that what it was doing with the brand's investment was correct.

Despite all the intelligence and creativity applied to this project, we affirm with conviction that the best and most efficient path between two points is courage. To have courage and to be bold when there is so much at stake is the most powerful force that can move someone from one point to another.

A toast to courage!

## Notes

1 Fenabrave: National Federation of Motor Vehicles. Online at: http://www.fenabrave.org.br
2 Quatro Rodas magazine: the most important car magazine in Brazil. Online at: http://quatrorodas.abril.com.br/
3 Ibope Monitor: national media investment database, outsourced by Ibope Research Institute. Online at: www.ibope.com.br
4 Meio & Mensagem magazine: the most important advertising magazine in Brazil. Online at: http://www.meioemensagem.com.br/

## Chapter 27

# The National Lottery

## How doing 'one hundred things one per cent better' helped Camelot achieve record sales

**By Simon Jenkins, MPG Media Contacts**
Contributing authors: Michael Salter, Andrew Deykin and Ben Dudley, MPG Media Contacts
Credited companies: Creative Agency: AMV BBDO; Media Agency: OMD; Client: Camelot

**Editor's summary**

This paper illustrates an amazing demonstration of long-term application and dedication to effectiveness from a unique brand. All lotteries generate vast excitement when they launch but go into steep sales decline as optimism inevitably fades. To address this, over the last seven years MPG Media Contacts has devised a successful rollover marketing formula, under-pinned by econometrics, to tame the inherent unpredictability of the lottery business. The strategy has involved minimising late-buying in TV, a focused spot-length strategy, and strategic message and channel deployment to maximise the payback potential of any jackpot scenario. This has provided the platform for managed long-term growth via brand diversification and new game development, and helped Camelot achieve record sales of £5.8bn in 2011 – bucking the global trend of declining lottery sales worldwide. Overall a very clever and brave solution that achieved clearly demonstrable results.

*It's not doing one thing 100 per cent better that makes the difference; it's doing one hundred things 1 per cent better.*

Dianne Thompson, Camelot Group CEO.[1]

You'd be forgiven for thinking it's easy to make 'advertising work' for The National Lottery. Everybody wants to be a millionaire, after all, and UK operator Camelot, has had the sole licence to run the lottery in the UK since 1994. However, it's not as straightforward as you might think.

All lotteries generate huge excitement when they launch – but tend to go into steep decline as the initial excitement wears off. Over the last seven years, Camelot has developed and implemented 'a proven strategy for long-term, responsible growth', which has culminated in record sales of £5.8bn in 2011.[2]

Success has been achieved by continually finding ways to keep the excitement going. New games, new ways to play and new marketing approaches – continuous innovation has underpinned genuine growth. Within this, MPG Media Contacts have adapted and consistently evolved Camelot's communications planning approach, putting a formula in place to tame the inherent 'unpredictability' of the business and harnessing ROI potential – to deliver ever-increasing advertising revenue contributions year after year.

This is unlike many IPA Effectiveness entries you may read. This paper is not about a 'silver bullet' solution that delivered a big step change. This is the story of seven years of hard graft, consistent learning, ruthless advertising and media optimisation – all of which is underpinned by econometric modelling. This is about lots of 'one per cent' improvements that have, cumulatively, made a massive £1.58bn difference to Camelot's sales revenues.[3]

In order to demonstrate where we have added genuine value, we need to take you on a journey through the history of The UK National Lottery.

## Background and context

The National Lottery (TNL) is Britain's biggest brand, with a total penetration of over 70%[4] of UK adults, with total sales five times bigger than the UK's acknowledged biggest grocery brand, Coca Cola.[5] In fact, total TNL sales are larger than the UK's top ten grocery brands' sales, combined.[6]

Camelot's primary remit, and the reason they were awarded a licence to run The National Lottery, is to maximise funds for National Lottery Good Causes in a socially responsible way. On average, 28p of every £1 sale goes directly to National Lottery Good Causes; benefiting projects which range from small local initiatives, to the London 2012 Olympics and Paralympic Games. Since its inception in 1994, TNL has raised over £27bn for National Lottery Good Causes (Figure 1).[7]

In line with the lottery licence, TNL sales are precisely divided. Beyond the 28% for Good Causes, over 50% will go directly back into prizes.[8] Marketing budgets are also fixed at 1.22% and directly linked to sales performance. Practically, this means that if sales fall, advertising budgets fall too. There is no margin for error.

Figure 1: Camelot has raised £27bn for National Lottery Good Causes

Understandably, ROI is the crucial KPI for advertising – with all activity scrutinised by Camelot's regulator the National Lottery Commission (NLC), who regulate that any marketing outlay is driving significant and measurable benefit to Good Causes.

## Lottery marketing is about fighting decline post launch

It is generally accepted in the lottery world that post-launch marketing is about managing sales decline efficiently. All lotteries tend to decline in both participation levels and sales after the excitement of launch fades and player optimism drifts away. Between 1994 and 2003, TNL sales were staying true to the rule.

The National Lottery launched in 1994, and immediately took the country by storm. Penetration peaked at a phenomenal 91%[9] and by year-end in 1998, sales peaked at a staggering £5.5bn. However, in line with the acknowledged global trend, sales soon began to slide. By year-end 2003, sales had reached an all-time low of £4.6bn (–20% from launch). See Figure 2 (Figure 3 for reference).

Camelot's strategy to address decline was to diversify – to launch new games and to give players fresh reasons to engage with the brand, with the aim of driving incremental sales. Between 1994 and 2003, TNL had launched a Scratchcards brand, Instants, re-branded the core lottery game to Lotto, and extended from a main Saturday draw to Wednesday too – as well as introducing new games, Thunderball, Lotto HotPicks and Lotto Extra.

The new games required advertising support from launch, providing us with an increasing number of brands to maintain on a limited budget – a budget which was now being closely scrutinised for ROI, as any sales decline is matched by decline in return to National Lottery Good Causes. New launches can also result in cannibalisation of sales, so portfolio management increasingly becomes a challenge.

Figure 2: Total TNL sales in decline 1993–2003: The National Lottery total annual sales

National Lottery revenue £m

6,000
5,000
4,000
3,000
2,000
1,000
0

Scratch cards
Launched Mar 1995

Wednesday
lotto
Launched Feb 1997

Thunderball
Launched Jun 1999

Lotto Extra
Launched Nov '00

lotto HotPicks
Jul 2002

1995/96 1996/97 1997/98 1998/99 1999/00 2000/01 2001/02 2002/03

Source: Camelot

Figure 3: US State Lotto games experienced significant decline 1998–2003

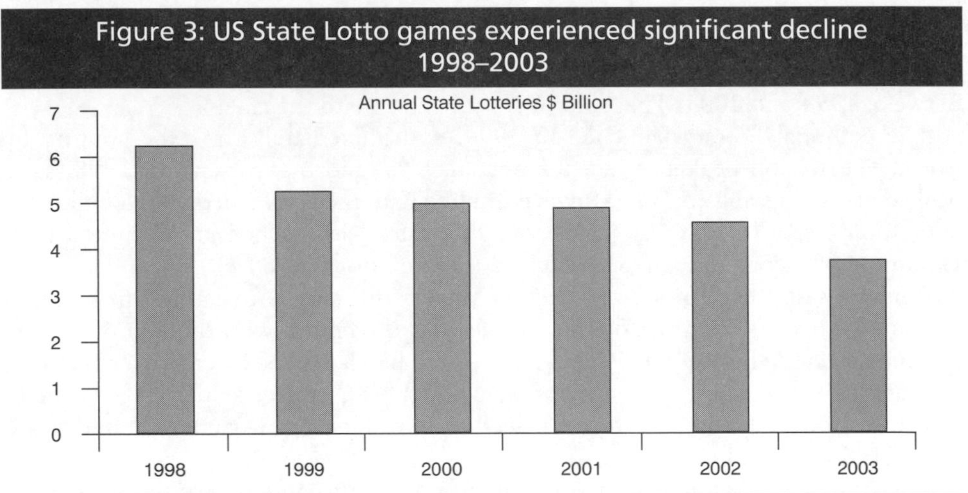


Source: Mizeur Whitepaper 2006 (La Fleurs)

## Rollover marketing is crucial to off-setting decline

Big jackpots represent the best opportunity to drive short-term incremental revenue. This is not only crucial to off-setting sales decline in the short-term, but a strong foundation of healthy revenue and engaged players is also essential if the business wants to launch and maintain new games – the proven tactic for long-term growth.

The 'Rollover' mechanic is designed to create big jackpots. For example, Lotto, the original 'rolling' game, is drawn on Wednesday and Saturday. If no player wins the jackpot on Saturday, it 'rolls over' to Wednesday, with the jackpot amount being carried over. If it is still not won on Wednesday, it 'rolls' on to Saturday (a Double Rollover), and so on, until we reach a 'Quadruple Rollover', where the jackpot 'rolls-down' if no-one matches all six numbers (see Figure 4).

Figure 4: Example of the Lotto 'Rollover' mechanic

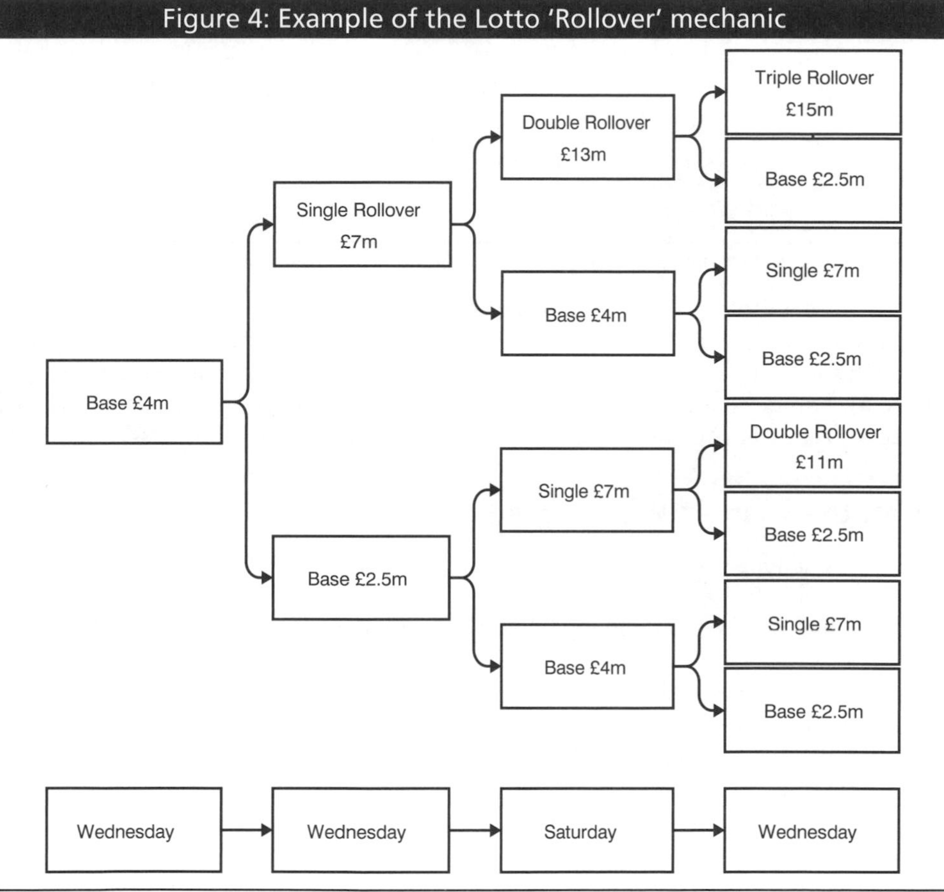


Rollovers are key revenue drivers as they act as triggers to bring 'occasional' players into the game,[10] due to increased jackpot size, and encourage 'weekly' players to increase their typical spend. Simply put, the bigger the jackpot, the greater the potential to drive incremental sales with advertising. The sales uplift from a rollover can range from +9%

above 'base' sales, on a single rollover, to +44% for a triple rollover (see Figure 5). With average Lotto sales in the region of £50m per week,[11] and with 25 rollovers per year,[12] sweating these 'margins' can make an important difference to the bottom line.

Figure 5: Average percentage sales uplift for Lotto rollovers

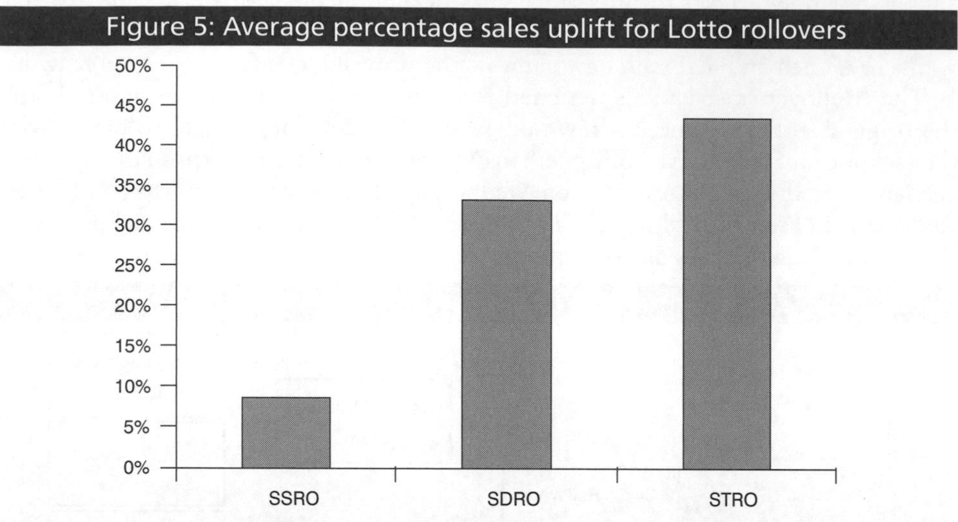


Source: Camelot (average uplifts based on 3 x previous non-rollover weeks (rolling))

Rollover advertising is also important for brand health, to keep players energised and enthusiastic about playing. Tracking data clearly demonstrate positivity and commitment to TNL increases during periods with significant rollover activity (see Figure 6). Similarly, we see reductions in the same scores during periods of rollover 'drought'. As such, rollovers really are the 'beating heart' of the business.

## Here's the snag – we can't predict the future

The main challenge we face with advertising rollovers is that we can't predict the future. So, while we have a good idea of the number of rollovers we can expect in a year, we have no way of knowing when they will arrive, and in what combination. Clearly, this makes efficient optimisation of a finite media budget a significant challenge. In real terms, this means when business closes on a Friday, we have no way of knowing what we'll be advertising on Monday morning.

Historically, we would react to rollovers as and when they arose. Practically, this meant buying media at the last minute to bring rollover advertising to market. This has massive implications both in terms of the cost and quality of inventory we can deliver. Pre-2004, up to 75% of the media budget was booked 'late'.[13] On TV, our strongest channel for driving sales,[14] this meant we were incurring a 45% premium for late-buying. Put another way, we were 'wasting' up to £7m per year in late penalties.[15]

At launch, while sales were flying, hefty premiums could be absorbed and we could still drive a healthy ROI. However, sliding base sales were putting increasing pressure on our ROIs. The 'last minute' reactive advertising plan was also labour intensive and a huge drain on marketing and agency team resources.

Figure 6: Tracking data demonstrates correlation between positivity and rollovers

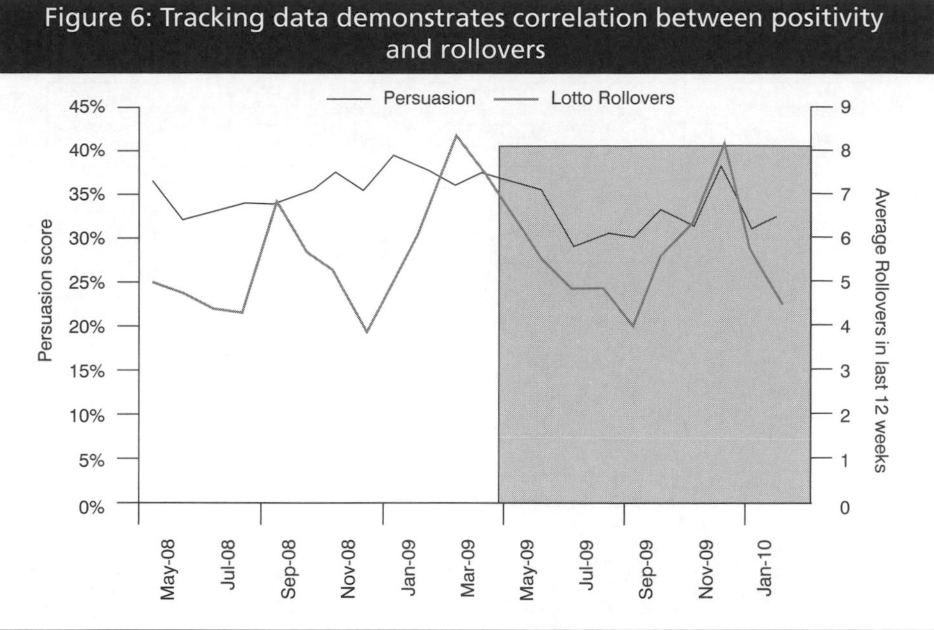


Source: Hall and Partners brand tracker

## 2004: The launch of EuroMillions would change everything

EuroMillions, launched in 2004 as a new Friday night draw, had the potential to be a game-changer, as it brought long-odds which meant huge jackpots that could exceed £150m.[16] While more big jackpots was great news, EuroMillions would also exacerbate the complexity and 'unpredictability' of jackpot marketing, by tripling the quantity of rollovers each year.[17]

When a budget is finite and ROI is crucial, it makes sense to invest behind the jackpots with the greatest ROI potential. However, because we are at the mercy of probability, EuroMillions would make budget management more like a game of poker; when do we stick, and when do we twist?

We could now be confident there would be four potential scenarios to contend with on Monday morning (see Figure 7), and that we would have less than 24 hours to bring a plan to market – which is not much time to optimise channel, weight and phasing, dependent on brand and jackpot size. There was increased risk we could waste even more time and money 'reacting to scenarios'.

Figure 7: Four potential Monday morning scenarios... Impossible to predict on Friday

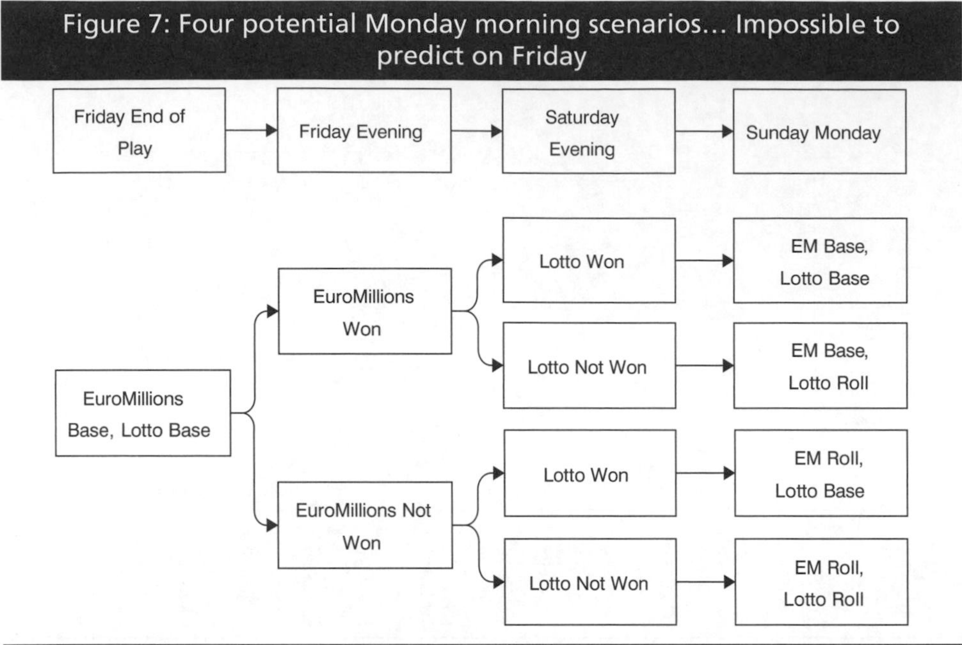


Plus we were launching a new, more expensive, game to an increasingly sceptical player, and EuroMillions was only forecast to secure a modest sales base initially – but we would have to over-invest to ensure a successful launch. This heaped additional pressure on the finite budget and declining ROIs.

We also had to find a way of ensuring that our two 'rolling' games didn't cannibalise sales from each other – ensuring that we grew EuroMillions from nothing while maintaining Lotto. This was the only way to deliver managed growth. To date, all previous launches had 'nibbled' at Lotto. EuroMillions brought 'even bigger' jackpots, so significantly increased the risk of cannibalisation.

We needed a solution to tame the increased 'unpredictability' of the new portfolio, make our budget work harder and increase the ROI potential of rollover advertising. We also needed a less labour intensive formula that would relieve pressure on marketing team time.

## Our solution: convert probability to certainty

While we were at the mercy of probability, we could be fairly certain about the number of rollovers we could expect in a fiscal. On Lotto alone, we knew we could expect up to 25 rollovers a year, which meant, on average, we needed to be in market every other week. The introduction of EuroMillions meant we would have circa 40 jackpots which warranted advertising support.[18] We could use this certainty to regain control of our ROI destiny.

Also, we were delivering simple but compelling jackpot messages to predisposed players. They just needed a 'nudge'. As such, a 10" ad could be as effective as a

30" spot but cost half the price – so was far more efficient.[19] Econometrics had also given us a good understanding of an efficient weekly weight range, where we could balance effective coverage and frequency and profit potential.

Our 'eureka' moment was when we realised we had reached a tipping point where, through smart streamlining of spot-lengths and weekly weights, we could actually afford to deliver a TV plan every week of the year for significantly less than it would cost us to late buy TV in a reactive fashion, every time we needed to support a rollover. We proposed a 52-week pre-booked 'portfolio TV strategy'.

This meant we could cover the vast majority of jackpot scenarios, improve the quality of our delivery, and save significant money in the process. In absence of rollovers, our burgeoning portfolio of games meant we had no shortage of messages to fill any 'gaps'. As such, we were also able to use the pre-booked platform to assist cross-sell of non-rolling TNL games, such as Thunderball and National Lottery Scratchcards.

Sounds easy? Don't underestimate the bravery of Camelot's marketing team to commit to such a single-minded strategy. Remember, advertising ROIs had been sliding in line with underlying sales decline,[20] and we were suggesting 'over-committing' and running ads every week, regardless of the jackpot scenario (so rollovers, or not). We were also proposing a 100% focus on punchy 10" spots, often perceived by marketers to be prohibitive to effective message delivery.

We worked closely with the client and creative agency, AMV BBDO, to develop a suite of hard-hitting 10" creative, including 'banker' ads for the non-time-sensitive games, which could run in non-rollover weeks (see Figure 8).

Figure 8: Example suite of 10" TV ads

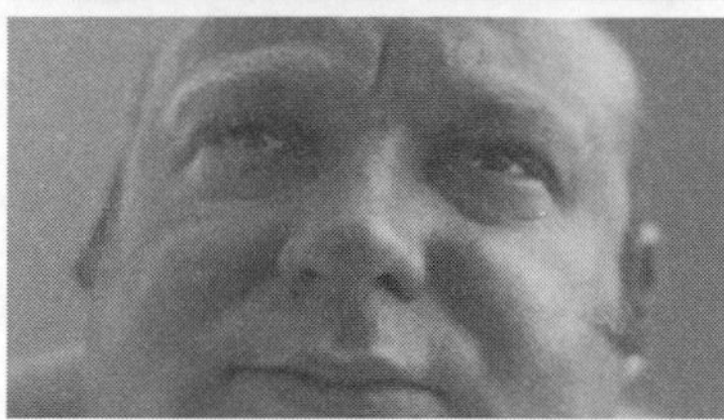

Beyond our pre-booked TV backbone, we retained a fund for late-buying additional media, such as radio, national press, digital formats, and outdoor (and, in exceptional cases, additional TV), which we could layer on, subject to the size of the jackpot (see Figure 9). Larger jackpots had greater sales and ROI potential and demanded greater coverage and frequency. These events were also great for brand health.

**Figure 9: Big jackpots upweighted with select multimedia formats**

## Portfolio management

Most importantly, we used econometric modelling to create pre-agreed principles for game support, message prioritisation and channel deployment. Econometrics helped us isolate and understand the drivers of sales, to create hierarchies of ROI by game, by creative execution, and by medium (see Figure 10).

Using these hierarchies, we could evaluate any of the potential jackpot combinations, and determine how to act to extract maximum ROI from any scenario. Our pre-determined 'rules' (see Figure 11) allowed us to objectively assess any number of scenarios, and remove unnecessary procrastination and reactive decision-making from our operating model. In real terms, we could leave work on a Friday, knowing what our most effective solution would be on Monday morning, regardless of whether jackpots were won, or rolled-over at the weekend.

## Figure 10: Hierarchies by game, media and message, used to maximise ROI

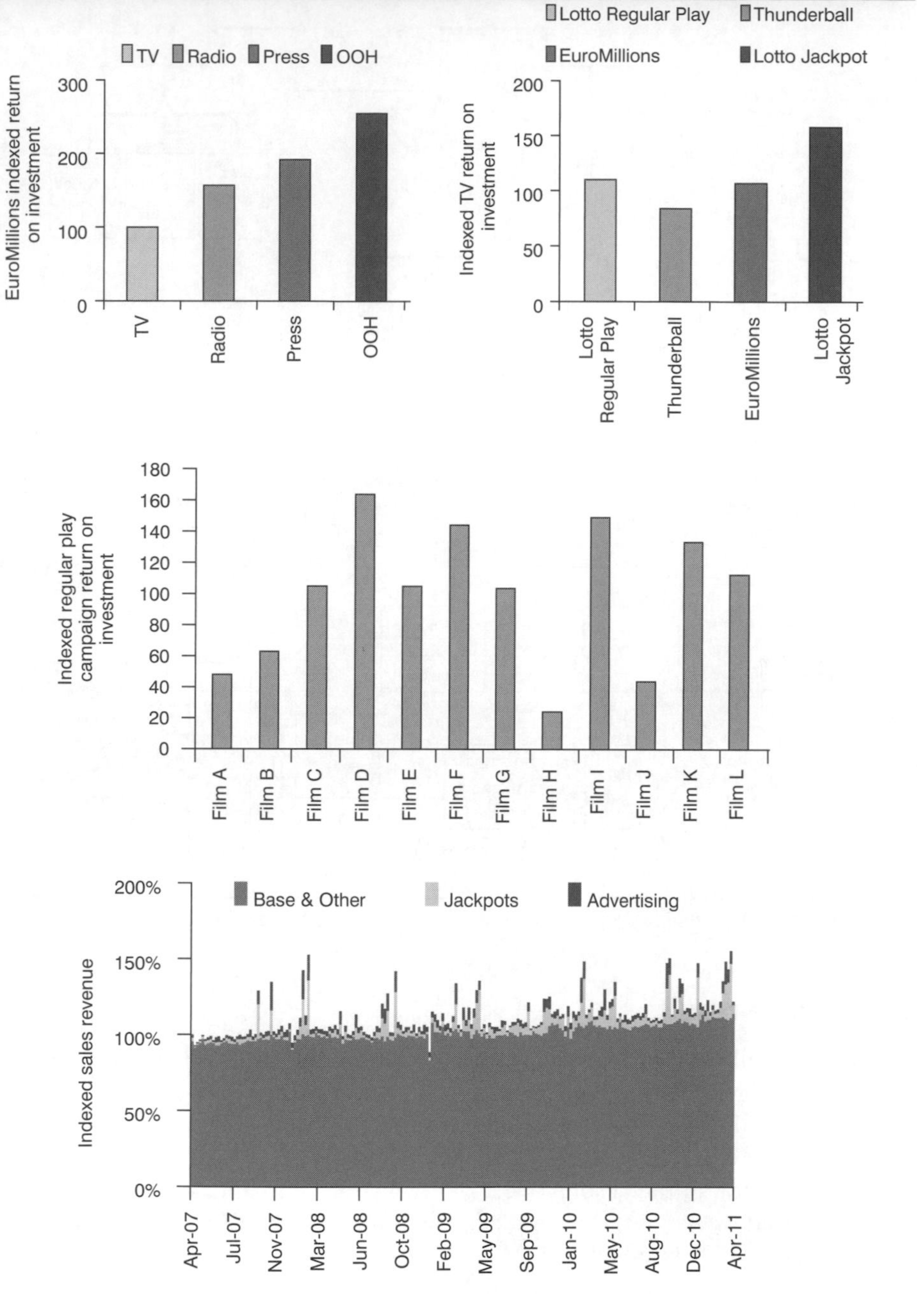

Source: MPG Econometrics

Figure 11: Example jackpot decision-making process

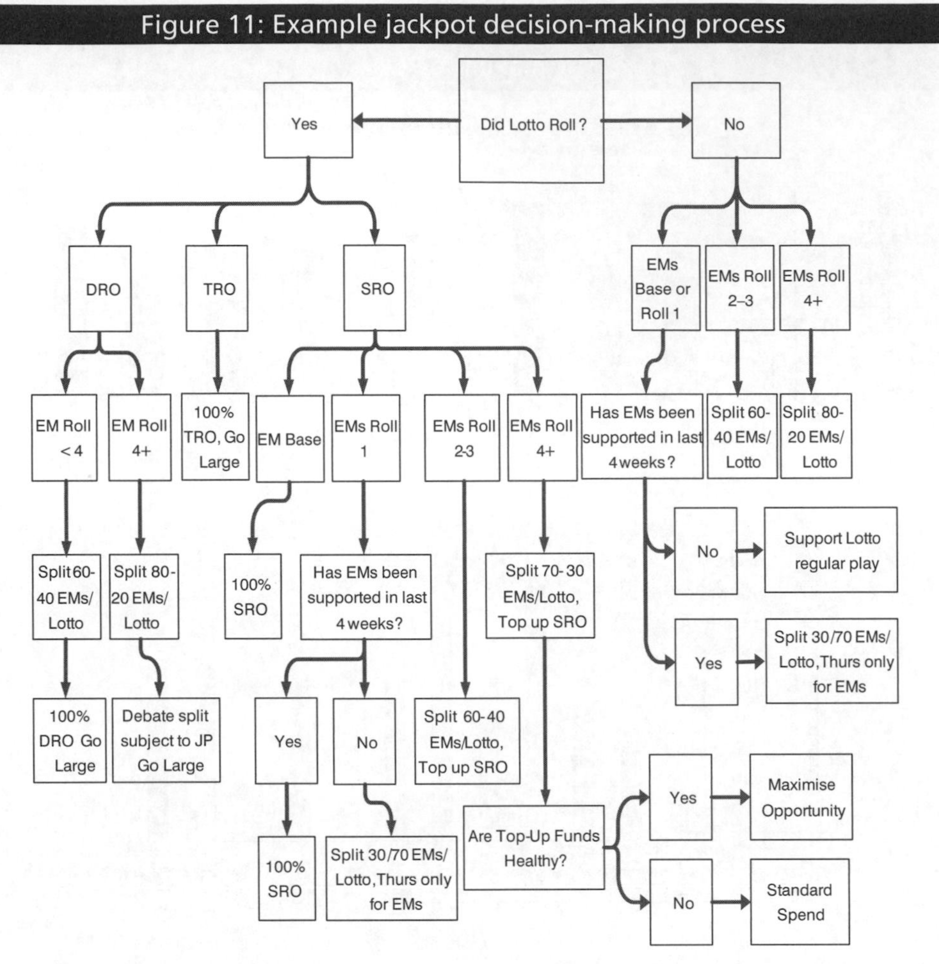


Source: MPG Econometrics

## Immediate results

In the first full year of employing the 'portfolio TV strategy' it saved circa £7m in media budget. We invested circa £15m in a 52-week pre-booked TV plan, to support 40 rollovers. This would have cost an estimated £22m using a late-booked TV approach.[21]

The reduction in the absolute cost of TV, via pre-booking, reduced spot-lengths, and optimised weekly weights, immediately improved the ROI of our Lotto rollover advertising by 13% (see Figure 12).

Figure 12: Positive shift in jackpot ROI after introduction of 'portfolio' strategy

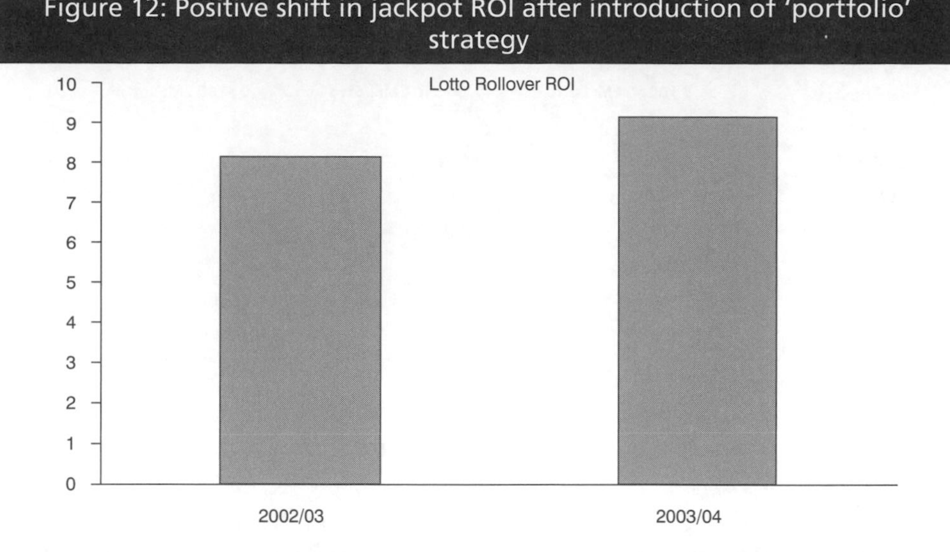


Source: MPG Econometrics

Funds released were re-allocated to support other games, such as Thunderball and National Lottery Scratchcards, previously the 'poor cousins' in terms of advertising support. This allowed us to drive new incremental revenue – and, crucially, gave us greater understanding about their ROI potential.

In total, as a result in our change of strategy, we were able to increase the contribution of advertising to sales by £50m year-on-year in year one.[22]

## Accelerated learning

But we didn't stop there. The ancillary benefit of running activity every week was rapid learning about what advertising support works best across a wide range of games. With more data points, our econometric modelling became richer.

### *Evolution 1: ongoing optimisation (2005/06–2010/11)*

We began to refine weekly weights by month based on fluctuating TV costs, underlying seasonality, and an understanding of diminishing returns – to over-invest in months with greater revenue potential and contracting in months with less. In time, we were able to set a minimum ROI threshold of £6 – a yield that we should never fall below – and could predict sales response to within 1% accuracy.

Where appropriate, we stopped simply supporting our strongest message *only*, and started supporting our two strongest messages. The principle being that we could provoke more incremental occasional sales with two compelling jackpot messages (see Table 1).

| Table 1: Subject to scenario, ROI potential improves by supporting multiple messages | | | |
|---|---|---|---|
| | **100 : 0 EM: Lotto** | **50 : 50 EM: Lotto** | **0 : 100 EM: Lotto** |
| EM Base | 100 | 96 | 86 |
| EM Roll 1 | 100 | 98 | 89 |
| EM Roll 2 | 100 | 113 | 109 |
| EM Roll 3 | 100 | 119 | 118 |
| EM Roll 4 | 100 | 129 | 133 |
| EM Roll 5 | 100 | 143 | 154 |
| EM Roll 6 | 100 | 163 | 182 |

Source: MPG Econometrics (ROI Index)

### *Evolution 2: from defence to offence and the importance of e-Commerce (2007/08–2010/11)*

We worked with the client and AMV BBDO to develop 'regular play' advertising that could fit into the portfolio strategy between rollovers. Initially, this was a 'defensive' measure. TNL sales annually dip over the summer months, as players' routines get disrupted (changing shopping patterns, school holidays, etc). As such, we created 10" 'play online' messaging, not only to drive players to Camelot's growing e-Commerce channel but also to offer players the chance to play in advance and never miss a draw.

We quickly discovered that 'regular play' advertising – especially TV which drove players to register for online play – could be more effective than rollover advertising. Firstly, because the eCRM benefits of online made digital players more valuable in the long-term. Secondly, because nudging, in absence of rollovers, can still be effective at generating incremental sales from occasional players. In fact, encouraging healthy routine has a net positive effect vs. driving lighter players towards sporadic big jackpots.

In isolation, our first burst of dedicated play online activity (June 2007) delivered an estimated 55% increase in natural registrations (i.e. those not directly attributed to online advertising) to national-lottery.co.uk (see Figure 13). By year end (March 2008), tracking data showed that spontaneous awareness of the ability to play online had risen from 19% to 32%; +68% increase.[23] In the short-term, this activity drove £23m in incremental revenue at an ROI of 11:1.[24]

With new non-time-sensitive weapons in our arsenal, we began to plan our regular play advertising 'offensively' – streamlining our 'portfolio strand' to the leanest effective level, in order to guarantee flexible jackpot support but also to free-up funds to deliver additional dedicated regular play activity when ROI potential was greatest.

Figure 13: Impact of 'regular play' TV on online registrations

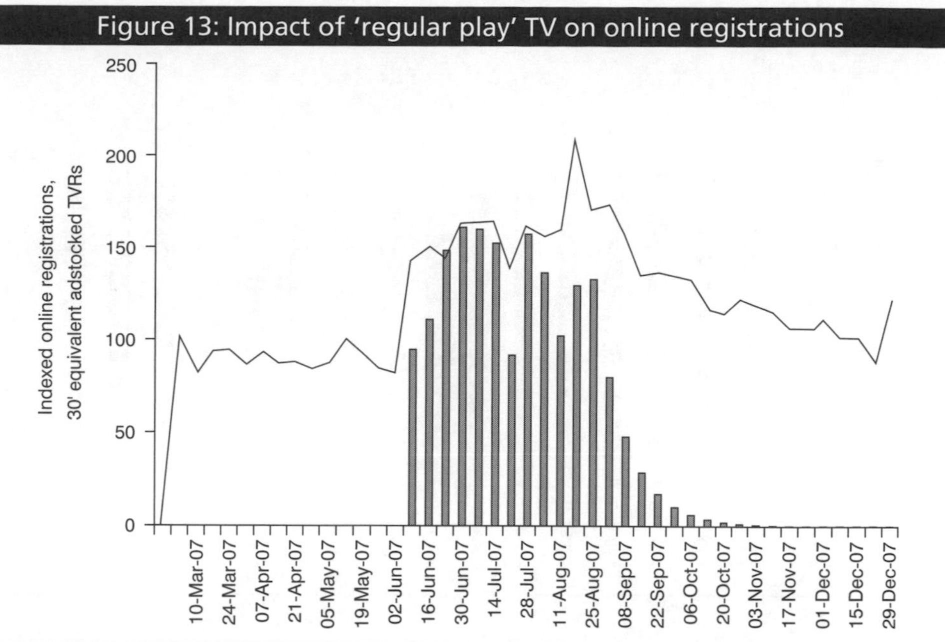


Source: MPG Econometrics/Camelot

*Evolution 3: super-charging the strategy via digital (2006 to date)*

As TNL's e-Commerce channel grew, so our investment in digital media increased. We were able to apply many of the same 'portfolio' principles that had served us so well 'off-line' to our on-line planning, but we had the added benefit of real-time digital optimisation and enhanced accountability.

Just like our 'traditional' media formula, we laid down a consistent layer of impacts, across which we played out a suite of creative messages (subject to jackpot scenario). Now message deployment was driven by algorithms to optimise based on real-time consumer demand, with trading agreements directly related to registrations driven.

## Summary of results

At year end (March) 2011, Camelot reported record annual sales of £5.8bn. This equated to a 6.8% increase year-on-year, and beat a previous record high of £5.5bn, set in March 1998. Even more impressively, this result confirmed that Camelot had successfully overturned the acknowledged downward trend for lotteries post launch.[25] The achievement was also delivered against a difficult economic background and a worldwide trend of slowing lottery sales (see Figures 14 and 15).[26]

Figure 14: Total National Lottery sales by year 1995/96–2010/11

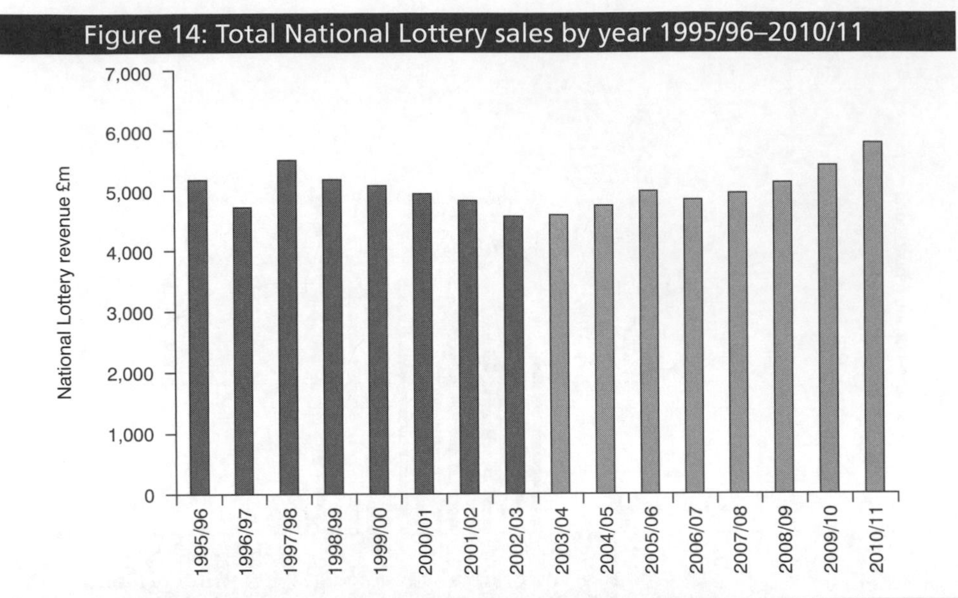


Source: Camelot

Figure 15: Camelot delivers record National Lottery sales

BBC News Sport Weather iPlayer TV Radio

NEWS BUSINESS

Home World UK England N. Ireland Scotland Wales Business Politics Health Education Sci/Environm

Market Data | Your Money | Economy | Companies

**3 June 2011** Last updated at 17:56

38 Share

**Camelot sets new lottery sales record**

**National Lottery operator Camelot has announced record ticket sales of £5.8bn in the year to March.**

That marked a 6.8% increase on a year ago and beat the previous record of £5.5bn set in 1997-98.

Seven of the world's 10 biggest lotteries have seen sales fall in the last year.

Source: bbc.co.uk

In fact, excluding China, The National Lottery is the fastest growing Lottery within the top 10 Lotteries in the world. TNL is also the only Lottery in the top 20 that has significantly accelerated and doubled its year-on-year growth vs. the long-term trend.[27]

Clearly, we cannot wholly attribute this up-turn in sales directly back to our jackpot management formula. In the 17 years since launch, advertising has accounted for an estimated 3–5% uplift in short-term sales in any given year.[28] Plus, Camelot's broader business strategy of product diversification, notably the launches of EuroMillions and National Lottery Scratchcards, have been significant drivers of growth. However, to reference Dianne Thompson, in The National Lottery world, little percentage shifts add up to a massive difference.[29] Over the last seven years, advertising has contributed an incremental £1.58bn to Camelot's bottom line.[30]

Within this, our jackpot management strategy has been fundamental to growth in four ways:

1. improved advertising ROI performance;
2. new learning and new revenue contributions;
3. kept players playing and minimised cannibalisation;
4. time back to facilitate managed growth.

### *1. Improved advertising ROI performance*

We can demonstrate that we have first stabilised, and then improved, jackpot advertising ROI performance since the conception of the 'portfolio strategy' in 2004. This has been achieved through a combination of minimising late-buying in TV, a focused spot-length strategy, and strategic message and channel deployment to maximise the ROI potential of any jackpot scenario. On average, our jackpot advertising ROI has improved 34% since the introduction of the portfolio strategy (see Figure 16).

**Figure 16: Improvements in average jackpot ROI since introduction of 'portfolio strategy'**

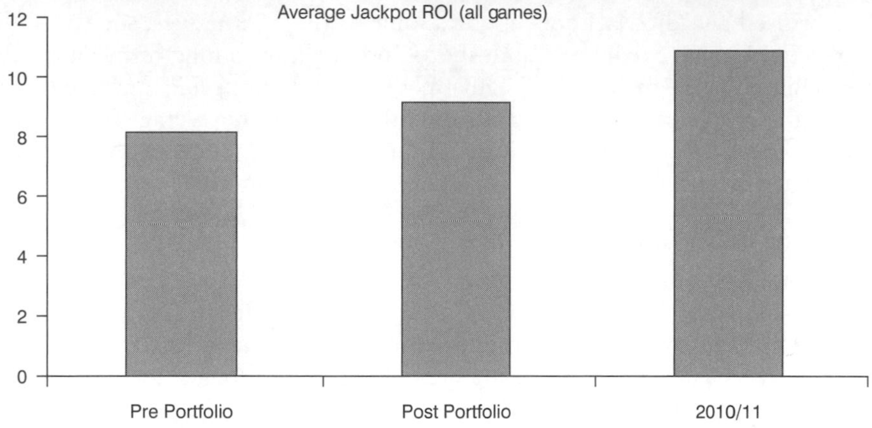

Source: MPG econometrics

Within this, it is worth noting that we have managed to protect and improve the ROI threshold of Lotto jackpot advertising, despite an underlying decline in Lotto jackpot uplifts. In real terms, after 15+ years of playing but not winning big, or often enough, rollovers have lost some of their natural appeal. However, advertising continues to work as hard as ever.

### 2. New learning and new revenue contributions

The other major benefit of our strategy is that streamlining our jackpot outlay frees up funds to invest in other profitable initiatives, such as 'regular play' activity. On a practical level, our pre-booking approach to TV has saved the client circa £20m in late-booked penalties over seven years (see Table 2). As such, we have been able to turn formerly 'wasted' money back into incremental sales.

**Table 2: Estimated media budget saved vs. late-booked approach on TV**

| | 2004/05 | 2005/06 | 2006/07 | 2007/08 | 2008/09 | 2009/10 | 2010/11 | Totals |
|---|---|---|---|---|---|---|---|---|
| TV advertising invested behind jackpots (pre-booked) (£m) | 15.6 | 13.4 | 4.7 | 3.6 | 3.5 | 4.7 | 3.3 | 48.8 |
| Estimated late booking penalty | 45% | 42% | 40% | 39% | 38% | 37% | 36% | |
| Projected late-booked cost for same jackpot TV advertising (£m) | 22.6 | 19.0 | 6.5 | 5.0 | 4.8 | 6.5 | 4.5 | 68.9 |
| Projected budget saving (£m) | 7.0 | 5.6 | 1.9 | 1.4 | 1.3 | 1.8 | 1.2 | 20.2 |

Source: FLE Audit/MPG estimates

'Regular Play' advertising, effectively a by-product designed to fill in the gaps for the portfolio strategy, has been the biggest beneficiary of this investment and has become an important and 'offensive' driver of extra sales. In some instances this has been prioritised ahead of jackpot support. Some of these initiatives, such as 'online-driving' activities, have delivered both short- and medium to long-term returns.

In combination, the inclusion of regular play activity – alongside improved jackpot advertising ROI – has enabled us to consistently improve the average ROI of TNL's advertising overall. Between 2004 and 2011, our ROIs have ranged from £6–£30+;[31] a staggering result in the context of FCMG averages, at sub -£2.[32]

### 3. Kept players playing and minimised cannibalisation

We mentioned that jackpots are the beating heart of the business. Our jackpot strategy has not only kept players motivated, by keeping more jackpots in market, but also allowed us to let Lotto and EuroMillions live in happy harmony alongside each other (see Figure 17). This has helped Camelot to protect Lotto penetration, whilst growing EuroMillions into a £1bn+ brand.[33]

Beyond this, being able to regularly support Lotto, alongside other new launches has helped to off-set underlying sales decline over time. Across the last five years, this equates to a projected £280m of incremental sales.

We also know that big jackpots equate to player positivity, which equates to healthy sales. By delivering a platform that ensures more big jackpots can be supported on a finite budget, notably, exciting EuroMillions jackpots, net TNL positivity has increased significantly over time (see Figure 18).

Figure 17: Total Lotto and EuroMillions penetration over time

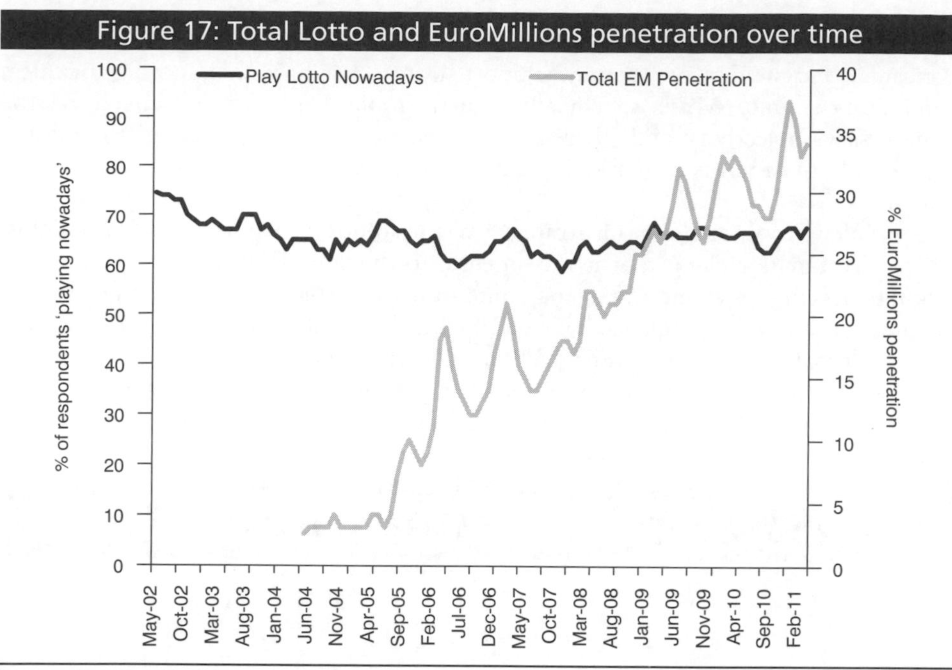


Source: Conquest Tracker

Figure 18: Growth in positivity towards The National Lottery

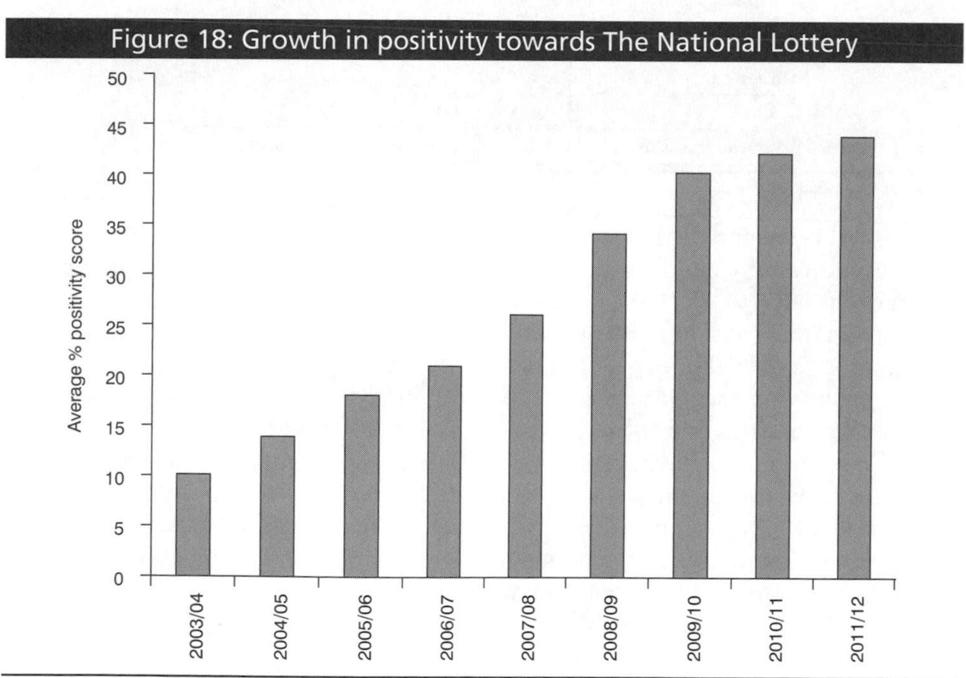


Source: Conquest Tracker

### 4. Time back to facilitate managed growth

We can also argue that our jackpot support strategy has provided another 'priceless commodity': time. More specifically, our formula has removed much of the unnecessary subjectivity and, therefore, wasted hours spent 'reacting' to rollover scenarios both in terms of marketing team hours, brand manager hours and agency hours.

So while we cannot claim our strategy was the solution to all Camelot's problems, we can legitimately claim that it was integral to the smooth day-to-day running of jackpots, freeing up client and agency time to deliver effective managed growth via medium- to long-term projects. This has included the introduction of the new look of Thunderball and launch of EuroMillions UK Millionaire Raffle.

It would be impossible to retrospectively log an accurate time-saving directly attributable to our strategy. However, we conservatively estimate that our approach has freed up over 10,000 hours over the last seven years (see Table 3).

**Table 3: Summary of estimated time-savings since introduction of portfolio strategy**

| | | | |
|---|---|---|---|
| Hours saved per week | Two hours saved, twice weekly.<br>Based on:<br>Front of week decisions<br>(Lotto Weds)<br>Back of week decisions<br>(EuroMillions Fri, Lotto Sat) | 4 | x |
| Marketers/Agency Staff | 2 x Brand Managers,<br>1 x Marketing Manager,<br>4 x Agency Staff | 7 | x |
| Weeks per year | April–March | 52 | x |
| Years | 2004/05–2010/11 | 7 | = |
| **Total hours saved** | | **10,192** | |

Source: MPG estimates

Without stretching virtuous circles too far, these reclaimed hours have helped Camelot successfully build a burgeoning portfolio, consisting of four of the top fast-moving consumer goods (FMCG) brands in the UK.

Back to the bottom line, this means we have been able to improve advertising's contribution to overall sales over time since 2004. Using econometrics, we can isolate the incremental impact of advertising directly linked to the portfolio strategy. We estimate this contribution to be £1.58bn between 2004 and 2011. This equates to around £442m of incremental funds raised for National Lottery Good Causes.[34]

As discussed, this is unlike other IPA Effectiveness papers you may read. This was not about a big creative idea. This is about seven years of making consistent improvements that, cumulatively, made a huge impact. It is our contribution to Dianne Thompson's 'doing one hundred things 1 per cent better that makes a difference'.

*A unique business model requires a unique communications strategy and MPG Media Contacts have helped us achieve just that. This entry demonstrates the power of client, media and creative agencies working together closely to harness the significant potential of an incredibly fluid brand. Using a combination of econometric modelling, a deep understanding of our players, and incredibly dynamic media planning and implementation, Camelot UK Lotteries have successfully delivered more money to National Lottery Good Causes year after year. Our jackpot management model is regarded as 'best practice' by other lotteries worldwide.*

Richard Bateson, Marketing Director Camelot

## Notes

1 Source: Thompson, D. (2011) Dianne Thompson: What ten years as CEO of Camelot have taught me. *The Telegraph*, 4 March. Online at: http://www.telegraph.co.uk/finance/businesslatestnews/8359834/Dianne-Thompson-What-ten-years-as-CEO-of-Camelot-have-taught-me.html
2 Source: Camelot.
3 Source: MPG Econometrics, based on April 2004–March 2011.
4 Source: Conquest Tracker.
5 Source: *The Grocer*/Nielsen, Britain's Biggest Grocery Brands, March 2012.
6 Source: *The Grocer*/Nielsen, Britain's Biggest Grocery Brands, March 2012.
7 Source: www.camelotgroup.co.uk
8 Source: www.camelotgroup.co.uk
9 Source: NFO Tracker.
10 'Occasional players' defined as playing The National Lottery less than once a week.
11 Source: Camelot. Rolling average uplifts based on three previous weeks of non-rollover (base) activity. Estimated Lotto sales average.
12 Source: Camelot. Based on Lotto rollovers 2006–2011.
13 Source: MPG/FLE estimates.
14 Source: MPG econometric modelling. TV has consistently been our strongest sales-driving channel.
15 Source: Fairbrother Lenz Eley.
16 Subject to exchange rates.
17 EuroMillions Friday launch added a further 52 additional jackpots in a 12-month period.
18 Not all EuroMillions jackpots would be supported.
19 Source: Based on MPG econometric models.
20 Lotto 'natural' (unrelated to advertising) average rollover uplifts were in decline, correlating with overall decline in underlying sales. See Figure 2 for reference.
21 Source: Fairbrother Lenz Eley audit 2005.
22 Source: MPG Econometrics.
23 Source: Camelot omnibus study.
24 Source: MPG Econometrics.
25 Several leading industry thinkers reference the long-term trend of decline in whitepapers, e.g. Mizeur (2006) 'Cure For The Common Lotto'.
26 Source: Lee Sienna, Camelot Chairman (extract from Chairman's Statement, Camelot website). For the period Camelot reported record sales, seven of the world's ten leading lotteries registered a decline in sales. Source: La Fleur's, December 2010. See also BBC Business report (2011) 'Camelot sets new lottery sales record', 3 June (www.bbc.co.uk) (Figure 15).
27 Source: La Fleur's, December 2010. Based on 2010 figures vs. previous five years GAGR average. China is a developing lottery market, so growth is exceptional vs. established lottery markets.
28 Source: MPG Econometrics (averages since modelling began).
29 Source: Thompson, D. (2011) Dianne Thompson: What ten years as CEO of Camelot have taught me. *The Telegraph*, 4 March. Online at: http://www.telegraph.co.uk/finance/businesslatestnews/8359834/Dianne-Thompson-What-ten-years-as-CEO-of-Camelot-have-taught-me.html
30 Source: MPG Econometrics.
31 Based on significant EuroMillions jackpots. Source: MPG Econometrics.
32 Source: MPG Econometrics/FMCG averages taken from Microsoft (2011) 'Check-out – An ROI analysis of the FMCG sector'. Online at: http://advertising.microsoft.com/europe/WWDocs/User/Europe/ResearchLibrary/ResearchReport/FMCG-Check-out-Research.pdf
33 Source: Camelot. EuroMillions full year sales at £1.05bn by year end (March 2011).
34 Based on estimated average 28% of total sales allocated to Good Causes.

## Chapter 28

# VO5 Extreme Style

## Building cred-stock for VO5 Extreme Style 2004–2011

**By Rebecca Moody and Andrew Quin, Euro RSCG London**
Contributing authors: Diana Caplinska, Euro RSCG London; Jonathan Fox, Holmes & Cook
Credited companies: Creative Agency: Euro RSCG London; Econometric modelling agency: Holmes & Cook; Client: Unilever

### Editor's summary

Since the birth of the teenager in the 1950s, males have rebelliously used their hair to create their identity, stir the envy of peers, cause parental scorn and get the girl. This paper tells how communications have helped VO5, an established ladies' haircare brand, to win over 16–24-year-old lads, build 'cred-stock' for VO5 Extreme Style, and become the number one hair styling range for men in the UK. Since 2004 the 'Break the mould' campaign has remained consistent with its message, whilst reinventing itself with new settings, music tracks and funky hairstyles. It has generated a payback of £1.75 for every £1 spent on advertising. The judges admired the brand's success at repositioning itself to appeal to a different audience without isolating their core female customers. An example of a strong brand idea that has successfully built long-term relationships with a new audience.

Since the birth of the teenager in the 1950s, lads have rebelliously used their hair to create their identity, stir the envy of peers, cause parental scorn and, above all, to get the girl.

How could an established ladies' haircare brand win over 16–24-year-old lads? How did VO5 Extreme Style loosen the apron strings to become the number one hair styling range for men in the UK?

This paper tells how communications has successfully built 'cred-stock' for VO5 Extreme Style with a life-time revenue ROI of £1.75 for every £1 spent on advertising.

## VO5: a brief history

Alberto VO5, beauty staple of the Fifties, was best known for its signature Hot Oil (with 5 vital oils) originally designed to repair Hollywood actresses' hair from the damage caused by fierce studio lights.

As the slogan said, 'Get hot!'

It had a solid shampoo and conditioner business, but at the turn of the millennium, with an older, primarily female user base, VO5 sought a fresh vision for growth.

## Growth potential: 'hair involved' male styling

Analysis of the UK styling market in the early Noughties revealed more products were being bought by 16–24-year-old men.

In terms of hairstyling, the '90s had turned out grungy for the lads. 'Teen Spirit' and Madchester epitomised a lazier, more 'bed hair' approach to styling. But with the advent of Pop Idol culture and a slicker British Indie scene, a swathe of more 'hair involved' chaps were looking for a better-tamed barnet.

Market mapping in 2002 suggested that there were three types of male hairstyling brands:

1. The 'evergreens': timeless brands (like Brylcreem and Dax), that ride the outer edges of the style roundabout waiting to capitalise on the next iconic regeneration of slicked back and sides.
2. The cool 'magnesium' niche brands that enjoy their brief time in the sun (like Fish), and are sold in trendy salons rather than supermarkets and thereby out of the reach of mass youth.
3. The enduring, 'try-hard' category leaders Shockwaves and Studio Line, with their penchant for cheesy teen Elvises singing into hairbrush microphones, described as 'plastic' and 'too extroverted' and only reluctantly purchased by our burgeoning crop of Johnny Borrells (Figure 1).[1]

It was clear that no hairstyling brand was successfully connecting with younger, mainstream guys or, more importantly, evolving quickly enough in the fashion stakes to reflect the ever-evolving style predilections of the average under 24-year-old.

Figure 1: Hairstyling review 2002: a mass-manufacture view of teens

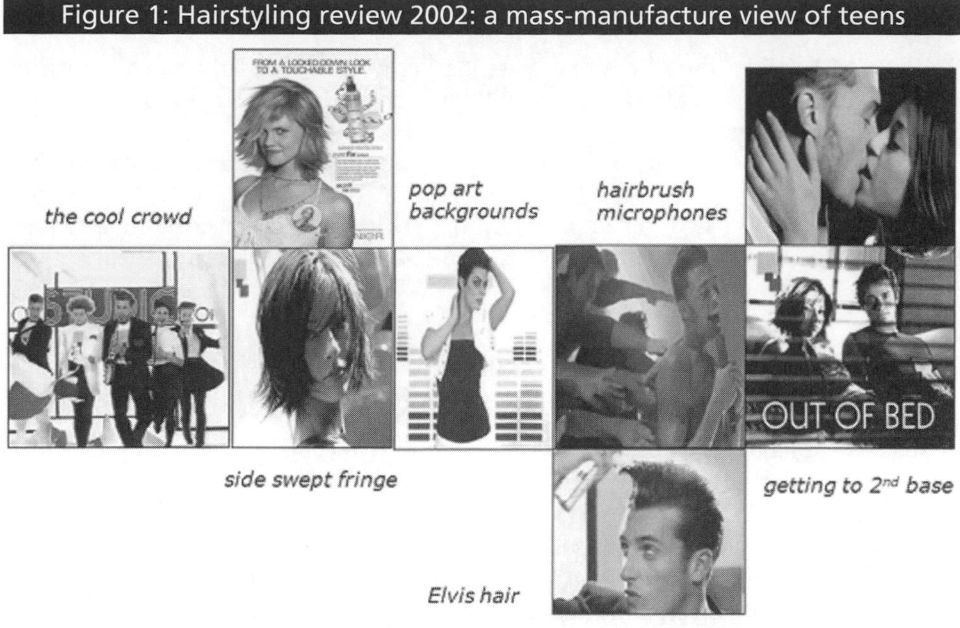


The category needed a rebel – one that would rip-up the rulebook by combining both the (albeit intermittent or fleeting) credibility of the 'evergreens' and 'magnesium' brands with the scale and endurance of the 'try-hards'… a credible mass-market youth brand that could be constantly relied upon to meet 16–24s ever-changing hairstyling needs: *a partner in style* (Figure 2).

Figure 2: The credibility gap – the opportunity

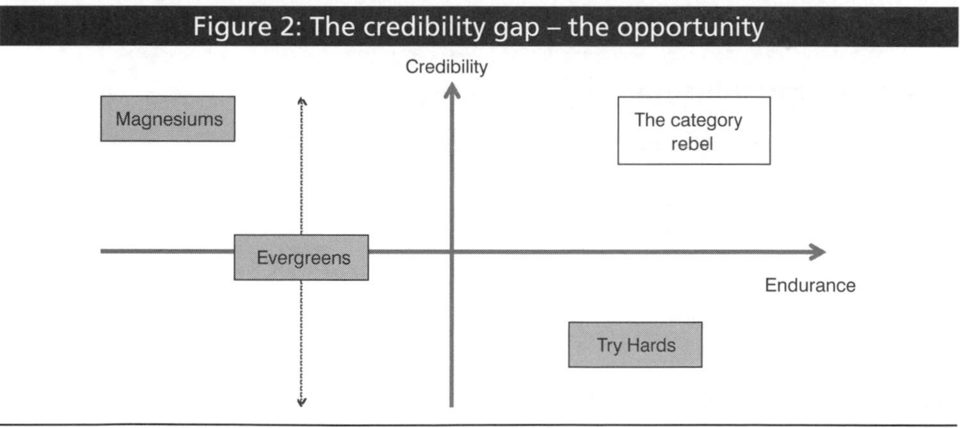

## Enter VO5 Extreme Style

While VO5 had introduced the first mass-market wax in 1987, the range of styling products on offer from the stable was still limited and by 2002 the brand had only 8.6% share of Styling & Hairspray.

The brainchild designed to meet the opportunity was a sub-range called VO5 Extreme Style.

Launched in 2003 with seven products, the goal was to drive *extraordinary sales* by becoming the go-to styling brand for 16–24-year-old males and secure *sector leadership* for the VO5 mother ship.

## The brand communications challenge

At first glance, this could be regarded as a simple story about target transition: an established female haircare brand diversifying into the male hair styling category. But to view it in this way underestimates the challenges VO5 Extreme Style faced in achieving this.

In 2003, the thought of asking young lads to seek hairstyling advice from VO5 was tantamount to asking their mum's best mate: attractive but not so cool.

In recognising this fact, and mixing in the learning from competitive pitfalls, we determined that the brand communications challenge for VO5 Extreme Style was two-fold:

- To *build a climate of credibility* for VO5 Extreme Style in a way that helped it loosen the apron strings from the mother ship – a potentially significant barrier to success.
- To *continuously set the style pace* in order to maintain credibility across the longer-term and to prevent the range from becoming yet another corporate 'try-hard', out of time and out of touch.

## The strategic solution

Taking a leaf out of our favourite mums' best mate's book – Madonna – we established that VO5 Extreme Style needed an enduring yet ever-changing communications idea that could adapt to changing tastes and trends but always stay true to its core brand promise.

Our strategy has therefore been to remain *'consistently inconsistent'*.

### *a) A consistent call to action built on a perennial youth insight*

To gain immediate credibility among the Inbetweeners,[2] VO5 Extreme Style needed to tap into the perennial and underlying motivation driving our consumers' desire for coolly-styled hair – no matter what the year, decade or prevailing hairstyle of the day.

Work with research company Duckfoot (Figure 3) showed that, whereas the key motivation of very young males is about fitting in, or belonging to, their gender peer group, the next stage in the Inbetweeners' image development, around 14–19 years old is actually about breaking away from peers and using their external appearance to help show off their emerging individuality.

This stage is about 'Launching Brand Me'.

Figure 3: The five stages of 'Brand Me' by Duckfoot

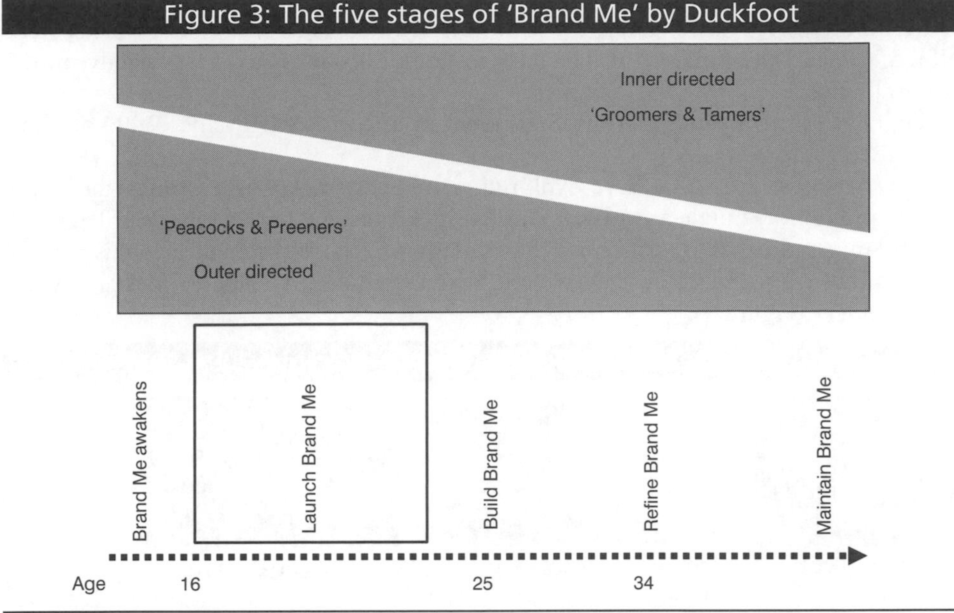


This is where cool hair comes in. It is the Inbetweener's crowning glory: their key style accessory – a constant work of art in progress where styling products play an important role as they peacock, preen and experiment with their identity.

And what drives this desire to break away from the pack and create differentiation is the belief that it will help them be more attractive to the opposite sex.

Simply put, being a teen rebel increases 'snog value' with teen girls.

It's a perennial insight that is expressed endlessly in popular culture: the dude who confidently breaks the rules always seems to get the girl. James Dean did it with his classic pompadour, as did Arctic Monkeys frontman Alex Turner with his own standout quiff in 2011.

Our value proposition, first developed in 2003, is therefore rooted in the Inbetweeners' rebellious streak: *'VO5 Extreme Style allows you to express your individuality by rebelling against conformity to attract the opposite sex.'*

And, by tapping into the key motivation behind having hair that expresses rebellious individuality we were able to create an ever-relevant and consistent call to action which has now run across all our VO5 Extreme Style communications since the brand campaign first broke in 2004: BREAK THE MOULD

### *b) Eight years of campaign 'inconsistency'*

'Break the Mould' isn't just our consumer-facing brand promise. It has been adopted as our mantra: to be prepared to be steadfastly 'inconsistent' in our approach to the campaign idea; to break the mould with each new iteration of the campaign in order to stay firmly on the style pulse.

While the controlling idea of 'Break the Mould' communications has remained consistent (rebel boy gets gal thanks to his extreme style), we have continuously reinvented the story by wrapping it with new settings, vanguard music tracks, fresh NPD news and the funkiest of hairstyles to make sure it always stays firmly on the cultural pulse.

The 'Break the Mould' platform has now run 'inconsistently' since 2004 and this is how we've done it:

*New Settings:* Six TVCs have explored settings as surreal as a Chinese boarding school and remote jungle army base. Our latest execution, 'The Pliktisijiteur Pageant', which launched in 2011, continues the strategy of youthful rebellion – this time in the confines of a small European village where 'same' is viewed as 'better' by the village elders (Figure 4).

**Figure 4: 'Break the Mould' campaign timeline, 2004–2011**

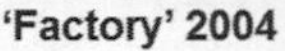

*New Sounds:* No two executions either look or sound the same. We have always kept our ears to the underground to break new groups and cool new choons like Chromeo's 'Fancy Footwork' and Santogold's 'Creator' in order to create an instant and credible connection with the target audience (Figure 5).

**Figure 5: Cool choons**

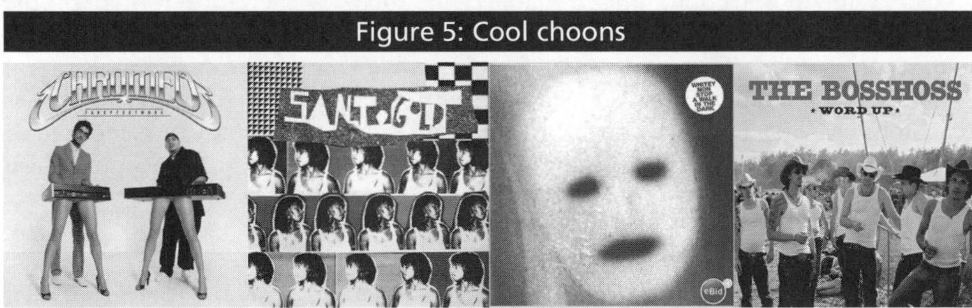

*New Styles:* Learning from the cautionary tales of competitors, we have also aimed to stay one step ahead of the fashion pace with this style-driven demographic.

The heart of the VO5 Extreme Style 'Break the Mould' philosophy continuously seeks out cutting-edge styling trends to hero in the advertising and, in collaboration with insight gurus Voodoo, we have religiously anticipated the breaking street hair trends since 2004 to help inform the latest looks ahead of the competition.

So, as mousses declined, we turned to showcasing new product forms like clays, gums and putties. Here's a flavour of styles from our most recent 2011 campaign 'The Pliktisijiteur Pageant' including groomingPomade for the vintage Broadwalk Empire look and sportsGel for 48 hours of hold (Figure 6).

Figure 6: 'Break the Mould' trend-driven hairstyle news 2011

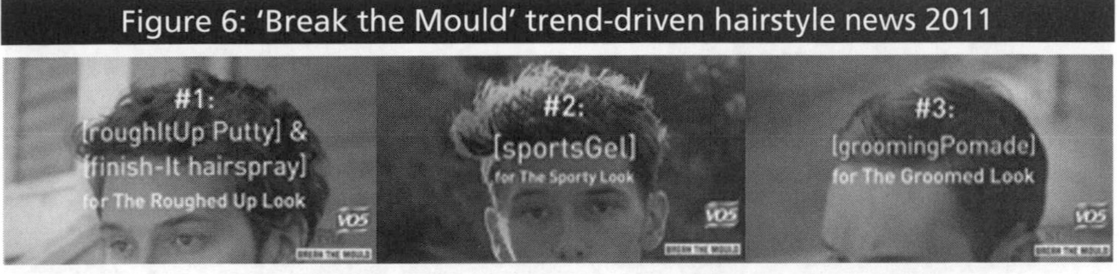


## The role of media: creating Source Credibility

From a media perspective, we have had to identify and create a credible context within which the brand can engage with these style-conscious lads and earn a place in their bathroom cabinets.

In the spirit of McLuhan's 'medium is the message', we knew we could further enhance the credibility of VO5 Extreme Style by taking an associative approach to our media planning – restricting people's exposure to the brand in only the most credible environments in the minds of Inbetweeners.

This would help build our Source Credibility – the theory developed by Yale University psychologist Carl Hovland – that highlights the importance of the perceived 'trustworthiness' and 'expertise' of the sender in mass communications.

Put simply, we would walk with the in-crowd – a journey which has evolved between 2004 and 2011 across three core media pillars:

### *1) 2004–2011: TV – targeting the Inbetweeners' 'water cooler' moments*

Since launch, TV has been the lead medium, and the 'in-crowd' strategy has been reflected in the way in which channels and programmes have been chosen. Credibility couldn't be expressed as underground as we had a commitment to the Multiples to create a mass youth brand. So, TV planning has evolved with two clear principles: 'provides social glue in the target's world' and 'influences their style'. All programming has to deliver against these principles (music programming like *X Factor*, dramas like *Skins*, *Entourage*, *TOWIE*, and comedies like *The Inbetweeners*, *Fresh Meat* and *Misfits*).

Figures 7a–c show three 'Break the Mould' TVC examples: 'China' (2006), 'Army' (2008–2009) and 'The Pliktisijiteur Pageant' (2011).

**Figure 7a: 'Break the Mould' 30" TVC: 'China' (2006)**

**Figure 7b: 'Break the Mould' 30" TVC: 'Army' (2008–2009)**

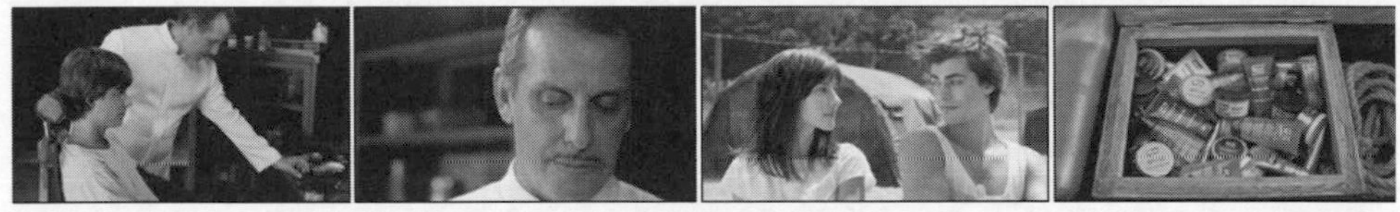

**Figure 7c: 'Break the Mould' 30" TVC: 'The Pliktisijiteur Pageant' (2011)**

Source: MVO: Alberto VO5 Extreme Style. Break the Mould

### 2) 2004–2011: FHM – creating a long-term partnership with a key 'in-crowd' style player

Being in with the in-crowd also relies on member endorsement. For our young fashion-conscious target, FHM is a style bible – they rely upon it to help them launch 'Brand Me'. From launch through to the present, we have therefore created a long-term, integrated partnership with FHM including sponsorship of the annual '100 Sexiest Women' special edition. By being in with this key influencer we have been able to behave more like a fashion brand, by creating editorial, brand, product and promotional activity across all FHM platforms (magazine, web, mobile, events and database) (Figure 8).

**Figure 8: Partnership with a high credibility source – FHM's 100 Sexiest Women (and our latest campaign work parody)**

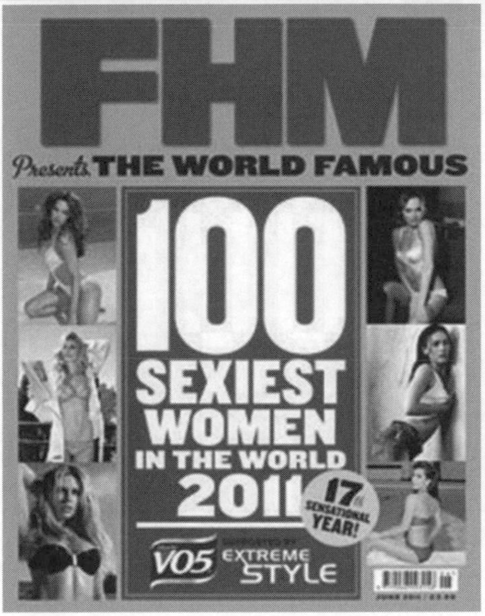


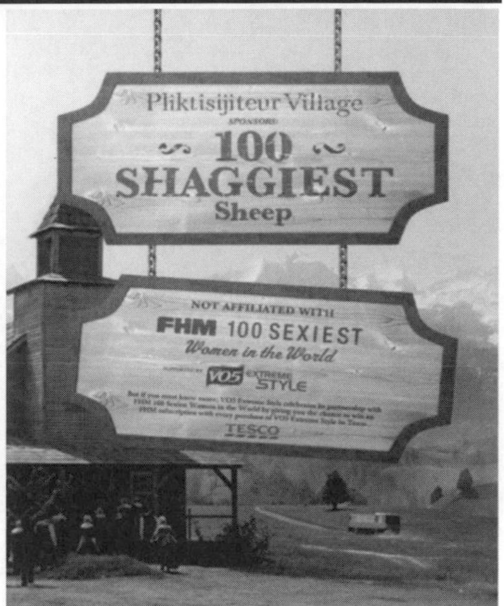


### 3) 2011: Social media – becoming part of the in-crowd's actual conversation

By late 2010 it was clear that the marketing and media ecosystem had fundamentally changed. Socially powered peer-to-peer recommendations are now a major driver of purchase decisions for young males. Today's social media and digital landscape has evolved Source Credibility theory further with friends' recommendations and 'the wisdom of the crowd' being the most trusted of all channels.

We therefore needed to ensure VO5 Extreme Style became *socially relevant*.

So for the 2011 campaign, 'The Pliktisijiteur Pageant', we reinvented our communications planning approach to provoke and facilitate conversation about VO5 Extreme Style around the TV core.

The evolved campaign had three phases:

1. *Pique interest for the TVC* with an unbranded online teaser film for a village pageant in the fictitious town of Pliktisijiteur, in social channels and on a dedicated website.
2. *Enrich the TVC story* using online films, out-takes and a 'Mockumentary'.
3. *Create conversations* using styling 'how to' videos and other grooming and style news with our fans, using social channels, in order to augment the TVC message (Figure 9).

Figure 9: 'The Pliktisijiteur Pageant' 2011 – creating social relevance

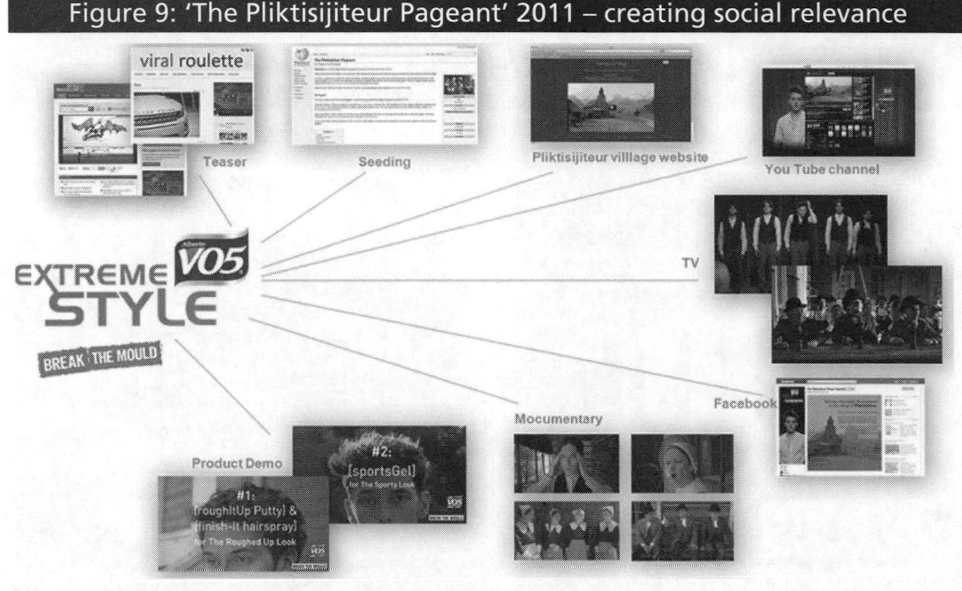


An estimated £7m was spent on media between 2009 and 2011 (Table 1).

## The business results

### *VO5 Extreme Style is now the number one Styling range for men in the UK*

The commercial objective set in 2003 was to achieve extraordinary sales growth. The range has fulfilled, and continues to fulfill, its original sales promise.

Between 2003 and 2011, VO5 Extreme Style grew +343% to become a £17.4m per annum range (Figure 10).[3]

Sales have consistently bucked the market trend. Between 2007 and 2011 alone, value sales of VO5 Extreme Style grew 23% against the backdrop of a 12.3% decline in Styling Aids.[4, 5]

Shockwaves and Studio Line, the original category leaders, have seen the most notable sales losses declining by 8.28% and 13.45% respectively since 2009.[6]

## Table 1: 2011 press, TV, cinema, digital activity laydown

| | Q1 | | | Q2 | | | Q3 | | | Q4 | | | Q1 2012 | | |
|---|---|---|---|---|---|---|---|---|---|---|---|---|---|---|---|
| | **Oct** | **Nov** | **Dec** | **Jan** | **Feb** | **Mar** | **Apr** | **May** | **Jun** | **Jul** | **Aug** | **Sep** | **Oct** | **Nov** | **Dec** |
| **VO5 Styling** | | | | | | | | | | | | | | | |
| **TV – VO5 Extreme (16–34 ads)** | 30" Headless & Tag | | | | | | | | | | | 30" | 30" | 30" | 30" |
| £000s net | | | | | | | | | | | | | | | |
| PO number | | | | | | | | | | | | | | | |
| TVRs | 80 | 140 | 150 | | | | | | | | | 200 | 170 | 165 | 80 |
| Est. 1+ cover/ OTS | 67% @ 5.6 | | | | | | | | | | | | | | |
| **IPTV – VO5 Extreme (16–34 ads)** | 30" | 30" | 10" | | | | | | | | | 30" | 30" | 30" | 30" |
| £000s net | | | | | | | | | | | | | | | |
| PO number | | | | | | | | | | | | | | | |
| TVRs | | | | | | | | | | | | | | | |
| **Press – VO5 Extreme range (1634M)** | Headless | | | | | News Int launch – Jam | New SKU sampling | | | | | Budget planned only at this stage | | | |
| £000s net | | | | | | | | | | | | | | | |
| PO number | PO 580254 | | | | | | | | | | | | | | |
| GRPs | 33 | 150 | 114 | | | | | | | | | | | | |
| Est. 1+ cover/ OTS | 74% @ 4 OTS | | | | | | 27% @ 1.3 OTS | | | | | | | | |
| **Cinema – VO5 (1634W)** | | | | | | | | | | | | | | | |
| £000s net | | | | | | | | | | | | | | | |
| PO number | | | | | | | | | | | | | | | |
| Admissions | | | | | | | | | | | | | | | |
| Est. 1+ cover/ OTS | | | | | | | | | | | | | | | |
| **Radio/ Digital – VO5 Extreme (16–34 ads)** | | | | | | Digital for *FHM* promo | Radio for *FHM* promo | | | | | | | | |
| £000s net | | | | | | | | | | | | | | | |
| PO number | | | | | | | | | | | | | | | |
| Est. 1+ cover/ OTS | | | | | | 2 weeks | 2 weeks | | | | | | | | |
| **Sponsorship** | | | | | *FHM* sponsorship | | | | | | | | | | |
| £000s net | | | | | | | | | | | | | | | |
| PO number | | | | | | | | | | | | | | | |
| Detail | | | | | Online traffic drivers, TV & radio promos, DPS marketing ADV in *Q* & *Zoo*, DPS advs *FHM*, Event | | | | | | | | | | |

Source: Alberto Culver UK

Figure 10: VO5 Extreme Style: 2003–2011 £ sales

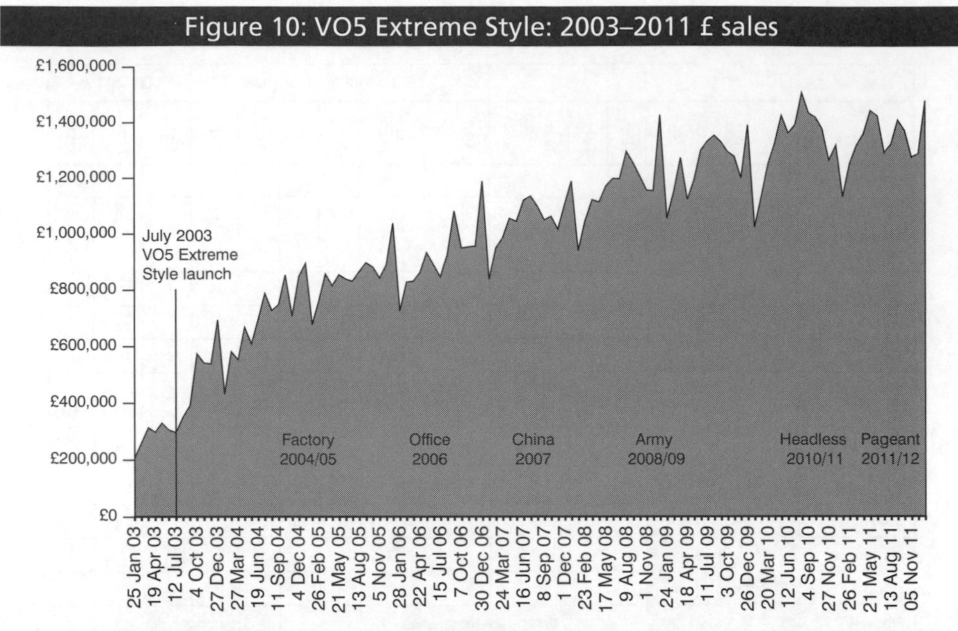


Source: VO5 Extreme Style value sales growth – IRI 4-week data 2003–2011

### *The range has helped power the success of the VO5 mother ship*

The VO5 Extreme Style launch, and subsequent focus on male styling, took VO5 to the No.1 position in Mass Styling & Hairspray – a position it has built on ever since: MAT value share of category has now reached 15.8% (Figure 11).[7]

Figure 11: VO5 growth within Mass Styling and Hairspray

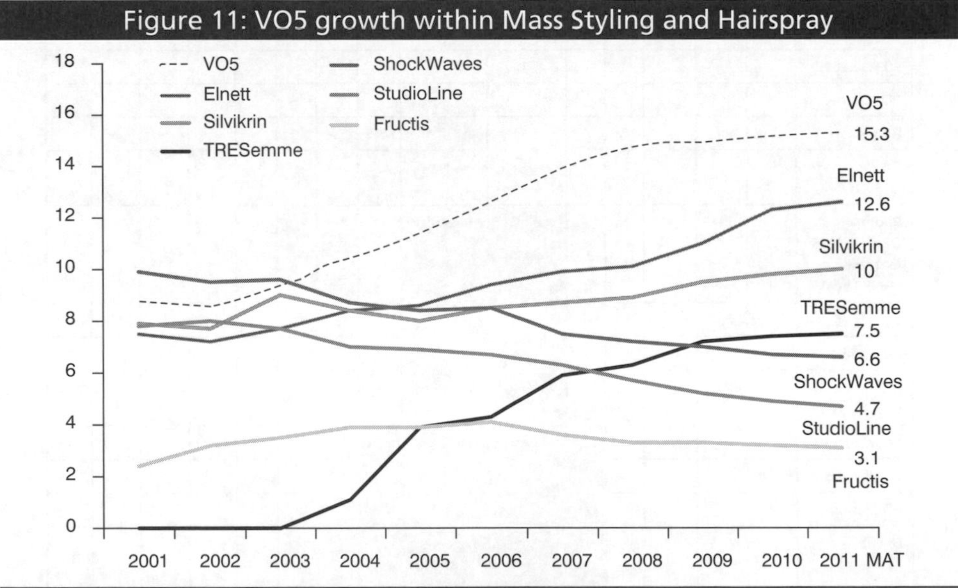


Source: VO5 Value Share of Mass Styling & Hairspray 2001–2011: IRI all outlets

VO5 Extreme Style contributed an average 46.2% value of total VO5 sales in Styling in 2011.[8]

### Business success has been driven by under 24-year-old men

VO5 Extreme Style has successfully enticed a reticent male audience to the VO5 stable:[9]

- 81% of all VO5 Extreme Style users are male compared with the 32% Styling category average.
- At the heart of the audience driving our success are under 24-year-olds. VO5 Extreme Style boasts 65% more under 24s than the Styling category average.

VO5 Extreme Style has gained its place in the Inbetweeners' bathroom cabinet.

## 'Break the Mould' TV: a major contributor to sales

While communications cannot claim all this success, econometric modelling, commissioned through Holmes & Cook, has evaluated the effect of VO5 Extreme Style advertising on total sales of VO5 Extreme Style between 2009 and 2011.

This model effectively strips out the effect of other key variables (such as a very active NPD programme) in order to isolate the extra growth generated solely by the advertising campaign.

The modelling was carried out using three years of four-weekly IRI data at Total Multiples level (including both Boots and Superdrug) between January 2009 and December 2011. Data allowing, we would have ideally gone right back to 2004 to examine the full contribution of 'Break the Mould'. Nonetheless, the three years' data that we have obtained shows a very positive advertising effect over the mature phase of the brand's life.

The findings conclude that 'Break the Mould' TV advertising contributed 27% of sales volume – a major contributing factor to sales success in the three-year period available to model.[10]

### *How the effect has worked*

In any given month, the model determined that 200 TVRs of VO5 Extreme Style activity produces a volume sales uplift of 2.3% in the month of airtime.

Furthermore, the cumulative TV effect identified by the modelling is very long lasting.

The 'Break the Mould' campaign claims an exemplary 97% adstock from month-to-month, which means that the same 200 TVRs will go on to generate a lifetime effect of the equivalent to 78% of an average week's volume (as demonstrated in Figure 12).

Thanks to a run of media data back to 2006, we have been able to obtain appropriate starting values for all adstocks. The longer-term effects of this carryover rate on volume sales (i.e. the lifetime incremental *sales difference* TV advertising has made) are shown in Figure 13.

Figure 12: 2.3% uplift, progress over time of a 97% adstock

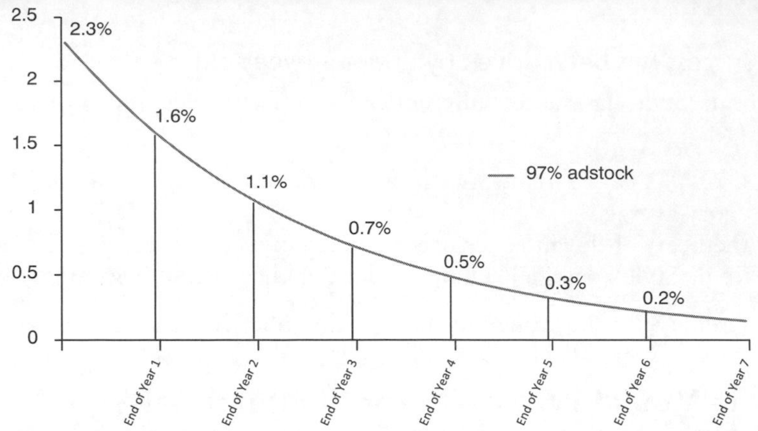

Source: Holmes & Cook VO5 Extreme Style model, April 2012

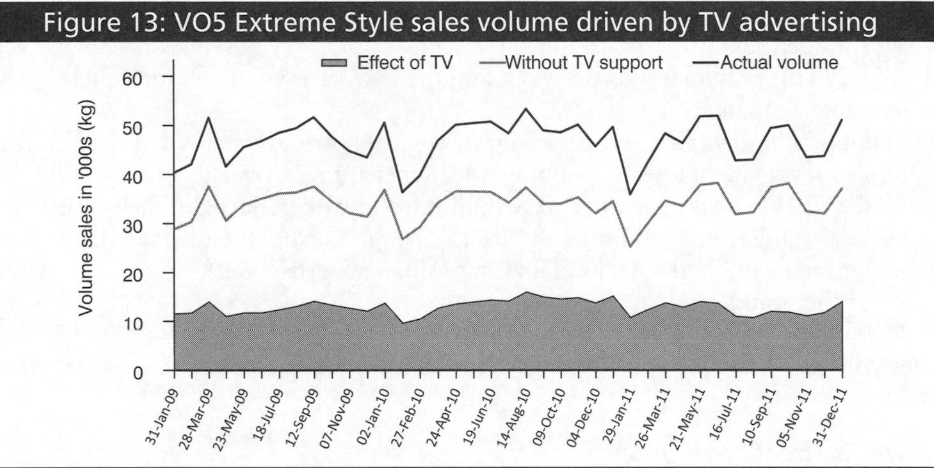


Figure 13: VO5 Extreme Style sales volume driven by TV advertising

Source: Holmes & Cook VO5 Extreme Style model, April 2012

Since January 2009 alone, Holmes & Cook estimates that the 'Break the Mould' films have contributed £14.25m incremental sales revenue to a total sales value of £50.9m during that period.

## How has communications achieved this success?

Over the last eight years, 'Break the Mould' has successively built what we call 'cred-stock'.

Not only does 97% adstock bear witness to this, but also the way our 'consistently inconsistent' campaign approach has successively continued to build affinity, belief and vital source credibility for VO5 Extreme Style, execution by execution, since 2004.

From mother's apron strings, VO5 Extreme Style has grown to become its own FMCG style icon.

And has achieved trusted 'mate status' among the Inbetweeners.

This is a snapshot of how this has been done.[11]

### *'Break the Mould' advertising has grabbed attention*

We have observed a growing link between 'Break the Mould' and VO5 Extreme Style since 2004 (Figure 14).

**Figure 14: A growing indelible link between 'Break the Mould' and VO5 Extreme Style**

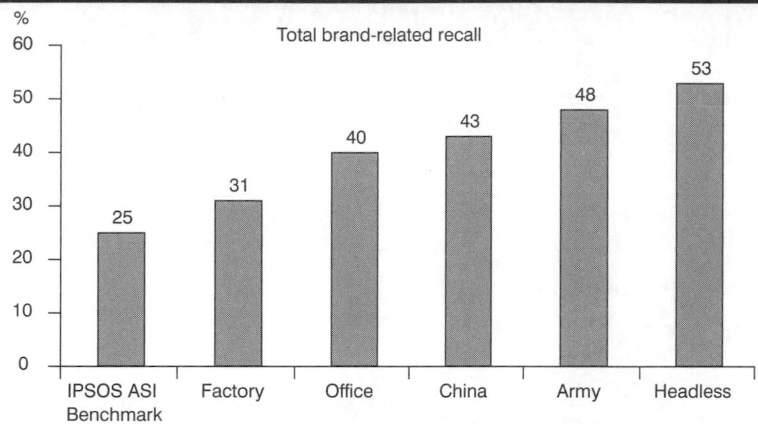


Source: IPSOS Pre-test; 'Break the Mould': total brand related recall, 2004–2010

The work has consistently held our target's attention – our audience is 36% more attentive (averaged across campaign) than study norms (Figure 15).

**Figure 15: Target highly attentive to the advertising**

Measured attention
(correct % based on aided recognition)

%
90
80
70
60
50
40
30
20
10
0
Not measured
IPSOS ASI Benchmark
Factory
Office
China
Army
Headless

Source: IPSOS Pre-test; 'Break the Mould': measured attention, 2004–2010

Our Inbetweeners are 'actively involved' in the executions (Figure 16).

**Figure 16: Active involvement – attention and engagement**

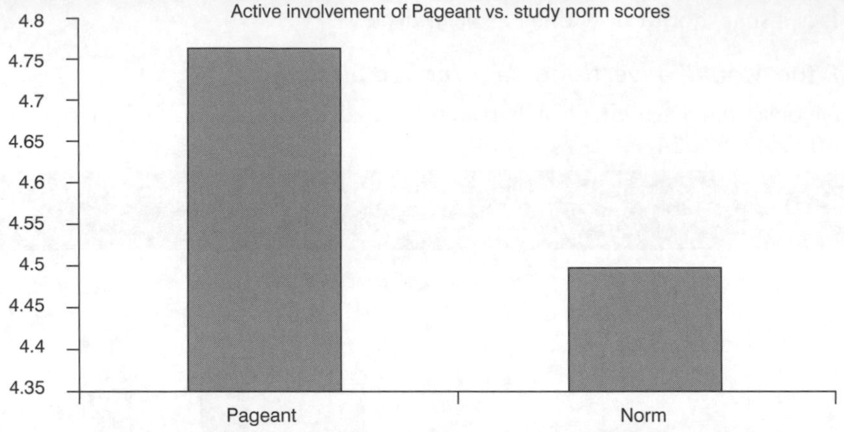

Source: Millward Brown LinkSelect; 'Break the Mould': active involvement for 'The Pliktisijiteur Pageant', 2011

Campaign cut-through in the real world is reflected in the high online viewing figures and interactions with our most recent 2011 campaign, 'The Pliktisijiteur Pageant':

- At the time of writing, the 90" film has 215,000 views on the VO5 Extreme Style channel, taking it to the top 2.7% of all YouTube content.[12]
- Furthermore, the 90" cut of the 'Pageant' film became the fourth most viewed UK comedy video on YouTube within five days of launch in October 2011. It's extremely rare for brands to break into this chart, so a good indication of cut-through and engagement.

Our target has consistently enjoyed the 'Break the Mould' campaign executions – likeability is on average 29% higher than benchmark norms (Figure 17).

### *'Break the Mould' has created a 'climate of credibility' for VO5 Extreme Style*

Referring back to Hovland, the root ingredients of credibility are perceived trustworthiness and expertise, and since 2004 we have witnessed a growing belief in the VO5 Extreme Style promise in line with the communications activity.

The advertising has delivered the promise of rebellious individuality (Figure 18).

Or as one young lad put it in a focus group last year, 'Break the Mould, VO5 will help you to look different and get the girl.'[13]

And we have created positive separation from the VO5 mother ship – a credible partner in style (Table 2).

And belief in the brand promise has continually gathered pace across the course of the campaign (Figure 19).

## Figure 17: Consistently high likeability scores

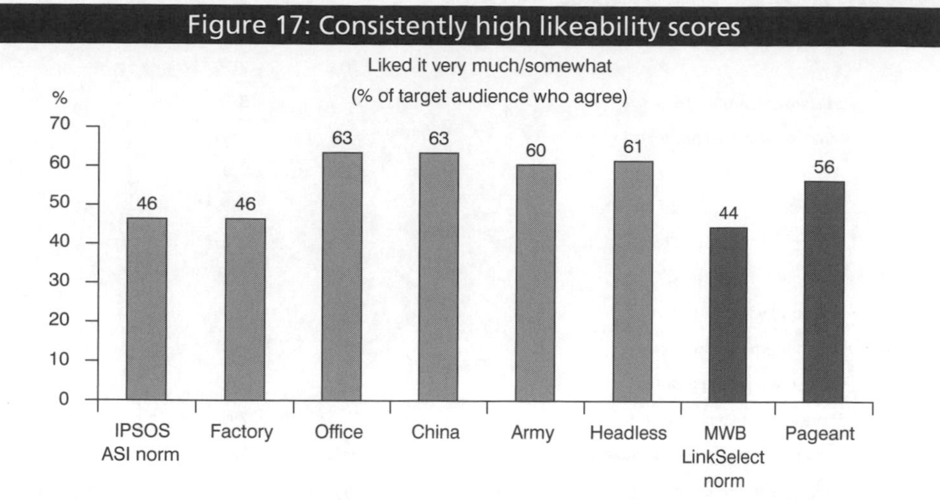


Source: IPSOS Pre-test data and Millward Brown LinkSelect; 'Break the Mould': likeability scores, 2004–2011

## Figure 18: Brand associations driven by the advertising (indexed against study norms)

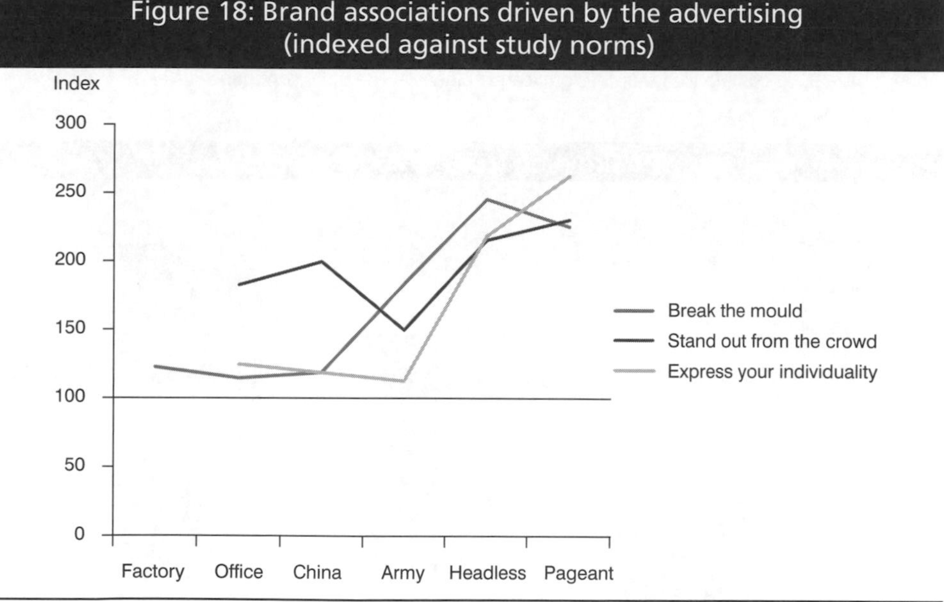


Source: IPSOS Pre-test and Millward Brown LinkSelect; 'Break the Mould': prompted key message Takeout, 2004–2011

## Table 2: VO5 Extreme Style brand attributes

| Statement applies to... | VO5<br>A | VO5 Extreme Style<br>B |
|---|---|---|
| Make professional products | 76% | 81% |
| Are trusted by stylists | 65% | 70% |
| Are worth paying a little more for | 46% | 58% ** |
| Have products that deliver what they promise | 70% | 81% ** |
| Are brands I really trust | 71% | 77% |
| Are good value for the money | 65% | 65% |
| Are modern and up-to-date | 67% | 88% * |
| Make great styling products | 77% | 81% |
| Have innovative products | 66% | 79% * |
| Help me express my individuality | 63% | 70% |
| Help give me confidence that I look my best | 64% | 72% |
| Have products that provide long-lasting hold | 74% | 88% * |
| Offer quick and easy ways to finish up my look | 75% | 80% |
| Keep my hair in place and well groomed | 73% | 81% |
| Help me achieve a variety of looks | 63% | 82% * |

Source: IPSOS Global Brand Equity Study 2009; base: aware of VO5 Extreme Style (n=115). * significantly higher at the 95% confidence level; ** significantly higher at the 90% confidence level

## Figure 19: Growing trust in VO5 Extreme Style

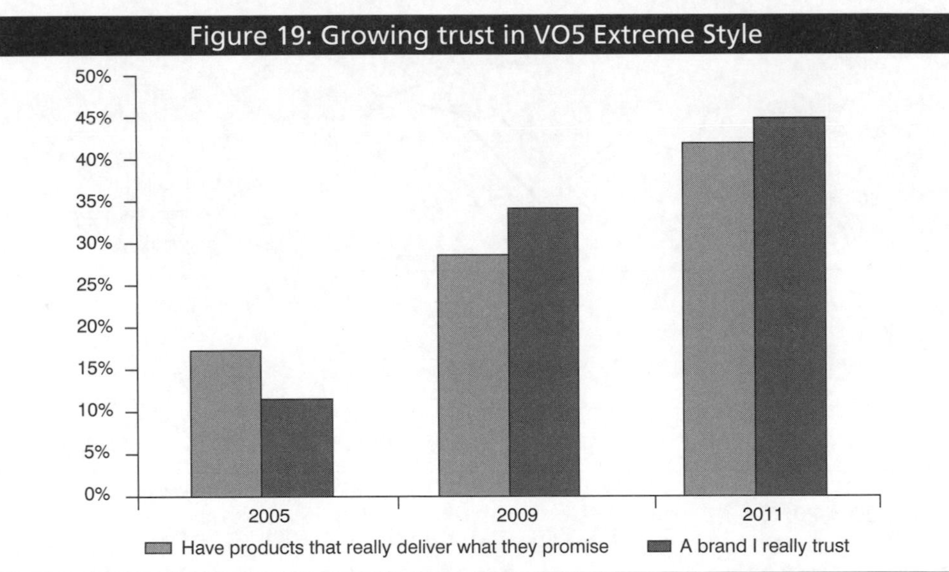


Source: IPSOS Global Brand Equity Study

There is now a clear value exchange between brand and the Inbetweener:

VO5 Extreme Style has been voted 'best hair styling range' at the FHM Grooming Awards every year since 2008 by FHM readers, our heartland – 16–24-year-old style-conscious males (Figure 20).

Figure 20: Perceived expertise – winning the FHM Grooming Awards 'best styling range'

*'Break the Mould' is increasingly persuasive*

We have witnessed an increasing propensity to purchase over time (Figure 21).

Figure 21: VO5 Extreme Style: propensity to purchase (% any agree)

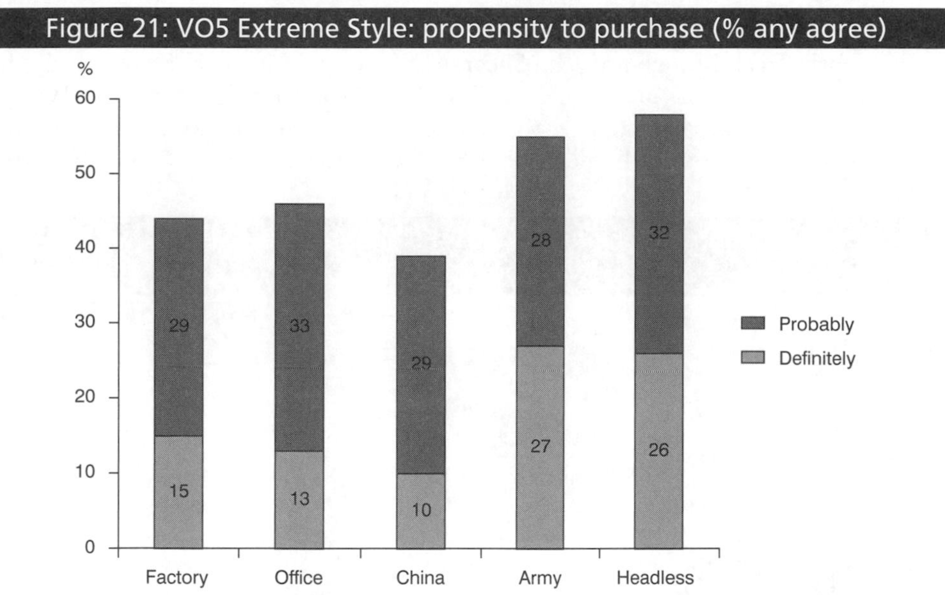


Source: IPSOS Pre-test; VO5 Extreme Style: propensity to purchase, IPSOS ASI 2004–2010

*'Break the Mould' has achieved 'mate's status'*

'High influence' Inbetweeners talk favourably about the brand (Figure 22).

As belief in VO5 Extreme Style has grown, so too has endorsement from some really influential places.

J1mmyb0bba, 'vlogger' and ultimate YouTube hair guru for our target audience, loves VO5 Extreme Style. With a subscriber base of 82,255 and over 5.8 million video views he is happy to wax (sorry!) lyrical about the virtues of VO5 Extreme Style.

**Figure 22: Online influencers advocating the brand – J1mmyb0bba**

*"This one is VO5 Extreme Style Texturising Gum, I've been using it religiously since high school and it's always in my little draw. It's under £3.50, it's a bargain! You can do anything you want that involves texture. It's so versatile, you can do any sort of style. And it smells nice too, which is one of the reasons why I like this brand. When you compare it to something like Shockwaves, their main competitors, I find this is much better quality, it lasts longer, and also they cater to more people. I love this stuff!"*

2012 Brit Breakthrough artist Ed Sheeran also recently name-checked 'VO5 (sic) wax for my ginger hair' in the lyrics of 'You Need Me, I Don't Need You' (Winner of Q Awards Best Single in 2011 – 10, 425,282 views on YouTube). He also tweeted about his reliance upon the brand to his 1.9 million followers on 27 September 2011 at 08.13 (Figure 23).

**Figure 23: High credibility sources – Ed Sheeran name-checking and tweeting about 'VO5'**

"From day one, I've been prepared with *VO5 wax for my ginger hair*"

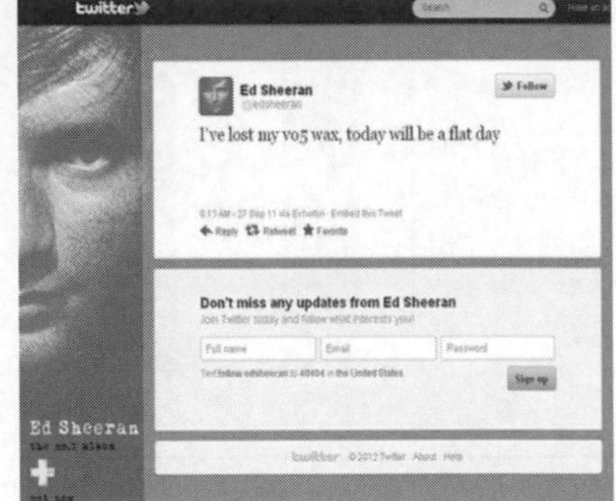


Social media is also starting to attract even wider advocacy.

It is early doors for our foray into the social web, but 'The Pliktisijiteur Pageant' has now received 10,000 mentions on blogs, forums, news channels and Twitter, and within one month ‘Pageant’ was embedded and endorsed by over 35,000 web properties willing to spread the brand love (Figure 24).

**Figure 24: Examples of ‘The Pliktisijiteur Pageant’ placement coverage on the Viral Ad Network**

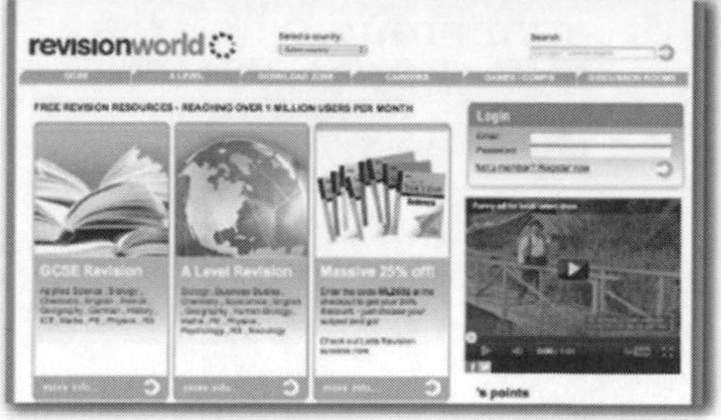


**Revision World**

http://revisionworld.co.uk/

**Insight:** Revision World is a free, easy to use online revision service for GCSE and A Level for students who are revising for exams...

**Spike Magazine**

http://www.spikemagazine.com/

**Insight:** SpikeMagazine.com is a books and culture site with hundreds of reviews, interviews and features...

This evidence points to ever-building ‘cred-stock’ for VO5 Extreme Style among its key users.

The climate of enduring credibility that we have originally sought to forge among under 24-year-old men for VO5 Extreme Style is alive and *still* kicking.

To quote Holmes & Cook’s more intellectual summary from the econometrics:

> *The modelling showed that the effects of ‘Break the Mould’ TV advertising were very long-lived and thus consistent with the advertising having generated repeat purchase and potentially word of mouth. This shows clearly that it has performed a brand building role.*
>
> Louise Cook, March 2012

## Acknowledging other success factors

While we have successfully demonstrated the *pure* TV effect, we are happy to illustrate the contribution of other potentially influential factors in the VO5 Extreme Style marketing mix.

We include these for the judges’ reference.

### *Innovations*

NPD is at the heart of the ‘consistently inconsistent’ strategy, and the ‘Break the Mould’ campaign has relied heavily on new product news to stay in touch. However, when new SKUs come in there is evidence of cannibalisation on existing SKUs, implying innovation is not all incremental, rather a way of injecting new style news and keeping up with the frenetic style pace (Figure 25).

Figure 25: Effect of NPD SKUs on VO5 Extreme Style ROS 2007 vs. 2006

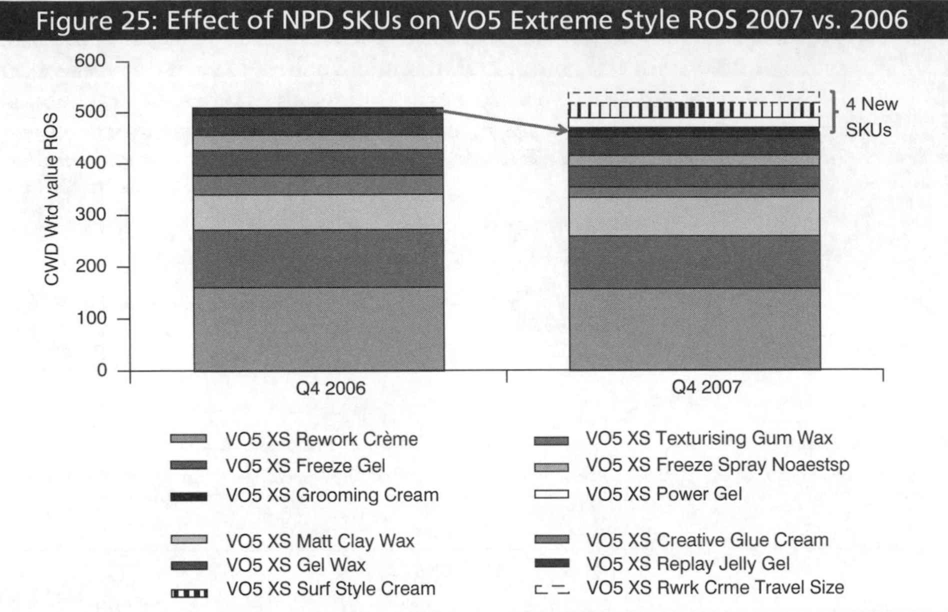


Source: Effect of new SKUs on ROS 2006 vs. 2007, IRI/Holmes & Cook

### *Distribution*

The model demonstrates that VO5 Extreme Style built distribution more quickly for new SKUs in the Multiples than Studio Line, Fructis and Shockwaves between 2009 and 2011 – this could be down to a number of marketing and sales factors but could equally provide evidence of positive brand communications equity with the Trade (Table 3).

Table 3: Average percentage distribution gains for new SKUs 2009–2011

| Styling brand | Average distribution attained by 2nd quarter after launch |
|---|---|
| Brylcreem | 83.6 |
| VO5 XS | 80.2 |
| Studio Line | 75.6 |
| Fructis | 71.2 |
| Shockwaves | 69.9 |

Source: IRI/Holmes & Cook

### *Price and promotions*

VO5 Extreme Style is becoming increasingly less reliant on price cuts for volume gain. The model has isolated an average 16.3% contribution from price cuts and promotions between 2009 and 2011, which is declining year-on-year (Table 4).

**Table 4: Percentage contribution of price cuts and promotions 2009–2011**

| | Actual volume | Volume gained due to price cuts & promotions | % contribution of price cuts and promotions |
|---|---|---|---|
| 2009 | 604,589 | 116,077 | 19.2% |
| 2010 | 619,331 | 101,723 | 16.4% |
| 2011 | 600,563 | 79,305 | 13.2% |
| Total | 1,824,483 | 297,105 | 16.3% |

Source: IRI/Holmes & Cook

Users paid an average £2.96 per pack vs. the Styling category average of £2.28 in 2011 suggesting that, with a clear value exchange, Inbetweeners are prepared to pay more to 'Break the Mould'.[14]

### *Summer and Christmas rutting seasons*

VO5 Extreme Style enjoys 'frisky' seasonal uplifts when a) the sun comes out and the shades go on, and b) during the Christmas party season. Uplifts in sales during these periods are duly discounted in the model.

## Calculating the advertising payback

In terms of actual advertising ROI, Holmes & Cook has calculated that the lifetime revenue ROI[15] of 'Break the Mould' TV between 2009 and 2011 is **£1.75** for every £1 spent (including Total Media).[16, 17]

Here are our workings (Table 5).

**Table 5: VO5 Extreme Style 'Break the Mould' lifetime revenue ROI calculation 2009–2011**

| | |
|---|---|
| Revenue generated from VO5 Extreme Style advertising from Jun 2009 to Dec 2011 | £5,820,704 |
| Future revenue as 97% adstock declines | £8,433,369 |
| Total lifetime revenue generated from VO5 XS advertising (aired Jun 2009 to Dec 2011) | £14,254,072 |
| Total cost of VO5 Extreme Style campaign including production (aired Jun 2009 to Dec 2011) | £8,167,456 |
| Incremental revenue after advertising costs | £6,086,616 |
| Lifetime revenue/cost of campaign | £1.75 : £1 |

Source: Holmes & Cook

This ROI compares very favourably with other recent winning IPA Personal Care cases (Dove deodorants £2.06:£1 in 2010) and 'smashes' the IRI average TV ROI of £0.52 to £1 typical for FMCG products.

In order to calculate the profit contribution made by the campaign, we now need to draw on publicly available Alberto-Culver Company (ACV) reports.[18] In Q1 2011, directly before its sale to Unilever in September 2011, ACV's gross profit margin was stated at 53.2%.

Using this 53.2% margin we are able to calculate that 'Break the Mould' made an incremental profit contribution of £3.2m between 2009 and 2011 *alone*.

Expressed as a percentage of the media budget this gives us 39p in profit for every £ spent on advertising (after the advertising has been paid for).

## And finally, here's to more 'Mould Breaking'

We conclude that, in creating a climate of credibility for VO5 Extreme Style among a ferociously critical male teenage audience through 'consistently inconsistent' brand communications, the 'Break the Mould' advertising property has been instrumental in embedding VO5 Extreme Style as a staple in the lives of hair-conscious young men.

Our restless, rebellious stance has subsequently had a powerful effect on the on-going sales success of a sub-range that needed to do more than cling on to its glamorous mum's apron strings.

This paper demonstrates that building 'cred-stock' has been absolutely vital to the range's success.

It is also interesting to note that between 2000 and 2010, VO5 Extreme Style was a crucial part of the portfolio that helped grow Alberto Culver from a £64.6m turnover company to £196.3m in the UK, which in turn had a role to play in the sale to Unilever for $3.7bn in September 2011.

VO5 Extreme Style was one of the jewels in the Alberto crown.

And we now look forward to many more years breaking the mould with Unilever at the helm.

## Notes

1 Source: Euro RSCG London focus groups.
2 Inbetweeners, as we now call our 16–24-year-old male target after the hit Channel 4 comedy show.
3 IRI all outlets total styling aids value sales MAT to December 2011 vs. 2003.
4 VO5 Extreme Style IRI value sales MAT 2011 vs. 2007.
5 Total Styling Aids IRI value sales MAT 2011 vs. 2007.
6 Total Styling Aids value sales MAT June 2011 vs. 2009.
7 IRI all outlets VO5 value share MAT to December 2011.
8 Holmes & Cook calculation based on IRI value sales.
9 VO5 Extreme Style demographics & penetration Kantar Worldpanel 12 m/e September 2011.
10 The use of four-weekly data (39 observations in total) means it has not been possible to separate out the effects of media other than the much larger effect of TV, i.e. FHM, print and digital.
11 Please note that Alberto Culver did not commission advertising tracking, instead favouring rigorous animatic pre-testing among men aged 16–24. We have therefore used IPSOS ASI (the testing method used for the first five TVCs 2004–2010) and Millward Brown LINK tests (the method used to test 'The Pliktisijiteur Pageant' TVC in 2011) as a proxy for 'real world' results where metrics and comparisons allow. We might also assume finished films would have performed even better than animatics.
12 TubeMogul: Digital Video Advertising Best Practices, 2011.
13 Male 20, Firefly (MWB) Qualitative Research Debrief, May 2011.
14 Kantar Wordpanel price per volume 52 w/e 22 January 2012.
15 ROI calculation assumes media effects are consistent on the remaining 3% of volume generated outside the multiples.
16 Please note: ROI is calculated using Addynamix spend, not actual spend which is likely to have shown a higher return.
17 Source: Addynamix, including production costs of £1.18m. Although the econometric model only shows TV effect, we have assumed this encompasses Total Media spend for the purpose of the ROI calculation.
18 Source: www.wikinvest.com

**SILVER AWARD: THE BROADBENT PRIZE FOR BEST DEDICATION TO EFFECTIVENESS**

## Chapter 29

# Waitrose

## The best ever Christmas

**By Debra Stephens and Michelle Gilson, Bartle Bogle Hegarty**

Contributing authors: Paddy Adams, Manning Gottlieb OMD and Diego Usai, BrandScience

Credited companies: Creative Agency: Bartle Bogle Hegarty; Media Agency: Manning Gottlieb OMD; Econometric Modelling Agency: BrandScience; Client: Waitrose



### Editor's summary

The judges loved this case study for its adoption of an incredibly brave strategy in a tough economic climate, in order to stay true to its brand. Waitrose was facing challenging market conditions, fiercer competition and no significant new news. To address this it made the tough decision to invest more in the brand, despite everything pointing to promoting price, and transformed its existing assets into a showcase to make the brand more magical and inclusive. The campaign attracted less frequent, lighter customers to Waitrose and created the best Christmas Waitrose ever had, delivering the highest growth in like-for-like sales in the grocery sector of more than 3.8%, and a net profit payback of £1.89 in just over eight weeks. This is a brilliant case around the persuasive power of creativity and creative execution and fully deserves a read.

## Management summary

This is the story of the best Christmas Waitrose has ever had, delivering the highest growth in like-for-like sales in the grocery sector (+3.8%).

It tells how communications attracted less frequent, lighter customers despite challenging market conditions, despite fiercer competition and despite no significant new news.

Marketing is often about making tough choices. Waitrose made the tough decision to invest more in brand, despite everything pointing to promoting price, and transformed their existing assets into a showcase to make the brand more magical and inclusive.

This delivered a net profit ROI of £1.89 over just eight weeks.

## Background

Waitrose is a relatively small player in the UK grocery market with 276 stores and 4.3% annual market share.[1] They are dwarfed by the mainstream supermarket giants of Morrisons, Asda, Tesco and Sainsbury's. Waitrose pride themselves on their approach to quality, service and CSR and are positioned towards the top end of the market with Sainsbury's and M&S. Their growth revenue has been delivered through a small but very loyal base of shoppers.[2]

Christmas 2010 was going to be a tough act to follow. Waitrose had a very successful Christmas in 2010 with total sales up 8.9% year-on-year (YOY) against market growth of 5.2%.[3]

## The opportunity in 2011: capitalise on an increased repertoire

Christmas is a valuable trading period worth £16.5bn.[4] Not only are people spending more over the Christmas period but they are also open to shopping in more places (therefore offering an opportunity for longer-term sales) (Figure 1).

Figure 1: Shopper repertoire in the grocery market

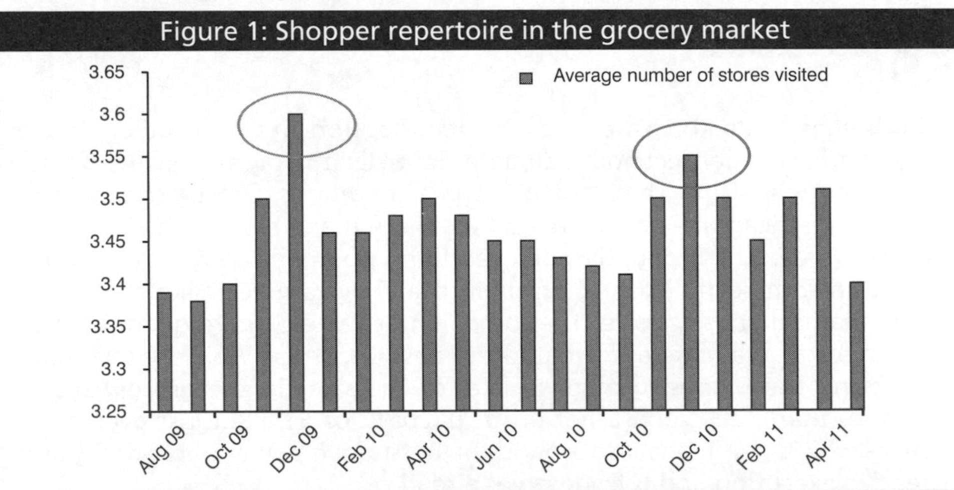


Source: Kantar Worldpanel total grovery, 4 w/e 26 June 2011

Waitrose set a tough target to generate a sales uplift of *over 8%* vs. 2010. Looking at where that growth could come from, the biggest opportunity in the market was to bring in less frequent, lighter customers.[5]

However, attracting lighter customers wasn't necessarily going to be easy. They spend as little as 10% or less of their grocery spend with Waitrose.[6]

Indeed when we looked back at Christmas 2010, Waitrose's most successful Christmas to date, sales had been delivered by their existing customers shopping more frequently with them (Figure 2).

**Figure 2: Contribution to Christmas 2010 sales growth year-on-year by percentage**

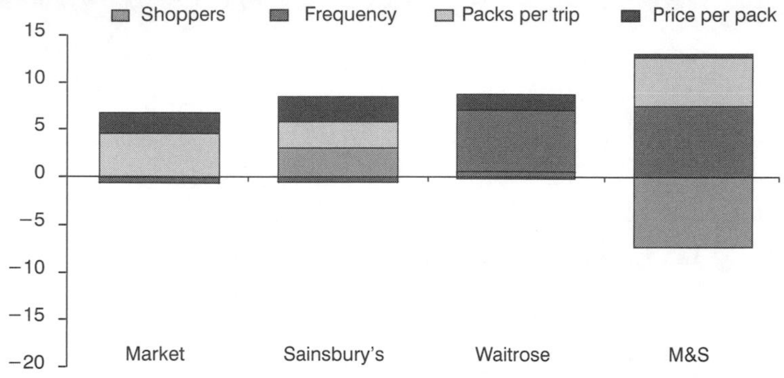

Shoppers Frequency Packs per trip Price per pack

15 10 5 0 −5 −10 −15 −20

Market Sainsbury's Waitrose M&S

Source: Kantar Worldpanel, 4 w/e 26 December 2010

On top of that, market conditions were challenging for all retailers.

## The challenge: market conditions had never been tougher

There were four big challenges to bringing in lighter customers in the Christmas 2011 period:

- difficult market conditions;
- fiercer competitors;
- people intending to spend less;
- no new marketing weapons of choice.

### *Difficult market conditions*

In the run up to Christmas 2011, retailers were facing major challenges and Waitrose, as a premium retailer, was as worried as any.

> *Roll up, roll up: it's the 'big price drop' – and not just at Tesco. Worried retailers across the high street are decking the aisles with discounts and it's not even December yet. This year's Christmas trading period is shaping up to be as tough as anything seen during the recession, as a year in which living costs have raced ahead of pay rises draws to a close.*
>
> Hard times on the high street mean an unhappy Christmas at the Treasury.
>
> *The Guardian*, November 2011

Families were feeling the squeeze as austerity and inflation took their toll on household budgets and disposable income continued to fall at an annualised rate of 3%.[7] As a result, consumer confidence was at an all-time low (Figure 3).

**Figure 3: Consumer Confidence Index falling year-on-year**

Source: Nationwide.co.uk/consumer_confidence

### *With ever fiercer competition*

The supermarkets were responding aggressively to these new market conditions and the price war began in earnest in 2011. Under their new 'Live well for less' idea, Sainsbury's had launched 'Brand Match' in October 2011, Tesco had launched the 'Big price drop' in September 2011, and M&S were continuing to focus on their successful 'Meal deals' (Figure 4).

**Figure 4: Competitors' value-led campaigns**

### *Therefore people were intending to spend less*

Over a third of the UK population were planning to spend less at Christmas this year (Figure 5).

Figure 5: How UK consumers planned to spend this Christmas compared to last

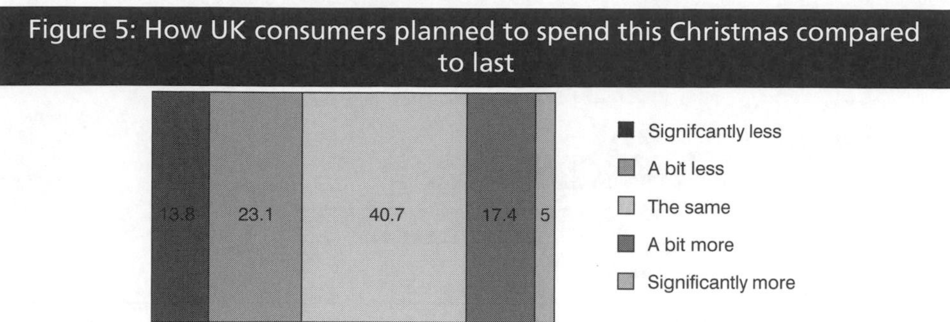


Source: Verdict. Base: Representative UK sample of 10,116

This was backed up in qualitative research when customers told us they were planning to shop around this Christmas in order to spend less. The qualitative researcher described their mind-set as:

'careful and considered' (The Source debrief, Waitrose Christmas 2011)

### *With no new marketing weapons of choice to bring them in*

Waitrose always create wonderful and interesting new products for Christmas, but clearly these products alone could not drive the significant growth Waitrose needed to hit the targets they had set.

- They were planning a similar Christmas design and store layout as the year before.[8]
- Delia and Heston were still the Waitrose brand ambassadors.
- There were new hero products from Delia and Heston, but from a customer point of view this Christmas innovation had reached a crescendo the year before when we first announced Heston's 'hidden orange Christmas pudding'.
- There were great new products within the Waitrose own branded dessert and party food range – but again these made up a small percentage of the total Christmas offering.
- There was the 'essential Waitrose' range but this had now been around for three years and was no longer news.

## The question: should Waitrose focus on price and offers this Christmas?

When we looked at the core barriers to lighter shoppers using Waitrose, the main reason was price. Compared to their heavy shoppers (gold customers) Waitrose don't score as highly as Sainsbury's and Tesco amongst their lighter shoppers (silver and bronze) on value perceptions (Figure 6).

Figure 6: Waitrose shoppers' view of grocer's value for money

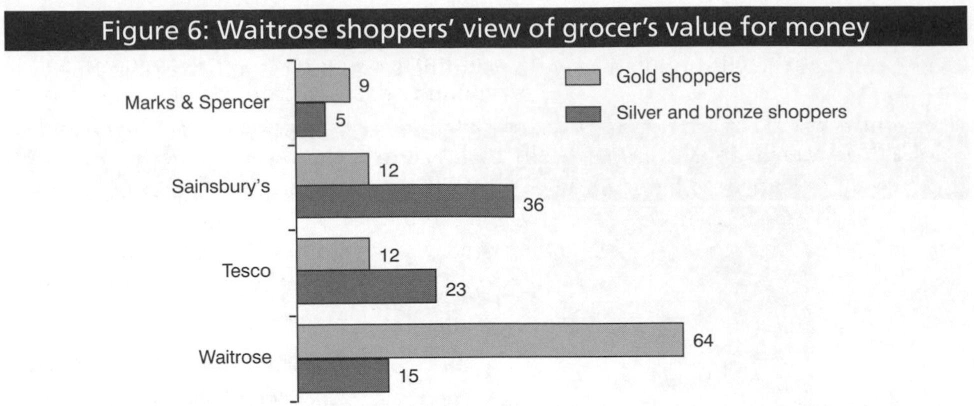


Source: Waitrose Brand Tracker, consumer insight. Base: Waitrose kitchen table panel: gold shoppers (74); other shoppers (39). NB: the difference between gold, silver and bronze customers is that gold customers tend to equate value to quality and price, whereas for bronze and silvers perception of value tends to just mean price

Even some of their heavy customers (gold) were planning to shop around in order to spend less this Christmas.

> *I'll still come to Waitrose for some of the nice things, but this year I'm going to shop around a bit more and try to spend less* – Waitrose heavy shopper.
>
> The Source debrief, Waitrose Christmas 2011

> *The economic climate is difficult right now. We all have to think about what we spend and on what* – Waitrose main shopper
>
> The Source debrief, Waitrose Christmas 2011

This placed Waitrose in a difficult situation. If Waitrose were to have another successful Christmas and continue to grow, should they address value perceptions or play to their biggest strength (quality)?

## The brave choice versus the logical choice

### *The logical choice: put the majority of Waitrose spend behind offers*

In 2011 Waitrose had made their offers more competitive within the marketplace and had increased their numbers – with good deals like half price on luxury biscuits, mince pies and champagne, and a third off 'essential Waitrose' meat.

However, as stated before, competition has never been fiercer and Waitrose do not promote as aggressively as some of their competitors.[9]

Even if we put Waitrose's total media budget (circa £6m) behind promoting offers, we estimated that we would have still been outspent by Sainsbury's on offers alone.[10]

Waitrose were not going to win in a price war alone.

### *The balanced choice: a balanced spend across brand and offers*

In 2010 Waitrose spread their media budget evenly across both offers and brand.[11] But in 2011, with only a 6% share of voice,[12] we were concerned that we would end up doing neither well.

When we looked back at Christmas 2010 the key competitor strategies were to own the middle ground (attracting customers trading up and trading down) for increased share of wallet (Figure 7).

**Figure 7: Sainsbury's 2010 focused on both premium and value spend of their customers**

Waitrose couldn't win against the mainstream grocers in this middle ground (putting high spend against value and premium). Fast forward to post Christmas 2011, and the middle ground is exactly where competitor Sainsbury's won.

> *That middle position, allowing customers [to trade up and down] has done well. It is the winning place to be.*
>
> Justin King, CEO J Sainsbury's on their Christmas 2011 performance.
> Source: *The Financial Times*

### *The brave choice: place the majority of the budget behind brand and put on a show*

Back in the summer of 2011, and in the middle of the recession, we took the decision that Waitrose had to stay true to themselves, focus on their 'shared love of food' and everything that makes Waitrose special. There were three arguments to back this up.

*First*, more than ever Waitrose had to defend their quality positioning and ensure their customers would not pick up the more premium products from competitors.

The other supermarkets were snapping at Waitrose's heels in terms of their quality and premium offering. Tesco were continuing to support their 'Finest' range; in 2010 Sainsbury's had re-launched and extended their 'Taste the difference' range from 150 lines to 1,141 products, and in 2011 Asda announced their tie up with the Leith school of cooking to launch their 'Extra special' range. Annual sales of both 'Finest' and 'Taste the difference' had broken the £1bn mark.

*Second*, you don't always take customer research at face value.

Of course we had to be competitive on price, but customers would come to Waitrose this year because they wanted to put on their own special Christmas. When we did qualitative research and dug deeper, our understanding was that a huge aim of Christmas was still to express love, feeling and emotion towards family and friends.[13] They would want to enjoy themselves over Christmas *because* it had been such a hard year.

> *You want people to know you care, of course you do* – Waitrose light shopper
> The Source debrief, Waitrose Christmas 2011

We took the view that the emotional side of our brain would take over the rational side as Christmas drew closer.

*Third,* we believed there was an opportunity to re-deploy our brand ambassadors (Delia and Heston) to take on M&S and Sainsbury's and broaden appeal to lighter shoppers.

When we looked over the research, a key missed opportunity for Waitrose was to put on more of a show over Christmas.

> *It's not really a spectacle is it* – Waitrose light shopper
> The Source debrief, Waitrose Christmas 2010

And an opportunity to put into effect Waitrose's longer-term goal of making the brand more inclusive, as they could be perceived as a bit posh and distant to lighter shoppers.

> *In Waitrose you get well groomed Mums with their kids Skye and Tarquin* – Waitrose light shopper
> Sense qualitative research, Waitrose light shopper 2010

Last year's campaign followed the successful cookery show format of their previous TV adverts (Figure 8).

**Figure 8: Last year's Waitrose Christmas TV ad**

This was in contrast to M&S who, alongside their dedicated food TV advertising, always put on a real Christmas spectacle (Figure 9).

Figure 9: Last year's M&S Christmas TV ad

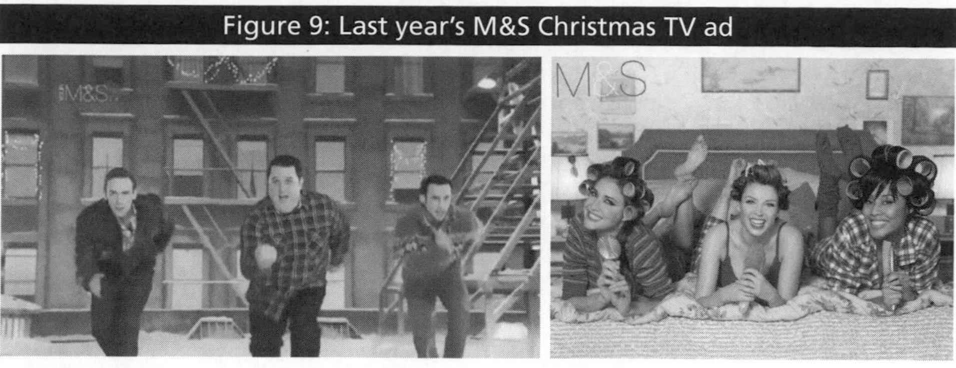


To bring lighter customers in we needed a creative idea that used our brilliant brand ambassadors in such a way that it felt big and inclusive. Based on these arguments, we took the brave decision to spend 70% of the media budget on 'brand' and 30% on 'offers'.

## The creative strategy: unlocking the magic

The key to unlocking this problem was the classic strategy of finding a way to match what customers really wanted with what Waitrose did best.

### *What Waitrose does best: magic in the product*

The one thing Waitrose had over other retailers at Christmas was its magical products, especially with chef Heston Blumenthal – such as his hidden orange Christmas pudding.

### *What consumers want: magic in the occasion*

Furthermore, through qualitative research we identified that Christmas isn't necessarily about being the best cook. It's about bringing sparkle and putting on a great show for your family and friends.[14] It's wanting to deliver the magic of Christmas that brings out the generous side in all of us.

### *What struck a chord in 2011: magic in the air*

Lastly, because we wanted the idea to feel big and mainstream, we looked to popular culture for inspiration. Summer 2011 saw the last of the Harry Potter films and the nation was gripped with magic (Figure 10).

Figure 10: Unlocking the creative idea

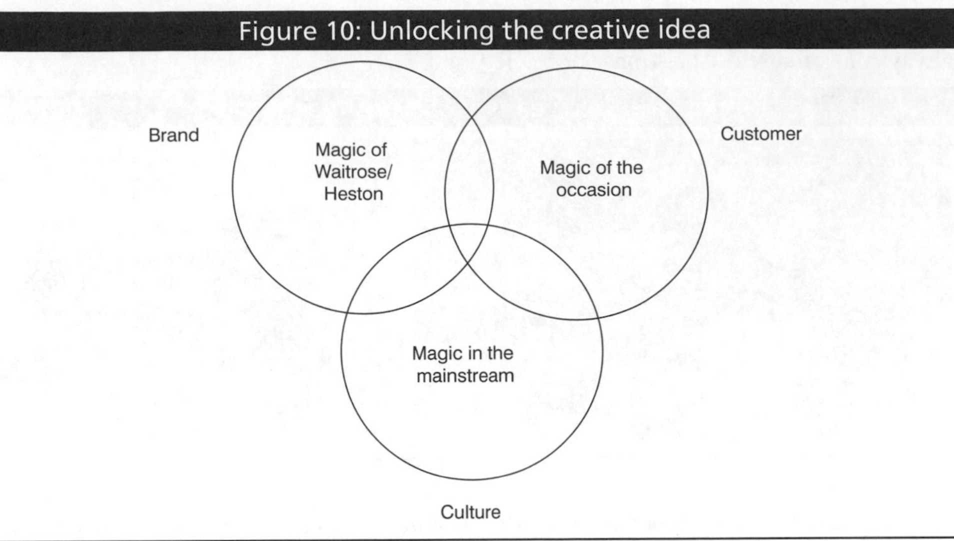


Source: BBH

We had our creative idea: the Waitrose 'School of magic'.

The 'School of magic' enabled us to break out of the studio format and showcase the most festive, show-stopping, edible treats Waitrose had to offer. Magic also enabled us to go beyond helping consumers be better cooks and tap into what everyone really wants to deliver at Christmas: magic and sparkle. Importantly the idea of a school made it easy for customers to create the magic themselves and helped us to make Waitrose feel more inclusive. This was delivered not only in the TV campaign but also through unique content (Figure 11).

## The media strategy: make it magical, make it easy

The approach to media was twofold. On the one hand, we had to make our advertising as *magical* as possible in order to create fame and emotional engagement amongst lighter customers. On the other hand, we recognised the need to make it as *easy* as possible for people to create a great Christmas for their loved ones. Both of these were necessary to make Waitrose more *inclusive* over the period. Where 2010 saw a 50:50 split between brand and offers,[15] 2011 saw 70:30.

### *Making it magical*

TV is the battleground for most advertisers at Christmas and none more so than the supermarkets. TV accordingly formed the backbone of our campaign, but it was used in a significantly different way to the previous Christmas.

We used 87% of our TV spend to support Waitrose 'brand' activity, with the remaining 13% being made up of 10" TV offer-led ads. The campaign kicked off with a 90" execution to maximise impact and stand-out (and thus excitement), which was followed by 30" and 40" cut-downs featuring one of our two chefs and highlighting a particular product (Delia's Christmas cake, roast turkey with trimmings, and Heston's pine-scented mince pies and 'feast of desserts').

Figure 11: The Waitrose 'School of magic' TV ad

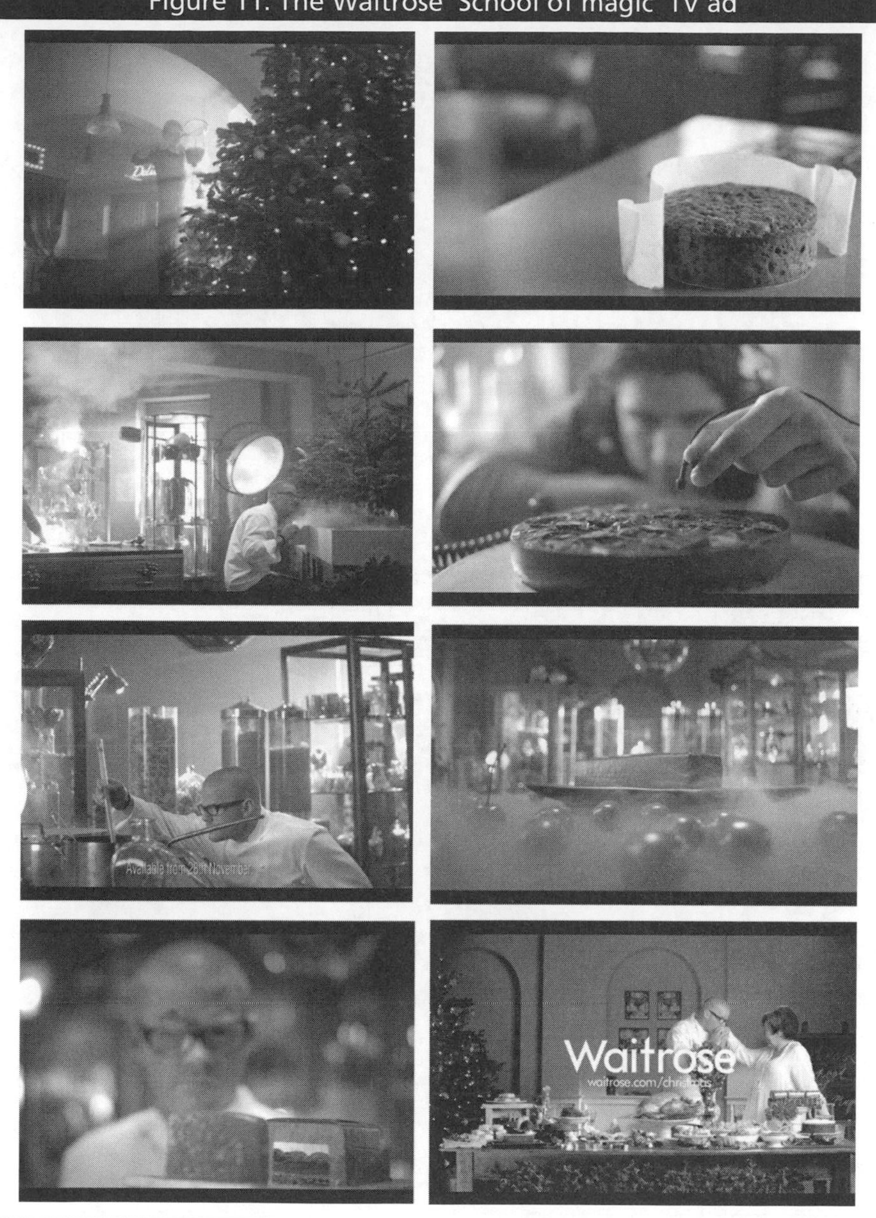


Waitrose were the only supermarket to run 90" ads during Christmas 2011, and spent the least behind offers within the sector (Figure 12).[16]

The campaign launched with a high-profile spot in X-Factor, with the channel mix focusing on ITV to deliver key family Christmas programming (Figure 13).

Figure 12: TV lengths of all retailers' Christmas advertising

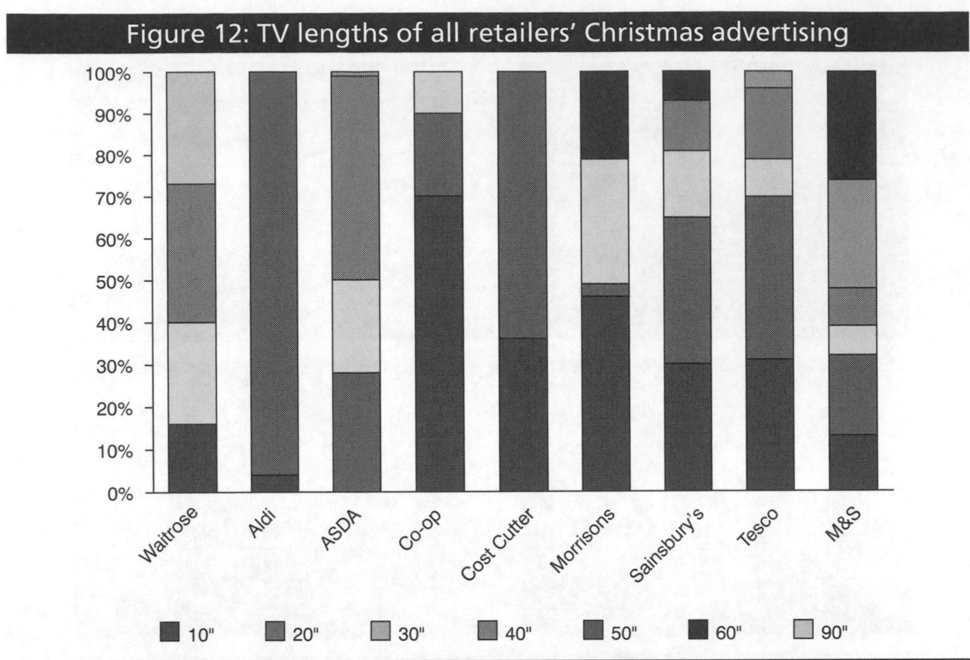


Source: Nielsen

Figure 13: Channel mix of Waitrose and competitors over the Christmas period

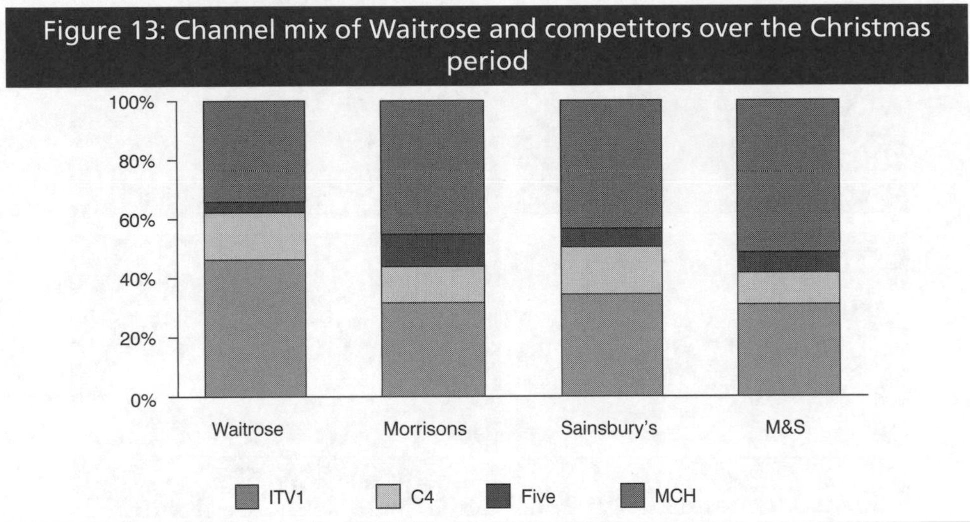


Source: Nielsen

We treated the TV ad as a piece of entertainment in its own right, and in order to generate as much excitement as possible around launch we started our activity before the first airing of the 90" ad, specifically:

- Engaged influential bloggers before the campaign launched to generate word of mouth for the new product launches.

- Premiered the TV ad on YouTube for the first time, generating 368,000 views in the first week, before launching on TV.
- Ran 24-hour roadblocks and skip-able pre rolls across mobile and YouTube to ensure consumers had a chance to watch the 90" ad on catch-up.

### *Making it easy*

In order to make the communication as inclusive as possible, all of the above activity acted as a gateway to further digital content, aimed at making it easy to create a great Christmas. We enabled users to be brought fully into the 'Waitrose School of Magic' no matter which touch-point they saw first.

- Across the TV ads we enabled 'green button' activity, which allowed users to record and access useful longer-form tutorials.
- In a TV media first we included the Blippar augmented reality graphic. At the end of the 90" 'School of Magic' ad, the viewer was invited to 'pause and blipp' their screen to access exclusive Heston or Delia content on their mobile or iPad (Figure 14).
- On the cover wrap of the *Metro*, readers were allowed to bring to life the magical Christmas products, and link through to recipes and Facebook and YouTube content, via the Blippar app on their mobiles.

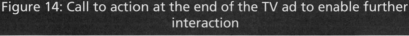

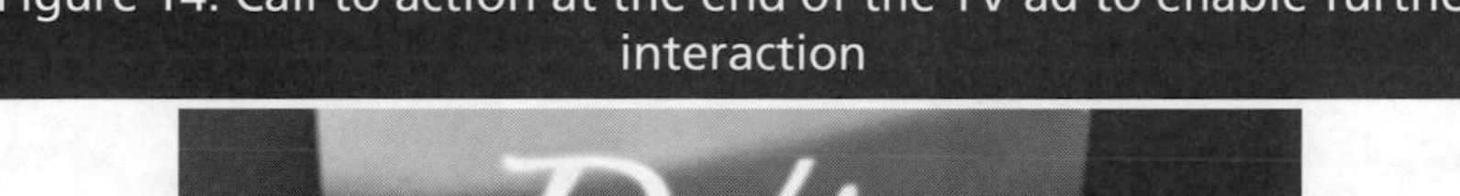
Figure 14: Call to action at the end of the TV ad to enable further interaction

Facebook became the hub of all 'School of Magic' content, and provided windows into everything throughout the whole period:

- live Q&As weekly with guest experts, including the Waitrose cookery school chefs;
- additional Delia and Heston recipe and how-to videos;
- a useful 'big day planner' which allowed consumers to plan their meal and calculate all the timings required. All of which was share-enabled.

Twitter enabled chef Dhruv Baker and wine expert Olly Smith to talk to Waitrose customers (23,000 followers) and their own 27,000 followers to prepare for the early Christmas party season.

Outside of social media we also ran:

- a live web-chat on Mumsnet with Delia Smith;
- Delia and Heston recipe content across the key foodie websites within banners.

Press was predominately used to deliver the offer message. Half page double-page spreads created stand-out and showcased the weekly offers in a format recognised as Waitrose (Figure 15).

Figure 15: The 'School of magic' through the line

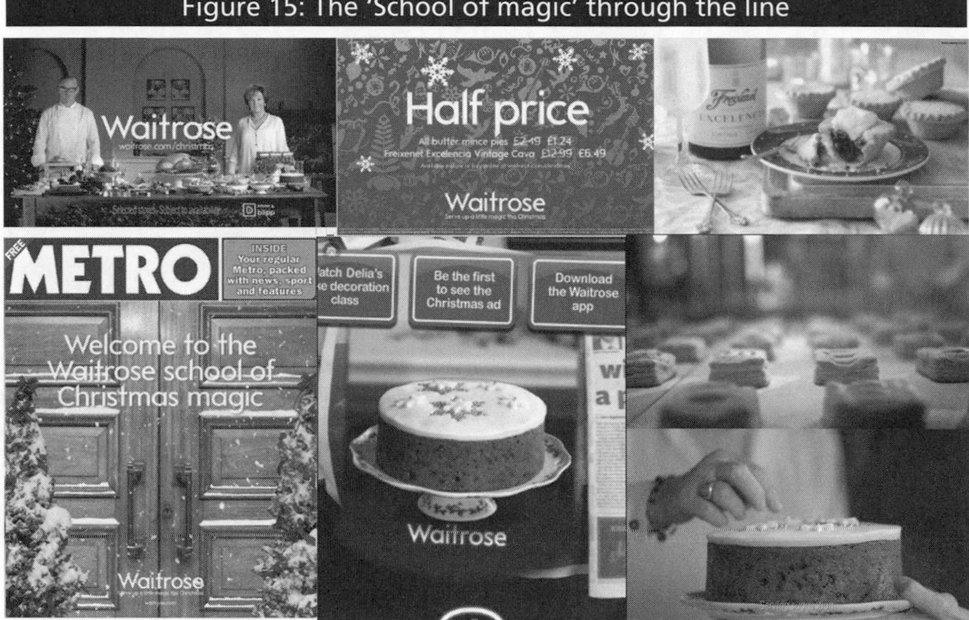


## Delivering the best Christmas ever

The overall market didn't continue to grow at the rate of Christmas 2010.[17] However, Waitrose delivered their best Christmas ever (Figure 16).

## Delivering a better Christmas than M&S and Sainsbury's

Waitrose grew sales more than their closest competitors, almost twice the rate of Sainsbury's and at twice the rate of the market. Not only this, but the only people to outperform us were the big discount retailers, Aldi, Iceland and Lidl (Figure 17).

Figure 16: Christmas sales from the model

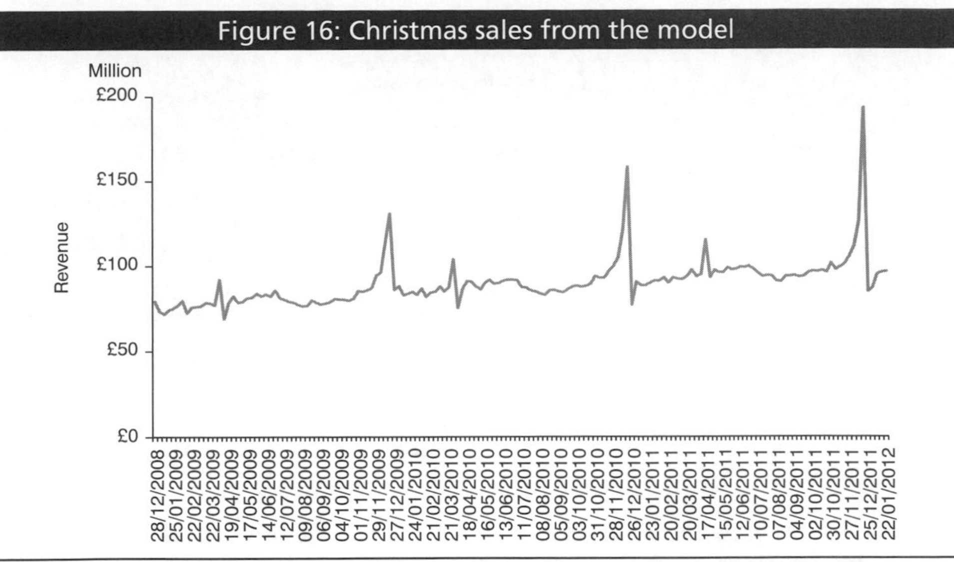


Source: Waitrose/BrandScience

Figure 17: Christmas sales across the grocery market

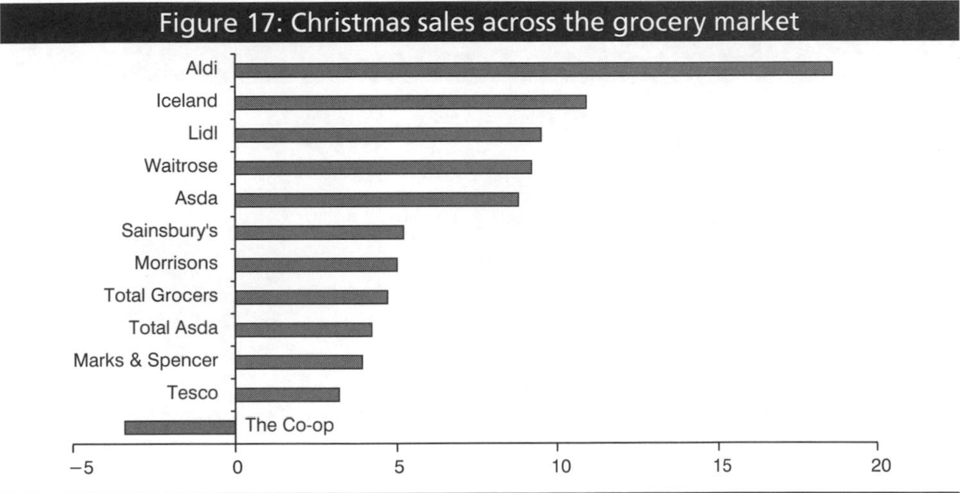


Source: Kantar Worldpanel, Total Food & Grocery, 12 w/e 25 December 2011

## Delivering the best like-for-like growth in the sector

From a marketing point of view, more importantly, Waitrose delivered the best like-for-like sales growth in the grocery market of 3.8%, ahead of M&S and Sainsbury's (Table 1).

**Table 1: Food retailers' performance Christmas 2011***

| | Like-for-like growth |
|---|---|
| Waitrose | 3.8% |
| M&S | 3.0% |
| Sainsbury's | 2.1% |
| Morrisons | 0.7% |
| Co-op | -0.2% |
| Tesco | -2.3% |

Source: Verdict
*Asda, Aldi, Iceland and Lidl have been excluded as they don't release their like-for-like growth figures

Having said what we achieved, now we'll explain how we did it.

## The communication punched above its weight

With the lowest spend in the market and only a 6% share of voice, Waitrose had to punch above their weight in order to cut through. The communication proved to be incredibly efficient and delivered the best awareness per £1 spent in the market with a ratio of 1:2.2 (Table 2).

**Table 2: Share of spend vs. share of total advertising awareness**

| | 2011 Christmas spend (Nov–Dec) | Share of spend (%) | Share of awareness (%) | Efficiency ratio |
|---|---|---|---|---|
| Asda | £25,445,942 | 25 | 15 | 1:0.6 |
| Tesco | £21,932,669 | 22 | 18 | 1:0.8 |
| Morrisons | £17,213,074 | 18 | 15 | 1:0.8 |
| Sainsbury's | £14,650,614 | 15 | 15 | 1:1.2 |
| M&S | £12,731,198 | 13 | 13 | 1:1.5 |
| Waitrose | £6,326,223 | 6 | 13 | 1:2.2 |

Source: Nielsen, and Waitrose Advertising and Brand Tracking study. Base: all respondents interviewed Christmas 2011: 4 November 2011–5 January 2012 (1,829)

## The communication was more inclusive

With 1.5 million views of our Christmas content across social channels, this placed Waitrose in the top ten YouTube branded channels on the site (with 3,000+ positive comments).[18]

- Waitrose had the highest interaction rate from Facebook page posts in the grocery sector peaking at 0.3%,[19] and at its peak, 36% of the fanbase were interacting.[20] Facebook fans and Twitter followers grew organically by 15% over the period.[21]

- Thirty-nine per cent of users who viewed banner video content viewed it in full. The industry average in retail is 6.4%, so engagement was five times the average. Also 18% of skippable ads on YouTube were viewed in full, 3% above average, and rich media average dwell time from mobile was an impressive 91 seconds.
- In total Waitrose had 42,000 'blipps' from 11,500 unique users, equating to an average frequency of 3.7.
- Waitrose was deemed the most successful supermarket in social media at Christmas in the UK with 92% of those interactions likely to buy from Waitrose at Christmas vs. just 82% on average for the sector.[22]

## The communication delivered magic and ease

The core message of inspiration and passion was cutting through most strongly with 74% of people agreeing that they are passionate about food. Importantly 67% of people also agreed that Waitrose has ideas to make Christmas easy (Figure 18).

Figure 18: Prompted impressions of Waitrose from the TV advertising

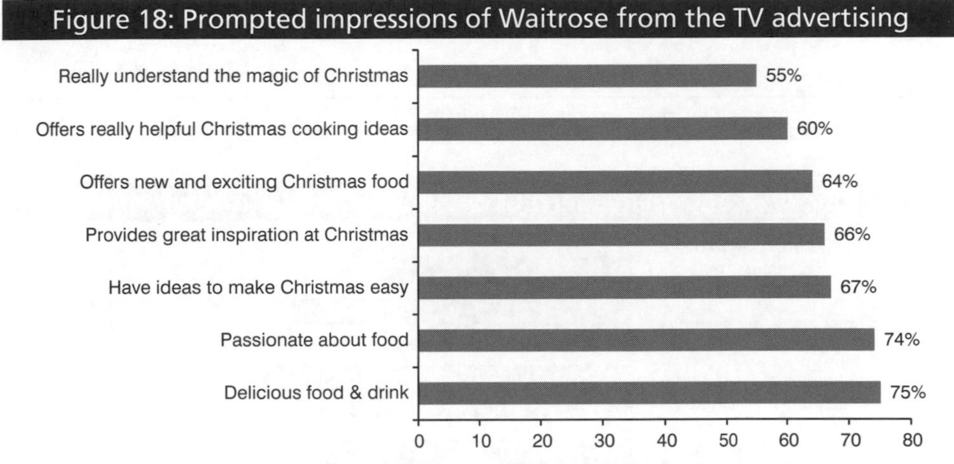


Source: Waitrose Brand and Advertising Tracking Study 2011. Base: all who recognise Waitrose advertising

Furthermore, verbatim comments demonstrate that the festive/magical tone of the advertising cut through and built anticipation around the festive period (Figure 19).

## The communication worked for all customers

Though our main aim this Christmas was to bring in lighter shoppers, the campaign was a success among Waitrose's customers (Figure 20).

## Figure 19: Quantitative research word cloud on what was liked about the TV advertising

**What was liked about TV advertising – Brand Ads**

*All those who are more likely to consider shopping at Waitrose as a result of the Brand TV advertising*

"The feel of it is almost like a Harry Potter class, which lends itself well to the Christmas theme. It is very homely and family-like."
*Secondary/ Bronze Shopper*

"It made me remember Christmases in the past, evoked good memories, made me want to cook the cake as well."
*Secondary/ Bronze Shopper*

christmas fun heston magic innovative really food like easy great style cakes captures looks different interesting idea magical modern informative something music cooking mince traditional advert delia christmassy ideas warm feel good love homely adverts feeling waitrose chef new exciting quality products feels look pies festive makes friendly product engaging theme warmth chefs shows spirit make

"That it was really magical and very Christmassy. Showed a lot of the food up close."
*Secondary/ Bronze Shopper*

I love the Harry Potter theme. The idea of the school of Christmas magic is great. I love the whole Christmas theme, the music is enchanting, the school is warm, cosy and exciting. The food is simply mouth-watering! Just leave you with a warm cosy feeling inside."
*Primary/ Gold Shopper*

"It's festive, fun, somewhat traditional but modern and the presence of Delia and Heston improves the credibility."
*Light/ Bronze Shopper*

Source: Consumer insight debrief, 775 people familiar with the advertising

## Figure 20: Brand image perceptions among all Waitrose shoppers

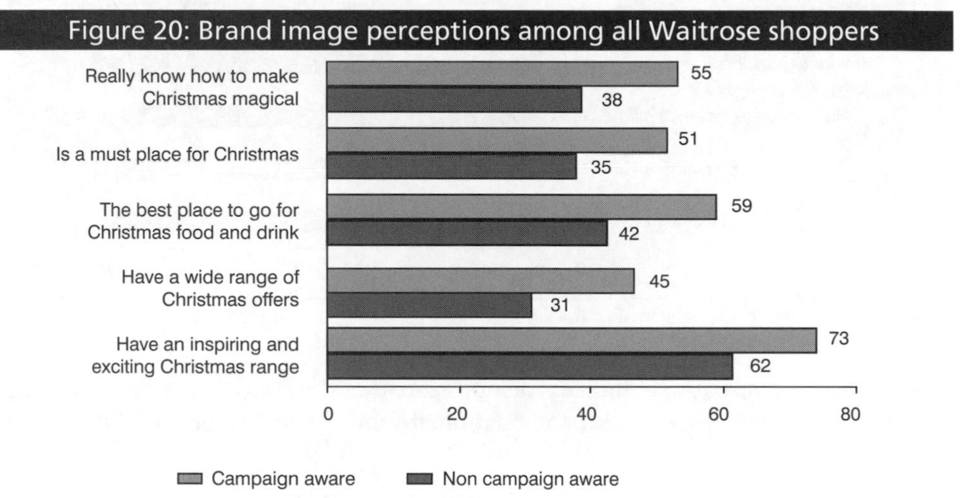

## The communication worked for lighter customers

Importantly, perceptions of Waitrose dramatically improved amongst lighter shoppers who were aware of the advertising, with half endorsing Waitrose as the best place to go for Christmas food and drink and believing that Waitrose is a 'must' place to go at Christmas (Figure 21).

Figure 21: Brand image perceptions among lighter Waitrose shoppers

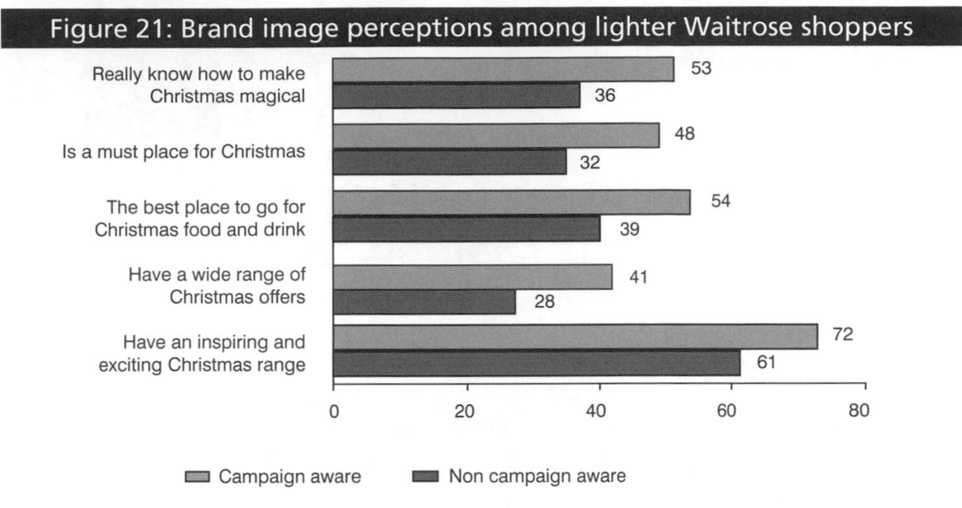


Source: Waitrose brand and tracking study. Base: medium/light Waitrose shoppers

## The communication brought in lighter customers

As we planned, over Christmas, growth was not driven by frequency but through attracting shopper volume (Figures 22a and b).

Figure 22a: 2011 Christmas sales were driven via shopper volume

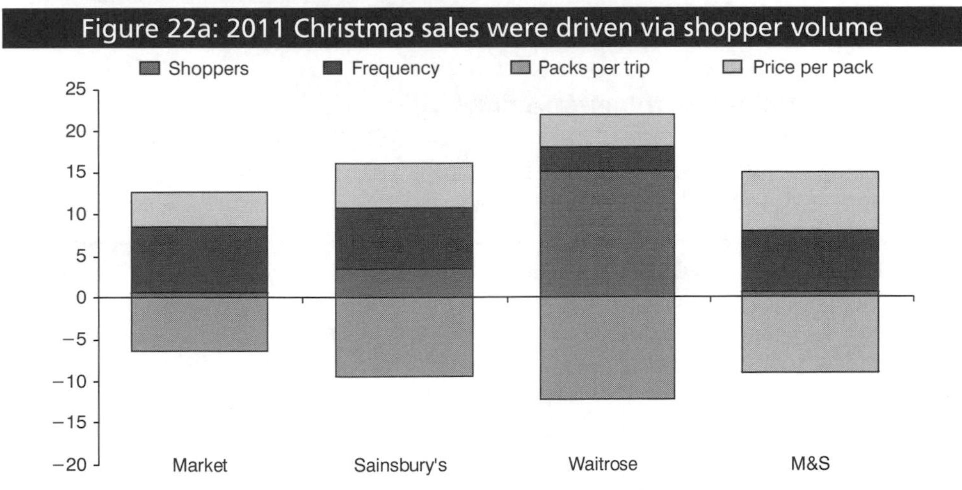


Source: Kantar Worldpanel, 4 w/e 26 December 2011

Figure 22b: 2010 Christmas sales were driven via shopper frequency

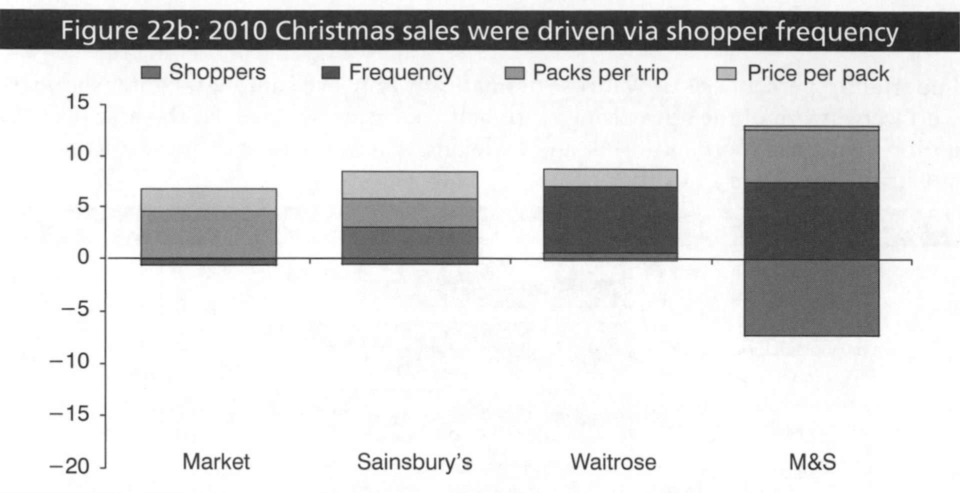


Source: Kantar Worldpanel, 4 w/e 26 December 2010

This was achieved by more people purchasing from Waitrose over the Christmas period (Figure 23).

And through Waitrose increasing their share of overall UK household wallets by 7%. Most importantly we grew share of wallet of our hardest (bronze) customers by 11% (Figure 24).

Figure 23: We increased the percentage of the population that purchased in Waitrose over Christmas

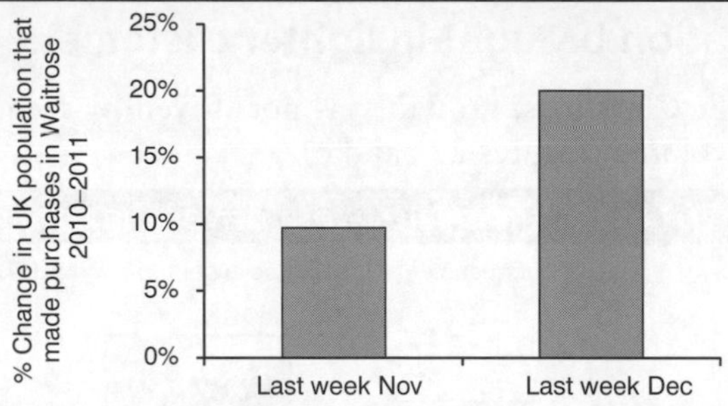


Source: Kantar Worldpanel

Figure 24: We increased our share of wallet with lighter shoppers

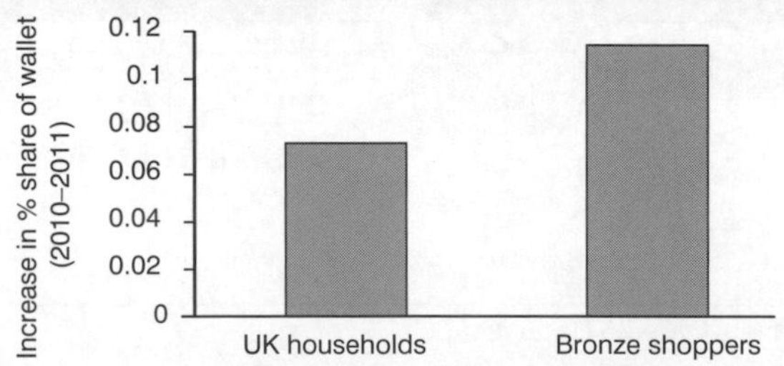


Source: Kantar Total Grocery 8 w/e data 26 December 2010 and 8 w/e data 25 December 2011

## Discounting other factors: nothing could have done it better than communications

### *The brand ambassadors*

Delia and Heston are great assets to the brand. However, these two brand ambassadors were used during the same Christmas period in 2010.

### *New store openings*

The figures in this paper have strictly been like-for-like, and all new stores or stores with sizable developments have been discounted in the BrandScience econometric model. Christmas design and store layouts were similar to the year before.

### *More products on promotion*

Waitrose increased their promotions from 2010 (as shown previously). The model has taken promotions into account and has found them to be a small percentage of the sales uplift.

### *NPD*

We would be the first to acknowledge that Waitrose has fantastic products. There were new hero products from Delia and Heston (stuffing kit, mince pies and a chocolate bouche). The part they played was accounted for in the model.

### *Competitive activity*

Not only were Waitrose outspent by their competitors but the other retailers also captured both value and quality in their advertising. For example, Sainsbury's 'Panto' extravaganza featured celebrity chef Jamie Oliver. M&S heroed their treat products including their Christmas pudding with edible gold dust. Morrisons had their 'Food market' and Asda majored on their partnership with Leith's cookery school (Figure 25).

**Figure 25: Christmas 2011 advertising**

### *Online sales*

Online sales are a relatively small proportion of the total sales and this has been taken into account in the model.

### *Inflation*

Inflation did affect food prices in the run up to Christmas.[23] However, Kantar data clearly shows that it was more shoppers and not increased prices that mainly drove sales. Also, inflation is taken into account in the econometric model.

Calculating the true effect of variables impacting on Waitrose revenue requires marketing-mix modelling, which BrandScience have built in order to understand the payback from the advertising.

## Calculating short-term payback

BrandScience have calculated the profit ROI to be £1.89 (by applying a 32% industry standard profit margin). Proving that advertising can pay back in the short term.

The model has been used by Waitrose for the last three years. The KPI used for the modelling is Waitrose weekly store sales revenue. Because we are modelling total revenue instead of like-for-like, the factors include effect of new store openings, price inflation, promotion, seasonality and underlying growth (Figure 26).

**Figure 26: Decomposition of Waitrose total revenue model**

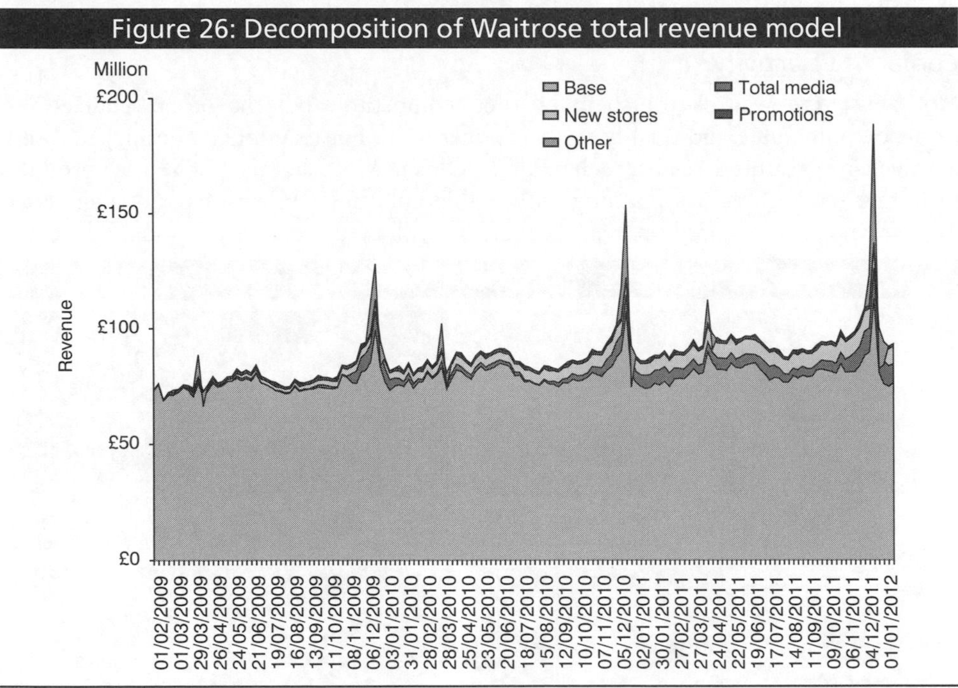


Source: Waitrose/BrandScience

## Lasting effects

It is too early to measure long-term effects of the advertising but we have seen an uplift in customers coming to Waitrose in the first quarter of 2012 compared to Q1 2011 (Figure 27).

Figure 27: Growth of customers year-on-year

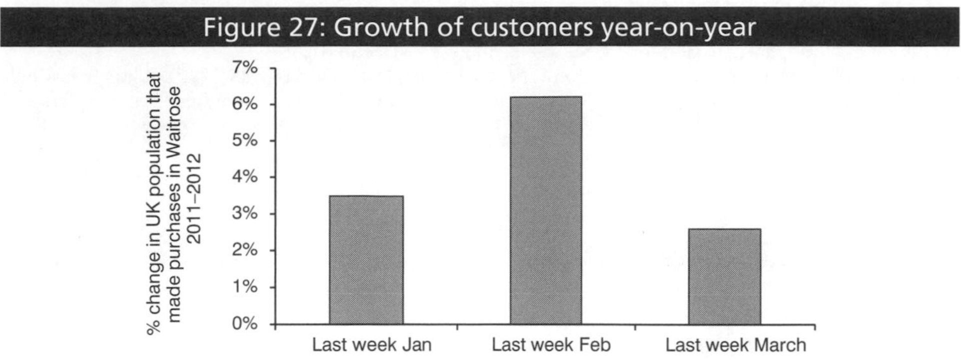


Source: Kantar Worldpanel

## In conclusion: the best Christmas for everyone

This is the story of how brave marketing decisions delivered the best Christmas Waitrose has ever had.

The brave decision to stay true to themselves and invest in brand when competitors would be spending heavily promoting their offers.

The brave decision to listen to what customers were saying (spend less) but deliver what they really wanted (a magical Christmas).

The brave decision to shift from a successful cookery show format to a 'School of magic' in order to reach out and make the brand more inclusive.

And, at the end of a hard year, help customers have their best Christmas.

> *The driving force behind Waitrose' increased sales for Christmas 2011 was the continuing consumer desire to trade up. This is particularly evident at Christmas where entertaining friends and family with indulgent foods is a priority. Consumers increased spend on entertaining at home to compensate for less disposable income in dining out over the festive season. The quality and added value associated with Waitrose' Christmas offer negated some of the shopper price sensitivity which has risen with inflation throughout 2011.*
>
> Cliona Lynch, senior retail analyst, Verdict

## Notes

1. Kantar till-roll data.
2. Waitrose and Kantar.
3. Kantar Worldpanel, Total Food & Grocery, 23 days, ending 23 December 2011.
4. Kantar, Total food and grocery market, 8 week ending 25 December 2011.

5 Waitrose categorise their customers as 'gold' (who spend 50% of their grocery shop in Waitrose), 'silver' (who spend 10–50% in Waitrose) and 'bronze' (who spend below 10% in Waitrose). In this paper Kantar data also refers to heavy/medium/light customers which is very similar as the split is 50% for heavy, 30% for medium and 20% for light. In this paper we refer to 'lighter' customers by which we mean those medium and light (or silver and bronze).
6 Kantar.
7 Office of National Statistics.
8 Waitrose.
9 Kantar Worldpanel, Total Grocery, 52 week ending 18 March 2012.
10 In 2010 Sainsbury's total media budget according to Nielson was £18,883,576. Looking over their 2010 campaign Manning Gottlieb OMD estimated roughly 61% went behind promoting offers and 39% went behind brand. This would have meant circa £11,518,981 spent on promoting offers alone.
11 Manning Gottlieb OMD.
12 Nielson.
13 The Source qualitative debrief, Christmas 2011.
14 The Source qualitative debrief, Christmas 2011.
15 Manning Gottlieb OMD.
16 Manning Gottlieb OMD estimation.
17 Kantar figures showed that while in 2010 year-on-year Christmas sales grew by 5.2%, 2011 year-on-year Christmas sales were 4.7%.
18 Manning Gottlieb OMD.
19 Allfacebookstats.
20 Facebook Insights.
21 Manning Gottlieb OMD.
22 Starcom SMBI.
23 ONS.

## Chapter 30

# Yorkshire Tea

## Taking Yorkshire Tea to the world: the story of Little Urn

**By Jamie Inman and Zoe Crowther, Beattie McGuinness Bungay**
Credited companies: Creative Agency: BMB; Media Agency: MediaCom Manchester; Research Agencies: The Nursery, Brainjuicer; Econometric modelling agency: Ebiquity Research; Client: Taylors of Harrogate

**Editor's summary**

Yorkshire Tea had a goal to become the number two brand in the tea market. To achieve this, their creative solution involved 'Little Urn', a van painted in the style of their iconic packaging. Led by Facebook fans, the van travelled from Britain to America, taking a 'proper brew' to the people who needed it most. Communications charted this Facebook-guided mission, which was then broadcast on television advertisements. In one year value sales increased in Yorkshire from £8.58m to £9.373m, a rise of 9.5%. In the rest of the country, sales rose by 11.6% – from 46.1m to £51.45m. Nationally, Yorkshire Tea market share rose from 12.06% to 13.79%. The judges loved the very simple truth around which this campaign is based; that the English mourn a decent brew when they're abroad. This brand displayed admirable originality; leveraging old and new media to physically bring the brand to life and spread the word to a brand new audience.

This is the story of how a small brand can overcome market inertia and achieve dynamic growth through the right advertising. It is also the story of the relationship between fandom and customer acquisition. It is also, therefore, a working example of the effective integration of social and broadcast communications. It is the story of a blend of 'traditional' television advertising and a 'modern' Facebook engagement platform.

Yorkshire Tea is a brand made to span the traditional and the modern. Based on its Yorkshire roots and incredibly vocal following, Yorkshire Tea had risen to become the number three tea brand in the UK.

Not satisfied with this heady achievement, Yorkshire Tea's owners set themselves an ambitious, long-term target to take the number two spot – presenting the tricky task of broadening our horizons without breaking faith with our traditional heartland.

We are helped by the fact that Yorkshire Tea is a 'proper brew' of acknowledged high quality that inspires consumption above market norms. People who like Yorkshire Tea really like it and drink a lot of it. But we also face considerable inertia to turn people on to Yorkshire Tea's superior qualities – put simply, most British people are happy with the cup of tea they have. And existing brand preferences are reinforced by some of the most established brand properties in British advertising – the tea folk, the monkey, and the 'oo' in Typhoo.

Achieving these lofty ambitions would require sending the brand 'away from home' in search of new customers. This is no easy challenge. Indeed the heart of our creative solution involved a journey, sending the brand on an epic, global adventure. And in doing so we not only attracted new customers from beyond our heartland, but also further increased our share within Yorkshire.

The Little Urn campaign commenced only a year ago, but the story so far includes one of the rarest of things in FMCG marketing – a return on investment in the short term.

## Let's have a proper brew

Yorkshire Tea is owned by Taylors of Harrogate, established in 1886 and to this day an independent family-run business.

Yorkshire Tea work hard to deliver a high quality cup of tea. Behind the scenes they have an army of tasters, buyers and blenders whose attention to detail is second to none, even making a blend specifically for hard water areas. They could be described as the Maître d's of tea – quietly yet passionately working to make sure their tea is top notch. This commitment to quality is summed up by the endline, 'Let's have a proper brew', a proper Yorkshire call to arms.

## At home in Yorkshire

Yorkshire Tea had grown slowly and steadily over many years to the point where it was number three in the market behind PG Tips and Tetley.

Yorkshire Tea has a strong presence in the north. Market share in its home county of Yorkshire was 18.68% by value at the beginning of this period (vs. a national share of 11.36%).

The iconography of the Yorkshire Tea box, featuring rolling hills, plays to the appeal of traditional Yorkshire and is their most recognisable asset (Figure 1).

Figure 1: Yorkshire Tea Standard Blend 80 pack

When we refer to Yorkshire Tea's heartland, we have this regional strength in mind. There is a demographic heartland as well, with the vast majority of sales coming from older shoppers (Figure 2).

Figure 2: Value sales by age (£000)

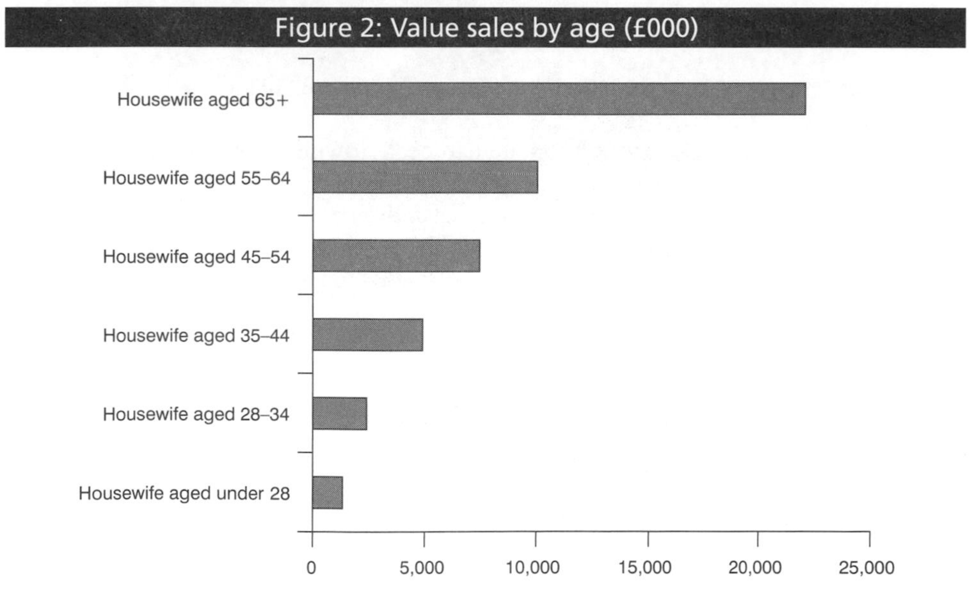


Source: Kantar, February 2011

Yorkshire Tea's heartland is loyal to the point that it is a rare exception to the Ehrenberg-Bass Double Jeopardy Law. This law (or 'generalisation') observes that brands with higher market share have far more buyers, and these buyers are slightly more loyal.

In 2010 Yorkshire Tea had a rather lower number of buyers than its share of sales would suggest, but they are much more loyal and drink a lot more Yorkshire Tea (Figure 3).

Figure 3: Penetration vs. volume by brand

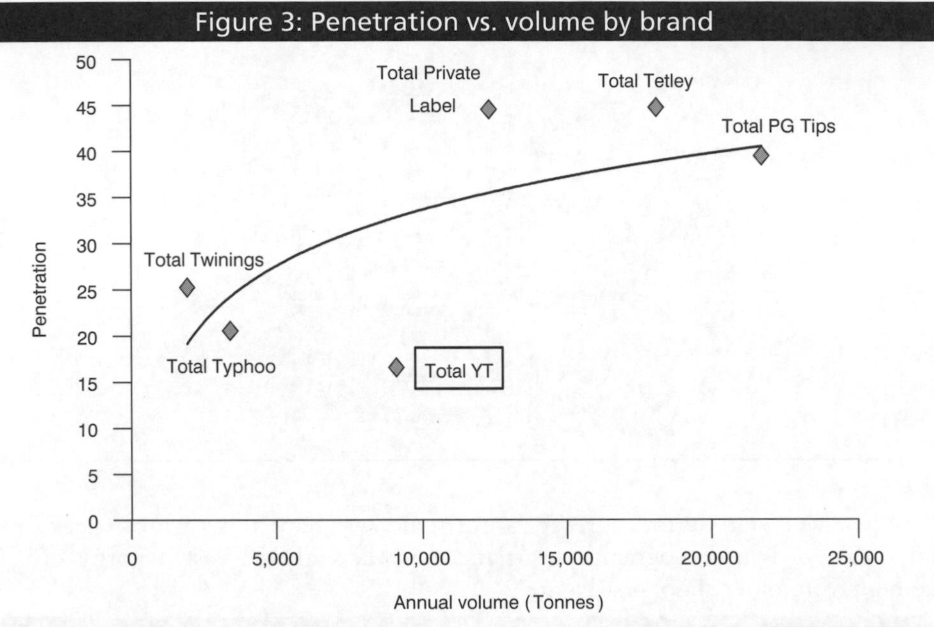


Source: Kantar, week ending 4 September 2011

And those buyers were buying much more Yorkshire Tea than market norms (Figure 4).

Much of Yorkshire Tea's growth to date had been down to word-of-mouth and the appeal of the pack. In the heartland, people 'got' Yorkshire Tea in a big way. Equally, lots of other people buying tea did not, or at least, did not yet. Yorkshire Tea is a small brand with a big following that could grow. If the passion of the fans could be shared with new audiences in the right way, there was room to grow.

## Big ambitions

At the end of 2010 Taylors of Harrogate set themselves a new long-term target – for Yorkshire Tea to become the number two brand in the market.

The marketing team would have to find a way to reach out to new audiences, both in the heartland and beyond, and excite them with the promise of a proper brew.

Figure 4: Average weight of purchase vs. volume by brand

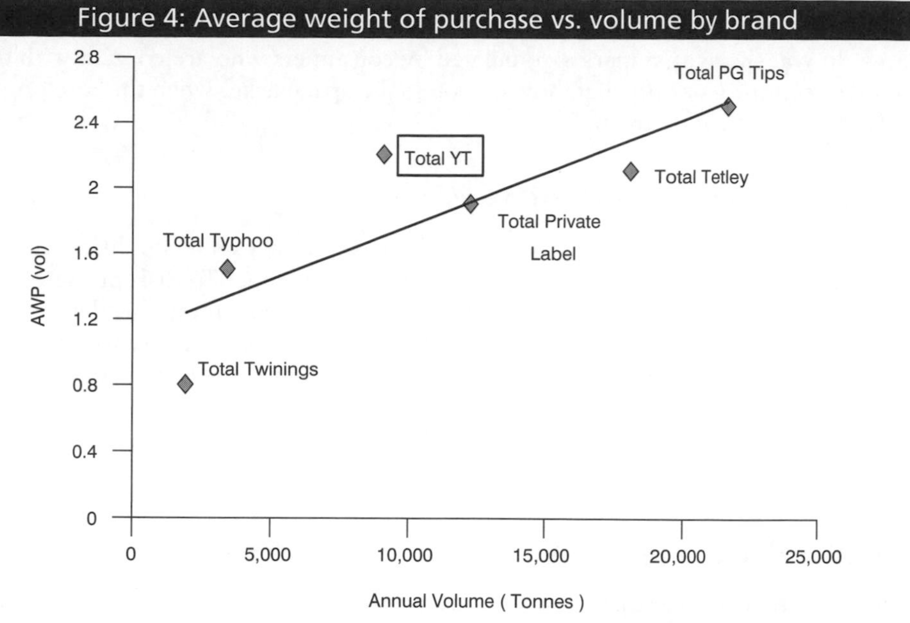


Source: Kantar, week ending 4 September 2011

We identified three barriers:

### 1. Taste

People tend to buy their tea very habitually – in effect they are in a 'tea trance', blind to the difference in quality between brands. For all that there are differences between different makes of tea, rational claims about superiority have limited value. Facts are unlikely to deliver a creative platform with sufficient scale and energy to break habits and establish new ones.

It is also tricky to assert that better quality tea will deliver better emotional benefits. The emotion of the tea moment is well-worn terrain for brands in the category. Without careful thought, the danger is that we find ourselves claiming that 'our' tea moment is better than 'their' tea moment. Why would a fan of PG Tips or Tetley find that to be more credible than the claim made by their own brand?

Yorkshire Tea needed a different approach to make people realise that not all tea is created equal.

### 2. Tradition

Yorkshire Tea values are a perfect fit for the category, but it is easy for them to be presented in a way that reinforces traditional, old-fashioned aspects of the brand. An earlier campaign for the brand had used John Shuttleworth to champion the wonders of Yorkshire. It worked reasonably well in business terms but less well in brand terms. In the heartland, Yorkshire people rejected what they perceived to be a stereotyped view of their county. Beyond the heartland, the campaign did not resonate strongly either.

We needed a fresh and contemporary vehicle, which nevertheless embodied Yorkshire Tea's timeless values.

*3. Tension (lack of)*

How do you shake up a market populated by consumers who are content with their brand selection? Not only that, how do you shake up a market when the core product benefit is in fact contentment?

## A proposition in search of a crisis

In a market premised on contentment and inertia, and consumers indifferent to the differences between products, we faced a mighty challenge. To disrupt the market, we would need to seek out some drama, where we could dramatise the merits of Yorkshire Tea, without losing sight of the essentially un-dramatic essence of tea.

We needed a bigger stage to showcase the power of a proper brew and to spread the fame of Yorkshire Tea. This led to the creative proposition:

Yorkshire Tea hates it when bad tea happens to good people.

But who were the good people and what was Yorkshire Tea going to do about it?

## A new relationship between loyal fans and new users

There is little evidence that growing a vibrant social media community can succeed as an acquisition strategy. The evidence, such as it is, suggests that social works better in rewarding existing users. The people at Yorkshire Tea have an intuitive understanding of this. Long ago, they would make a point of replying to customer letters on the same day they arrived. Each response would be handwritten with a fountain pen. Fast-forward to the era of Facebook. Yorkshire Tea are participating in a lively conversation with Yorkshire Tea fans.

In the conversation between Yorkshire Tea and its fans we discovered the raw materials for our campaign. A large proportion of the 12,000 group members were British people living outside the UK, not a huge group in Facebook terms but hugely inspirational in creative terms. These people would praise Yorkshire Tea to the skies. They would do it, however, from a position of some distress. They lived in places where a proper brew was impossible to come by. This was a real world experiment in deprivation research. The passion of the fan abandoned by circumstance, communicated to Yorkshire Tea in social media, could fuel a broader conversation with new users.

Meanwhile, the people at Yorkshire Tea had been travelling around Britain making tea in a little ice cream van, painted in the livery of their iconic packaging. The van is known affectionately amongst staff as 'Little Urn'. It symbolises many of the things that are good about Yorkshire Tea. It is humble. It is plucky, never deterred from its task. And it is a real, physical example of Yorkshire Tea's mission to come to the rescue of people deprived of a proper brew.

## A heroic mission

We decided to send Little Urn to the place where people needed him most, a place where Brits who knew all about the pleasures of a proper brew had to go without, a place where it is universally acknowledged that you cannot get a good cup of tea.

We sent Little Urn to … the tea desert that is the United States of America.

### *Little Urn in America*

In constructing the full route for the TV campaign we relied on our social media fans to direct us. We asked British people in America (or their friends or family here at home) to alert us to their tea crisis, whereupon we would race to the rescue with a proper cup of tea.

We purposely placed gaps in the story so that tea fans back at home could get involved using Facebook, YouTube and Twitter. For example, with a few hours to spare in sunny San Francisco our Facebook fans challenged us to get Little Urn up San Francisco's steepest hill (Figure 5).

The energy for the adventure would come from social media. But the scale would be delivered by the TV.

We had a rough route in place and we could also seek out some appropriate places for relevant product stories. For example, Nevada has some of the hardest water in the world, which allowed us to create content about our hard water blend.

**Figure 5: Facebook app for Little Urn's trip**

At all times, Yorkshire Tea staff would drive the van. Three TV ads were made in total (Figure 6).

## Figure 6: TV creative

**Nevada**

Little Urn heads to Nevada to rescue Brits from terrible tea. After a night in Las Vegas, the ad climaxes in a little tea party by the Grand Canyon.

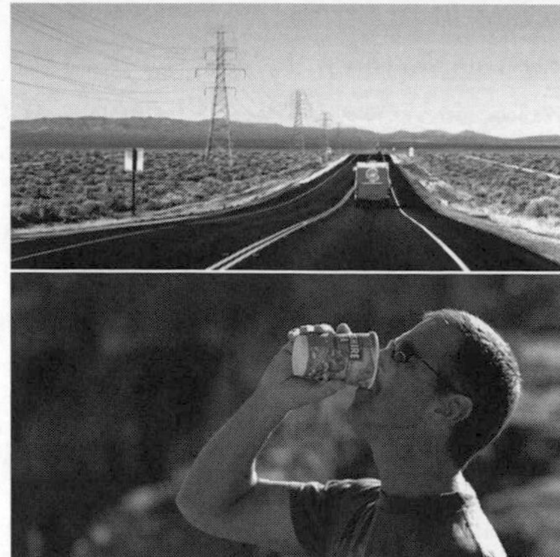

**Florida**

Florida is home to half a million Brits, all of them making do with terrible tea. Little Urn heads to the rescue.

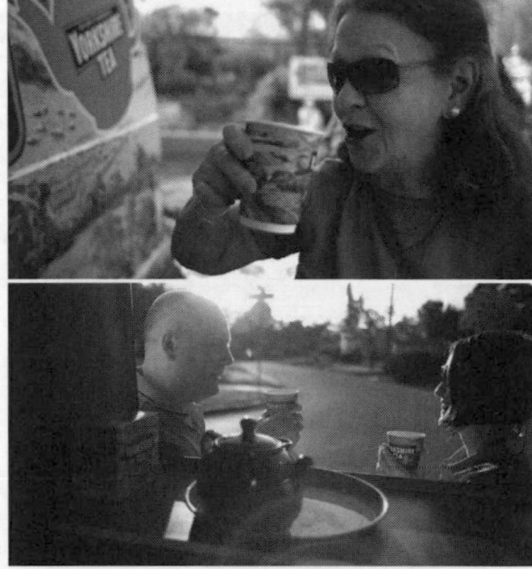

**Best Bits**

Best Bits is a montage ad featuring the best bits from the previous two ads and highlights from all the other footage.

In addition to the ads, we produced seven long-form films to document each leg of their stateside journey, documenting the wonderful and eccentric Brits abroad who requested a proper brew. From a car salesman from Essex to the owners of 'Tea and Sympathy', an original British Tea shop in New York. On top of these longer docs, we produced countless ad hoc video snippets for our 'Brew Tube' page and Facebook, so fans could follow our journey every step of the way. These video snippets allowed followers to interact with our journey – from deciding where we went next, to votes and dares.

The campaign ran on TV in four bursts with additional spend supporting the activity on Facebook (Table 1).

Table 1: Media schematic

| | Feb | Mar | April | | June | | Aug | | Feb | Mar |
|---|---|---|---|---|---|---|---|---|---|---|
| TV | | | | | | | | | | |
| Facebook support | | | | | | | | | | |

Source: A new burst began on 27 February 2012, too late to be covered by this paper

## A powerful campaign vehicle

Sending Little Urn to America (Figure 7) was an unusual advertising approach for the tea category. But it was an idea that, once conceived, had an extraordinary capacity to unlock new meaning for Yorkshire Tea (Table 2).

Above all, it separated Yorkshire Tea from the rest, helping to spread its fame.

We disrupted the seemingly undisruptable British tea convention of a cosy, comforting, quintessentially British tea moment, while maintaining a strong emotional connection with the essence of tea. Sending Little Urn abroad allowed Yorkshire Tea to present their commitment to a proper brew to new audiences in a highly original way.

Figure 7: Little Urn hits the road

Source: Launch TV commercial

| Table 2: Shifts delivered by the campaign | |
|---|---|
| **From** | **To** |
| Yorkshire brand | Yorkshire brand representing all Britain |
| Familiar old-world imagery | Unexpected new-world imagery |
| Traditional | 21st century |
| Inward looking | Open-minded exploration |
| Subjective tea claim | Universally recognised tea crisis |
| Third in the UK | Number one in the world |

## In summary – our objectives

We wanted to grow market share by increasing penetration amongst all audiences. We would achieve this by growing the fame of Yorkshire Tea and their commitment to a proper brew.

## So what happened? The results to date

We will review the performance of the campaign from launch (7 February 2011) to the end of February 2012.

### *Value sales for Yorkshire Tea grew in the heartland and beyond*

- Value sales increased in Yorkshire from £8.58m to £9.373m, a rise of 9.5%.
- In the rest of the country, sales rose by 11.6% – from £46.1m to £51.45m (Figure 8).

Figure 8: Value sales Yorkshire Tea (£)

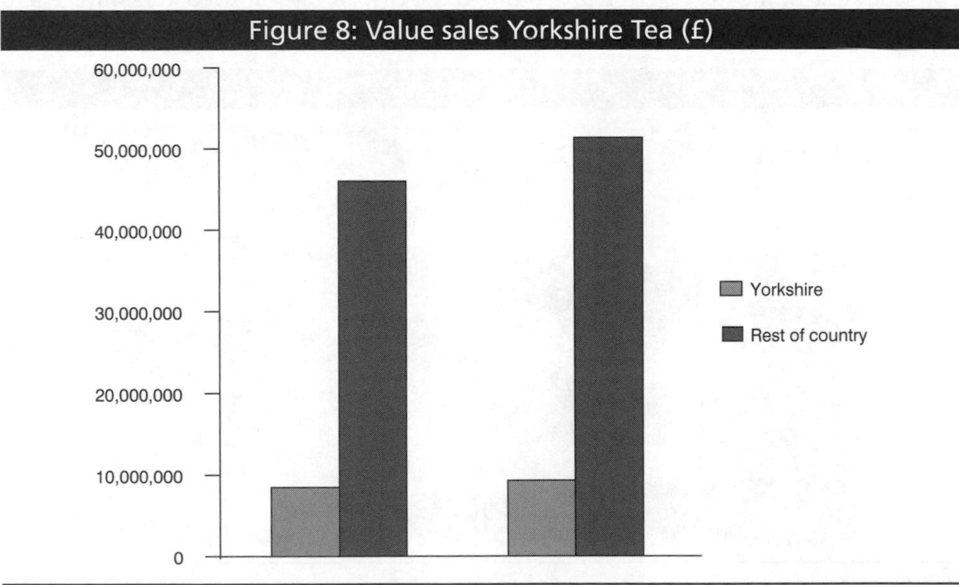


Source: AC Nielsen

*Competitor value sales declined across the board*
(Figure 9)

Figure 9: Value sales by brand (£)

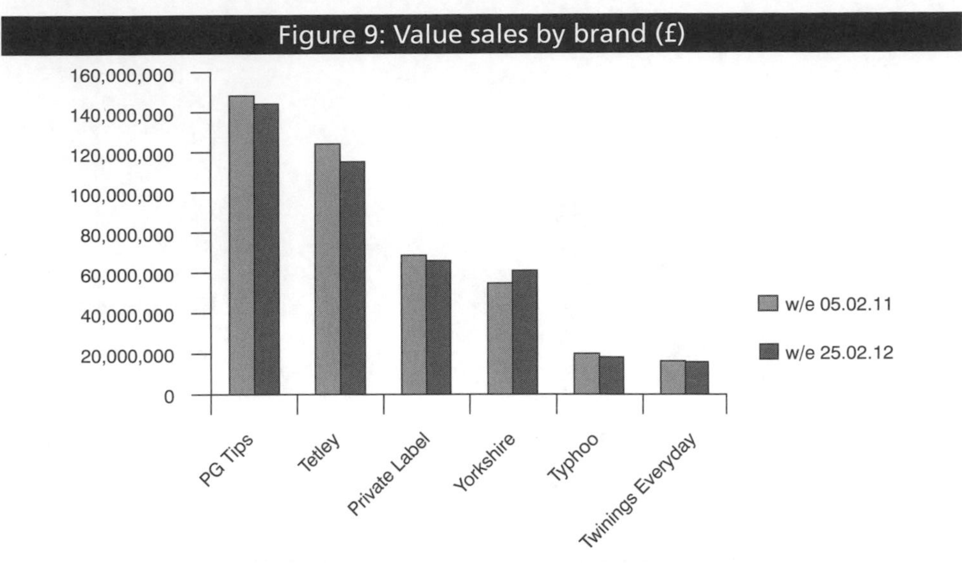


Source: AC Nielsen

*Penetration increased for Yorkshire Tea (and declined for most competitors)*
(Figure 10)

Figure 10: Weighted penetration (%)

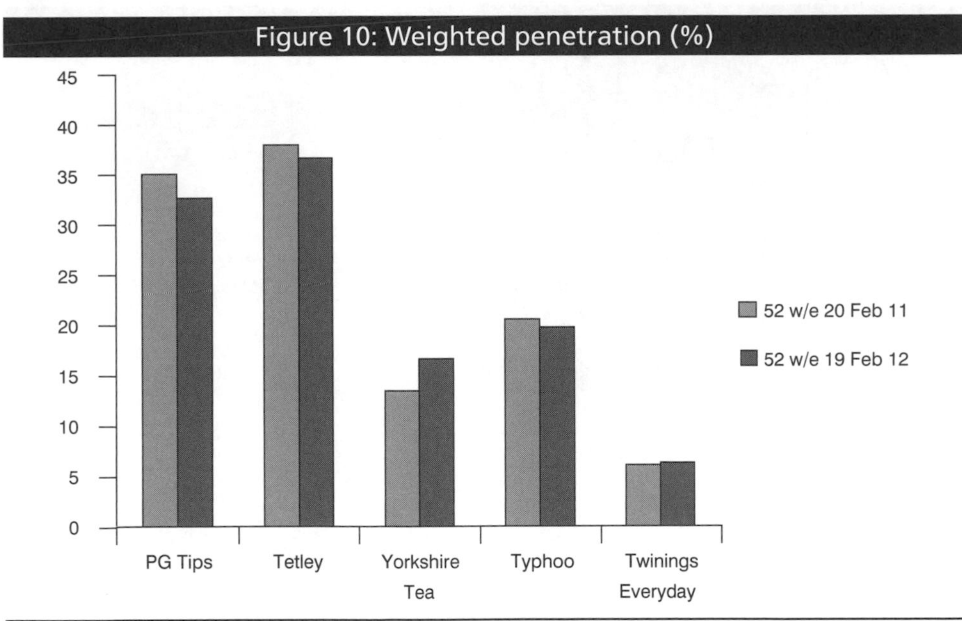


Source: Kantar

*This delivered an increase in market share in Yorkshire ...*

Yorkshire Tea market share in Yorkshire rose from 18.68% to 21.22% (Figure 11).

Figure 11: Market share standard teabags (£)

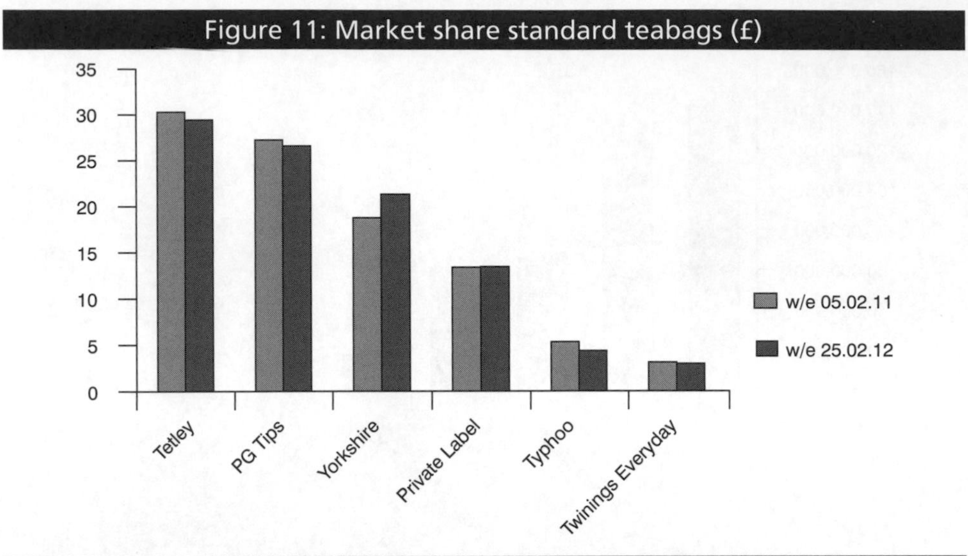


Source: AC Nielsen

*.. and an overall increase in market share nationally*

Yorkshire Tea market share nationally rose from 12.06% to 13.79% (Figure 12).

Figure 12: Market share standard teabags (£)

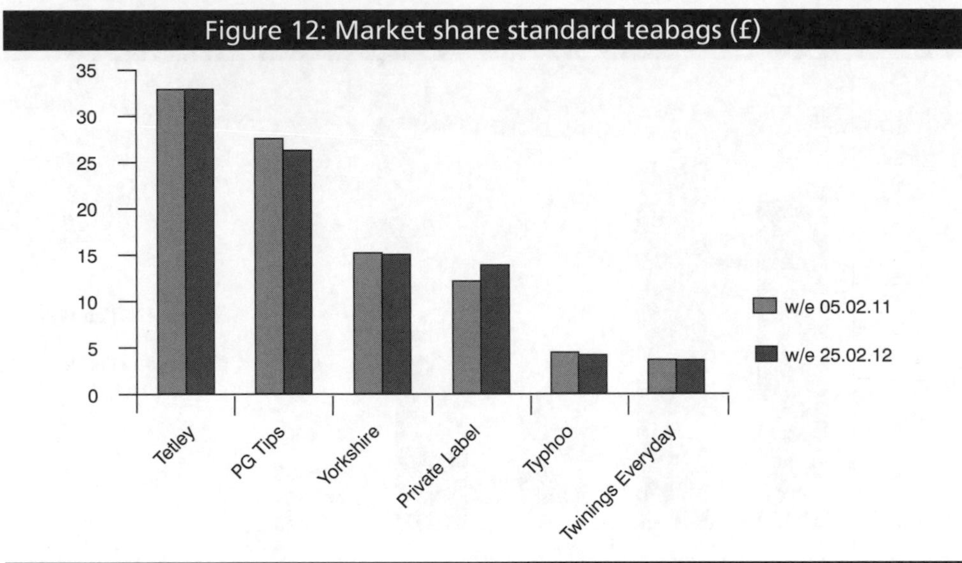


Source: AC Nielsen

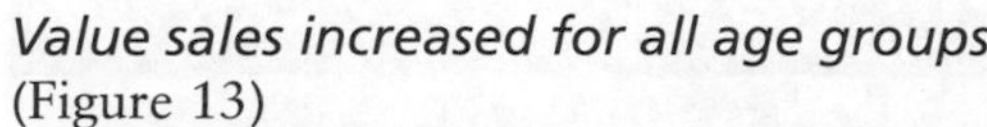

*Value sales increased for all age groups*
(Figure 13)

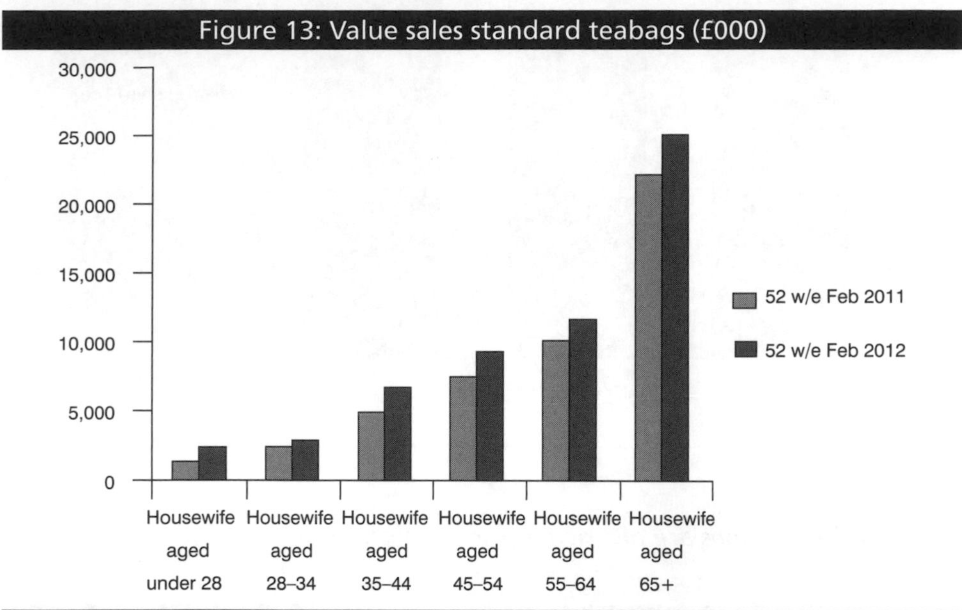


Source: Kantar

*Growth was particularly strong amongst younger shoppers*

Thirty-four per cent of the growth in value sales was delivered by people 44 and under, and the majority, 54%, by people 54 and under.[1]

*Tracking diagnostics show growing brand strength*[2]

Little Urn has delivered Yorkshire Tea's highest ever ad recognition, both for Yorkshire Tea and non-Yorkshire Tea drinkers.

Little Urn ad recognition:
Yorkshire Tea drinkers – 52%
Other Tea drinkers – 41%[3]

*And for ad recognisers, brand attribution is excellent for all audiences*
(Figure 14)

Figure 14: Brand attribution (March 2012)

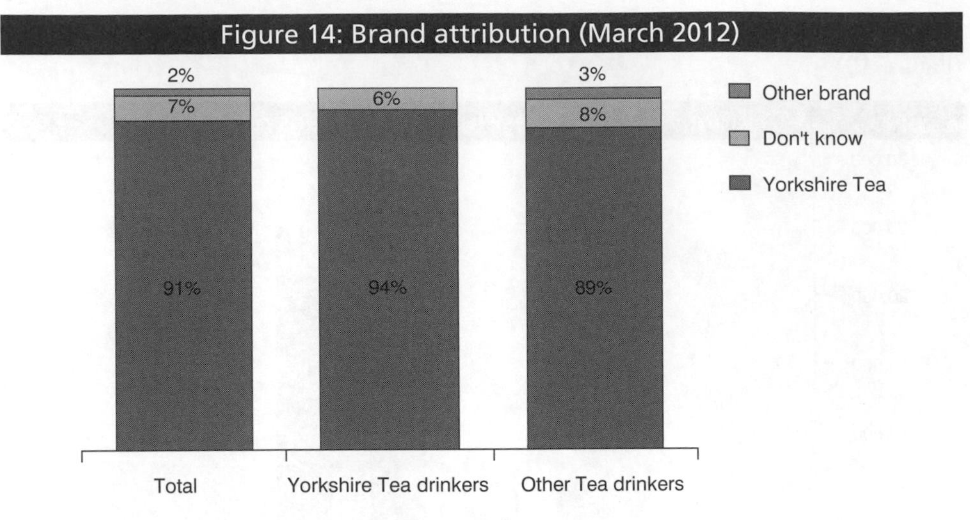


Source: The Nursery

*All the TV executions are distinctive and memorable …*
(Figure 15)

Figure 15: Ad diagnostics (Recognisers)

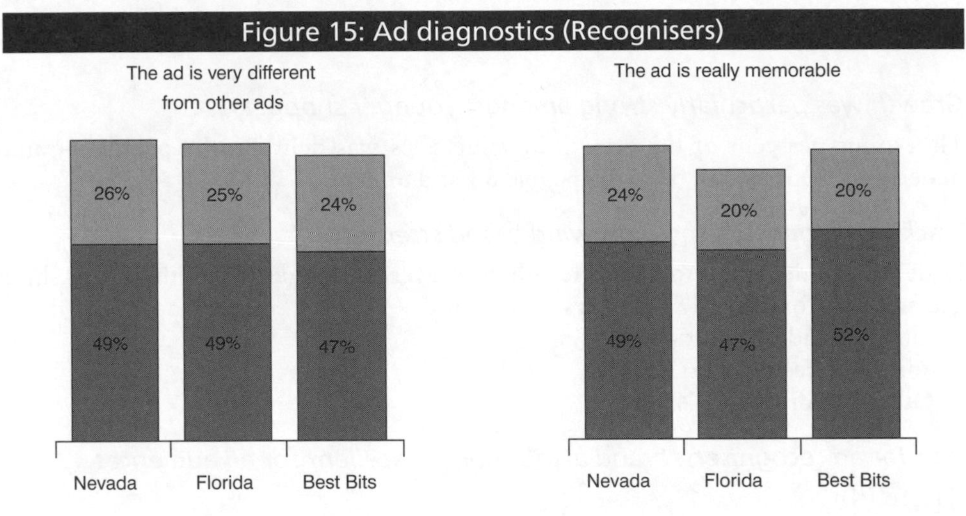


Source: The Nursery

*... and bring joy to the category*
(Figure 16)

Figure 16: Ad diagnostics (Recognisers)

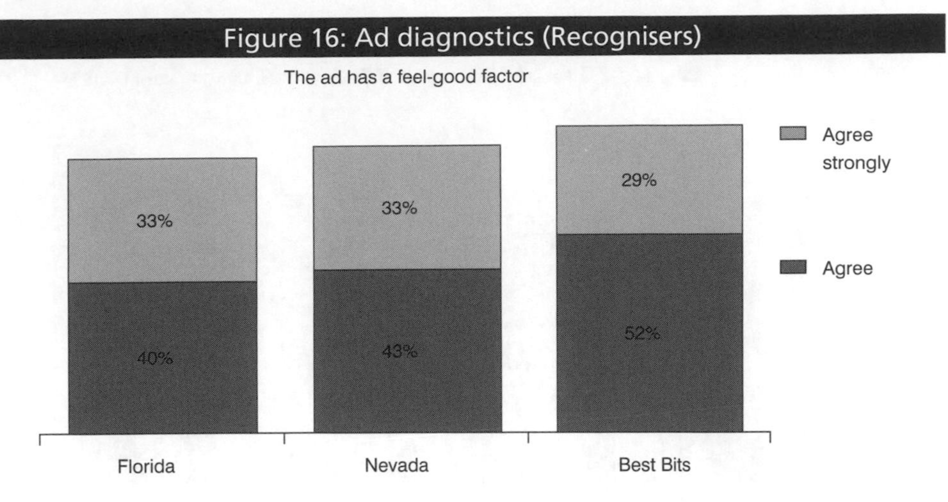


Source: The Nursery

*Spontaneous awareness has grown year-on-year*
(Figure 17)

Figure 17: Spontaneous awareness (first mentions)

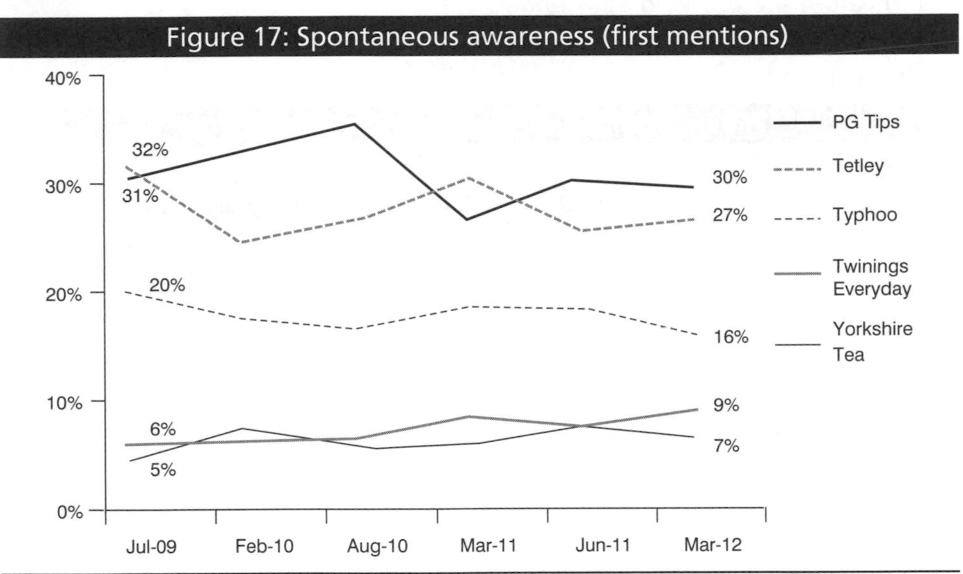


Source: The Nursery

*Successive bursts have delivered category-leading brand momentum*
(Figure 18)

Figure 18: Brand momentum

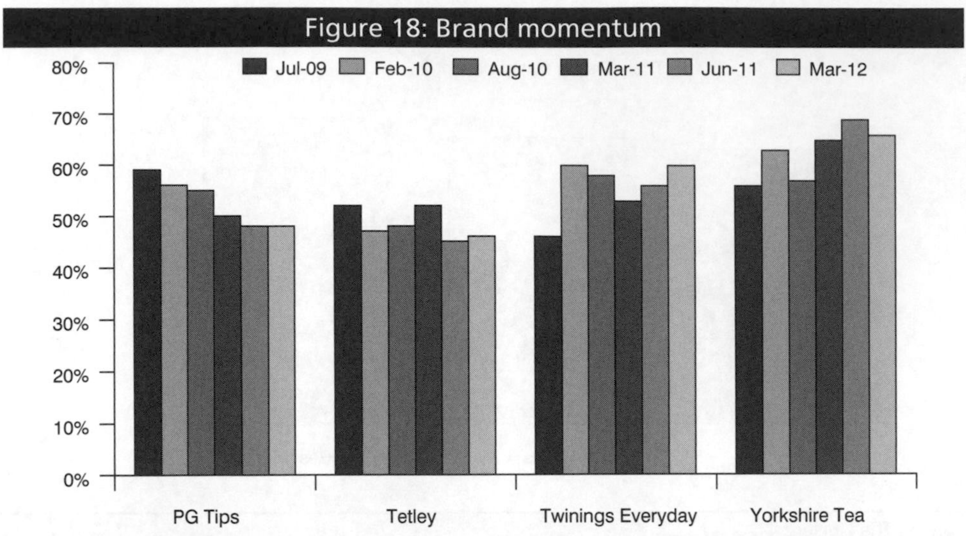


Source: The Nursery. Q5: 'We would now like you to indicate whether you think the following brands are on the way up or on the way down'

*Brand values are evolving as intended*

Yorkshire Tea is building perceptions of modernity without eroding heritage (Figure 19).

Figure 19: Brand values (top 2 box agreement)

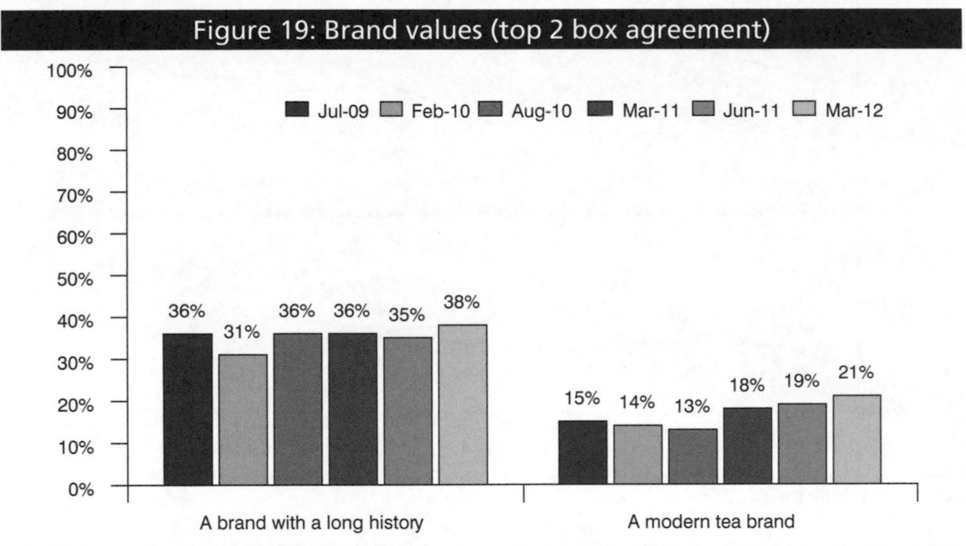


Source: The Nursery

*Taste and quality credentials are on the rise*
(Figure 20)

Figure 20: Brand values (top 2 box agreement)

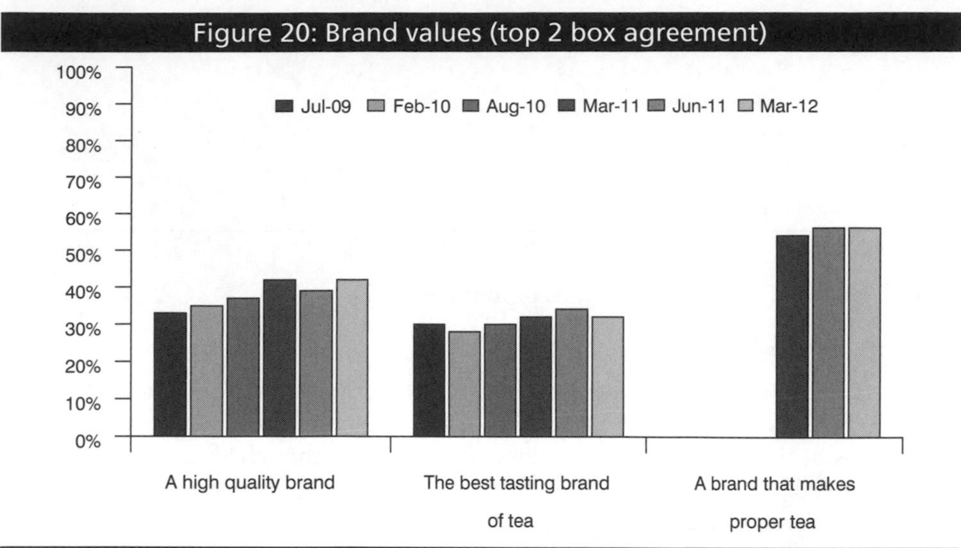


Source: The Nursery

## What else was going on – other influential factors

There were other factors impacting on sales, some of which were helpful but by no means fully explain the growth we have seen to date. Ultimately the advertising effect can only be disentangled by our econometric model, which follows shortly. But it is useful to briefly explore these other factors first.

*Distribution, already good, increased slightly*
(Table 3)

Table 3: Yorkshire Tea distribution

| | |
|---|---|
| WE 5 February 2011 | 78.08% |
| WE 25 February 2012 | 79.54% |

Source: AC Nielsen

*Premium pricing maintained*

Yorkshire Tea maintains premium pricing, although the average price premium versus the market (which takes account of price promotions too) has slightly decreased (Table 4).

**Table 4: Yorkshire Tea distribution, price per tonne**

| | Price | |
|---|---|---|
| **Product range** | **WE 5 February 2011** | **WE 25 February 2012** |
| Typhoo | 4.52 | 4.70 |
| Twinings Everyday | 7.71 | 7.95 |
| Tetley | 5.93 | 5.82 |
| Yorkshire | 7.37 | 6.91 |
| PG Tips | 6.43 | 6.72 |

Source: AC Nielsen

This has been fully taken account of in the model.

*Advertising investment*

Increased investment behind its number two target meant that Yorkshire Tea's share of voice increased from 16% in 2010 to 25% in 2011. This is also partly due to the success of the campaign. A new burst was added to the schedule for November/December following the success of the campaign and ROIs observed earlier in the year. Again the model takes account of this.

## Econometrics can help us disentangle the impact of Little Urn from these effects

Ebiquity has been providing Yorkshire Tea with econometric analysis since 2008. Ebiquity use a rolling three-year sample period of analysis, with the most recent review covering the period between 2009–2011. The model looks at all product variants, price, seasonality, distribution, promotions, advertising and many other factors.

*Little Urn TV has driven incremental volume across all variants of Tea*

(with the majority of volume coming from standard bags, Figure 21)

*In aggregate, Little Urn TV contributed an additional 10% to sales* (Figure 22)

### The model indicates...

The Little Urn TV advertising effect on sales was found to decay very slowly. The retention rate of the advertising effect is 98% per week.

The longevity of the advertising effect is at the top end of Ebiquity's benchmarks and is a crucial element of Yorkshire Tea advertising effectiveness (Figure 23).

*Part of the advertising contribution is delivered through enhancing the impact of promotions* (Figure 24)

## Figure 21: Volume uplifts delivered by Little Urn (by product)

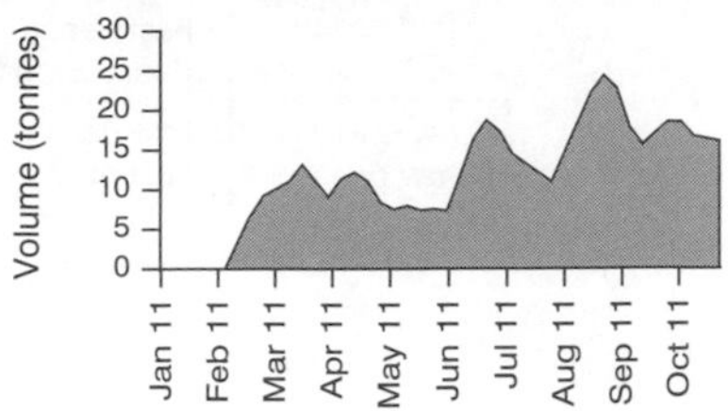


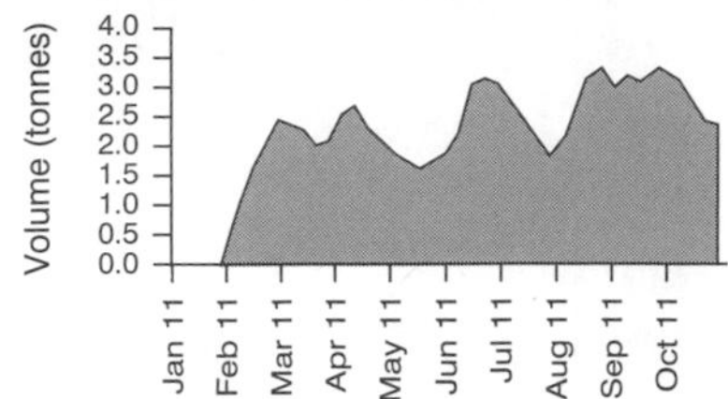


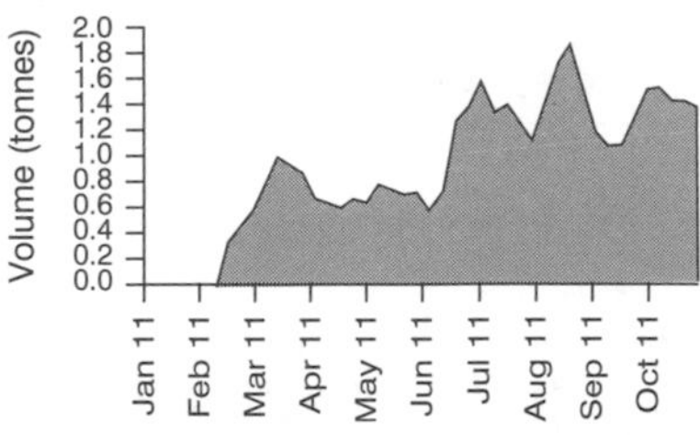


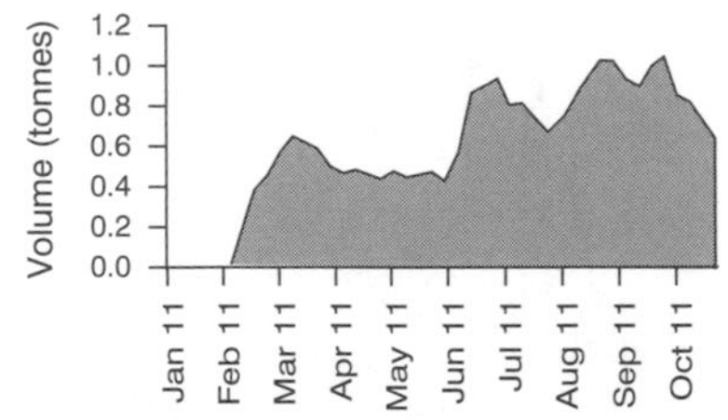


Source: Ebiquity Econometric Modelling

## Figure 22: Sales volume contribution due to Little Urn TV and % uplift of total volume uplift

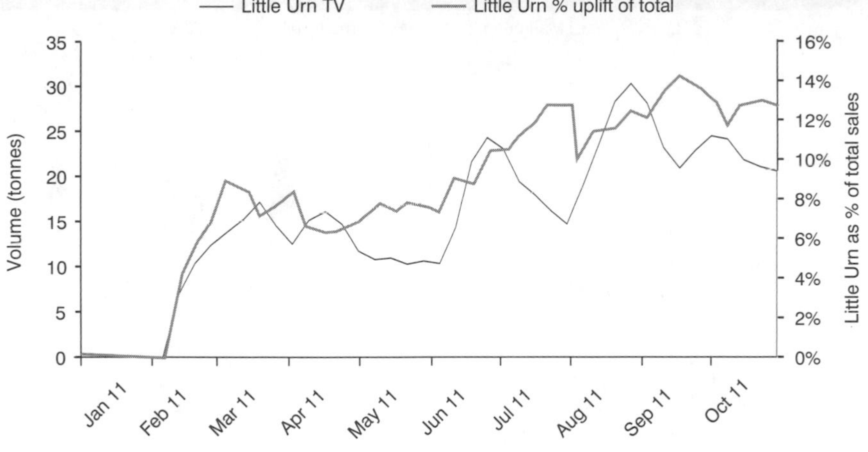


Source: Ebiquity Econometric Modelling

## Figure 23: Advertising effect – decay rate vs. benchmarks

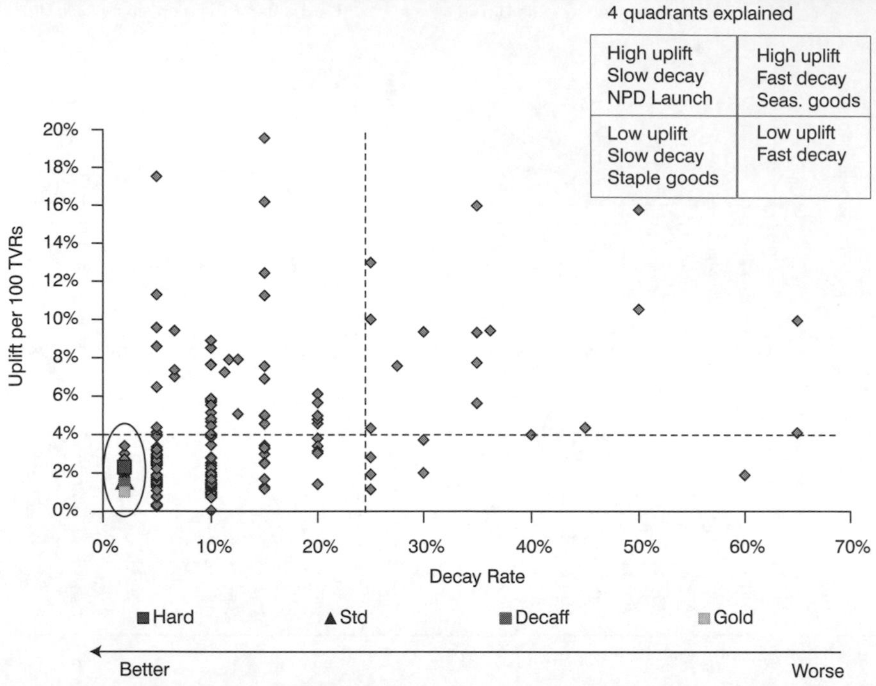

4 quadrants explained

| High uplift<br>Slow decay<br>NPD Launch | High uplift<br>Fast decay<br>Seas. goods |
|---|---|
| Low uplift<br>Slow decay<br>Staple goods | Low uplift<br>Fast decay |

Uplift per 100 TVRs

20%
18%
16%
14%
12%
10%
8%
6%
4%
2%
0%

0% 10% 20% 30% 40% 50% 60% 70%

Decay Rate

Hard ▲Std Decaff Gold

Better Worse

Source: Ebiquity Econometric Modelling

## Figure 24: The additional (multiplicative) impact of advertising on promotions

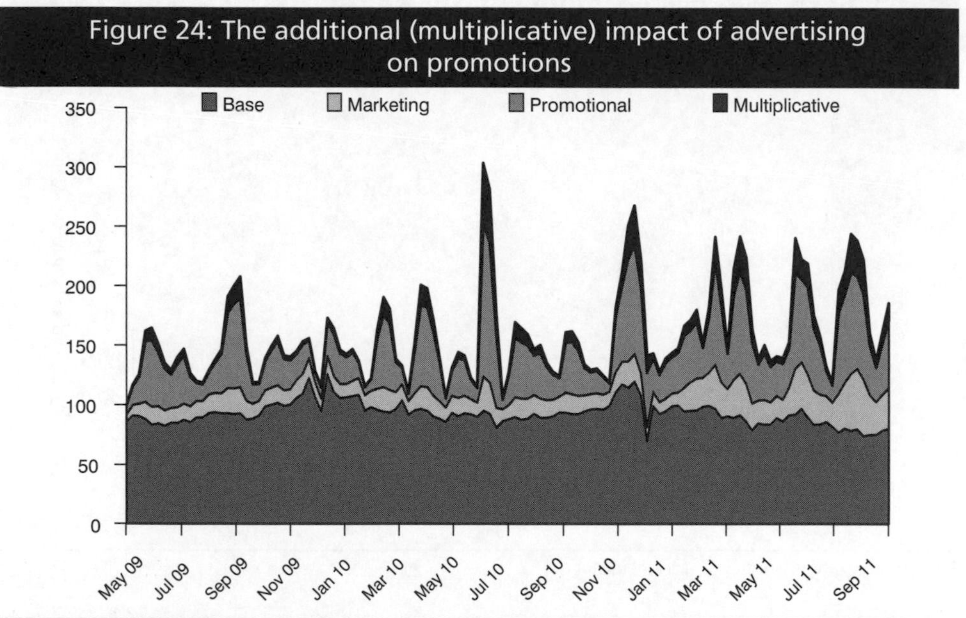


Source: Ebiquity Econometric Modelling

*Little Urn delivered £1.74 in payback (incremental gross profit) for every £1 spent on advertising*

Most FMCG brands do not see a positive return on advertising. Analysis done by Ebiquity research for Thinkbox found that the average ROI for FMCG brands was £0.61 (Figure 25).

Ebiquity have only modelled the impact of the February, June and August bursts of TV. Nevertheless, the profit after marketing costs is £2,043,119. The figure for the entire period covered by this paper will be higher.

Figure 25: Ebiquity Database/Thinkbox

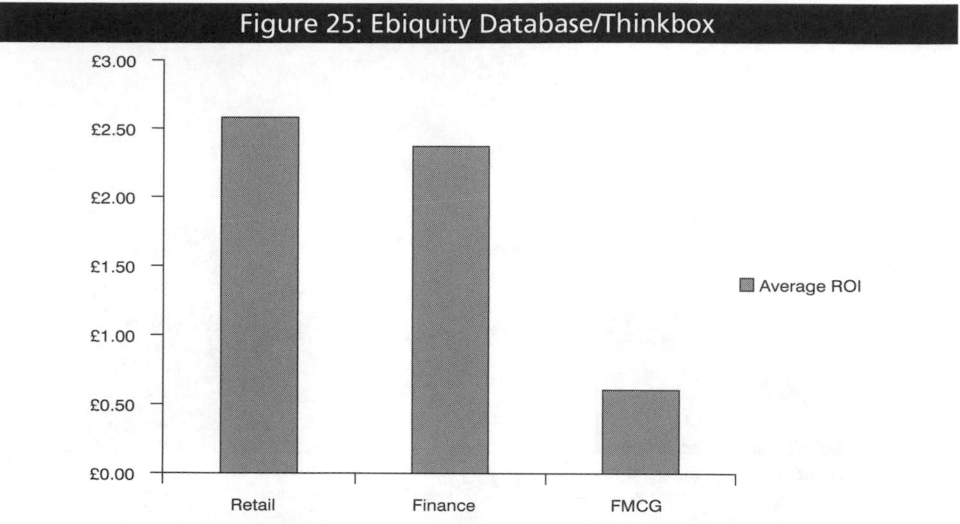


Source: Ebiquity Econometric Modelling

## Longer-term effects

We are only 12 months into the campaign and the effects observed are inevitably short-term. The strong growth on brand measures provides confidence that growth will be sustainable and that the longer-term return on investment will also grow.

The Ebiquity model does attempt to capture long-term impact via carryover measurements already discussed. These are high for the campaign and indeed contribute to the unusually high ROIs (for FMCG) already achieved. But only a much longer run of the campaign will truly reveal its long-term impact, which could well be in excess of its (still very profitable) impact observed to date. The broad-based PWC/Thinkbox research in 2008 suggested that the average TV campaign (and Little Urn is very much above average!) generates 45% of its incremental value after Year One. Similarly the 2010 IPA Grand Prix winner, Hovis, referenced a long-term effect of 2.5x the Year One effect.[4]

Intriguing work by research company BrainJuicer suggests another potential source of long-term value.

Figure 26 shows improved emotional response to Yorkshire Tea and selection of brand at any price among non-brand buyers exposed to the campaign.

**Figure 26: Exposure to campaign improves emotional response and reduces price sensitivity even among brand non-buyers**

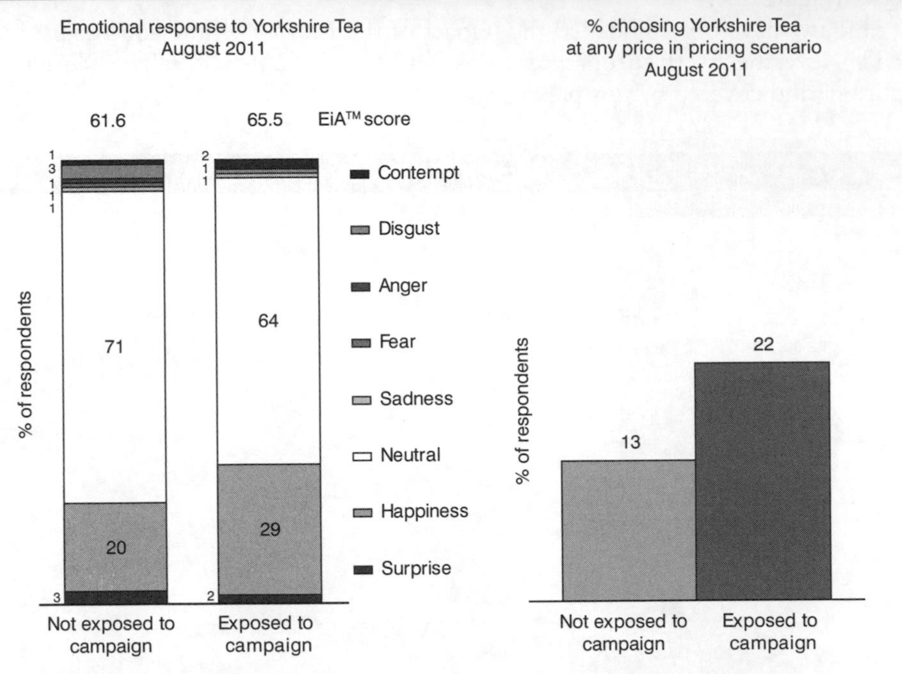


Source: BrainJuicer Labs

The figure shows how non-buyers of Yorkshire Tea who recognise the campaign have an improved emotional response to the brand (increased happiness and a higher Emotion-into-Action™ score – BrainJuicer's measure of brand strength) and are also more likely to select it at any price in a competitive price scenario exercise. The scenario-based pricing exercise suggested a drop in price sensitivity for Yorkshire Tea among both brand and non-brand buyers.[5] We haven't yet seen evidence for this in the econometrics, but the research findings hint at an even more profitable business in the future.

## Engagement

Yorkshire Tea's social presence goes from strength to strength. Facebook likes on 1 February 2011 were at 19,670. Facebook likes were 82,893 on 29 February 2012. Yorkshire Tea was more frequently and positively talked about on Facebook, Twitter, forums, blogs and online news sites than the market leader PG Tips.[6] People did not just 'engage' with Facebook. Their participation shaped Little Urn's route across America.

As we took Yorkshire Tea to new audiences, it was essential we did not erode the strength of existing relationships. For many people it is their 'discovered' brand of tea. In the last few months, celebrities have tripped over themselves to endorse Yorkshire Tea – including global superstars like Noel Gallagher, Louis Tomlinson from One Direction,[7] and the character Damien Lewis plays in *Homeland* (Figures 27 and 28). Given the challenge of introducing younger people to the pleasures of tea, Louis' ongoing endorsement is particularly valuable. While we cannot claim these as direct effects of the campaign, we feel certain that had Little Urn hit the wrong note, we could very well have lost their advocacy.

Figure 27: Noel Gallagher's guide to making tea – 'must be Yorkshire Tea'

Source: *The Sun*, 7 June 2011

## Conclusion

Yorkshire Tea took the slow-moving tea market by storm. Little Urn's heroic trip across America, bringing a proper brew to Brits who needed it most, elevated Yorkshire Tea into the 'big league' of established tea advertisers. The campaign is continuing to build brand strength, while delivering a positive return on investment in its first year, rare for the FMCG sector. The profit generated by the campaign is significantly higher than £2m. For small brands in big categories, Little Urn has a particular message. They should take heart and have the courage to establish their own, unique voice. With that, they can cut through the clutter of their rivals and establish valuable, new consumer behaviour. The world, or some of it, is there for the taking.

Figure 28: Louis Tomlinson (One Direction) on tour in America, as shown in *The Sun*

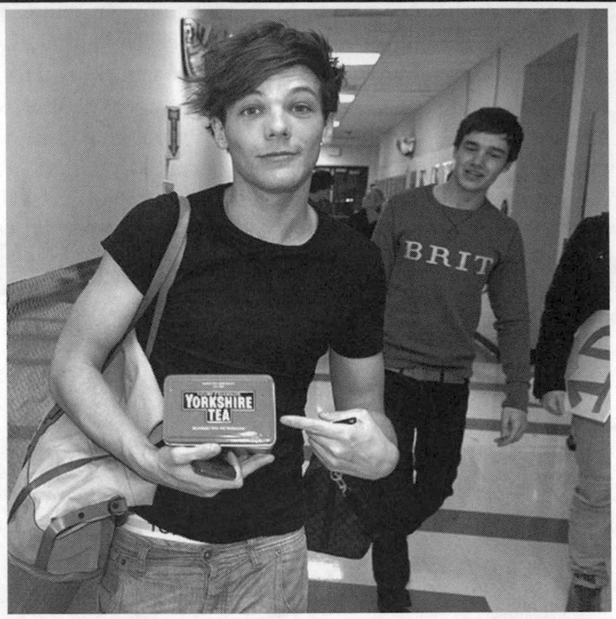


Source: *The Sun*, 12 March 2012

## Notes

1 Source: Kantar.
2 The March 2012 dip was in field after the TV burst in February.
3 Source: The Nursery.
4 Source: Broadbent, T. (2001) How advertising pays back. *Admap*, 422, November.
5 The research was undertaken in early August 2011, six months on from the campaign launch. Respondents were shown 80-bag packs of the five main tea brands at their undiscounted price and at a set of other prices (from +10% to -10% of current) and asked to select which brand they would choose. Exposure to campaign was determined by showing all major elements of the campaign to the sample and asking whether they had seen the advertising before.
6 Source: Sysomos Social Media Tracker.
7 1990 Indie fans may prefer the endorsement of Charlatans singer, Tim Burgess.

SECTION 5

# Bronze winners

# Audi

## The Audi A1: a big idea, condensed

**By James Mitchell and Ross Berthinussen, Bartle Bogle Hegarty**
Contributing authors: Ida Siow and Daryl Frost, Bartle Bogle Hegarty
Credited companies: Creative Agency: Bartle Bogle Hegarty; Digital Agencies: Razorfish and Pirata; Media Agency: Mediacom; Visual Effects: Framestore; Production Company: Passion Pictures; Client: Audi

### Editor's summary

This paper details the next chapter in the story of Audi and 'Vorsprung durch Technik'. In 2010 Audi made a leap that no other prestige car brand had done; it launched a small car, the Audi A1. The opportunity was great, but the risk of sacrificing the prestige of VdT was greater. By understanding that Audi is as much a technology brand as car marque, its small size was turned from a weakness into a benefit. Communications were spread across the biggest media formats available, representing 'small' as a hallmark of superiority and modernity. The campaign attracted new customers and helped the A1 exceed its sales targets, returning £4.40 for every £1 spent. The judges appreciated the sophisticated analysis of how the car market is segmented, and strategic thinking around where the opportunity for Audi lay. They were also impressed by Audi's ability to preserve the core attributes of the brand, whilst achieving a more courageous agenda for the new A1.

**BRONZE AWARD**

# Boots

## Keeping the girls coming in

**By Laurence Horner, Mother**
Contributing authors: Jane Christian, MediaCom Business Science; Jon Hildrew, Boots; Peter Pereira, IPSOS ASI
Credited companies: Creative Agency: Mother; Design Agency: Jupiter Design; Digital Agency: Grand Union; Direct Marketing Agency: LIDA; Media Agency: OMD UK; Publishing: Redwood; Client: Boots UK

**Editor's summary**

In 2007, Boots' UK market share was under pressure from new competitors in the health and beauty market. To address this problem Boots embarked on a journey to identify and understand its most valuable customers: 25- to 44-year-old women, and developed a strategy to secure their loyalty. The resulting campaign, 'Here come the girls' really resonated with these women, arresting the share decline and maintaining Boots' position as market leader.

The client judging panel genuinely felt that for a market leader in any category to take the decision to focus on retention at the expense of acquisition and, more importantly, to concentrate on a core segment, was brave. Boots acknowledged that their share was going to decline within the aggress; they chose to unapologetically and single-mindedly focus on their most valuable segment. To great effect.

# BT

## How understanding the ordinary can achieve extraordinary results

**By Steve Hopkins and Pippa Morris, Abbott Mead Vickers BBDO**

Contributing authors: Matt Turnbull, Abbott Mead Vickers BBDO; James Campbell, MAXUS; Alfredo Garicoche, BT

Credited companies: Creative Agency: Abbott Mead Vickers BBDO; Media Agency: MAXUS; Client: BT

### Editor's summary

This paper outlines how BT constructed a soap-opera style campaign to sell their broadband service to ordinary people living ordinary lives. The judges were drawn by the move into using social media to engage the audience directly in the story of Adam and Jane. Whilst other brands in the category designed campaigns to appeal to technologically hungry 'early adopters', BT realised the opportunity to explain to a more mass-market, technologically sceptical group of consumers how broadband could help keep their everyday lives on an even keel. The paper outlines how adoption theory was used to help construct the campaign to produce £874m in incremental revenue to BT, a gross profit payback of £3.36 per £1 spent on advertising. All-in-all the judges loved the great channel integration with obvious and considered objectives for each.

BRONZE AWARD

# Dove Hair

## Favourite things

**By Kate Smither and Warwick Cairns, Ogilvy & Mather**

Contributing author: John Stuart, Ogilvy & Mather

Credited companies: Creative Agency: Ogilvy & Mather Paris; Media Agency: Mindshare; Client: Unilever

**Editor's summary**

Dove had established fame and success with its 'Real beauty' campaign, but this success wasn't being reflected in the hair care category. This paper demonstrates how Dove went from decline to growth in the Latin American market where mistreating hair was the norm. The 'Favourite things' campaign showed how women mistreat their hair in the course of living, enjoying life and having fun, and the ways that Dove could put things right.

The judges were impressed that Dove achieved growth in a highly fragmented market with 216 products in direct competition, where the product was undifferentiated, and priced at a premium. They developed good customer and cultural insight, giving the product distinctiveness at a comparably lower competitor spend. This paper also outlines a classic media channel strategy with reach and emotional engagement delivered through TV, emotional and functional benefits through magazines, deep engagement through Internet, point of sale messaging through in-store and an inventive social media strategy.

# Gordon's

## Shall we G&T down to business?

**By Richard Helyar and Tass Tsitsopoulos, Bartle Bogle Hegarty**
Contributing authors: Vishal Patel, Sunny Sandhu and Katherine Munford, Data2Decisions
Credited companies: Creative Agency: Bartle Bogle Hegarty; Media Agency: Carat; Research Agency: Nielsen; Client: Diageo

**Editor's summary**

In 2010, gin was a category in decline. It was losing out to wine as people's opening drink and wasn't seen as contemporary. Rather than pick a fight over quality and battle for the Christmas drinking market, Gordon's restated the role of gin as the best way to start any evening and established Gordon's as the definitive brand in the category. The campaign was built around two well-known actors, Philip Glenister and Emilia Fox, cast as themselves, to personify the 'kick' and 'bubbly' character of a G&T. The campaign delivered sales of £8.42m with a payback of £3.95 per marketing pound spent.

The judges argued hotly over this paper as some felt that the brand problem was too big, the campaign weight too low and the competitive context too difficult to achieve the sales results shown. We looked at pricing, promotions, distribution, etc., but in the end decided that it was 'case proven'. This paper is a good demonstration of the power of insight plus strong creative delivery to deliver effectiveness when the odds are stacked against you.

**BRONZE AWARD**

# Gü

## Give in to the power of TV. Give in to Gü.

**By Clare Dowen, DDB, and Nick Smith, DDB Matrix**
Contributing authors: Les Binet, DDB Matrix; Sarah Carter, DDB
Credited companies: Creative Agency: DDB UK; Media Agency: John Ayling and Assosciates; Client: Gü

**Editor's summary**

This paper is a great example of the way a premium brand managed to create appeal and engagement in a time of austerity, and on a low budget. For the first few years, Gü's desirable image had drawn women in, unable to resist its luxurious and distinctive chocolate taste; however, due to increased competition entering the category and the perception that it was aloof, Gü sales began to stall. The challenge was to take Gü off its pedestal and allow women to feel like it was an innocent pudding for any occasion, whilst keeping its premium price. Through a TV ad that changed women's perceptions of it, which was supported on Facebook and outdoor posters, sales increased by 24% in one year, generating £6.5m in sales.

# LV=

## The power of love

**By Miriam Mainwood, Designate, and John O'Sullivan, 24-7 Ideas.com**
Contributing authors: Sarah Bulling, Guy Hedger and Nick Whitnell, LV=
Credited companies: Creative Agencies: Designate and 24-7ideas.com; Media Agency: Carat; Client: LV=

**Editor's summary**

In 2006, Liverpool Victoria was a business in trouble that was rapidly losing customers. The insurance business was in terminal decline, and due to FSA solvency requirements it was predicted that if this continued they would have had to cease trading personal insurance by 2011. In 2007 the company was rebranded to LV= and the advertising was transformed into a contemporary, modern appealing brand. The impact and results of the LV re-launch in 2007 enabled LV= to reach number three in the market by 2010, from 9th in 2006, and grew annual sales by 696% in five years.

This is a solid case study, in a market where many brands fail to differentiate. The scale of the task faced by Liverpool Victoria was huge, with the company under threat of insolvency under FSA rules. By reinventing Liverpool Victoria as LV= they survived in a cut-throat market.

BRONZE AWARD

# Shangri-La Hotels & Resorts

## It's in our nature

**By Clarissa Tam, Ogilvy & Mather Hong Kong**
Contributing authors: Catherine Moustou and Tim Broadbent, Ogilvy & Mather Hong Kong
Credited companies: Creative Agency: Ogilvy & Mather Hong Kong; Media Agency: Maxus; PR Agency: Ogilvy Impact; Others: Quad Productions; Client: Shangri-La Asia

**Editor's summary**

Shangri-La, like other luxury hotels, suffered in the 2008–2009 recession. Rather than cutting prices, it used creativity to restore growth. The objective was to return to 2008 sales levels by acquiring ten extra stays per night per hotel, without price discounting. Against the category trend of rational claims, the campaign delivered by touching both the traveller audience via a TV campaign, and the internal staff audience via internal launch events at every hotel, reminding them of their importance to the brand. Sales increased above target and faster than competitors, delivering an estimated sales payback of 14:1, a profit payback of 6:1, and a shareholder value of payback of 35:1.

This entry is similar to John Lewis in many ways. It demonstrates the importance of staff as key stakeholders in re-framing a brand in your consumer's mind. Success for Shangri-La depended on loyalty, and this could not be achieved without informed, motivated and empowered staff.

# Ta Chong Bank

## Dream rangers

**By Oliver Tsai, Ogilvy & Mather Taipei**
Contributing authors: Tim Broadbent and Minguay Yeh, Ogilvy & Mather Taipei
Credited companies: Creative Agency: Ogilvy & Mather Taipei; Client: Ta Chong Bank

### Editor's summary

The judges appreciated the bravery and boldness behind the strategy in such a highly risk-averse sector; a bank that didn't talk about banking in its communications, but instead tried to humanise it. Following the 2008–2009 financial crisis, the banking community had a poor reputation. The challenge for Ta Chong Bank was three-fold: to stimulate interest in the bank, to attract new customers and to boost the morale of its staff. The 'Dream ranger' campaign launched with the longest commercial ever shown on TV in Taiwan, 180 seconds, showing a group of aged men together for one last bike ride, an experience easily relatable for the Taiwanese people. The campaign generated 24 million complete online views from around the world, tripling the growth of the bank and paying back approximately 134 times for every dollar spent. This paper demonstrated the benefit of great commitment to the power of salience and emotional strategies.

BRONZE AWARD

# Velvet

## Sustainability sells – Velvet Three Trees

**By Tom Goodwin and Isabelle O'Sullivan, Fallon London**

Contributing authors: Sam Veitch and Federico Forti, BrandScience

Credited companies: Creative Agency: Fallon London; Design Agency: Tynan D'Arcy; Direct Marketing Agency: Publicis Chemistry; Media Agency: Carat; PR Agency: Haygarth; PR Agency: Myriad; Econometric modelling agency: BrandScience; Client: SCA



### Editor's summary

Velvet struggled as the number two brand in the toilet paper market. To address this it set out to make caring for the environment an important purchase decision criterion, changing the rules of the category from 'soft, strong and long' to 'soft, strong, long and sustainable'. By putting its environmental credentials at the heart of advertising, Velvet's three trees advertising more than doubled the short-term effectiveness of its communications to achieve a payback of £1.84.

Whilst this paper may have been entered a little 'early' (and we may see it again), the judges still felt that the brand team realised that the time has come to move beyond softness as the key category descriptor and were also brave enough to take on the thorny issue of sustainability. However, they achieved this in a simple way and are starting to see an effect which will hopefully continue to grow over time.

# Virgin Trains

## Don't go zombie, go Virgin Trains

**By Paul Becque, Elvis and Zehra Chatoo, Manning Gottlieb OMD**

Contributing authors: Federico Forti and Sam Veitch, BrandScience; Anita Wilkins, Manning Gottlieb OMD; Tom Duckham, Elvis

Credited companies: Creative Agency: Dare; Integrated Agency: Elvis; Media Agency: Manning Gottlieb OMD; Econometric modelling agency: BrandScience; Client: Virgin Trains

### Editor's summary

In 2009–2010, 16 million fewer journeys were taken via train, and in 2010 cars accounted for 64% of all trips. To address this, the campaign for Virgin Trains encouraged people to re-evaluate their mode of transport choice by highlighting the stressful and often miserable reality of car and plane travel. This was dramatized by the creative idea that travelling by car or plane was a poor, zombie-like decision, particularly when there was the option of taking a Virgin Train instead. This message was communicated via television advertising to champion Virgin Trains, by outdoor and radio to reflect and interrupt consumers' behaviour, and by Streetview, a Facebook game, eCRM, and digital display to build campaign longevity. The judges hailed this paper as an impressive example of a solid channel strategy across a range of interesting platforms. Faced with the task of convincing consumers to reappraise using trains, this campaign adopted a solid and impressive channels strategy across a range of interesting platforms which altered people's consideration of Virgin Trains to a great effect.

# How to access the IPA Effectiveness Awards Databank

The IPA Databank represents the most rigorous and comprehensive examination of marketing communications working in the marketplace, and in the world. Over more than 30 years of the IPA's Effectiveness Awards competition, we have collected over 1,200 examples of best practice in advertising development and results across a wide spectrum of marketing sources and expenditures. Each example contains up to 4,000 words of text and is illustrated in full by market, research, sales and profit data.

## IPA Effectiveness Awards Search Engine (EASE)

You can use the EASE search engine at www.ipa.co.uk/ease to interrogate over 1,200 detailed case studies from the IPA Databank. You can search the case studies by keywords and/or filter by any parameter from questions asked in the Effectiveness Awards Entry Questionnaire. EASE is free to use and is the first search engine on the web which allows you to do this. IPA members can also contact the Information Centre directly where more complex searches can be commissioned and the results supplied by e-mail.

## Purchasing IPA case studies

Member agencies are entitled to download a maximum of 12 case studies in any given calendar year, free of charge, after which they can download additional case studies from the IPA website at www.ipa.co.uk/cases for £25 each. Alternatively members can sign up to warc.com (see overleaf) at a beneficial IPA rate and can then download case studies as part of that subscription. Non IPA members can purchase case studies from the IPA website (www.ipa.co.uk/cases) at £40 per copy.

## Further information

For further information, please contact the Information Centre at the IPA,
44 Belgrave Square, London SW1X 8QS
Telephone: +44 (0)20 7235 7020
Fax: +44 (0)20 7245 9904
Website: www.ipa.co.uk
Email: info@ipa.co.uk

## warc.com

Warc is the official publisher of the IPA Effectiveness Awards' case histories. All IPA case studies are available at warc.com, alongside thousands of other case studies, articles and best practice guides, market intelligence and industry news and alerts, with material drawn from over 50 sources across the world.

Warc.com is relied upon by major creative and media agency networks, market research companies, media owners, multinational advertisers and business schools, to help tackle any marketing challenge.

IPA members can subscribe at a 10% discount. To find out more, request a trial at www.warc.com/trial.

## www.ipaeffectivenessawards.co.uk

On our dedicated Awards website you can find out everything you need to know about the annual IPA Effectiveness Awards competition, including how to enter, and who's won what since 1980.

As well as viewing case study summaries and creative work, you'll also find a series of over 25 brand films from over 30 years of the Awards including:

- HSBC
- Hovis
- Cadbury Dairy Milk
- PG Tips
- Tesco

# IPA Databank case availability

* Denotes winning entries
** Denotes cases published in *Area Works* volumes 1–5
S Denotes cases published in *Scottish Advertising Works* volumes 1–4

**NEW ENTRIES 2012**

2012 2011 Census
2012 Admiral
2012 Aldi*
2012 American Golf
2012 Art Fund*
2012 Audi*
2012 Aviva
2012 Axe
2012 B&Q
2012 Barclays
2012 Barnardo's
2012 Bombay Sapphire
2012 Boots*
2012 British Gas*
2012 BT*
2012 Cadbury Dairy Milk*
2012 Danone Activia*
2012 Department for Transport*
2012 Digital UK*
2012 Dove Hair*
2012 Dove*
2012 Europcar
2012 Ford C-Max
2012 Gordon's*
2012 Gü*
2012 Health Promotion Board Singapore*
2012 Homebase
2012 IBM*
2012 John Lewis*
2012 Ladbrokes
2012 LateRooms.com
2012 Lights by TENA
2012 LV=*
2012 Magnum Gold?!*
2012 McCain
2012 McDonald's*
2012 Mercedes-Benz
2012 Mercedes-Benz (Germany)
2012 Metropolitan Police Service*
2012 Motorola
2012 Nikon*
2012 Nissan*
2012 Odol-med3
2012 Post Office
2012 Pringles
2012 Remember a Charity
2012 Ryvita
2012 Sainsbury's
2012 Shangri-La Hotels & Resorts*
2012 Sky
2012 Snickers*
2012 Ta Chong Bank*
2012 Talk Talk
2012 The National Lottery*
2012 TOTAL 0% Greek Yoghurt
2012 TV Licensing
2012 Velvet Toilet Tissue*
2012 Virgin Atlantic*
2012 Virgin Media
2012 Virgin Trains*
2012 VO5 Extreme Style*
2012 Volkswagen Passat
2012 Waitrose*
2012 Walkers*
2012 Which?*
2012 Yorkshire Tea*

**NUMERICAL**

2003 55 Degrees North**
2006 100.4 smooth fm
2000 1001 Mousse*
2012 2011 Census

**A**

2004 AA Loans*
1982 Abbey Crunch
1990 Abbey National Building Society
1990 Abbey National Building Society
1980 Abbey National Building Society Open Bondshares
1990 Aberlour Malt Whisky*
2004 Ackermans (SA)
2008 Acquisition Crime*
2006 Actimel*

2012 Admiral
1996 Adult Literacy*
2002 Aerogard Mosquito Repellent (Australia)
1999 Agri Plan Finance**
1986 AGS Home Improvements*
1988 AIDS
1994 AIDS*
1986 Air Call
2010 Albert Bartlett Rooster Potatoes
2012 Aldi*
1990 Alex Lawrie Factors
1980 All Clear Shampoo*
1988 Alliance & Leicester Building Society*
1990 Alliance & Leicester Building Society*
1992 Alliance & Leicester Building Society*
1984 Alliance Building Society
1990 Allied Dunbar
1984 Allinson's Bread
1984 Alpen
1990 Alton Towers
2003 Alton Towers 'Air'**
1999 Alton Towers 'Oblivion'**
2010 Always
2012 American Golf
1990 Amnesty International*
1992 Amnesty International
2009 Ancestry.co.uk
1990 Anchor Aerosol Cream
1988 Anchor Butter
1994 Anchor Butter
2011 Anchor Squirty Cream
1986 Andrex*
1992 Andrex
1994 Andrex Ultra
1986 Anglia Building Society
1996 Anglian Water
2006 Anti-Drugs (Scottish Executive)
2007 Anti-Drugs (Scottish Executive)*
2002 Anti-Drink Driving*
1997 Anti-Drink Driving (DoE Northern Ireland)**
1990 Anti-NHS Reform Campaign (BMA)
1994 Anti-Smoking
2011 Aquafresh Kids*
2007 Aqua Optima*
2000 Archers*
2006 Ariel
2007 Army Cadet Force
1998 Army Recruitment*
2004 Army Recruitment*
2005 Arriva Buses*
1996 Arrol's 80
2012 Art Fund*
1994 Arthur's (cat food)
2005 ATS Euromaster*
1988 Audi
1990 Audi*
1998 Audi*
2006 Audi
2008 Audi*
2010 Audi*
2012 Audi*
1982 Austin Metro*
1980 Austin Mini*
1990 *Auto Express*
1996 Automobile Association*
2012 Aviva
2006 Axe
2012 Axe

**B**

2002 B&Q
2004 B&Q
2012 B&Q
1988 Baby Fresh
1988 Babycham
1996 Bacardi Breezer
1998 Bacardi Breezer
1992 Bailey's
2002 Bakers Complete*
2005 Bakers Complete*
2006 Bakers Complete*
2005 Bank of Ireland
1988 Barbican
1990 Barbican Health & Fitness Centre
1992 Barclaycard
1996 Barclaycard*
2010 Barclaycard*
2010 Barclays*
2012 Barclays
1998 Barclays Bank Current Account
2006 Barclays Global Investors (iShares)
2010 Barclays Wealth*
2002 Barnardo's*
2012 Barnardo's
1994 Batchelors
1998 Batchelors Supernoodles*
2005 Baxters Soup[S]
2008 BBC iplayer
2004 Beck's Bier (Australia)
2005 Belfast City
2001 Belfast Giants**
1998 Bell's Whisky
2002 Benadryl*
2006 Bendicks

2009 Benecol
1986 Benylin*
2010 Berocca*
2006 Bertolli
2007 Big Plus, The (Improving Scotland's adult literacy and numeracy)
1990 Billy Graham's Mission 89
1986 Birds Eye Alphabites*
1992 Birds Eye Country Club Cuisine
1994 Birds Eye Crispy Chicken
1982 Birds Eye Oven Crispy Cod Steaks in Batter*
1999 Birmingham, City of**
1988 Birmingham Executive Airways
2010 Bisto*
1990 Black Tower
1996 Blockbuster Video
2005 Blood Donation*
1982 Blue Riband
2000 Bluewater*
2005 bmi baby
1994 BMW*
2004 BMW Films – The Hire*
1994 Boddington's*
2012 Bombay Sapphire
2008 Bonfire Night
2003 Bonjela**
1994 Book Club Associates
2012 Boots*
1998 Boots Advantage Card
1988 Boots Brand Medicines
2004 Bounty (paper towels)*
1994 Boursin
1998 Boursin
1986 Bovril
2000 Bowmore
2008 Bradesco
1986 Bradford & Bingley Building Society*
1990 Bradford & Bingley Building Society
2006 Branston Baked Beans*
1980 Braun Shavers
1982 Bread Advisory Council*
1982 Breville Toasted Sandwichmaker
2002 Britannia Building Society*
1994 British Airways*
1996 British Airways
2004 British Airways*
1984 British Airways Shuttle Service
1994 British Diabetic Association*
1980 British Film Institute*
2012 British Gas*
1994 British Gas Central Heating
1988 British Gas Flotation*
2006 British Heart Foundation* (Anti Smoking)
2009 British Heart Foundation – Watch Your Own Heart Attack*
2009 British Heart Foundation – Yoobot*
1988 British Nuclear Fuels
1988 British Rail Young Person's Railcard
1982 British Sugar Corporation
1980 British Turkey Federation
2005 Broadband for Scotland*[S]
2006 Brother
2007 Brother*
1992 BT
2008 BT
2009 BT
2010 BT
2012 BT*
2004 BT Broadband*
2005 BT Broadband (Consumer)
1994 BT Business
1996 BT Business*
2000 BT Business
1992 BT Call Waiting*
2002 BT Cellnet*
1986 BT Consumer*
2001 BT Internet (Northern Ireland)**
1999 BT Northern Ireland**
1986 BT Privatisation*
2002 BT Retail*
2007 BT Total Broadband
2010 BT Total Broadband*
1998 Bud Ice
1988 Budweiser
2002 Budweiser*
2006 Bulldog 2004
1980 BUPA
2000 BUPA
2002 BUPA
2004 BUPA
1996 Butter Council

C

1996 Cable Television
2008 CABWISE (Transport for London)*
2008 Cadbury Dairy Milk
2010 Cadbury Dairy Milk (India)
2010 Cadbury Dairy Milk*
2012 Cadbury Dairy Milk (India)*
2008 Cadbury's Biscuits*
1994 Cadbury's Boost*
1992 Cadbury's Caramel
1984 Cadbury's Creme Eggs
1988 Cadbury's Creme Eggs
1998 Cadbury's Creme Eggs
1992 Cadbury's Crunchie

1984 Cadbury's Curly Wurly*
1980 Cadbury's Dairy Box
2004 Cadbury's Dream (SA)
1982 Cadbury's Flake
1984 Cadbury's Fudge*
1994 Cadbury's Highlights
1999 Cadbury's Jestives**
1990 Cadbury's Mini Eggs
1994 Cadbury's Roses*
1986 Cadbury's Wispa
1988 Café Hag
2009 California Travel & Tourism Commission
2011 California Travel & Tourism Commission
1996 Californian Raisins
1980 Campari*
1992 Campbell's Condensed Soup
1988 Campbell's Meatballs*
1994 Campbell's Soup
1996 Cancer Relief Macmillan Fund
1984 Canderel
2008 Capital One
1994 Car Crime Prevention
1992 Caramac
1997 Carex**
1998 Carex
2003 Carex**
2007 Carex*
2008 Carex
2010 Carling
1994 Carling Black Label
1996 Carling Black Label
1984 Carousel
1998 Carrick Jewellery
1986 Castlemaine XXXX*
2006 Cathedral City*
1992 Cellnet Callback
1988 CenterParcs
2004 Central London Congestion Charge*
1992 Central Television Licence Renewal
2010 Change4Life
2000 Channel 5
1990 Charlton Athletic Supporters Club*
1980 Cheese Information Service
1996 Cheltenham & Gloucester Building Society
1988 Chessington World of Adventures
1998 Chicago Town Pizza
2002 Chicago Town Pizza
2003 Chicago Town Pizza**
1994 Chicken Tonight
2000 Chicken Tonight Sizzle and Stir*
2007 Child Protection on the Internet (Home Office)
1994 Child Road Safety
1992 Childhood Diseases Immunisation
2004 Children's Hearings (Scottish Executive)*
2005 Children's Hearings System*
1990 Children's World
2001 Chiltern Railways (Clubman Service)**
1984 Chip Pan Fires Prevention*
1990 Choosy Catfood*
1992 Christian Aid
1998 Christian Aid*
2007 Churchill Square (Shopping Centre)
1994 CICA (Trainers)*
1992 Citroen Diesel Range
2010 Civic
1988 Clairol Nice n' Easy
1988 Clarks Desert Boots*
1996 Classic Combination Catalogue
1994 Clerical Medical
1992 Clorets
1984 Clover
1988 Clover
2007 Coca-Cola Zero*
1980 Cointreau
1998 Colgate Toothpaste*
1990 Colman's Wholegrain Mustard
2010 Comfort Fabric Conditioner*
2010 Commonwealth Bank
2000 Confetti.co.uk*
2005 Consensia/Police Service of Northern Ireland
2000 Co-op*
2004 Co-op Food Retail
1994 Cooperative Bank*
1996 Cooperative Bank
1990 Copperhead Cider
2007 Cornwall Enterprise
2010 Corsodyl*
1982 Country Manor (Alcoholic Drink)
1986 Country Manor (Cakes)
1984 Cow & Gate Babymeals*
1982 Cracottes*
2004 Cravendale (Milk)*
2000 Crime Prevention
2003 Crimestoppers Northern Ireland**
1980 Croft Original
1982 Croft Original
1990 Croft Original*
2011 CrossCountry Trains
1999 Crown Paint**
2002 Crown Paint
2003 Crown Paint**

2000 Crown Paints*
2004 Crown Paints
1990 Crown Solo*
1999 Crown Trade**
1999 Crown Wallcoverings**
1984 Cuprinol*
2007 Curanail
1999 Cussons 1001 Mousse**
1986 Cyclamon*
2009 Cycling Safety*

D
1996 Daewoo*
1982 *Daily Mail**
2002 Dairy Council (Milk)*
2000 Dairylea*
1992 Danish Bacon & Meat Council
2008 Danone Activia*
2012 Danone Activia*
1980 Danum Taps
2003 Data Protection Act
1990 Data Protection Registrar
2008 Dave*
1980 Day Nurse
1994 Daz
2006 Daz*
2008 De Beers*
1996 De Beers Diamonds*
2002 Debenhams
1980 Deep Clean*
2005 Deep River Rock - Win Big
2000 Degree
2003 Demand Broadband**
2011 Department for Transport
2012 Department for Transport*
2011 Depaul UK*
2006 Dero*
2008 Dero
1980 Dettol*
2009 Dextro Energy
2002 DfES Higher Education
2010 DH Hep (C)
1984 DHL Worldwide Carrier
2012 Digital UK*
1998 Direct Debit
2004 Direct Line*
1992 Direct Line Insurance*
2008 Direct Payment*
2007 Direct Payment (Department of Work and Pensions)*
2006 Disability Rights Commission
2003 District Policing Partnerships (Northern Ireland)
1990 Dog Registration
2006 Dogs Trust
2000 Domestic Abuse*
2002 Domino's Pizza*
2009 'Don't be a Cancer Chancer'*
2011 Doro Mobile Phones
2008 Dove*
2012 Dove*
2010 Dove Deodorant*
2012 Dove Hair*
2002 Dr Beckmann Rescue*
2001 Dr Beckmann Rescue Oven Cleaner**
1980 Dream Topping
1988 Drinking & Driving
1998 Drugs Education*
1994 Dunfermline Building Society
1980 Dunlop Floor Tiles
1990 Duracell Batteries
1980 Dynatron Music Suite

E
1988 E & P Loans*
2007 E4 Skins (Channel 4)*
2011 East Midlands Trains*
2004 East of England Development Agency (Broadband)*
2000 easyJet*
2009 Eden and Blighty*
1994 Edinburgh Club*
1990 Edinburgh Zoo
1980 Eggs Authority
2004 Electoral Commission (Northern Ireland)
2003 Electoral Commission/COI (DoE Northern Ireland)
1992 Electricity Privatisation
2009 Elephant Chakki Gold (ECG)
2009 Ella's Kitchen
1980 Ellerman Travel & Leisure
1996 Emergency Contraception
1986 EMI Virgin (records)*
1980 English Butter Marketing Company
1986 English Country Cottages
1992 Enterprise Initiative
2003 Equality Commission of Northern Ireland
1992 Equity & Law
2007 Erskine*
2010 essential Waitrose*
1990 Eurax (Anti-Itch Cream)
2012 Europcar
1999 EuroSites (continental camping holidays)**
2004 Eurostar*
2006 Eurostar
2008 Eurostar

1994 *Evening Standard* Classified Recruitment
2010 Everest*
2004 Evergood Coffee (Norway)
1984 Exbury Gardens

F
2008 Fairy Liquid
2008 Fairy Non Bio
1990 Family Credit
1998 Famous Grouse, The
2006 Famous Grouse, The*
1982 Farmer's Table Chicken
1996 Felix*
2000 Felix*
2006 Felix*
1980 Ferranti CETEC
1990 Fertilizer Manufacturers' Association
2011 Fiat*
1982 Fiat Auto UK
1980 Findus Crispy Pancakes
1988 Findus French Bread Pizza & Crispy Pancakes
1992 Findus Lasagne
1982 Fine Fare*
1984 Fine Fare
2005 Fire Authority for Northern Ireland*
2005 First Choice*
1996 First Choice Holidays
1998 first direct*
1992 first direct
2004 first direct
2011 first direct*
2005 First Great Western and First Great Western Link
2007 First Scotrail
2003 Fisherman's Friend**
1992 Flowers & Plants Association
2002 Flowers & Plants Association
2003 Flymo Turbo Compact**
1994 Fona Dansk Elektrik
2012 Ford C-Max
1980 Ford Fiesta
1998 Ford Galaxy*
1986 Ford Granada*
1982 Ford Model Range
2010 Forevermark*
1984 Foster's
1995 Fox's Biscuits**
2005 Fox's Rocky*
1998 French Connection
2000 Freschetta*
1999 Freschetta Pizzas**
2009 FRijj*
1982 Frish*
1996 Frizzell Insurance*
2002 Fruitopia
1994 Fruit-tella
2000 ft.com*
2005 Fybogel

G
1997 Gala Bingo Clubs**
1999 Gala Bingo Clubs**
2004 Garnier
1986 General Accident
2003 George Foreman Grills
2009 ghd*
1992 Gini (Schweppes)*
2010 Ginsters
2007 Glasgow City
1986 Glasgow's Lord Provost
1986 GLC's Anti 'Paving Bill' Campaign*
2000 Glenmorangie*S
1995 Glow-worm Boilers (Hepworth Heating)**
1996 Glow-worm Central Heating
2001 GoByCoach.com (National Express)**
1996 Gold Blend*
1988 Gold Spot
1984 Golden Wonder Instant Pot Snacks*
1980 Goodyear Grandprix
2012 Gordon's*
1984 Grant's Whisky
1992 Green Giant
1988 Green Science
1988 Greene King IPA Bitter
1990 Greenpeace
2012 Gü*
1982 *Guardian, the*
2004 *Guardian, the**
1990 Guinness (Draught) in Cans
1996 *Guinness Book of Records*

H
1990 H. Samuel
1992 Haagen-Dazs*
2009 Halifax*
2006 Halifax Bank of Scotland
1982 Halifax Building Society
1992 Halifax Building Society
1994 Halifax Building Society
2002 Halifax Building Society*
1980 Halifax Building Society Convertible Term Shares
1994 Halls Soothers*
1982 Hansa Lager

1999 Hartley's Jam**
2007 Hastings Hotels
2002 Hastings Hotels (Golfing Breaks)*
2001 Hastings Hotels (Golfing Breaks in Northern Ireland)**
2000 Health Education Board for Scotland
2012 Health Promotion Board Singapore*
1994 Heineken Export
2010 Heinz*
2008 Heinz Beanz Snap Pots
1980 Heinz Coleslaw
1984 Hellman's Mayonnaise*
1982 Henri Winterman's Special Mild
1996 Hep30 (Building Products)
1990 Herta Frankfurters
1992 Herta Frankfurters
2008 Hewlett Packard Personal Systems Group (PSG)
2005 Hidden Treasures of Cumbria*
2005 Highlands and Islands Broadband Registration Campaign
2011 Hiscox
2007 Historic Scotland*
2006 HM Revenue & Customs (Self Assessment)*
1980 Hoechst
1992 Hofels Garlic Pearles
1984 Hofmeister*
1982 Home Protection (Products)
1984 Home Protection (Products)
2006 Homebase
2012 Homebase
1990 Honda
2004 Honda*
1986 Horlicks
1994 Horlicks
2006 Horlicks
1986 Hoverspeed
1992 Hovis
1996 Hovis
2002 Hovis*
2010 Hovis*
2010 HSBC*
1984 Hudson Payne & Iddiols
1996 Huggies Nappies
1994 Hush Puppies

I

1996 I Can't Believe It's Not Butter!*
2012 IBM*
2008 Iceland
1992 Iceland Frozen Foods
1980 ICI Chemicals
1984 ICI Dulux Natural Whites*
1992 IFAW*
1998 Imodium
2001 Imperial Leather**
2002 Imperial Leather
2003 Imperial Leather**
2004 Imperial Leather*
1990 Imperial War Museum
1998 Impulse
1988 *Independent, the*
2006 ING Direct*
1998 Inland Revenue Self Assessment
2005 Inland Revenue Self Assessment*
1988 Insignia
1982 International Business Show 1981
1990 International Wool Secretariat
1992 IPA Society
2005 *Irish News, The*
2007 *Irish News, The* (Recruitment)
1992 Irn-Bru
2009 Irn-Bru
2007 Irn-Bru 32
2003 Ironbridge Gorge Museums**
1994 Israel Tourist Board
2010 It Doesn't Have to Happen

J

2006 Jamie's School Dinners*
1998 Jammie Dodgers
1994 Jeep Cherokee
2001 Jeyes Bloo**
2002 Jeyes Bloo
1992 Jif
1999 JJB Super League**
1988 Job Clubs
2012 John Lewis*
2002 John Smith's Ale
1982 John Smith's Bitter*
1994 John Smith's Bitter*
2006 Johnnie Walker
2008 Johnnie Walker*
2011 Johnnie Walker
1998 Johnson's Clean & Clear*
2011 Jungle Formula*
2010 Juvederm Ultra

K

1992 K Shoes*
1995 K Shoes (Springers)**
1992 Kaliber
1996 Kaliber
2010 Kärcher Pressure Washers*
1990 Karvol
1980 Kays Catalogue
1992 Kellogg's All Bran*

| | |
|---|---|
| 1984 | Kellogg's Bran Flakes* |
| 1984 | Kellogg's Coco Pops* |
| 1994 | Kellogg's Coco Pops |
| 2000 | Kellogg's Coco Pops* |
| 1982 | Kellogg's Cornflakes |
| 1980 | Kellogg's Frozen Waffles |
| 2000 | Kellogg's Nutri-Grain* |
| 2002 | Kellogg's Real Fruit Winders* |
| 1980 | Kellogg's Rice Krispies* |
| 1982 | Kellogg's Super Noodles* |
| 2005 | Kelso Racecourse |
| 1998 | Kenco |
| 2010 | Kenco |
| 1986 | Kensington Palace* |
| 2009 | Key 103 |
| 1984 | KFC |
| 1998 | KFC |
| 2008 | KFC* |
| 2010 | KFC* |
| 2000 | KFC USA |
| 1988 | Kia Ora* |
| 2004 | Kiwi (SA) |
| 1984 | Kleenex Velvet |
| 2007 | Knife Crime (Police Service of Northern Ireland) |
| 2009 | Knorr* |
| 1990 | Knorr Stock Cubes* |
| 2010 | Kodak* |
| 1988 | Kodak Colour Print Film |
| 1984 | Kraft Dairylea* |
| 1994 | Kraft Dairylea |
| 1980 | Krona Margarine* |
| 1986 | Kronenbourg 1664 |
| 2006 | Kwik-Fit* |

L

| | |
|---|---|
| 1990 | Lada |
| 2012 | Ladbrokes |
| 2004 | Lamb (Meat & Livestock Australia)* |
| 2010 | Lamb (Meat & Livestock Australia) |
| 2005 | Lancashire Short Breaks* |
| 1990 | Lanson Champagne* |
| 2012 | LateRooms.com |
| 2005 | Lay Magistrates |
| 1992 | Le Creuset |
| 1982 | Le Crunch |
| 1986 | Le Piat D'or |
| 1990 | Le Piat D'or |
| 1996 | Le Shuttle |
| 1980 | Lea & Perrin's Worcestershire Sauce |
| 1990 | Lea & Perrin's Worcestershire Sauce* |
| 2008 | Learndirect* |
| 1988 | Leeds Permanent Building Society |
| 1988 | Lego |
| 2004 | Lego Bionicle |
| 1984 | Leicester Building Society |
| 1996 | Lenor |
| 2002 | Levi Strauss Engineered Jeans (Japan) |
| 1980 | Levi Strauss UK |
| 1992 | Levi Strauss UK* |
| 1988 | Levi's 501s* |
| 2005 | Lift Off |
| 2012 | Lights by TENA |
| 1990 | Lil-lets* |
| 1996 | Lil-lets |
| 1996 | Lilt |
| 1992 | Limelite* |
| 1980 | Limmits |
| 1999 | Lincoln Financial Group** |
| 2000 | Lincoln Insurance |
| 2000 | Lincoln USA |
| 1980 | Lion Bar |
| 1988 | Liquorice Allsorts |
| 1992 | Liquorice Allsorts |
| 1980 | Listerine |
| 1988 | Listerine* |
| 2004 | Listerine |
| 1998 | Littlewoods Pools |
| 2011 | Liverpool ONE |
| 1984 | Lloyds Bank* |
| 1992 | Lloyds Bank |
| 2010 | Lloyds TSB* |
| 1999 | Local Enterprise Development Unit (NI)** |
| 1990 | London Buses Driver Recruitment |
| 2009 | London Business School* |
| 1982 | London Docklands |
| 1984 | London Docklands* |
| 1990 | London Philharmonic |
| 1992 | London Transport Fare Evasion |
| 1986 | London Weekend Television |
| 1980 | Lucas Aerospace* |
| 1996 | Lucky Lottery |
| 1980 | Lucozade* |
| 1992 | Lucozade |
| 2008 | Lucozade Sport* |
| 1988 | Lurpak |
| 2000 | Lurpak* |
| 2008 | Lurpak |
| 2012 | LV=* |
| 2002 | Lynx* |
| 2011 | Lynx* |
| 2004 | Lynx Pulse* |
| 1994 | Lyon's Maid Fab |
| 1988 | Lyon's Maid Favourite Centres |

**M**
2004 M&G
1988 Maclaren Prams
2003 Magna Science Adventure Centre**
2007 Magners Irish Cider*
1999 Magnet Kitchens**
2004 Magnum
2012 Magnum Gold?!*
2009 Make Poverty History
2006 Make Poverty History (Comic Relief)
1990 Malibu
2006 Manchester City*
1999 Manchester City Centre**
2001 Manchester City Centre**
2002 *Manchester Evening News* (Job Section)*
2003 *Manchester Evening News* Job Section**
2003 ManchesterIMAX**
1982 Manger's Sugar Soap*
1988 Manpower Services Commission
2011 Marie Curie Cancer Care*
1994 Marks & Spencer
2006 Marks & Spencer*
2004 Marks & Spencer Lingerie*
1998 Marmite*
2002 Marmite*
2008 Marmite*
2011 Marmite XO
1998 Marmoleum
1988 Marshall Cavendish Discovery
1994 Marston Pedigree*
2001 Maryland Cookies**
2006 Mastercard
2008 Mastercard
2009 Maximuscle*
1986 Mazda*
1986 Mazola*
2008 McCain
2012 McCain
2011 McCain Wedges*
1996 McDonald's
1998 McDonald's
2010 McDonald's
2012 McDonald's*
2008 McDonald's Eurosaver
1980 McDougall's Saucy Sponge
1988 Mcpherson's Paints
1990 Mcpherson's Paints
2000 McVitie's Jaffa Cakes
2004 McVitie's Jaffa Cakes
2010 Medicine Waste
2012 Mercedes-Benz
2012 Mercedes-Benz (Germany)
1992 Mercury Communications
2005 Metrication
1988 Metropolitan Police Recruitment*
2012 Metropolitan Police Service*
2003 Microbake
1988 Midland Bank
1990 Midland Bank
1992 Miele
1988 Miller Lite*
2000 Moneyextra*
2010 Monopoly
2006 Monopoly Here & Now*
2006 More4*
1999 Morrisons**
2008 Morrisons*
2009 Morrisons*
2010 Morrisons
1988 Mortgage Corporation*
2008 Motorola*
2012 Motorola
2002 Mr Kipling*
1984 Mr Muscle
2010 MTR*
1995 Müller Fruit Corner**
1994 Multiple Sclerosis Society
2010 Munch Bunch
1996 Murphy's Irish Stout*
2000 Myk Menthol Norway*

**N**
2005 Nambarrie Tea[S]
2000 National Code and Number Change
1980 National Dairy Council - Milk
1992 National Dairy Council - Milk
1996 National Dairy Council - Milk*
1992 National Dairy Council - Milkman*
1996 National Lottery (Camelot)
1999 National Railway Museum**
1996 National Savings
1984 National Savings: Income Bonds
1982 National Savings: Save by Post*
2007 National Trust (Northern Ireland)
1986 National Westminster Bank Loans
1982 Nationwide Building Society
1988 Nationwide Flex Account
1990 Nationwide Flex Account
2006 Naturella*
1990 Navy Recruitment
1988 Nefax
1982 Negas Cookers
1982 Nescafé
2000 Network Q
1992 Neutrogena
1982 New Man Clothes

1994 New Zealand Lamb
1980 New Zealand Meat Producers Board
2003 Newcastle Gateshead Initiative
2001 NHS Missed Appointments**
2006 Nicorette*
1994 Nike
1996 Nike
2012 Nikon*
2012 Nissan*
1994 Nissan Micra*
2000 No More Nails*
1986 No.7
2005 Noise Awareness*
1988 Norsk Data
1998 North West Water
1997 North West Water (drought)**
1998 North West Water (drought)
2007 Northern Bank
2007 Northern Ireland Fire and Rescue Service
2009 Northern Ireland Fire and Rescue Service
2005 Northern Ireland Office Community Safety Unit*
2003 Northern Ireland Social Care Council
2003 Northern Ireland Tourist Board
2004 Northern Ireland Tourist Board
1998 Norwich Union
2002 Norwich Union Pensions
1990 Nouvelle Toilet Paper
2000 NSPCC*
2006 NSPCC
1990 Nurofen
1986 Nursing Recruitment
2009 Nutella*
1994 Nytol

O
2004 $O_2$*
2006 $O_2$*
2010 $O_2$*
2008 $O_2$ UK
1980 *Observer*, the – French Cookery School Campaign
2002 Ocean Spray*
1988 Oddbins*
2012 Odol-med3
1998 Olivio*
2002 Olivio/Bertolli*
1998 Olympus
1982 Omega Chewing Gum
1998 One2One*
2005 onlineni.net
1992 Optrex*
2010 Oral-B
2005 Oral Cancer*
1996 Orange*
1998 Orange*
2010 Orange*
2000 Orange International
2000 Orange Just Talk*
1984 Oranjeboom
2007 Organ Donor Recruitment (Scottish Executive)*
2011 Organ Donor Register*
2007 Original Source*
1990 Otrivine
2001 Our Dynamic Earth Visitor Attraction**
2011 Ovaltine*
1988 Oxo
1990 Oxo
1992 Oxo*
1998 Oxo Lamb Cubes

P
2007 P&O Cruises
2007 P&O Ferries
1986 Paignton Zoo
2000 Pampers South Africa*
2011 Panasonic Toughbook
1988 Paracodol*
1984 Paul Masson California Carafes
2005 Payment Modernisation Programme
1982 Pedal Cycle Casualties*
1998 Penguin
1994 Peperami*
2011 PepsiCo Walkers*
1994 Pepsi Max
1986 Perrier
1990 Perrier
2000 Persil*
2006 Petits Filous
1990 PG Tips*
2000 PG Tips*
1996 Philadelphia*
1994 Philadelphia
1988 Phileas Fogg
1988 Phileas Fogg
1994 Phileas Fogg
2010 Philips
1980 Philips Cooktronic
1980 Philips Video
2003 Phoenix Natural Gas
2003 Phones 4u**
1998 Physical Activity Campaign (HEB Scotland)
2009 Pilgrims Choice

2007 Pilkington Activ*
1990 Pilkington Glass
1992 Pilsner
1986 Pink Lady
1984 Pirelli
1986 Pirelli
1990 Pirelli
1996 Pirelli
1994 Pizza Hut
1996 Pizza Hut
1998 Pizza Hut*
1990 Plax
2010 Plenty
1980 Plessey Communications & DataSystems
1998 Polaroid*
2007 Police Community Support Officers
1994 Police Federation of England and Wales
2004 Police Officer Recruitment (Hertfordshire Constabulary)*
2002 Police Recruitment*
2002 Police Recruitment (Could You?)
2002 Police Recruitment Northern Ireland
2001 Police Service of Northern Ireland**
2007 Police Service of Northern Ireland (Recruitment)
1996 Polo Mints
1984 Polyfoam
2007 Pomegreat
1986 *Portsmouth News*
2002 Post Office*
2012 Post Office
1980 Post Office Mis-sorts
1986 Post Office Special Issue Stamps
2004 Postbank (Post Office SA)
1998 Pot Noodle
1996 Potato Marketing Board
2008 Power of One
1984 Presto
1980 Pretty Polly*
2010 Pringles
2012 Pringles
2006 Privilege Insurance
2011 Program of Humanitarian Attention to the Demobilised*
2005 Progressive Building Society – Financial Services
2011 Promote Iceland*
1992 Prudential
2008 Public Awareness Campaign for Helmet Wearing*

Q

1984 QE2
2003 Qjump.co.uk
1988 Quaker Harvest Chewy Bars*
1982 Qualcast Concorde Lawn Mower*
1986 Quatro
1986 Quickstart
1996 Quorn Burgers

R

1982 Racal Redec Cadet
1990 Radio Rentals
1994 Radio Rentals
1990 Radion Automatic*
2008 Radley*
1980 RAF Recruitment*
1996 RAF Recruitment
2004 Rainbow (evaporated milk)*
1994 Range Rover
2000 Reading and Literacy*
1992 Real McCoys
2000 Rear Seatbelts*
1984 Red Meat Consumption
1998 Red Meat Market*
1988 Red Mountain*
1996 Reebok*
1990 Reliant Metrocabs
1994 Remegel
2010 Remember a Charity*
2012 Remember a Charity
1998 Renault
1990 Renault 19*
1986 Renault 5
1992 Renault Clio*
1996 Renault Clio*
1984 Renault Trafic & Master
2009 Resolva 24H*
2005 ResponsibleTravel.Com
2010 Retail OTP
1982 Ribena*
1996 Ribena
2001 right to read (literacy charity)**
2001 rightmove.co.uk**
2002 Rimmel*
1986 Rimmel Cosmetics
2008 Road Safety*
2009 Road Safety
2006 Road Safety – Anti-Drink Driving (DoE Northern Ireland)
2006 Road Safety --THINK! (Department of Transport)
1999 Road Safety (DoE Northern Ireland)**
2003 Road Safety (DoE Northern Ireland)

2004 Road Safety (DoE Northern Ireland)*
2007 Road Safety (Republic of Ireland Road Safety Authority/DoE Northern Ireland)
2010 Robinsons Fruit Shoot*
1996 Rocky (Fox's Biscuits)
1988 Rolls-Royce Privatisation*
2004 Roundup
2005 Roundup Weedkiller*
1988 Rover 200
1982 Rowenta
1990 Rowntree's Fruit Gums
1992 Royal Bank of Scotland
1986 Royal College of Nursing
2002 Royal Mail
1986 Royal Mail Business Economy
1997 Royal Mint**
1990 Royal National Institute for the Deaf
1996 RSPCA
2011 Rubicon
1988 Rumbelows
2012 Ryvita
2006 Ryvita Minis
2007 Ryvita Minis*

S
2004 s1jobs
1994 S4C
1988 Saab*
2004 Safer Travel at Night (GLA)*
1996 Safeway
2002 Sainsbury's* (Jamie Oliver)
2002 Sainsbury's* (Promotion)
2006 Sainsbury's
2008 Sainsbury's*
2010 Sainsbury's*
2012 Sainsbury's
2008 Sainsbury's magazine
2001 Salford University**
2003 Salvation Army, the**
1996 Samaritans
1980 Sanatogen
1986 Sanatogen
1988 Sandplate*
1986 Sapur (Carpet Cleaner)
1992 Save the Children*
1988 Schering Greene Science
2001 Scholl Flight Socks**
2000 scoot.com*
1980 Scotcade
2005 Scotch Beef [S]
1984 Scotch Video Cassettes
1992 Scotrail
1992 Scottish Amicable*
2008 Scottish Government: Teacher Recruitment
2005 Scottish Power*
1998 Scottish Prison Service
2005 Scruffs Hard Wear
2002 Seafish Industry Authority
2006 Seeds of Change (Masterfoods)
1980 Seiko
2010 Self Assessment*
1992 Sellafield Visitors Centre
2001 Senokot**
2002 Senokot
2005 Senokot
1999 Seven Seas Cod Liver Oil**
1980 Shake 'n' Vac
1984 Shakers Cocktails*
2012 Shangri-La Hotels & Resorts*
2009 Shell
2002 Shell Optimax
1999 Shippam's Spread**
1980 Shloer*
1986 Shredded Wheat
1990 Silent Night Beds*
2005 Silent Night My First Bed*[S]
2009 Simple
2002 Skoda*
1982 Skol
1992 Skol
2008 Sky
2012 Sky
1999 Slazenger (cricket bats)**
2009 Slendertone*
1980 Slumberdown Quilts
1990 Smarties
1980 Smirnoff Vodka
1980 Smith's Monster Munch
1982 Smith's Square Crisps
1992 Smith's Tudor Specials
1992 Smoke Alarms
1994 Smoke Alarms*
2011 Smokefree North West
2012 Snickers*
1996 So ...? (Fragrance)
2006 Sobieski (Vodka)
1986 Soft & Gentle
1996 Soldier Recruitment
1995 Solpadol**
1994 Solvent Abuse
1996 Solvite
1999 Solvite**
2000 Solvite*
1988 Sony
1992 Sony
2006 Sony BRAVIA

1992 Sony Camcorders
2006 Sony DVD Handycam
2006 Sony Ericsson K750i/W800i*
2004 Sony Ericsson T610*
1996 Springers by K (Shoes)
2006 Sprite
1984 St Ivel Gold*
2004 Standard Bank (SA)
2005 Standard Life[S]
2009 Stanley Tools UK
2000 Star Alliance
1992 Stella Artois*
1996 Stella Artois*
1998 Stella Artois
2000 Stella Artois*
2002 Stella Artois*
2002 Strathclyde Police
1994 Strepsils*
2010 Stroke Awareness*
1990 Strongbow
2009 Strongbow
2007 Subway*
1982 Summers the Plumbers
1980 Sunblest Sunbran
1990 Supasnaps
2000 Surf*
2010 Surf*
1980 Swan Vestas*
1984 SWEB Security Systems
1992 Swinton Insurance
2009 Swinton Taxi Division*
1996 Switch
1998 Switch
2003 Syndol (painkillers)**

T
2012 Ta Chong Bank*
2012 Talk Talk
1992 Tandon Computers
1990 Tango
2010 Tango
1986 TCP*
2010 TDA Teacher Recruitment*
2006 Teacher Recruitment*
2001 Teacher Training Agency**
2003 Teacher Training Agency**
1986 Teletext
1986 Territorial Army Recruitment
2000 Terry's Chocolate Orange*
1980 Tesco
2000 Tesco*
2002 Tesco*
2007 Tesco (Green Clubcard)
1990 Tetley Tea Bags
2010 The Army
2010 The Co-operative Food*
1992 *The Economist**
2002 *The Economist**
2011 *The Economist**
2010 The Happy Egg Co.
2012 The National Lottery*
2004 The Number 118 118*
2010 thetrainline.com*
2010 THINK!*
1984 Thomas Cook
2008 Thomas Cook
1990 Tia Maria
1992 Tia Maria
1990 *Times, The*
1994 Tizer
2005 Tizer*
1980 Tjaereborg Rejser*
2010 T-Mobile*
2004 Tobacco Control (DH)*
2010 Tobacco Control*
1980 Tolly's Original
2002 Tommy's: The Baby Charity*
1984 Torbay Tourist Board*
1986 Toshiba*
2012 TOTAL 0% Greek Yoghurt
1986 Touche Remnant Unit Trusts
1992 Tower of London
2004 Toyota Corolla
1996 Toyota RAV4
2008 Toyota Yaris
1982 Trans World Airlines
2003 Translink CityBus
2007 Translink Metro
2003 Translink Smartlink
2005 Travelocity.co.uk*
2006 Travelocity.co.uk*
1984 Tri-ac (Skincare)
2009 Tribute Ale
2008 Trident*
2007 Trident (Metropolitan Police)*
2004 Tritace
1980 Triumph Dolomite
2006 Tropicana Pure Premium*
1986 TSB*
1988 TSB*
1994 TSB
2004 TUI (Germany)
1982 Turkish Delight*
1986 TV Licence Evasion*
2006 TV Licensing*
2012 TV Licensing
2000 Twix Denmark

U
1984 UK Canned Salmon

1986 Umbongo Tropical Juice Drink
2003 UniBond
1999 UniBond No More Nails**
2005 UniBond Sealant Range*
2005 University of Dundee*S
1998 UPS
2003 UTV Internet
1990 Uvistat*

V
1988 Varilux lenses
1994 Vauxhall Astra
1990 Vauxhall Cavalier
1996 Vauxhall Cavalier
1999 Vauxhall Network Q**
1996 Vegetarian Society
2006 Vehicle Crime Prevention (The Home Office)*
2004 Vehicle Crime Reduction (The Home Office)
2012 Velvet Toilet Tissue*
2001 Vimto**
1986 Virgin Atlantic
2008 Virgin Atlantic*
2010 Virgin Atlantic*
2012 Virgin Atlantic*
2012 Virgin Media
2004 Virgin Mobile*
2004 Virgin Mobile Australia*
2004 Virgin Trains*
2006 Virgin Trains*
2010 Virgin Trains
2012 Virgin Trains*
1994 Visa
2006 Visit London
2012 VO5 Extreme Style*
1986 Vodafone
1998 Volkswagen*
2002 Volkswagen (Brand)*
2004 Volkswagen Diesel*
2006 Volkswagen Golf*
2006 Volkswagen Golf GTI Mk5*
2002 Volkswagen Passat*
2012 Volkswagen Passat
2008 V-Power
1992 VW Golf*

W
1980 Waistline
2002 Waitrose*
2007 Waitrose*
2008 Waitrose*
2012 Waitrose*
2003 Wake Up To Waste (Northern Ireland)**
1992 Wales Tourist Board
2010 Walkers
2012 Walkers*
1996 Walkers Crisps*
2002 Walkers Crisps*
1980 Wall's Cornetto
2006 Wall's Sausages
1984 Wall's Viennetta*
1996 Wall's Viennetta
1998 Wallis
1984 Walnut Whips
2003 Warburtons
1990 Warburtons Bread*
2005 Waste Awareness
1984 Websters Yorkshire Bitter
2004 Weetabix*
2007 Weetabix*
1988 Weight Watchers Slimming Clubs
2002 West End Quay
2005 West Midlands Hub of Museums*
1990 Westwood Tractors
2012 Which?*
1992 Whipsnade Wild Animal Park*
1980 Whitegate's Estate Agents*
2010 Wickes
1990 Wilson's Ultra Golf Balls
1988 Winalot Prime*
2010 Wispa*
2006 Women's Aid*
1994 Wonderbra*

Y
2000 Yellow Pages Norway
1980 Yeoman Pie Fillings
1980 Yorkie
1982 Yorkshire Bank
2002 Yorkshire Forward/Yorkshire Tourist Board
2012 Yorkshire Tea*
2008 Yorkshire Tourist Board – Make Yorkshire Yours

Z
1984 Zanussi*
1994 Zovirax

In compiling this list the IPA has made every effort to ensure an accurate record of all cases currently available in the IPA Databank. However, there may be instances where cases are currently missing from file and as a result have not been listed here.

# Index